HOMICIDE

HOMICIDE

A Sourcebook of Social Research

M. Dwayne Smith
Margaret A. Zahn
Editors

For information:

SAGE Publications, Inc.
2455 Teller Road
Thousand Oaks, California 91320
E-mail: order@sagepub.com

SAGE Publications Ltd.
6 Bonhill Street
London EC2A 4PU
United Kingdom

SAGE Publications India Pvt. Ltd.
M-32 Market
Greater Kailash I
New Delhi 110 048 India

Printed in the United States of America

Library of Congress Cataloging-in-Publication Data

Main entry under title:

Homicide: A sourcebook of social research /
edited by M. Dwayne Smith and Margaret A. Zahn.
p. cm.
Includes bibliographical references and index.
ISBN 0-7619-0765-3 (cloth : acid-free paper)
1. Homicide–United States. 2. Homicide. I. Smith, M. Dwayne. II. Zahn, Margaret A.
HV6529 .H675 1998
364.15′2′0973–ddc21 98-25350

This book is printed on acid-free paper.

00 01 02 03 04 10 9 8 7 6 5 4 3 2

Acquiring Editor: C. Terry Hendrix
Production Editor: Wendy Westgate
Production Assistant: Nevair Kabakain
Typesetter/Designer: Rose Tylak

Contents

PART VI PREVENTING HOMICIDE: PROPOSED SOLUTIONS

Acknowledgments

A number of persons have contributed to the preparation of this volume. First, our thanks are extended to C. Terry Hendrix, senior editor at Sage, for his patience with and support of this undertaking, and to Alison Binder, copyeditor, and Wendy Westgate, production editor, who gave new meaning to the terms patience and perserverance in guiding this volume through the various stages of production. Also, we owe a considerable debt of gratitude to the contributing authors for their perseverance and graciousness in addressing our many requests. A hearty "thank you" is extended to three persons at the University of North Carolina at Charlotte who assisted in chapter editing. Susan Masse, Smith's departmental administrative assistant, provided valuable editorial suggestions for a number of revisions to early versions of the manuscripts. Graduate assistant Natalie Hicks was extremely helpful in the early stages of the project; graduate assistant Terina Roberson was simply wonderful in helping to bring the project to its conclusion, especially as she repeatedly combed through the chapters in search of those elusive departures from APA style! Finally, one of us (Smith) is especially appreciative for the personal and professional support offered by Sondra Fogel; quite simply, my dear, I couldn't have done it without you.

A Dedication to Marvin E. Wolfgang (1924–1998)

When we began the project of outlining and assembling this volume, we asked Professor Marvin Wolfgang to write a foreword and were pleased that he graciously agreed to do so. Unfortunately, by the time the chapters were ready for review, Professor Wolfgang had become seriously ill; sadly, he died several months later. It is our loss not to have his thoughtful commentary; it is our privilege instead, however, to dedicate this volume to him.

There is no more fitting person to dedicate this effort to than Marvin Wolfgang, whose classic works, *Patterns in Criminal Homicide* (1958) and *Subculture of Violence: Toward an Integrated Theory in Criminology* (1967; with Franco Ferracuti), directly inspired many of the authors in this book and have left a lasting legacy in the field of homicide studies. I (Zahn) feel a particular debt to him because I adopted his work as a guide for my own work on homicide in Philadelphia. Throughout the years, we shared a keen appreciation for homicide detectives, a commitment to primary data collection, a hope for a sociologically informed public policy, and a genuine affection for the city of Philadelphia.

We hope that the chapters of this book meet the standards of empirical rigor and thoughtful interpretation that informed Professor Wolfgang's work and that our dedication is a fitting acknowledgment of the intellectual debt owed to him as a contemporary founder of the social study of homicide.

Margaret A. Zahn
M. Dwayne Smith

PART I

Introduction

CHAPTER 1

A Sourcebook for the Study of Homicide

■ *M. Dwayne Smith & Margaret A. Zahn*

Homicide is a topic that fascinates academic researchers as well as the public. A search of references using the key words *murder* or *homicide* produces an incredible volume and array of citations. Unfortunately, the "facts" contained in the vast literature concerning homicide are complex, confusing, and, at times, simply contradictory. Understanding this wealth of material and using it to develop viable recommendations for public policy are a daunting task, one made even more difficult by a lack of comprehensive sources of information concerning recent homicide research.

Recognizing these difficulties has motivated and guided the development of *Homicide: A Sourcebook of Social Research,* as well as a companion volume, *Studying and Preventing Homicide: Issues and Challenges.* Although *Homicide* is intended for professionals, especially those engaged in various facets of research and public policy, *Studying and Preventing Homicide: Issues and Challenges* is a shorter version that has been edited and condensed to make it accessible to a larger audience.

Our goal in preparing these volumes was to provide a resource of current information on a variety of topics pertinent to the study of homicide from a *social* perspective.[1] To aid in pursuing this goal, we have been fortunate to obtain the contributions of a group of outstanding scholars whose own work is quite prominent within literatures that their chapters address. In some cases, the literature these authors discuss is large and complex; in other cases, it is, so far, rather limited. Regardless of their topic, however, the contributors have provided summaries of the existing research, interpretations of the major findings to emerge from this literature, and an identification of issues that await further study. A few chapters present original research that was conducted for this publication.

The literature covered in this collection of chapters is vast and diverse. Therefore, as an aid to readers, both end-of-chapter references *and* a comprehensive list of references included in all chapters have been provided. We believe that the latter feature contains a substantial portion of the scholarly literature pertaining to homicide as a social phenomenon, especially that published in the United States during the past 50 years.

The chapter following this introduction provides a framework for the remaining contributions. Margaret Zahn and Patricia McCall begin with an overview of homicide trends in the United States during the 20th century. The general trends they discuss have been the object of much research, and explanations for these trends have often been controversial. Zahn and McCall point out, however, that trends involving total rates of homicide often conceal considerable shifts in *patterns* of homicide that are embedded within these broad trends. Consequently, they present analyses of changes in patterns of age, circumstance, and victim-offender relationship, concluding that a full understanding of homicide in the United States requires us to comprehend the trends displayed by various populations and changes in the general dynamics of homicide that have occurred during this century. As they note, however, the *causes* of these shifts remain the subject of much debate.

Part II is devoted to a review of the most prominent social theories of homicide. In Chapter 3, Steven Messner and Richard Rosenfeld discuss perhaps the most enduring theoretical social approach to homicide, the social-structural perspective. The authors review and summarize the large body of research exploring various facets of this perspective, then conclude with an assessment of the major findings to emerge from the literature. Their review leads to a particularly profound and timely conclusion that "the social production of homicide *can* be tempered when people have the collective will to do so."

Chapter 4, by Jay Corzine, Lin Huff-Corzine, and Hugh Whitt, is devoted to the role of cultural and subcultural theories in expanding our understanding of homicide. The authors discuss at length one of the most contested questions in the study of homicide—whether a subcultural perspective can be used to explain the historically higher rates of homicide that have marked the southern region of the United States. They suggest that the answer may be dependent on the definition of *South* that is employed in research, and readers are provided with the demarcation of a "cultural" South that Corzine, Huff-Corzine, and Whitt have found useful in addressing this issue. The authors recommend that extending this approach may present a wealth of opportunities for the study of homicide and other cultural and subcultural groupings.

Although social-structural and cultural/subcultural perspectives tend to dominate the current homicide literature, Martin Daly and Margo Wilson provide a provocative argument in Chapter 5 for the efficacy of sociobiological explanations of homicide. The authors maintain that well-known patterns of homicide are in many ways quite predictable, reflecting as they do the biological and anthropological mandates that influence much of *homo sapiens'* behavior. Aggressive male responses to perceived competition for resources and victimization patterns that predominate among family homicides (e.g., the high risk to stepchildren) are but a few of the topics they find wholly explainable from an socioevolutionary perspective. Daly and Wilson stress, however, that their argument should not be interpreted as undermining the theories discussed in the previous chapters; indeed, they stress that social conditions can—and do—greatly affect the manner in which biological forces manifest themselves among different populations. Daly and Wilson warn, however, that the tendency to dismiss sociobiological factors has left a gap in our knowledge of the causes and correlates of homicide.

The topics of Part III pertain to a number of methodological issues that must be confronted when engaging in homicide research. Marc Riedel begins this section in Chapter 6 with a discussion of the major sources of homicide data. Although homicide data are considered to be among the most complete and accurate crime information available to researchers, they are far from ideal. Through comparisons of widely used sources of information regarding homicide offending and victimization, Riedel reviews the data's strengths and weaknesses. A careful reading of Riedel's chapter will assist readers in becoming more informed consumers of homicide information and more facile users of homicide data.

Robert Flewelling and Kirk Williams have been at the forefront in arguing for the study of disaggregated rates of homicide. In Chapter 7, they reiterate their earlier calls for more specific examinations of trends and patterns of homicide. The authors provide a particularly useful summary of studies that have employed a disaggregated approach in homicide research. As well, they discuss some of the more serious problems to be confronted when engaging in disaggregated analyses and suggestions for how these may be addressed.

Karen Parker, Patricia McCall, and Kenneth Land discuss another controversy in Chapter 8: When seeking to ascertain social-structural correlates of homicide, does the unit of analysis influence the outcome? Addressing this question, Parker, McCall, and Land present an extensive review of research concerning social-structural correlates of homicide; readers will find the summary table and accompanying appendix to be a useful index to this body of literature. The authors conclude that if some troublesome methodological (largely statistical) issues are properly dealt with, then levels of analysis *will not* matter and that a reasonably invariant set of social-structural factors can effectively predict homicide rates across a broad spectrum of social spaces.

Although the chapters of this volume concentrate almost exclusively on homicide in the United States, Gary LaFree reminds us in Chapter 9 that considerable homicide research has been conducted on a cross-national basis. As he discusses at length, a host of methodological issues complicate this research as well as present challenges to interpreting the literature. Nevertheless, a considerable number of studies have explored the cross-national correlates of homicide, and LaFree has prepared a table that paints a vivid picture of nearly four decades of this research. He organizes his discussion around this table that both synthesizes and summarizes the major findings from this literature, concluding with his thoughts on the directions that cross-national research should now take.

The chapters in Part IV discuss topics whose literatures are particularly complex and/or have generated considerable controversy. Angela Browne, Kirk Williams, and Donald Dutton point out in Chapter 10 that intimate partner homicide has particular implications for women because a substantial proportion of female victims are killed by men with whom they have (or have had) personal relationships. Recent years have seen an expansion of the intimate partner concept to include such couplings as boyfriend-girlfriend and former lovers. This expansion alters both the pattern and trend of homicides in which persons, especially women, are killed by perpetrators who can be classified as intimate partners. The trend itself is complex; married partner homicides seem to have declined, but homicides among nonmarried intimate partners appear to have increased. Equally perplexing is another trend whereby the killing of men by female intimate partners has declined during the past two decades, yet the reverse situation (the killing of women by male intimates) has shown little change. Browne, Williams, and Dutton analyze these multifaceted trends and speculate on what accounts for them. They also offer suggestions regarding the research needed to more adequately address the questions that remain in this area.

James Alan Fox and Jack Levin begin Chapter 11 by noting that recent public attention has focused on a small subset of homicides, those committed by serial killers. A spate of television shows and motion pictures have featured serial killers/killing as a central theme, and uninformed observers could easily conclude that this variety of murder is a rather common occurrence. Addressing this misperception, along with nine other myths regarding serial killers/killing, Fox and Levin provide an overview of more recent academic research, the thrust of which departs considerably from what have become popular, but erroneous, beliefs.

In Chapter 12, Robert Nash Parker and Kathleen Auerhahn tackle the difficult subject of the role played by drugs and alcohol in the commission of homicide. Various models of drug and alcohol use are explored in the chapter, with an emphasis placed on uncovering their direct and indirect links to homicide. In answering the question "Is there a homicide-drugs/alcohol linkage?" Parker and Auerhahn offer a definite "yes." Their response to the question is qualified throughout the chapter, however, as they suggest *multiple* pathways by which homicide can be related to drug and alcohol use. These pathways, even when empirically verifiable, are far from straightforward. Parker and Auerhahn conclude with a discussion of the necessity of sorting through these complexities when attempting to formulate reasonable, effective public policy initiatives.

The chapters of Part V deal with the manifestation of homicide among different social groups. Joining the argument made in earlier chapters, Darnell Hawkins maintains in Chapter 13 that the story told by national trends of homicide may be an informative but incomplete tale. Hawkins proceeds to demonstrate why it is important to disaggregate national data by focusing on trends and patterns of homicide among African Americans, a group that suffers particularly high rates of homicide in the United States, both as offenders and as victims. Through analyses of race-specific data that move beyond simple comparisons with Whites, African American homicide is shown to be at once different because of its prevalence and predictable in the forces that appear to drive it. This point is reinforced by the author's analysis of county rates of homicides and the dominant ethnic groups within those counties. Hawkins urges the understanding that African American homicide is a diverse phenomenon demanding separate study to fully develop significant public policy.

In Chapter 14, Ramiro Martinez Jr. and Matthew Lee echo Hawkins's contention by making a case for the separate study of Latino homicide. The authors note that Latinos are frequently classified as "White" in both offending and victimization data. Yet an emerging literature based on more precise ethnic group categorizations finds Latino homicide to have its own distinct characteristics. Furthermore, with an argument similar to that of Hawkins's concerning African Americans, Martinez and Lee maintain that Latino homicide is resistant to simple generalizations because considerable variations in levels and patterns of homicide can be found among the diverse groups that constitute this broad ethnic grouping. Martinez and Lee conclude with their thoughts on research issues that if properly addressed can expand our knowledge of homicide among an increasingly prominent segment of the U.S. population.

Few aspects of homicide have caused more alarm than an apparent downward shift in the age of offenders, as well as the increased representation of juveniles among the victims of homicide. The furor surrounding these shifts has contributed to federal and state laws aimed at juveniles, many of which, arguably, are ill conceived and potentially counterproductive. Kathleen Heide takes on the difficult task of addressing this controversial topic in Chapter 15. In doing so, she employs a multidisciplinary approach that unlike most of the other chapters in this volume, assesses the psychological as well as sociological literature in her exploration of juvenile murderers. In addition, she considers a sociobiological literature that she finds largely undeveloped, but as maintained in the chapter by Daly and Wilson, it is an area that cannot be capriciously discarded. Although conceding the daunting challenge involved, Heide offers her summary of the factors most pertinent to the incidence—and changes in that incidence—of murder by youths.

In Chapter 16, Cheryl Maxson concludes this section with a consideration of a unique form of homicide—that committed by members of gangs. Maxson reviews the difficult problems faced by gang researchers, beginning with the deceptively simple issue of what constitutes a "gang" homicide. From there, we learn of the complexities that appear to make some cities with gangs prone to high levels of violence, whereas others are reasonably immune to these dramatic manifestations of gang activity. That is, gang presence, in and of itself, does not necessarily mean that a city will have high rates of homicide. Further, a relative absence of gang activity does not ensure low rates. Maxson presents original research that aids in sorting out these and other issues regarding the relationship between gangs and homicide.

The final section of the book, Part VI, contains a set of chapters discussing possible remedies that if successful, could be expected to prevent and therefore reduce the incidence of homicide. The policies selected for discussion represent differing ends of the political spectrum. This section begins with a consideration of the effects of the death penalty, a response favored by political conservatives who see punitive responses as essential for deterring people from crime. In Chapter 17, William Bailey and Ruth Peterson consider the impact of the death penalty in serving as a general deterrent to crime, a controversy that figures prominently in the homicide literature. Bailey and Peterson's careful assessment of a vast array of literature leads them to conclude that the deterrence hypothesis remains unsupported. That is, the weight of the evidence suggests that use of the death penalty has little connection to levels of homicide, especially across differing states of the United States. At the same time, Bailey and Peterson find somewhat tenuous support for the competing hypothesis of a "brutalization effect" thought to increase the incidence of homicide, a counterposition frequently offered by death penalty opponents. As an additional contribution, the authors consider the possibility that capital punishment may have a more pronounced impact on an understudied population, female offenders. Engaging in a careful analysis of capital punishment on female homicide, they report results that suggest a minor deterrent effect on one type of female-perpetrated murder. However, the overall thrust of the literature leads them to conclude that significant efforts to reduce homicide will have to be expended in areas other than the use of capital punishment.

When advocating ways to reduce homicide, conservative fervor for the death penalty is easily matched by the faith that political liberals place in restrictions on the sale and possession of firearms. Liberals will therefore take heart with the conclusions of Philip Cook and Mark Moore in Chapter 18. Following an exhaustive review of yet another large, complicated body of research, Cook and Moore find the weight of evidence to support the notion that selected controls on firearms can bring about a reduction in homicide. They warn, however, that the values underlying effort to achieve such legislation clash bitterly with other sets of values; for many people, the trade-off in reduced homicide rates is simply not worth the loss of rights necessary to achieve that goal. In such an atmosphere, Cook and Moore maintain that it is especially important to decipher "what works," and they furnish readers with a contemporary assessment of gun control programs that show promise for achieving the specific goals to which they are directed.

Few responsible persons argue that significant reductions in homicide can be achieved via legislation alone. Instead, the effort will require an investment of considerable social and financial resources across a broad array of areas. There is a seemingly endless list of places, however, where such investments should be made. In the book's last chapter (Chapter 19), James Mercy and Rodney Hammond outline a *public health* approach, one that they maintain strives to be comprehensive in addressing the multiple factors contributing to homicide. In essence, homicide is approached from the perspective of a disease model, one for which an integration of multiple solutions is appropriate. Mercy and Hammond explore various options in developing the framework for a comprehensive program aimed at homicide reduction. Echoing Messner and Rosenfeld's concluding thoughts in Chapter 3, Mercy and Hammond are firm in their belief that a notable reduction in U.S. homicide rates is entirely possible with a thoughtful application of the approach they describe.

Overall, this sourcebook represents some of the best, most comprehensive information available on the subject of homicide. It is designed to serve as a guide for current research and as a blueprint for the work that remains to be done in the social study of homicide. Sound research that guides carefully constructed public policy offers our best hope for achieving a significant reduction in what Marc Riedel has appropriately termed the "rare but exceedingly tragic crime of homicide." It is our sincere wish that this volume is used to advance our knowledge and inform public policy so that homicide becomes an even rarer event.

■ *NOTE*

1. Although several chapters mention and even offer overviews of some aspects of a psychological or socio-biological literature, the major focus of this volume is on research whose topics address the larger social dynamics that influence levels of homicide across time, geographic space, and social groups.

CHAPTER 2

Trends and Patterns of Homicide in the 20th-Century United States

Margaret A. Zahn & Patricia L. McCall

This chapter reviews trends and patterns of homicide in the United States for almost a full century, from 1900 to 1996.[1] It presents an analysis of changing trends, a portrait of the dominant types of homicide in different periods of American history, and some analysis of the populations that are differentially affected through time by this type of violent death. Because no fully national databases exist for the entire century, the portrait of American homicide that follows is a composite derived from national sources, when available, and a review of major studies in different periods.

HOMICIDE DATA SOURCES

In Chapter 6, Marc Riedel will discuss at length the sources of data that are used in the study of homicide. Several of those sources, however, have provided reliable information for only the latter half of this century. Therefore, establishing a national portrait of homicide through the entire 20th century poses a variety of problems. One is in how homicide is defined. In some studies, for instance, justifiable homicides—killings by officers of the law or those occurring in self-defense—are included. In other studies, these types of homicides are not included in the database. Generally, studies in the 1920s seem more likely to include justifiable homicides than do those in the 1960s.[2] As another example, in some periods, abortion, infanticide, or both are included as separate types of homicide, whereas at other times, they are excluded or are simply not defined as homicide.

A particularly troublesome issue is that many studies have discussed the type of relationship between a homicide victim and his or her aggressor, but there has been no consistent definition across studies of the various types of victim-offender relationship (e.g., what constitutes an acquaintance or a stranger). In much of the research on this issue, no precise definitions

AUTHORS' NOTE: We thank Karen Acree and Carolyn Bunn for their secretarial support, as well as graduate students Shawn Hutton and Travis Preslar for their work on various components of this chapter.

are offered at all. (For excellent discussions of this issue see Decker, 1993, and Chapter 7 in this volume.) Further, some studies have focused only on cases in which the offender is known, whereas others consider homicides with both known and unknown offenders. Especially confusing is that some homicide studies focus on rates of offending, whereas, more commonly, others focus on victimization; all too often, it is not clear which of these is the object of the research. In short, there are many ways in which the available studies are not comparable and thus difficult to analyze in a comparative manner. Given these methodological difficulties, findings about patterns in homicide at various times must be viewed as suggestive, rather than definitive.

Additional problems involving data sources include their availability at different times and biases that are specific to each source. Although these sources are discussed at length in subsequent chapters, it is worthwhile to briefly consider some of the problems that their use poses for historical analyses.

■ *DATA SOURCES FOR THE STUDY OF 20TH-CENTURY HOMICIDE TRENDS*

Two primary sources of data on homicide rates are available in published form. They are *Vital Statistics,* collected by the National Center for Health Statistics (NCHS), and the *Uniform Crime Reports* (*UCR*) compiled by the Federal Bureau of Investigation (FBI) through reports from law enforcement agencies across the United States. Neither data set is fully national prior to the early 1930s. The information provided by these sources is discussed in the sections below.

Mortality Data

Mortality data are produced by coroners' and/or medical examiners' offices that forward their results, via death certificates, to the Vital Statistics Division of the NCHS. As with law enforcement agencies, patterns and practices of the coroners' offices will affect data collected by them. For example, the coroner, an appointed or elected official, is responsible for determining cause and/or manner of death. Coroners, in contrast to medical examiners, are not required to have medical training. In some places, the only requirement for holding office is that they be of legal age to hold office. Early in the century, following late 19th-century practice, a fee-for-service system among coroners directly affected their reporting of homicides. Coroners received a set fee for each death that they investigated and for which they established cause of death. The fee paid was the same no matter how much difficulty the case involved, and the fee was, in cases of murder, often to be collected from the convicted offender. If it was likely that the offender would not be apprehended, as when a victim was found with a slit throat on the highway or if the victim was an infant, these deaths were not likely to be reported as homicides; instead, means of death was likely to be ruled as a ruptured aorta in the case of the slit throat or suffocation for the infant (Lane, 1979).

Further, the thoroughness of the investigation and detailed determination of cause of death are directly affected by the size, training, and funding of coroners' and medical examiners' staffs. Doing autopsies, as well as establishing and maintaining toxicology units, is expensive. Some offices, such as large medical examiner offices, have the necessary equipment to conduct sophisticated blood tests to determine if the cause of death is drug related or some other less obvious means. Quite simply, many smaller units cannot make such distinctions.

The factors noted above affect data collection at the local level; others affect reporting at the national level, that is, in the *Vital Statistics* reports. Changes in definition and coding have occurred. For example, if the medical examiner cannot determine whether a suspicious death is an accident or a homicide, he or she may report it as "undetermined." Prior to 1968, however, *Vital Statistics* did not allow for such a possibility. If a medical examiner was unsure, the case was assigned, through a series of complex procedures, to either the "accident" or "homicide" categories.[3] The impact of such shifts in coding schemes on homicide rates is unclear, but it is certainly plausible that such changing classification procedures add error to the data produced.

A greater problem is that states entered the national reporting system at different times. Although *Vital Statistics* data were available for some states from around 1900, they did not become fully national until the 1930s. Prior to the 1930s, the data available depended on which states and cities were included. Boston was the first entrant and, in general, there were data from East Coast cities quite early. Boston had death data in 1880, Pennsylvania in 1906, and Washington, D.C., in 1880. Other states, however, for example, Georgia and Texas, entered the registry much later, in 1922 and 1933, respectively. In establishing the national homicide trend, then, we have difficulty with obtaining national data prior to 1930 and, throughout the century, there are the data-reporting difficulties discussed earlier that affect the quality and the nature of the data. For additional discussions of this problem and attempted resolution using an econometric forecasting approach, see Eckberg (1995).

Data From Law Enforcement Agencies

Law enforcement data also have numerous problems. Review of the literature on police statistics indicates that these statistics may reflect as much about the activity and size of the police force, ability to do detective work (Hindelang, 1974; Savitz, 1978),[4] and tolerance level of the community (Center & Smith, 1973; Lane, 1979) as they do about the actual criminal phenomenon itself. For example, lack of systematic investigation may result from a law enforcement judgment that the community does not want the investigation done or from low morale because police feel that their work will not result in prosecution. It seems credible that official police data may be fairly accurate on the actual occurrence of a homicide event. We have virtually no idea, however, how many homicides go undetected and may be falsely considered accidents or death by natural causes. Our understanding of the types and motives of homicide may also be influenced by the size of the force, the connections its investigative units have to the community, the definitions of events that the department uses, and other organizational variables. Such local problems may be exacerbated when the data are gathered by the FBI and published in the *UCR*.

National-level law enforcement data began to be compiled in 1933. Those early years, however, were not inclusive of all jurisdictions and represented only portions of the United States (Savitz, 1978).[5] Furthermore, the sampling and extrapolation procedures used by the FBI were problematic and underwent a number of revisions; thus, time-series comparisons through the 1950s are not entirely reliable (see Cantor & Cohen, 1980, for a detailed analysis of these issues.[6]) Although there are numerous problems with the data at both the local and national levels, it is somewhat reassuring to note that *UCR* and *Vital Statistics* rates of homicide have been found to be reasonably similar through time and to move consistently in the same direction. It also is evident that in general, *Vital Statistics* rates are usually somewhat higher than the *UCR* for the same year. This is largely because *Vital Statistics* data use a medical definition of homicide, that is, all cases in which there is the intentional taking of another's life, whereas the *UCR* data use a legal definition ("murder and involuntary manslaughter"), that is, the willful killing of another under illegal circumstances. Consequently, justifiable homicides are included in *Vital Statistics* but are not in the *UCR*.

A major discontinuity occurs from 1933 to 1935 because of problems with the *UCR*. For this reason, this chapter presents data from the *UCR* only from 1935 to 1996. Data from *Vital Statistics* are considered highly reliable from 1933 onward, but less reliable data are available from the beginning of the century. Trends discussed in the subsequent section are based on these data sources. The discussion that follows is devoted to trends in homicide victimization.

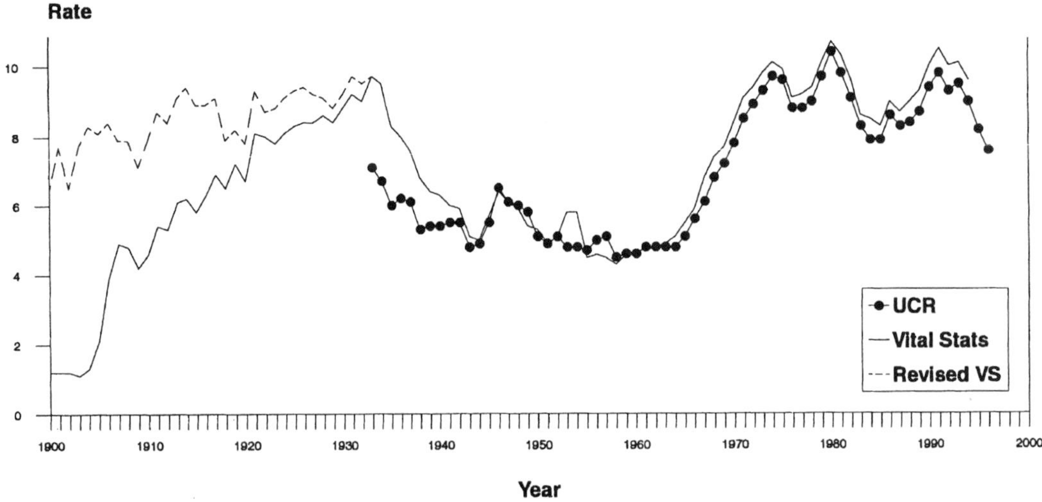

Figure 2.1. Trends in U.S. Homicide Rates, 1900 to 1996: Rates per 100,000 Population

SOURCE: Federal Bureau of Investigation, *Crime in the United States: Uniform Crime Reports* (Annual); National Center for Health Statistics, *Vital Statistics of the United States* (Annual).

■ *NATIONAL HOMICIDE TRENDS IN THE 20TH CENTURY*

Trends in national homicide victimization rates are presented in Figure 2.1. Separate rates are shown from data in the *UCR* and in *Vital Statistics.* Rates from *Vital Statistics* for 1900 to 1933, however, should be viewed with extreme caution; in particular, the exaggerated upward trend during this period is due in large measure to the entry of the high homicide rates of western and southern states into the NCHS registration system. In addition, Eckberg (1995) argues that this "false impression of dramatic increases in homicide rates" (p. 7) is a result of underreporting because most homicides were misclassified as accidental deaths. In a careful forecasting estimation procedure, Eckberg has generated revised homicide rates for 1900 to 1933. These data are based on a detailed history of U.S. death registration provided in the first volume of *Mortality Statistics* published in 1906. After adjusting the underreported early homicide counts and estimating the homicide rates for states that were not included in the registration area until 1933, Eckberg proposes that the homicide rates of the first three decades of this century portray a "moderate increase during the first five years of the century, six years of 'random walk' stability, another increase, then general stability again" (p. 12).[7]

To provide a more accurate portrayal of early homicide trends, we have included Eckberg's (1995) revised rates for 1900 to 1933 in Figure 2.1. If we compare Eckberg's estimates with the original homicide rates published by *Vital Statistics,* we see that his estimates are higher but that the trends, in general, are comparable. Both series display rates that fluctuate through time but show a general increase, peaking in 1906, 1921, and 1931. The result of this reanalysis suggests that the United States began the 20th century with homicide rates around 6 per 100,000 population, which climbed to around 9.5 per 100,000 by the 1930s.

Local studies of eastern and midwestern cities during this period also generally show increases. Sutherland and Gehlke (1933), using arrest data from Baltimore, Buffalo, Chicago, Cleveland, St. Louis, and the state of Massachusetts, found increasing homicide rates from 1900 to the late 1920s with the peak for the five cities occurring in 1928. For Massachusetts, the peak was in 1925. Overall, then, the general trends suggested by national data are confirmed by local data from several different cities.

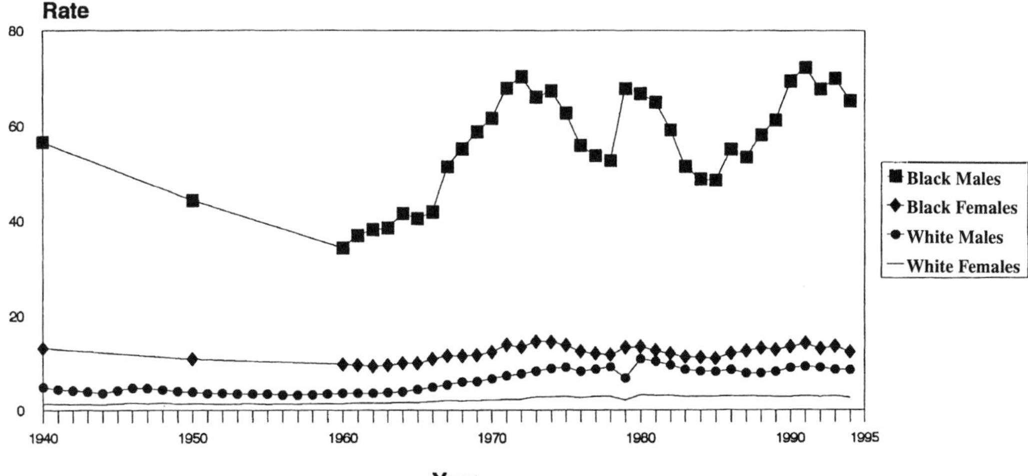

Figure 2.2. Race- and Sex-Specific Homicide Victimization Rates for Whites and Blacks From 1940 to 1994
SOURCE: National Center for Health Statistics, *Vital Statistics of the United States* (Annual).

After the mid-1930s, both mortality and law enforcement data are increasingly reliable. Together, the rates from these sources show a U-shaped trend between 1933 and 1974. The homicide rate declines through 1964, although the trend is interrupted by a short spurt of increase in the 3 years immediately after World War II. After 1964, the rate begins to rise, from 5.9 per 100,000 in 1966 (*Vital Statistics*) to 10.2 in 1974 and an all-time high of 10.7 in 1980. The national homicide rate doubled in the 20 years between the mid-1950s and 1980. Since 1980, a fluctuating trend is seen for homicide rates, dipping to 8.3 in 1985, increasing again to 10.0 in 1990, then declining until the mid-1990s. The *Uniform Crime Reports* data show the homicide rate dropping to 7.4 in 1996.[8] In summary, the highest homicide rates of the century occurred during the last two decades, whereas the lowest rates appeared in the late 1950s.

Trends in Race and Sex Patterns of Homicide

When homicide rates are disaggregated by race and sex as seen in Figure 2.2,[9] we find that the changes occurring in recent years have not affected all population groups equally. Although Black males continue to have much higher rates than other groups, the victimization rate for Black males (and females) has actually decreased since the 1970s and into the 1980s, whereas the rates for White males and females have been increasing. Since the mid-1980s, however, the rates for Black males have climbed dramatically to a high of 72 per 100,000 Black males. Along with Black male victimization rates, Black female victimization rates have steadily increased; although much lower than rates for Black males, their rates range between approximately 11 and 14.5 (per 100,000 Black females) from the mid-1970s into the 1990s. White male and female homicide victimization rates also increased from 1960 until 1980; at approximately 11 and 3 homicides per 100,000 males and females, respectively, these rates were the highest levels since race and gender figures have been systematically recorded. The victimization rates for all four groups have maintained these relatively high and stable rates since 1980, although Black male victimization trends have shown more fluctuation.[10]

Trends in Age Patterns of Homicide

When we disaggregate the homicide victimization rates by age, we discover some startling

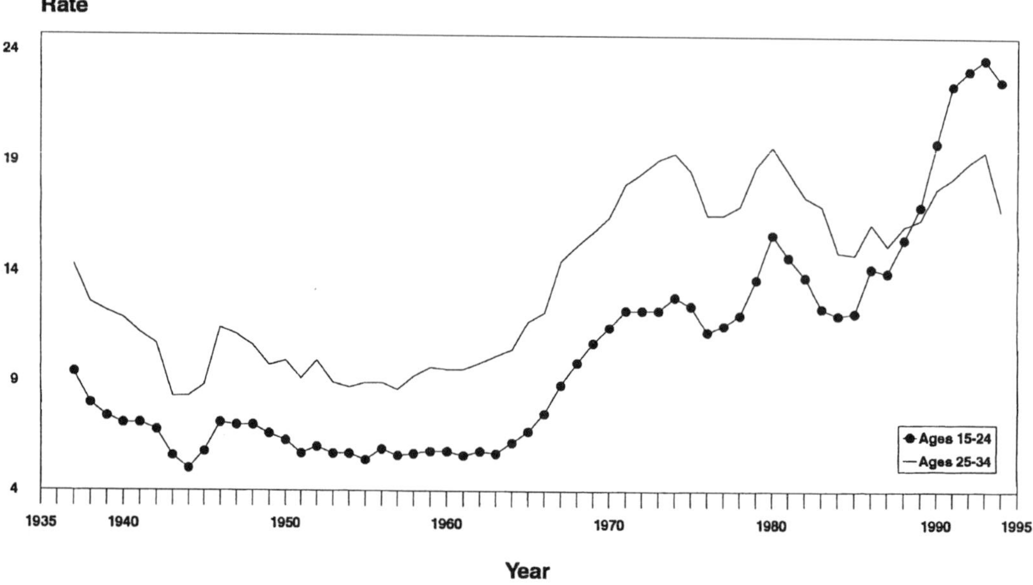

Figure 2.3. Homicide Victimization Rates for Ages 15 to 24 and 25 to 34 From 1937 to 1994
SOURCE: National Center for Health Statistics, *Vital Statistics of the United States* (Annual).

patterns. As can be seen in Figure 2.3, the rates for most age groups declined during the 1990s; victimization rates for the age groups 15 to 24 and 25 to 34, however, continued to climb. Traditionally, these two age groups have homicide rates substantially above the national rate, although the rate for 15- to 24-year-olds has been 4 to 6 homicides per 100,000 lower than that for the 25- to 34-year-old youths. Both groups' homicide victimization rates are shown to steadily increase since 1985, but surprisingly, the rate for the 15- to 24-year-old youths converges with and then surpasses the older group's rate in 1989. By 1993, the homicide rate for 15- to 24-year-olds was approximately 23.5 (per 100,000 persons in that age group) and 19.5 for 25- to 34-year-olds. This shift in the age structure of homicide may be one of the most significant changes in the demographics of homicide during this century. For an in-depth discussion of youth homicide and the factors associated with it, see Chapter 15 by Kathleen Heide. An additional commentary can be found in Blumstein (1995).

■ *TRENDS IN HOMICIDE TYPES*

Although the description of changing rates is important, knowledge of the relationships that spawn homicide in different eras and of the circumstances that trigger them tells us more about the social organization of homicide than rates can. Unfortunately, data on victim-offender relationship and motive for the homicide are particularly difficult to obtain and to interpret. This is caused by a lack of definitional consistency between studies and also because the motive for a homicidal event and the interpretation of the circumstances surrounding it are often attributions made by officials, usually police, rather than actual descriptions by participants. Nonetheless, studies that provide description of the participants, their relationship to each other, and some attributed reasons for the lethal violence will tell us something about the nature of homicides and how they change through time. The following discussion of types of homicides through time is based on both

UCR data from 1963 to 1996 and an analysis of major studies done in the respective periods.

Homicide: 1900 to the 1930s

Because there were no national data on victim-offender relationships prior to 1963, an analysis of victim-offender types relies solely on specific studies until that time. Two major studies of early 20th-century homicide, one by H. C. Brearley (1932) and the other by Frederick Hoffman (1925), found a steady increase in homicide rates from 5.0 in 1906 to 8.5 in 1929. Higher victimization rates existed among Blacks, among the young, and among men. The South and its northern neighbors (Ohio and West Virginia) had the highest rates, whereas the New England states and the northern part of the Midwest had the lowest. The majority (71.5%) of homicides were committed with a gun, with the general tendency being toward an increase in the use of guns throughout the early 1900s.[11]

As to types of motives, only Boudouris's study (1970) of Detroit homicides from 1926 to 1968 and Lashly's (1929) description of Chicago homicides consider this issue for this early period. Boudouris found that Detroit in the late 1920s had a higher homicide rate than any of the other periods he studied. He classified victim-offender relationships into (a) domestic and love affairs; (b) friends and acquaintances; (c) business relationship, for example, landlord-tenant and prostitute-pimp; (d) criminal transaction, that is, homicide resulting from violation of the law, for example, bootlegging; (e) noncriminal, that is, killing of a felon by police or private citizen; (f) cultural-recreational-casual; (g) subcultural-recreational-casual; (h) other; and (i) unknown. Boudouris found that for 1926 to 1933, the largest percentages of homicides were listed as justifiable (noncriminal), that is, killings of felons by police officers or killings by private citizens that were ruled as self-defense.

Aside from justifiable homicides, Boudouris (1970) found almost equal proportions of homicide involving domestic relations (18.2%), friends and acquaintances (18.2%), and criminal transactions (16.6%). Of the criminal transaction homicides during 1926 to 1934, 30.1% (71 of 236) were related to gang wars to control bootlegging (Prohibition was repealed in 1933). An additional 18 homicides were police killed in the line of duty, often in the process of enforcing Prohibition law.

Lashly's (1929) analysis of 883 homicides in Chicago for 1926 to 1927 showed a similar pattern. As in Detroit, a large percentage of homicides during this period were justifiable. Although the Chicago data do not separate out criminal transactions as a type of homicide, the data do suggest that when "justifiables" are removed from the analysis, the two major categories of homicide were gang and criminal related (approximately 33.3%) and altercations and brawls (30.4%). Domestic homicides were infrequent, appearing as only 8.3% of the total.[12]

These two sources suggest that there was not one modal type of urban homicide during the first third of the century. Friends or acquaintances often killed each other in arguments; homicides resulting from criminal transactions and those considered justifiable—both assumedly related to bootlegging and enforcement of Prohibition[13]—were of equal, if not greater importance, however, in at least two large cities. The importance of family-related homicides varied with the city studied, being almost as common as criminal and friend homicides in Detroit but of lesser importance in Chicago.

Homicide: The 1940s and 1950s

A number of studies of this period examined the relationships in which people were killed in both southern and northern cities, including Birmingham (Harlan, 1950), Houston (Bullock, 1955), Cleveland (Bensing & Schroeder, 1970), Detroit (Boudouris, 1970, 1974), and Wolfgang's (1958) classic study of Philadelphia. All these studies show that domestic and love-related homicides became a more important category than in the preceding years, whereas males killing males in quarrelsome situations continued to be an important form of homicide. In contrast, homicides related to criminal transactions decreased to a small percentage.

One of the major research efforts during this period was Harlan's (1950) study of homicide in Birmingham, Alabama. In an analysis of 500 cases of criminal homicide from 1937 to 1944, he found that the majority of the victims were Black males (67.8%) and that the modal type of homicide was a Black man killing another Black man while arguing in a private residence. Arguments (for example, about gambling or money) were the prime circumstance surrounding homicides in Birmingham; marital discord, jealousy, and quarrels over lovers ranked next in frequency as the basis for murder.

Bullock (1955), using police records for the 489 cases of criminal homicide in Houston during 1945 to 1949, found the highest rates of homicide to be clustered among low-income, Black, and Hispanic persons, 67% of whom were laborers and domestic servants. The homicides occurred most frequently between people who knew each other (in 87% of the cases, the victim and offender were acquainted with each other), and arguments were the prime precipitating factors. Bullock did not indicate the number killed in domestic quarrels but reports that marital discord was the third most important reason for death. The three most frequent patterns precipitating homicide were (a) arguments originating from a variety of situations, (b) love triangles and jealousy between friends, and (c) marital discord. The most frequent place of death was a rooming house (42.1% of the victims were killed there), followed by a tavern (28.6%) and the street (21.1%).

In the northern cities of Cleveland and Detroit, a similar pattern prevailed. Using 662 cases of homicide from 1947 to 1953 in Cleveland, Bensing and Schroeder (1970) found that the majority of homicides involved Black males who knew each other. In only 4.5% of the cases were the victim and offender unknown to each other. Although Bensing and Schroeder's study does not specify the predominant motive for homicide, they do list these three circumstances as important: (a) quarrels of a petty nature, (b) marital discord, and (c) love or sex disputes in which the deceased was slain by someone other than a spouse or common-law mate.

The importance of marital and love disputes is further documented in Boudouris's (1970, 1974) study of Detroit. Analysis of his data shows the 1940s and especially the 1950s to be a time when domestic relations and love affairs claimed most of the homicide deaths. Recomputing his data to combine domestic relations and love affairs into one category, we find that in the 1920s, 21.9% of the homicides were domestically related, a figure that rose to 29.3% in the 1930s, to 32.6% in the 1940s, and to a high of 38.4% in the 1950s.[14] Friend and acquaintance homicides were consistently second to domestic and love homicides in Detroit during the 1940s and 1950s.

Wolfgang's (1958) research further demonstrates the importance of close relationships in homicide during this era. He examined all 588 criminal homicides that occurred in Philadelphia from 1948 to 1952, relying primarily on police records that included investigation reports of the police homicide unit, witnesses' statements, and the like. The data for this period indicated an overall criminal homicide rate of 5.7 per 100,000. When age, race, and age-specific homicide rates were compared, however, the rates of Blacks and males were found to be considerably greater than for Whites and females; Black males had a rate of 36.9 per 100,000, Black females 9.6, White males 2.9, and White females 1.0. Those aged 25 to 34 were the most likely to be victims, whereas offenders were most likely to be in the 20 to 24 age group. Regarding homicide settings, Wolfgang found that the predominant place in which homicides occurred was inside a home (50.5% of the victims were slain there).

Wolfgang (1958) classified homicide cases both by victim-offender relationships and by motive recorded by the police for the slaying. Regarding victim-offender relationships, 25% of the homicides occurred within the family, with an additional 10% involving sexual intimates who were not family members; 42% occurred between acquaintances and/or close friends; and only 12% involved people who

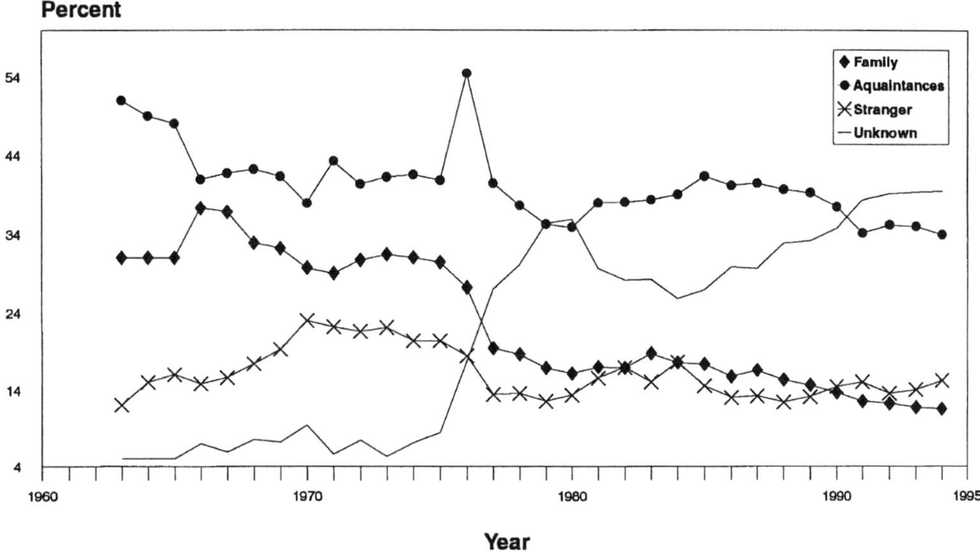

Figure 2.4. Homicide in Four Types of Victim-Offender Relationships as a Percentage of All Homicides Between 1963 and 1994

SOURCE: Federal Bureau of Investigation, *Crime in the United States: Uniform Crime Reports* (Annual).

were strangers to each other. The most common motives recorded by police included altercations of a "relatively trivial origin" (35.0%), domestic quarrels (14.1%), jealousy (11.6%), and altercations about money (10.5%). Robbery accounted for only 6.8% of homicides; revenge, for another 5.3%.

In sum, the 1940s and (especially) 1950s were a time with a relatively low and stable homicide rate. It was a time, further, when two types of murder seemed most prevalent, that between family members—usually husband and wife or lovers—and that between two males known to each other who were involved in an argument. In some cities, the family and love relationship murder was predominant, whereas in other places, deadly arguments between males were more frequent. But in all instances, these two types were the dominant ones and, unlike an earlier period, the family and love relationship murder became a more dominant form.

Homicide: The 1960s to the 1990s

Homicide types from the 1960s through the 1990s have been studied in a variety of ways; these analyses have included in-depth studies of different homicide types in single cities (e.g., Block, 1974, 1977; Lundsgaarde, 1977), studies of different types in multiple cities (e.g., Curtis, 1974; Riedel & Zahn, 1985), and in-depth studies of selected types of homicide such as drug related, gang related, stranger robbery, or spousal homicide.[15]

For this chapter, we analyzed *UCR* data from 1963 to 1995, classifying homicides into four general categories—family, acquaintance, stranger, and unknown. As indicated in Figure 2.4, throughout most of the last 30 years, acquaintance homicides dominated, varying from a high of 51% of homicides in 1963 to a low of 32% in 1995. The percentage of homicides involving acquaintances, although always a major category, dropped during the 30 years and, since 1990, has been superseded in national figures by those of unknown relationship. In addition to a decline in the percentage of acquaintance homicides, there has been a steep decline in family-related homicides from 31% of the total in 1963 to 11% in 1995.[16] Also, the percentage of homicides with known offenders—and thus, knowledge of the victim-offender relationship—has declined; indeed, there has

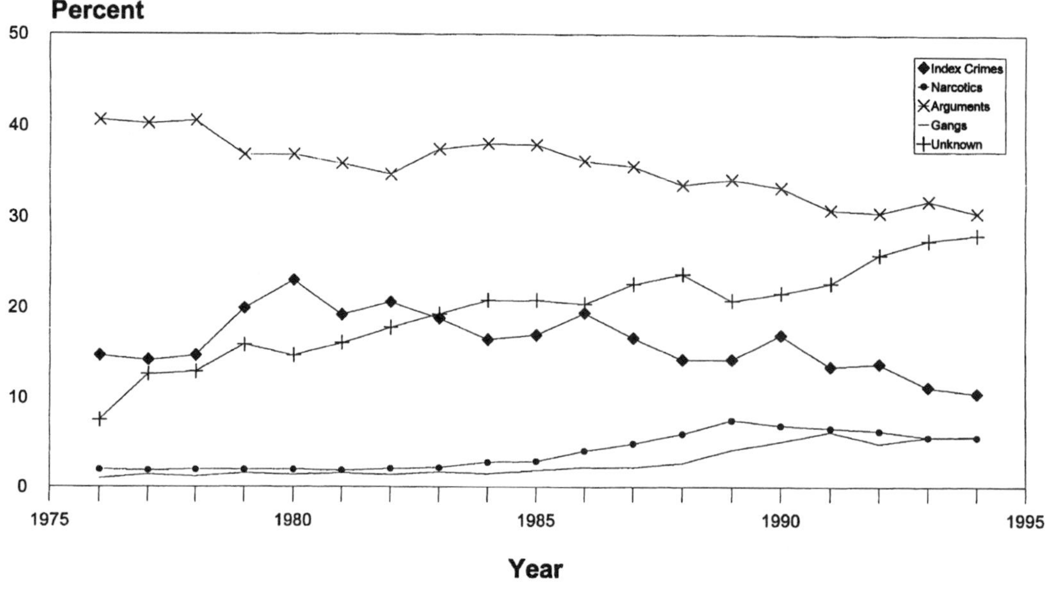

Figure 2.5. Homicides in Five Types of Circumstances as a Percentage of All Homicides Between 1976 and 1994

SOURCE: Federal Bureau of Investigation, *Crime in the United States: Uniform Crime Reports* (Annual).
NOTE: Index crimes include rape, robbery, and burglary.

been a pronounced increase in "unknown" relationships from 6% in 1963 to 39% in 1995. Individual city studies, using direct police-level data, confirm the general trends of decreasing family homicides and increasing unknowns, although in many of these studies (Curtis, 1974; Decker, 1993; Riedel & Zahn, 1985), the percentage of unknowns is smaller, sometimes substantially so, than that reported for those cities by the FBI.

In addition to relationship, we also classified homicides according to the circumstance surrounding the event. For reasons that will be discussed below, classifying homicides in this manner can be problematic, but we have attempted to group homicides into five general categories to analyze broad trends in these types. The types into which homicides have been categorized are (a) arguments; (b) those related to the commission of the index crimes of rape, robbery, and burglary; (c) narcotics related; (d) gang related; and (e) homicides with unknown origins. Trends through time in the distribution of these types of homicides are displayed in Figure 2.5. Throughout the 30 years, arguments remained the dominant precipitating event, although dropping in proportion during the period. The second most common precipitating factor in the 1970s and early 1980s was homicides associated with other felonies, especially robbery. These have become supplanted since 1983 by homicides occurring for unknown reasons (but see note 16). Given the attention afforded the issue, it is interesting that although narcotics-related homicides increased from 1985 to 1995, in no year did these types of homicides equal more than 6% of the total number of homicides in the country. Similarly, although gang-related homicides increased from 1988 to 1995, they also represent only a small fraction of U.S. homicides in any given year.

Supplemental Homicide Reports

One of the important developments during this period was the emergence of a new source of national-level homicide data. Beginning in 1961, the FBI began to collect annual data on homicides; this effort was termed the Supplemental Homicide Reports (SHR). Included in the data are relationship and circumstances for each homicide that has been reported to the FBI. These were the data used in the analyses and illustrative figures that have been discussed above.

Although problems with SHR data will be discussed in detail in other chapters (see especially Chapters 6 and 7), it is worth noting here some of the issues facing researchers who work with this source of information. One shortcoming is that events having multiple victims or offenders have relationship and circumstance codes that reflect only the first, arbitrarily selected, victim and offender combination. For example, in an event in which a woman kills her children and husband, the code of "son" may be listed for all victims. For this reason, SHR research is often limited to those cases involving a single offender with a single victim (e.g., Messner & Golden, 1992; Peterson & Krivo, 1993; Williams & Flewelling, 1988).

Another problem with the SHR program is that it is voluntary; thus, agencies may not submit monthly reports. Chicago, for example, did not submit its supplemental information at all during 1984 and 1985 and provided data for only 1 month in 1987, 6 months in 1990, and 9 months in 1986 (Williams & Flewelling, 1987).

The final problem to be mentioned here involves the consistency—or lack thereof—of definitions across law enforcement agencies. The potential for different interpretations of the circumstance and relationship in homicide events is significant. Given the number of agencies submitting information and the range of options available with respect to these variables, it is likely that classifications of "brawl under the influence of alcohol" in one jurisdiction, for example, may be coded as an "argument over money" in another. The circumstances codes are not strictly mutually exclusive and may be used differently across jurisdictions or even within agencies as different personnel maintain reporting responsibilities through time. Coupled with a general overuse of the circumstance category "other," such definitional confusion may lead to serious misrepresentations of the patterns and correlates of homicide events on a national basis. For these reasons, in-depth city studies using primary data collection remain a major data source whereby detailed and potentially accurate descriptions of specific types of homicide can be generated.

City-Level Studies

For 1960 to 1990, several major multicity studies focus on homicide relationship types (e.g., Curtis, 1974; Lattimore, Trudeau, Riley, Leiter, & Edwards, 1997; Riedel & Zahn, 1985). A variety of single-city studies also do so. Among cities studied, three have been the sites of extensive research—Chicago (Block, 1974), St. Louis (Decker, 1993; Rosenfeld, 1997), and Philadelphia (Riedel & Zahn, 1985; Zahn, 1997). Each of these will be discussed below.

As in preceding decades, researchers failed to use standard categorization schemes for data on victim-offender relationship or for circumstances precipitating the event. Two major multicity studies, however, do allow for comparison. A study using police records in eight cities in 1978 (Riedel & Zahn, 1985) found there was substantial intercity variation as to prevalence of types of homicide. Nevertheless, in all cities, acquaintance homicide was the most frequent type, followed by stranger homicide, with family homicide the least frequent. Further, approximately one fourth (25%) of homicides were felony related, with robbery being the most frequent felony link.

A decade later, a study sponsored by the National Institute of Justice (Lattimore et al., 1997), using a different set of eight cities—Atlanta, Detroit, Indianapolis, Miami, New Orleans, Richmond, Tampa, and Washington, D.C.—again found a great deal of between-city variation. Concentrating on 1985 to 1994, their general findings included a reduction in the number of female victims, a continuing predominance of Black male victims, and an increasing rate of offending for young men. Although not all eight cities showed decreases in intimate family homicides, most did. Some cities showed increases in homicides associated with crack cocaine use; perceptions of city officials regarding the relationship between drug use and homicide, however, often varied substantially from actual drug trends. Gangs were not linked to homicide in any significant way in any of the eight cities during the study.

Individual cities have also been studied extensively during the 1960 to 1990 time frame. The Chicago homicide data set is the largest, most detailed data set available for any individual city. On the basis of a number of analyses from this project (e.g., Block, 1974, 1977; Block & Christakos, 1995a, 1995b), from 1965 to 1990, the dominant relationship type of homicide in Chicago was "acquaintance" for every year except 1970 and 1987. From 1991 to 1995, the dominant type of relationship became the "unknown" relationship or "mystery" category. Mystery or unknown relationship as a type increased tremendously, going from 5% in 1965 to 25% in 1995 and, as of 1991, became the dominant type of relationship between victim and offender.

Spousal homicide decreased from 23% in 1965 to 6% in 1995, while child-parent and other family relationships remained stable during this period. The "friends" category also experienced some major changes in the past three decades, decreasing from a high of 16% in 1966 to 3% in 1995. Further, "rival gang" homicide increased substantially from 1.5% in 1965 to 20% of homicides in 1995; "illegal business" also rose sharply and remained high from 1988 to 1994, although decreasing significantly in 1995. Finally, homicide between strangers increased as a proportion of homicides in the 1970s and early 1980s. Since 1987, however, the proportion has returned to previous levels.

Overall, the trends of homicide relationships in Chicago from 1965 to 1995 seem to be away from intimate or personal relationships to more informal relationships or unknown relationships. Spousal, friend, and acquaintance homicides have decreased in importance, whereas the homicide categories of rival gangs, illegal business, and unknown relationships have become more prominent.

Although types varied, the homicide victimization rate by race/ethnicity revealed a consistent picture. The non-Latino White victimization rate was by far the lowest and remained stable from 1970 to 1993 (Block, 1993). The Latino rate was consistently higher than the non-Latino White rate. The Latino rate peaked in 1979 when it nearly approached the non-Latino Black rate. The non-Latino Black rate was by far the highest, a situation that has not changed.

Like the Chicago data set, the St. Louis homicide project has continuing data collection from police records that stem from 1960 to the present. In victim-offender relationship type, acquaintance homicide remained the dominant type, with stranger homicide a strong second type, accounting for approximately a fourth of homicide in all periods. The major change in frequency of homicide types was the drop in marital partner homicide, a drop that was particularly substantial for African American men and women as well as for White men (Rosenfeld, 1997).

Decker (1993), when cross-tabulating motives with victim-offender relationship type, found *expressive* motives dominant in 53% of all homicides, whereas 47% were of an *instrumental* quality (i.e., to gain material advantage). Changes in motives through time were not investigated, although given the strong association between expressive motivation and family or intimate partner homicide, one might expect some decline in expressive homicides through time.

On the basis of data collected for 1980 to 1994 (Zahn, 1997), acquaintance homicide in Philadelphia remained the dominant form, claiming, on average, 47% of the deaths in that city. This was followed by unknowns and stranger events, each accounting for 20% of deaths in each of the 14 years. Only family homicides showed a trend during this period, with family homicides decreasing from 16% of all homicides in 1980 to 11% in 1994.

With regard to circumstances surrounding the event, drug-related homicides were rare in Philadelphia in 1978 (7% of victims had drugs in their systems at time of death; see Riedel & Zahn, 1985) but increased greatly in the late 1980s and into the 1990s. Eleven percent of the homicides were drug related in 1980, compared with 21% in 1990. Domestic homicide decreased from 13% to 7%, and argument homicide decreased from 40% to 29%. Victims of a felony increased slightly from 15% to 18%, but at no time in the 1980s and 1990s was the victimization during a felony (usually a robbery) as great as in 1978 when it accounted for 25%

of all homicides in Philadelphia (Riedel & Zahn, 1985).

Taken together, the major city studies show considerable variation in their findings, indicating that homicide is strongly influenced by local events. Nevertheless, some commonalities can be detected; in particular, all three cities showed a decrease in spousal killings from the 1960s to 1990s and a continuation of young male acquaintance homicide as a dominant type of homicide.

■ *SUMMARY*

A review of homicide trends for the 20th-century United States shows that the highest rates have occurred during the last two decades, whereas the lowest rates occurred in the 1950s. Throughout this entire period, young Black males have had much higher levels of victimization than other groups. In the most pronounced shift in trends, victims became younger toward the end of the century, with 15- to 24-year-olds becoming the group most at risk of homicide victimization.

Although it is difficult to accurately assess homicide types and precipitating circumstances for such a long period, it appears that arguments between young males is a dominant type of circumstance through time. Family homicides, particularly spouse homicides, seem to have proportionately decreased as a specific type, especially in the last part of the century (but see Chapter 10 for discussion of an increase in nonmarital, intimate relationship homicides). At some specific times and in specific locales, drug- and/or robbery-related homicides increase as a percentage of the total. Gang-related homicides, although rare in the national picture, tend to affect only certain cities such as Los Angeles or Chicago (see Chapter 16 for an extensive discussion of gang homicides).

The purpose of this chapter has been to sensitize readers to both the continuities and changes in patterns of homicide in the United States during the 20th century. The remaining chapters in this book attempt to answer many of the questions that arise regarding the causes of these patterns and the reasons for their change.

■ *NOTES*

1. This chapter is a substantial revision and update of earlier chapters; "Homicide in the Twentieth Century United States" originally appeared in Inciardi and Faupel (1980) and later as "Homicide in the Twentieth Century United States: Trends, Types and Causes" in Gurr (1989).

2. This difference is at least partially attributable to differences in data sources. In the 1920s, *Vital Statistics* data on causes of death were used for national homicide studies; this source includes justifiable homicides within the overall homicide statistic. Law enforcement data (e.g., *Uniform Crime Reports*), which are used more frequently in later studies, do not include justifiable homicide under the category of murder and nonnegligent manslaughter.

3. Information regarding this classification change was obtained from a telephone conversation with the former head of the Mortality Unit of Vital Statistics. His name was not recorded.

4. See Savitz (1978) and Hindelang (1974).

5. This article and other sources indicate that the number of police agencies cooperating in the voluntary UCR Program has changed through time from 400 in 1930 to 8,500 in 1968, the latter representing 92% of the national population. Consequently, national data are not available from police sources until well after the 1930s, which makes establishing the homicide trend for the early part of the century difficult.

6. Cantor and Cohen (1980), who compared the two measures on homicide for 1933 to 1975, conclude that the two time series are highly correlated ($r = .97$) from 1936 to 1973.

7. We thank Douglas Eckberg for permitting us to incorporate his estimates into our figure of homicide trends.

8. A paper presented by Blumstein and Rosenfeld (1998) suggests that on the basis of UCR trends during the first half of 1997, the rate for 1997 will drop to about 6.7.

9. Race, age, and sex-specific homicide rates are available only from *Vital Statistics,* and, as of this printing, the latest available figures are for 1994.

10. These differences also are analyzed by Farley (1980), Klebba (1975), and O'Carroll and Mercy (1986).

11. Gun homicide data are from Brearley (1932, p. 68).

12. For detailed analysis of the Chicago data, see Arthur V. Lashly (1929). Also, see a reanalysis of Chicago data by Block and Block (1980).

13. For a discussion of how violence became associated with bootlegging, see Haller (1989).

14. Data for the 1920s do not encompass a whole decade but only 1926 to 1929. All figures represent an average of the percentages.

15. Many studies have been done on types of homicide in the past 30 years. Illustrations of drug-related homicide studies include Brownstein and Goldstein (1990); Goldstein (1989); Goldstein, Bellucci, Spunt, and Miller (1991); Zahn and Bencivengo (1973); and Zahn and Snodgrass (1978); gang homicides, Maxson and Klein (1990); and spousal homicide, Browne and Williams (1993) and Wilson and Daly (1992). As well, an entire issue of *Journal of Criminal*

Law and Criminology (Riedel, 1987) was devoted to stranger violence; see especially Zahn and Sagi (1987). For examples of studies dealing with robbery murders, see Block (1977), Cook (1983, 1987), and Zimring (1979).

16. The apparent trend of an increase in the proportion of unknown offenders should be viewed with caution. Many aspects of homicide cases may be originally coded by law enforcement agencies as "unknown" because those cases had not yet been cleared—that is, no arrests had been made by the end of the reporting year. If arrests are made in later years, however, details of the case are not corrected in the earlier reports. Thus, in any given year, the actual proportion of cases in which the offender (and thus, other aspects of the case) *remains unknown* may be considerably lower than the proportion of cases originally coded as unknown. See Decker (1993) and Riedel (1998) for further discussions of what may be an erroneous sense of a significant increase in uncleared cases.

■ *REFERENCES*

Bensing, R. C., & Schroeder, O., Jr. (1970). *Homicide in an urban community.* Springfield, IL: Charles C Thomas.

Block, C. R. (1993). Lethal violence in the Chicago Latino community. In A. V. Wilson (Ed.), *Homicide: The victim/offender connection* (pp. 267-342). Cincinnati, OH: Anderson.

Block, C. R., & Block, R. L. (1980). *Patterns of change in Chicago homicide: The twenties, the sixties, and the seventies.* Chicago: Statistical Analysis Center, Illinois Law Enforcement Commission.

Block, C. R., & Christakos, A. (1995a). Intimate partner homicide in Chicago over 29 years. *Crime & Delinquency, 41,* 496-526.

Block, C. R., & Christakos, A. (1995b). *Major trends in Chicago homicide: 1965-1994* (Research Bulletin). Chicago: Illinois Criminal Justice Information Authority.

Block, R. L. (1974, November). *Homicide in Chicago: A ten-year study, 1965-1974.* Paper presented at the annual meeting of the American Society of Criminology, Chicago.

Block, R. L. (1977). *Violent crime.* Lexington, MA: Lexington Books.

Blumstein, A. (1995). Youth violence, guns, and the illicit-drug industry. *Journal of Criminal Law and Criminology, 86,* 10-36.

Blumstein, A., & Rosenfeld, R. L. (1998, March). *Explaining recent trends in U.S. homicide rates.* Paper presented at Conference on Decreasing Crime Rates, Northwestern University Law School, Evanston, IL.

Boudouris, J. (1970). *Trends in homicide: Detroit, 1926-1968.* Unpublished doctoral dissertation, Wayne State University, Detroit, MI.

Boudouris, J. (1974). A classification of homicides. *Criminology, 11,* 525-540.

Brearley, H. C. (1932). *Homicide in the United States.* Chapel Hill: University of North Carolina Press.

Browne, A., & Williams, K. R. (1993). Gender, intimacy, and lethal violence: Trends from 1976 through 1987. *Gender & Society, 7,* 78-98.

Brownstein, H. H., & Goldstein, P. (1990). Research and the development of public policy: The case of drugs and violent crime. *Journal of Applied Sociology, 7,* 77-92.

Bullock, H. A. (1955). Urban homicide in theory and fact. *Journal of Criminal Law, Criminology and Police Science, 45,* 565-575.

Cantor, D., & Cohen, L. E. (1980). Comparing measures of homicide trends: Methodological and substantive differences in the Vital Statistics and Uniform Crime Report time series (1933-1975). *Social Science Research, 9,* 121-145.

Center, L. J., & Smith, T. G. (1973). Criminal statistics: Can they be trusted? *American Criminal Law Review, 11,* 1046-1086.

Cook, P. J. (1983). *Robbery in the United States: An analysis of recent trends and patterns.* Washington, DC: National Institute of Justice.

Cook, P. J. (1987). Robbery violence. *Journal of Criminal Law and Criminology, 78,* 357-376.

Curtis, L. A. (1974). *Criminal violence.* Lexington, MA: Lexington Books.

Decker, S. (1993). Exploring victim-offender relationship in homicide: The role of individual and event characteristics. *Justice Quarterly, 10,* 585-612.

Eckberg, D. (1995). Estimates of early twentieth-century U.S. homicide rates: An econometric forecasting approach. *Demography, 32,* 1-16.

Farley, R. (1980). Homicide trends in the United States. *Demography, 17,* 179-188.

Federal Bureau of Investigation. (Annual). *Crime in the United States: Uniform crime reports.* Washington, DC: Government Printing Office.

Goldstein, P. J. (1989). Drugs and violent crime. In N. A. Weiner & M. E. Wolfgang (Eds.), *Pathways to criminal violence* (pp. 16-48). Newbury Park, CA: Sage.

Goldstein, P. J., Bellucci, P. A., Spunt, B. J., & Miller, T. (1991). Volume of cocaine use and violence: A comparison between men and women. *Journal of Drug Issues, 21,* 345-367.

Gurr, T. (Ed.). (1989). *Violence in America: Vol. 1. The history of crime.* Newbury Park, CA: Sage.

Haller, M. H. (1989). Bootlegging: The business and politics of violence. In T. Gurr (Ed.), *Violence in America: Vol. 1. The history of crime* (pp. 146-162). Newbury Park, CA: Sage.

Harlan, H. (1950). Five hundred homicides. *Journal of Criminal Law, Criminology and Police Science, 40,* 736-752.

Hindelang, M. (1974). The Uniform Crime Reports revisited. *Journal of Criminal Justice, 2,* 1-17.

Hoffman, F. (1925). *The homicide problem.* San Francisco: Prudential Press.

Inciardi, J. A., & Faupel, C. E. (Eds.). (1980). *History and crime: Implications for criminal justice policy.* Beverly Hills, CA: Sage.

Klebba, A. (1975). Homicide trends in the United States, 1900-1974. *Public Health Reports, 90,* 195-204.

Lane, R. (1979). *Violent death in the city: Suicide, accident, and murder in nineteenth century Philadelphia.* Cambridge, MA: Harvard University Press.

Lashly, A. V. (1929). Homicide (in Cook County). In J. H. Wigmore (Ed.), *The Illinois crime survey* (pp. 589-640). Chicago: Illinois Association for Criminal Justice and Chicago Crime Commission.

Lattimore, P. K., Trudeau, J., Riley, K. J., Leiter, J., & Edwards, S. (1997). *Homicide in eight U.S. cities: Trends, context, and policy implications* (NCJ-167262). Washington, DC: U.S. Department of Justice.

Lundsgaarde, H. P. (1977). *Murder in space city.* New York: Oxford University Press.

Maxson, C. L., & Klein, M. W. (1990). Street gang violence: Twice as great, or half as great? In C. R. Huff (Ed.), *Gangs in America* (pp. 71-100). Newbury Park, CA: Sage.

Messner, S. F., & Golden, R. M. (1992). Racial inequality and racially disaggregated homicide rates: An assessment of alternative theoretical explanations. *Criminology, 30,* 421-447.

National Center for Health Statistics. (Annual). *Vital statistics of the United States* (Vol. 2: Mortality, Pt. A). Washington, DC: Government Printing Office.

O'Carroll, P. W., & Mercy, J. A. (1986). Patterns and recent trends in Black homicide. In D. F. Hawkins (Ed.), *Homicide among Black Americans* (pp. 29-42). Lanham, MD: University Press of America.

Peterson, R. D., & Krivo, L. J. (1993). Racial segregation and Black urban homicide. *Social Forces, 71,* 1001-1026.

Riedel, M. (1998). Counting stranger homicides: A case study of statistical prestidigitation. *Homicide Studies, 2,* 206-219.

Riedel, M. (Ed.). (1987). Symposium on stranger violence: Perspectives, issues, and problems [Special issue]. *Journal of Criminal Law and Criminology, 78*(2).

Riedel, M., & Zahn, M. A. (1985). *National Institute of Justice research report: The nature and patterns of American homicide.* Washington, DC: Government Printing Office.

Rosenfeld, R. L. (1997). Changing relationships between men and women: A note on the decline in intimate partner homicide. *Homicide Studies, 1,* 72-83.

Savitz, L. D. (1978). Official police statistics and their limitations. In L. D. Savitz & N. Johnston (Eds.), *Crime in society* (pp. 69-82). New York: John Wiley.

Sutherland, E. H., & Gehlke, C. E. (1933). Crime and punishment. In W. C. Mitchell (Ed.), *Recent social trends in the United States* (pp. 1114-1167). New York: McGraw-Hill.

Williams, K. R., & Flewelling, R. L. (1987). Family, acquaintance, and stranger homicide: Alternative procedures for rate calculations. *Criminology, 25,* 543-560.

Williams, K. R., & Flewelling, R. L. (1988). The social production of criminal homicide: A comparative study of disaggregated rates in American cities. *American Sociological Review, 53,* 421-431.

Wilson, M. I., & Daly, M. (1992). Who kills whom in spouse killings? On the exceptional sex ratio of spousal homicides in the United States. *Criminology, 30,* 189-215.

Wolfgang, M. E. (1958). *Patterns in criminal homicide.* Philadelphia: University of Pennsylvania Press.

Zahn, M. A. (1997, November). *Changing patterns of homicide and social policy.* Paper presented at the annual meeting of the American Society of Criminology, San Diego.

Zahn, M. A., & Bencivengo, M. (1973). Violent death: A comparison between drug users and non-drug users. *Addictive Diseases, 1,* 183-296.

Zahn, M. A., & Sagi, P. C. (1987). Stranger homicides in nine American cities. *Journal of Criminal Law and Criminology, 78,* 377-397.

Zahn, M. A., & Snodgrass, G. (1978). Drug use and the structure of homicide in two U.S. cities. In E. Flynn & J. Conrad (Eds.), *The new and old criminology* (pp. 134-150). New York: Praeger.

Zimring, F. (1979). Determinants of the death rate from robbery: A Detroit time study. In H. M. Rose (Ed.), *Lethal aspects of urban violence* (pp. 31-50). Lexington, MA: Lexington Books.

PART II

Social Theories of Homicide

CHAPTER 3

Social Structure and Homicide

Theory and Research

Steven F. Messner & Richard Rosenfeld

This chapter describes social-structural approaches to the study of homicide, distinguishes them from cultural approaches, and reviews key research on the structural sources of lethal violence. The structural perspective is based on the premise that the killings of one person by another are not simply idiosyncratic, individual acts of violence. Rather, they are "social facts" that are distributed in patterned ways.[1] Our description of structural approaches situates them within a broader conception of social organization. Within this conceptual framework, we subdivide structural influences on homicide into two basic types: (a) *control influences*—structural weaknesses or ruptures that free or release people to engage in violence, and (b) *strain influences*—structural forces that push or pressure persons into violence.[2]

We begin by describing the concept of social organization and its attendant components and explaining the theoretical linkages of this concept to homicide. Next, we review theory and research on the major structural correlates of homicide—class, gender, race, and age. The chapter concludes with a brief discussion of important issues for future research on homicide and social organization.

THE COMPONENTS OF SOCIAL ORGANIZATION AND STRUCTURAL THEORIES OF HOMICIDE

Social structure is commonly understood as one of the two basic components of social organization, the other being *culture*.[3] Social structure describes the social positions or statuses people occupy (e.g., parent, employee, and student) and the behavioral expectations attached to them (e.g., prepare meals, show up for work, and take tests). Because social positions and the role expectations attached to them are relatively enduring and patterned features of social life, explanations of behavior based on them are referred to as *structural.* Such explanations may be contrasted with those from *cultural* or *subcultural* theories, which account for behavioral variation through the values, norms, and beliefs held by members of a group or subgroup (see Chapter 4 for an extended discussion of cultural theories of homicide).

An important bridging concept in this view of social organization is *social institution.* Institutions refer to the relatively stable configurations of statuses, roles, values, and norms that emerge from the basic functional requirements of a society. They can be thought of as the pillars of a society, rooted in the social structure and supporting the culture. Examples include the economy, which organizes the production and distribution of goods and services; the family, which socializes members in the values and beliefs of the society; and the political system, which mobilizes resources for collective goal attainment and distributes power across social positions.

Institutions are integrated to a greater or lesser degree to reflect and reinforce cultural values, resulting in particular forms of social organization that distinguish groups and societies from one another. Whatever the particular institutional makeup of a society, however, and despite the varying functional purposes of different institutions, all institutions share two basic functions: regulating members' behavior in terms of the normative patterns of the society and facilitating members' access to necessary and desired resources and rewards. These defining aspects of social institutions are directly relevant to structural theories of homicide. The first informs theory and research that link homicide and other crime to the erosion of *social control.* The second underlies explanations that attribute homicide to increases in *social strain.*

Formally, social control refers to efforts to channel behavior according to the essential values and norms of a society (cf. Horowitz, 1990, pp. 8-11). When the control functions of an institution weaken, persons are to some degree released from the social bonds that produce conformity to norms. They are freed to deviate and, under certain conditions, to engage in violence. This is the essential insight of *control* theories of deviance and crime (Hirschi, 1969; Kornhauser, 1978). *Social disorganization* theories of crime apply this insight to the level of communities, positing that crime results when community controls are weakened by residential turnover, population heterogeneity, and economic deprivation (Bursik, 1988; Shaw & McKay, 1969).

In addition to social control, another common function of institutions is to facilitate access to the material and social resources needed for physical survival and for meeting the conditions of full social membership as defined by the norms of a particular society. In standard sociological use, by regulating access to wealth, power, and prestige, institutions determine the *life chances* of a population. This institutional function is relevant to homicide because constraints on life chances are potential sources of motivation for aggression and violence. According to *strain* theories, crime and violence result from structural conditions that deprive people of the resources and rewards that they need, expect, or desire.[4]

Applying this general conceptual framework, the research on homicide and social stratification has focused on two interrelated substantive questions: (a) Why do levels of homicide vary across positions that are differentially located within a given form of social organization? and (b) Why do levels of homicide vary across social collectivities (e.g., communities, cities, and societies) that are organized in different ways?

The first issue involves an examination of the social demographic correlates of homicide. The basic logic of this type of structural approach is to argue that persons who occupy different statuses (i.e., persons with different social demographic characteristics) confront different life experiences and life chances. These differences in life experiences and life chances ultimately determine the distribution of the psychological states or *psychological fields* that are the proximate causes of homicide (Cohen, 1985). The nature of the intervening psychological processes varies according to whether persons are viewed as pushed or pressured into violence, as posited by strain theories, or freed to engage in violence, as stipulated by control perspectives.[5]

The second substantive focus for social-structural research considers the implications of different patterns of social organization for the overall level of homicide in a social collectivity. In some cases, the theorizing about social organization and homicide is essentially a direct extrapolation from arguments about the social demographic correlates of homicide; in essence, collectivities have high homicide rates if they contain relatively large numbers of persons with a high potential for homicide. This type of approach is a *compositional* one; groups vary in their level of homicide according to the social demographic composition of their populations. An alternative approach to the explanation of homicide directs attention to social-structural arrangements that alter the context of action for all members of a collectivity. These arrangements influence the *motivational fields* for the population at large and thus promote or discourage homicide throughout the social structure. Given its emphasis on the characteristics of the social context in which homicide is produced, this approach may be termed a *contextual* explanation of homicide.

Whether they direct attention to compositional or contextual influences, or adopt a control or strain perspective, structural approaches to homicide have focused primarily on the stratification system for explaining the social distribution of homicide. Stratification refers to the hierarchical ranking of statuses such that some positions are advantaged relative to others with respect to wealth, power, or prestige. Multiple social characteristics serve as the basis for social stratification in contemporary societies. The most important of these for the research on homicide are social class, race, gender, and age. These characteristics are discussed at length in the sections that follow.

■ *MAJOR CORRELATES OF HOMICIDE RELATED TO SOCIAL STRATIFICATION*

Social Class

Social class stratification most commonly refers to inequality in the possession of, and access to, economic resources.[6] Speculations about the possible link between economic conditions and criminal activity can be traced back as far as antiquity (McDonald, 1976). The 19th-century "moral statisticians" such as Quetelet and Guerry conducted systematic inquiry relating socioeconomic characteristics of areas with levels of crime (Radzinowicz, 1966). A large body of contemporary research has continued this tradition and has examined the relationship between homicide and two particularly important features of economic stratification: poverty and income inequality.

Poverty is generally understood to represent economic deprivation in an absolute sense. It refers to a situation wherein persons have difficulty securing the basic necessities for a healthy life. Poverty thus conceptualized is likely to produce the strain that can push or pressure people to commit acts of lethal violence. As Williams and Flewelling (1988) explain, "it is reasonable to assume that when people live under conditions of extreme scarcity, the struggle for survival is intensified. Such conditions are often accompanied by a host of agitating psychological manifestations, ranging from a deep sense of powerlessness and brutalization to anger, anxiety, and alienation. Such manifestations can provoke physical aggression in conflict situations" (p. 423).

The deprivation associated with meager economic resources has also been related to a weakening of the social controls that inhibit the violent expression of hostile impulses. According to this argument, extreme economic deprivation is *de*moralizing; it undermines the legitimacy of the conventional order and the controls associated with it (e.g., Fiala & LaFree, 1988).

Support for the hypothesized relationship between poverty and homicide comes from evidence indicating that persons serving time in prison for homicide and other conventional crimes in the United States are drawn disproportionately from the unemployed and the low-income population (Bureau of Justice Statistics, 1993). This negative association between economic status and criminal homicide has been reported for other nations and other periods as well (see Chapter 9 by Gary LaFree). The picture becomes somewhat more clouded, however, when research on the relationship between the relative size of the poverty population and the homicide rate for social aggregates is examined. In these studies, a measure of the prevalence of poverty (e.g., percentage below the official poverty line) is typically included in multiple regression equations predicting homicide rates along with controls for other structural characteristics of collectivities (e.g., indicators of family structure, demographic structure, and population turnover). A significantly positive coefficient for the poverty measure is then interpreted as evidence of the criminogenic impact of the presence of relatively large numbers of poor persons, net of other factors.

The results of this research have been inconsistent. Some studies detect the theoretically expected positive effect of poverty on homicide rates, whereas others do not.[7] These inconsistencies in the research on poverty and homicide rates have often been attributed to a variety of methodological difficulties (e.g., Bailey, 1984; Land, McCall, & Cohen, 1990; Loftin & Parker, 1985; Williams, 1984). More consistent findings emerge in studies that combine indicators of the presence of low-income populations with other social conditions that usually occur in combination with poverty, such as low educational attainment, high infant mortality, inadequate housing, and family breakdown (e.g., Flango & Sherbenou, 1976; Harries, 1974, 1976; Land et al., 1990; Loftin & Hill, 1974; Parker & Smith, 1979). At the least, then, poverty appears to be an important component of the correlated causes that consistently accompany high aggregate levels of homicide.

A slightly different approach to the study of economic conditions and homicide is to focus on the relative, rather than the absolute, lack of material resources, that is, to consider *inequality* rather than poverty. This approach is based on the premise that the subjective experience of deprivation either motivates or frees individuals to engage in criminal violence (see Patterson, 1991). As the level of inequality for a given type of social collectivity increases, feelings of *relative deprivation* should become more pervasive and more acute, and rates of homicide should rise accordingly.

The inequality hypothesis has been tested with data on income distributions and homicide for varying types of population aggregates (neighborhoods, cities, metropolitan areas, states, and entire nations). For subnational units, the evidence is once again mixed, and it is difficult to reach unambiguous conclusions about the effects of income inequality on homicide rates. Some studies show the hypothesized positive association between indicators of income inequality and homicide when other conditions are controlled, whereas others show no significant effect (Blau & Blau, 1982; Blau & Golden, 1986; Blau & Schwartz, 1984; Braithwaite, 1979; Messner, 1982, 1983; Messner & Tardiff, 1986; Rosenfeld, 1986; Sampson, 1985; Williams, 1984; see also see Patterson, 1991, for a review). Research at the level of nation-states, in contrast, has been remarkably consistent. A fairly large number of studies report that nations with high levels of income inequality tend to exhibit high homicide rates, controlling for other national characteristics. Much of this research, however, involves similar observations (overlapping samples, data sources, and periods), and thus the studies cannot be considered as independent replications of a general pattern.

The vast majority of studies of income inequality and homicide rates have employed cross-sectional designs. A recent exception to this generalization is the work by LaFree and Drass (1996). They examine the effect of changes in levels of income inequality on changes in race-specific, national arrest rates for homicide (along with other offenses) in a time-series analysis for 1957 to 1990 in the United States. Their findings, consistent with theoretical expectations, were that increases in income inequality are related to increases in homicide arrest rates for both Blacks and Whites.

Race

As the LaFree and Drass (1996) study reveals, the class dimension of stratification is sometimes combined with the racial dimension of stratification in research on homicide. Race is also a strong sociodemographic correlate of homicide. Members of disadvantaged minority groups are overrepresented as both offenders and victims of homicide. For example, African Americans compose roughly 12% of the U.S. population but contributed 51% of the homicide victims and 56% of the known offenders in 1993 (Federal Bureau of Investigation, 1994, Table 2.6). To explain this overrepresentation, some researchers have directed attention to inequality between racial groups. The general hypothesis informing this research is that inequalities rooted in ascribed characteristics such as race are likely to be a particularly potent source of criminal violence.

The most influential formulation and test of the racial inequality hypothesis are those of Blau and Blau (1982; see also Blau & Schwartz, 1984). The Blaus cite multiple reasons for anticipating a relationship between racial inequality and criminal violence, although the causal mechanisms are not fully explicated (Messner & Golden, 1992). Nevertheless, the general thrust of their thesis is that racial inequality leads to strong pressures to commit acts of criminal violence and to weak social controls against doing so. Both of these processes derive from the inherent contradiction between ascriptive inequality and democratic values. A fundamental principle in democratic societies is that rewards should be distributed in accordance with merit and effort. Given such democratic value orientations, persons who receive meager rewards because of their race are likely to develop feelings of resentment, frustration, and hostility. These feelings are likely to be expressed through aggression that is typically directed toward convenient targets. In addition, the very illegitimacy of the stratification system threatens to undermine the general social order—people are unlikely to remain committed to rules that help sustain a fundamentally unjust social system.

The Blaus (1982) report evidence indicating that racial inequality is positively related to official murder rates for a sample of metropolitan areas in the United States. A number of studies have attempted to replicate the Blaus' findings using similar procedures but have obtained mixed results (Balkwell, 1990; Blau & Golden, 1986; Golden & Messner, 1987; Simpson, 1985; Williams, 1984). Some subsequent studies have modified the Blaus' approach and examined race-specific homicide rates. This approach is based on the reasoning that the effects of racial inequality should be manifested primarily among the racial minority. Despite this methodological refinement, ambiguities remain in the literature; conflicting results have also been reported in studies using racially disaggregated data on homicide (cf., e.g., Corzine & Huff-Corzine [1992] and Messner & Golden [1992] with Harer & Steffensmeier [1992]; see also Sampson, 1985, 1986).[8]

Indicators of economic deprivation appear to have weaker effects on homicide rates for Blacks than for Whites in studies using race-specific data (Messner & Golden, 1992; Peterson & Krivo, 1993; Smith, 1992; Smith, Devine, & Sheley, 1992). In addition, LaFree and Drass (1996) observe complex interactions between income inequality, educational attainment, and race-specific homicide arrest rates. For African Americans, increasing educational attainment is associated with rising arrest rates, whereas for Whites, increasing educational attainment is associated with lower crime rates during periods of declining inequality. Both these relationships, however, depend on trends in income inequality.

Most structural approaches to the relationship between race and crime have focused on economic deprivation, either between or within racial groups. In addition to this research, some studies have examined the potential criminogenic consequences of racial residential segregation. Segregation has been linked theoretically with homicide via two mechanisms. One is a deprivation argument that is similar to the thesis relating racial economic inequality with violent crime. According to this approach, segregation is essentially regarded as another form of ascriptive inequality that entails deprivation for the racial minority, especially Blacks. Blacks are restricted to communities that provide inferior resources and social opportunities for their residents. Hence, segregation is likely to lead to the same types of feelings of resentment, frustration, and hostility that racial income inequality produces (cf. Logan & Messner, 1987).

A second theoretical argument calls attention to the *social isolation* of segregated minority groups and the implications of such isolation for social control. As Peterson and Krivo (1993) explain, "Residential segregation implies isolation from mainstream society, an isolation that ties blacks into a local setting of multiple disadvantages" (p. 1005; see also Shihadeh & Flynn, 1996). These disadvantages are likely to undermine the capacity of communities to exert both formal control (e.g., to obtain adequate police protection) and informal control (e.g., to mobilize community residents for crime prevention). It follows, then, that high levels of racial residential segregation should be associated with high homicide rates, especially among the Black population. Although this hypothesis has been evaluated in only a limited number of studies, the results are generally supportive of it (Logan & Messner, 1987; Peterson & Krivo, 1993; Rosenfeld, 1986; Shihadeh & Flynn, 1996; Smith, 1992; but see Sampson, 1985).

Gender

Gender is another key feature of social stratification that is related to violence and homicide. For this dimension of inequality, however, the pattern of offending and victimization is opposite to that observed for class and race. For the latter, low-status and deprived groups (e.g., racial minorities and the poor) exhibit high involvement in criminal homicide as both offenders and victims. For gender, in contrast, the relatively disadvantaged group (females) is generally underrepresented in homicide incidents. According to data from the Supplementary Homicide Reports, for example, in 1993, females composed 23% of the homicide victims in the United States while constituting about half of the total population. For incidents with known offenders, females constituted only 9% of the offenders (calculated from data in Federal Bureau of Investigation, 1994, Tables 2.5 and 2.6).

Stratification processes nevertheless have been identified as important structural causes of gender patterns in homicide. The most common approach is to shift the focus of attention away from offending to victimization and to apply a conflict-oriented variant of the control argument. In essence, female homicide victimization is viewed as an expression of the control efforts of the dominant group. In one formulation of this argument, a high female victimization rate simply represents an extreme form of domination of women by men. In a somewhat different formulation, homicide represents inadequacies or defects in male domination, which result in the resort to violence to maintain control. Both perspectives, however, attribute female homicide victimization to gender stratification (Bailey & Peterson, 1995; Gartner, Baker, & Pampel, 1990).[9]

An illustration of this approach is provided in the work of Bailey and Peterson (1995), who investigate two general hypotheses. One hypothesis is that female homicide victimization is inversely related to the status of women in an absolute sense. This hypothesis is based on the assumption that women "are afforded greater protection against lethal assault" when they have higher levels of educational, occupational, employment, and income attainment (p. 177). The other hypothesis directs attention to the status of women relative to men. Drawing on the general feminist position, Bailey and Peterson hypothesize that greater gender inequality "invites victimization" (p. 177) of the subordinate group—women. In essence, men are "freer" to use violence against women when men are in a more dominant social position.[10]

Bailey and Peterson (1995) assess these hypotheses with data on female homicide victimization and status indicators for a sample of 138 U.S. cities in 1980. They find no support for the hypothesis concerning absolute status. Objective indicators of educational, income, occupational, and employment status of women are not significantly related to rates of female homicide victimization. In contrast, some measures of the status of women relative to men have the expected effects on some types of homicide. For example, the "rate of women being killed by their husbands is significantly higher in cities where the college education gap between males and females is greater, and where women experience higher levels of unemployment than men" (p. 202). The general pattern of results, however, is ambiguous. Several of the indicators of relative status fail to exhibit significant effects, and one (occupational gender inequality) is significantly related to female homicide victimization in the "wrong" direction—cities with higher levels of occupational inequality between women and men exhibit *lower* rates of female homicide victimization. Moreover, subsequent research by Brewer and Smith (1995) fails to support the gender inequality hypothesis. They estimate a comprehensive baseline model of the general structural determinants of homicide and discover that the addition of measures of gender inequality does not improve the explanation of rates of female homicide victimization beyond that provided by the baseline model. They conclude that it is the "overall economic distress of a community in which women live, rather than the specific dynamics of gender inequality, that most influences their risk of victimization" (p. 187; see also Smith & Brewer, 1992).

Gartner et al. (1990) also examine the relationship between gender stratification and homicide, focusing on the "gender gap" in homicide victimization: the differential between male and female homicide rates. They argue that greater status resources for women provide them with more protection from male offenders. This should lead to a larger gender gap because female victimization will decrease relative to male victimization. They report evidence in support of this hypothesis in a pooled time-series analysis of 18 advanced capitalist nations. They also find that the gender gap decreases along with the adoption of nontraditional roles by women, which they interpret with reference to changes in the situational context and associated opportunities for the victimization of women.

Significant attention has also been devoted to homicide situations involving *intimate partners,* that is, incidents in which the victim and offender are married, separated, divorced, or nonmarital cohabitants.[11] In addition to the theoretical arguments that have been applied to male-female homicide in general, the research on intimate partner violence incorporates a strong focus on prevention policy. Of particular note is the possible impact on intimate partner homicide of shelters for battered women, domestic violence hotlines, legal resources, and related facilities and services developed in recent years to address the problem of partner violence. Evidence based on data from U.S. states suggests that such programs are associated with a decline in intimate partner homicide, although the greatest decrease is observed in the victimization rates for *male* partners (Browne & Williams, 1989, 1993). Evidently, the availability of prevention resources has enabled women, in essence, to escape from violent relationships without having to kill their way out.[12] Definitive conclusions regarding the effect of policy interventions on intimate partner homicide must await further research, especially studies using social aggregates smaller than states as units of analysis (see Dugan, Nagin, & Rosenfeld, 1997). The work to date, however, illustrates the policy relevance of structural explanations of homicide.

Like the research on female victimization, studies of the structural determinants of *child homicide* also place strong emphasis on the strains produced by gender stratification. Female labor force participation and measures of social welfare spending emerge as consistent predictors of child homicide rates in cross-national studies of developed nations. Fiala and

LaFree (1988) found that nations with relatively high rates of social welfare expenditures and low levels of female participation in the labor force tend to exhibit low rates of homicide victimization for both infants and children between 1 and 4 years old. Measures of economic inequality, unemployment, and social change are not consistently associated with child homicide rates in their study, and the significant effects found for women's labor force participation and welfare expenditures are limited to the more developed nations.

For the developed nations, Fiala and LaFree (1988) interpret the labor force participation and state spending effects from a perspective combining both strain and control arguments. High levels of female labor force participation, they suggest, increase economic stress and role strain for working women with families. Where these pressures are ameliorated or curbed by increased levels of governmental support for working parents and their families, rates of child abuse and homicide will remain low. Nations that do not respond in such ways to the strains of increased economic participation of women, however, experience correspondingly higher rates of child victimization.

Gartner's (1991) study of child homicide in 17 developed nations also shows significant effects for female labor force participation and government social spending. In addition, Gartner's research indicates that these relationships exist through time as well as across nations. Increases in the economic participation of women contribute to increases in child homicide. These effects, however, are conditioned by social spending. The impact of women's labor force participation on changes in child homicide rates is smaller in nations in which social welfare expenditures are high or rising compared with nations in which spending is more limited (see also Gartner, 1990).

Finally, Gartner's (1991) study also reveals significant effects of family structure on child homicide rates and indicates that these effects, like those of female labor force participation, are conditioned by welfare spending. Rates of infant homicide are greater in nations with high rates of birth to teenage mothers, and the homicide rates of young children are greater where divorce rates, illegitimacy rates, and teenage birthrates are higher. The level of and changes in child homicide are reduced in nations with high or increasing social expenditures.

Like Fiala and LaFree (1988), Gartner (1991) suggests that increased social spending reduces a nation's level of child homicide by mitigating the economic stress associated with women's participation in the labor force. She also interprets the effects on child homicide of rates of divorce, illegitimacy, and teenage births—and the role of social spending in mitigating these effects—in terms of the "resource constraints" imposed by such family structures (p. 237).

Age

Age is a final dimension of stratification with important implications for structural explanations of homicide. These implications, however, have received considerably less attention in the research literature than that devoted to the relationships between homicide and class, race, and gender. To be sure, the general relationship between age and criminality has been the subject of significant commentary and debate, but the research on that relationship focuses primarily on property crimes. An issue that has received notable attention from homicide researchers, however, is the relationship between the relative size of age cohorts and age-specific homicide rates. It is useful to situate the research on this topic in the more general controversy about the nature of the age-crime connection.

Travis Hirschi and Michael Gottfredson (1983) touched off considerable debate several years ago when they published an article asserting that the relationship between age and crime is *invariant* with respect to social and economic circumstances (see also Gottfredson & Hirschi, 1990, pp. 123-144). Hirschi and Gottfredson do not question the age-crime relationship itself; rather, they reject standard sociological interpretations of it. Specifically, they assert that the relationship between age and criminal behavior cannot be accounted for by any of the standard factors thought to influence criminality in general, and the age-crime relationship in particular. The age-crime relationship is invariant with respect to gender, race, and other demographic distinctions. It is unaffected by income, employment, marriage and family formation, or any of the other economic or social strains or restraints assumed to be associated with the process of *maturational reform,* the aging out of crime typically observed during late adolescence and extending through adulthood (Gottfredson & Hirschi, 1990, pp. 134-144; see Matza, 1964, for a discussion of delinquency and maturational reform).

What, then, does account for the observed decline in criminal offending with age? Having rejected all situational, structural, and cultural interpretations, Gottfredson and Hirschi (1990) are left with only one answer—age itself. "Since this decline cannot be explained by change in the person or by his exposure to anticriminal institutions," they write, "we are left with the conclusion that it is due to the inexorable aging of the organism" (p. 141).

This invariance hypothesis has been vigorously challenged (Greenberg, 1985; Steffensmeier, Allan, Harer, & Streifel, 1989; Tittle, 1988). Little disagreement exists, however, about the basic form of the relationship between age and crime.[13] Age-specific rates of both criminal offending and victimization tend to rise with increasing age during childhood and early adolescence, peak in the late teens or early 20s, and then fall rapidly thereafter. In 1992, for example, the age-specific arrest rate for homicide in the United States was less than 1 per 100,000 population for persons age 12 and under, rose steeply during the teens to a peak of 52 per 100,000 population at age 18, and declined to one half the peak rate by age 24 (Federal Bureau of Investigation, 1993, p. 25). Although this curvilinear pattern to the distribution of crime through age characterizes both property and violent crime, the age-crime curve for violent offenses tends to be somewhat flatter, peaking at a later age and declining less rapidly.

David Greenberg (1977, 1981) has offered an influential structural interpretation of the relationship between age and crime, one that Hirschi and Gottfredson (1983) challenged directly in their original statement of the invariance hypothesis. Greenberg's argument combines elements of both strain and control theories of crime. Levels of delinquency and crime, including "nonutilitarian" forms of violent offending, peak in the middle to late teens, according to Greenberg, because adolescents experience difficulties achieving socially approved goals through conventional means and are free from the confinements of childhood and the restraining influences of adulthood. Teenagers' precarious position in the labor market does not generate the resources necessary to fulfill the heightened consumption demands of contemporary adolescent subcultures. The resulting economic strain leads working- and lower-class teenagers in particular to engage in illegal income-producing activities. Many adolescents, especially males, find schools to be alienating and degrading environments and engage in compensatory nonutilitarian forms of deviance to restore a sense of autonomy and self-respect.

The gender role system also contributes to male delinquency, in Greenberg's (1981) terms, by provoking "masculine status anxiety" in young men, resulting in assaultive violence and violence against women to "provide a sense of potency that is expected and desired but not achieved in other spheres of life" (p. 131). Finally, the pronounced and increasing age segregation in advanced industrial societies reinforces the isolation of adolescents from conventional patterns of behavior and reduces stakes in conformity to adult-dominated institutions.

Greenberg's explanation brings together in a single explanatory framework virtually all the major sociological perspectives, and much of the relevant research, on adolescent crime and delinquency. His detailed description of the varied mechanisms linking adolescent status and roles to crime stands in striking contrast to the invariance hypothesis. Looking at much the same age-crime curve, he sees a different process at work. Gottfredson and Hirschi view criminal behavior as essentially embedded in the biological process of aging. For Greenberg (1981), "If age is relevant to criminality, the link should lie primarily in its social significance" (p. 119). From such a perspective, the age-crime relationship is not immutable but is highly contingent on the changing social position of adolescents. Gottfredson and Hirschi (1990) reject this position, suggesting that social factors play a trivial role in accounting for the age effect. "In our view," they write, "the question for criminology is whether the glass is 97 percent full or 3 percent empty" (p. 134).

We wish not to join in the debate about the age-crime relationship but rather to use it as a backdrop for discussing the comparatively limited research on homicide and age structure. At the macrolevel, this research has directed attention to the contribution of the postwar baby boom to the increasing rates of homicide and other forms of crime beginning in the middle 1960s and to the declining crime rates of the early 1980s (Cohen & Land, 1987; Fox, 1978; Steffensmeier & Harer, 1991; Wellford, 1973). As the large birth cohorts of the late 1940s and 1950s began reaching middle adolescence in the 1960s, they exerted strong upward pressures on aggregate crime rates. As the baby-boom cohorts began to age out of the crime-prone years in the late 1970s and were replaced by the smaller cohorts born in the 1960s, demographic pressure on crime rates waned.

Demographic accounts linking changes in overall levels of crime with changes in age structure are compatible with both sides of the age-crime debate. Whether rooted in social structure or biology, all else equal, the age effect on crime will result in higher overall rates of crime when the youthful population is growing and in lower crime rates when it is shrinking. This type of effect of age structure on crime rates is a purely *compositional* one. Aggregate crime rates increase or decrease simply as a function of changes in the age composition of the population. If the proportion of the population in the age groups with high crime rates grows (declines), total crime rates will increase (decrease) as a result, even if no change occurs in age-specific rates. Put simply, teenagers' rates of offending do not have to increase for overall crime rates to go up when the teenage segment of the population is growing.

The compositional interpretation of the effect of age structure on crime rates can be contrasted with a *contextual* interpretation that emphasizes the influence of changes in the size of age groups on age-specific crime rates. The contextual perspective, prominently associated with the work of economist Richard Easterlin (1987), hypothesizes that changes in the relative size of birth cohorts alter the economic and social context within which young people grow up, resulting in positive or negative outcomes depending on the nature of contextual influences. Easterlin focused on the consequences of the large baby boom cohorts for the social and economic welfare of their members (pp. 97-111). Other things equal, moving through the life course as a member of a large cohort, especially through adolescence and the young adult years, reduces economic opportunities and weakens the capacity of institutions to perform vital social control functions. Unemployment rates increase and incomes decline when labor markets are crowded with large numbers of new entrants. Adults have difficulty imposing discipline and instilling conventional values in crowded families, schools, and other institutions of social control. The results of the increased economic strain and diminished social control associated with large birth cohorts include heightened levels of mental stress, drinking and drug use, suicide, crime, and violence.

The Easterlin hypothesis, therefore, predicts that the crime rate will change as a function of both compositional and contextual influences associated with change in relative cohort size. Like the compositional effect of age on crime, the contextual effect predicted by Easterlin is consistent with the social-structural explanation of the age-crime relationship; it incorporates many of the strain and control influences summarized by Greenberg (see Easterlin, 1987, p. 211, n.). It is not consistent, however, with the Hirschi-Gottfredson (1983) invariance hypothesis. There is little reason to expect that change in relative cohort size will influence age-specific crime rates, if the age effect is limited to the biological changes inherent in the aging process. Labor market crowding and overburdened institutions may have some influence on crime rates, but they do not account for the age effect as understood by Gottfredson and Hirschi.

Easterlin's (1987) relative cohort size hypothesis has been evaluated in several studies of crime, including homicide, and the results have been mixed. Some studies have found appreciable cohort-size effects on age-specific homicide rates (pp. 101-104; Smith, 1986), whereas others have found small or inconsistent effects (Maxim, 1985; O'Brien, 1989). One recent study reports a small but *negative* association between cohort size and arrest rates for homicide and other offenses for younger age groups and a *positive* effect for older persons (Steffensmeier, Streifel, & Shihadeh, 1992). This result contradicts Easterlin's contention that the negative outcomes of growing up in large cohorts will be aggravated for adolescents and young adults. From a somewhat different perspective, Smith and Feiler (1995) contrast the observed increase in the homicide arrest rates of the baby boom cohorts during the late 1960s with the much steeper increase exhibited by the smaller teenage cohorts of the late 1980s. They note that "for all of the attention accorded them at one time, baby boomer youths were rather tame in comparison to more recent cohorts of youths, at least in terms of their involvement in arrests for murders" (p. 331).

Tests of Easterlin's relative cohort size hypothesis have been limited primarily to the United States. In part, this is due to problems of data availability and comparability that plague cross-national investigations of crime in general. The focus on American society also reflects Easterlin's argument that the contextual effects of age structure should be most pronounced in the United States, which experienced substantially greater upswings in birthrates following World War II than did most other nations. Cross-national studies generally have shown weak or nonexistent relationships between the age structure of the population, specifically the relative size of the youthful cohorts, and aggregate homicide rates (Gartner, 1990; Gartner & Parker, 1990). A recent investigation of 18 industrial nations by Pampel and Gartner (1995), however, showed that the effect of age structure on homicide rates is contingent on the presence of "institutions for collective social protection" (p. 243). Although they did not examine the effect of relative cohort size on age-specific homicide rates, they do refer explicitly to Easterlin's arguments concerning the contextual influences of relative cohort size on crime. They found that the effect of age structure on homicide rates is attenuated in nations that ease labor market dislocations for young workers and reduce age segmentation by promoting a sense of collective, class-based solidarity. The impact of age structure on homicide is greater in those nations lacking such protective and "collectivist" policies and social structures.

■ *NEW DIRECTIONS FOR THE SOCIAL-STRUCTURAL STUDY OF HOMICIDE*

The research reviewed in this chapter demonstrates the utility of the structural perspective for understanding the social forces that produce homicide. It reveals that persons with different sociodemographic characteristics exhibit distinctive levels of involvement in homicide as both victims and offenders. It also shows that variation in homicide rates across social collectivities can be accounted for, at least in part, by features of the social organization of these collectivities.

Despite the extensive work on the social-structural sources of homicide during recent decades, important tasks need to be confronted in future research. One such task is to explain the more curious anomalies in the literature. As noted above, poverty (and the correlates of poverty) emerge as major determinants of homicide offending for Whites but not for Blacks. Researchers have identified other factors that help explain levels of Black offending, such as residential segregation, but the question still remains why the effects of poverty vary so dramatically across racial groups. Similarly, the reversal of the normal pattern of the effects of inequality on homicide for the gender dimension of stratification requires more systematic theoretical attention. Recall that two common explanations for the homicide victimization of females by males are that the superior power of men "frees" them to act violently against women and that men inflict violence against women to protect their dominant status. But why are such processes limited to gender? Why doesn't economic inequality free rich persons to kill poor persons? Why doesn't racial inequality lead to high rates of Whites killing Blacks?

Another important task for future theorizing and research is to integrate structural and cultural factors in explanations of homicide. Indeed, many structural arguments presuppose cultural dynamics, but these dynamics simply are left implicit. For example, the strain tradition emphasizes the extent to which structural location is associated with relative deprivation, which can generate motivations for lethal violence. For people to experience relative deprivation, however, they must have some end state that they anticipate that they will be unable to attain because of structural impediments. These end states are, in the final analysis, determined by culture.

Similarly, there is an important role for culture in control explanations of homicide. Control theories explain how breakdowns in the functioning of social institutions weaken the controls against violence. Yet it seems likely that the functioning of institutions reflects the cultural orientations that prevail in a society. Hence, major institutional changes that threaten to weaken control and increase the probability of homicide, such as changes in the structure of families or the supervisory capacity of local schools, are undoubtedly linked with broad changes in the larger culture. A comprehensive theory of homicide and institutional control must specify the cultural preconditions for the effective or ineffective functioning of institutions of social control.[14]

It is also important for researchers to broaden their structural focus in future work on homicide. Much of the research within the structural tradition concentrates on either a single social institution or the additive effects of several institutions. Given that institutions are interdependent, however, it is critical to consider the ways in which the effects of institutions work in combination to generate or suppress homicide. Examples of this type of multi-institutional focus can be found in the research reviewed earlier on gender stratification and child homicide and on age structure and homicide. These studies reveal that the criminogenic consequences of certain forms of stratification, such as the stresses associated with female labor force participation and the pressures associated with large birth cohorts, are mitigated when other, protective social institutions are operating.[15]

Despite the limitations associated with the social-structural tradition in the study of homicide, this approach contains an important implication for efforts to deal with the problem of lethal violence. If a given level of homicide reflects to a significant extent features of the social structure, it need not be an inevitable (nor invariant) fact of life. Social structures are ultimately created, sustained, and altered by the members of a society. The structural strains and controls that influence the rate of homicide are mediated, as research described in this chapter has shown, by public policies that protect people from economic dislocations, strengthen social institutions, and promote norms of collective obligation. The social production of homicide *can* be tempered when people have the collective will to do so.

■ *NOTES*

1. Durkheim (1895/1964) defines *social facts* in the *Rules of Sociological Method* and applies the idea to what is commonly viewed as an individual act in *Suicide* (1897/1966).

2. A third type of structural influence is predicted by *routine activity* and *opportunity* perspectives, which explain the distribution of criminal activity as a function of the confluence in time and space of motivated offenders, suitable targets, and the absence of capable guardians (see Cantor & Land, 1985; Cohen & Felson, 1979; Felson & Cohen, 1980). These conditions, particularly guardianship, are treated for the purposes of this discussion as part of a broader set of control influences on crime and violence. For applications of this approach in research on cross-national differences in homicide, see Gartner (1990) and Kick and LaFree (1985).

3. We have referred to the conceptual framework discussed here as the *sociological paradigm.* See Messner and Rosenfeld (1997a, pp. 44-57) for an extended discussion of the elements of social organization and of how the sociological paradigm informs the major theoretical orientations in criminology.

4. The preeminent strain theorist is Robert K. Merton (1938). Merton's thesis links crime to the disjuncture between society's success goals and the institutionalized means for achieving them. Agnew (1992) has elaborated the

social-psychological mechanisms underlying structural strain in his general strain theory of crime.

5. See Goldstein (1986) for an extended discussion of psychological instigators and inhibitors of aggression and violence.

6. Some of the material in this section draws on Messner (1982, 1988).

7. See Land et al. (1990) for a comprehensive review of this research.

8. Messner (1989) has applied the Blaus' general theoretical framework in an analysis of the effect on national homicide rates of economic discrimination. Economic discrimination is positively related to the national homicide rate in his multivariate analyses with controls for other national characteristics.

9. See Gartner (1990) for a routine activity interpretation of female homicide victimization.

10. Similar arguments have been put forth concerning a potential link between gender inequality and forcible rape (e.g., Baron & Straus, 1989).

11. For a review and extension of this area of research, see Chapter 10 by Angela Browne, Kirk R. Williams, and Donald G. Dutton.

12. See Gillis (1996) for a similar interpretation of the role of liberalized divorce laws in the decline in marital homicide in France during the 19th century.

13. See Britt (1992) for a mathematical assessment of the age-crime function and its stability through time.

14. We offer one such explanation of how anomic cultural orientations undermine the control functions of major social institutions (Messner & Rosenfeld, 1997a).

15. For additional examples of homicide research that adopts a multi-institutional focus, see Sampson (1987) and Shihadeh and Steffensmeier (1994). These studies analyze the direct and indirect effects on race-specific homicide rates of economic conditions and family structure. A cross-national study (Messner & Rosenfeld, 1997b) found a relationship between an indicator of social welfare policies and aggregate homicide rates, which the authors interpreted in terms of the "institutional balance of power" (p. 1396) in market societies.

■ *REFERENCES*

Agnew, R. (1992). Foundations for a general strain theory of crime and delinquency. *Criminology, 30,* 47-87.

Bailey, W. C. (1984). Poverty, inequality, and city homicide rates: Some not so unexpected findings. *Criminology, 22,* 531-550.

Bailey, W. C., & Peterson, R. D. (1995). Gender inequality and violence against women. In J. Hagan & R. D. Peterson (Eds.), *Crime and inequality* (pp. 174-205). Stanford, CA: Stanford University Press.

Balkwell, J. W. (1990). Ethnic inequality and the rate of homicide. *Social Forces, 69,* 53-70.

Baron, L., & Straus, M. A. (1989). *Four theories of rape in American society: A state-level analysis.* New Haven, CT: Yale University Press.

Blau, J. R., & Blau, P. M. (1982). The cost of inequality: Metropolitan structure and criminal violence. *American Sociological Review, 47,* 114-129.

Blau, P. M., & Golden, R. M. (1986). Metropolitan structure and violent crime. *Sociological Quarterly, 7,* 15-26.

Blau, P. M., & Schwartz, J. E. (1984). *Crosscutting social circles.* New York: Academic Press.

Braithwaite, J. (1979). *Inequality, crime, and public policy.* London: Routledge & Kegan Paul.

Brewer, V. E., & Smith, M. D. (1995). Gender inequality and rates of female homicide victimization across U.S. cities. *Journal of Research in Crime and Delinquency, 32,* 175-190.

Britt, C., III. (1992). Constancy and change in the U.S. distribution of crime: A test of the "invariance hypothesis." *Journal of Quantitative Criminology, 8,* 75-187.

Browne, A., & Williams, K. R. (1989). Exploring the effect of resource availability and the likelihood of female-perpetrated homicides. *Law and Society Review, 23,* 75-94.

Browne, A., & Williams, K. R. (1993). Gender, intimacy, and lethal violence: Trends from 1976 through 1987. *Gender & Society, 7,* 78-98.

Bureau of Justice Statistics. (1993). *Survey of state prison inmates, 1991.* Washington, DC: U.S. Department of Justice.

Bursik, R. J., Jr. (1988). Social disorganization and theories of crime and delinquency: Problems and prospects. *Criminology, 26,* 519-551.

Cantor, D., & Land, K. C. (1985). Unemployment and crime rates in the post-World War II United States: A theoretical and empirical analysis. *American Sociological Review, 50,* 317-323.

Cohen, A. K. (1985). The assumption that crime is a product of environments: Sociological approaches. In R. F. Meier (Ed.), *Theoretical methods in criminology* (pp. 223-243). Beverly Hills, CA: Sage.

Cohen, L. E., & Felson, M. (1979). Social change and crime rate trends: A routine activity approach. *American Sociological Review, 44,* 588-608.

Cohen, L. E., & Land, K. C. (1987). Age structure and crime: Symmetry versus asymmetry and the projection of crime rates through the 1990s. *American Sociological Review, 52,* 170-183.

Corzine, J., & Huff-Corzine, L. (1992). Racial inequality and Black homicide: An analysis of felony, nonfelony, and total rates. *Journal of Contemporary Criminal Justice, 8,* 150-165.

Dugan, L., Nagin, D., & Rosenfeld, R. (1997). *Explaining the decline in intimate partner homicide: The effects of changing domesticity, women's status, and domestic violence resources* (Working paper No. 2.). Pittsburgh, PA: Carnegie Mellon University, National Consortium on Violence Research.

Durkheim, E. (1964). *The rules of sociological method.* New York: Free Press. (Original work published 1895)

Durkheim, E. (1966). *Suicide: A study in sociology.* New York: Free Press. (Original work published 1897)

Easterlin, R. A. (1987). *Birth and fortune: The impact of numbers on personal welfare* (2nd ed.). Chicago: University of Chicago Press.

Federal Bureau of Investigation. (1993). *Age-specific arrest rates and race-specific arrest rates for selected offenses, 1965-1992.* Washington, DC: U.S. Department of Justice.

Federal Bureau of Investigation. (1994). *Crime in the United States 1993: Uniform crime reports.* Washington, DC: Government Printing Office.

Felson, M., & Cohen, L. E. (1980). Human ecology and crime: A routine activity approach. *Human Ecology, 32,* 389-406.

Fiala, R., & LaFree, G. (1988). Cross-national determinants of child homicide. *American Sociological Review, 53,* 432-445.

Flango, V. E., & Sherbenou, E. L. (1976). Poverty, urbanization, and crime. *Criminology, 14,* 331-346.

Fox, J. A. (1978). *Forecasting crime data.* Lexington, MA: Lexington Books.

Gartner, R. (1990). The victims of homicide: A temporal and cross-national comparison. *American Sociological Review, 55,* 92-106.

Gartner, R. (1991). Family structure, welfare spending, and child homicide in developed democracies. *Journal of Marriage and the Family, 53,* 231-240.

Gartner, R., & Parker, R. N. (1990). Cross-national evidence on homicide and the age structure of the population. *Social Forces, 69,* 351-371.

Gartner, R., Baker, K., & Pampel, F. C. (1990). Gender stratification and the gender gap in homicide victimization. *Social Problems, 37,* 593-612.

Gillis, A. R. (1996). So long as they both shall live: Marital dissolution and the decline of domestic homicide in France, 1852-1909. *American Journal of Sociology, 101,* 1273-1305.

Golden, R. M., & Messner, S. F. (1987). Dimensions of racial inequality and rates of violent crime. *Criminology, 25,* 525-554.

Goldstein, J. H. (1986). *Aggression and crimes of violence* (2nd ed.). New York: Oxford University Press.

Gottfredson, M. R., & Hirschi, T. (1990). *A general theory of crime.* Stanford, CA: Stanford University Press.

Greenberg, D. (1977). Delinquency and the age structure of society. *Contemporary Crises, 1,* 189-224.

Greenberg, D. (1981). *Crime and capitalism.* Palo Alto, CA: Mayfield.

Greenberg, D. (1985). Age, crime, and social explanation. *American Journal of Sociology, 91,* 1-21.

Harer, M. D., & Steffensmeier, D. (1992). The differing effects of economic inequality on Black and White rates of violence. *Social Forces, 70,* 1035-1054.

Harries, K. (1974). *The geography of crime and justice.* New York: McGraw-Hill.

Harries, K. (1976). Cities and crime: A geographic model. *Criminology, 14,* 369-386.

Hirschi, T. (1969). *Causes of delinquency.* Berkeley: University of California Press.

Hirschi, T., & Gottfredson, M. R. (1983). Age and the explanation of crime. *American Journal of Sociology, 89,* 552-584.

Horowitz, A. V. (1990). *The logic of social control.* New York: Plenum.

Kick, E. L., & LaFree, G. (1985). Development and the social context of murder and theft. *Comparative Social Research, 8,* 37-58.

Kornhauser, R. R. (1978). *Social sources of delinquency: An appraisal of analytic models.* Chicago: University of Chicago Press.

LaFree, G., & Drass, K. A. (1996). The effect of changes in intraracial income inequality and educational attainment on changes in arrest rates for African Americans and Whites, 1957 to 1990. *American Sociological Review, 61,* 614-634.

Land, K. C., McCall, P. L., & Cohen, L. E. (1990). Structural covariates of homicide rates: Are there any invariances across time and social space? *American Journal of Sociology, 95,* 922-963.

Loftin, C., & Hill, R. H. (1974). Regional subculture and homicide: An examination of the Gastil-Hackney thesis. *American Sociological Review, 39,* 714-724.

Loftin, C., & Parker, R. N. (1985). An errors-in-variable model of the effect of poverty on urban homicide rates. *Criminology, 23,* 269-285.

Logan, J. R., & Messner, S. F. (1987). Racial residential segregation and suburban violent crime. *Social Science Quarterly, 68,* 510-527.

Matza, D. (1964). *Delinquency and drift.* New York: John Wiley.

Maxim, P. (1985). Cohort size and juvenile delinquency: A test of the Easterlin hypothesis. *Social Forces, 63,* 661-679.

McDonald, L. (1976). *The sociology of law and order.* Boulder, CO: Westview.

Merton, R. K. (1938). Social structure and anomie. *American Sociological Review, 3,* 672-682.

Messner, S. F. (1982). Poverty, inequality, and the urban homicide rate: Some unexpected findings. *Criminology, 20,* 103-114.

Messner, S. F. (1983). Regional and racial effects on the urban homicide rate. *American Journal of Sociology, 88,* 997-1007.

Messner, S. F. (1988). Research on cultural and socioeconomic factors in criminal violence. *Psychiatric Clinics of North America, 16,* 511-525.

Messner, S. F. (1989). Economic discrimination and societal homicide rates: Further evidence on the cost of inequality. *American Sociological Review, 54,* 597-611.

Messner, S. F., & Golden, R. M. (1992). Racial inequality and racially disaggregated homicide rates: An assessment of alternative theoretical explanations. *Criminology, 30,* 421-447.

Messner, S. F., & Rosenfeld, R. (1997a). *Crime and the American dream* (2nd ed.). Belmont, CA: Wadsworth.

Messner, S. F., & Rosenfeld, R. (1997b). Political restraint of the market and levels of criminal homicide: A cross-national application of institutional-anomie theory. *Social Forces, 75,* 1393-1416.

Messner, S. F., & Tardiff, K. (1986). Economic inequality and levels of homicide: An analysis of urban neighborhoods. *Criminology, 24,* 297-319.

O'Brien, R. M. (1989). Relative cohort size and age-specific crime rates: An age-period-relative cohort size model. *Criminology, 27,* 57-78.

Pampel, F., C., & Gartner, R. (1995). Age structure, socio-political institutions, and national homicide rates. *European Sociological Review, 16,* 243-260.

Parker, R. N., & Smith, M. D. (1979). Deterrence, poverty, and type of homicide. *American Journal of Sociology, 85,* 614-624.

Patterson, E. B. (1991). Poverty, income inequality, and community crime rates. *Criminology, 29,* 755-776.

Peterson, R. D., & Krivo, L. J. (1993). Racial segregation and Black urban homicide. *Social Forces, 71,* 1001-1026.

Radzinowicz, L. (1966). *Ideology and crime.* New York: Columbia University Press.

Rosenfeld, R. (1986). Urban crime rates: Effects of inequality, welfare dependency, region, and race. In J. M. Byrne & R. J. Sampson (Eds.), *The social ecology of crime* (pp. 116-130). New York: Springer-Verlag.

Sampson, R. J. (1985). Race and criminal violence: A demographically disaggregated analysis of urban homicide. *Crime & Delinquency, 31,* 47-82.

Sampson, R. J. (1986). Crime in cities: The effects of formal and informal social control. In A. J. Reiss, Jr., & M. Tonry (Eds.), *Communities and crime* (pp. 271-311). Chicago: University of Chicago Press.

Sampson, R. J. (1987). Urban Black violence: The effect of male joblessness and family disruption. *American Journal of Sociology, 93,* 348-382.

Shaw, C. R., & McKay, H. D. (1969). *Juvenile delinquency in urban areas.* Chicago: University of Chicago Press.

Shihadeh, E. S., & Flynn, N. (1996). Segregation and crime: The effect of Black social isolation on the rates of Black urban violence. *Social Forces, 74,* 1325-1352.

Shihadeh, E. S., & Steffensmeier, D. (1994). Economic inequality, family disruption, and urban Black violence: Cities as units of stratification and social control. *Social Forces, 73,* 729-751.

Simpson, M. E. (1985). Violent crime, income inequality, and regional culture: Another look. *Sociological Focus, 18,* 199-208.

Smith, M. D. (1986). The era of increased violence in the United States: Age, period, or cohort effect? *Sociological Quarterly, 27,* 239-251.

Smith, M. D. (1992). Variations in correlates of race-specific urban homicide rates. *Journal of Contemporary Criminal Justice, 8,* 137-149.

Smith, M. D., & Brewer, V. E. (1992). A sex-specific analysis of correlates of homicide victimization in United States cities. *Violence and Victims, 7,* 279-286.

Smith, M. D., Devine, J. A., & Sheley, J. F. (1992). Crime and unemployment: Effects across age and race categories. *Sociological Perspectives, 35,* 551-572.

Smith, M. D., & Feiler, S. M. (1995). Absolute and relative involvement in homicide offending: Contemporary youth and the baby boom cohorts. *Violence and Victims, 10,* 327-333.

Steffensmeier, D., & Harer, M. D. (1991). Did crime rise or fall during the Reagan presidency? The effects of an "aging" U.S. population on the nation's crime rate. *Journal of Research in Crime and Delinquency, 28,* 330-359.

Steffensmeier, D., Allan, E. A., Harer, M. D., & Streifel, C. (1989). Age and the distribution of crime. *American Journal of Sociology, 94,* 803-831.

Steffensmeier, D., Streifel, C., & Shihadeh, E. S. (1992). Cohort size and arrest rates over the life course: The Easterlin hypothesis reconsidered. *American Sociological Review, 57,* 306-314.

Tittle, C. R. (1988). Two empirical regularities (maybe) in search of an explanation. *Criminology, 26,* 75-85.

Wellford, C. (1973). Age composition and the increase in recorded crime. *Criminology, 16,* 61-70.

Williams, K. R. (1984). Economic sources of homicide: Reestimating the effects of poverty and inequality. *American Sociological Review, 49,* 283-289.

Williams, K. R., & Flewelling, R. L. (1988). The social production of homicide: A comparative study of disaggregated rates in American cities. *American Sociological Review, 53,* 421-431.

CHAPTER 4

Cultural and Subcultural Theories of Homicide

■ *Jay Corzine, Lin Huff-Corzine, & Hugh P. Whitt*

Cultural theories of homicide have a long history. André-Michel Guerry (1833), one of the first scholars to conduct a systematic statistical analysis of official crime data, was struck by the high rates of violent crimes in the south of France. Guerry thought the regional variations he found might reflect cultural differences left over from tribal settlement patterns in ancient times. France, he argued, was made up of several distinct nations, each with its own language, manners, customs, and traditional prejudices. Because of these cultural differences, residents of different regions would behave differently in similar situations.

A generation later, Italian political and intellectual leaders agonized over what to do about the "southern question" or "southern problem" (Mack Smith, 1969)—the presence within the newly unified nation of a "barbarian" region, in which, as a result of "hatreds, vendettas, and outlawries, we have an official list of 1,500 homicides in two years, and the real figure would be more like a thousand a year" (Govone, 1968, p. 372). Some argued at the time that there was no need for scientific study of the southern problem because it was obviously due to the culturally ingrained "sloth and corruption" of Neapolitans, Calabrians, and Sicilians (Mack Smith, 1969, p. 229). Others attributed it to social-structural factors such as southern poverty or the extreme level of social and economic inequality in the south.

Redfield's (1880) groundbreaking study of the United States showed that homicide was concentrated in the southern region, just as it was in France and Italy. Other patterns of violence suggestive of a cultural influence have been identified (e.g., Wolfgang's [1958] *Patterns in Criminal Homicide*), and there are few conflicts over the empirical regularities that are reflected in homicide data.[1] Offending rates are higher for males, younger persons, African Americans, Hispanics, and southerners. Regardless of recent attention focused on violence in the workplace, homicides more often occur during leisure time, with higher rates during the

AUTHORS' NOTE: Our contributions as authors are equal. Our names are listed alphabetically.

evening hours and on weekends. Situational elements that increase the odds of a confrontation escalating into a killing include alcohol consumption (Parker, 1995) and the use of a gun or knife (Felson & Messner, 1996).

Any consensus among researchers dissolves, however, when they turn from establishing the nature of homicide patterns to providing explanations for them. Although social-structural and cultural theories of homicide are not mutually exclusive, debates between advocates of these perspectives have been common (see Corzine & Huff-Corzine, 1989; Dixon & Lizotte, 1987; Ellison & McCall, 1989; Gastil, 1971; Hackney, 1969; Loftin & Hill, 1974). Early investigators of homicide, including Guerry (1833), Redfield (1880), and Brearley (1932), viewed both structural and cultural characteristics as important in understanding variations in homicide rates. Likewise, although promoting the position that cultural factors influence homicide rates, we do not view ourselves as opponents of other perspectives. It is apparent to us that economic disadvantage is related to violence, including killing, although the linkages may be more complex than many investigators assume (for attempts to unravel the relationships, see Land, McCall, & Cohen, 1990; Sampson, 1987). Our position is that a consideration of social-structural variables is necessary but *not sufficient* to provide an explanation of homicide, and theories that include cultural differences between groups offer a promising avenue for advancing our understanding of killing (Unnithan, Huff-Corzine, Corzine, & Whitt, 1994).

Our previous research supports cultural as well as social-structural interpretations of high homicide rates in the American South (Huff-Corzine, Corzine, & Moore, 1986, 1991; Nelsen, Corzine, & Huff-Corzine, 1994; Whitt, Corzine, & Huff-Corzine, 1995), and we rely heavily on the literature linking regional homicide to a southern subculture of violence in this chapter. In the following sections, we will (a) review theoretical positions linking culture and violence, including homicide; (b) introduce Swidler's (1986) idea of culture as a "tool kit" as the most useful conceptualization of how culture affects action; (c) present a model that integrates cultural and structural variables in explaining variations in rates of lethal violence; (d) discuss recent studies that provide advances in understanding the influence of regional culture on homicide in the United States; and (e) suggest avenues for future research.

■ *CULTURES, SUBCULTURES, AND VIOLENCE*

Theoretical and empirical work has focused on the role of cultural (or subcultural)[2] differences in explaining rates of violence committed by women (Ogle, Maier-Katkin, & Bernard, 1995); high school boys (Felson, Liska, South, & McNulty, 1994); hockey players (Faulkner, 1974); Native Americans (Bachman, 1992); Latin Americans (Neapolitan, 1994); African Americans (Cao, Adams, & Jensen, 1997; Curtis, 1975; Harer & Steffensmeier, 1996); and southerners (Hackney, 1969). Most recent theoretical work on cultural factors in violence implicitly or explicitly traces its ancestry to the insights of Thorsten Sellin (1938), Albert Cohen (1955), Walter Miller (1958), Gresham Sykes and David Matza (1957), or the subculture of violence thesis formulated by Marvin Wolfgang and Franco Ferracuti (1967). Despite their common intellectual ancestry, theorists and researchers differ among themselves over what aspects of cultures and subcultures produce heightened levels of violence.

The core idea in Wolfgang and Ferracuti's (1967) work is that some subcultures among groups (e.g., men, African Americans, southerners, and Colombians) provide greater normative support than others for violence in upholding such values as honor, courage, and manliness. In other words, some people engage in violent acts because they hold facilitative attitudes or values (i.e., they approve of violence). As an example of research on this, Dixon and Lizotte (1987) measure membership in a subculture of violence through a "violent attitudes scale" designed to be "indicative of the set of violent values Wolfgang and Ferracuti (1967) deem the defining characteristic of subcultures of violence" (p. 396).

A serious flaw in *some* studies grounded in the Wolfgang and Ferracuti (1967) thesis is the implicit assumption that members of some groups kill or injure others because their subculture approves of violence *in general.* Although it is probably true that every society includes some unsocialized individuals who place a high positive value on violence across the board (Athens, 1989), violence, and especially violence against one's group, is seldom positively sanctioned in any and all situations. Persons who are indiscriminately violent are viewed as dangerous, and societies and members of subcultures find formal and informal ways of controlling them. If approved at all, violence is deemed acceptable only in some situations (e.g., violations of the code of honor in organized crime families).

John Shelton Reed (1982) views southern culture in the United States as defining a range of situations in which violence is accepted or required, although it is sometimes regarded as regrettable rather than a "good thing." According to Reed,

> Sometimes people are violent because they want to be and there is nothing to stop them. But sometimes people are violent, even though they *don't* want to be, because there will be penalties (disgrace is a very effective one) for *not* being violent. (p. 147)

Reed's conceptualization suggests that southerners will be more predisposed to violence than nonsoutherners only in situations defined by subcultural tradition as requiring violent responses (e.g., to right a wrong or exact retribution against a person who has offended one's honor). It therefore becomes necessary to identify the specific content of a cultural or subcultural tradition to predict not only the conditions under which homicide will occur but also the nature of these homicides (for an excellent example of this approach, see Montell, 1986).

Research in the subculture of violence tradition has not been limited to the cultural and subcultural normative legitimation of violence, but several studies in addition to Dixon and Lizotte (1987) have explored this normative component of subcultures defined by age, gender, race, and social class, with varying results (see Baker & Ball, 1969; Ball-Rokeach, 1973; Erlanger, 1974; Hartnagel, 1980; Heimer, 1997; Shoemaker & Williams, 1987). Markowitz and Felson (1998), however, argue that it is misleading and inaccurate to regard differences in attitudes between social-demographic categories such as race or class as reflecting subcultural differences. Although their work is derived from the subculture of violence tradition, Markowitz and Felson offer the term *attitude mediation thesis* in place of *subculture of violence thesis* because in their words,

> The notion of a subculture implies a degree of consensus within a group, and differences between groups, that rarely exists. Such a pattern may exist in small groups where members interact with each other, but it is unlikely to be observed for large aggregates of people (Felson et al., 1994). For example, to say that poor people belong to a subculture of violence—based on small statistical differences between social classes—is to overstate the case. (pp. 117-118)

Whether one excludes differences across aggregates as subcultural, the subculture of violence tradition extends well beyond the strictly normative tradition emphasized by Wolfgang and Ferracuti (1967). Miller's (1958) classic article on lower-class culture as a generating milieu for gang delinquency identified a number of themes—trouble, toughness, smartness, excitement, fate, and autonomy—none of which involves explicit norms legitimating violence. Instead, these focal concerns involve values, expectations, beliefs, and explanatory styles (Seligman, 1990, 1992) that reflect conditions of life in poverty areas and increase the probability of involvement in violence quite apart from any norms requiring or permitting violent behavior.

Similarly, Curtis (1975) defines culture "as consisting of values, behaviors, outlooks, imagery, expectations, definitions of reality, and meanings specific to a community that shares them" (p. 7). A similar view is presented by Hannerz (1969). This broader conceptualization of culture and subculture underlies much of the recent work in this area, including our own.

Curtis points out that culture may affect even the ways in which persons assign meanings to situations (e.g., how they understand the causes of negative situations and events and how they assign blame for them). As symbolic interactionism suggests, the way persons interpret situations has implications for how they act. Similarly, if behavior is included in the definition, culture can be seen as influencing homicide in less direct ways. For example, firearms and alcohol are situational contingencies that increase the odds of an altercation resulting in a death (Felson & Messner, 1996), and cultural differences in propensity to drink to excess or to carry a gun for protection or to keep one in the house may prove to be a partial explanation for regional differences in homicide rates (Bankston & Thompson, 1989).

Research on the emergence of a ghetto underclass consisting disproportionately of minorities in some neighborhoods within the inner cities of Rust Belt metropolitan areas demonstrates how broader subcultures may influence levels of violence. As developed by William Julius Wilson (1987, 1996), Elijah Anderson (1990, 1994), and others, this research focuses on how changes in the U.S. economy, especially the major loss of manufacturing jobs and their partial replacement by low-paying service jobs, affect African American communities in central cities. The basic thesis is that the loss of well-paying manufacturing jobs, exacerbated by the continuing effects of racism and other factors, has produced a high level of social disorganization in many inner-city areas. This is exemplified in several aspects of community life, including the substantial decrease in two-parent families, high rates of out-of-wedlock births to teenage mothers, a generational schism between older and younger African Americans, chronic poverty, and high rates of violent crime and drug abuse.

Although Wilson (1996) interprets many of the behaviors associated with the underclass as situational adaptations that do not reflect a distinct cultural perspective, Anderson (1990, 1994), Bernard (1990), and Rose and McClain (1990, 1998) assert that an *oppositional subculture* rejecting many middle-class values related to family, work, and the appropriateness of violence has become established among some segments of the underclass, particularly young African American males. On the basis of ethnographic research on inner-city neighborhoods, Anderson (1994) identifies a "code of the streets" that includes a heightened sensitivity to personal affronts by others and a strong emphasis on maintaining honor, that is, "respect," at all costs, including one's life. Because of the ambiguous nature of much interaction in both public and private places, such as the appropriateness of maintaining eye contact, adherents of the code of the streets are predisposed to violence. Inner-city residents maintaining a "decent" orientation may also become involved in violent altercations because they cannot avoid dealing with persons who have a "street" orientation.

Rose and McClain (1990, 1998) assign a prominent role to oppositional subculture in their investigations of African American homicides. Specifically, both increases in the homicide rate, especially among younger males, and a shift from *expressive* to *instrumental* killings are attributed to the rise of an oppositional subculture in northern cities. Rose and McClain's work points to the complexity of using cultural and subcultural approaches to violence because they see homicide patterns among African Americans influenced by both a waning southern subcultural tradition and the emergent oppositional subculture.

■ *CULTURE AS A TOOL KIT*

In our view, the most persuasive argument on how culture influences action has been developed by Ann Swidler (1986). Instead of relying on the concept of values as transituational goals to which action is oriented, she offers the idea of culture as a collection of resources that actors use in shaping "strategies of action" (p. 273), a viewpoint that is congruent with Reed (1982). In this perspective, culture provides persons with repertoires of ideas, definitions of types of situations, material products, and other factors that may be combined in numerous ways in developing actions. In Swidler's words,

> The alternative analysis of culture proposed here consists of three steps. First, it offers an image of culture as a "tool kit" of symbols, stories, rituals, and world-views, which people may use in varying configurations to solve different kinds of problems. Second, to analyze culture's causal effects, it focuses on "strategies of action," persistent ways of acting through time. Third, it sees causal significance not in defining ends of actions, but in providing cultural components that are used to construct strategies of action. (p. 273)

In a broad sense, cultural explanations for behaviors try to explain "why different actors make different choices even in similar situations" (Swidler, 1986, p. 274). By linking cultural differences to violent acts, we are asking why some persons respond to situations violently, whereas others with the same or similar economic and demographic characteristics do not. In part, those faced with similar situations will adopt different responses because their cultural repertoires, the contents of their tool kits, are dissimilar.

Swidler's (1986) conceptualization of culture as a tool kit suggests at least two paths by which cultural differences across groups might be expected to affect levels of violence. The first involves knowledge of weapons—how to identify them, how to use them, and so on. Assuredly, it does not require a sophisticated cultural repertoire to make use of some types of weapons available to the human species for thousands of years. Virtually everyone, for example, grasps the concept of picking up a hard object and striking someone on the head. On the other hand, knowledge of firearms and experience in their use differentiate the cultural tool kits typically accessible to men and women in many societies, including the United States, and undoubtedly provide part of the explanation for sex differences in committing both homicide and suicide. It is doubtful, however, if difference in access to weapons or in experience with their use is an important linkage between culture and racial or regional differences in homicide rates, at least in the United States. It is possible, however, that part of the increase in homicide rates among young, minority males in urban areas during the late 1980s and early 1990s is attributable to the availability of more sophisticated and lethal firearms that accompanied the introduction of crack cocaine in inner cities (Blumstein, 1995).

The second path for exploring cultural linkages to violence suggested by Swidler's (1986) work is that culture provides ways of organizing sensory experiences and identifying situations, that is, of answering the question, "What is going on here?" Our view is that culture's primary influence on violence, such as homicide, is through "definitions of the situation," "frames," and/or "attributional styles" that affect the likelihood that an actor will define a situation as one in which physical assault, perhaps with the intent to kill an opponent, is appropriate or even demanded. This is not a new idea. It is implicit in the works of Luckenbill (1977), Lundsgaarde (1977), Reed (1982), and others, but until recently, it has not played a central role in debates about cultural explanations of violence. The notion that actors must "make sense" of their circumstances before deciding on proper lines of action is central to theoretical perspectives focused on the microlevel of social life, including symbolic interactionism and ethnomethodology, but in our view, *attribution theory* provides the most promising foundation for linking culture and homicide at the macrolevel. The following section outlines a provisional integrated theory of homicide and suicide that incorporates attribution theory, as well as cultural and social structural variables, in explaining differences in rates of lethal violence.

■ *AN INTEGRATED MODEL OF HOMICIDE AND SUICIDE*

Although homicide and suicide are typically examined independently (Unnithan et al., 1994), researchers have noted that the rates of these two types of lethal violence usually vary inversely (Ferri, 1925/1934; Guerry, 1833; Henry & Short, 1954; Morselli, 1879/1903; Whitt, Gordon, & Hofley, 1972). Hackney (1969) noted that the pattern of violence characteristic of the American South is best described as a juxtaposition of high homicide and low suicide rates. Unfortunately, Hackney's observation has been ignored by most investigators, who have restricted their attention to the high level of homicide in the region.

Elsewhere, we have proposed an integrated model of lethal violence, that is, homicide and suicide, that provides a different way of thinking about the relationship between culture, social structure, and homicide (Unnithan et al., 1994). As a modified version of Henry and Short's (1954) theory, it conceptualizes both suicide and homicide as violent acts with similar origins. To envision how we view the integrated model operating, imagine a river of violence rushing downstream. The size of the stream is a function of forces of production, which are mainly social-structural factors such as poverty and inequality. These variables are responsible for the overall level of lethal violence in a society or group. Forces of direction, which are mainly cultural, divide the stream into two channels, one representing homicidal, and the other suicidal, behavior. The task of researchers using the integrated model is to identify these two sets of variables. Forces of production, which affect the total volume of lethal violence, would typically be sought in socially patterned (i.e., structural) sources of frustration, stress, or negative life events. Structurally patterned negative life events considered in this way are viewed as the major source of violent acts, whether the target is the self or others.

The integrated model operationalizes the size of the stream of violence in a group or aggregate as the lethal violence rate (LVR), defined as

$$\text{LVR} = (S + H)$$

where S is the suicide rate and H is the homicide rate. Theoretically, the LVR is a function of forces of production. The ebb and flow of both homicides and suicides, therefore, determine the LVR. Hypothetically, if one region of a nation has a relatively high homicide rate and a relatively low suicide rate, its LVR may be similar or identical to another region that has the converse pattern of a relatively high suicide rate and a relatively low homicide rate.

Mathematically, the integrated model's operationalization of the direction of lethal violence, or what Henry and Short (1954) called the "choice between suicide and homicide" (p. 101), is the suicide-homicide ratio, or SHR, which is calculated by dividing the suicide rate by the sum of the suicide and homicide rates (i.e., the LVR). Thus,

$$\text{SHR} = (S/LVR)$$

The SHR represents the proportion of violent deaths in a population that are suicides, rather than homicides. The integrated model links the propensity to express violence as homicide rather than suicide to the concept of attributional (explanatory) styles as developed in the literature on the stress-diatheses (hopelessness) model of depression (e.g., Abramson, Metalsky, & Alloy, 1988; Alloy, Abramson, Metalsky, & Hartlage, 1988; Seligman, 1990, 1992). As a result, the SHR is a product of situational and cultural factors that contribute to the development of explanatory styles and attributions of blame or responsibility for negative life events (Unnithan et al., 1994). Culturally based explanatory styles that emphasize external attributions of blame or responsibility tip the balance of lethal violence toward homicide, thereby lowering the SHR. Although psychologists have examined attribution as an intrapsychic process, several studies show that attributional patterns vary across groups (e.g., Miller, 1984).

There is some evidence that the integrated model provides a useful perspective for understanding the pattern of southern violence. It has been shown (Huff-Corzine et al., 1991) that *southernness,* measured as the percentage of the population born in the census South, is negatively related to the SHR for both Whites and African Americans at the state level. In other words, higher percentages of violent deaths in the South are homicides. More recently, Whitt et al. (1995) found that the SHR is lower in both nonmetropolitan and metropolitan counties in the South than in other regions. Unfortunately, these studies do not include measures of cultural elements apart from region and, therefore, provide no direct evidence on what it is about the South that may predispose its residents toward external violence. They are, however, important in providing support for Hackney's (1969) contention that the distinctiveness of southern violence includes both high homicide rates and low suicide rates. In addition, most research on high homicide rates in the South has assumed that cultural influences affect White southerners *only* (Gastil, 1971; Hackney, 1969), but the findings by Huff-Corzine et al. (1991) support the existence of a regional influence affecting both Whites and African Americans.

■ *RECENT STUDIES AND DIRECTIONS FOR FUTURE RESEARCH*

Although there are exceptions, the majority of studies show that with social-structural variables controlled, southernness increases the homicide rate and lowers the SHR. Opponents of the southern subculture of violence thesis have argued that unmeasured structural variables may account for the apparent relationship between region and homicide (Loftin & Hill, 1974; Parker, 1989). This position is correct, but it is equally plausible that some of the significant relationships between structural variables and levels of violence may be "explained away" once unmeasured cultural differences linked to region are controlled. A third possibility, which we suspect is correct, is that structural conditions such as poverty and inequality encourage the development of culturally based explanatory styles featuring the external attribution of blame. If so, culture would hold the status of an intervening variable useful in explaining how and why structural conditions lead to homicide.

As it has been framed until recently, the structure versus culture debate in research on southern violence is unlikely to be productive. Nonetheless, "it is incumbent upon proponents of the cultural perspective to identify and measure those aspects of Southern culture that affect regional patterns of violence in order that more precise tests can be accomplished" (Huff-Corzine et al., 1991, p. 728). The same task is equally important for explaining distinctive levels of violence among other groups. For example, high levels of violent acts among African Americans that are unexplained by structural variables are often attributed to subcultural differences between the races, although no measures of culture are included in the models (e.g., Harer & Steffensmeier, 1996). In the following section, however, we will limit our review to research that advances our understanding of the interconnections between culture, region, and violence.

Specifying Southern Violence

Although the idea that southerners or others who may hold tolerant views toward violence will be more violent without regard to particular sets of circumstances (e.g., Dixon & Lizotte, 1987) has been criticized (Corzine & Huff-Corzine, 1989; Ellison & McCall, 1989; Reed, 1982), most studies of the linkage between the level of killings and southernness have used total homicide rates for population groups as dependent variables. In a recent examination of the circumstances surrounding homicide incidents recorded in the Federal Bureau of Investigation's Supplementary Homicide Reports, however, Rice and Goldman (1994) show important regional differences in the characteristics of killings. Specifically, southern homicides are more likely than those in other regions to arise from arguments rather than from other types of precipitating incidents. They also more often involve persons who know each other instead of strangers than do killings in the non-South. Furthermore, these relationships are consistent across areas with different population sizes, suggesting that the rural character of the South does not account for these regional patterns.

Homicide events are not homogeneous, and different typologies of homicide, for example, felony versus nonfelony and instrumental versus expressive, have been proposed (Block, 1986; Smith & Parker, 1980; Williams & Flewelling, 1988). For instance, McCall, Land,

and Cohen (1992) show that a regional impact on violent crimes exists for murder but not for other violent offenses. Because robberies include an instrumental component, that is, the desire for money, and felony homicides are more likely to arise from robberies than from other offenses, it is reasonable to predict that expressive and nonfelony homicide rates would reflect a regional influence. These hypotheses are consistent with the view that the increment in southern homicides reflects a regional cultural perspective emphasizing personal honor (Nisbett, 1993), but evidence has been mixed. A positive and significant relationship has been reported between the percentage of the population born in the South and both felony and nonfelony homicide rates for Whites in standard metropolitan statistical areas (Corzine, Huff-Corzine, & Wilson, 1992). On the other hand, Williams and Flewelling (1988) report that a regional variable (the Confederate South) augments city homicide rates in nonconflict situations between family members but has no effect on the level of killings involving other victim-offender relationships. Finally, Smith and Parker (1980) find no evidence of a southern influence on primary or nonprimary homicide rates at the state level.

It is difficult to interpret the significance of these conflicting findings because the studies use different typologies of homicides, units of analysis, and measures for the southern region. Future investigations should devote more attention to developing the linkages between the specific content of the southern cultural tradition and specific types of violence, including homicide. It is likely that studies employing total rates of violence provide only crude tests of cultural and perhaps structural explanations.

Mapping the South

Despite the many efforts to test the southern subculture of violence thesis, few researchers offer theoretical rationales for their measures of southernness. These studies typically allocate cities, metropolitan areas, or states to regions by equating the South with the former Confederacy or by relying on the census classification for the South.[3] Nonetheless, neither the Confederate South nor the census South corresponds to what most people mean when they think about where southern culture begins and ends. Some states that are generally considered culturally southern (Kentucky, Oklahoma, and perhaps West Virginia) lie outside the Confederate South; conversely, the census South includes Delaware and Maryland, states that arguably have more in common with the Northeast than with Mississippi and Alabama. Florida, which is in but perhaps not of the South, presents a problem for both operationalizations. To compensate for this, some researchers using data for states have measured southernness by the percentage of the population born in the South or Gastil's (1971, 1975) Southernness Index, which is based on both historical settlement patterns and more recent population movements.

None of these operationalizations of the South are ideal. Scholars from a variety of disciplines have grappled for more than half a century with the problem of defining the boundaries of the cultural regions of the United States (e.g., Carver, 1987; Gastil, 1975; Kniffin, 1965; Kurath, 1949; Markwardt, 1957; Odum, 1936; Odum & Moore, 1938/1966; Reed, 1976, 1993; Thomas, 1958; Zelinsky, 1951, 1961, 1973). Their regional boundaries have been based on everything from linguistic patterns to the percentage of mules in the draft animal population and from expenditures for cornmeal and lard to the limits of where kudzu grows.

The most comprehensive efforts to delineate cultural regions of the United States are those of Odum (1936; Odum & Moore, 1938/1966), Zelinsky (1973), and Gastil (1975). Odum divided the United States into six major regions. As shown in Figure 4.1, his divisions split the South into two regions—the Southeast and the Southwest—which he claims have more in common with each other than either has with other regions.

Odum's regions are a cleaner way of delineating the limits of southern culture than using the Confederate South or the census South. As Odum recognized, however, any regional classification following state lines faces ambiguities in the classification of Florida and the border states.

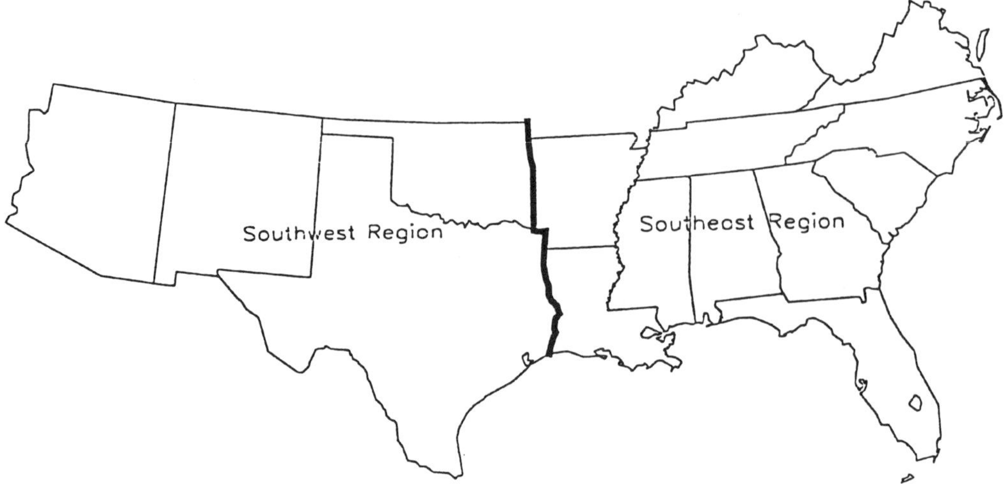

Figure 4.1. Odum's Southern Regions
SOURCE: Odum & Moore (1938/1966).

Because cultural areas do not conveniently coincide with state lines, Zelinsky (1973) and Gastil (1975) have used historical settlement patterns and other cultural factors (e.g., religion and linguistic patterns) to trace regional boundaries that cross state and sometimes even county lines. Attempting to compensate for these difficulties, both have proposed their own boundary schemes, diagrams of which are shown in Figures 4.2 and 4.3.

Odum's regions are probably adequate for use with state-level data. Nonetheless, the extension of southern culture into parts of the border states leads us to prefer Gastil and Zelinsky's finer-grained approach, which allows us "to draw cultural lines along the county lines where they are ultimately most useful" (Gastil, 1971, pp. 425-426). In preliminary research (Whitt et al., 1995), we have used county boundaries to construct three southern subregions—the Eastern South, Western South, and Interior Southwest—using Gastil's and, to a lesser extent, Zelinsky's free-flowing boundaries as a guide. These subregions are displayed in Figures 4.4 and 4.5.

Homicide rates are higher and suicide-homicide ratios are lower in both metropolitan and nonmetropolitan counties in these three subregions than in any other region or subregion of the United States. Moreover, the three southern subregions are ranked on these variables in the order we expect on the basis of the dominance of traditional southern cultural patterns (e.g., membership in the Southern Baptist Church), which declines as one moves west. We believe this approach to measuring southernness has considerable promise, but it fails to answer the question of what it is about southern culture that leads to a predisposition for lethal violence.

Regional Attitudes Toward Violence

Recent investigations have provided some clarity in the identification of regional attitudes toward violence. Using data from the General Social Surveys, Dixon and Lizotte (1987) constructed two scales measuring "violent" and "defensive" attitudes. The Violent Attitudes Scale consists of four questions asking respondents if they approve of an adult male striking or punching another man who committed a minor and, in three cases, nonphysical, provocation; the Defensive Attitudes Scale inquired about the propriety of the same response in three situations—an adult man beating up a woman, striking the man's child, and breaking into his home.

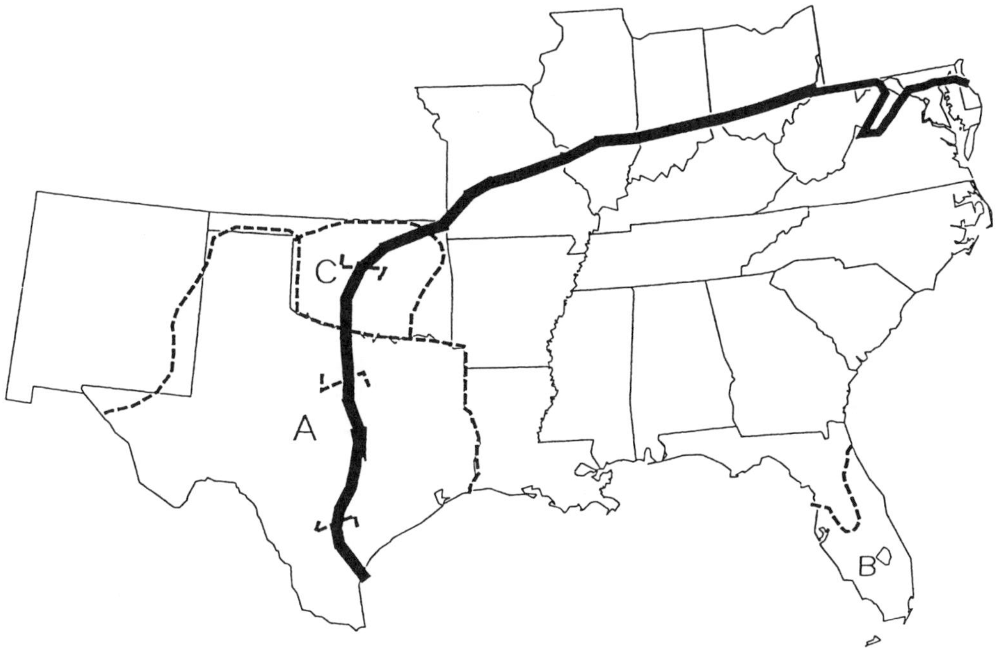

Figure 4.2. Zelinsky's Southern Regions (Note: Texas, Peninsular Florida, and Oklahoma have uncertain status)
SOURCE: Zelinsky (1973).

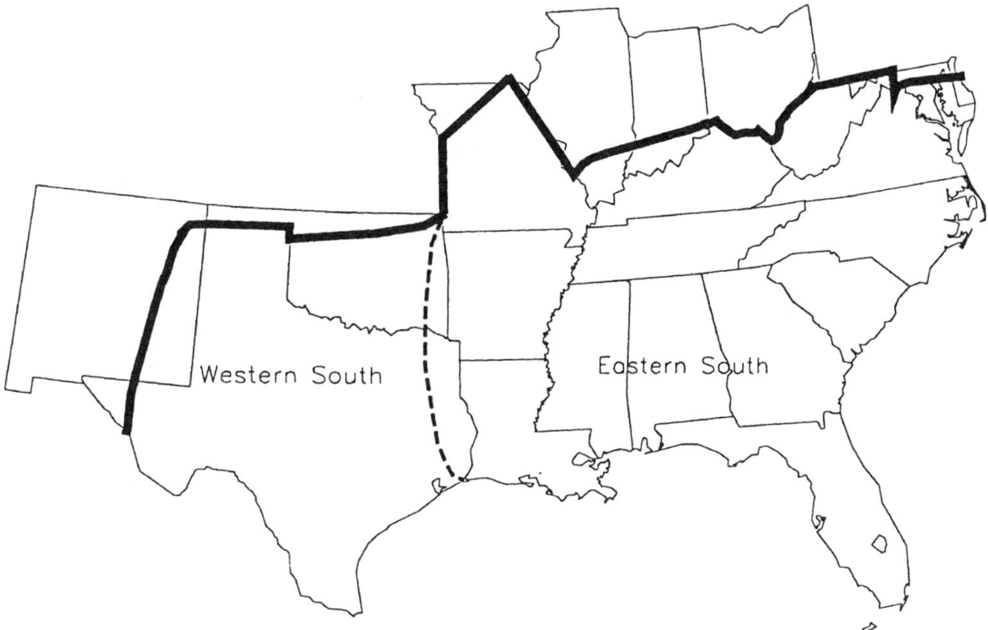

Figure 4.3. Gastil's Southern Regions
SOURCE: Gastil (1975).

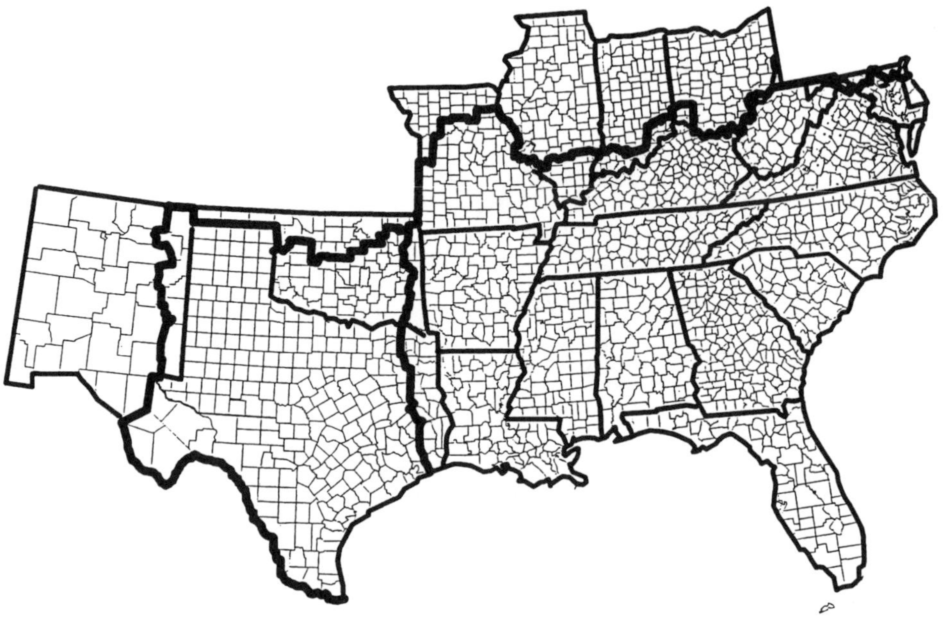

Figure 4.4. Whitt, Corzine, and Huff-Corzine's Southern Regions Using County Boundaries: The Eastern and Western South

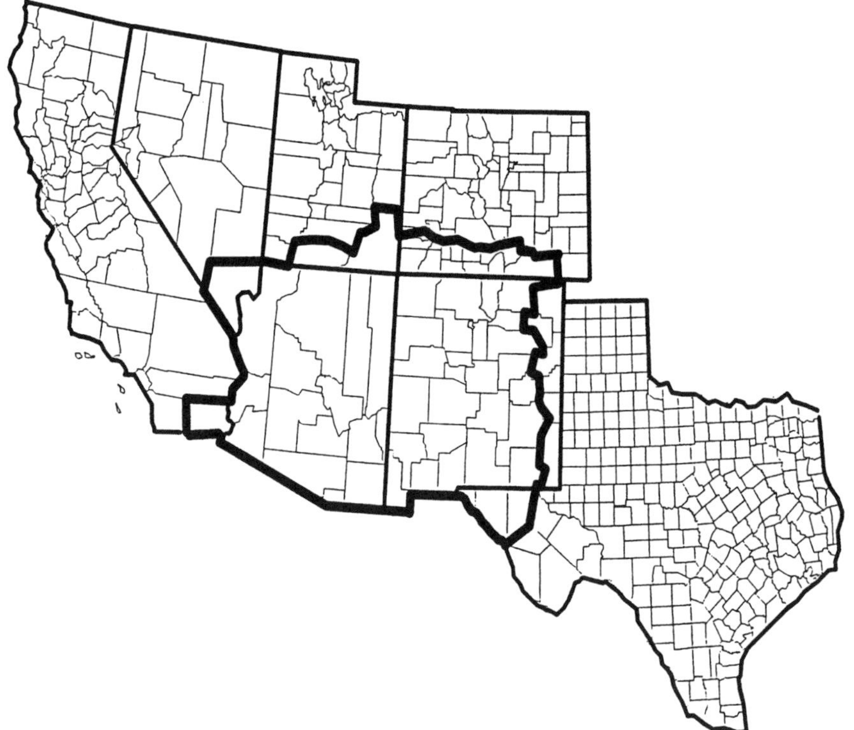

Figure 4.5. Whitt, Corzine, and Huff-Corzine's Southern Regions Using County Boundaries: The Interior Southwest

Although those raised in the South and currently living there scored higher on the Defensive Attitudes Scale than others, Dixon and Lizotte conclude that their study offers no support for the existence of a southern subculture of violence. A more logical interpretation is that southerners are no more likely than others to approve of hitting others in response to minor transgressions but have less hesitancy about using violence against people who pose a serious physical threat to their safety or that of others (Corzine & Huff-Corzine, 1989; Ellison & McCall, 1989).

In perhaps the most important work on regional differences in attitudes toward violence, Ellison (1991) replicates Dixon and Lizotte's finding that southerners are indeed more approving of defensive violence. Moreover, he shows that regional background interacts with gender so that in his words, "Native southern females exhibit fewer inhibitions about the use of physical force than their counterparts elsewhere" (p. 1231).

In addition to specifying cultural content, it is important to specify the mechanisms by which distinctive attitudes, values, attributional styles, and worldviews are transmitted across generations. Ellison (1991) suggests that southern religion may play a pivotal role in maintaining regional views toward violence. Specifically, among southerners, increased church attendance and holding a "hierarchical image of God" (p. 1229) consistent with fundamentalist theology are positively related to support for defensive violence.

The Protestant fundamentalism that is more popular in the South than in other regions (although its influence is growing nationally) may be linked to high levels of homicide through a second mechanism. Lupfer, Hopkinson, and Kelley (1988) conclude that fundamentalists are more likely to attribute intentionality to the acts of others because they emphasize the role of internal characterological traits in guiding behavior. Similarly, Grasmick, Davenport, Chamlin, and Bursik (1992) infer that a tendency to rely on dispositional (i.e., characterological) explanations for the actions of others may explain fundamentalists' support for retribution in judging the appropriateness of criminal sanctions. Further investigation of the relationship of fundamentalist religious beliefs to attributional tendencies and defensive and retributive violence (e.g., "an eye for an eye") holds substantial promise for unraveling the connections between regional culture and the level of killing.

Cultural Products

Beyond research on fundamentalist religious beliefs, studies of the relationship between elements of southern culture and violence have been sparse. The notable exception is the flurry of recent investigations of the effects of country music. Stack and Gundlach's (1992) finding that country music was positively related to suicide rates sparked considerable debate (Maguire & Snipes, 1994; Snipes & Maguire, 1995; Stack & Gundlach, 1994, 1995).

Several characteristics of country music point to its potential effect on violent attitudes and acts. Originating among the White lower class in the rural South, it was originally a badge of southern "ethnic" identity that gradually diffused into the White working- and lower-middle classes in areas settled by southern migrants (Killian, 1970; Peterson & DiMaggio, 1975). Thus, the roots of country music are indisputably southern.

Second, although Stack and Gundlach (1992) linked country music to suicide by emphasizing its traditional emphasis on hard times (e.g., suffering a broken heart or losing oneself in the bottle), the violent acts portrayed in country music are typically directed at others in retaliation for wrongs. This is the type of defensive or retributive violence supported by southerners (Ellison, 1991). As Kenny Rogers points out in "The Coward of the County," when you've been done wrong or the honor of the woman you love has been offended, "sometimes you've got to fight to be a man." Moreover, from Reba McEntire's "The Night the Lights Went Out in Georgia," to "Independence Day" by Martina McBride, country music lyrics describe women as both willing and able to exact homicidal revenge for serious wrongs.

We have argued (Corzine, Huff-Corzine, & Whitt, 1995) that in the context of the integrated model, country music's most likely influence on violence would be to increase the level of homicide by providing cultural legitimation for retaliatory violence. With controls for the percentage of the population born in the South and several structural and demographic characteristics included in multivariate models, however, we report that country music is significantly and negatively related to both suicide and homicide rates at the county level. Although the contention that country music contributes to high levels of lethal violence has received scant support in the literature, further research on the influence of cultural elements characteristic of the South should receive a high priority in research on regional homicide rates.

■ *CONCLUSION*

This chapter, like much of the protracted debate on structural versus cultural factors explaining homicide, has concentrated on cultural theories of southern violence in the United States. Nonetheless, there is a need to extend theory and research to other settings. As we noted above, beginnings have been made in identifying cultural sources of violence among African Americans, Native Americans, Hispanics, and athletes in the United States.

Cross-national research (e.g., Hitson & Funkenstein, 1959; Straus & Straus, 1953; Unnithan & Whitt, 1992; Whitt et al., 1972), some of it in the context of the integrated model, links culture to lethal violence through such variables as child-rearing practices, religion, economic development, and culturally based intolerance of differences. Some of this research is now quite old, and it only scratches the surface of the types of cultures and subcultures of violence similar to those identified by Wolfgang and Ferracuti (1967). As only one example, the concentration of crimes against persons in southern France identified by Guerry in 1833 still calls for an explanation.

■ *NOTES*

1. Guerry's (1833) data are for crimes against persons, rather than homicides per se.

2. The terms *culture* and *subculture* have been used in multiple ways by sociologists, anthropologists, and others. Rather than add our own definitions to those already in the literature, it should be sufficient to note that our preference is for broader definitions of culture (e.g., Curtis, 1975), and we disagree with efforts to identify subcultural adherence or membership *only* on the basis of differences in attitudes or norms (e.g., Dixon & Lizotte, 1987). Subcultures reflect a lack of homogeneity in complex societies (Fine & Kleinman, 1979) and are typically defined in reference to a more inclusive level of social organization, for example, region (subculture) versus nation (culture). In our view, the distinction is not important for understanding how culture (subculture) shapes action in particular contexts but acquires meaning in reference to different rates of behavior across group boundaries.

3. The states of the former Confederacy are Alabama, Arkansas, Florida, Georgia, Louisiana, Mississippi, North Carolina, South Carolina, Tennessee, Texas, and Virginia. The census designation of the South includes these 11 states plus Delaware, Kentucky, Maryland, Oklahoma, and West Virginia.

■ *REFERENCES*

Abramson, L. Y., Metalsky, G. I., & Alloy, L. B. (1988). The hopelessness theory of depression: Does the research test the theory? In L. Y. Abramson (Ed.), *Social cognition and clinical psychology* (pp. 33-65). New York: Guilford.

Alloy, L. B., Abramson, L. Y., Metalsky, G. I., & Hartlage, S. (1988). The hopelessness theory of depression: Attributional aspects. *British Journal of Clinical Psychology, 27,* 5-21.

Anderson, E. (1990). *Streetwise: Race, class, and change in an urban community.* Chicago: University of Chicago Press.

Anderson, E. (1994, May). The code of the streets. *Atlantic Monthly, 273,* 81-94.

Athens, L. (1989). *The creation of dangerous violent criminals.* New York: Routledge & Kegan Paul.

Bachman, R. (1992). *Death and violence on the reservation: Homicide, family violence and suicide in American Indian populations.* New York: Auburn House.

Baker, R. K., & Ball, S. J. (1969). *Mass media and violence: Report to the National Commission on Causes and Prevention of Violence.* Washington, DC: Government Printing Office.

Ball-Rokeach, S. J. (1973). Values and violence: A test of the subculture of violence thesis. *American Sociological Review, 38,* 736-749.

Bankston, W. B., & Thompson, C. Y. (1989). Carrying firearms for protection: A causal model. *Sociological Inquiry, 59,* 75-87.

Bernard, T. J. (1990). Angry aggression among the truly disadvantaged. *Criminology, 28,* 73-96.

Block, C. R. (1986). *Homicide in Chicago.* Chicago: Loyola University, Center for Urban Policy.

Blumstein, A. (1995). Youth violence, guns, and the illicit-drug industry. *Journal of Criminal Law and Criminology, 86,* 10-36.

Brearley, H. C. (1932). *Homicide in the United States.* Chapel Hill: University of North Carolina Press.

Cao, L., Adams, A., & Jensen, B. J. (1997). A test of the Black subculture of violence thesis: A research note. *Criminology, 35,* 367-379.

Carver, C. M. (1987). *American regional dialects: A word geography.* Ann Arbor: University of Michigan Press.

Cohen, A. K. (1955). *Delinquent boys: The culture of the gang.* New York: Free Press.

Corzine, J., & Huff-Corzine, L. (1989). On cultural explanations of southern homicide: Comment on Dixon and Lizotte. *American Journal of Sociology, 95,* 178-182.

Corzine, J., Huff-Corzine, L., & Whitt, H. P. (1995, November). *Country music and lethal violence.* Paper presented at the annual meeting of the American Society of Criminology, Boston.

Corzine, J., Huff-Corzine, L., & Wilson, J. K. (1992, November). *Mean streets: Poverty, race, and homicide in metropolitan areas.* Paper presented at the annual meeting of the American Society of Criminology, New Orleans.

Curtis, L. A. (1975). *Violence, race, and culture.* Lexington, MA: D. C. Heath.

Dixon, J., & Lizotte, A. J. (1987). Gun ownership and the southern subculture of violence. *American Journal of Sociology, 93,* 383-405.

Ellison, C. G. (1991). An eye for an eye? A note on the southern subculture of violence thesis. *Social Forces, 69,* 1223-1239.

Ellison, C. G., & McCall, P. L. (1989). Region and violent attitudes reconsidered: Comment on Dixon and Lizotte. *American Journal of Sociology, 95,* 174-178.

Erlanger, H. S. (1974). The empirical status of the subculture of violence thesis. *Social Problems, 22,* 280-292.

Faulkner, R. R. (1974). Making violence by doing work: Selves, situations, and the world of professional hockey. *Sociology of Work and Occupations, 1,* 288-304.

Felson, R., Liska, A., South, S., & McNulty, T. (1994). The subculture of violence and delinquency: Individual vs. school context effects. *Social Forces, 73,* 155-174.

Felson, R., & Messner, S. F. (1996). To kill or not to kill? Lethal outcomes in injurious attacks. *Criminology, 34,* 519-545.

Ferri, E. (1934). *Omicidio-suicidio* [Homicide-Suicide] (4th ed.) (C. Pena, Trans.). Madrid, Spain: Editorial Review. (Original work published 1925)

Fine, G. A., & Kleinman, S. (1979). Rethinking subculture: An interactionist analysis. *American Journal of Sociology, 85,* 1-20.

Gastil, R. (1971). Homicide and a regional culture of violence. *American Sociological Review, 36,* 412-427.

Gastil, R. (1975). *The cultural regions of the United States.* Seattle: University of Washington Press.

Govone, G. (1968). Speech to parliament by General Govone after leaving his military command in Sicily, December 3, 1863. In D. Mack Smith (Ed.), *The making of Italy, 1796-1870* (pp. 371-373). New York: Walker.

Grasmick, H. G., Davenport, E., Chamlin, M. B., & Bursik, R. J., Jr. (1992). Protestant fundamentalism and the retributive doctrine of punishment. *Criminology, 30,* 21-45.

Guerry, A. (1833). *Essai sur la statistique morale de la France* [Essay on the moral statistics of France]. Paris: Chez Crochard.

Hackney, S. (1969). Southern violence. *American Historical Review, 39,* 906-925.

Hannerz, U. (1969). The roots of Black manhood. *Transaction, 6,* 12-21.

Harer, M. D., & Steffensmeier, D. J. (1996). Race and prison violence. *Criminology, 34,* 323-355.

Hartnagel, T. F. (1980). Subculture of violence: Further evidence. *Pacific Sociological Review, 23,* 217-242.

Heimer, K. (1997). Socioeconomic status, subcultural definitions, and violent delinquency. *Social Forces, 75,* 799-833.

Henry, A. F., & Short, J. F., Jr. (1954). *Suicide and homicide: Some economic, sociological, and psychological aspects of aggression.* Glencoe, IL: Free Press.

Hitson, H. M., & Funkenstein, D. H. (1959). Family pattern and paranoidal personality structure in Boston and Burma. *International Journal of Social Psychiatry, 5,* 182-190.

Huff-Corzine, L., Corzine, J., & Moore, D. C. (1986). Southern exposure: Deciphering the South's influence on homicide rates. *Social Forces, 64,* 906-924.

Huff-Corzine, L., Corzine, J., & Moore, D. C. (1991). Deadly connections: Culture, poverty, and the direction of lethal violence. *Social Forces, 69,* 715-732.

Killian, L. M. (1970). *White southerners.* New York: Random House.

Kniffin, F. B. (1965). Folk housing: Key to diffusion. *Annals of the Association of American Geographers, 55,* 549-577.

Kurath, H. (1949). *A word geography of the eastern United States.* Ann Arbor: University of Michigan Press.

Land, K. C., McCall, P. L., & Cohen, L. E. (1990). Structural covariates of homicide rates: Are there any invariances across time and space? *American Journal of Sociology, 95,* 922-963.

Loftin, C., & Hill, R. H. (1974). Regional subculture and homicide: An examination of the Gastil-Hackney thesis. *American Sociological Review, 39,* 714-724.

Luckenbill, D. F. (1977). Criminal homicide as a situated transaction. *Social Problems, 25,* 176-186.

Lundsgaarde, H. P. (1977). *Murder in space city.* New York: Oxford University Press.

Lupfer, M., Hopkinson, P. J., & Kelley, P. (1988). An exploration of the attributional styles of Christian fundamentalists and authoritarians. *Journal of Scientific Study of Religion, 27,* 389-398.

Mack Smith, D. (1969). *Italy: A modern history.* Ann Arbor: University of Michigan Press.

Markowitz, F. E., & Felson, R. B. (1998). Social-demographic attitudes and violence. *Criminology, 36,* 117-138.

McCall, P. L., Land, K. C., & Cohen, L. E. (1992). Violent criminal behavior: Is there a general and continuing influence of the South? *Social Science Research, 21,* 286-310.

Maguire, E. R., & Snipes, J. B. (1994). Reassessing the link between country music and suicide. *Social Forces, 72,* 1239-1243.

Markwardt, A. H. (1957). Principal and subsidiary dialect areas of the north-central states. *Publications of the American Dialect Society, 27,* 3-15.

Miller, J. G. (1984). Culture and the development of everyday social explanation. *Journal of Personality and Social Psychology, 46,* 961-978.

Miller, W. B. (1958). Lower class culture as a generating milieu in gang delinquency. *Journal of Social Issues, 14,* 5-19.

Montell, W. L. (1986). *Killings: Folk justice in the upper South.* Lexington: University Press of Kentucky.

Morselli, H. (1903). *Suicide: An essay in comparative moral statistics.* New York: Appleton. (Original work published 1879)

Neapolitan, J. L. (1994). Cross-national variation in homicides: The case of Latin America. *International Criminal Justice Review, 4,* 4-22.

Nelsen, C., Corzine, J., & Huff-Corzine, L. (1994). The violent West reexamined: A research note on regional homicide rates. *Criminology, 32,* 149-161.

Nisbett, R. E. (1993). Violence and U.S. regional culture. *American Psychologist, 48,* 441-449.

Odum, H. W. (1936). *Southern regions of the United States.* Chapel Hill: University of North Carolina Press.

Odum, H. W., & Moore, H. E. (1966). *American regionalism.* Glouster, MA: Peter Smith. (Original work published 1938)

Ogle, R. S., Maier-Katkin, D., & Bernard, T. J. (1995). A theory of homicidal behavior among women. *Criminology, 33,* 173-193.

Parker, R. N. (1989). Poverty, subculture of violence, and type of homicide. *Social Forces, 67,* 983-1007.

Parker, R. N., & Rebhun, L. (1995). *Alcohol and homicide: A deadly combination of two American traditions.* Albany: State University of New York Press.

Peterson, R. A., & DiMaggio, P. (1975). From region to class: The changing focus of country music. *Social Forces, 53,* 497-506.

Redfield, H. V. (1880). *Homicide, North and South.* Philadelphia: J. B. Lippincott.

Reed, J. S. (1976). The heart of Dixie: An essay in folk geography. *Social Forces, 54,* 925-939.

Reed, J. S. (1982). *One South: An ethnic approach to regional culture.* Baton Rouge: Louisiana State University Press.

Reed, J. S. (1993). *My tears spoiled my aim and other reflections on southern culture.* Columbia: University of Missouri Press.

Rice, T. W., & Goldman, C. R. (1994). Another look at the subculture of violence thesis: Who murders whom and under what circumstances. *Sociological Spectrum, 14,* 371-384.

Rose, H. M., & McClain, P. D. (1990). *Race, place, and risk: Black homicide in urban America.* Albany: State University of New York Press.

Rose, H. M., & McClain, P. D. (1998). Race, place, and risk revisited: A perspective on the emergence of a new subcultural paradigm. *Homicide Studies, 2,* 101-129.

Sampson, R. J. (1987). Urban Black violence: The effect of male joblessness and family disruption. *American Journal of Sociology, 93,* 348-382.

Seligman, M. E. P. (1990). *Learned optimism.* New York: Pocket.

Seligman, M. E. P. (1992). *Helplessness: On development, depression and death.* New York: Freeman.

Sellin, T. (1938). *Culture conflict and crime.* New York: Social Science Research Council.

Shoemaker, D. J., & Williams, J. S. (1987). The subculture of violence and ethnicity. *Journal of Criminal Justice, 15,* 461-472.

Smith, M. D., & Parker, R. N. (1980). Type of homicide and variation in regional rates. *Social Forces, 59,* 136-147.

Snipes, J. B., & Maguire, E. R. (1995). Country music, suicide and spuriousness. *Social Forces, 74,* 327-329.

Stack, S., & Gundlach, J. (1992). The effect of country music on suicide. *Social Forces, 71,* 211-218.

Stack, S., & Gundlach, J. (1994). Country music and suicide: A reply to Maguire and Snipes. *Social Forces, 72,* 1245-1248.

Stack, S., & Gundlach, J. (1995). Country music and suicide—individual, indirect and interaction effects: A reply to Snipes and Maguire. *Social Forces, 74,* 331-335.

Straus, J. H., & Straus, M. A. (1953). Suicide, homicide and social structure in Ceylon. *American Journal of Sociology, 58,* 461-469.

Swidler, A. (1986). Culture in action. *American Sociological Review, 51,* 273-286.

Sykes, G. M., & Matza, D. (1957). Techniques of neutralization. *American Sociological Review, 22,* 664-670.

Thomas, C. K. (1958). The linguistic Mason and Dixon line. In D. C. Bryant (Ed.), *The rhetorical idiom: Essays in rhetoric, oratory, language, and drama* (pp. 251-255). Ithaca, NY: Cornell University Press.

Unnithan, N. P., Huff-Corzine, L., Corzine, J., & Whitt, H. P. (1994). *The currents of lethal violence: An integrated model of suicide and homicide.* Albany: State University of New York Press.

Unnithan, N. P., & Whitt, H. P. (1992). Inequality, economic development and lethal violence: A cross-national analysis of suicide and homicide. *International Journal of Comparative Sociology, 33,* 182-195.

Whitt, H. P., Corzine, J., & Huff-Corzine, L. (1995). Where is the South? A preliminary analysis of the southern subculture of violence. In C. R. Block & R. L. Block (Eds.),

Trends, risks, and interventions in lethal violence (pp. 127-148). Washington, DC: National Institute of Justice.

Whitt, H. P., Gordon, C. P., & Hofley, J. R. (1972). Religion, economic development and lethal aggression. *American Sociological Review, 37,* 193-201.

Williams, K. R., & Flewelling, R. L. (1988). The social production of criminal homicide: A comparative study of disaggregated rates in American cities. *American Sociological Review, 53,* 421-431.

Wilson, W. J. (1987). *The truly disadvantaged: The inner city, the underclass, and public policy.* Chicago: University of Chicago Press.

Wilson, W. J. (1996). *When work disappears: The world of the new urban poor.* New York: Knopf.

Wolfgang, M. E. (1958). *Patterns in criminal homicide.* Philadelphia: University of Pennsylvania Press.

Wolfgang, M. E., & Ferracuti, F. (1967). *The subculture of violence.* London: Tavistock.

Zelinsky, W. (1951). Where the South begins: The northern limit of the CIS-Appalachian South in terms of settlement landscape. *Social Forces, 30,* 172-178.

Zelinsky, W. (1961). An approach to the religious geography of the United States: Patterns of church membership in 1952. *Annals of the Association of American Geographers, 51,* 139-193.

Zelinsky, W. (1973). *The cultural geography of the United States.* Englewood Cliffs, NJ: Prentice Hall.

CHAPTER 5

An Evolutionary Psychological Perspective on Homicide

■ *Martin Daly & Margo Wilson*

Spend some time perusing an archive of homicide cases, and you are likely to find that certain conflict typologies, characteristic of particular victim-killer relationship categories, are common. Barroom interactions among unrelated men became heated contests concerning dominance, deference, and face, and escalated to lethality. Women seeking to exercise autonomy were slain by proprietary ex-partners. Thieves killed victims they feared might cause them trouble later. Children were fatally assaulted by angry caretakers.

How are we to understand why certain recurring types of conflicts of interest engender passions that are sometimes so intense as to motivate these prototypical sorts of homicides? A satisfactory answer to this question seems to require an understanding of what interpersonal conflicts of interest are fundamentally about, and such an understanding must itself be predicated on a basic theory of the sources and substance of individual self-interests. Fortunately, scientists have been developing, testing, and refining the requisite body of theory for decades, with the result that it is now sufficiently complex, nonintuitive, and well verified to be of real value to criminologists and other social scientists. The area of intellectual endeavor to which we refer has come to be called *evolutionary psychology* (Barkow, Cosmides, & Tooby, 1992; Bock & Cardew, 1997; Daly & Wilson, 1988a, 1988b, 1995, 1997; Simpson & Kenrick, 1997; Wright, 1994). This chapter is intended to provide an overview of this perspective and to demonstrate its utility for enhancing the understanding of homicide.

AUTHORS' NOTE: We thank the following agencies for financial support of the work cited in this chapter: the Social Sciences and Humanities Research Council of Canada, the Harry Frank Guggenheim Foundation, the Natural Sciences and Engineering Research Council of Canada, the North Atlantic Treaty Organization, the John Simon Guggenheim Foundation, the Center for Advanced Study in the Behavioral Sciences, Health and Welfare Canada, the McMaster University Arts Research Board, and the John D. and Catherine T. MacArthur Foundation.

■ *A SHORT INTRODUCTION TO EVOLUTIONARY PSYCHOLOGY*

The evolutionary view is that the basic perceptions of self-interest shared by all normal members of a given species are products of a long history of natural and sexual selection and thus may be expected to exhibit "design" for promoting *fitness* (genetic posterity) in ancestral environments. The phrase "perceptions of self-interest" should be interpreted broadly. We intend that it should encompass appetites and aversions both for relatively specific pleasures and pains and for such intangibles as social status and self-esteem, and even that it should encompass processes that are not psychological in any ordinary sense of that word. Our immune systems and cell membranes, for example, operate outside our awareness, but they participate in perceiving and defending our interests nonetheless.

In this view, it is often useful to analyze an individual organism into its constituent adaptations, that is, components with specific functions. A human being, for example, is a complex integrated system in which distinct tasks such as respiration, learning, digestion, visual scene analysis, killing parasitic microorganisms, and so forth are carried out by distinct bits of anatomical, biochemical, and psychological machinery. The properties of these bits of machinery are largely to be understood in terms of their separate functions, but a fuller understanding requires consideration of how they fit into the functionally integrated, higher-order agenda of the whole organism. From an evolutionary perspective, the essence of that higher-order agenda is the manufacture of additional, similar creatures, because reproductive posterity is the sole criterion by which all that complex functionality was accumulated through generations. Darwinian selection is the only source of functional design in evolution, and *selection* is nothing more or less than the differential reproductive success of alternative attributes (phenotypes) within populations and within each sex. It follows that selection favors any attribute that enables individuals to outreproduce others of the same sex and species, and it also follows that these reproductively efficacious attributes are the constituent adaptations referred to above.

Adaptationist reasoning about the functional designs of the organism's component parts and processes is a ubiquitous and inescapable element of all life sciences (Mayr, 1983). Assumptions and hypotheses about adaptive function pervade psychology for the same reason that they pervade physiology—because the mechanisms under study are obviously organized in such a way as to achieve something (Daly & Wilson, 1995). Psychological research is guided by conceptions of what that "something" might be; this includes objectives such as signal detection, social comparison, the reduction of frustration, and the maintenance of self-esteem. Unfortunately, adaptationist thinking in psychology has often been naive because of failures to make use of contemporary understandings of evolution by selection, the process that creates adaptations. Had Freud better understood the implications of Darwinism, for example, the world might have been spared such fantastic notions as "death instincts" and "Oedipal" desires.

Psychologists have long been aware of hierarchies of function. Lateral inhibition in the retina, for example, is interpreted as a means to the end of edge detection, which is a means to the end of object recognition, which is a means to such ends as finding food and avoiding predators, which are means to the ends of energy accrual and survival. Psychologists who lack an evolutionary overview, however, have wandered down innumerable garden paths by imagining that the summit to this hierarchy of functions—the end to which one's immediate objectives are subsidiary—is homeostatic quietude, personal growth, longevity, the reproduction of the species, or even death. What people and other organisms are organized to achieve is, of course, none of these. It is *fitness:* the expected value (in the statistical sense) of a phenotypic design's success in promoting the replicative success of its bearer's genes relative to their alleles (alternative variants at the same genetic locus), in the environment(s) in which that phenotypic design evolved.

The implication is that psychological phenomena—appetites and aversions, attentional priorities, memory systems, time horizons, thrill seeking, maternal love, and so forth—have all evolved to facilitate behavioral choices with the best expected fitness consequences in ancestral environments. Sweet tastes acquired their appeal because they were useful indicators of the presence of valuable nutrients. Infidelity of one's mate is aversive because of the threats to fitness that it has entailed.

We stress *ancestral environments* because the evolved psychology and physiology of any species are historical artifacts, designed by a natural selective process that required persistent relationships between cue and consequence through many generations. When environments change rapidly, evolved psychological mechanisms will not necessarily promote fitness, even on average (Symons, 1990; Tooby & Cosmides, 1990). Mechanisms whose function is the detection of nutrients can be deceived by evolutionarily novel substances such as saccharine. Mechanisms whose function is the assessment of a potential mate's fertility can be deceived by evolutionarily novel cosmetic interventions. The point here is not that an evolved psyche is a simple stimulus-response machine, which it clearly is not, but simply that fitness is not itself a goal that people and other animals could have evolved to monitor or pursue. Our most basic aims are things that led to fitness in past environments, and they do not necessarily do so in the present environment. Thus, although we will not repeat the phrase "ancestral environments" whenever we speak of such things as "statistically expected fitness consequences," the reader should assume that meaning.

It is easy to accept the idea that such psychophysiological phenomena as sweetness detection exist and take their present forms by virtue of their past contributions to survival and reproduction. Where readers are more likely to balk is at the notion that selection has also imparted complex structure to the seemingly more voluntary and rational psychological processes by which people choose and execute the means to gain their ends. Introspection and folk psychology can be misleading in these matters, however, and we maintain that a more subtle evolutionary psychological conception better reflects the diversity of processes that actually mediate "choice" among behavioral alternatives.

What is the essence of decision making? Evolutionists routinely model the costs and benefits of alternative decision rules about such matters as how many eggs a bird should lay before incubating them and rearing the chicks, or when a plant should stop putting all its accumulated energy into further growth and start putting some into reproduction. To everyday folk psychology, this use of the term *decision* is likely to sound metaphorical; *real* decisions are surely the products of deliberation by conscious human beings! Unfortunately for this folk conception, however, experimental psychologists have demonstrated repeatedly that people do not necessarily enjoy privileged insight into the determinants of their own decisions and that the phenomenology of deliberation and reasoned choice can be illusory and reconstructive (Kahneman, Slovic, & Tversky, 1982; Nisbett & Ross, 1980). People provide and defend sincere, coherent explanations for their own choice behavior that are demonstrably incorrect (e.g., Nisbett & Wilson, 1977), and this retrospective theorizing about the reasons for our actions not merely leads us to misunderstand why we did what we did but even makes us misrecall the actions themselves, sometimes rather dramatically. Some researchers in this area have concluded that human decision making and the inferential procedures that inform it are inept, but that is not our intended point here. (Human inference and choice procedures apparently deal with naturalistic inputs very well; see Cosmides & Tooby, 1995; Gigerenzer & Hoffrage, 1995.) Rather, the point we stress is that decision processes are not so transparent to introspection as one might suppose. A great deal of inaccessible information processing, carried out by complex evolved machinery designed by selection specifically to make such decisions, is involved.

This complex evolved machinery includes the emotions, which are readily interpreted as functional operating modes whose specific elements are design features facilitating effective response to the situations that arouse them (Nesse, 1990). Anger, for example, entails physiological mobilization that clearly represents preparation for violent action. Jealousy directs attention to specific types of subtle social cues. Thus, to an evolutionist, the popular notion that emotion is the antithesis and enemy of rationality misconstrues both. If fear, anger, jealousy, and other emotional states interfered with our capacities to make decisions that furthered our interests, we would have evolved to be affectless zombies. That humans have not done so is testimony to the functionality of emotional states, as is the incapacity of people whose emotional mechanisms are operating abnormally (Nesse, 1990).

Once the complexity of the psychological machinery generating even our "rational" choices is acknowledged, it no longer seems odd to speak of a physiological "decision" about when to ovulate or to refer to "choice" points in growth and development, using the same language that we apply to the process that selects among behavioral options. In all these cases, certain courses of action are selected over alternatives by elaborate and only partially understood procedures that use evolved information-processing machinery to respond to some combination of contemporary extrinsic inputs and trace representations of past experience. And it is in this sense of decision making that evolutionary psychologists address such problems as how the human mind assesses prospective costs and benefits, discounts the future, responds to cumulative and immediate social inputs, and . . . opts for committing murder.

■ *HOMICIDE AS A CONFLICT ASSAY*

The proposition that expected fitness is the currency underlying perceptions of self-interest entails an implicit theory about where interests intersect and where they diverge. If the exigencies that enhance person A's expected fitness enhance person B's, too, then we may expect that the two will perceive their interests as harmonious, and each will ordinarily be happy to let the other pursue his or her aims unobstructed. An example is the case of monogamous mates with a shared interest in the welfare of their offspring. Conversely, two creatures are likely to perceive their interests as discordant, and hence to experience conflict, to the degree that the exigencies that raise one's expected fitness diminish the other's. Each party suffers when the other actively promotes its self-interest, and inclinations to thwart one another are likely. An example is the case of rivals for the same mate.

Clearly, where interpersonal violence is a response to apprehended conflict, this conceptual framework has implications about who is likely to use violence against whom and about the circumstances that will exacerbate or mitigate the risk of violence in particular relationship categories. That has been the unifying idea behind our evolutionary psychological approach to the epidemiology of homicide (Daly & Wilson, 1988a, 1988b, 1997; Wilson & Daly, 1985, 1993a, 1996). Any theory of the nature of human conflict ought to shed some light on who is likely to kill whom, when, why, and under what circumstances.

Homicides are extreme manifestations of interpersonal conflict and, for that reason, are detected and recorded in a more reliable, less biased way than more frequent but less extreme types of conflict behavior such as assaults and slanders. An *assay,* such as the color change that an acid induces in litmus paper or the ovulatory behavior that a pregnant woman's urine induces in a frog, is a conspicuous manifestation of some otherwise cryptic quantity of interest. Because they are relatively reliably detected and recorded, homicides provide a *conflict assay*—an index of relationship-specific, demographic, and situational variations in the intensity of interpersonal conflict.

It must be emphasized that using homicides as an assay of the evolved psychology of interpersonal conflict does not presuppose that killing is (or even that it necessarily ever was) an effective way to promote one's fitness. There may or may not be aspects of the human psyche that have been shaped by selection to deal specifically with lethal intraspecific conflict, but that is immaterial for present purposes. Regardless of whether killing is interpreted as effective self-interested action or as an overreactive "mistake," we may expect that the factors that exacerbate or mitigate conflict will raise or lower the likelihood of homicide accordingly. Insofar as killings represent the extreme tail of a distribution—rare products of psychological processes whose more usual, nonlethal manifestations have useful social effects such as successful resource expropriation, deterrence of infidelity, coercion, and intimidation—then factors that influence the likelihood of violence in the pursuit of these valuable social outcomes may be expected to affect the risk of homicide, too.

Although homicides are often, perhaps typically, overreactions whose net effects are not in the perpetrators' interests, it does not follow that violence is a pathology. Pathologies are failures of anatomical, physiological, and psychological entities and processes, reducing their effectiveness in achieving the adaptive functions for which they evolved (Nesse & Williams, 1994; Williams & Nesse, 1991). Violence cannot be dismissed as a mere by-product of such failures because people and other animals possess psychological and physiological machinery that is clearly *designed for* the production and regulation of violence (Archer, 1988; Daly & Wilson, 1997; Huntingford & Turner, 1987). The evidence for this claim is broad. For example, violent inclinations are aroused in contexts in which they are likely to be useful, such as in response to the usurpation of valued resources, and the motivational states of readiness for violence entail complex psychophysiological and postural mobilization for effective agonistic action. There are morphological structures that function solely or primarily as intraspecific weapons, and they are often sexually differentiated and characteristic of delimited life stages. There is neural machinery dedicated to aggression, and this too is often sexually differentiated. Moreover, the sexual differentiation of physical aggression is itself variable across species, and the magnitude of sex differences in both overt weaponry and in intrasexual aggressive behavior is systematically related to the breeding system (Daly & Wilson, 1983). These facts are testimony to the potency of Darwinian selection in shaping the anatomy and psychology of aggression.

The mistaken idea that human violence is merely pathological has perhaps been reinforced by the modern conviction that it is a product of disadvantaged backgrounds and environments. But this association is by no means universal. In face-to-face societies without central authority, violent capability and action are prevalent among the most successful men, too, and contribute to their success (see, for example, Betzig, 1986; Chagnon, 1988, 1996). In modern state societies, the welfare of most people no longer depends on their personal violent capability or that of their allies, and violent action is therefore relatively likely to reflect psychological pathology (but see Furlow, Gangestad, & Armijo-Prewitt, 1998). However, a disproportionate number of violent offenders are drawn from precisely those groups who lack access to the opportunities and protective state services available to more fortunate citizens and who therefore find themselves in "self-help" circumstances much like those experienced by most of our human ancestors. It is not at all clear that violence in such circumstances is usefully deemed pathological, and even in those cases in which the perpetrator suffers from a defect, there remains a functional organization to violence's contingent controls.

Thus, although evolutionary psychological hypotheses about risk factors for homicide do not presuppose that killing per se is an evolved adaptation, they *are* predicated on the assumption that the arousal of violent inclinations is systematically and functionally related to self-interest and interpersonal conflict.

■ *EVOLVED NEPOTISM AND FAMILY VIOLENCE*

One hundred fifty years ago, the adaptive complexity of living creatures could be interpreted only as a reflection of the incomprehensible aesthetic preferences of one or more creators. Darwin (1859) radically reinterpreted biological adaptations as components of *reproductive strategies,* a view that remained essentially unchanged for more than a century, until

Hamilton (1964) pointed out that personal reproductive success is not really the fundamental criterion of success or failure in the evolutionary sweepstakes. The more basic criterion is one's impact on the replicative success of one's phenotypic and genotypic elements, whether in one's descendants (one's *direct fitness effects*) or in other kin (*indirect fitness effects*).

Imagine a woman we shall call Ego. Any one of Ego's genes has a 50% chance of having a descendant copy in her daughter, D. Each such gene also has a 50% chance of being represented in Ego's sister, S, by virtue of descent from the same parental gene. D and S are equally related to Ego and equally likely to share any of her heritable traits. Any child produced by S would provide exactly the same expected contribution to Ego's long-term genetic posterity as would a child of D. Hence, it is at least possible for selection to favor sororal as well as maternal beneficence. Whether it will do so in any given species depends on its ecology and on the average effects of alternative ways of allocating one's efforts.

Hamilton's (1964) *inclusive fitness* theory formalized and generalized this *nepotistic* logic, providing the single most important stimulus to recent theory and research on social evolution (for an elaboration, see Cronin, 1991). By extending the concept of fitness to include indirect as well as direct fitness effects, he solved the problem of accounting for the evolution of altruistic actions that reduce the actor's expected reproductive success while enhancing someone else's. In the process, Hamilton replaced the classical Darwinian conception of organisms as evolved *reproductive strategists* with the notion that they have evolved to be *nepotistic strategists* (Alexander, 1979).

One implication of this theory is that any socially complex species is likely to possess psychological adaptations tending to soften potentially costly conflicts among genetic relatives. If the rival in a contest for a limited resource is my brother, for example, it makes less difference to my fitness who wins than if the rival were unrelated, so the benefit of victory is diminished. Moreover, the cost of using dangerous competitive tactics is higher in the case of fraternal rivalry because injury to either party damages the fitness of both. One implication is that evolved social psychologies are likely to be structured such that they respond to cues indicative of close kinship by turning down the heat of conflict, and a large body of research on nonhuman animals has confirmed this expectation. For example, in some species of fig wasps, coresidency inside a fig is a reliable cue of probable brotherhood, and males engage in a nonviolent scramble competition for mating opportunities, whereas in related species in which coresidency is not indicative of kinship (because females move between each act of oviposition), males fight to the death (Hamilton, 1967). In ground squirrels, adult females treat younger adult females who were seen affiliating with their own mothers relatively tolerantly because the affiliation is a cue that they are at least maternal half-sisters, but they also favor littermate full sisters over littermate half-sisters (those with different fathers as a result of polygamous mating by the mother), probably on the basis of odor cues of kinship (Holmes & Sherman, 1982).

The general rule is that the intensity of conflict is adjusted nepotistically in relation to available cues of kinship. There is no obvious reason why human beings should be an exception. Nevertheless, that is how our species is sometimes portrayed. Even the professional literature on family violence often implies that rather than being relatively subdued, conflicts with close kin are especially violent. According to Gelles and Straus (1985), for example,

> With the exception of the police and the military, the family is perhaps the most violent social group, and the home the most violent social setting, in our society. A person is more likely to be hit or killed in his or her home by another family member than anywhere else or by anyone else. (p. 88)

To an evolutionary psychologist, these assertions are too surprising to escape critical scrutiny. The first concept needing scrutiny is *family*. Following Wolfgang (1958), homicide researchers have commonly partitioned the victim-killer relationship into three categories: stranger, acquaintance, and relative. But the third of these is far too general, encompassing relationships whose qualitative distinctions greatly surpass those distinguishing "strangers" from "acquaintances." Within the family, the evolutionary psychological basis of the parent-child relationship is different from that characterizing the marital relationship because parent and child are genetic relatives with an indissoluble overlap in expected fitness, whereas a comparable overlap in the expected fitness of marriage partners is predicated on reproduction and sexual fidelity. It follows that the specific potential sources of conflict in these two family relationships are likely to be quite different, and indeed they are (Daly & Wilson, 1988a).

The proposition that social motives are functionally nepotistic implies mitigated conflict among blood (but not necessarily marital) relatives. Testing the hypothesis that kinship softens conflict is trickier than it may first appear, however, because one must somehow take account of the differential opportunities for interaction that characterize different relationships as a result of routine activities and social organization. One way to control for opportunity, at least in part, is to consider only within-household relationships, for which the numbers at risk in a relevant population at large can be derived from census or survey information. We conducted such an analysis of within-household homicides in Detroit (Daly & Wilson, 1982), and the results strongly upheld the distinction between genetic and marital relatives; specifically, rates of homicide by victim-killer relationship category were vastly higher both for spouses and for other coresiding persons who were not genetic relatives than for any category of blood kin.

A second way to control for opportunity while testing for nepotistic discrimination is to compare the distribution of victim-killer relationships with that of co-offender relationships. Although opportunity variables presumably influence the two in parallel, the distributions are always different; close genetic relationships are far more prevalent among collaborators in violence than among victim and killer in each of a wide variety of human societies, whereas the reverse is consistently true about inlaws (Daly & Wilson, 1988b). Even in patrilineal social systems in which brothers are one another's principal rivals for familial lands and titles, there is evidence that close genealogical relationship softens otherwise equivalent conflicts and reduces the incidence of violence.

We have discussed opportunity models as if they were alternatives to Hamiltonian nepotism, but they need not be. Kinship cannot be apprehended magically; nepotistic allocations of benefits depend on *cues* of kinship, and those cues might in principal be the ones invoked as determinants of behavior in an opportunity model. Many animals indeed "recognize" their kin on the basis of mere exposure, for example, but that usually means exposure at a specific life stage (Hepper, 1991). If one's nest mates are reliably one's siblings in a given species, then selection may favor learning the individual identities of putative siblings in infancy and continuing to treat such early nest mates preferentially throughout life. The effect will be nepotistic discrimination in favor of close genetic relatives unless some mishap (such as an evolutionarily unforeseen cross-fostering by an experimenter) has uncoupled genetic relatedness from infantile familiarity. Familiarity in general (that is, regardless of life stage), however, is unlikely to be an even remotely reliable cue of kinship, and it is certainly not the basis of familial solidarity in *Homo sapiens* (Daly, Salmon, & Wilson, 1997).

Child Homicide

Evolutionary thinking led to the discovery of the most important risk factor for child homicide—the presence of a *stepparent* (Daly & Wilson, 1996). Parental efforts and investments are valuable resources, and selection favors those parental psyches that allocate effort effectively to promote fitness. The adaptive problems that challenge parental decision making include both the accurate identification of one's offspring and the allocation of one's resources among them with sensitivity to their needs and abilities to convert parental investment into fitness increments. A mistake in identification can obviously incur a huge natural selective penalty, and countless animals have been found to be sensitive to species-appropriate cues that help parents avoid squandering resources on nonrelatives. Nevertheless, parents can be deceived, especially because selection is also acting on those unrelated usurpers to evolve means of bypassing parental defenses, as is dramatically illustrated by cuckoos and other brood parasites that lay eggs (which often mimic those of their hosts) in the nests of other species.

More puzzling than such deception are instances in which adults who have access to reliable cues of nonparenthood take on parental duties nonetheless. In the animal kingdom, this happens mainly after forming a new mateship with a mate that already has dependent young. In many species, such young are likely to be killed, but in species in which the single parent has some leverage, the replacement mate may assume the role of stepparent, with varying degrees of effort and enthusiasm. The human animal is clearly such a species: New mates make pseudoparental investments in their predecessors' children as part of the reciprocal exchange involved in courting and establishing a relationship with the widowed or divorced parent.

Human stepparents invest considerable effort and may even come to love their wards. But it would be surprising if the psychology of genetic parenthood were fully engaged, with full commitment, in this situation. It is adaptive and normal for genetic parents to accept nontrivial risks to their own lives in caring for their young, but selection is likely to have favored much lower thresholds of tolerable cost in stepparenting. Stepchildren were seldom or never so valuable to one's expected fitness as one's own offspring would be, and those parental psyches that were easily parasitized by just any appealing youngster must always have incurred a selective disadvantage. It is little wonder, then, that the exploitation and mistreatment of stepchildren are thematic staples of folktales all around the world (Thompson, 1955). And little wonder, too, that stepparental obligation demonstrably enters into remarriage decisions as a cost, not a benefit, with dependent children from past unions both detracting from the single parent's marriage market value and raising the chance that the remarriage will fail (White & Booth, 1985).

In light of these considerations, one might suppose that child abuse researchers hardly needed an evolutionary perspective to wonder about the factual basis of Cinderella stories. Are parents really more likely to neglect, assault, exploit, and otherwise mistreat their stepchildren than their genetic children, and if so, just how important a risk factor is this? Surprisingly, however, in the explosion of child abuse research that followed the proclamation of a battered-child syndrome in 1962, this seemingly obvious question was not raised. The first published study addressing it was Wilson, Daly, and Weghorst's (1980) demonstration that stepchildren constituted an enormously higher proportion of child abuse victims in the United States than their numbers in the population-at-large would warrant. Subsequent research by many workers has shown that this excess risk is crossnationally and cross-culturally ubiquitous and is most extreme with respect to the most severe outcomes, namely, child homicide (Daly & Wilson, 1996).

Homicides perpetrated by stepfathers differ from those by genetic fathers not just in their incidence but in qualitative attributes, too. In both Canada and Great Britain, for example, a substantial proportion of children killed by genetic fathers, but virtually none of those killed by stepfathers (Daly & Wilson, 1994), are slain in the context of a suicide, and the distraught father may even construe the homicide as a "rescue" (Wilson, Daly, & Daniele, 1995). By contrast, steppaternal cases are especially likely to involve a violent, assaultive rage reaction; whereas most small children killed by stepfathers are beaten to death, genetic fathers are relatively likely to have disposed of the child by gunshot or asphyxiation (Daly & Wilson, 1994). These contrasts support the evolutionary psychological theorizing that led to their discovery.

Infants are taxing. They wail and soil themselves and can be hard to soothe. But the very commotions that can grate on the nerves of bystanders are likely to evoke only attentive concern from a committed parent. Potentially damaging, angry responses are inhibited by parental love, an evolved psychological adaptation that makes the efforts of child rearing tolerable and even delightful. Stepparents assuredly vary in their degrees of personalized affection for the children, as do genetic parents, but it is equally sure that the average stepparent loves the child less. As we anticipate from the argument that excess risk derives ultimately from the stepparent's lesser commitment to that individual child's welfare, stepparents are overrepresented in all forms of child maltreatment, including neglectful as well as assaultive cases, and in sexual misuse, too. The higher rates of homicide incurred by stepchildren are the most dramatic, but by no means the only, consequences of a difference in the distributions of parental and stepparental affection, supporting the proposition that homicides may be used as a "tip-of-the-iceberg" assay of the differences between relationships in their degrees and types of conflict.

Because parental care is costly in time and resources, evolutionists expect parental psychologies to have evolved to allocate investments even in one's own genetic offspring with sensitivity to the young's needs and capabilities (Clutton-Brock, 1990). A compelling selectionist model of parent-offspring conflict was outlined by Trivers (1974), who noted that an asymmetry of relatedness within the family makes such conflict inescapable. From the perspective of any particular offspring, one's self is twice as valuable as a potential generator of inclusive fitness as a sibling, all else equal, whereas the two young have equal value from the maternal perspective. It follows that each party will have a different optimum when a familial resource is divided, and this chronic conflict explains the existence of such wasteful and even dangerous phenomena as weaning conflict and tantrums, as well as accounting for a number of otherwise puzzling phenomena in pregnancy (Haig, 1993).

Wilson and Daly (1993b) used this theoretical framework to generate a set of predictions about the patterning of maternal and paternal solicitude as a function of the time since birth and the parents' ages, and confirmed that rates of parentally perpetrated homicide exhibit the patterns that would be expected if such killings are deemed a *reverse assay* of parental solicitude. Voland (1984) used an extension of the same theory (see Trivers & Willard, 1973) to generate hypotheses about parental discrimination in relation to the child's sex and found support for his model in patterns of sex-differential child mortality in historical data. Parentally perpetrated filicide, although rare and perhaps seldom an adaptive means of reallocating parental efforts, does seem to be exacerbated by a number of circumstantial factors that detract from the expected fitness consequences of continued investment (Daly & Wilson, 1988b, 1995).

Marital Homicide

We noted earlier that the Hamiltonian view of organisms as evolved nepotists implies that blood kinship is likely to be psychologically distinct from other sorts of relationship. Mateship is another qualitatively distinct category of relationship, with some similarities to blood kinship. By the production of shared fitness vehicles, namely children, mates forge a deep commonality of interest. Indeed, in a species in which most reproductive effort is parental (as opposed to investment in collateral kin), the fitnesses of long-term mates are more highly correlated than those of even the closest genetic relatives. Any state of affairs that promotes or damages one partner's expected fitness will affect the other's identically, and this situation inspires a convergence of perspectives, as is often conspicuous in long-standing marriages (Alexander, 1987). But although the indissolubility of blood kinship is a force favoring forgiveness of breaches and reconciliation, the marital relationship is fragile, especially if the couple is still childless. Most notably, the basis for marital solidarity is undermined by adulterous inclinations, perhaps especially those of the wife, because the risks of misattributing parenthood and investing one's parental efforts in a rival's offspring are sexually asymmetrical (Wilson & Daly, 1992a). These considerations suggest that a crucial arena of potential conflict in the marital arena will be sexual entitlements and fidelity, a proposition that is upheld by a variety of studies addressing the ostensible motives and perceived grievances precipitating cases of spousal homicides (Campbell, 1992; Daly & Wilson, 1988b; Polk & Ranson, 1991; Wilson & Daly, 1996).

To predict and understand risk factors for marital homicide, we have explored the joint implications of two propositions: first, that marital conflict and violence are largely the results of male sexual proprietariness and female efforts to escape male control, and second, that homicides usually represent the tip of the iceberg of coercive control rather than a motivationally distinct phenomenon. These considerations have motivated explorations of such issues as the risk of uxoricide in the aftermath of separation (Wilson & Daly, 1993c), the relevance of age and age disparity (Wilson & Daly, 1992b; Wilson, Daly, & Wright, 1993), the social determinants of variation in the relative risk of lethality for wives versus husbands (Wilson & Daly, 1992b), the effects of stepchildren on uxoricide risk (Daly, Wiseman, & Wilson, 1997), the social-structural and ecological correlates of cross-cultural variations in marital violence (Wilson & Daly, 1993a), and the similarities and differences in demographic risk patterns between lethal and nonlethal violence against wives (Wilson, Johnson, & Daly, 1995).

■ *HOMICIDE OUTSIDE THE FAMILY*

We have devoted much of our attention to the minority of homicides that are intrafamilial, precisely because they have seemed the most challenging from a Darwinian perspective. But most killers are not related to their victims, neither by blood nor marriage, and an evolutionary psychological approach sheds considerable light on these cases, too.

Perhaps the most conspicuous fact about such violence is that it is sexually differentiated. Men kill unrelated men vastly more often than women kill unrelated women, everywhere (Daly & Wilson, 1988b, 1990). Tales of exotic societies in which this sex difference is reversed are fantasies. It is no use attributing this cross-culturally universal difference to local aspects of particular societies, as many criminologists have done (e.g., Wolfgang, 1978), or to construct explanatory theories (e.g., Hagan, 1990) premised on assumptions about sex role socialization that are known to be false (see Daly & Wilson, 1988b, 1997). A more promising approach is to try to understand the psychological design differences between the sexes in the light of evolutionary understandings of the male-female phenomenon.

Sex-differential violence appears to be one of many manifestations that the human male psyche has evolved to be more risk accepting in competitive situations than is the female psyche (Daly & Wilson, 1990; Wilson & Daly, 1985). The sex difference in intrasexual violence is one that humans share with other species with "effectively polygynous" mating systems: species in which the variance in fitness among males exceeds that among females. The evidence that human beings evolved under a mild degree of effective polygyny is abundant and consistent, and the natural selective link between such a mating system and sex differences in competitive violence is well understood and noncontroversial (Daly & Wilson, 1983). Basically, greater fitness variance selects for greater acceptance of risk in the pursuit of scarce means to the end of fitness. Furthermore, "recklessly" life-threatening risk proneness is especially likely to evolve where staying alive by opting out of competition promises to yield no fitness at all and is therefore the natural selective equivalent of death.

Lethal violence between unrelated men is transparently competitive. *Competition* refers to any conflict of interests in which one party's possession or use of a mutually desired resource precludes another party's possession or use of the same. Robbery homicides are unequivocal instances, as are many "sexual triangle" cases. More subtle examples are the "face" and "status" disputes that constitute a large proportion (perhaps the majority) of all homicides in the United States; the social resources contested in these cases are limited means to the end of more tangible resources. Not all conflicts are competitive. For instance, if a woman spurns one suitor for another, then she and the rejected suitor have a conflict of interest, but they are not competitors, whereas the male rivals are. In general, competition is predominantly a same-sex affair because same-sex individuals are usually more similar in the resources they desire than are opposite-sex individuals.

The rate at which men kill unrelated men is the most variable component of the overall homicide rate (Daly & Wilson, 1988b). The incidence of such male-male killings in a given time and place can be interpreted as a reflection of the local severity of male-male competition. One attractive hypothesis that has yet to receive a good test is that conditions or policies that promote stable monogamy will tend to reduce both the gross homicide rate and the sex difference. A better established hypothesis is that inequity in the distribution of material resources is an important source of variation in homicide rates (Hsieh & Pugh, 1993; Krahn, Hartnagel, & Gartrell, 1986). The United States has by far the most inequitable income distribution in the modern West and by far the highest homicide rate; moreover, in comparisons among the 50 states of this highly homicidal country, inequity measures predict homicide rates even more highly than they predict other components of mortality rates (Kennedy, Kawachi, & Prothrow-Stith, 1996).

There is considerable evidence that persons who engage in risky criminal activities discount the future relatively steeply (Wilson & Herrnstein, 1985). Such inability to delay gratification is usually interpreted as a sign of immaturity and pathology, but this seems to us unduly pejorative. The psychological and behavioral tendencies that are disparaged as indicative of a "lack of impulse control" sound instead a lot like adaptive adjustment of risk acceptance. Steep discounting of the future is just what a properly functioning evolved psyche might be expected to do in the sorts of social and material circumstances that are especially likely to foster violent crime (Daly & Wilson, 1988b).

One sort of information that ought to affect discounting of the future is information bearing on the likelihood that the future will ever come. Reason to doubt that one will be alive tomorrow is reason to grab what one can today. An increase in mortality in one's reference group increases the appeal of risky action in pursuit of quick returns, especially if the sources of that excess mortality are independent of the actor's choices. But what sort of evidence would bear on such risk adjustment? One possibility is some sort of semistatistical apprehension of the distribution of local life spans. This need not be so complex as it sounds. If a young man's grandfathers were both dead before he was born, and more than a couple of his primary school classmates are already dead too, and gray-haired men stand out in his neighborhood by virtue of their rarity, there may be something going on that he should attend to. In Chicago, there are large variations in life expectancy between neighborhoods, and expected future life span is a good predictor of neighborhood-specific homicide rates, even if expected life span is computed with the mortality effects of homicide itself removed (Wilson & Daly, 1997). Of course, more traditional measures of poverty are highly correlated with both expected life span and homicide, but expected life span is at least as good a predictor as any other. Whether readiness to commit violence is indeed affected by the sorts of "life expectancy cues" suggested above is a question deserving considerable future research.

In this context, the common misconception that evolutionary thinking has reactionary implications is ironic. *Evolutionary psychological theory and research come down firmly in support of the proposition that inequity and desperation are the principal, remediable causes of crime and violence.* This is true not only because people are obsessive about social comparison and escalate their competitive tactics when they are losing out but also because purely punitive crime control, without remediation of inequity and desperation, actually invites increased recklessness. More generally, there is no basis for social Darwinism in evolutionary biology, and there never was. Those seeking ideological support for policies whose beneficiaries are the rich and privileged will have to look elsewhere.

A Final Comment About the Generation of Evolution-Minded Hypotheses

Like other scientists, evolutionists frequently formulate alternative hypotheses that cannot simultaneously be true. When we began studying spousal homicide, one of us (Daly) proposed that wives would incur increasing risk as they aged because their declining reproductive value would make their husbands value them less. The other (Wilson) hypothesized instead that uxoricides are largely to be understood as maladaptive by-products of coercive and proprietary motives and emotions that husbands feel most extremely when their wives are young. Although it has proved difficult to separate the effects of female age from the correlated effects of male age, marital duration, and parity, it is now clear that Wilson's hypothesis was much closer to the facts than Daly's. Young wives incur the greatest risk, and this is not an incidental consequence of their tendency to be married to young husbands (Wilson et al., 1993).

In correspondence in the journal *Science,* Harcourt (1988) accused us of engaging in untestable pseudoscience because our brand of "evolutionary social psychology" could accommodate these alternative hypotheses. But of course, the fact that evolutionists can and do generate conflicting hypotheses is not an embarrassment, any more than is the fact that one can generate alternative neurophysiological or sociological hypotheses. The source of confusion seems to be that evolutionary psychology has sometimes been portrayed, by enthusiasts as well as critics, as another addition to the Babel of rival psychological theories and systems. It is not. We know, as surely as scientists know anything, that living things and their attributes have evolved and that insofar as those attributes exhibit complex functionality, their properties have been shaped through many generations by selection (Dawkins, 1986).[1] Thus, when an enthusiastic Darwinist refers to some particular pet idea as "the evolutionary prediction" and professes to test it against "nonevolutionary" alternatives, this framing misstates what is actually being done. The proposition that the psyche evolved under the influence of selection and exhibits functional organization for the promotion of fitness is not itself being tested, nor is it even controversial. Although removed from direct observation and highly abstract, this proposition is a "fact" in the same sense as it is a fact that "information" is "transmitted" across synapses in the nervous system or that "molecules" are composed of "atoms."

Whatever the results of research in the behavioral sciences, we can be sure that evolved psychological adaptations are involved. The question is not whether this is so, but "so what?" Just as one may ask whether learning some neuroscience is a good intellectual investment for a psychological scientist, the question here is simply whether paying serious attention to theory and research in evolutionary biology can help psychologists and other social scientists do their own scientific work better. It is increasingly clear that the answer is a most definite *yes.*

■ *NOTE*

1. The only alternative yet proposed is that an unconstrained supernatural power simply "created" everything, a proposition that is devoid of empirical or practical implications until supplemented by additional supernatural revelations, as it invariably is. *This* is pseudoscience.

■ *REFERENCES*

Alexander, R. D. (1979). *Darwinism and human affairs.* Seattle: University of Washington Press.

Alexander, R. D. (1987). *The biology of moral systems.* Hawthorne, NY: Aldine.

Archer, J. (1988). *The behaviourial biology of aggression.* New York: Cambridge University Press.

Barkow, J., Cosmides, L., & Tooby, J. (Eds.). (1992). *The adapted mind.* New York: Oxford University Press.

Betzig, L. L. (1986). *Despotism and differential reproduction: A Darwinian view of history.* Hawthorne, NY: Aldine de Gruyter.

Bock, G., & Cardew, G. (Eds.). (1997). *Characterizing human psychological adaptations.* Chichester, UK: Wiley.

Campbell, J. (1992). "If I can't have you, no one can": Power and control in homicide of female partners. In J. Radford

& D. E. H. Russell (Eds.), *Femicide: The politics of woman killing* (pp. 99-113). New York: Twayne.

Chagnon, N. A. (1988). Life histories, blood revenge, and warfare in a tribal population. *Science, 239,* 958-992.

Chagnon, N. A. (1996). Chronic problems in understanding tribal violence and warfare. In G. Bock & J. Goode (Eds.), *Genetics and crime* (pp. 202-236). Chichester, UK: Wiley.

Clutton-Brock, T. H. (1990). *The evolution of parental care.* Princeton, NJ: Princeton University Press.

Cosmides, L., & Tooby, J. (1995). Are humans good intuitive statisticians after all? Rethinking some conclusions of the literature on judgment under uncertainness. *Cognition, 58,* 1-73.

Cronin, H. (1991). *The ant and the peacock.* Cambridge, UK: Cambridge University Press.

Daly, M., Salmon, C., & Wilson, M. (1997). Kinship: The conceptual hole in psychological studies of social cognition and close relationships. In J. A. Simpson & D. Kenrick (Eds.), *Evolutionary social psychology* (pp. 265-296). Mahwah, NJ: Lawrence Erlbaum.

Daly, M., & Wilson, M. (1982). Homicide and kinship. *American Anthropologist, 84,* 372-378.

Daly, M., & Wilson, M. (1983). *Sex, evolution, and behavior* (2nd ed.). Belmont, CA: Wadsworth.

Daly, M., & Wilson, M. (1988a). Evolutionary social psychology and family homicide. *Science, 242,* 519-524.

Daly, M., & Wilson, M. (1988b). *Homicide.* Hawthorne, NY: Aldine de Gruyter.

Daly, M., & Wilson, M. (1990). Killing the competition. *Human Nature, 1,* 83-109.

Daly, M., & Wilson, M. (1994). Some differential attributes of lethal assaults on small children by stepfathers versus genetic fathers. *Ethology and Sociobiology, 15,* 207-217.

Daly, M., & Wilson, M. (1995). Discriminative parental solicitude and the relevance of evolutionary models to the analysis of motivational systems. In M. S. Gazzaniga (Ed.), *The cognitive neurosciences* (pp. 1269-1286). Cambridge: MIT Press.

Daly, M., & Wilson, M. (1996). Violence against stepchildren. *Current Directions in Psychological Science, 5,* 77-81.

Daly, M., & Wilson, M. (1997). Crime and conflict: Homicide in evolutionary psychological perspective. *Crime and Justice, 18,* 251-300.

Daly, M., Wiseman, K. A., & Wilson, M. (1997). Women with children sired by former partners incur excess risk of uxoricide. *Homicide Studies, 1,* 61-71.

Darwin, C. (1859). *On the origin of species by means of natural selection, or, the preservation of favored races in the struggle for life.* London: John Murray.

Dawkins, R. (1986). *The blind watchmaker.* Harlow, UK: Longman.

Furlow, B., Gangestad, S. W., & Armijo-Prewitt, T. (1998). Developmental stability and human violence. *Proceedings of the Royal Society of London: Series B, 265,* 1-6.

Gelles, R. J., & Straus, M. A. (1985). Violence in the American family. In A. J. Lincoln & M. A. Straus (Eds.), *Crime and the family* (pp. 55-110). Springfield, IL: Charles C Thomas.

Gigerenzer, G., & Hoffrage, U. (1995). How to improve Bayesian reasoning without instruction: Frequency formats. *Psychological Review, 102,* 684-704.

Hagan, J. (1990). The structuration of gender and deviance: A power-control theory of vulnerability to crime and the search for deviant exit roles. *Canadian Review of Sociology and Anthropology, 27,* 137-156.

Haig, D. (1993). Genetic conflicts in human pregnancy. *Quarterly Review of Biology, 68,* 495-532.

Hamilton, W. D. (1964). The genetical evolution of social behaviour. *Journal of Theoretical Biology, 7,* 1-52.

Hamilton, W. D. (1967). Extraordinary sex ratios. *Science, 156,* 477-488.

Harcourt, A. H. (1988). Letter to the editor. *Science, 243,* 462-463.

Hepper, P. G. (Ed.). (1991). *Kin recognition.* Cambridge, UK: Cambridge University Press.

Holmes, W. G., & Sherman, P. W. (1982). The ontogeny of kin recognition in two species of ground squirrels. *American Zoologist, 22,* 491-517.

Hsieh, C., & Pugh, M. D. (1993). Poverty, income inequality, and violent crime: A meta-analysis of recent aggregate data studies. *Criminal Justice Review, 18,* 182-202.

Huntingford, D., & Turner, A. (1987). *Animal conflict.* London: Chapman & Hall.

Kahneman, D., Slovic, P., & Tversky, A. (Eds.). (1982). *Judgment under uncertainty.* New York: Cambridge University Press.

Kennedy, B. P., Kawachi, I., & Prothrow-Stith, D. (1996). Income distribution and mortality: Cross sectional ecological study of the Robin Hood index in the United States. *British Medical Journal, 312,* 1004-1007.

Krahn, H., Hartnagel, T. F., & Gartrell, J. W. (1986). Income inequality and homicide rates: Cross-national data and criminological theories. *Criminology, 24,* 269-295.

Mayr, E. (1983). How to carry out the adaptationist program? *American Naturalist, 121,* 324-334.

Nesse, R. M. (1990). Evolutionary explanations of emotions. *Human Nature, 1,* 261-289.

Nesse, R. M., & Williams, G. C. (1994). *Why we get sick.* New York: Random House.

Nisbett, R. E., & Ross, L. (1980). *Human inference: Strategies and shortcomings of social judgment.* Englewood Cliffs, NJ: Prentice Hall.

Nisbett, R. E., & Wilson, T. D. (1977). Telling more than we can know: Verbal reports on mental processes. *Psychological Review, 84,* 231-259.

Polk, K., & Ranson, D. (1991). The role of gender in intimate homicide. *Australia and New Zealand Journal of Criminology, 24,* 15-24.

Simpson, J. A., & Kenrick, D. (Eds.). (1997). *Evolutionary social psychology.* Mahwah, NJ: Lawrence Erlbaum.

Symons, D. (1990). Adaptiveness and adaptation. *Ethology and Sociobiology, 16,* 427-444.

Thompson, S. (1955). *Motif-index of folk literature.* Bloomington: University of Indiana Press.

Tooby, J., & Cosmides, L. (1990). The past explains the present: Emotional adaptations and the structure of ancestral environments. *Ethology and Sociobiology, 16,* 375-424.

Trivers, R. L. (1974). Parent-offspring conflict. *American Zoologist, 14,* 249-264.

Trivers, R. L., & Willard, D. (1973). Natural selection of parental ability to vary the sex-ratio of offspring. *Science, 179,* 90-92.

Voland, E. (1984). Human sex-ratio manipulation: Historical data from a German parish. *Journal of Human Evolution, 13,* 99-107.

White, L. K., & Booth, A. (1985). The quality and stability of remarriages: The role of stepchildren. *American Sociological Review, 50,* 689-698.

Williams, G. C., & Nesse, R. M. (1991). The dawn of Darwinian medicine. *Quarterly Review of Biology, 66,* 1-22.

Wilson, J. Q., & Herrnstein, R. J. (1985). *Crime and human nature.* New York: Simon & Schuster.

Wilson, M. I., & Daly, M. (1985). Competitiveness, risk-taking and violence: The young male syndrome. *Ethology and Sociobiology, 6,* 59-73.

Wilson, M. I., & Daly, M. (1992a). The man who mistook his wife for a chattel. In J. Barkow, L. Cosmides, & J. Tooby (Eds.), *The adapted mind* (pp. 289-322). New York: Oxford University Press.

Wilson, M. I., & Daly, M. (1992b). Who kills whom in spouse killings? On the exceptional sex ratio of spousal homicides in the United States. *Criminology, 30,* 189-215.

Wilson, M. I., & Daly, M. (1993a). An evolutionary psychological perspective on male sexual proprietariness and violence against wives. *Violence and Victims, 8,* 271-294.

Wilson, M. I., & Daly, M. (1993b). The psychology of parenting in evolutionary perspective and the case of human filicide. In S. Parmigiami & F. vom Saal (Eds.), *Infanticide and parental care* (pp. 73-140). Chur, Switzerland: Harwood Academic.

Wilson, M. I., & Daly, M. (1993c). Spousal homicide risk and estrangement. *Violence and Victims, 8,* 3-16.

Wilson, M. I., & Daly, M. (1996). Male sexual proprietariness and violence against wives. *Current Directions in Psychological Science, 5,* 2-7.

Wilson, M. I., & Daly, M. (1997). Life expectancy, economic inequality, homicide, and reproductive timing in Chicago neighborhoods. *British Medical Journal, 314,* 1271-1274.

Wilson, M. I., Daly, M., & Daniele, A. (1995). Familicide: The killing of spouse and children. *Aggressive Behavior, 21,* 275-291.

Wilson, M. I., Daly, M., & Weghorst, S. J. (1980). Household composition and the risk of child abuse and neglect. *Journal of Biosocial Science, 12,* 333-340.

Wilson, M. I., Daly, M., & Wright, C. (1993). Uxoricide in Canada: Demographic risk patterns. *Canadian Journal of Criminology, 35,* 263-291.

Wilson, M. I., Johnson, H., & Daly, M. (1995). Lethal and nonlethal violence against wives. *Canadian Journal of Criminology, 37,* 331-361.

Wolfgang, M. E. (1958). *Patterns in criminal homicide.* Philadelphia: University of Pennsylvania Press.

Wolfgang, M. E. (1978). Family violence and criminal behavior. In R. L. Sadoff (Ed.), *Violence and responsibility* (pp. 87-103). New York: Spectrum.

Wright, R. (1994). *The moral animal.* New York: Pantheon.

PART III

Methodological Issues in the Study of Homicide

CHAPTER 6

Sources of Homicide Data

A Review and Comparison

■ *Marc Riedel*

Homicide is a statistically rare event. It occurs less frequently than other violent crimes, which are themselves uncommon. For example, in 1993, there were 24,456 murders in a population of 257,908,000 people in the United States. This amounts to 0.00948% of the population being victims of a murder. In contrast, there were 1,135,099 victims of aggravated assault, the most common of other serious violent crimes, including robbery and rape; this figure represents 0.44%, or less than ½ of 1% of the population (Federal Bureau of Investigation [FBI], 1994).

This comparison is not intended to minimize the substantial human, economic, and social costs associated with homicide. Instead, it is meant to suggest that homicide researchers operate under a severe constraint from the outset; given its rarity, researchers are unlikely to directly observe the subjects of their studies. Instead, researchers interested in the quantitative analysis of homicide have to depend on secondary data, that is, information gathered for some other purpose. Because of the character of secondary data, information about homicide events are filtered through layers of recorders and reporters who answer to the demands of organizations that may or may not be concerned with the criteria for research data. Further, subsets of information are transmitted from local to state and national data collection programs, all of which have their attendant problems.

The purpose of this chapter is to describe and evaluate national sources of homicide data. The discussion focuses mainly on murder and nonnegligent manslaughter data from the Uniform Crime Reporting (UCR) Program of the FBI and homicide data from the mortality files of

AUTHOR'S NOTE: I would like to thank a number of people who have given advice, suggestions, and data in the preparation of this chapter. They are Ann Cibulskis, Chicago Police Department; Vicki Major, Harvey M. Rosenthal, and Ken Candell, UCR Program; John Peddicord, Stephen P. James, and Linda Saltzman, Centers for Disease Control; Steve Galeria, Bonnie Collins, and Tricia Clark, California Criminal Justice Statistics Center; and Bernard Auchter, National Institute of Justice.

the National Center for Health Statistics (NCHS). Also, the National Incident-Based Reporting System (NIBRS) and its relation to the UCR Program are described. Following a description of each program, studies using various *intrasource* comparisons to examine the data's reliability and validity are discussed. As well, a section is devoted to reviewing research that considers *intersource* comparisons to determine similarities and differences between NCHS and UCR data. The discussion begins with a description of the official manner in which homicide data are collected in the United States.

■ *COLLECTING HOMICIDE DATA: AN OVERVIEW*

Homicide is the only offense for which there are two nationwide reporting systems that gather detailed information on the entire population of events. An overview of the dual reporting system is provided in Figure 6.1. As shown there, both the police (or appropriate law enforcement agency) and county medical examiners or coroners begin an investigation when a suspected homicide is reported. The two offices determine independently whether a homicide has occurred. During this determination, files are generated concerning identification of the victim, relatives, family members, medical cause of death, circumstances, and possible offenders. Medical examiners are charged with assigning a cause of death and judging whether medical evidence indicates that the death occurred by the actions of another person. The records they produce include autopsy results and related materials. Although limited to victim characteristics, medical examiner records are especially useful to answer questions about, for example, the presence of drugs or alcohol in the victim's body at the time of the killing.

Police, on the other hand, have legal responsibilities. They conclude whether a criminal homicide has occurred and, if so, develop records to facilitate the investigation, arrest, and prosecution of offenders. Police records are the most frequent source of data on homicides be-

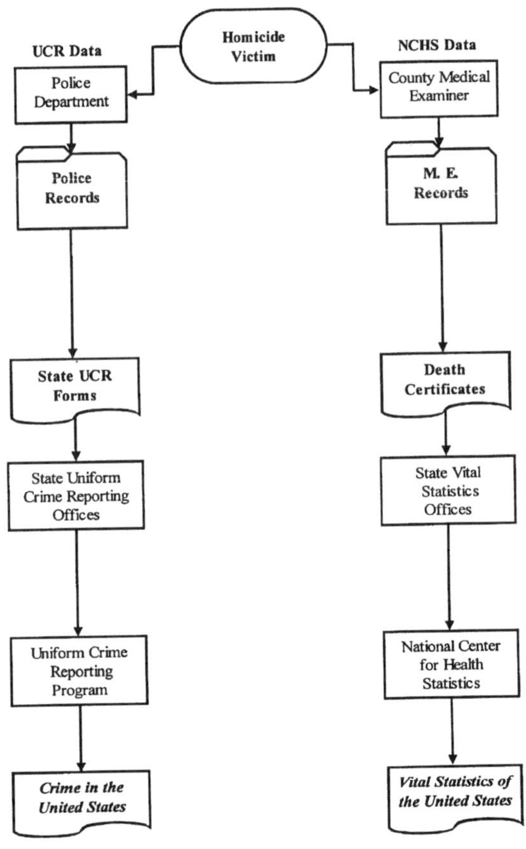

Figure 6.1. Nationwide Sources of Homicide Data

cause they include information about offenders and arrests as well as victim characteristics.

To satisfy the demands of national reporting programs, a subset of information is extracted from both medical examiner and police records and forwarded to state reporting agencies. As shown in Figure 6.1, all states have vital statistics offices to which death certificates are forwarded. To simplify matters, Figure 6.1 assumes that all police data are reported to state level agencies; as will be discussed, however, some police jurisdictions report directly to the UCR Program.

Periodically, the information collected at the state level is transmitted to national reporting programs. Police-based data go to the UCR Program, whereas copies of death certificates go to the Vital Statistics Division of the NCHS. The

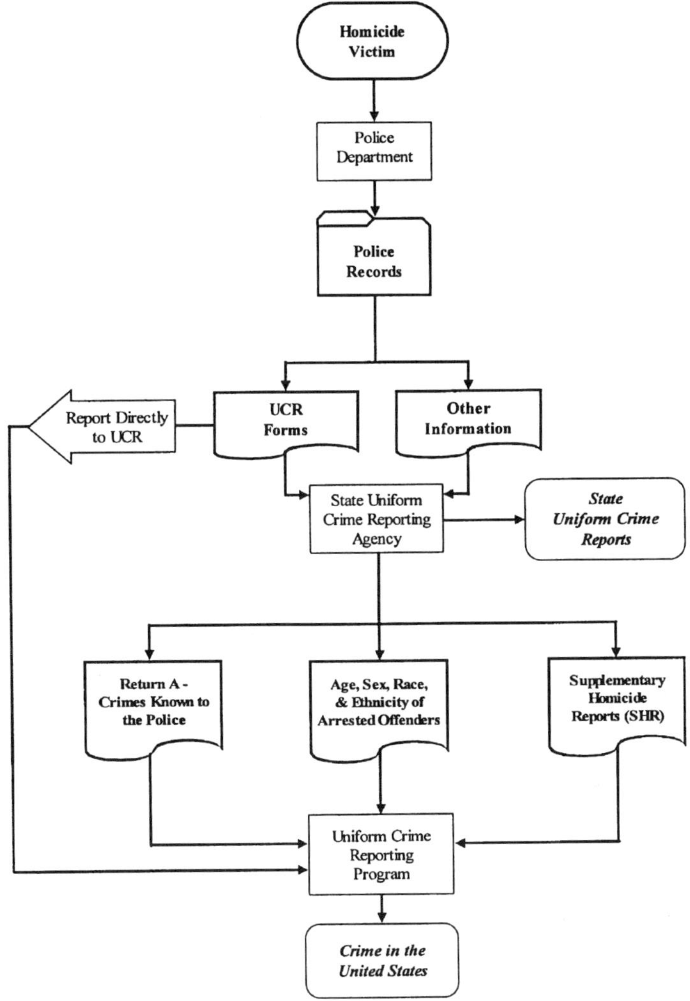

Figure 6.2. Uniform Crime Reporting Program

following sections will describe at length these two sources of homicide data.

■ *THE UNIFORM CRIME REPORTING PROGRAM*

The UCR Program began in the late 1920s following recognition by the International Association of Chiefs of Police that a system of national crime statistics was needed. In January 1930, Congress authorized the attorney general to gather crime information; the attorney general, in turn, designated the FBI to serve as the national clearinghouse for data collected (FBI, 1994).

Initially, the UCR Program depended on compliance by individual agencies, but this method did not prove to be effective. The UCR Program soon moved to a model of reporting that had been successful in collecting national vital statistics data whereby *state agencies* are established with mandatory reporting requirements. As of 1993, 44 states and the District of Columbia had reporting systems (FBI, 1994). The remaining jurisdictions report directly to the UCR Program. Data collected by the UCR Program are analyzed, organized for presentation, then reported in annual editions of *Crime in the United States: Uniform Crime Reports.* Referred to often as simply *Uniform Crime Reports,* this publication has become the most widely used source of information concerning crime in the United States.[1] To illustrate the process by which UCR Program data eventually get reported, a flow chart is displayed in Figure 6.2.

The UCR Program establishes standards for a state reporting system and has been known to exclude data from jurisdictions for reporting violations. Many states have legislation designating a specific agency to which reporting is required. California, for example, has a legislatively designated state-level agency and has achieved complete compliance in reporting. Illinois also has mandatory reporting but recently listed 9 of 879 law enforcement agencies in the state as not in compliance (Illinois State Police, 1995).

Although state agencies collect the data that are part of the national reporting system, they may also collect additional information. For example, in addition to available computer tapes, the California Bureau of Criminal Information and Analysis publishes *Homicide in California* (Division of Law Enforcement, 1994), which provides detailed information on offender dispositions as well as characteristics of homicide and justifiable homicides.

There is no doubt that considerable variation in reporting practices and data availability among state agencies exists, although research on this topic is severely limited. In one of the few studies to address this issue, Rokaw, Mercy, and Smith (1990) found that the NCHS reports 50% or more homicides than the UCR Program in some states. No other research known to me indicates to what extent state programs implement reporting standards, what sanctions are available and imposed for noncompliance, and how states vary according to what is available in their reporting system.

In general, homicide researchers have not explored the many opportunities for analysis offered by state-level statistics. The first of two exceptions is the Victim Level Murder file available through the Statistical Analysis Center of the Illinois Criminal Justice Information Authority. It consists of murders reported to the official state crime statistics agency, the Illinois State Police, from 1971 through 1991. The data were evaluated to remove inconsistencies in the number of cases and reformatted so that the victim, rather than the event, is the unit of analysis (Miller & Block, 1983).

Another exception is the work of Keppel, Weis, and LaMoria (1990), who have developed the federally funded Homicide Information and Tracking System (HITS) to obtain information on all homicides in the state of Washington. This data set contains information on crime evidence, victim and offender characteristics, geographic locations, and other variables. Data for the most recent National Institute of Justice report consist of all *solved* murders from 1981 through 1986 and are available from the National Archives of Criminal Justice Data (1998; http://www.icpsr.umich.edu/nacjd/). HITS continues in Washington under state financial support and has expanded to include other states. Information on uncleared homicides and homicides after 1986 are not available for investigative and proprietary reasons (J. Weis, personal communication, October 10, 1996).

Definitions and Data Collected

The UCR Program collects information on murder and nonnegligent manslaughter, negligent manslaughter, and justifiable homicides. The category of *murder and nonnegligent manslaughter* is defined as the "willful (nonnegligent) killing of one human being by another" (FBI, 1984, p. 6). As a general rule, any death due to injuries received in a fight, argument, quarrel, assault, or commission of a crime is counted as a murder or nonnegligent manslaughter. Suicides, accidental deaths, assaults to kill, and attempted murders are not included in the category.

Manslaughter by negligence includes the killing of another through gross negligence by the offender. Traffic fatalities are excluded, although recent legislation concerning driving while intoxicated may change that practice. *Justifiable homicide* is defined as the killing of a person by a peace officer in the line of duty. The definition also includes the killing by a private citizen of a person who is engaging in a felony crime (FBI, 1984). Negligent manslaughter data are collected but not reported, whereas information on justifiable homicides by weapon and perpetrator (police or civilian) has been reported in *Uniform Crime Reports* since 1991.

UCR Program Forms Used in Data Collection

In the following discussion of UCR Program forms, two general characteristics of these forms have an impact on homicide research. First, the UCR Program continues to follow the "hierarchy rule." That is, except for arson, only the most serious offense is classified in a multiple offense situation. The rank order of seriousness is criminal homicide, forcible rape, robbery, aggravated assault, burglary, larceny-theft, motor vehicle theft, and arson. Although the hierarchy rule has been vigorously debated, a 1984 study of Oregon indicated that only 1.2% of Part I offenses are lost (Akiyama & Rosenthal, 1990).

Second, no common identifier links information on one form with information on another form at the level of specific cases. For example, there is no way to link victim information on the Supplementary Homicide Reports (SHR; discussed below) with Return A to determine if the case was cleared.

Return A: Crimes Known to the Police

As the name implies, this form contains the following information:

1. Offenses reported or known
2. Founded or unfounded complaints
3. Number of actual offenses (founded complaints)
4. Total number cleared by arrest or exceptionally cleared (described below)
5. Number of clearances for persons under 18

A number of characteristics of data drawn from this form should be noted. First, because not all jurisdictions report, the numbers of criminal homicides that are given in annual editions of *Uniform Crime Reports* are *estimates* based on Return A reports. An *imputation methodology* used to arrive at the estimates is described in detail in Schneider and Wiersema (1990); except for some small changes that users should discuss with the UCR Program, this description generally represents current procedures.

Second, numbers drawn from Return A are aggregated monthly. They provide no information on specific cases; that type of information is available only from the SHR, a source described at length in a later section.

Third, the number of *arrest clearances* refers to the number of offenses for which an arrest was made, not the number of offenders arrested. One arrest can clear many crimes, and the arrest of many people may clear only one crime. *Exceptional clearances* refer to the administrative closing of cases for a variety of circumstances beyond the control of police departments. When cases have been adequately investigated, some of the reasons for not effecting an arrest include offenders who committed suicide, died from accidents or natural causes before being arrested, made deathbed confessions, or were killed by police or citizens. Other reasons include confessions by offenders prosecuted for other crimes in other jurisdictions, denial of extradition to the jurisdiction in which the crime occurred, and refusal of the district attorney to prosecute.

Exceptional clearances can account for a substantial number of cases. In an unpublished analysis of murders in Chicago, I determined that exceptional clearances accounted for 15.9% of the 1,665 cleared cases from 1988 through 1990. Notably, arrest clearance statistics reported by the UCR Program include those cases cleared by both arrest *and* exceptional means.

Arrest clearances pose a major problem for homicide researchers interested in offender data because clearance rates have been declining steadily since at least 1960. In that year, 93% of the murders were cleared by arrest; since then, the clearance rate has steadily declined to 65% in 1995 (FBI, 1962, 1996). The extent to which generalizations about offenders are biased because about one third of the offender information is missing is unclear; it does appear, however, that arrest clearances are less likely for homicides involving felonies (Riedel & Rinehart, 1996).

Age, Race, and Ethnic Origin of Persons Arrested

There are two basic forms of this type, one for adults and the other for persons under 18. The two forms are the same except that the juvenile form requests information about curfew violations and runaways. Unlike the clearance measure for offenses, this form asks for the number of arrested offenders.

Offenders are classified into four racial groups: White, Black, American Indian, and Asian or Pacific Islander. Ethnicity is coded as Hispanic or Not Hispanic. *Hispanic* refers to Mexicans, Puerto Ricans, Cubans, Central and South Americans, and any persons of "Spanish culture or origin, regardless of race" (FBI, 1984, p. 58); in actuality, however, ethnicity is recorded by investigating officers who may use a variety of definitions. Given the difficulty of establishing ethnicity, and because Hispanic murders have increased in recent years, this variable should be used by researchers with caution until more research is done to determine its reliability.

Supplementary Homicide Reports

Although Return A and Age, Sex, Race, and Ethnic Origin of Persons Arrested forms represent aggregated monthly and annual information, the SHR form provides information on each recorded case of murder and nonnegligent manslaughter. This form was introduced in 1961; that year, information was collected on 6,991 murders (82.0%) of an estimated total of 8,530 cases. Because of incomplete coverage and coding difficulties, however, the SHR did not become a useful source of research data until 1964. That year, the number of homicides reported was 85.6% of those estimated from Return A submissions.

From 1962 through 1975, the SHR was primarily a record of the age, race, and gender of victims; weapon used; and circumstances of the offense. Readers interested in the detailed changes in the SHR during that period are referred to my earlier work (Riedel, 1990).

Beginning with information reported in 1976, the SHR underwent a major revision that substantially improved its usefulness as a data source. The following changes occurred.

1. The handbook and coding guides became more congruent because many of the codes used in preparing the form were given to law enforcement personnel preparing the form.
2. Information was collected on offenders so that victims and offenders could be linked together for specific events.
3. Rather than using homicide victims as the unit of analysis, the SHR became an event-based system requiring information on multiple victims and/or multiple offenders.
4. Victim-offender relationships were no longer coded as part of the circumstances variable; they became a separate variable with detailed codes.
5. Circumstances were divided into codes for types of felonies and nonfelonies and a code for suspected felonies.

Two additional changes were implemented in 1980. Race codes were made highly specific with codable instructions; also, an ethnicity code was added (FBI, 1980).

The current version of the SHR contains the following information:

1. A situation code indicating combinations of single or multiple victims and single, multiple, or unknown offenders
2. Age, sex, race, and ethnicity of all victims and offenders involved in the event
3. Weapons used
4. Victim-offender relationships
5. Circumstances including type of involvement in other felony crimes associated with the homicide

Intrasource Comparisons

A number of studies have considered the consistency in reporting between the various components of the UCR Program. These are discussed in the sections below.

Return A Estimates

The UCR Program covers law enforcement jurisdictions that account for 95% of the United States population. Claims for this level of coverage are based on Return A requests; the percentage of SHR received is somewhat lower.

Incomplete coverage through Return A necessitates estimation. Historically, methods to estimate the total number of homicides have varied considerably. In their examination, Cantor and Cohen (1980) suggest that the most generally useful series of homicide estimates are those from 1933 to 1972 published by the Office of Management and Budget. They also suggest that UCR data should not be used prior to 1958 because of variations in estimation practices.

In their discussion of imputation methodology, Schneider and Wiersema (1990) attempted to reproduce the estimates that were published in the 1980 *Uniform Crime Reports.* They found that for 40 of 51 state-level observations, the resulting offense estimates were within one percentage point of the comparable figures published in the *Uniform Crime Reports.* With two exceptions, the estimates for other states were within 7.5% of what was published. For the two states that were exceptions (Vermont and Connecticut), data coding inconsistencies or the misidentification of comparable agencies may have accounted for large errors. Despite this relatively positive result, Schneider and Wiersema suggest a need for improvement in and further validation research of UCR Program data.

Police Reports and the SHR

The total number of homicides reported by police departments agrees reasonably well with the numbers reported by the SHR. Information from police records for 1978 was compared with the SHR for seven cities—Philadelphia, Newark, St. Louis, Memphis, Dallas, Oakland, and "Ashton" (a pseudonym; Zahn & Riedel, 1983). The amount of agreement was measured by dividing the SHR frequency by the frequency recorded by the city police. The mean agreement ratio for the seven cities was 0.99, close to complete agreement (1.00). Within a range of 0.97 to 1.07, five of the seven cities had a tendency to report more homicides than the SHR, but the differences were small. For example, Philadelphia (0.97) reported 362 cases, whereas the SHR reported 353 cases. At the other extreme, Newark (1.07) reported 102 cases, whereas the SHR reported 109 cases.

The study also examined the amount of agreement between police department records and the SHR for gender, race, and age of victims and weapon used. For demographic variables, the smallest discrepancies between the two data sources existed for gender, followed by race and age.

For male victims, the agreement ratios ranged from 0.95 to 1.02. For female victims, the range was from 0.96 to 1.29 with a slight tendency for the SHR to report more female victims. Because Hispanics were coded as Whites in 1978, comparisons for only Black victims were done. The range of differences was from one in Ashton to nine cases in St. Louis, where the SHR reported more Black victims than were recorded by police.

Although ages were grouped in 10-year intervals, the agreement between police records and the SHR was not high. The pattern of discrepancy is difficult to summarize because of the variation among the cities. Oakland, for example, had almost complete agreement in the youngest ages but less agreement as age increased. Ashton, by contrast, had fairly high levels of agreement with the SHR except for the 60 to 69 and 70 to 79 age groups.

For weapons, the level of agreement was more than 90% in five of seven cities. This was especially true for knives and guns; discrepancies between the two data sources were greater for other types of weapons.

In general, although there are differences in the numbers recorded by the police and reported by the SHR, the differences are small. What may be more important is that there is no systematic pattern among the cities in the discrepancies between the two data sources.

Stranger Homicides and Missing Data

One consistent finding emerges from comparisons between police records and SHR: In different cities at the same time, and the same cities at different times, the SHR data contain fewer stranger homicides and more unknown relationships than are reflected in police files. Although there are variations among cities, the highest level of agreement between the two data sources occurs for homicides within families, followed by homicides involving friends and acquaintances.

The consistency in underreporting of stranger homicides between police records and the SHR is probably attributable to a lag in reporting. Because stranger homicides take longer to clear by arrest, relationships are reported as "unknown" when submitted to SHR. Subsequent investigation and arrests lead to corrections in police records; the updates, however, are not forwarded to the UCR Program and, therefore, are not reflected in their records (Riedel, 1993).

To compensate for this problem, Williams and Flewelling (1987) developed a circumstance-adjusted procedure based on the strong relationship between robbery murders and stranger involvement. Using robbery information from more completely recorded circumstances, they estimated that stranger homicides made up 25% of all homicides, which is substantially above the 13% to 15% range reported by the UCR through the years.

Reasons for the focus on the proportion of stranger homicides are twofold. First, it is necessary to counteract misinformation about the involvement of strangers in murder (Riedel, 1998). Claims that stranger homicides are as high as 53% of all homicides have been reported in the popular press (Walinsky, 1995). As discussed in detail (Riedel, 1998), this feat of statistical prestidigitation is accomplished by adding together two categories of homicides: (a) those in which relationships are unknown to the police because they are uncleared offenses and (b) those reported by police as actually involving strangers. Nevertheless, the claim of large numbers of stranger homicides was given additional credence by ambiguous wording in an addendum report to the 1994 edition of *Uniform Crime Reports* (FBI, 1994).

Second, an interest in stranger homicides is an avenue to gain a better understanding of the large number of uncleared cases for which offender, as well as victim-offender relationship, information is missing. For instance, through intensive classification efforts of 794 police homicide records from St. Louis, Decker (1993) was able to reduce the unknown category to 4%. On the basis of his calculations and projection to national figures, he concluded that 19% of all murders involved strangers, a far cry from the 53% mentioned above. Decker concludes, "This finding suggests that stranger homicides may not account for the bulk of those events which remain unclassified, and that missing data from an unsolved homicide case may not distort the distribution of cases across victim-offender relationships" (p. 608).

Summary

Perhaps the most general summary of UCR Program homicide data is that much more needs to be done but that what is available is not discouraging. As a rule, more recent data are more reliable than older data; in particular, there are substantial disagreements for homicide data based on Return A estimates before 1960. Further, the imputation methodology provides reproducible results in a large number of instances, although disparities exist for unknown reasons.

Research has revealed disagreements in comparisons between police records and SHR reports for specific variables, although the differences are not large. The most puzzling of these discrepancies is victim age. Given the wide interval (10 years) used as a basis of comparison, the two data sources should show greater agreement.

The most vexing current problem is the large amount of information not available on offenders because of uncleared murders. Decker's (1993) research suggests that these cases are not characterized by disproportionate stranger involvement, but little else is known about uncleared homicides.

One problem contributing to the clearance issue may be endemic to the system. The UCR Program will accept homicide reports from agencies for up to 1 year after a report is published. Thereafter, unless there is a major change, such as a large city turning in a missing month of data about homicides, the master files are unchanged. Although this policy leads to a comprehensive data set, it means that published figures, particularly by other sources, are characterized by small shifts in numbers. It is advisable, therefore, that homicide researchers using SHR data get the most current data from that source and expect that there will be some variation from published UCR figures.

Useful in coping with this problem would be a practice in which annual report figures are taken as a baseline. Thereafter, any changes would be logged and a record of the changes made available to researchers using the data. These changes could be incorporated into data from the UCR Program that are currently available on compact disks or as downloadable files from the National Archives of Criminal Justice Data.

■ *THE NATIONAL CENTER FOR HEALTH STATISTICS*

Homicide data from the Vital Statistics Division of the NCHS is part of a nationwide collection of mortality data. The death registration system includes the 50 states, the District of Columbia, New York City (with its own registration system), Puerto Rico, the U.S. Virgin Islands, Guam, American Samoa, and the Trust Territory of the Pacific Islands. In this discussion, the United States refers to the 50 states, New York City, and the District of Columbia (NCHS, 1996).

Information on homicide is collected through the use of standardized death certificates that are completed by some medico-legal officer (such as a medical examiner) in the case of violent deaths. The preparation of death certificates essentially follows the process displayed in Figure 6.1. When completed, death certificates are given to local registrars who are usually county health officers; they verify the certificates' completeness and accuracy, make records of them, and forward copies to state registrars. Personnel at state vital statistics offices check death certificates for incomplete or inconsistent information, then send them to the NCHS. At the NCHS, cases are classified according to categories in the *International Classification of Diseases* (*ICD*) and entered into a national mortality data set.

The death certificates received by the NCHS are sent by states who are members of death registration areas and can demonstrate that the data submitted include at least 90% of all events that occurred. The NCHS assumes complete coverage since 1933; no estimates are used, and all published data are considered final and not subject to revision (Cantor & Cohen, 1980). By 1985, national officials concluded "that over 99% of the birth and deaths occurring in this country are registered" (NCHS, 1985, p. 15).

The *ICD* is published by the World Health Organization, a body that supports a worldwide vital statistics reporting system (see U.S. Department of Health and Human Services, 1991). The classifications contained in this publication are revised approximately every 10 years in a meeting of participating nations. The various *ICD* causes of death used in homicide are prefixed with the letter *E* for "External Causes" and have three-digit codes. Beginning in 1979, a fourth digit was added for more detail.

The most recent *ICD* homicide codes are listed in Table 6.1. Also shown are the years when the codes were added to the collection system. Beginning in 1949, criminal homicides

Table 6.1 Homicide Cause of Death ICD Codes (E960-E969)

Year Started	*Codes*	*Cause of Death*
1968	E960	Fight, brawl, rape
1979	960.0	Unarmed fight or brawl
1979	960.1	Rape
1968	E961	Corrosive or caustic substance
1948	E962	Poisoning
1979	962.0	Drugs and medicinal substances
1979	962.1	Other solid and liquid substances
1979	962.2	Other gases and vapors
1979	962.9	Unspecified poisoning
1968	E963	Hanging and strangulation
1968	E964	Drowning
1933*	173	Firearms
1948	E965	Firearms and explosives
1979	965.0	Handgun
1979	965.1	Shotgun
1979	965.2	Hunting rifle
1979	965.3	Military firearms
1979	965.4	Other unspecified
1979	965.5	Antipersonnel bomb
1979	965.6	Gasoline bomb
1979	965.7	Letter bomb
1979	965.8	Other specified
1979	965.9	Unspecified explosive
1933	E966	Cutting and piercing instrument
1979	E967	Child battering and maltreatment
1979	967.0	By parent
1979	967.1	By other specified person
1979	967.9	By unspecified person
1933	E968	Assault by other unspecified
1979	968.0	Fire
1979	968.1	Pushing from high places
1979	968.2	Blunt or thrown object
1979	968.3	Hot liquid
1979	968.4	Criminal neglect
1979	968.8	Other specified
1979	968.9	Other unspecified
1933	E969	Late effects of injury

SOURCE: U.S. Department of Health and Human Services, October, 1991, *International Classification of Diseases* (9th rev., 4th ed., Vol. 1) (DHHS Publication No. PHS 91-1260), Washington, DC: Government Printing Office.
* Changed to an E-code in the sixth revision.

(E960-E969) were distinguished from legal intervention homicides (E970-E978). Homicides by firearms were collected from 1933 until 1948; then, firearms and explosives were joined together as one category. Three-digit codes continue to be used, but since 1979, it is possible to distinguish firearms from explosives by four-digit codes. Information on infanticides (deaths of children under 1 year of age) was collected from 1933 until 1948. The category reappeared in 1979 with four-digit codes under "Child Battering and Maltreatment." "Pushing From High Places" was given a three-digit code beginning in 1968 (E967) but was subsequently reclassified in the ninth revision as a four-digit code under "Assault by Other and Unspecified Means" (Riedel, 1990).

The Death Certificate

Information on homicide and other deaths is collected using either a standard death certificate or one approved by the NCHS. Although periodically revised, the current standard form was approved for state use on January 1, 1989. The relevant items include

1. Age, race, gender, and ethnicity of victims
2. Whether victims were in the armed forces and social security numbers
3. Birthplaces, marital statuses, occupations, education, residences, and places of death
4. Places and manners of disposition and whether autopsies were performed
5. Parents' names and addresses
6. Times, places, and causes of death and whether they occurred at work

Unfortunately, not all death certificates sent to the NCHS are received; further, not all that are received find their way into reported mortality figures. As a case in point, the 1964 deaths for Massachusetts were never received by the NCHS, affecting figures for the United States and the New England region. Also, records of deaths in Alabama, Alaska, and New Jersey for 1992 were amended because of errors, but the

NCHS did not receive copies of the amended records (NCHS, 1996).

Although the NCHS endeavors to create and maintain complete data sets, omissions, underreporting, and the necessity for sampling inevitably occur. These are discussed in detail in technical appendixes each year. For example, mortality statistics for 1972 were based on a 50% sample of all records, rather than all records as occurred in previous years. The sample design and error estimates are given in the technical appendix for 1972 (NCHS, 1976).

Intrasource Comparisons

Comparability Between Revisions

Because the *ICD* is revised approximately every 10 years, a question arises about the comparability between classifications. To determine the effect of classification revisions, the NCHS uses comparability ratios that are based on dual codings of a single set of death certificates. For example, to construct comparability ratios for the seventh and eighth revisions, a sample of death certificates is coded using both revisions.

The ratios are obtained by dividing the numbers of deaths assigned to a particular cause of a death category in the eighth revision by the number of deaths assigned to the most nearly comparable cause in the eighth revision. The resulting ratios measure the net effect of changes in the classification, rules for selecting the underlying cause of death, and NCHS procedures. A comparability analysis done by the NCHS indicated a ratio of 0.9969 for the category of "homicide" between the seventh and eighth revisions (Klebba, Dolman, & Dolman, 1975), a high level of agreement.

Medical Certification

None of the forms used by the UCR Program or the NCHS are going to be any better than the quality of decisions made by police and medical examiners. Regarding this issue, research on NCHS data is sparse and not encouraging, whereas that on the UCR Program is nonexistent. In a report prepared by the NCHS (1982) of 128 cause-of-death validation studies through 23 years, it was concluded that the "most striking finding is that so little is known about the quality of medical certification and its effect on diagnostic statistics in general and national cause-of-death statistics in particular" (p. iii).

In a sharp critique of NCHS data, Sherman and Langworthy (1979) contend that there is "apparently widespread lack of the coroners' awareness of, support for, and legal obligation to comply with the system's request for the full information necessary to code the causes of death according to ICD categories" (p. 548). One problem noted by Sherman and Langworthy is that the instructions for completing the death certificate are vague. Only small spaces are available on the form to describe how the injury occurred, and respondents are encouraged to be complete while "using as few words as possible" (p. 549).

In other research, Moriyama, Baum, Haenszel, and Mattison (1958) found that 30% of a sample of Pennsylvania death certificates was based on sketchy diagnostic information. Also, James, Patton, and Heslin (1955) studied clinical information, protocols, and laboratory reports on 1,889 autopsies in Albany, New York, and concluded that 57% of the homicide and suicide deaths were possibly misclassified as to circumstances of death.

One index of the quality of reporting is the proportion of death certificates using codes of symptoms, signs, and ill-defined conditions instead of specific causes of death. Use of these codes had remained stable from 1981 through 1987 but have declined slightly in recent years to a record low of 1.1%, indicating fewer errors and misclassifications (NCHS, 1996).

Age

Hambright (1968) compared ages given on the death certificates with those available from self-reports of ages on census records from May through August, 1960. For more than 199,000 records, she found an agreement of 68.8% for all causes for single-year comparisons, 85.9% for 5-year intervals, and 90.3% for 10-year intervals. In general, there was substantially less age agreement between NCHS and census figures for non-White males and females.

For the category of accidents, which includes E codes for homicide, the level of agreement was much higher. Using 10-year intervals, decedents under 35 years of age showed much higher agreement than those over 35 years. For those under 35 years, the agreement ranged from 86% for non-White males and females to 93.9% for White males and females. For those aged 35 to 99, there was substantially greater agreement for White males (92.6%) and White females (90.6%) than for non-White males (79.2%) and non-White females (77.2%). The net difference agreement between the two data sources showed that death certificates tended to report fewer deaths in the older non-White category, thereby making the age-specific death rate lower than what would be obtained from census figures. The greater agreement between data sources for accidents is explained by the greater likelihood that medico-legal officers fill in the death certificate and do so on the basis of such documents as driver's licenses. This may also hold true for homicides.

In examining age-specific homicide rates for infanticide, Jason, Carpenter, and Tyler (1983) noted a precipitous decline of 25% in 1968 that continued until 1970. One factor affecting this decline was the introduction in 1968 of the code "injuries undetermined whether accidentally or purposely inflicted." Another change was the addition of an "undetermined" in the cause of death categories for the death certificate. Moving the latter cases to the homicide category, as well as recoding cases in New York, led Jason et al. to conclude that the drop in infanticides was artifactual and associated with coding and certificate changes occurring in 1968.

Lapidus, Gregorio, and Hansen (1990) compared the homicide classifications on 161 death certificates in Connecticut with supplementary information from the state chief medical examiner's files that included the results of police investigations. They found an overreporting (29%) of homicides for the 0 to 19 age group on death certificates, primarily in the category of hit-and-run incidents. Errors were less common among the 15 to 19 age group, especially when compared with older decedents.

Race

A number of studies have examined the reliability of racial classification, although none have specifically focused on homicides. Hambright (1969) compared 340,000 death certificates with census records for a 4-month period in 1960. There was 99.8% agreement for White decedents, and 98.2% for Black decedents. The agreement was lowest for smaller minority groups including Filipino (72.6%), American Indian (79.2%), and Chinese (90.3%). Research by Sorlie, Rogot, and Johnson (1992) and the NCHS (1996) revealed similar patterns.

Ethnicity

Hispanic mortality data were published for the first time in 1984 but must be viewed with some caution. For instance, two states, New Hampshire and Oklahoma, were excluded from the 1992 tabulations because their death certificates did not identify persons of ethnic origin. Also, a number of Hispanic deaths occurring in Connecticut in 1991 were determined to be erroneously coded (NCHS, 1996).

In one of the few studies to examine the coding of Hispanic origin in mortality data, Sorlie et al. (1992) compared reports of Hispanic origin on 43,520 death certificates with those reported on 12 current population surveys for 1979 to 1985. Agreement was 89.7% for any report of Hispanic origin. Further analysis indicated an underreporting on death certificates of 1.07% when compared with self-reports made to the U.S. Bureau of the Census.

Research is also available on the reliability of other variables on the death certificates. McCarthy (1968) compared classification of place of residence on death certificates and matching census records. In addition to age and race, Hambright (1969) compared marital status, nativity, and country of origin on the death certificate with matching census records. Sorlie et al. (1992) also compared death certificates with current population surveys for race, ethnicity, gender, place of birth, and veteran status. In general, the agreement for major racial groups and other groups was above 95%.

Summary

The mortality reporting system of the NCHS is clearly much simpler than the system used by the UCR Program. It relies on one form (the death certificate) and claims complete reporting since 1933. For the NCHS, the most important source of information—a dead victim—is at hand, so it is not plagued with the unknown information problem in regard to offenders found with the UCR Program. Complete vital statistics reports, however, are released 2 or 3 years (even longer in recent years) after the reporting year; in contrast, the UCR Program has no more than a 1-year lag in releasing its information.

The addition of four-digit codes in the ninth revision of the *ICD* contributes much to the utility of NCHS data. Homicide researchers can manipulate three- and four-digit codes to create a variety of data sets. In addition, in recent decades, the NCHS has added a number of variables to the death certificate that are useful to homicide researchers, especially information concerning ethnicity, location, occupation, and education. Similarly, the availability of comparability ratios helps ensure continuity between revisions of the *ICD*.

The NCHS also maintains an active commitment to assessing the value of death certificates as a measurement tool. As the prior section indicated, a steady stream of research is evaluating the validity and reliability of the data. The reliability of death certificate items such as age, race, and ethnicity has been found to be surprisingly high for the cause of death classifications used. Unfortunately, there is little research indicating the reliability of these variables for the specific category of homicides.

The major shortcoming of NCHS homicide data is one that affects the UCR Program as well—the lack of clear indications of the reliability and validity of initial decisions. Ultimately, no matter how sophisticated the data collection *after* the death certificate is completed, accuracy in making initial classification decisions is crucial to the value of the information provided by this source.

NCHS data on homicides are available from annual publications of *Vital Statistics of the United States*. Mortality data can also be downloaded from the National Archives of Criminal Justice Data (1998; http://www.icpsr.umich.edu/nacjd/). Special mention needs to be made of the Centers for Disease Control and Prevention's (1998) CDC WONDER (http://wonder.cdc.gov/rchtml/Convert/data/AdHoc.html), an Internet web site that gives the user the opportunity to construct a data file on-line and receive it by e-mail in a number of different formats. At this time, homicide data sets can be constructed from mortality files from 1979 through 1994 for years; states; counties; age, race, and gender of victim; and cause of death. Because of the extremely large size of NCHS files and the time needed to download them, CDC WONDER is a useful solution that needs to be expanded to cover more years and variables.

■ *INTERSOURCE COMPARISONS*

A pressing issue is whether there is a reasonable level of agreement between the two main sources of homicide data that are available to researchers. Generally, there is agreement that the UCR Program category of murders and nonnegligent manslaughters is most comparable with the combined NCHS categories of E960-E969.9 (Cantor & Cohen, 1980; Hindelang, 1974; Rokaw, Mercy, & Smith, 1990) and that figures from the two sources should be similar. Thus, much of the research to be discussed below has used these categories when attempting to assess the two sources' comparability. Little is known, however, regarding the comparability between NCHS codes and the UCR categories of justifiable homicides and negligent manslaughters. In one of the few studies addressing this issue, Rokaw et al. (1990) note that justifiable homicides are comparable with the NCHS codes E970-E978 (legal intervention homicides).

National Comparisons

One of the earliest studies of the agreement between homicide data sources was Hindelang's (1974) comparison of UCR murder and nonnegligent manslaughter rates with NCHS

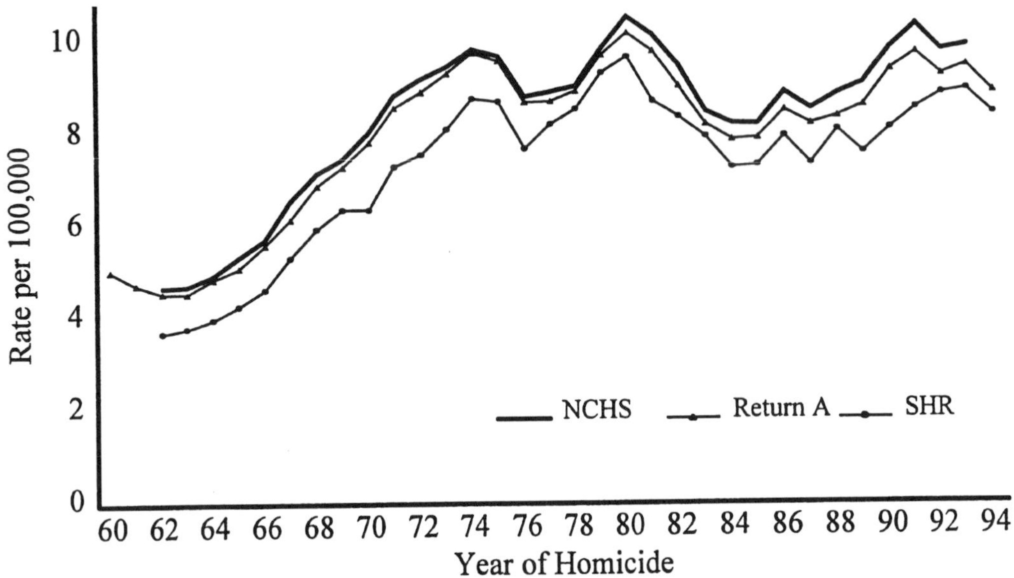

Figure 6.3. Trends for NCHS, Return A, and SHR Homicide Rates

homicide rates (excluding legal intervention homicides) from 1935 through 1970. For 1940 through 1970, he concluded that the agreement was "generally good. Indeed the similarity in the shapes of the curves is striking" (p. 3).

Cantor and Cohen (1980) did a more extensive investigation, analyzing the agreement among eight time series compiled by the NCHS, the UCR Program, and the Office of Management and Budget. They found the best available series from the UCR Program to be homicides reported annually from 1958 through 1976. Prior to 1958, Cantor and Cohen suggest using a series compiled by the Office of Management and Budget. They concluded that results of analyses can be substantially affected by the period chosen, leading them to recommend caution in interpreting time-series results. One possible strategy they suggest is to use both UCR and NCHS series when conducting longitudinal analyses.

For purposes of this chapter, I have supplemented the existing literature by making comparisons for 1960 through 1994 among rates of homicide generated from NCHS homicide reports (E960-E969) and two UCR sources, Return A estimates and SHR (murder and nonnegligent manslaughter). The trends displayed by these sets of homicide rates are shown in Figure 6.3.

To aid in their interpretation, a numerical indication of agreement between the sources used in Figure 6.3 was obtained by dividing the annual number of homicides in one source by the number of homicides in another. Using this method and data available for both measures, the mean agreement ratio for NCHS homicides divided by Return A estimates was 1.04 (*SD* = 0.01) for 1962 to 1993. In other words, the NCHS reported 4% more homicides than found in Return A estimates. The mean and standard deviation did not change for the series from 1976 through 1993, but there was a slight increase (1.05) in the mean ratio for 1986 through 1993 as the rates diverged a bit more than in the past.

Although there is no research, FBI statistician G. Gee (personal communication, October 22, 1996) suggests that the discrepancy between sources can be accounted for by the police initially recording on Return A that the deaths of children younger than 3 years old were accidents. On further investigation by medical examiners and police, if the cause of death is found to be homicide, it is recorded as such on death certificates and the SHR. Gee

Table 6.2 Mean Agreement Ratios and Standard Deviations for Comparisons Between NCHS, SHR, and Demographic Categories (1976–1982)

Comparisons	*Mean Ratio*	*SD*	*Comparisons*	*Mean Ratio*	*SD*
NCHS ÷ SHR*	1.11	0.04	NCHS ÷ SHR**	1.09	0.03
Female	1.06	0.03	All Black	1.07	0.03
Male	1.10	0.03	Female	1.04	0.04
All White	1.12	0.03	Male	1.07	0.03
Female	1.07	0.03	All other	1.14	0.21
Male	1.14	0.04	Female	1.11	0.27
			Male	1.15	0.20

*Comparison excludes legal intervention and justifiable homicides.
**NCHS-SHR comparison and comparisons between NCHS and SHR for demographic categories are taken from Rokaw, Mercy, and Smith (1990, p. 452).

also believes that at present, police tend to inquire more carefully into the circumstances of death, especially those of children.

With the same method of deriving ratios, the mean agreement ratios for NCHS and SHR annual data show the greatest discrepancy among the sources for both the 32-year series (M = 1.17, SD = 0.06) and for the years since 1976 (M = 1.13, SD = 0.05). Dividing Return A estimates by SHR annual counts resulted in a mean ratio of 1.12 (SD = 0.06) for the 32-year series and 1.08 (SD = 0.04) since 1976. Overall, it can be seen that agreement between NCHS rates and Return A estimates have not shown much change through the series; in contrast, agreement between NCHS and SHR frequencies has increased, as has agreement between Return A and SHR frequencies.

Expanding the comparisons to include race and sex categories, Rokaw et al. (1990) compared totals and demographic categories for NCHS and SHR for 1976 through 1982. In doing so, they included legal intervention homicides in their NCHS data and justifiable homicides in the UCR data. A summary of their results is presented in Table 6.2 by using the comparison strategy described above (i.e., ratios). For purposes of further comparison, the first entry on the left side of Table 6.2 contains results from my analysis of the data with legal intervention and justifiable homicides excluded from the associated data sources. The remaining entries are derived from Rokaw et al.'s analyses.

Across categories, the mean agreement ratio (1.11) and standard deviation (0.04) for the reanalyzed data is slightly higher than that reported by Rokaw et al. (M = 1.09, SD = 0.03). This is most likely attributable to the differential treatment of legal intervention and justifiable homicides. Sherman and Langworthy (1979) found that fewer homicides (legal interventions) by police are reported in NCHS than in the UCR Program. Because the NCHS generally reports more homicides in general, a decrease through time in NCHS police legal intervention homicides, coupled with an increase in UCR justifiable police homicides, would produce the smaller mean ratio in Rokaw et al.'s results.

In general, the mean ratios for demographic categories show little variability. The greatest amount of underreporting for the SHR occurs for White males (1.14) and males of other racial groups (1.15). To the extent that they exist, Rokaw et al. (1990) attribute the variations in agreement ratios to

1. Differences in the coverage of the U.S. population
2. Differences in the practices or rules governing the reporting of homicide deaths to the NCHS and the FBI
3. Differences in the criteria used in defining a case as a homicide
4. Differences in the categories used and the rules employed to classify people among demographic subgroups (p. 451)

State and City Comparisons

National comparisons between data sources may not hold true for state or county comparisons. In addition to their analysis of national data, Rokaw et al. (1990) also computed mean ratios for states. Although many of the state NCHS counts agreed with SHR figures, there was a general pattern of underreporting in the SHR, sometimes by large amounts. Georgia (1.51), Montana (6.18), New Mexico (7.26), North Dakota (1.69), South Dakota (2.73), and Vermont (2.46) had especially high mean ratios, indicating that many more cases were reported to the NCHS than to the UCR Program.

Keppel et al. (1990) found a similar pattern of underreporting in the SHR while working with the HITS project. After a careful examination of information on homicides from the NCHS, the UCR Program, and local offices of police and medical examiners, Keppel et al. concluded that there were 1,309 actual homicides in the state of Washington from 1980 to 1986. Using this figure as a base for comparison, they found that local offices of the medical examiners and coroners (-21.3%) and the NCHS (-16.0%) were characterized by considerable underreporting. In contrast, the UCR underreported by 4.7%, whereas local police and sheriff's offices underreported by only 0.5%. The HITS project attributed the discrepancies to several factors, including failure to update death classification records, errors in coding, incorrectly identifying the victim, and underreporting of multiple-victim homicides. Consideration of this research in conjunction with the variations in state reporting indicated by Rokaw and his colleagues (1990) suggests that high levels of national agreement between UCR sources and NCHS may disguise a large amount of intrastate variation.

As discussed earlier, Sherman and Langworthy (1979) found that a larger number of homicides by police (legal interventions) were reported by the UCR than by the NCHS. Providing more detail, these researchers compared data from two heavily urban states (California and New Jersey), six less urban states (Alaska, Nebraska, Oregon, South Carolina, Vermont, and Wisconsin), and five New York counties. They found that NCHS data accounted for only 25% of legal intervention homicides from 1971 through 1975. Taking account of underreporting and omission of some years in jurisdictions, Sherman and Langworthy concluded that police homicides were about 26% higher than reported by the NCHS. In conducting an analysis of police homicides, however, they reported that both measures generated similar results.

The seven-city study mentioned earlier (Zahn & Riedel, 1983) compared police records with medical examiner data. The level of agreement for total number of homicides was 95% or better. The two local data sets were also compared for agreement on victims' sex, gender, and age, as well as victim-offender relationships. Gender agreement, not unexpectedly, was high at 99.5% or better in each city. For race, the level of agreement was 75.6% or higher, with discrepancies occurring mostly in the coding of Hispanic ethnicity. In general, police departments classified some victims as Hispanic, whereas medical examiners classified them as "other races."

Using age differences of 1 year, the range of agreement between police and medical examiners was above 80%, with five of the cities having agreements of 90% or higher. The level of agreement for victim-offender relationships was relatively low, ranging from 52.2% to 80.6%. This low level of agreement resulted largely from medical examiners completing their records and forwarding death certificates before the police had made arrests. Because of this practice, agreement between the two data sources was also high for domestic slayings but low for stranger and acquaintance killings, for which more time is required to effect an arrest.

As a summary of intersource comparisons, the preceding discussion suggests that national comparisons have generally shown relatively high agreements. These results, however, may provide a measure of false comfort because the agreement may depend on what level of analysis is compared. Larger numbers of cases and simpler classifications that characterize national-level studies have tended to generate respectable levels of the agreement between the two data sources. In contrast, when more refined comparisons are made using specific variables, there is considerable variation; few specific explanations are able to account for these variations, especially at levels of analysis such as states or cities.

■ *THE NATIONAL INCIDENT-BASED REPORTING SYSTEM*

Although this chapter has concentrated on a discussion of the two most commonly used data sources in the study of homicide, the recently implemented NIBRS deserves mention. The NIBRS originated as the outcome of an effort in 1982 by a FBI/Bureau of Justice Statistics task force to do a comprehensive evaluation and redesign of the UCR Program. The first two phases of a grant awarded to Abt Associates were focused on what changes were needed; a third phase was devoted to implementing the recommended changes (Akiyama & Rosenthal, 1990; Poggio, Kennedy, Chaiken, & Carlson, 1985).

Except for the SHR, the traditional UCR system relies on counts of incidents and arrests. The NIBRS is designed to gather detailed information on 46 "Group A" offenses in 22 categories such as robbery, types of homicides, assaults, sex offenses, fraud, and stolen property offenses. Group A offenses were selected, in part, because of their seriousness, frequency, prevalence, and visibility to law enforcement. "Group B" offenses consist of 11 less serious offense categories, including bad check offenses, curfew violations, disorderly conduct, and drunkenness. For Group A crimes, a detailed incident report is filed, whereas only an arrest report is filed for Group B crimes (FBI, 1992). Because homicides fall into Group A crimes, subsequent discussion will be limited to that category.

When fully implemented, the NIBRS will provide much more data and in greater detail than are currently available from the SHR and summary data sources. Among the most important additions are these:

1. Each incident contains information on 52 variables covering characteristics of offenses, victims, offenders, and arrestees (Jarvis, 1992).
2. All segments of the incident will be linked together with originating agency identifiers, incident numbers, and sequence numbers where multiple victims and offenders are involved.
3. The hierarchy rule is no longer used; information on up to 10 offenses, 99 victims, and 99 offenders will be gathered.
4. Information will be available on offenses cleared and exceptionally cleared, offenses attempted and completed, drug and/or alcohol use, bias crime involvement, type of premise entry, and property crime characteristics.
5. Victim data will include resident status, type of victims and injuries, and specific relationship to each offender in multiple victim/offender cases.
6. In addition to age, race, ethnicity, and gender of arrestees, offender information will include dates of arrest, codes to distinguish arrests for each offense, whether arrestees were armed and weapon, resident status, and disposition of arrestees under 18.
7. Incident reports will be indicated as initial or supplemental, which permits updating of the files. (FBI, 1992)

The NIBRS data are not generally available in NIBRS format because the process of their development and implementation is still under way; available data from participating states, however, are currently incorporated in UCR publications. In conjunction with the development program, Chilton (1996) used data from 10 participating states to conduct research on domestic homicides. His study demonstrates the flexibility and variety of questions that can be answered using NIBRS data. Reaves (1993) provides a description of the NIBRS, discusses technical problems associated with its use, and uses NIBRS data from three states to examine nonlethal violent crime. Snyder (1995), studying violent crime in South Carolina, has provided a detailed discussion of the formidable problems associated with processing a large complex data set such as the NIBRS.

■ *CONCLUSIONS*

In general, the intrasource agreement for NCHS and UCR data is higher than the intersource agreement. Regarding the UCR Program, agreement between total homicides available from the UCR Program and what appears in the SHR is reasonably high. The imputation (i.e., estimation) methodology used by the UCR Program has received confirmation by outside researchers, but much more needs to be done to justify full confidence in the results. Comparison of social and demographic categories, excluding stranger homicides, shows some variation among cities, although not in a consistent pattern. The underreporting of stranger homicides and overreporting of unknown relationships by the UCR Program most probably reflect a reporting lag and the larger problem of declining clearance rates.

For NCHS data, I know of no studies of comparisons between local records and national records of death certificates. Perhaps because of the quality control procedures used by the NCHS, the assumption is that such comparisons are not needed. Comparisons of death certificates with other populations have been made and indicate substantial agreement on totals, social, and demographic variables. Disagreements are found, however, in the recording of homicides among young victims and among non-White and minority victims. Although there is generally an acceptable level of reliability for many variables of interest to homicide researchers, the research examining intrasource agreement for the *ICD* homicide category is sparse.

The more important question involves the validity of the data provided by the two sources, as least as can be measured by intersource agreement. One way to view validity in relation to data sources is to relate it to the actual number of homicides. Just as there is no "true" crime rate, there are only estimates of the "true" number of homicides because in neither case can they be measured directly (Gove, Hughes, & Geerken, 1985). Because all measures contain error, the next best test is to compare one flawed measure with another. To the extent they agree and share no biases in the same or opposite directions, the agreement is an estimate of their validity. On those grounds, the high level of agreement between Return A estimated rates and NCHS homicide rates nationally is rather strong evidence that supports their validity (see Figure 6.3). Considering the amount of resources expended, that this degree of validity holds true only for comparatively recent data, and that there remains substantial and unexplained variation in more specific comparisons, however, this overall record is hardly one that constitutes a stellar achievement.

In attempting to understand why the overall level of compatibility between the two data sources is not what researchers might wish, the cogent summary by Rand (1993) is worth noting. In attempting to match death certificates to SHR, Rand concluded that

> differences between cases in the files are to a great degree the result of differences in the two programs' purposes and procedures. Basically, the UCR measures crimes, of which death is one outcome. The Mortality System measures deaths, of which crime is one cause. (p. 112)

In this statement, Rand (1993) summarizes that the two sources are different in three fundamental ways. First, data collection and dissemination are the major mission of the NCHS, whereas the UCR Program is a small part of an organization devoted to federal law enforcement. The difference in orientation means fewer resources are devoted to the UCR Program for data collection, monitoring, and evaluation of the resulting data. Second, although the NCHS has mandatory reporting in 50 states, the UCR Program has mandatory reporting in only 44 states with no independent evaluation of the amount of compliance. Finally, the NCHS program is a victim-based system. By contrast, the

UCR Program not only collects information on victims but also coordinates collection of information on offenders, which may or may not be available. Given these considerations, what is surprising is not that NCHS data are of high quality but that UCR homicide data are as good as they are.

Still, we are left with problems that cannot be explained by the preceding factors. Foremost among them is the relative absence of information about the validity of the initial classifications in either source. There is little encouraging research about the accuracy of medical classification of homicide and none about the accuracy of police decisions.

Also, differences in organizational goals and procedures do not explain the substantial variations in state-level reporting. As discussed earlier, research by Rokaw et al. (1990) indicates that in several states, the NCHS reported approximately 50% more homicides than the SHR. The work by Keppel et al. (1990), however, found substantial amounts of underreporting in Washington State vital statistics data, serving as a reminder that the numbers reported by the NCHS are not more valid simply because they are generally larger.

On a positive note, the majority of studies examining *patterns* and *trends* of homicide generally show similar results across both data sources and when using different parts of the same data source. The major caution here is that there is greater agreement among more recent data (Cantor & Cohen, 1980).

Two developments bode well for the future of research using both UCR and NCHS data sources. First, the greatest potential for extensive nationwide data on homicide remains with the development and further implementation of the NIBRS. Time-consuming and formidable problems are associated with implementing it in police agencies and developing a capacity for users. It is clear, however, that the FBI has made a major commitment to revising the UCR reporting system and replacing it with the NIBRS.

Second, many of the data from both the NCHS and the UCR Program are or are becoming generally available in various places on the Internet and/or the National Archives of Criminal Justice Data. This technological development provides an opportunity for research that is only beginning to be explored. Making homicide data easily accessible gives researchers increased opportunity to examine their strengths and limitations; explore different criminological problems; and propose alternative uses, classifications, and measurement tools. All told, given the richness of NIBRS data and an increasing availability of various forms of data, it appears quite possible that we will be able to do a better job in the future of understanding and controlling the statistically rare but exceedingly tragic crime of homicide.

■ *NOTE*

1. The term "Uniform Crime Reports" has become virtually synonymous with this publication. Unless shown in italics, Uniform Crime Reports (or UCR) is used throughout this chapter to refer to the data-gathering effort supported by the FBI.

■ *REFERENCES*

Akiyama, Y., & Rosenthal, H. M. (1990). The future of the Uniform Crime Reporting Program: Its scope and promise. In D. L. MacKenzie, P. J. Baunach, & R. R. Roberg (Eds.), *Measuring crime: Large-scale, long-range efforts* (pp. 49-74). Albany: State University of New York Press.

Cantor, D., & Cohen, L. E. (1980). Comparing measures of homicide trends: Methodological and substantive differences in the Vital Statistics and Uniform Crime Report time series (1933-1975). *Social Science Research, 9,* 121-145.

Centers for Disease Control and Prevention. (1998). CDC WONDER [On-line]. Available: http://wonder.cdc.gov/rchtml/Convert/data/AdHoc.html

Chilton, R. (1996). Can the National Incident-Based Reporting System (NIBRS) contribute to our understanding of domestic violence? In M. Riedel & J. Boulahanis (Eds.), *Lethal violence: Proceedings of the 1955 meeting of the Homicide Research Working Group* (pp. 195-205). Washington, DC: Government Printing Office.

Decker, S. H. (1993). Exploring victim-offender relationships in homicide: The role of individual and event characteristics. *Justice Quarterly, 10,* 585-612.

Division of Law Enforcement. (1994). *Homicide in California, 1994.* Sacramento, CA: Bureau of Criminal Justice Information and Analysis.

Federal Bureau of Investigation. (1962). *Crime in the United States 1961: Uniform crime reports.* Washington, DC: Government Printing Office.

Federal Bureau of Investigation. (1980). *Uniform crime reporting handbook.* Washington, DC: Government Printing Office.

Federal Bureau of Investigation. (1984). *Uniform crime reporting handbook.* Washington, DC: Government Printing Office.

Federal Bureau of Investigation. (1992). *Uniform crime reporting handbook: National Incident-Based Reporting System edition.* Washington, DC: Government Printing Office.

Federal Bureau of Investigation. (1994). *Crime in the United States 1993: Uniform crime reports.* Washington, DC: Government Printing Office.

Federal Bureau of Investigation. (1996). *Crime in the United States 1995: Uniform crime reports.* Washington, DC: Government Printing Office.

Gove, W. R., Hughes, M., & Geerken, M. (1985). Are Uniform Crime Reports a valid indicator of index crimes? An affirmative answer with some minor qualifications. *Criminology, 23,* 451-501.

Hambright, T. Z. (1968). Comparability of age on the death certificate and matching census record: United States—May-August, 1960. *Vital and health statistics: Data evaluation and methods research* (Series 2, No. 29). Rockville, MD: National Center for Health Statistics.

Hambright, T. Z. (1969). Comparability of marital status, race, nativity, and country of origin on the death certificate and matching census record: United States—May-August, 1960. *Vital and health statistics: Data evaluation and methods research* (Series 2, No. 34). Rockville, MD: National Center for Health Statistics.

Hindelang, M. J. (1974). The Uniform Crime Reports revisited. *Journal of Criminal Justice, 2,* 1-17.

Illinois State Police. (1995). *Crime in Illinois: 1994.* Springfield: State of Illinois.

James, G., Patton, R. E., & Heslin, A. S. (1955). Accuracy of cause of death statements on death certificates. *Public Health Reports, 70,* 39-51.

Jarvis, J. P. (1992). The National Incident-Based Reporting System and its application to homicide research. In C. R. Block & R. L. Block (Eds.), *Questions and answers in lethal and non-lethal violence: Proceedings of the homicide research working group* (pp. 81-85). Washington, DC: Government Printing Office.

Jason, J., Carpenter, M. M., & Tyler, C. W., Jr. (1983). Underrecording of infant homicide in the United States. *American Journal of Public Health, 73,* 195-197.

Keppel, R. D., Weis, J. G., & LaMoria, R. (1990). *Improving the investigation of murder: The Homicide Information and Tracking System (HITS)* (National Institute of Justice Final Report No. 87-IJ-CX-0026). Washington, DC: Government Printing Office.

Klebba, A., Dolman, J., & Dolman, A. B. (1975). Comparability of mortality statistics for the seventh and eighth revision of the International Classification of Diseases: United States. *Vital and health statistics: Data evaluation and methods research* (Series 2, No. 66). Rockville, MD: National Center for Health Statistics.

Lapidus, G. D., Gregorio, D. I., & Hansen, H. (1990). Misclassification of childhood homicide on death certificates. *American Journal of Public Health, 80,* 213-214.

McCarthy, M. A. (1968). Comparison of classification of place of residence on death certificates and matching census records. *Vital and health statistics: Data evaluation and methods research* (Series 2, No. 30). Washington, DC: National Center for Health Statistics.

Miller, L. S., & Block, C. R. (1983). *Illinois murder victim data 1973-1981: Guide to quality, availability, and interpretation.* Chicago: Illinois Criminal Justice Information Authority.

Moriyama, I. M., Baum, W. S., Haenszel, W. M., & Mattison, B. F. (1958). Inquiry into diagnostic evidence supporting medical certifications of death. *American Journal of Public Health, 48,* 1376-1387.

National Archives of Criminal Justice Data. (1998). Mortality data [On-line]. Available: http://www.icpsr.umich.edu/nacjd/

National Center for Health Statistics. (1976). *Vital statistics of the United States 1975* (Vol. 2, Mortality, Pt. A). Washington, DC: Government Printing Office.

National Center for Health Statistics. (1982). Annotated bibliography of cause-of-death validation studies: 1958-1980. *Vital and health statistics* (Series 2, No. 89). Washington, DC: Government Printing Office.

National Center for Health Statistics. (1985). *Vital statistics of the United States 1980* (Vol. 2, Mortality, Pt. A, Tech. Appendix). Washington, DC: Government Printing Office.

National Center for Health Statistics. (1996). *Vital statistics of the United States 1992* (Vol. 2, Mortality, Pt. A, Tech. Appendix). Washington, DC: Government Printing Office.

Poggio, E. C., Kennedy, S. D., Chaiken, J. M., & Carlson, K. E. (1985). *Blueprint for the future of the Uniform Crime Reporting Program: Final report of the UCR study.* Boston: Abt Associates.

Rand, M. R. (1993). The study of homicide caseflow: Creating a comprehensive homicide data set. In C. R. Block & R. L. Block (Eds.), *Questions and answers in lethal and non-lethal violence: Proceedings of the homicide research working group* (pp. 103-118). Washington, DC: Government Printing Office.

Reaves, B. A. (1993). *Using NIBRS data to analyze violent crime* (Bureau of Justice Statistics Tech. Rep. NCJ-144785). Washington, DC: Government Printing Office.

Riedel, M. (1990). Nationwide homicide data sets: An evaluation of the uniform crime reports and National Center for Health Statistics data. In D. L. MacKenzie, P. J. Baunach, & R. R. Roberg (Eds.), *Measuring crime: Large-scale, long-range efforts* (pp. 175-205). Albany: State University of New York Press.

Riedel, M. (1993). *Stranger violence: A theoretical inquiry.* New York: Garland.

Riedel, M. (1998). Counting stranger homicides: A case study of statistical prestidigitation. *Homicide Studies, 2,* 206-219.

Riedel, M., & Rinehart, T. A. (1996). Murder clearances and missing data. *Journal of Crime and Justice, 19,* 83-102.

Rokaw, W. M., Mercy, J. A., & Smith, J. C. (1990). Comparing death certificate data with FBI crime reporting statistics on U.S. homicides. *Public Health Reports, 105,* 447-455.

Schneider, V. W., & Wiersema, B. (1990). Limits and use of the Uniform Crime Reports. In D. L. MacKenzie, P. J. Baunach, & R. R. Roberg (Eds.), *Measuring crime: Large-scale, long-range efforts* (pp. 21-48). Albany: State University of New York Press.

Sherman, L. W., & Langworthy, R. H. (1979). Measuring homicide by police officers. *Journal of Criminal Law and Criminology, 70,* 546-560.

Snyder, H. N. (1995). NIBRS and the study of juvenile crime and victimization. In C. R. Block & R. L. Block (Eds.), *Trends, risks, and interventions in lethal violence: Proceedings of the homicide research working group* (pp. 309-315). Washington, DC: Government Printing Office.

Sorlie, P. D., Rogot, E., & Johnson, N. J. (1992). Validity of demographic characteristics on the death certificate. *Epidemiology, 3,* 181-184.

U.S. Department of Health and Human Services. (1991, October). *International classification of diseases* (9th rev., 4th ed., Vol. 1) (DHHS Publication No. PHS 91-1260). Washington, DC: Government Printing Office.

Walinsky, A. (1995, July). The crisis of public order. *Atlantic Monthly, 276,* 39-54.

Williams, K. R., & Flewelling, R. L. (1987). Family, acquaintance, and stranger homicide: Alternative procedures for rate calculations. *Criminology, 25,* 543-560.

Zahn, M. A., & Riedel, M. (1983). National versus local data sources in the study of homicide: Do they agree? In G. P. Waldo (Ed.), *Measurement issues in criminal justice* (pp. 103-120). Beverly Hills, CA: Sage.

CHAPTER 7

Categorizing Homicides

The Use of Disaggregated Data in Homicide Research

Robert L. Flewelling & Kirk R. Williams

Roughly 20,000 homicides are perpetrated in the United States each year. No two of them are alike. If we were to dig deep enough and had access to all the relevant background information on the perpetrator, the victim, the setting, and the circumstances, we would find that each homicide has its unique characteristics and history. As any mystery writer knows, the complexities of human behavior and the multiple influences and motivations that guide our actions are rarely so evident as in the unfolding of the events that ultimately lead to the intentional killing of one person by another. Most real-life homicides are probably even more complicated than what is typically reflected in mystery novels or any other forms of mass media.

Despite the uniqueness of each individual incident, homicides do need to be counted for purposes of surveillance and quantitative research. Furthermore, it is often useful, if not essential, to distinguish various types of homicides in this process. All homicides are not alike, but some are more alike than others. This may be so with respect to the circumstances surrounding the homicide event, the motives of the perpetrator, the relationship between the victim and perpetrator, and the various characteristics of the individuals involved. A key issue encountered by homicide researchers is how to best categorize homicides into significant and relatively homogeneous types, under the assumption that different types of homicide may have different patterns and causes.

The choice of classification strategy depends ultimately on the underlying purpose of the research. Nevertheless, a worthwhile but so far elusive goal for homicide researchers has been to develop a typology of homicide that is useful across a wide range of research questions and theoretical perspectives. Much homicide research in the past has focused on the overall homicide rate, either for the nation as a whole or for geographic units within the nation. There are purposes for which this approach is both reasonable and productive. Much of the sociological research on homicide, however, has sought to elucidate the explanatory role of various structural, cultural, and situational factors with respect to geographic and/or temporal variations in homicide rates. Because different types of homicide may be influenced by different factors, or at least influenced to varying degrees by these variables, results of studies that focus on the overall homicide rate have important limitations that need to be acknowledged. They may also appear to contradict each other or behave in a manner that is inexplicable unless the underlying composition of homicide types is considered.

During the past two decades, a small but convincing body of evidence has accumulated that demonstrates the importance of disaggregating homicide rates into more significant and homogeneous subcategories. In this chapter, we review various classification strategies that have been proposed and examined by homicide researchers and the results of several studies that support the utility of this approach. Although the importance of developing and applying a typology of homicides has received strong support, there does not appear to be any optimal or uniformly agreed-on strategy. The needs for standardization of classification systems must be balanced against both the specific purposes and needs of individual projects and the availability of data. Clearly, however, the use of common classification systems across studies would greatly enhance our ability to interpret and synthesize the findings from multiple studies and thereby advance our knowledge regarding the causes and correlates of homicide.

Given the complexity of the phenomenon and the number of variables that are available for consideration, it is not surprising that no optimal or even commonly accepted classification strategy has emerged. In general, the science of identifying homogeneous classes of entities, or *clustering,* has produced a large assortment of classification strategies that vary widely, both conceptually and analytically. The famous "Fisher-Anderson Iris data" (Fisher, 1936) have been subjected to dozens, if not hundreds, of various statistical procedures, the object of which is to distinguish specific subspecies within a sample of irises. This classic problem entails only four variables, all precisely measured, yet yields an assortment of different clustering "solutions" (see Mezzich & Solomon, 1980). Certainly, then, no one should expect an easy solution to the problem of classifying homicides, for which there are many more potential characteristics to consider and for which the measurement of characteristics is often far from precise.

■ *THE NEED FOR CLASSIFICATION: A CONCEPTUAL JUSTIFICATION*

The first concerted and systematic attempt to categorize and cross-tabulate homicide events with respect to several conceptually important dimensions was Marvin Wolfgang's (1958) classic study *Patterns in Criminal Homicide.* Although Wolfgang examined a number of variables, his 11-category classification of the victim-offender relationship was an especially significant step that has exerted a major influence on subsequent research and surveillance systems. Wolfgang also introduced the concept of victim-precipitated homicides, referring to those events in which the homicide victim was "the first to commence in the interplay of resort to physical violence" (p. 252). This concept, although difficult to operationalize, was important because it focused attention on the fact that many homicides do represent the ultimate act in an escalating cycle of violence between persons who know each other, as distinguished from homicides in which the victim was uninvolved in any prior conflict with the perpetrator.

Since Wolfgang's classic study, the notion that homicides should not be treated as a homogeneous group, and that different types of homicides may indeed have different patterns, correlates, and causes, has gradually taken root. This was certainly one of the primary themes that emerged from a collection of articles published in 1991 honoring Wolfgang's contributions to the field (Block & Block, 1991; Cheatwood, 1991; Zahn, 1991). For example, Zahn lists as one of the four pressing needs for homicide researchers "to delineate clearly the types of homicide that exist, for homicide is indeed a multidimensional, not unidimensional, phenomenon" (p. 17). During the past two decades, a number of researchers have also voiced this same fundamental concern (e.g., Block & Zimring, 1973; Boudouris, 1974; Brewer & Smith, 1995; Cornell, 1989; Harries, 1993; Parker & Smith, 1979; Williams & Flewelling, 1988; Wright & Davis, 1977). The importance of disaggregation was recognized even before Wolfgang's study by Durkheim (1897/1951), who stated that "homicide, therefore, like suicide is not a single, indivisible criminological entity, but must include a variety of species very different from one another" (p. 358). Many of the studies described in this chapter are based on this premise.

Two important objectives may be realized by operationalizing conceptually relevant classification systems in homicide research. The first, as touched on earlier, is to more clearly establish correlational and ostensibly causal relationships between antecedent variables and homicide. These variables may be either individual-level characteristics or attributes of geographic units and include various structural and cultural indicators. In either case, there are both theoretical justification and empirical data to support the notion that different types of homicide are influenced by varying degrees or even different constellations of causal factors. Without disaggregating homicides into more homogeneous groups, potentially important determinants of one type of homicide could easily be missed. Conversely, analytic findings based on the overall homicide rate do not necessarily generalize to subtypes. Of equal importance is the potential for studies conducted at different places or at different times to yield different results based on their relative mixes of homicide subtypes. Without explicitly recognizing this possibility, it will be difficult, if not impossible, to accurately interpret findings across studies and advance our knowledge through comparative research.

A second objective is a more pragmatic one. Public awareness, policy options, and prevention strategies regarding homicide and other forms of violence are to some extent guided by empirical data. Statistics about the overall number or rate of homicides cannot help define specific subgroups at highest risk for homicide, nor do they shed any light on the particular types of homicide that may be most prevalent. Traditional epidemiologic approaches tend to classify homicides according to the age category, race, and gender of the victim. This is a necessary first step, but there are other important defining aspects of homicide events that are critical for better understanding the nature of these events and how they might be prevented. It has often been noted that the public commonly misperceives homicides as typically committed by persons unknown to the victim, usually connected with some dramatic circumstances such as robbery, rape, drug dealing, or gangs. Homicides actually occur most often among persons who know each other, usually within the context of escalating and emotionally charged arguments. Both public perceptions and policy responses must be driven by accurate data regarding the nature of homicides for intervention and prevention efforts to be effectively tailored and accurately targeted.

■ *APPROACHES TO THE CLASSIFICATION OF HOMICIDES*

Classification approaches for homicides have ranged from one extreme—no disaggregation whatsoever—to the other—extremely fine typologies based on detailed clinical or personal interview data. In many aggregate-level sociological studies, the dependent variable is the overall homicide rate for cities, states, or other geographical units (e.g., Blau & Blau, 1982; Land, McCall, & Cohen, 1990; Messner, 1983; Williams, 1984). Some researchers have even suggested the possible use of expanding the definitional boundaries to include other forms of violent deaths such as suicide, injury deaths, and deaths that may be attributable to white-collar crime and other social injustices (Wilson, 1993).

Clearly, studies that have examined the overall rate of homicide are important and useful, provided the results are interpreted in a prudent manner. As we have noted (Williams & Flewelling, 1988), the total rate of homicide is a useful indicator for the overall levels of lethal interpersonal violence, just as the Dow Jones Industrial Average provides an overall gauge of the strength of the securities market in the United States. Findings from research using overall rates, however, need to be interpreted cautiously and in light of the relative composition of homicide types that compose the total, especially if used in comparative research. Furthermore, the absence of significant associations between particular constructs and the overall rate does not necessarily mean that they are irrelevant, as their effects may be unique to a specific form of homicide.

A different body of research focuses on detailed information obtained from perpetrators of homicide through clinical evaluation or in-depth interviews. Typically, the focus of these studies is the psychological attributes of the killer, the intent of which is to identify and better understand distinct psychological profiles of homicide offenders. Some of these studies have also examined patterns and correlates of typologies that are based on psychological data (e.g., Cornell, Benedek, & Benedek, 1989; Rasche, 1993; Toupin, 1993). Because of the different goals and methods of these studies and the focus of many of them on only a specific form of homicide, however, a review of this research is beyond the scope and intent of this chapter.

Between the global "Dow Jones Average" approach and the case study are a number of strategies that have grouped homicides into a small number of distinct and significant subcategories. Two variables, the *victim-offender relationship* and the *circumstance of the event,* have received the most attention, although other classification criteria have also been used. Again, it should not be inferred that there is necessarily a single correct typology or "gold standard" approach. Different research questions and data needs may require different classification systems.

A number of typologies used in recent studies are displayed in Table 7.1. We have chosen to focus on classification variables that appear to hold significant theoretical interest and that are amenable to a variety of possible alternative definitions. This does not imply that classification strategies based on more readily defined and agreed-on variables such as weapon used or the demographic characteristics of the victim and/or offender are less important. Indeed, categorization of homicides based on age, gender, and race/ethnicity, along with geographic unit, form the mainstay of an epidemiologic surveillance system that provides valuable information. The identification of the dramatic surge in youth homicide perpetrations and victimizations in the past decade is a case in point, as is the documentation of different trends in partner homicide by gender (see Chapter 10 by Angela Browne, Kirk Williams, and Donald Dutton). Categorizations based on gender, race, and age have also been useful in exploring theoretical issues regarding structural determinants of homicide (e.g., LaFree & Drass, 1996).

There is, however, a strong and distinct tradition in homicide research that has examined the absolute and relative influence of various cultural and structural indicators on homicide rates. A primary impetus for these studies was the assertion that higher rates of homicide in the southern states could be attributed to a greater cultural acceptance of violence in that region of the country (Gastil, 1971). This tradition of research stimulated efforts to disaggregate the overall homicide rates into constituent elements. Led by the early work of Parker and Smith (1979), the focus of this effort has centered primarily on attributes of the homicide event as defined by the victim-offender relationship and the circumstances surrounding the incident.

The fundamental distinction in the classification of homicides based on victim-offender relationship has been between those incidents in which the victim and the perpetrator knew each other and those in which they were strangers (e.g., Parker & Smith, 1979; see also Smith & Parker, 1980). Subsequent categorizations based on relationship have focused on finer gradations of the "known" category, starting with the distinction between family and nonfamily. Even within the family and acquaintance groups, other researchers have stressed the im-

Table 7.1 Homicide Classification Strategies

Classification Variable(s)	*Typology*	*Source*
Victim-offender relationship	1. Family and acquaintance (primary) Stranger (nonprimary)	Parker & Smith (1979); Smith & Parker (1980)
	2. Family Acquaintance Stranger	Riedel & Przybylski (1993); Rojek & Williams (1993)
	3. Family intimate Family nonintimate Primary intimate Primary nonintimate	Parker & Toth (1990) (family/acquaintance only)
	4. Stranger Acquaintance Friend Other relative Romantic link	Decker (1993)
	5. Married Cohabiting Divorced/ex Dating	Rodriguez & Henderson (1995) (partner homicides only)
Circumstance	1. Co-occurrence with another crime (secondary) Non-co-occurrence (primary)	Jason, Strauss, & Tyler (1983); Harries (1989)
	2. Robbery type Criminal killed Victim-precipitated (argument) Other	Wright & Davis (1977)
Relationship and circumstance	1. Family, conflict Family, other Acquaintance, conflict Acquaintance, other Stranger, conflict Stranger, other	Williams & Flewelling (1988)
	2. Robbery Other felony Intimate Other family Acquaintance nonfelony	Parker (1995); see also Loftin & Parker (1985); Parker (1989)
	3. Family Acquaintance Stranger felony Stranger nonfelony	Zahn & Sagi (1987)
Relationship and gender of victim	1. Male, married Male, not married Female, married Female, not married	Browne & Williams (1993) (partner homicides only)
Circumstance and psychopathology of perpetrator	1. Psychotic Crime Conflict	Cornell, Benedek, & Benedek (1989)
Motivation of perpetrator	1. Expressive Instrumental Rape Street gang Other Mystery	Block (1993); C. R. Block & R. L. Block (1992)
Drug relatedness	1. Pharmacologic Instrumental Systemic	Goldstein, Brownstein, & Ryan (1992)
	2. Nonfelony drug-related Felony-type drug-related Drug used as weapon	Harries (1993)
Alcohol relatedness	1. Alcohol intoxication by victim or offender (yes or no)	Przybylski & Block (1991)

NOTE: This table provides an illustrative, rather than a comprehensive, depiction of the variety of homicide classification strategies used in aggregate-level research studies. Typologies based on age, race, and sex of the victim and perpetrator, and other more objectively defined variables such as weapon, are not included.

portance of differentiating between homicides involving spouses or romantic partners and other relationships. As depicted in Table 7.1, Rodriguez and Henderson (1995) subdivided intimate relationships even further into specific attributes of these relationships. A more detailed historical review of categorization strategies for the victim-offender relationship is provided by Decker (1993).

Approaches to categorizations of homicides based on circumstance have exhibited a range in specificity. Again, one fundamental distinction has been widely recognized—in this case, whether the homicide occurred during the commission of another crime such as a robbery. Both conceptually and empirically, there is an implicit correspondence between this typology and the primary-nonprimary distinction in victim-offender relationship. That is, homicides committed in the context of another crime are typically thought of as involving strangers, whereas those that arise from other circumstances, such as arguments, are much more likely to involve individuals who know each other. This conceptual overlap has to some extent obscured the difference between classification approaches based on circumstance and those based on relationship, as evidenced in the blending of terminology in the typology used by Parker (1995).

On the other hand, an earlier study (Williams & Flewelling, 1988) retained separate dimensions for circumstance and victim-offender relationship by employing a typology based on the cross-classification of these two constructs. One finding from that study was that atypical categories, that is, nonconflict family and acquaintance homicides and conflict stranger homicides, were not as rare as might have been expected. In this study, nonconflict homicides were defined primarily as those committed in the context of some other crime, whereas conflict homicides lacked any apparent connection with other criminal activity. Other studies have demonstrated fundamental differences in the characteristics of homicides that have been simultaneously disaggregated by both circumstance (defined by whether the incident was felony related) and relationship (Riedel & Przybylski, 1993; Zahn & Sagi, 1987).

Although a number of variations or alternatives to classifications based on relationship and circumstance have been proposed, their implementation may be constrained by the availability and the quality of the source data. The source for many studies that have disaggregated homicide rates has been the FBI's Supplemental Homicide Reports (SHR) file. This database includes the vast majority of homicides that occur in the United States and provides a fairly detailed categorization of both homicide circumstance and victim-offender relationship. One of the shortcomings of the SHR data, however, is their reliance on readily available information at the time of the initial investigation and consequent lack of more complete or detailed information about the incident. A number of studies around the country have implemented procedures for obtaining additional and more complete information about each homicide and have developed alternative and/or complementary approaches to characterizing homicide events.

One of the best examples of this approach is the Chicago Homicide Project. On the basis of thorough reviews of more than 18,000 homicides between 1965 and 1989, C. R. Block and R. L. Block (1992) have developed a typology of homicide "syndromes" based on the underlying motivation for the homicide. In this typology, homicides are classified according to whether the underlying motive is determined to be *expressive* (i.e, the homicide begins as an interpersonal confrontation) or *instrumental* (begins as a predatory attack). Several additional syndromes include mixed motives (rape and street gang-related homicides), other motives, and unknown. Although this typology bears a noticeable resemblance to those based on circumstance codes in the SHR, the use of thorough record reviews and the focus on perpetrator's internal motivation rather than situational characteristics distinguish the approach from other strategies that rely on the SHR. A description of other variables that have also been developed to characterize homicides in the Chicago Homicide Project may be found in Block and Block (1992).

■ *VALIDITY AND RELEVANCE OF TYPOLOGIES: EMPIRICAL EVIDENCE*

A primary purpose of disaggregation is to identify different constellations of possible causal factors for homicide. Thus, one important criterion on which to assess the utility of any given classification is whether rates for different types are associated with different predictor variables. Results of studies that have ex-

Table 7.2 OLS Regression Coefficients Obtained for Each Predictor in Models Applied to Relationship/Circumstance-Specific Homicide Rates and the Overall Homicide Rate in U.S. cities (100,000 population or more), 1980 to 1984

Predictors	*Family Conflict*	*Family Other*	*Acquaintance Conflict*	*Acquaintance Other*	*Stranger Conflict*	*Stranger Other*	*Total Rate*
Percentage poor	.255***	.355***	.542***	.512***	.277***	.407***	.691***
Percentage Black	.140***	.055	.254***	.169***	.057	.215***	.259***
Justifiable homicide ratio	.054*	.010	.089***	-.011	.060**	.075	.088**
Confederate South	.035	.052*	.042	.050	.000	-.048	.045
Divorce rate	.296***	.341***	.385***	.620***	.170	.566***	.656***
Population density	-.015	-.028	.035	.166***	.020	.253***	.118**
Constant	-.370	-.405	-.821	-1.442	-.441	-1.719	-1.131
R^2	.468	.343	.692	.501	.278	.468	.735

SOURCE: Adapted from Williams and Flewelling (1988).
NOTES: All rates and variables are logarithmically transformed (base 10), except Confederate South.
$*p \leq .05$, one-tailed test of statistical significance.
$**p \leq .025$, one-tailed test of statistical significance.
$***p \leq .005$, one-tailed test of statistical significance.

amined the influence of various structural and cultural constructs have generally found support for the hypothesis that disaggregated rates are differentially influenced by presumed causal factors. For example, the early work in this area based on state-level analyses by Parker and Smith (1979) and Smith and Parker (1980) showed a significant effect of poverty on *primary* but not *nonprimary* homicides, whereas the opposite was observed for urbanicity. Results of subsequent studies continued to demonstrate support for the differential effects of hypothesized predictors, although the pattern of associations were not always as expected (Parker, 1989; Parker & Toth, 1990). Some results, such as the relative effects of poverty on primary and nonprimary homicide rates, have been inconsistent.

A study based on similar methods (Williams & Flewelling, 1988) also observed different patterns of predictors for homicide rates in U.S. cities defined according to a cross-classification of victim-offender relationship and circumstance. A summary of the findings from this regression analysis is presented in Table 7.2. The size and the significance of the estimated effect for each indictor (i.e, independent variable) were found to vary across homicide types and also to differ between each specific type and the overall rate. Most of the differences observed were consistent with the underlying hypotheses regarding the relative influences of structural and cultural variables on specific forms of homicide rates. Two predictors, *percentage poor* and the *divorce rate,* showed strong and consistent effects on all or nearly all the specific homicide categories, and both these variables had stronger effects for the total rate than for any specific subtype. The implications of these patterns are explored further in the discussion section below.

Other studies that have disaggregated homicides into subgroups also provide support for the argument that different forms of homicides have different underlying causes. Results from the Chicago Homicide Project indicate that the various homicide syndromes have different profiles based on the demographic characteristics of the victim and offender and that their rates also vary differentially across neighborhoods. For example, Block and Block (1992) reported that expressive homicides tended to occur primarily in residential areas, whereas instrumental homicides were much more likely to occur in commercial areas and public housing complexes. Although the focus of this research has not been the identification of causal factors per se, the differential patterns associated with the syndromes, especially with respect to neighborhood, lend strong support to the hypothesis that these homicide subgroups may be influenced by different causal processes. Clearly, these findings have implications for programmatic and policy responses to the homicide problem. Block's (1993) study on homicides among Latinos in Chicago provides a lucid example of how analysis of disaggregated rates can be extremely useful for better understanding and potentially addressing violence among high-risk subgroups.

The work on juvenile homicides by Cornell et al. (1989), which was done at the individual level and involved careful case histories regarding the perpetrators, is also relevant. Findings from this research showed that the juvenile perpetrators of *crime-type* homicides were much more likely than juvenile perpetrators of *conflict-type* homicides to have histories of prior delinquency and school failure, whereas the conflict-type group reported higher levels of stressful life events prior to the homicide. The findings are consistent with the argument that homicides committed during conflict are actually more similar to nonfatal assaults than to crime-related homicides, that is, they are "sibling" crimes (Block & Block, 1991; Harries, 1989). Conversely, crime-related homicides have more in common with other nonfatal crimes (e.g., robberies) than with homicides arising from conflict situations.

■ *IMPLICATIONS FOR THE STUDY OF HOMICIDE*

Among those who study homicide, especially from a macrolevel perspective, there is generally broad support for the utility of categorizing homicides into more specific and homogeneous subgroups. Common themes on how best to accomplish this have focused primarily on the victim-offender relationship and the somewhat loosely and flexibly defined construct of circumstance. Researchers have proposed a variety of specific typologies, however, and as yet there does not seem to be one approach that is commonly supported or used. As research findings accumulate, it is possible that a particular typology or set of typologies that is especially useful across a range of theoretical perspectives and research questions will emerge. How likely this will be remains to be seen; at least initially, it may be more reasonable to expect consensus only on some broad categories and basic variables and perhaps also on what criteria should be used in assessing the usefulness of any particular approach.

There almost certainly is no Holy Grail waiting at the end of the search for those involved in developing homicide classification strategies. There will always be some heterogeneity among homicides within categories, and it is also likely that there will be some degree of similarity and overlap in determinants and patterns across different homicide types. Furthermore, different research questions will sometimes require, by design, different ways of disaggregating homicide. These concerns should not diminish the possibility and potential importance of developing a standard terminology and a basic set of fairly broad groupings to define fundamentally different sorts of homicides. As stated earlier, such an accomplishment would be especially important in enhancing opportunities for comparative research. Beyond that goal, however, are many additional needs for even finer or axiomatically different classification systems as dictated by the specific research questions being posed.

Affecting the development, use, and assessment of any system of classifying homicides for research purposes are a number of extremely important methodological issues. We have touched briefly on the limitations of the SHR, perhaps the most commonly used national database that includes information on individual homicide events. SHR records are completed by the investigating law enforcement officers at the time of or shortly after the initial response to each incident is made. A substantial proportion of the records may contain incomplete or unknown information. Information fields that require the judgment of the investigating officer, such as circumstance, may be prone to both inaccuracies because of the lack of available information and biases that reflect current areas of emphasis or concern (e.g., drug-related or gang-related homicides). Therefore, any research using homicide typologies that are based on SHR files must be especially attuned to the possible implications of measurement error in this data set. For this reason, it is probably not warranted to develop extremely fine categories based on circumstance or to interpret unquestionably the time trends in specific circumstance codes such as "gang-related" (see Chapter 16 by Cheryl Maxson for a discussion of the difficulties involved in coding homicides that involve gang members). Some researchers have advocated that circumstance be coded as a multiple choice checklist rather than a single forced-choice item (Loftin, 1986; Maxfield, 1989), thus raising the possibility of using overlapping rather than mutually exclusive categories. It is also recommended that researchers make an effort to deal constructively with the problem of unknown information, rather than simply exclude such cases from the analyses or assume that they follow the same overall distribution as the known cases (see Williams & Flewelling, 1987).

A second concern about the SHR and probably most other sources of homicide data is the handling of incidents with multiple victims and/or offenders. Such cases pose difficulties for classification systems based on characteristics of the victim, the offender, and especially the victim-offender relationship. As currently structured, the SHR records provide information on the relationship of each offender to only the first victim identified in the record. Consequently, it is not possible to enumerate all the pertinent victim-offender relationships in multiple victim incidents, and dealing with incidents that have multiple victims or offenders raises questions as to how to count such events. Many studies that examine victim-offender relationship have avoided these problems by including only homicides that have single victims and offenders. The exclusion of such cases, however, has resulted in a significant proportion of homicides that have received relatively little attention in studies that examine victim-offender relationships.

A third methodological issue that is extremely pertinent to research on disaggregated rates is the difficulty in interpreting findings based on rates calculated from small numbers of incidents. As homicides are broken into finer subgroups, the number of incidents in each subgroup can become small, especially when done for specific geographic units such as cities or neighborhoods. Rates based on small numbers of incidents tend to be unstable through time, and the significance of any specific rate becomes questionable. Measurement error in the source data will exacerbate this problem. In this context, different patterns and correlates of disaggregated rates are bound to emerge—whether the differences obtained are significant or replicable is another question. Homicide researchers need to examine critically the number of homicides on which disaggregated rates are calculated. This consideration may play a role in determining the level of detail in any topology that is employed.

The above methodological issues are all important considerations for studies that disaggregate the overall homicide rate into specific categories. Another consideration, more conceptual in nature, is also worth mentioning. The focus in studies that examine disaggregated rates has generally been on identifying differences across subcategories with respect to their structural and cultural predictors. Because of the underlying objective of these studies, less attention has been directed to commonalities that may also exist *across* homicide subgroups. This lack of attention may be unfortunate because it is not unreasonable to expect that some determinants may exhibit a broad-ranging influence across many categories of homicide, whereas others may be limited to specific types. In the results displayed in Table 7.2, the poverty indicator exerts a statistically significant influence on all six subcategories, and the percentage divorced variable has a significant effect on five of these six, although the relative strength of the effects varies. Furthermore, the effects of these two predictors are larger for the total homicide rate than any of the disaggregated rates,[1] and the percentage of total variation explained by the prediction model is highest for the total homicide rate.

These findings suggest that factors such as deprivation and social or familial disruption may exhibit a pervasive influence across a range of violent behaviors and raise the question of whether different forms of lethal interpersonal violence might, to some extent, reflect different responses to fundamentally similar circumstances. The higher levels of explained variance (R^2) for the total homicide models are consistent with a model that recognizes a generalized influence of certain key constructs such as deprivation while also recognizing that the specific form of the response variable may be determined, or differentially influenced, by other more selective factors. This type of explanation does not diminish the argument that homicides are heterogeneous and need to be disaggregated to advance our understanding of the phenomenon. It does serve as a reminder, however, that the search for specific types and causes of homicide should not ignore the possibility that there may also be underlying or root causes that help create the foundation from which various specific forms of lethal violence emerge.

In conclusion, it is clear that despite the significant advances that have been made in our understanding of homicide during the past two decades as a consequence of disaggregation, substantial work remains. Important conceptual issues regarding how disaggregation is approached and operationalized (e.g., identification of the key dimensions and categories) still need to be resolved, and several significant methodological issues require more attention than they have received to date. The likelihood for further advances in this area will depend to a large extent on whether researchers are able to develop and agree on theoretically significant classification systems and whether the necessary data are available to support such strategies. Nonetheless, there is already sufficient evidence to begin thinking about the potential applications of this area of research to homicide prevention and to begin working more closely with those directly involved in the development of programs and policies dedicated to this objective.

■ *NOTE*

1. This was true for both the unstandardized coefficients (shown in Table 7.2) and the standardized coefficients (not shown).

■ *REFERENCES*

Blau, J. R., & Blau, P. M. (1982). The cost of inequality: Metropolitan structure and violent crime. *American Sociological Review, 47,* 114-129.

Block, C. R. (1993). Lethal violence in the Chicago Latino community. In A. V. Wilson (Ed.), *Homicide: The victim/offender connection* (pp. 267-342). Cincinnati, OH: Anderson.

Block, C. R., & Block, R. L. (1991). Beginning with Wolfgang: An agenda for homicide research. *Journal of Crime and Justice, 14,* 31-70.

Block, C. R., & Block, R. L. (1992). Overview of the Chicago homicide project. In C. R. Block & R. L. Block (Eds.), *Questions and answers in lethal and non-lethal violence: Proceedings of the first annual workshop of the homicide research working group* (pp. 97-122). Washington, DC: National Institute of Justice.

Block, R. L., & Block, C. R. (1992). Homicide syndromes and vulnerability: Violence in Chicago community areas over 25 years. *Studies on Crime and Crime Prevention, 1,* 61-87.

Block, R. L., & Zimring, F. E. (1973). Homicide in Chicago, 1965-1970. *Journal of Research in Crime and Delinquency, 10,* 1-7.

Boudouris, J. (1974). A classification of homicides. *Criminology, 11,* 525-540.

Brewer, V. E., & Smith, M. D. (1995). Gender inequality and rates of female homicide victimization across U.S. cities. *Journal of Research in Crime and Delinquency, 32,* 175-190.

Browne, A., & Williams, K. R. (1993). Gender, intimacy, and lethal violence: Trends from 1976 through 1987. *Gender & Society, 7,* 78-98.

Cheatwood, D. (1991). Doing the work of research: Wolfgang's foundation and beyond. *Journal of Crime and Justice, 14,* 3-15.

Cornell, D. G. (1989). Causes of juvenile homicide: A review of the literature. In E. P. Benedek & D. G. Cornell

(Eds.), *Juvenile homicide* (pp. 3-36). Washington, DC: American Psychiatric Press.

Cornell, D. G., Benedek, E. P., & Benedek, D. M. (1989). A typology of juvenile homicide offenders. In E. P. Benedek & D. G. Cornell (Eds.), *Juvenile homicide* (pp. 59-84). Washington, DC: American Psychiatric Press.

Decker, S. H. (1993). Exploring victim-offender relationships in homicide: The role of individual and event characteristics. *Justice Quarterly, 10,* 585-612.

Durkheim, E. (1951). *Suicide* (J. A. Spaulding & G. Simpson, Trans.). Glencoe, IL: Free Press. (Original work published 1897)

Fisher, R. A. (1936). The use of multiple measurements in taxonomic problems. *Annals of Eugenics, 7,* 179-188.

Gastil, R. (1971). Homicide and a regional culture of violence. *American Sociological Review, 36,* 412-427.

Goldstein, P. J., Brownstein, H. H., & Ryan, P. J. (1992). Drug-related homicide in New York: 1984 and 1988. *Crime & Delinquency, 38,* 459-476.

Harries, K. (1989). Homicide and assault: A comparative analysis of attributes in Dallas neighborhoods, 1981-1985. *Professional Geographer, 41,* 29-38.

Harries, K. (1993). A victim ecology of drug-related homicide. In A. V. Wilson (Ed.), *Homicide: The victim/offender connection* (pp. 397-414). Cincinnati, OH: Anderson.

Jason, J., Strauss, L. T., & Tyler, C. W., Jr. (1983). A comparison of primary and secondary homicides in the United States. *American Journal of Epidemiology, 117,* 309-319.

LaFree, G., & Drass, K. A. (1996). The effect of changes in intraracial income inequality and educational attainment on changes in arrest rates for African Americans and Whites, 1957 to 1990. *American Sociological Review, 61,* 614-634.

Land, K. C., McCall, P. L., & Cohen, L. E. (1990). Structural covariates of homicide rates: Are there any invariances across time and social space? *American Journal of Sociology, 95,* 922-963.

Loftin, C. (1986). The validity of robbery-murder classifications in Baltimore. *Violence and Victims, 1,* 191-204.

Loftin, C., & Parker, R. N. (1985). An errors-in-variable model of the effect of poverty on urban homicide rates. *Criminology, 23,* 269-285.

Maxfield, M. G. (1989). Circumstances in supplementary homicide reports: Variety and validity. *Criminology, 27,* 671-695.

Messner, S. F. (1983). Regional and racial effects on the urban homicide rate: The subculture of violence revisited. *American Journal of Sociology, 88,* 997-1007.

Mezzich, J. E., & Solomon, H. (1980). Cluster analysis of iris specimens. In P. H. Rossi (Ed.), *Taxonomy and behavioral science: Comparative performance of grouping methods* (pp. 84-107). New York: Academic Press.

Parker, R. N. (1989). Poverty, subculture of violence, and type of homicide. *Social Forces, 67,* 983-1007.

Parker, R. N. (1995). Bringing "booze" back in: The relationship between alcohol and homicide. *Journal of Research in Crime and Delinquency, 32,* 3-38.

Parker, R. N., & Smith, M. D. (1979). Deterrence, poverty, and type of homicide. *American Journal of Sociology, 85,* 614-624.

Parker, R. N., & Toth, A. T. (1990). Family, intimacy, and homicide: A macro-social approach. *Violence and Victims, 5,* 195-210.

Przybylski, R. K., & Block, C. R. (1991, November). *Drug-related homicides in Chicago: Trends over twenty-five years.* Paper presented at the annual meeting of the American Society of Criminology, San Francisco.

Rasche, C. E. (1993). Given reasons for violence in intimate relationships. In A. V. Wilson (Ed.), *Homicide: The victim/offender connection* (pp. 75-100). Cincinnati, OH: Anderson.

Riedel, M., & Przybylski, R. J. (1993). Stranger murders and assault: A study of a neglected form of stranger violence. In A. V. Wilson (Ed.), *Homicide: The victim/offender connection* (pp. 359-382). Cincinnati, OH: Anderson.

Rodriquez, S. F., & Henderson, V. A. (1995). Intimate homicide: Victim-offender relationship in female-perpetrated homicide. *Deviant Behavior, 16,* 45-57.

Rojek, D. G., & Williams, J. L. (1993). Interracial vs. intraracial offenses in terms of the victim/offender relationship. In A. V. Wilson (Ed.), *Homicide: The victim/offender connection* (pp. 249-266). Cincinnati, OH: Anderson.

Smith, M. D., & Parker, R. N. (1980). Type of homicide and variation in regional rates. *Social Forces, 59,* 136-147.

Toupin, J. (1993). Adolescent murders: Validation of a typology and study of their recidivism. In A. V. Wilson (Ed.), *Homicide: The victim/offender connection* (pp. 135-156). Cincinnati, OH: Anderson.

Williams, K. R. (1984). Economic sources of homicide: Reestimating the effects of poverty and inequality. *American Sociological Review, 49,* 283-289.

Williams, K. R., & Flewelling, R. L. (1987). Family, acquaintance, and stranger homicide: Alternative procedures for rate calculation. *Criminology, 25,* 543-560.

Williams, K. R., & Flewelling, R. L. (1988). The social production of criminal homicide: A comparative study of disaggregated rates in American cities. *American Sociological Review, 53,* 421-431.

Wilson, N. K. (1993). Gendered interaction in criminal homicide. In A. V. Wilson (Ed.), *Homicide: The victim/offender connection* (pp. 43-64). Cincinnati, OH: Anderson.

Wolfgang, M. E. (1958). *Patterns in criminal homicide.* Philadelphia: University of Pennsylvania Press.

Wright, R. K., & Davis, J. H. (1977). Studies in the epidemiology of murder: A proposed classification system. *Journal of Forensic Science, 22,* 464-470.

Zahn, M. A. (1991). The Wolfgang model: Lessons for homicide research in the 1990s. *Journal of Crime and Justice, 14,* 17-30.

Zahn, M. A., & Sagi, P. C. (1987). Stranger homicides in nine American cities. *Journal of Criminal Law and Criminology, 78,* 377-397.

CHAPTER 8

Determining Social-Structural Predictors of Homicide

Units of Analysis and Related Methodological Concerns

■ *Karen F. Parker, Patricia L. McCall, & Kenneth C. Land*

Homicide researchers long have studied the question of why cities, metropolitan areas, and states in the United States possess differing rates of homicide.[1] This question has stimulated a debate about which level of aggregation is the most theoretically relevant when examining the effects of structural factors on homicide. Messner (1982), for instance, claimed that *standard metropolitan statistical areas* (SMSAs) are more appropriate units of analysis than are cities because SMSAs are bound by county lines and reflect genuine communities. Bailey (1984) questioned, however, whether SMSAs provide a relevant frame of reference when examining the relationship between total homicide and poverty or income inequality. He concluded that cities are much more theoretically appropriate because of their greater homogeneity with respect to crime rates. More recently, noting the inconsistencies that exist across aggregate-level analyses of homicide rates, Land, McCall, and Cohen (1990) claim that the debate regarding the theoretical relevance in the level of aggregation may be specious. Specifically, they argue that the use of proper methodological techniques should generate consistent findings, regardless of the units of analysis employed.

In this chapter, we address whether the level of aggregation implemented in homicide studies is worthy of the attention it has generated. In our efforts to address the methodological issues surrounding units of analysis, we offer a systematic review that examines the effects of structural factors on aggregated, disaggregated, and time-series homicide studies. Of central concern is the comparison of theoretically relevant structural variables employed in homicide studies across various levels of analysis. We propose that this review will enable us to address not only the debate about unit of analysis but also the inconsistencies in findings that often mark homicide research.

We begin with a summary of criminological approaches and the identification of those theoretical variables that we will compare across studies. Specifically, we focus on three theoretical approaches most commonly employed in the study of homicide: social disorganization theory, strain/deprivation theory, and the southern subculture of violence thesis (for extended discussions of these theories, see Chapters 3 and 4 in this volume). Next, we summarize the salient empirical research that has examined covariates of homicide rates during various periods and across various levels of aggregation. Finally, we explain inconsistent findings across these studies by examining statistical characteristics of these data that may account for these discrepancies. Our concluding remarks provide recommendations that may help researchers avoid the production of erroneous substantive inferences in future research.

■ *THEORIES OF CRIME CAUSATION*

One of the most fundamental approaches to the study of crime, known as *social disorganization,* emanates from the Chicago school research of Shaw and McKay (1942). As defined by Bursik (1988), social disorganization refers to the inability of a community structure to realize the common values of its residents and maintain effective social control. Key to social disorganization is the idea that structural barriers impede development of the formal and informal ties that promote the community's ability to solve common problems. Social and economic changes in a community tend to lead to the deterioration of group solidarity and to a breakdown in social control mechanisms, producing conflict and increasing the potential for crime. Numerous empirical analyses have offered support for social disorganization theory (e.g., Petee & Kowalski, 1993; Sampson, 1991; Sampson & Groves, 1989; Smith & Brewer, 1992; Smith & Jarjoura, 1988). Structural variables such as racial heterogeneity, unit population size, density, percentage of young, and percentage of divorced persons have often been taken as indicative of disruption in community social organization in these studies.

According to classical *strain/deprivation theory,* limited or blocked economic opportunities are accompanied by feelings of injustice and resentment (Merton, 1938). As economically deprived persons become aware of their blocked economic resources and grow resentful of what they perceive as an unjust system, so grows their potential for violence. Strain/deprivation theorists also attempt to explain the response of certain racial groups to unfulfilled promises of justice and equity by suggesting that minority groups are more likely to be blocked from educational and employment opportunities. This approach explains the linkage between economic conditions and violence, whereby the economically deprived group is presumed to experience relative deprivation from these blocked opportunities that engenders frustration and, ultimately, results in violence. In accord with this approach, measures of economic and racial inequality are offered as indicative of strain/deprivation. In recent studies, researchers also have employed various component indexes that include measures of poverty, unemployment, income inequality, racial inequality, racial segregation, and the percentage of Black residents as indicators of strain/deprivation.

In perhaps the most cited work in the study of violence, *The Subculture of Violence: Toward an Integrated Theory in Criminology,* Wolfgang and Ferracuti (1967) have applied a cultural model to homicide by suggesting that subcultural patterns that exist among southern populations can account for higher homicide rates in the South. The *subculture of violence* thesis argues that southerners have a greater predisposition for violence because southern regional culture permits or demands violent responses to situations in which one's honor, family, or possessions are challenged or assaulted. Evidence of southerners' greater tendency for physical aggression has been set forth in research examining the high rates of homicide within the southern region (Gastil, 1971; Hackney, 1969). Messner's (1982, 1983a) finding that the southern region has a positive effect on the homicide rate independent of economic conditions has been interpreted by many as support for the subculture of violence hypothesis. The tendency toward violence as an attribute unique to cultural or subcultural traditions that persist in the South has been the contention of many scholars (Pettigrew & Spier, 1962; Simpson, 1985; Wolfgang & Ferracuti, 1967). In efforts to estimate the impact of southern regional culture on homicide rates, studies have used various measures, which include southern region, percentage of persons born in the South, Gastil's Southernness Index, and other region measures (e.g., West and non-South).

Opponents of the subcultural interpretation of homicide propose that rather than culture, structural factors, such as economic deprivation, are the driving forces behind regional differences in homicide rates. A large body of research offers support for theoretical frameworks that emphasize structural versus cultural explanations (Blau & Blau, 1982; Loftin & Hill, 1974; Parker, 1989). Measurement and design weaknesses leave the debate unsettled.

Criminologists' efforts to test the influence of these mainstream theoretical approaches (including structure versus culture, absolute versus relative deprivation, and characteristics of social disorganization) account for the majority of studies of homicide that have been conducted in recent decades. The results from many of these studies will be summarized below.

■ *A REVIEW OF RECENT STUDIES ON HOMICIDE*

Extant research has accumulated during the past two decades that examines these three theoretical perspectives, primarily through estimating the effects of structural factors on homicide rates in social units at different levels of aggregation in the United States. To address the issues related to level of aggregation, we summarize the results produced in 44 empirical studies of homicide. To facilitate this review, we organize studies into three general categories: aggregated, disaggregated, and time series. The results of 26 studies employing various theoretical variables thought to have an effect on aggregated (as opposed to disaggregated) homicide rates are shown in Table 8.1. The empirical findings for 14 studies examining the effects of structural covariates on disaggregated homicide rates are presented in Table 8.2. Finally, the results of four time-series studies of homicide are displayed in Table 8.3. In each table, variables traditionally identified with one of the three theoretical perspectives discussed above are listed; accompanying entries denote whether the effect of each variable was reported to be significantly positive (+), significantly negative (-), or statistically null (0). We provide details (e.g., operational alternatives and variable transformation) for each study in the appendix.

We do not claim that this review has identified *every* study of structural factors of homicide rates in the United States. We believe, however, that the research we discuss here represents a large proportion of statistical studies of this type that have been published in readily available sources during the past several decades.

Not surprisingly, the findings cataloged in Tables 8.1 through 8.3 reveal a number of inconsistencies across homicide research. Variance across findings, usually in the form of reversals of algebraic sign and/or variations in levels of significance, appear in homicide studies examining major theoretical issues from social disorganization and strain/deprivation theories. In particular, this is characteristic of the findings across strain/deprivation studies of the absolute versus relative deprivation argument. Specifically, depending on the study, the relationship between the Gini index of income inequality measure (relative deprivation) and homicide rates is positive and statistically significant or null, whereas the relationship between the poverty measure (absolute deprivation) and homicide rates is positive, negative, or

Table 8.1 Summary of Studies Using Aggregated Homicide Rates (*N* = 26)

					Findings					
Source		*Unit of Analysis*	*N*	*Period*	*Social Disorganization*		*Strain/ Deprivation*		*Subculture of Violence*	
Messner & Golden (1992)		Cities	154	1980	Percentage divorced	+	Resource Deprivation Index	+	South	0
					Population Index	+	Racial Inequality Index	+		
					Percentage aged 15-29	0	Sex ratio	+		
Land, McCall, & Cohen (1990)		Cities	896	1980	Percentage divorced	+	Resource Deprivation Index	+	South	+
					Population Structure Index	+	Unemployment rate	0		
					Percentage aged 15-29	–				
Chamlin (1989)	(Model 1)	Cities	109	1980	Percentage female-headed households	0	Poverty	–	South	
					Population size	–	Income inequality	0		
					Population mobility	0	Percentage Black population	0		
	(Model 2)	Cities	109	1980	Percentage female-headed households	0	Poverty	0	——	
					Population size	+	Income inequality	+		
					Population mobility	0	Percentage Black population	0		
Williams & Flewelling (1988)		Cities	168	1980	Percentage divorced	+	Poverty	+	South	0
					Population density	+	Percentage Black population	+		
Sampson (1986)		Cities	171	1980	Percentage divorced	+	Income inequality	+	West	+
					Population size	+	Percentage Black population	+		
Parker (1989)		Cities	299	1970	Population size	+	Structural Poverty Index	+	South	+
					Population density	–	Income inequality	0		
					Percentage aged 20-34	0	Percentage Black population	0		
Land, McCall, & Cohen (1990)		Cities	722	1970	Percentage divorced	+	Resource Deprivation Index	+	South	+
					Population structure	+	Unemployment rate	0		
					Percentage aged 15-29	0				
Sampson (1985)		Cities	55	1970	Population size	+	Poverty	+	——	
							Racial inequality	0		
							Unemployment rate	–		
							Percentage Black population	+		
Loftin & Parker (1985)		Cities	49	1970	Population size	0	Poverty	0	South	0
					Population density	0	Proportion non-White	+		
					Proportion aged 18-24	–				
Bailey (1984)	(Model 1)	Cities	153	1970	Population size	+	Poverty	+	South	0
					Population density	0	Income inequality	0		
					Percentage aged 15-29	–	Percentage Black population	+		
	(Model 2)	Cities	153	1970	Population size	+	Poverty	+	South	0
					Population density	0	Percentage Black population	+		
					Percentage aged 15-29	–				
	(Model 3)	Cities	153	1970	Population size	+	Income inequality	0	South	0
					Population density	0	Percentage Black population	+		
					Percentage aged 15-29	–				
Land, McCall, & Cohen (1990)		Cities	526	1960	Percentage divorced	+	Resource Deprivation Index	+	South	+
					Population structure	+	Unemployment rate	0		
					Percentage aged 15-29	0				
Bailey (1984)	(Model 1)	Cities	73	1960	Population size	0	Poverty	+	South	0
					Population density	0	Income inequality	0		
					Percentage aged 15-29	0	Percentage Black population	+		
	(Model 2)	Cities	73	1960	Population size	0	Poverty	+	South	0
					Population density	0	Percentage Black population	+		
					Percentage aged 15-29	0				
	(Model 3)	Cities	73	1960	Population size	0	Income inequality	0	South	+
					Population density	0	Percentage Black population	+		
					Percentage aged 15-29	0				

Table 8.1 Continued

Source	Unit of Analysis	N	Period	Findings: Social Disorganization		Strain/ Deprivation		Subculture of Violence	
Harer & Steffensmeier (1992)	SMSAs	125	1980	Population size	0	Poverty	0	South	0
				Percentage aged 15-24	0	Income inequality	+		
						White-Black income difference	0		
						Percentage Black population	0		
Land, McCall, & Cohen (1990)	SMSAs	257	1980	Percentage divorced	+	Resource Deprivation Index	+	South	+
				Population structure	+	Unemployment rate	–		
				Percentage aged 15-29	0				
Land, McCall, & Cohen (1990)	SMSAs	186	1970	Percentage divorced	+	Resource Deprivation Index	+	South	+
				Population structure	+	Unemployment rate	+		
				Percentage aged 15-29	0				
Blau & Golden (1986)	SMSAs	125	1970	Population size	+	Poverty	+	South	+
				Percentage divorced	+	Racial inequality	0		
						Percentage Black population	+		
Rosenfeld (1986)	SMSAs	125	1970	Population size	0	Income inequality	+	——	
						Unemployment rate	0		
						Percentage Black population	+		
Simpson (1985) (Model 1)	SMSAs	125	1970	Population size	0	Poverty	0	South	0
				Percentage divorced	+	Income inequality	+		
				Percentage aged 15-29	0	Racial inequality	+		
						Percentage Black population	+		
(Model 2)	SMSAs	125	1970	Population size	0	Poverty	0	South	+
				Percentage divorced	0	Income inequality	+		
				Percentage aged 15-29	0	Racial inequality	+		
						Percentage Black population	+		
Williams (1984) (Model 1)	SMSAs	125	1970	Percentage divorced	+	Poverty	+	——	
				Population size	0	Income inequality	0		
						Racial inequality	+		
						Percentage Black population	+		
(Model 2)	SMSAs	125	1970	Population size	+	Poverty	+	South	0
				Population density	0	Income inequality	0		
						Percentage Black population	+		
Messner (1983a) (Model 1)	SMSAs	204	1970	Population size	+	Structural Poverty Index	+	South	+
				Population density	0	Income inequality	0		
				Percentage aged 20-34	0	Percentage Black population	+		
(Model 2)	SMSAs	204	1970	Population size	+	Structural Poverty Index	+	Southernness Index	+
				Population density	0	Percentage Black population	+		
				Percentage aged 20-34	–	Income inequality	0		
Messner (1983b) (Model 1)	SMSAs	256	1970	Population size	+	Poverty	0		
				Population density	0	Income inequality	0		
				Percentage aged 15-29	0	Percentage Black population	+		
(Model 2)	SMSAs	256	1970	Population size	+	Poverty	0		
				Population density	0	Percentage Black population	+		
				Percentage aged 15-29	0				
(Model 3)	SMSAs	256	1970	Population size	+	Income inequality	0		
				Population density	0	Percentage Black population	+		
				Percentage aged 15-29	0				
(Model 4)	SMSAs	91	1970	Population size	+	Poverty	+		
				Population density	0	Income inequality	0		
				Percentage aged 15-29	0	Percentage Black population	+		
(Model 5)	SMSAs	91	1970	Population size	+	Poverty	+		
				Population density	0	Percentage Black population	+		
				Percentage aged 15-29	0				
(Model 6)	SMSAs	91	1970	Population size	+	Income inequality	0		
				Population density	0	Percentage Black population	+		
				Percentage aged 15-29	0				

(continued)

Table 8.1 Continued

Source		Unit of Analysis	N	Period	Findings: Social Disorganization		Findings: Strain/ Deprivation		Findings: Subculture of Violence	
Blau & Blau (1982)		SMSAs	125	1970	Percentage divorced	+	Income inequality	+	-----	
					Population size	0	Racial inequality	+		
							Percentage Black population	+		
Messner (1982)	(Model 1)	SMSAs	204	1970	Population size	+	Poverty	–	South	+
					Population density	–	Income inequality	0		
					Percentage aged 15-29	0	Percentage Black population	+		
	(Model 2)	SMSAs	204	1970	Population size	+	Poverty	–	South	+
					Population density	–	Percentage Black population	+		
					Percentage aged 15-29	0				
	(Model 3)	SMSAs	204	1970	Population size	+	Income inequality	0	South	+
					Population density	–	Percentage Black population	+		
					Percentage aged 15-29	0				
Crutchfield, Geerken, & Gove (1982)		SMSAs	65	1970	Population size	0	Impoverished	0	——	
					Mobility	+	Unemployed	–		
					Young males	–	Median years of education	0		
							Percentage Black population	+		
Land, McCall, & Cohen (1990)		SMSAs	182	1960	Percentage divorced	+	Resource Deprivation Index	+	South	+
					Population structure	0	Unemployment rate	–		
					Percentage aged 15-29	0				
Land, McCall, & Cohen (1990)		States	50	1980	Percentage divorced	+	Resource Deprivation Index	+	South	0
					Population structure	+	Unemployment rate	0		
					Percentage aged 15-29	+				
Land, McCall, & Cohen (1990)		States	50	1970	Percentage divorced	+	Resource Deprivation Index	+	South	0
					Population structure	+	Unemployment rate	–		
					Percentage aged 15-29	+				
Huff-Corzine, Corzine, & Moore (1986)	(Model 1)	States	48	1970	Percentage rural	0	Structural Poverty Index	+	South	0
					Percentage aged 20-34	0	Income inequality	0		
							Percentage non-White	+		
	(Model 2)	States	48	1970	Percentage rural	0	Structural Poverty Index	+	Southernness Index	+
					Percentage aged 20-34	0	Income inequality	0		
							Percentage non-White	+		
Parker & Smith (1979)		States	48	1970	Percentage urban	+	Structural Poverty Index	+	South	0
					Percentage aged 20-34	0	Percentage non-White	0		
Smith & Parker (1980)		States	50	1970	Percentage urban	0	Poverty	+	Non-South	0
					Percentage aged 20-34	0	Income inequality	0		
							Percentage non-White	0		
Land, McCall, & Cohen (1990)		States	50	1960	Percentage divorced	+	Resource Deprivation Index	+	South	+
					Population structure	+	Unemployment rate	0		
					Percentage aged 15-29	+				
Loftin & Hill (1974)	(Model 1)	States	48	1960	Percentage rural	0	Structural Poverty Index	+	South	0
					Percentage aged 20-34	+	Income inequality	+		
							Percentage non-White	0		
	(Model 2)	States	48	1960	Percentage rural	0	Structural Poverty Index	+	Southerness Index	0
					Percentage aged 20-34	+	Income inequality	+		
							Percentage non-White	0		
Gastil (1971)		States	48	1960	Population size	0	Median income	–	South	+
					Percentage aged 20-34	+	Median years of educ.	–		
					Percentage urban	0	Percentage Black population	+		

\+ Positive statistically significant coefficient.
\- Negative statistically significant coefficient.
0 Not statistically significant.

null.[2] The summaries in Tables 8.1 and 8.2 reveal that component indexes are capable of producing invariant findings across studies of homicide rates; an exception is the null effect indicated in two studies of disaggregated homicide rates.[3]

Most indicators of the concepts underlying social disorganization theory, such as percentage of young, population size, and density, also exhibit relationships to the homicide rates that vary across studies. An exception is found for the social disorganization variable "percentage of divorced persons," for which consistent results are found across virtually all aggregated homicide studies shown in Table 8.1 in which this variable appears. Invariance for the percentage divorced measure, however, does not persist in studies of disaggregated homicide rates; as can be seen in Table 8.2, the divorce indicator exhibits either a positive or null relationship to the homicide rates.

As seen in Table 8.1, studies have indicated differential findings for the effect of southern region on homicide rates, regardless of the level of aggregation employed.[4] For example, our review suggests that some studies find that South—an indicator of southern subculture of violence thesis—has a null effect, whereas others indicate southern culture increases the aggregate homicide rate at the city, metropolitan, and/or state levels (e.g., Chamlin's, 1989, aggregate homicide analysis reports a negative effect of southern region). In the more recent studies of disaggregated homicide rates presented in Table 8.2, mixed results are also exhibited. In the one time-series analysis (Table 8.3) that includes a southern region measure, a direct significant effect is found.

In brief, discrepancies in algebraic sign or significance levels of parameter estimates are found across studies examining the effects of structural covariates on homicide rates for cities, metropolitan areas, and states summarized in Tables 8.1 through 8.3. We find that a structural variable can have a statistically positive effect on homicide rate at one level of analysis but that the same covariate can also exhibit a statistically negative or null relationship to the homicide rate at another level of analysis. This general pattern of inconsistency is found within and across time periods, sample sizes, and different types of homicide.

It has been suggested that a general theory of homicide should be capable of accommodating all levels of analysis. The question of why there is such considerable variance in findings produced in homicide research has been addressed by Land et al. (1990). We pursue here the argument put forth in that work that the observed variance in findings from social-structural analyses of homicide are not due to differences in units of analysis across these studies. Rather, we maintain that the discrepancies appearing in the studies that we have summarized can most likely be accounted for by methodological difficulties commonly encountered in homicide research. Moreover, we propose that these inconsistencies can be reduced when models are properly specified and estimated. Such procedures are discussed in the sections that follow.

■ *ACCOUNTING FOR STATISTICAL INCONSISTENCY IN HOMICIDE STUDIES*

In the past two decades, numerous empirical studies have aimed at understanding the effects of social and economic forces on homicide offending. The bulk of this research has focused on comparable sets of structural covariates, as indicated in the above section, while producing dissimilar results. Given this, attention to the reasons for conflicting findings is a research priority. To address the issue of inconsistencies in homicide studies, we offer a discussion of the following research design obstacles to consistent statistical inferences: a focus on urban areas, outliers and extreme cases, problems associated with collinearity including multicollinearity, and the presence of the partialing fallacy.

The Predominance of Urban Areas as Sites of Homicide Studies

Current knowledge of the correlates of homicide is based primarily on studies of urban areas (central cities) and/or SMSAs (in later years, termed metropolitan statistical areas [MSAs]). Regardless of the reasons for the general exclusion of rural areas (e.g., ease in data collection), there is the potential of excluding

Table 8.2 Summary of Studies Using Disaggregated Homicide Rates ($N = 14$)

Unit of Disaggregation, by Source	*Unit of Analysis*	*N*	*Period*	*Findings*					
				Social Disorganization		*Strain/ Deprivation*		*Subculture of Violence*	
African-Americans									
Shihadeh & Maume (1997)	Cities	103	1990	Population size	+	Poverty[a]	0	North	0
				Percentage aged 15-34[a]	0	Unemployment rate[a]	0		
						Education[a]	+		
						Centralization[a]	0		
						Unevenness	0		
						Job access[a]	–		
						Proportion Black	0		
Shihadeh & Flynn (1996)	Cities	151	1990	Population size	+	Poverty[a]	0	North	0
				Percentage aged 15-34[a]	0	Employment rate[a]	–		
				Percentage female-headed households	+	Education[a]	0		
						Black isolation	–		
						Unevenness	0		
Parker & McCall (1997)	Cities	164	1980	Population size	+	Resource Deprivation Index[a]	+	South	0
				Percentage divorced[a]	+	Racial Inequality Index	0		
Peterson & Krivo (1993)	Cities	125	1980	Population size	0	Segregation	+	South	0
				Percentage divorced[a]	0	Poverty[a]	0		
				Percentage aged 15-34[a]	0	Racial inequality	0		
						Income inequality[a]	0		
						Percentage Black population	–		
Smith (1992)	Cities	129	1980	Population size	+	Segregation	+	South	0
				Percentage divorced[a]	0	Poverty[a]	0		
				Percentage aged 20-34[a]	0	Percentage unemployment[a]	0		
						Income inequality	0		
						Proportion Black	0		
						Sex ratio	0		
Messner & Golden (1992)	Cities	154	1980	Population Index	+	Resource Deprivation Index[a]	0	South	0
				Percentage divorced					
				Percentage aged 15-29[a]	+	Racial Inequality Index	+		
					0	Sex ratio	0		
Messner & Sampson (1991)	Cities	153	1980	Population size	+	Employment rate	+	West	+
				Population density	0	Sex ratio	+		
				Median aged	+				
				Percentage female-headed households	+				
Sampson (1985)	Cities	55	1980	Population size	0	Poverty	+	——	
						Racial inequality	–		
						Unemployment rate	0		
Harer & Steffensmeier (1992)	SMSAs	125	1980	Population size	0	Poverty[a]	0	South	0
				Percentage aged 15-24[a]	0	Income inequality[a]	0		
						Percentage Black population	0		
Corzine & Huff-Corzine (1992)0	SMSAs	149	1980	Population size	+	Percentage poor[a]	0	South	0
				Population density	–	Income inequality	+		
				Percentage aged 20-34[a]	–				
				Population change	+				
Huff-Corzine, Corzine, & Moore (1986) (Model 1)	States	48	1970	Percentage rural	–	Structural Poverty Index	0	South	0
				Percentage aged 20-34	+	Income inequality	+		
						Percentage non-Black	–		
(Model 2)	States	48	1970	Percentage rural	–	Structural Poverty Index	0	Southernness Index	+
				Percentage aged 20-34	+	Income inequality	0		
						Percentage non-Black	–		

Table 8.2 Continued

Unit of Disaggregation, by Source		*Unit of Analysis*	*N*	*Period*	*Findings: Social Disorganization*		*Findings: Strain/ Deprivation*		*Findings: Subculture of Violence*	
Whites										
Parker & McCall (1997)		Cities	168	1980	Population size	+	Resource Deprivation Index[a]	+	South	+
					Percentage divorced[a]	+				
Smith (1992)		Cities	129	1980	Population size	+	Segregation	0	South	0
					Percentage divorced[a]	+	Poverty[a]	+		
					Percentage aged 20-34[a]	–	Percentage unemployment[a]	0		
							Income inequality	–		
							Proportion White	–		
							Sex ratio	0		
Messner & Golden (1992)		Cities	154	1980	Population Index	+	Resource Deprivation Index[a]	+	South	0
					Percentage divorced	+	Racial Inequality Index	+		
					Percentage aged 15-29[a]	0	Sex ratio	0		
Messner & Sampson (1991)		Cities	153	1980	Population size	+	Employment rate	0	West	+
					Population density	0	Sex ratio	+		
					Median aged	+				
					Percentage female-headed households	+				
Sampson (1985)		Cities	55	1980	Population size	0	Poverty	+	——	
							Racial inequality	0		
							Unemployment rate	0		
Harer & Steffensmeier (1992)		SMSAs	125	1980	Population size	0	Poverty[a]	+	South	0
					Percentage aged 15-24[a]	0	Income inequality[a]	+		
							Percentage Black population	0		
Huff-Corzine, Corzine, & Moore (1986)	(Model 1)	States	48	1970	Percentage rural	0	Structural Poverty Index	0	Percentage born in South	+
					Percentage aged 20-34	+	Income inequality	0		
	(Model 2)	States	48	1970	Percentage rural	–	Structural Poverty Index	+	Southerness Index	+
					Percentage aged 20-34	0	Income inequality	0		
Hackney (1969)		States	48	1940	Urbanization	0	Income	0	South	+
					Median age	–	Median years of education	0		
							Percentage unemployment	0		
Interracial										
Parker & McCall (1997)	(Black-White Model)	Cities	101	1980	Population size	+	Resource Deprivation Index[a]	0	South	–
							Racial Inequality Index	–		
							Segregation	–		
	(White-Black Model)	Cities	97	1980	Population size	+	Resource Deprivation Index[a]	+	South	0
							Racial Inequality Index	0		
							Segregation	0		
Messner & Golden (1992)		Cities	154	1980	Population Index	+	Resource Deprivation Index[a]	+	South	0
					Percentage divorced	+	Racial Inequality Index	0		
					Percentage aged 15-29[a]	0	Sex ratio	+		
Messner & South (1992)	(Model 1)	Cities	154	1980	Population size	+	Segregation	–	——	
					Population density	0	Racial inequality	–		
							Employment rate	+		
	(Model 2)	Cities	154	1980	Population size	+	Segregation	–	——	
							Racial inequality	–		
							Employment rate	+		

(continued)

Table 8.2 Continued

Unit of Disaggregation, by Source		*Unit of Analysis*	*N*	*Period*	*Findings: Social Disorganization*		*Findings: Strain/ Deprivation*		*Findings: Subculture of Violence*	
	(Model 3)	Cities	154	1980	Population density	+	Segregation	–	——	
							Racial inequality	–		
							Employment rate	+		
Males										
Brewer & Smith (1995)		Cities	177	1980	Population size	+	Unemployment rate	0	South	0
					Percentage divorced	+				
					Population density	0				
					Percentage aged 15-29	–				
Sampson (1985)	(Model 1)	Cities	55	1980	Population size	0	Poverty	+	——	
							Racial inequality	–		
							Unemployment rate	–		
							Percentage Black population	0		
	(Model 2)	Cities	55	1980	Population size	0	Poverty	+	——	
							Racial inequality	0		
							Unemployment rate	0		
							Percentage Black population	0		
Females										
Brewer & Smith (1995)		Cities	177	1980	Population size	+	Unemployment rate	0	South	0
					Percentage divorced	+				
					Population density	0				
					Percentage aged 15-29	–				

a. Denotes race-specific measures.
+ Positive statistically significant coefficient.
- Negative statistically significant coefficient.
0 Not statistically significant.

factors that differentially affect urban versus rural homicide offending. Many aggregate-level studies of homicide restrict their focus to those "largest" cities with populations of 250,000 or more.

Researchers who have examined race-, age-, or sex-specific homicide rates using a larger set of urban areas (e.g., those with populations of 100,000 and more) have found that some factors that are statistically significant in the largest urban settings are not significant when "smaller" urban settings are included. This may be accounted for by the wider variation in key theoretical indicators found in diverse geographic locations. Statistically, the greater the sample variance of a regressor, the greater the standard error of its associated coefficient that reduces the t value. Although invariant results in cities with populations of 10,000 or larger have been found (Land et al., 1990), the question remains whether such invariant relationships would be found if disaggregated homicide rates were analyzed. Further research exploring the nature of homicide offending in smaller urban areas and rural areas is warranted.

The Influence of Outliers and Extreme Cases

Because criminological literature suggests that homicide is a relatively rare event, extreme cases (limiting samples to a small number of the largest cities or SMSAs that inflate parameter coefficients and/or excluding cases with extreme values) also are related to the inconsistent findings in homicide research. Although univariate distributions and bivariate scatterplots provide useful information on outliers and nonlinear relationships in the data, these methods are ineffective in detecting potential problems in advanced statistical analysis. In multivariate

Table 8.3 Summary of Time-Series Studies of Homicide Rates ($N = 4$)

Source		*Unit of Analysis*	*N*	*Period*	*Findings*				
					Social Disorganization		*Strain/Deprivation*		*Subculture of Violence*
LaFree & Drass (1996)	(Model 1)	Annual, U.S.	34	1957-1990	Δ Percentage aged 14-29[a]	0	Economic Index[a]	0	———
							Δ Family income[a]	+	
							Δ Median years of education[a]	0	
	(Model 2)	Annual, U.S.	34	1957-1990	Δ Percentage aged 14-29[a]	+	Economic Index[a]	0	———
							Δ Family income[a]	+	
							Δ Median years of education[a]	–	
Fowles & Merva (1996)		Biannual, MSA	28	1975-1990	Population density	+	Poverty	+	South +
					Percentage aged 16-21	0	Wage inequality	+	
							Δ Unemployment	+	
LaFree, Drass, & O'Day (1992)	(Model 1)	Annual, U.S.	32	1957-1988	Δ Percentage aged 14-29[a]	0	Δ Percentage female-headed households[a]	0	———
							Δ Family income[a]	+	
							Δ Median years of education[a]	0	
	(Model 2)	Annual, U.S.	32	1957-1988	Δ Percentage aged 14-29[a]	0	Δ Percentage female-headed households[a]	0	———
							Δ Family income[a]	0	
							Δ Median years of education[a]	–	
Smith, Devine, & Sheley (1992)	(Model 1)	Annual, U.S.	29	1959-1987	-----		Δ Unemployment	+	———
	(Model 2)	Annual, U.S.	29	1959-1987	-----		Δ Unemployment	–	———
	(Model 3)	Annual, U.S.	29	1959-1987	-----		Δ Unemployment	–	———

a. Denotes race-specific measures.
+ Positive statistically significant coefficient.
- Negative statistically significant coefficient.
0 Not statistically significant.
Δ Denotes change measures.

analyses, it is important to identify the extent to which the presence of outliers affects the regression coefficient estimates, standard errors, and test statistics (Belsley, Kuh, & Welsch, 1980, p. 7). Partial regression plots provide the researcher a visual display of outliers that would not be apparent in bivariate scatterplots. In examining these residuals, Belsley et al. argue that studentized residuals are preferable because they have equal variance and are often distributed closely to the t distribution (p. 9). Further, although ordinary regression residuals may have substantially different variances, studentized residuals adjust the ordinary residuals to take into account their differences in sampling error. Nonetheless, although studentized residuals provide vital information on some influential cases, potential outliers with relatively small studentized residuals could be overlooked. Given this, it is also important to examine the changes that occur in the regression coefficients as a result of removing a single observation. Procedures for this are available in some statistical packages.

Collinearity

Collinearity is no stranger to researchers using aggregate data. A collinearity problem exists when there is a high correlation between two or more covariates included in an analysis. Evidence of collinearity among covariates is associated with (a) a change in regression coefficient estimates when a variable is either added or deleted from the model and when an observation is altered or deleted in some way, (b) nonsignificant test statistics and algebraic signs opposed to those predicted from theoretical arguments and previous findings, and (c) instability occurring among the regression coefficient estimates from sample to sample. When the problem of collinearity is encountered, the sampling errors in the observed correlations are magnified in the process of estimating parameters, and, therefore, the estimates are inefficient and unreliable (Heise, 1975, p. 187). Although previous studies of homicide rates recognize the potential for problems with collinearity among regressor variables, few studies make attempts to correct for its presence among covariates in multiple regression analysis. Attention to the issue of collinearity, as an influence on the pattern of inconsistent findings across studies, is essential in homicide research.

Partialing Fallacy

Perhaps more troubling than the problems associated with collinearity are those related to the partialing fallacy—harmful collinearity that occurs when the intercorrelations of regressor variables are greater than the correlations of those regressors with the dependent variable (the homicide rate in the current discussion). Land et al. (1990) provide a convincing argument that many previous homicide analyses are plagued by the partialing fallacy, the result of which is the allocation of all explained variance to that regressor among an intercorrelated set that possesses the (possibly very slightly) higher correlation with the dependent variable (see Gordon, 1967). A potential result of model estimation under these conditions is a significant test statistic for only one of the two regressors in question when if it were not for this partialing fallacy, the researcher would find that both factors are contributing explained variance to the homicide rate and that there is no theoretical reason for assigning all explained variance to only one of the regressors. The substantive implication is that a regressor that is an important social or economic force on homicide offending may be dismissed as not contributing to our understanding of homicide.

Many of the inconsistent findings in homicide studies are products of research generated before Land et al. (1990) drew attention to collinearity/partialing fallacy problems that were, by and large, responsible for the variance in findings across these studies. Collinearities among regressors such as poverty, income inequality, percentage Black, and southern region impair statistical programs from accurately attributing the unique explained variance of each regressor to the homicide rate (this is also known as a *suppressor effect*). Since Land et al.'s contribution, some researchers have applied statistical techniques to reduce collinearity and the associated risk of partialing fallacies among regressor variables, resulting in a greater consistency of inferences about the effects of regressor variables across studies (e.g., Messner & Golden, 1992).

■ *CONCLUSION AND IMPLICATIONS FOR HOMICIDE RESEARCH*

In our review of recent studies that examine the effect of structural factors on homicide rates across time and social space, we find an abundance of inconsistent and variant findings. These discrepancies materialize in homicide studies that examine theories pivotal to criminology, specifically those of social disorganization, strain/deprivation, and the subculture of violence thesis. Unmasking the reasons for variance in findings has been the priority of this chapter. Having reviewed a number of potential causes, we posit that the unit of analysis *is not* a relevant concern for studies of homicide rates. Rather, the statistical discrepancies among results of homicide analyses stem from problems related to research design.

Recent methodological advances provide statistical innovations to correct for methodological weaknesses and the inconsistencies in past research. Land et al. (1990) have argued that no theoretical rationale exists for restricting data analysis to larger (S)MSAs and/or cities. Further, they suggest that principal components analysis is suitable for eliminating the obstacles associated with the partialing fallacy and collinearity problems because it reduces the regressor space of the covariates. In essence, principal components analysis is a data reduction technique that enables the researcher to determine the underlying dimensions of relationships among a set of independent variables. This statistical technique allows independent variables to cluster into one or more composite indexes, often representing a particular latent social or economic concept (Kim & Mueller, 1985, p. 4). A limitation of this approach, however, is that it prevents researchers from testing competing theories when using highly correlated conceptual measures.

In conclusion, we find evidence that any general theory of homicide should generate empirical invariant findings regardless of the level of analysis examined. We argue that those interested in examining aggregated, disaggregated, time-series, or other category-specific homicide rates should direct their attention to issues of statistical inferences, particularly those of collinearity and partialing of explained variance among regressor variables. Future aggregate-level studies exploring issues related to homicide will continue to produce substantively questionable findings unless statistical diagnostics and techniques are employed to eliminate collinearity and problems resulting from the partialing fallacy.

■ *NOTES*

1. We are aware that a number of studies have employed other levels of analysis, including census tracts (Avakame, 1997; Krivo & Peterson, 1996; Morenoff & Sampson, 1997; Schuerman & Kobrin, 1986); American Indian reservations (Bachman, 1991); and counties (Kposowa & Breault, 1993). For the purpose of comparability, however, we limit our attention to the bulk of research that has accumulated at the levels discussed in this chapter.

2. In a response to the presence of collinearity among the relative (Gini index of income inequality) and absolute (poverty) deprivation indicators, some studies provide separate statistical homicide models for these variables (e.g., Bailey, 1984; Messner 1982, 1983b). Nevertheless, in review of these separate models, reversals of algebraic sign or levels of significance emerge for the poverty measure, whereas the Gini index of income inequality exhibits a null effect consistently across studies.

3. Messner and Golden (1992) found a null relationship between the resource deprivation index and the African American homicide rate. They found the racial inequality index exhibited a null effect on the interracial homicide rate, as well. For the structure of poverty index, Huff-Corzine, Corzine, and Moore (1986) found it had a null effect on the rates of African American homicide in both statistical models.

4. Southern regional culture usually is operationalized as an indicator (dummy) variable for cities, metropolitan areas, and states located in the South; other indicators, however, such as Gastil's Southernness Index and the percentage of the unit's population that is southern born, have been employed. See the appendix for details on each study as to which measure of southern regional culture is used.

■ *REFERENCES*

Avakame, E. F. (1997). Urban homicide: A multilevel analysis across Chicago's census tracts. *Homicide Studies, 1,* 338-358.

Bachman, R. (1991). An analysis of American Indian homicide: A test of social disorganization and economic deprivation at the reservation county level. *Journal of Research in Crime and Delinquency, 28,* 456-471.

Bailey, W. C. (1984). Poverty, inequality, and city homicide rates: Some not so unexpected findings. *Criminology, 22,* 531-550.

Belsley, D. A., Kuh, E., & Welsch, R. E. (1980). *Regression diagnostics: Identifying influential data and sources of collinearity.* New York: John Wiley.

Blau, J., & Blau, P. M. (1982). The cost of inequality: Metropolitan structure and violent crime. *American Sociological Review, 47,* 114-129.

Blau, P. M., & Golden, R. M. (1986). Metropolitan structure and criminal violence. *Sociological Quarterly, 27,* 15-26.

Brewer, V. E., & Smith, M. D. (1995). Gender inequality and rates of female homicide victimization across U.S. cities. *Journal of Research in Crime and Delinquency, 32,* 175-190.

Bursik, R. J., Jr. (1988). Social disorganization and theories of crime and delinquency: Problems and prospects. *Criminology, 26,* 519-551.

Chamlin, M. B. (1989). A macro social analysis of the change in robbery and homicide rates: Controlling for static and dynamic effects. *Sociological Focus, 22,* 275-286.

Corzine, J., & Huff-Corzine, L. (1992). Racial inequality and Black homicide: An analysis of felony, nonfelony and total rates. *Journal of Contemporary Criminal Justice, 8,* 150-165.

Crutchfield, R. D., Geerken, M. R., & Gove, W. R. (1982). Crime rate and social integration. *Criminology, 20,* 467-478.

Fowles, R., & Merva, M. (1996). Wage inequality and criminal activity: An extreme bounds analysis for the United States, 1975-1990. *Criminology, 34,* 163-182.

Gastil, R. (1971). Homicide and a regional culture of violence. *American Sociological Review, 36,* 412-427.

Gordon, R. A. (1967). Issues in multiple regression. *American Journal of Sociology, 78,* 592-616.

Hackney, S. (1969). Southern violence. *American Historical Review, 74,* 906-925.

Harer, M. D., & Steffensmeier, D. (1992). The differing effects of economic inequality on Black and White rates of violence. *Social Forces, 70,* 1035-1054.

Heise, D. R. (1975). *Causal analysis.* New York: Wiley-Interscience.

Huff-Corzine, L., Corzine, J., & Moore, D. C. (1986). Southern exposure: Deciphering the South's influence on homicide rates. *Social Forces, 64,* 906-924.

Kim, J., & Mueller, C. W. (1985). *Introduction to factor analysis: What is it and how to do it.* Beverly Hills, CA: Sage.

Kposowa, A. J., & Breault, K. D. (1993). Reassessing the structural covariates of U.S. homicide rates: A county level study. *Sociological Focus, 26,* 27-46.

Krivo, L., & Peterson, R. D. (1996). Extremely disadvantaged neighborhoods and urban crime. *Social Forces, 75,* 619-648.

LaFree, G., & Drass, K. A. (1996). The effect of changes in intraracial income inequality and educational attainment on changes in arrest rates for African Americans and Whites, 1957 to 1990. *American Sociological Review, 61,* 614-634.

LaFree, G., Drass, K. A., & O'Day, P. (1992). Race and crime in postwar America: Determinants of African-American and White rates, 1957-1988. *Criminology, 30,* 157-188.

Land, K. C., McCall, P. L., & Cohen, L. E. (1990). Structural covariates of homicide rates: Are there any invariances across time and social space? *American Journal of Sociology, 95,* 922-963.

Loftin, C., & Hill, R. H. (1974). Regional culture and homicide: An examination of the Gastil-Hackney thesis. *American Sociological Review, 39,* 714-724.

Loftin, C., & Parker, R. N. (1985). An errors-in-variable model of the effect of poverty on urban homicide rates. *Criminology, 23,* 269-285.

Merton, R. K. (1938). Social structure and anomie. *American Sociological Review, 3,* 672-682.

Messner, S. F. (1982). Poverty, inequality, and the urban homicide rate: Some unexpected findings. *Criminology, 20,* 103-114.

Messner, S. F. (1983a). Regional and racial effects on the urban homicide rate: The subculture of violence revisited. *American Journal of Sociology, 88,* 997-1007.

Messner, S. F. (1983b). Regional difference in the economic correlates of the urban homicide rate: Some evidence of the importance of culture context. *Criminology, 21,* 477-488.

Messner, S. F., & Golden, R. M. (1992). Racial inequality and racially disaggregated homicide rates: An assessment of alternative theoretical explanations. *Criminology, 30,* 421-447.

Messner, S. F., & Sampson, R. J. (1991). The sex ratio, family disruption, and rates of violent crime: The paradox of demographic structure. *Social Forces, 69,* 693-713.

Messner, S. F., & South, S. J. (1992). Interracial homicide: A macrostructural-opportunity perspective. *Sociological Forum, 7,* 517-536.

Morenoff, J. D., & Sampson, R. J. (1997). Violent crime and the spatial dynamics of neighborhood transition: Chicago, 1970-1990. *Social Forces, 76,* 31-64.

Parker, K. F., & McCall, P. L. (1997). Adding another piece to the inequality-homicide puzzle: The impact of structural inequality on racially disaggregated homicide rates. *Homicide Studies, 1,* 35-60.

Parker, R. N. (1989). Poverty, subculture of violence, and type of homicide. *Social Forces, 67,* 983-1007.

Parker, R. N., & Smith, M. D. (1979). Deterrence, poverty, and type of homicide. *American Journal of Sociology, 85,* 614-624.

Petee, T. A., & Kowalski, G. S. (1993). Modeling rural violent crime rates: A test of social disorganization theory. *Sociological Focus, 26,* 87-89.

Peterson, R. D., & Krivo, L. J. (1993). Racial segregation and Black urban homicide. *Social Forces, 71,* 1001-1026.

Pettigrew, T. F., & Spier, R. B. (1962). The ecological structure of Negro homicide. *American Journal of Sociology, 67,* 621-629.

Rosenfeld, R. (1986). Urban crime rates: Effects of inequality, welfare dependency, region and race. In J. M. Byrne & R. J. Sampson (Eds.), *The social ecology of crime* (pp. 116-130). New York: Springer-Verlag.

Sampson, R. J. (1985). Race and criminal violence: A demographically disaggregated analysis of urban homicide. *Crime & Delinquency, 31,* 47-82.

Sampson, R. J. (1986). Crime in cities: The effects of formal and informal social control. In A. J. Reiss, Jr., & M. Tonry (Eds.), *Communities and crime* (pp. 271-311). Chicago: University of Chicago Press.

Sampson, R. J. (1991). Linking the micro- and macrolevel dimensions of community social organization. *Social Forces, 70,* 43-64.

Sampson, R. J., & Groves, W. B. (1989). Community structure and crime: Testing social disorganization theory. *American Journal of Sociology, 94,* 774-802.

Schuerman, C. E., & Kobrin, S. (1986). Community careers in crime. In A. J. Reiss, Jr., & M. Tonry, *Communities and crime* (pp. 67-100). Chicago: University of Chicago Press.

Shaw, C. R., & McKay, H. (1942). *Juvenile delinquency and urban areas.* Chicago: University of Chicago Press.

Shihadeh, E. S., & Flynn, N. (1996). Segregation and crime: The effects of Black social isolation on the rates of Black urban violence. *Social Forces, 74,* 1325-1352.

Shihadeh, E. S., & Maume, M. O. (1997). Segregation and crime: The relationship between Black centralization and urban Black homicide. *Homicide Studies, 1,* 254-280.

Simpson, M. E. (1985). Violent crime, income inequality, and regional culture: Another look. *Sociological Focus, 18,* 199-208.

Smith, D. A., & Jarjoura, G. R. (1988). Social structure and criminal victimization. *Journal of Research in Crime and Delinquency, 25,* 27-52.

Smith, M. D. (1992). Variations in correlates of race-specific urban homicide rates. *Journal of Contemporary Criminal Justice, 8,* 137-149.

Smith, M. D., & Brewer, V. E. (1992). A sex-specific analysis of correlates of homicide victimization in United States cities. *Violence and Victims, 7,* 279-286.

Smith, M. D., Devine, J. A., & Sheley, J. F. (1992). Crime and unemployment: Effects across age and race categories. *Sociological Perspectives, 35,* 551-572.

Smith, M. D., & Parker, R. N. (1980). Type of homicide and variation in regional rates. *Social Forces, 59,* 136-147.

Williams, K. R. (1984). Economic sources of homicide: Reestimating the effects of poverty and inequality. *American Sociological Review, 49,* 283-289.

Williams, K. R., & Flewelling, R. L. (1988). The social production of homicide: A comparative study of disaggregated rates in American cities. *American Sociological Review, 53,* 421-431.

Wolfgang, M. E., & Ferracuti, F. (1967). *The subculture of violence: Toward an integrated theory in criminology.* London: Tavistock.

Appendix

Notes on Studies Listed in Tables 8.1 Through 8.3

Studies in Table 8.1

Bailey (1984): For 1970, the sample consists of 153 cities with a population of 100,000 or more; for 1960, the sample includes 73 large cities within SMSAs with a population of 250,000 or more; Model 1 includes both relative and absolute deprivation measures; Model 2 presents absolute deprivation; Model 3 displays relative deprivation; natural log transformations were performed on 1970 homicide, population size, and population density.

Blau and Blau (1982): Sample consists of the largest SMSAs with populations of 250,000 or more in 1970 (*N* = 125); base 10 log transformation was performed on dependent variable.

Blau and Golden (1986): Sample consists of 125 largest SMSAs in 1970 (see Blau & Blau, 1982, description); all variables are logarithmically transformed; South refers to percentage southern born; arrests/crimes measure was also included in the model (*NS*).

Chamlin (1989): The sample consists of 109 cities, with 60% of the cities having populations of 100,000 or more and all but five cities having populations of at least 50,000 as of 1980; the aggregate homicide rate and population size measures were transformed by natural logarithm.

Crutchfield, Geerken, and Gove (1982): Sample consists of 65 SMSAs with populations greater than 500,000 in 1970 to achieve detailed migration data on SMSA sample.

Gastil (1971): Sample consists of 48 states of continental United States in 1960; other measures in model that were not presented in Table 8.1 include hospital beds per 1000, percentage in cities greater than 300,000, and measure of physicians per 1000; South denotes Southernness Index that is based on the persistence of southern cultural traditions that emerged in the pre-Civil War era (see article for details).

Harer and Steffensmeier (1992): Sample consists of the largest SMSAs for 1980 (*N* = 125); the aggregated model shown in Table 8.1 is for arrest rates as opposed to the aggregated offense rate; a measure of police was also included in the model (*NS*); the dependent variable has been transformed logarithmically.

Huff-Corzine, Corzine, and Moore (1986): Sample consists of 48 states in 1970; natural logarithmic transformations given for percentage born in South measure; normalized ridge regression (NRR) also employed for each model, but it is not presented here (refer to article for details); findings for hospital beds per 100,000 not shown; in Model 1, South refers to percentage of southern born, whereas Model 2 employs the Southernness Index.

Land, McCall, and Cohen (1990): Sample consists of 528 cities and 182 SMSAs in 1960; for 1970, the sample includes 729 cities and 187 SMSAs; for the 1980 sample, 904 cities and 259 SMSAs are selected; a sample of all 50 states was employed in the 1960, 1970, and 1980 models; natural log transformations were performed on the dependent variable, population size, population density, and median family income measures.

Loftin and Hill (1974): Sample consists of the 48 states of continental United States in 1960; hospital beds per 100,000 also included in models; Model 1 displays the findings when South is measured as the Confederate South, and Model 2 presents the findings for Southernness Index.

Loftin and Parker (1985): Sample consists of the 49 largest cities in 1970 with no specific sample selection criteria given; South is a dummy variable (South = 1, others = 0); population density is measured as the proportion of housing units with greater than 1.0 persons per room; OLS parameter estimations given only.

Messner (1982): Sample consists of 204 SMSAs in 1970; natural logarithmic transformation were performed on population size and density measures; South measure is a dummy variable (SMSAs located in the South = 1, otherwise = 0).

Messner (1983a): Sample consists of 204 SMSAs with no selection criteria given; in Model 1, South refers to the Confederate South; Model 2 presents the findings when Southernness Index is employed.

Messner (1983b): Total sample consists of 347 cities, whereby 256 of those cities are nonsouthern and 91 are cities located in southern region; natural logarithmic transformation on population size and population density measures; Models 1 through 3 display the findings based on the 256 nonsouthern cities, whereas Models 4 through 6 display the findings based on the 91 southern cities.

Messner and Golden (1992): Sample consists of cities with populations of 100,000 or more (*N* = 168); of the 168 cities, an additional selection of those cities with Black population of 1,000 or more led to the final sample of 154 cities.

Parker (1989): Sample consists of 299 central cities from the 204 SMSAs analyzed in Messner's (1982) article; logarithmic transformation were performed on population size and density measures; in this study, Parker also provides models for average homicide rate (1969-1971) and (1973-1975), other felony homicides, robbery, and primary nonintimate and family intimate homicides.

Parker and Smith (1979): Sample consists of 48 states; measures of severity and certainty of punishment are included in model; authors also examine nonprimary and primary homicide rates; South is a dummy variable (South = 1, other = 0).

Rosenfeld (1986): Sample consists of 125 SMSAs in 1970; other models were provided in this study, but they are not presented here.

Sampson (1985): Sample consists of the largest cities with populations of 250,000 or more (*N* = 55); relative deprivation is measured using the ratio of White to Black median income; arrest/offense ratio measure was also included in the model.

Sampson (1986): Sample consists of cities with populations of 100,000 or more (*N* = 171); the relative deprivation variable is measured as those defined by Sampson (1985) above; occupational status (+), police aggressiveness (0), local incarceration risk (0), and state prison risk (+) measures were also included in the model.

Simpson (1985): A sample of SMSAs with populations of 250,000 or more was used (*N* = 125); log base 10 transformation has been applied to the dependent variable; the logit form of the percentage Black population and percentage divorced is used in both models; the logit form or age structural variable (White males ages 15-29) squared were not included in Table 8.1.

Smith and Parker (1980): Hospital beds per 100,000 was also included in the model (*NS*); primary and nonprimary homicide models were also provided.

Williams (1984): Sample consists of 125 SMSAs with populations of 250,000 or more in 1970; the homicide rates, poverty, population size, population density, and racial inequality measures were transformed logarithmically (base 10); percentage Black population (squared) was also included in the models.

Williams and Flewelling (1988): Sample consists of 168 cities with populations of 100,000 or more; all variables were transformed logarithmically (base 10); only the total homicide rate model is presented here; see original article for the effects of these variables on victim-offender relationship by precipitating incident-specific homicide rate models; South refers to Confederate South measure; a measure of justifiable homicide ratio is included in model but not shown in Table 8.1.

Studies in Table 8.2

Brewer and Smith (1995): Sample consists of central cities with populations of 250,000 or more (*N* = 177); male and female homicide victimization rates across cities are examined; logarithmically transformed variables include the population size and population density measures; other measures included in the models (not displayed in Table 8.2) include differences in high school education, differences in college education, differences in full-time employment, differences in median income, and differences in professional occupations; other models are included—see original article for details.

Corzine and Huff-Corzine (1992): Sample includes 149 SMSAs with population of 250,000 or more in 1980; in some SMSAs in which there were relatively few felony-related killings of Blacks, the authors calculated the mean annual rate per 100,000 population for the 5 years from 1978 to 1982; only the total Black homicide model has been presented here; see original article for findings related to felony and nonfelony related Black homicide models; natural log transformations were performed on the following indicators: population size, population density, percentage aged 20 to 34, percentage South, and income inequality; measures included in analyses but not shown here include the number of hospital beds per 100,000 residents (HOSPBEDS), percentage of persons under the age 18 living in two-parent families (%TWOPARENTS), and the percentage of Black residents residing in the central city (%CITY).

Hackney (1969): Sample consists of 48 contiguous U.S. states in 1940; urbanization measure reflects the percentage of the population in towns of 2,500 or more; income is measured by per capita personal income in dollars; South is dummy variable (former Confederate states = 1, other states = 0); measure of wealth (state's per capita income in dollars) also included in model but not displayed in Table 8.2.

Harer and Steffensmeier (1992): Sample consists of the largest SMSAs for 1980 (*N* = 125); a measure of police was also included in the model (*NS*); Black and White aggregate arrest rates have been transformed logarithmically.

Huff-Corzine, Corzine, and Moore (1986): Sample consists of 48 states in 1970; natural logarithmic transformations given for percentage born in South measure; normalized ridge regression (NRR) also employed for each model, but it is not presented here (refer to article for details); findings for hospital beds per 100,000 not shown; Model 1 consists of non-Whites that are southern born; Model 2 employs the Southernness Index measure for the non-White model.

Messner and Sampson (1991): Sample consists of 171 cities that had a population of greater than 100,000 in 1980; an additional criterion was used to select those cities with a Black residential population of at least 1,000 (*N* = 153); the racially disaggregated homicide rates and population size measure have been transformed logarithmically; the employment rate measure refers to males only; all measures are race-specific with the exception of population size, density, and region (West) measures; per capita income and public assistance measures were also included in the models but not presented here.

Messner and South (1992): Initial sample size composed of 168 cities with populations of 100,000 or more; analysis presented in Table 8.2 is based on a selected sample of those cities with a minimum of 1,000 Blacks (*N* = 154); a logit transformation was imposed on the dependent variable; also, log transformations were employed on the population size and population density measures; measures included in the models but not presented in Table 8.2 include racial heterogeneity and nonhousehold activity ratio.

Parker and McCall (1997): Sample includes the 168 cities with a population of greater than 100,000 in 1980; an additional criterion was used to select those cities with a Black residential population of 10% or more in the Black and White interracial homicide models; Black-White model refers to Black offender-White victim homicide rates, and White-Black model refers to White offender-Black victim homicide rates; other measure included in the interracial models was percentage change in unemployment in 1980 and 1970.

Peterson and Krivo (1993): Sample includes the central cities of SMSAs with a central city population of 100,000 or more and a Black residential population of at least 5,000 (*N* = 125); only Black homicide rates are examined; other measures presented in model include professionals and education; population size measure is logarithmically transformed; percentage aged 15 to 34 measure consists of Black males only.

Sampson (1985): Sample consists of the largest cities with populations of 250,000 or more ($N = 55$); arrest/offense ratio measure was included in the models; under the African American subcategory, author examines non-White homicide rates; under the male subcategory, Model 1 consists of all non-White males, and Model 2 includes White males only; in an additional model, author also examines the effects of racial residential segregation and South on race-specific homicide rates.

Shihadeh and Flynn (1996): This sample is selected from cities with populations of 100,000 or more and a Black residential population of 5,000 or more in 1990; "Black isolation" refers to the probability of Black to White interactions; "unevenness" was measured using the index of dissimilarity; aged 15 to 34 measure refers to the proportion of Black males aged 15 to 34; logarithmic transformations were performed on the Black homicide rate and Black isolation measure; only the full homicide model (Model #5 in their study) is presented here; refer to original article for details on other models and analyses of robbery rates; measures included in model but not presented in Table 8.2 include renters, vacant households, youth attachment, and political empowerment.

Shihadeh and Maume (1997): The unit of analysis in this study included 103 cities with populations of 100,000 or more and cities that had at least 5,000 Black residents in 1990; "centralization" refers to an index reflecting Black residential centralization relative to Whites; "unevenness" was measured using the index of dissimilarity; "job access" was measured as the ratio of the number of jobs with low-skill employment to the number of Blacks with a high school diploma or less aged 25 and older; "proportion Black" refers to the proportion of Black population; only the full model (authors' Model 3) is presented in Table 8.2; other measures included in the study are offense/arrest ratio and Black homeowners.

Smith (1992): Sample consists of 126 central cities in 1980 in which the African American population was at least 11.6% (approximate national average); log transformations were performed on population size and sex ratio measures; percentage divorced measure also includes percentage separated.

Table 8.3

Fowles and Merva (1996): Biannual sample consists of 28 large MSAs to ensure adequate sample size for the wage inequality measure; whether logarithmic transformation were preformed on the dependent or independent variables is not specified; a control variable ("year") and percentage of the population with at least a college education were also included in the model; South is a dummy variable (South = 1; otherwise = 0).

LaFree and Drass (1996): Annual U.S. rates for 1957 to 1990 (34 years); Δ refers to the "first difference of variable (X_1 - X_{t-1})"; the Δ family income, Δ median education of males aged 25 and older, and Δ percentage aged 14 to 29 and race-specific dependent variables were transformed logarithmically; Model 1 displays findings for African Americans, and Model 2 presents the findings for White population; variables included in models (but not shown in Table 8.3) are Δ log consumer price index, Δ log prison rate, and Δ log criminal opportunity index.

LaFree, Drass, and O'Day (1992): Annual U.S. rates for 1957 to 1988 (32 years); Δ refers to the "first difference of variable (X_1 - X_{t-1})"; Δ family income, Δ median education of males aged 25 and older, and Δ percentage males aged 14 to 29, and race-specific dependent variables were transformed logarithmically; Model 1 displays findings for African Americans, and Model 2 presents the findings for White population; variables included in models (but not shown in table) are: Δ log consumer price index, Δ log prison rate, and Δ log criminal opportunity index.

Smith, Devine, and Sheley (1992): Annual U.S. rates for 1959 to 1987 (29 years); Model 1 displays total homicide rate, whereas Model 2 presents findings for African Americans and Model 3 for White population.

CHAPTER 9

A Summary and Review of Cross-National Comparative Studies of Homicide

■ *Gary LaFree*

Modern efforts to develop international crime statistics can be traced back to the General Statistical Congress, convened in Brussels in 1853 (Campion, 1949). Conference participants were clearly convinced of the need for international crime statistics but, at the same time, were wary of the formidable impediments. In particular, they regarded the differences in legal definitions of crime between countries as a seemingly insurmountable obstacle (Vetere & Newman, 1977).

A similar ambivalence toward the collection of international crime statistics clouded the first International Congress on the Prevention and Repression of Crime, held in London in 1872. One of the primary purposes of the congress was to collect reliable international crime statistics (Pears, 1872). Differences between countries with regard to police and court organization, definitions of legal terms, and the collection and reporting of crime statistics, however, effectively discouraged systematic efforts at international crime comparisons for several more decades.

Not until 1949 did the United Nations convene an international group of experts to establish a plan for collecting international crime statistics (Vetere & Newman, 1977). A memorandum prepared for this group recommended that efforts be made to develop a standard classification of offenses and that the collection and publication of criminal statistics be limited to three major offenses: homicide, aggravated assault, and a combined tally of robberies and burglaries (Ancel, 1952). In 1950, the United Nations published a *Statistical Report on the State of Crime 1937-1946* that also contained an examination of the difficulties of collecting international crime statistics. From this modest beginning in the early 1950s, international crime statistics gradually have become

AUTHOR'S NOTE: Send correspondence to Gary LaFree, Director, Institute for Social Research, University of New Mexico, 2808 Central SE, Albuquerque, New Mexico 87106; 505-277-4257 (phone); 505-277-4215 (fax); lafree@unm.edu (e-mail).

more widely available and, increasingly, the object of systematic empirical study.

Because homicide is generally regarded as offering the most valid and reliable data for international comparisons (Archer & Gartner, 1984; Huang & Wellford, 1989; Lynch, 1995), efforts to collect international crime data have emphasized homicide. Consequently, there undoubtedly are more cross-national studies that focus on homicide than on any other type of crime. This focus reflects the fact that compared with other crimes, homicides are more likely to be reported to police, that police are more likely to record homicides than other crimes, and that legal systems generally spend more time and resources solving homicides than other crimes (Riedel, 1990; Sellin & Wolfgang, 1964).

The purpose of this chapter is to review post-World War II cross-national comparative research on homicide. To simplify the task, the focus will be on 34 quantitative studies that have attempted to explain variations in the homicide rates of different countries. Summarized in Table 9.1, these studies all are published in English and include cross-national homicide rates as a dependent variable. The list does not include theoretical reviews (e.g., Lynch, 1995; Neuman & Berger, 1988), studies of homicide rates that exclude independent variables (e.g., Bennett & Lynch, 1990; Messner, 1992), or longitudinal studies of single nations (e.g., Gartner & McCarthy, 1991; Landau & Pfeffermann, 1988). The studies are listed in order of publication date, oldest to most recent.

As an aid to readers, the following information has been provided for each study listed in Table 9.1: citation, data sources, sample sizes, analytical technique, dependent variables, and independent variables used. The discussion of this research begins with an examination of available data sources for international homicide rates, then moves to a consideration of methodological issues associated with conducting quantitative cross-national research on homicide. I then consider the major theoretical perspectives that have been used to develop an understanding of variations in cross-national homicide rates. Finally, a summary of the empirical evidence regarding correlates of international homicide rates is provided.

■ *SOURCES OF DATA FOR CROSS-NATIONAL STUDIES OF HOMICIDE*

Sources for the homicide data examined in the 34 studies are listed in the second column of Table 9.1. Five sources are shown, including the International Criminal Police Organization (Interpol), the World Health Organization (WHO), the United Nations (UN), the Comparative Crime Data File (CCDF), and the Human Relations Area Files (HRAF).[1] At present, Interpol and the UN (which also collects WHO data) are the only international organizations that collect annual crime statistics from a large number of countries. WHO compiles annual data on causes of death, including homicide, from public health agencies. The CCDF was assembled by Archer and Gartner (1984) and represents the most extensive set of international crime data yet collected by private researchers. The HRAF is a cross-cultural anthropological data set that includes a sample of 60 societies representative of major world cultural regions. The origins and nature of each of these data sources are considered in the following sections.

Interpol

Interpol is the data source most commonly used by these studies, responsible for 21 (61.8%) of the studies summarized in Table 9.1. Interpol crime data generally have been collected annually but published biennially.[2] The first Interpol report was approved in 1954 and included statistics for 1950 and 1951. Since then, data have been released every 2 years. Data are based on total crime reported to police in each nation. In addition to "willful murder," Interpol reports include data on sexual offenses, major and minor larcenies, various types of fraud, counterfeiting, and drug-related offenses. Interpol reports also include national-

(text continued on p. 133)

Table 9.1 Summary of Cross-National Homicide Studies, 1965 to 1997

Study	*Crime Data Source*	*Sample Size*	*Type Analysis*	*Dependent (1) and Independent (2) Variables*	*Relation to Homicide*
Quinney (1965)[a]	World Health Organization	48	Tabular (measures of central tendency)	1. Homicide and suicide rates	
				2. Industrialization	– ?
				Urbanization	– ?
Wolf (1971)[b]	Interpol	17	Tabular classifications	1. Murder/larceny ratio	
				2. High infant mortality	+ ?
				High percentage of labor force in agriculture	+ ?
				Low adult literacy rate	+ ?
				Low GNP, per capita	+ ?
				Low newspapers, per capita	+ ?
				Low telephones, per capita	+ ?
				Low urbanization	+ ?
				Non-Westernized countries	+ ?
Wellford (1974)[b]	Interpol	75	Bivariate	1. Murder, major larceny, and total crime rates	
				2. GNP, per capita	– ?
				Political orientation	– ?
				Population size	– ?
McDonald (1976)[c]	Interpol	40	OLS regression	1. Murder, juvenile crime, theft, property offense, and total offenses	
				2. GNP, per capita	–
				Governmental stability	+
				Intersectoral inequality	+
				Linguistic heterogeneity	+
				Population increase	+
				Bureaucracy	
				Data collection index	
				Executive stability	
				Family size	
				Labor force participation	
				Land inequality	
				Newspapers, per capita	
				Police force	
				Political representation	
				Racial heterogeneity	
				Radios, per capita	
				Religious heterogeneity	
				School enrollment	
				Unemployment	
				Voting proportion	
				Urbanism	
Krohn (1976)[d]	Interpol	24	Zero-order correlations	1. Homicide, property, and total crime rates	
				2. Energy consumption, per capita	– ?
				GNP, per capita	– ?
				Income inequality	+ ?
				Percentage unemployed	+ ?
Krohn & Wellford (1977)[b]	Interpol	59	OLS regression, various models	1. Homicide, property, and total crime rates	
				2. GNP, per capita	– ?
				Political orientation	– ?
				Population	– ?
		32		1. GNP, per capita change	
				2. Population change	+ ?
Krohn (1978)[b]	Interpol	33	OLS regression	1. Homicide, property, and total crime rates	

(continued)

Table 9.1 Continued

Study	*Crime Data Source*	*Sample Size*	*Type Analysis*	*Dependent (1) and Independent (2) Variables*	*Relation to Homicide*
				2. Division of labor	+ ?
				Energy consumption, per capita	− ?
				Population	− ?
				Systematic frustration	+ ?
				Urbanism	− ?
Braithwaite (1979)[e]	World Health Organization	20, 29	Bivariate	1. Homicide rates	
				2. Income inequality	+
				Social security/GNP	−
Braithwaite & Braithwaite (1980)[f]	Interpol	31	Stepwise multiple regression	1. Average homicide rates	
				2. Ethnic fractionalization index	+ ?
				Income inequality	+ ?
				Political freedom index	− ?
				Protein grams, per capita	− ?
				Freedom of the press index	
				GDP, per capita	
				GNP, per capita	
				Type of political system	
				Urbanization	
Messner (1980)[g]	Interpol	39	OLS regression, various models	1. Murder rates (log)	
				2. Income inequality	+
				GDP, per capita	
				Population density	
				Population size	
				Urbanism	
Hansmann & Quigley (1982)[h]	United Nations	58, 40	OLS regression, various models	1. Homicide rate	
				2. Ethnic heterogeneity	+
				Income inequality	+
				Linguistic heterogeneity	−
				Religious heterogeneity	−
				Youth	+
				GNP, per capita	
				Population density	
				Urbanism	
Hartnagel (1982)[i]	Interpol	40	OLS regression	1. Female homicide, larceny, theft, and fraud rates	
				2. Economic index	
				Education index	
				Female labor force participation	
				Fertility	
				GNP, per capita	
				Illiteracy	
				Marriage rates	
				Occupational stratification	
				Urbanism	
				Years of suffrage	
Messner (1982)[j]	Interpol	39	OLS regression, various models	1. Homicide rates (log)	
				2. Income inequality	−
				Population growth	+
				GDP, per capita	
				Population density	
				Population size	
				Percentage Protestant	
				Urbanism	
Landau (1984)[b]	Interpol	14 countries, 1965-1980	Comparison of trends	1. Homicide, robbery, major larceny, rape, suicide, and total offenses	

Table 9.1 Continued

Study	*Crime Data Source*	*Sample Size*	*Type Analysis*	*Dependent (1) and Independent (2) Variables*	*Relation to Homicide*
				2. Inflation	+?
				Births to unmarried mothers	+?
				Marriage/divorce ratio	−?
				Mental health contacts	+?
Conklin & Simpson (1985)[j]	World Health Organization	52	OLS regression	1. Homicide rates (log)	
				2. Infant mortality rate (log)	+
				Percentage males aged 15-29 (log)	+
				Persons per square mile (log)	+
				Population (log)	+
				Percentage urbanism (log)	−
				Energy consumption per capita	
				Gross school enrollment ratio	
				Life expectancy	
				Sex ratio	
				Telephones per 100 inhabitants	
Groves, McCleary, & Newman (1985)[k]	United Nations	50	LISREL	1. Homicide rates	
				2. Judges ratio	+
				Agricultural worker ratio	
				Catholic predominant	
				GDP, per capita	
				Income inequality	
				Infant mortality rate	
				Moslem predominant	
				Protestant predominant	
				School enrollment ratio	
Kick & LaFree (1985)[j]	Comparative Crime Data File	40	OLS regression, various models	1. Murder rates and theft rates (log)	
				2. Development index	−
				Income inequality	+
				Persons per household	+
				Urbanism	
Messner (1985)[l]	Interpol	29	OLS regression, various models	1. Homicide rates for women and men	
				2. Income inequality	+
				Percentage never married	+
				GDP, per capita (log)	
				Population (log)	
Avison & Loring (1986)[g]	World Health Organization	32, 27	OLS regression, various models	1. Homicide rates	
				2. Ethnic heterogeneity	+
				Income inequality	+
				Labor force participation, males	−
				Income inequality × ethnic heterogeneity	+
				Energy consumption, per capita	
				Population density	
				Youths, 15-24	
Krahn, Hartnagel, & Gartrell (1986)[g]	Interpol	65	OLS regression, various models	1. Homicide rates (log)	
				2. Democracy index	+
				Income inequality	+
				Population growth rate	+
				Percentage agriculture, males	
				Capital formation/GDP	
				Collective violence	
				Defense expenditures/GNP	
				Divorce rate	
				Ethnic and linguistic fractionalization	
				GDP growth rate	

(continued)

Table 9.1 Continued

Study	Crime Data Source	Sample Size	Type Analysis	Dependent (1) and Independent (2) Variables	Relation to Homicide
				GDP, per capita (log)	
				Internal security force	
				Percentage literate	
				Percentage mining and manufacturing, male	
				Population density	
				School enrollment	
				Percentage urban	
				Percentage youths aged 15-19, 20-24, 25-29, 30-34	
LaFree & Kick (1986)[g]	Comparative Crime Data File	47	OLS regression	1. Murder and theft rates (log)	
				2. Economic development index	–
				Income inequality	+
				Population growth	+
				Population (log)	
				Urbanism	
Fiala & LaFree (1988)[g]	World Health Organization	15-40	OLS regression with intercept and slope dummy variables, various models	1. Homicide rate for children less than 1 year old and 1 to 4 years old	
				2. Female share labor force	+
				Female-to-male professionals	–
				Government revenue/GDP	–
				Social security/GDP	–
				Social security family expenditures/GDP	–
				Percentage tertiary female students	–
				GNP, per capita	
				GNP growth	
				Homicide rate	
				Income inequality	
				Persons per household	
				Physicians per 100,000	
				Unemployment rates	
				Urban growth rates	
Messner (1989)[g]	Interpol/ World Health Organization	52, 32	OLS regression, various models	1. Murder rates (log)	
				2. Economic discrimination	+
				Income inequality	+
				Population less than 15 years old	+
				Percentage urban	–
				Democracy index	
				Development index	
				Ethnolinguistic heterogeneity	
				Percentage males 15-29 years old	
				Population (log)	
				Population density (log)	
Steffensmeier, Allan, & Streifel (1989)[g]	Interpol	69	OLS regression and decomposition effects	1. Female percentage of homicide, major property, and minor property arrests	
				2. Years of arrest data	+
				Energy, per capita (log)	
				Percentage female university students	
				Occupational segregation	
				Radios, per capita (log)	
Gartner (1990)[g]	World Health Organization	18 at 7 time points, 1950-1980	Pooled time-series analysis using modified generalized least squares procedures, various models	1. All males	
				All females	
				Males greater than 14 years old	
				Females greater than 14 years old	
				Children 5-14 years old	

Table 9.1 Continued

Study	*Crime Data Source*	*Sample Size*	*Type Analysis*	*Dependent (1) and Independent (2) Variables*	*Relation to Homicide*
				Children 1-4 years old	
				Infants less than 1 year old (log)	
				2. Battle deaths	+
				Death penalty	+
				Divorce rate	+
				Ethnic heterogeneity	+
				Female workers/households	+
				Income inequality	+
				Welfare spending	–
				Percentage youths 15-29 years old	
Gartner, Baker, & Pampel (1990)[m]	World Health Organization	18 at 7 time points, 1950-1980	Pooled time-series analysis using modified generalized least squares procedures	1. Gender gap in homicides, measured by orthogonal regression	
				2. Female share college enrollments	–
				Female share labor force	+
				Female share unmarried	+
				Illegitimacy rate	+
				Divorce rate	
				Female share population	
				Occupational desegregation	
Shichor (1990)[g]	Interpol	44	Bivariate; various years	1. Homicide rates	
				2. Infant mortality	+
				Newspapers/1,000 population	–
				Population change	+
				Population/hospital beds	+
				Population/physicians	+
				Population size	
				Public education expenditure	
Bennett (1991a)[g]	Interpol	38 countries, 1960-1984	Pooled time series, various models	1. Homicide and theft rates	
				2. Juvenile proportion	–
				GDP manufacturing/GDP agriculture	+
				Income inequality	
				Level of development	
Bennett (1991b)[g]	Interpol	43 countries, 1960-1984	Pooled time-series	1. Homicide and theft rates	
				2. Educational inequality	–
				Percentage urban	+
				Female labor force participation	
				GDP manufacturing/GDP	
				GDP per capita	
				Juvenile proportion	
Rosenfeld & Messner (1991)[g]	Human Relations Area Files	32	Bivariate	1. Classification of homicides as frequent or infrequent	
				2. Drunken brawling	+
				Military authority	–
				Political authority	–
				Political oppression	–
				Total population	–
				Typical settlement size	–
				Wife beating	+
				Caste stratification	
				Change in moral codes	
				Change in traditional authority	
				Change in subsistence occupation	
				Class stratification	
				Divorce	
				Internal population density	
				Judicial authority	

(continued)

Table 9.1 Continued

Study	*Crime Data Source*	*Sample Size*	*Type Analysis*	*Dependent (1) and Independent (2) Variables*	*Relation to Homicide*
				Organizational complexity	
				Relative deprivation	
				Size of largest place	
				Technological complexity	
Ortega, Corzine, Burnett, & Poyer (1992)[g]	Interpol	51 countries, 1969-1982	Pooled time-series analysis	1. Homicide and theft rates	
				2. African continent	–
				Asian continent	–
				European continent	–
				North American continent	–
				Oceania continent	–
				GNP, per capita	+
				Percentage middle-aged	–
				Percentage urban	–
				Year	–
				Percentage youths	+
Neapolitan (1994)[g]	Interpol/ World Health Organization	64-106	OLS regression, various models	1. Homicide rates	
				2. Economic discrimination	+
				GDP, per capita (log)	–
				Income inequality	+
				Latin American countries	+
				Population size (log)	–
				Population density (log)	
				Population under 15 years old	
Neapolitan (1996)[g]	Interpol/ World Health Organization/ United Nations	58-105	OLS regression, various models	1. Murder and theft rates (log)	
				2. GDP, per capita	–
				Income inequality	+
				Population size (log)	–
				Population density (log)	
Messner & Rosenfeld (1997)[n]	World Health Organization	39-45	OLS regression, various models	1. Homicide rates	
				2. Decommodification index	–
				Development index	–
				Economic discrimination index	+
				Sex ratio (log)	–
				Income inequality	

NOTES:

a. Quinney presents no tests of statistical significance but argues for a relationship based on simple classifications.

b. No significance tests provided.

c. Based on McDonald (1976, pp. 172-174); $p < .05$, one-tailed tests.

d. Based on Krohn (1976, Table 3); no significance tests were included.

e. Spearman rank order correlation, $p < .05$, one-tailed tests.

f. Significance tests were presented for various models, not for individual variables; see Braithwaite & Braithwaite (1980, pp. 50-52).

g. Significant at $p < .05$, two-tailed tests.

h. Variables marked significant were significant in at least one of six models; $p < .05$, one-tailed tests.

i. Taken from Hartnagel (1982, p. 483); no variable significant at $p < .05$, two-tailed tests.

j. Significant at $p < .05$, one-tailed tests.

k. Significance tests based on direct effects model, Groves et al. (1985, p. 69).

l. Income inequality significant (parameter twice standard error) for male homicide rates only; percentage never married females significant (parameter twice standard error) for female homicide rates only.

m. Based on results for full sample (Gartner et al., 1990, p. 606); significant at $p < .05$, one-tailed tests.

n. Unstandardized coefficient at least 1.5 times standard errors.

level data on number and type of offenses, number and type of offenders (by gender and adult/juvenile), and total cases solved. In constructing the international forms to be used by member nations, Interpol (1960) devised four rules:

1. The forms only refer to several broad categories of crime more or less universally recognized and indictable in ordinary law.
2. The definitions of these categories are very broad in order to allow the use of national crime statistics without too many modifications.
3. Each state is allowed a certain amount of latitude in the interpretation of these definitions; the nature of the crime is determined according to the legislation of each state.
4. The forms are intended to show crime trends rather than its actual extent. (p. vii)

Although Interpol currently provides the most widely used source of international data for homicide researchers, the use of this data set is severely limited by the method through which Interpol data are collected. First, Interpol relies on the unvalidated data supplied by member nations. It appears that Interpol simply reports data submitted to the agency without attempting to verify it. For example, in its 1993 report, Interpol shows that Argentina—a country whose population was estimated to be 33 million—had just 24 homicides (p. 4). Instead of working to improve the quality of the data published, Interpol simply includes a warning that the statistics derived from these data should be interpreted with caution.

Second, Interpol data are published several years after the crimes have occurred. At the time this chapter was prepared, the most recent Interpol data available were nearly 4 years old.

Third, because of the voluntary nature of the Interpol data collection effort, a large number of the world's nations do not participate. Kalish (1988) reports that in 1984, Interpol had a membership of 145 nations, but from 1980 to 1984, no more than 85 (58.6%) nations reported their statistics in any single year. Not surprisingly, Interpol data are most often reported by industrialized, Western-styled democracies.

Fourth, since beginning data collection efforts more than 40 years ago, Interpol appears to have made few systematic efforts to standardize legal definitions across countries. The reports produced in the early 1990s are nearly identical in form and content to the reports first produced in the early 1950s. The lack of standardized legal definitions is undoubtedly less of a problem with homicide than with other crimes, but as discussed in greater detail below, it still reduces the validity of the available data.

Finally, Interpol collects only aggregate-level data from member nations. This severely limits the types of analyses that can be conducted. For instance, it is impossible to determine who has killed whom from Interpol data.

World Health Organization

The second most common source of data for the homicide studies summarized in Table 9.1 is the United Nation's World Health Organization, used in 11 of the studies. WHO has collected annual data from participating countries on total deaths and their causes since 1951. These statistics have usually included separate homicide estimates. The data are not ambiguous with regard to classifying attempted homicides because, by definition, only total deaths are included. WHO data, however, do not distinguish between intentional and unintentional homicides and provide no information for crimes other than homicide. For some years, WHO data include deaths that resulted from police activities, but legal executions have always been excluded. Further, earlier WHO reports combined homicides with war-related casualties (Vigderhous, 1978).

At present, WHO data probably represent the most valid option for researchers interested in studying cross-national homicide. In the 1995 report, WHO data were available for 47 nations for various years from 1986 to 1993. These data allow researchers to study homicide rates disaggregated by the victim's age and gender and have fewer categorization difficulties than any of the other cross-national homicide data sets currently available.

Unfortunately, WHO data include only completed homicides from nations willing and able to supply cause of death information. In general, WHO, like all other cross-national data sources on homicide, is most likely to include information from developed, Western-styled democracies.

United Nations Surveys

Only three of the studies summarized in Table 9.1 relied on UN data. Although the UN had an early interest in international crime statistics, for many years the UN ignored the collection of common data on crimes, concentrating instead on examining commonalities in penal law across member nations (Vetere & Newman, 1977). As recently as 1965, UN officials concluded that "the technical and theoretical problems of international cross-cultural comparisons are, at present, so large and the utility of any results which might be obtained in such doubt that priority should not be given to studies of this kind" (United Nations, 1966, p. 26).

As a result of this reasoning, comparative crime statistics were not collected by the UN from member nations until the 1970s (United Nations, 1977). Initially, the 146 member countries were sent a questionnaire that requested data on homicide and seven other offenses for 1970 to 1975, but only 50 nations returned usable information. Three subsequent UN international crime surveys were completed for 5-year periods, 1975 to 1990. A fifth UN survey is under way and will include the years 1990 to 1994. Of those countries responding, sources of data for the most part are official publications and handbooks of participating nations. In a few cases, the data are from unpublished official documents.

In many ways, the UN is the most logical international organization to collect reliable cross-national data on homicide and other crimes. Unfortunately, the UN has thus far not lived up to this expectation. As this chapter was being prepared, the most recent UN data on homicide were nearly 6 years old. The 5-year cycle now used by the UN for its surveys guarantees that data will already be dated by the time they are available to researchers. Validity and reliability problems remain and, compared with Interpol, the UN data thus far include fewer nations. That the UN has now succeeded in collecting crime data during a 25-year period is an encouraging development.

Comparative Crime Data File

Two of the studies summarized in Table 9.1 used homicide data originally collected by Archer and Gartner (1984), whose CCDF includes crime data for 110 nations and 44 cities, for all or part of the years 1900 through 1970. Archer and Gartner collected these data through (a) correspondence with national and metropolitan governments in each nation, (b) annual statistical reports and official documents from each nation, and (c) secondary examination of records kept by other national and international agencies (p. 12). Unlike the other international data collection efforts listed above, Archer and Gartner did not attempt to provide common definitions of crimes but instead asked officials to report the offense categories employed in their own nations. Thus, unlike the other data sources, which attempt to standardize information received by asking countries to classify offenses into broad and uniform classes, Archer and Gartner report different types of homicide for each country and rely on *post facto* classification procedures.

In considering this source, it is worth noting that by the mid-1970s, two independent researchers, with little outside funding, had collected a more extensive data set on cross-national crime than had been collected to date by any international agency. Without a continuing data collection organization, however, such individual efforts quickly become dated. The CCDF is now more than 20 years old. Moreover, the fact that the CCDF does not standardize crime categories for the information collected has probably reduced its utility.

Human Relations Area Files

A final study summarized in Table 9.1 draws homicide data from the HRAF, a sample of small, nonindustrial societies representative of major world cultural regions. The HRAF data are useful because they include a set of societies that are excluded by every other study summarized in Table 9.1. The measures of homicide and other variables available in the HRAF are so different from the other cross-national studies of homicide, however, that comparisons with other data sets are problematic (Rosenfeld & Messner, 1991).

■ *METHODOLOGICAL ISSUES IN CROSS-NATIONAL COMPARATIVE STUDIES OF HOMICIDE*

The information shown in Table 9.1 is presented as an overview of the methods used to study cross-national homicide rates. For instance, sample sizes range from a low of 15 observations (Fiala & LaFree, 1988) to a high of 1,075 (Bennett, 1991b, using pooled time-series techniques). Earlier studies more often relied on simple classifications or measures of central tendency. Of the 10 earliest studies summarized in Table 9.1, 7 did not report significance tests for individual variables. Through time, however, the studies have employed increasingly sophisticated multivariate methods, including multiple regression analysis, pooled time-series analysis, and LISREL. Further, the numbers of variables used as controls have increased substantially in more recent studies. To facilitate comparisons, I list the statistically significant independent variables first, followed by other variables examined in the study.

The research summarized in Table 9.1 uses homicide or murder rates as at least one of the dependent variables. In general, definitions of murder used by Interpol are similar to definitions of homicide used by WHO and the UN. Many of these studies report analyses based on homicide rates averaged for 3- or 5-year periods. This strategy is used as a method for reducing missing data; by using a multiyear measure, countries with incomplete data periods can be included.[3]

The studies listed in Table 9.1 faced a formidable set of methodological problems in conducting their analyses. These can be divided into general problems that are common to most comparative research and those that are specific to the study of cross-national homicide data collection.

General Problems

Most of the general difficulties facing comparative research using nations as the unit of analysis are related to problems of directly transferring common statistical analysis techniques to an analysis environment in which the available sample is severely limited. For example, most common statistical analysis techniques are based on the assumption that the cases being analyzed are randomly sampled from a larger population. But comparative cross-national studies of homicide generally have been based not on random samples but instead on simple data availability. This has at least four important implications:

1. Samples are intrinsically biased in that not all nations of the world are equally likely to be studied. In general, comparative cross-national studies more commonly have included developed, Western-styled democracies and less commonly have included developing nations and nations of the former Soviet bloc.
2. Because the total number of nations with available data is relatively small, sample sizes analyzed are also small. Small sample sizes mean that results may be highly dependent on only a few cases. In the analysis of cross-national homicide rates, a single outlier can sometimes change conclusions.
3. In part as a consequence of data availability and in part as a consequence of small sample sizes, the range of variables that can be included in models also is limited. In many cases, adding or deleting a single variable can substantially change results.

4. Because of sample size limitations, analyses based on common statistical techniques are severely limited. For example, problems of multicollinearity cannot be solved by increasing the size of the sample. Moreover, statistical techniques generally are limited to relatively simple direct effects models.

Specific Problems

In addition to problems that are common to most cross-national comparative research, several problems are more specific to cross-national studies of homicide. Perhaps the most basic of these is the problem of classifying homicides in a consistent fashion across nations. Although there is widespread agreement that among all crimes, definitions of homicide are most nearly similar across nations, classification problems persist. This is evident in comparing definitions for the three sources of homicide data collected by international agencies:

Interpol: "Murder: Any act performed with the purpose of taking human life, in whatever circumstances. This definition *excludes abortion,* but *includes infanticide*" (emphasis in original; International Criminal Police Organization, 1993, p. 16).

WHO: "Homicide and other (lethal) injury purposely inflicted by other persons" (World Health Organization, 1994, Table B-1).

UN: "Intentional homicide: Death purposely inflicted by another person including infanticide" (Kalish, 1988, p. 4).

In general, Interpol's definition of murder is similar to homicide definitions from WHO and the UN. Given that both Interpol and the UN purport to measure crimes known to police, these two estimates should be similar. However, because Interpol and the UN surveys use separate organizations to compile data and do not appear to consult each other to verify the data compiled, statistics reported by the two sources are known to differ, sometimes substantially.

Classification differences between Interpol and UN data are especially likely to occur in three areas—attempted and completed homicides, intentional and unintentional homicides, and homicides that are accompanied by other crimes. Interpol and the UN ask nations to include attempted homicides in their counts of total homicides. The Interpol survey then asks respondents to report the percentage of total homicides that were attempts; the UN survey asks respondents to report separately on attempted homicides. Many nations, however, do not report attempted homicides as a separate category (Neapolitan, 1996). For example, of the 80 nations that supplied Interpol data in 1993, 39 (48.7%) did not report the percentage of attempted homicides. Many of these problems could be solved if Interpol and the UN did more vigorous data validity checks. For example, in a comparison of Interpol, UN, and WHO data, Kalish (1988) found that some countries in the UN survey reported a larger number of attempted homicides than total homicides (attempted plus completed crimes). Presumably, some of these cases could be addressed by contacting each nation and explaining more thoroughly the precise nature of the questions being asked, then requesting a corrected figure.

Not all the classification problems surrounding distinctions between attempted and completed homicide can be traced to misunderstandings of what was being asked, however. For example, the definition of homicide used by the *Uniform Crime Reports* in the United States *excludes* attempted homicides, treating them instead as assaults (Federal Bureau of Investigation, 1995). In contrast, Japan classifies assaults that result in death as assaults, not homicides, but it classifies as homicide both unsuccessful preparations for homicide and assistance with suicide (Kalish, 1988). WHO data do not face this problem; because WHO data are based on death certificates, homicide attempts are, by definition, excluded.

Another source of classification difficulty is the distinction between intentional and unintentional homicides. All three data sources explicitly ask for information only on intentional homicides. Many countries distinguish between intentional and unintentional homicides in their own crime statistics but do not necessarily report these distinctions consistently to the various international agencies that request their data, however. Thus, in a comparison of crime statistics from Interpol, the UN, and WHO, Kalish (1988) found that some countries reporting homicide to Interpol and the UN routinely combined intentional and unintentional homicides, whereas others did not. WHO data, based on death certificates, can make no distinction between intentional and unintentional homicides.

A final and undoubtedly more minor classification problem has to do with how individual nations count several offenses that are part of a single act. For example, Interpol asks participating countries to count only the most serious offense when several offenses are identified in a single act. Given that homicide is generally the most serious crime, this should have limited impact on homicide estimates. Kalish (1988), however, reports that Czechoslovakia classifies rape that results in the death of the victim as rape, not as homicide. It is not certain to what extent other similar anomalies exist.

The potential variability of data on homicide is perhaps best illustrated by the Archer and Gartner (1984) data because they simply record data collected in the same format as the country that supplied it. Their data show that countries varied considerably in the legal distinctions they made between types of homicides (e.g., murder and manslaughter). Also, many countries changed their classification strategies from 1900 to 1970.

The validity of homicide statistics may also be related to the stability of the regime that produces them (Vigderhous, 1978). Even assuming the good intentions of official agents to accurately record and report homicide statistics, separating homicides from other casualties may be complex or impossible in nations experiencing civil or foreign wars, or even widespread civil unrest. This is not necessarily a trivial point; among the 80 nations reporting homicide cases to Interpol in 1993 were Croatia, Lebanon, and Syria.

The utility of current cross-national homicide data is also limited because the available data are highly aggregated. The most reliably disaggregated information on homicide at present is WHO data, which are compiled for different categories of the gender and age of the victim. Interpol asks participating nations to provide the percentages of total murders that are committed by women, by juveniles, and by noncitizens. Definitions of *juvenile* vary across nations, however, and, in any event, few nations consistently supply information on gender and age. No international data currently available allow for disaggregation beyond the victim's gender and age.

■ *COMPARING SOURCES OF DATA*

Given these methodological difficulties, how closely do the different sources of cross-national homicide data resemble one another? Bennett and Lynch (1990) compared Interpol, WHO, and CCDF homicide data for 25 nations from 1960 to 1972. Also, they compared homicide data for 31 nations from Interpol, WHO, and the UN for 1975 to 1980. The authors found considerable differences among the four data sets, both in actual rates and rankings. The main exception was for comparisons of Interpol and United Nations data, which did not differ significantly from 1975 to 1980.

Similarly, in cross-sectional comparisons of homicide rates for 1970 and 1980 from different sources, Huang and Wellford (1989) found the greatest similarity between Interpol and UN data. Correlations between Interpol and UN homicide data with WHO and CCDF data were consistently lower. Given what researchers know about these data sets, this outcome is logical; both WHO and CCDF data should report lower homicide rates than either Interpol or the UN because WHO excludes attempted homicides and because the CCDF allows nations to use their own categories, which frequently distinguish completed from attempted homicides (for further discussions, see Gurr, 1977; Kalish, 1988).

Bennett and Lynch (1990) also found that all four data sets provided consistent results when used to assess the direction of change in homicide rates through time and across nations. They concluded that summary statistics used to describe total homicide rates yielded similar results regardless of data set chosen.

To summarize, because of the relatively unambiguous way that homicides are recorded by medical professionals, at present WHO offers the most valid data for homicides. For other crimes, Interpol remains by far the most extensive data source. Regardless of the international data source used, however, great caution is necessary. As Kalish (1988) observes, "It is risky to quote a crime rate for a particular country for a particular year without examining rates for other years, and, whenever possible, rates from other sources" (p. 8).

■ *A LISTING OF CROSS-NATIONAL HOMICIDE RATES*

Having discussed the sources of homicide data, I turn now to a discussion of what these data reveal about the incidence of homicide from a cross-national perspective. Shown in Table 9.2 are homicide rates for 52 nations that were included in WHO statistics for 1991. Again, that WHO records the total number of completed homicides in a country makes it the most valid current source for international data in this category. The average annual homicide rate for these countries is 6.1 per 100,000 residents. The highest rate shown is for Colombia, one nearly 300 times greater than for Malta, the country with the lowest rate. Also, Colombia's homicide rate is nearly four times higher than that of the next highest nation, Puerto Rico.

Two features of Table 9.2 are worth mentioning. First, some regions of the world are nearly excluded from this set of countries, whereas others are greatly overrepresented. The island of Mauritius, for example, is the only representative from the entire continent of Africa. Similarly, Argentina and Colombia are the only representatives included from South America, whereas Costa Rica, Mexico, Puerto Rico, and Trinidad-Tobago are the only nations from Central America. Even more telling, the list includes only five Asian nations (Australia, Hong Kong, Japan, New Zealand, and Singapore). In contrast, 38 (73%) of the nations included are from Europe.

Second, because of the countries included, a strong regional pattern in the crime rates is evident. None of the 10 highest homicide rate

Table 9.2 Cross-National Homicide Rates, 1991

Country	*Rate per 100,000 Residents*
Colombia	89.5
Puerto Rico	22.5
Mexico	17.5
Russian Federation	15.3
Kazakhstan	12.1
Latvia	11.5
Estonia	10.8
Belarus	10.5
U.S.A.	10.4
Lithuania	9.1
Ukraine	8.7
Trinidad-Tobago	7.6
Uzbekistan	5.6
Northern Ireland	4.8
Romania	4.5
Argentina	4.3
Albania	4.1
Costa Rica	4.1
Bulgaria	4.0
Hungary	4.0
Mauritius	3.2
Finland	3.1
Poland	2.9
Italy	2.8
Slovenia	2.5
Canada	2.3
Luxembourg	2.3
Tajikistan	2.3
Australia	2.0
Iceland	1.9
New Zealand	1.9
Czech Republic	1.8
Hong Kong	1.8
Singapore	1.8
Portugal	1.6
Norway	1.5
Scotland	1.5
Denmark	1.4
Greece	1.4
Sweden	1.4
Switzerland	1.4
Armenia	1.3
Austria	1.3
Israel	1.2
Netherlands	1.2
France	1.1
Germany	1.1
Spain	0.9
England/Wales	0.6
Ireland	0.6
Japan	0.6
Malta	0.3

SOURCE: World Health Organization (1995).

countries are from Western Europe. Four are from North or South America (Colombia, Puerto Rico, Mexico, and the United States), whereas the other 6 are new nations from the former Soviet Union (Russian Federation, Kazakhstan, Latvia, Estonia, Belarus, and Lithuania). At the other end of the spectrum, 8 of 10 of the lowest homicide rate countries are in Western Europe. The two exceptions are Israel and Japan.

■ *THEORETICAL PERSPECTIVES ON CROSS-NATIONAL HOMICIDE*

How can the considerable differences in national rates of homicide shown in Table 9.2 be explained? Given the methodological difficulties faced by cross-national comparative studies of homicide, it is not surprising that theoretical development thus far has been relatively modest. Small sample sizes and missing data generally have limited analyses to a few independent variables and to direct effects models. It is clear, however, that theoretical arguments are growing more sophisticated through time. Although there is considerable variation, the major theoretical arguments found in the 34 studies listed in Table 9.1 can be divided into three main categories: (a) modernization, (b) economic stress, and (c) situational perspectives. Brief discussions of these theoretical perspectives are provided in the next sections.

Modernization/Social Disorganization

Modernization/social disorganization theories have probably been the earliest and most common perspectives explored in cross-national studies. Modernization/social disorganization perspectives can be traced to Durkheim's (1893/1947) assessment of the transition to a modern industrial society. According to this view, crime results when there is a breakdown or disruption in a prior, stable normative order. The disruption of established systems of role allocation and the emergence of new roles not yet fully institutionalized and integrated into society make normative guidelines ambiguous and may disrupt traditional support mechanisms.

This perspective usually assumes that crime will be more likely in societies undergoing rapid social change, particularly when traditional patterns have been disrupted through economic growth, urbanization, and the shift from agricultural to industrial and service economies. Urbanization is thought to be related to these processes because modern values are generally stronger and social control mechanisms are less effective in urban areas.

Many of the studies outlined in Table 9.1 offer partial tests of this general perspective. Specifically, Bennett (1991a); Groves, McCleary, and Newman (1985); Hansmann and Quigley (1982); Hartnagel (1982); Krohn (1978); Krohn and Wellford (1977); Messner (1982); Ortega, Corzine, Burnett, and Poyer (1992); Quinney (1965); Shichor (1990); Steffensmeier, Allan, and Streifel (1989); Wellford (1974); and Wolf (1971) all examine related aspects of this argument.

Economic Stress

Closely related to modernization models is the argument that crime results from the stress caused by economic hardships associated especially with inequality, poverty, and unemployment. Although modernization theorists emphasize the impact that economic conditions have on population heterogeneity and turnover (Bursik, 1988), economic stress perspectives focus on the direct impact of economic conditions on aggregate crime rates. Partial tests of economic stress perspectives are found in many of the studies summarized in Table 9.1, especially Avison and Loring (1986); Braithwaite and Braithwaite (1980); Krahn, Hartnagel, and Gartrell (1986); Landau (1984); Messner (1989); and Messner and Rosenfeld (1997). Cross- national investigations of child homicide and its relation to economic stress are found in two studies (Fiala & LaFree, 1988; Gartner, 1990).

Economic stress perspectives are closely related to elements of "radical" criminology

(Bernard, 1981; Greenberg, 1981) and world systems theory (Chirot, 1977; Wallerstein, 1974). In a review of cross-national crime research, Neuman and Berger (1988) argue that incorporating these other theoretical traditions into cross-national crime studies could advance research by explicitly considering the uneven spread of economic production modes and social relations across the globe.

Situational Perspectives

Situational perspectives are most consistent with the recent work of Cohen, Felson, and their associates (see in particular, Cohen & Felson, 1979; Cohen, Felson, & Land, 1980). They argue that development in the United States has brought about changes in "routine activities," increasing the dispersion of activities away from the home and consequently heightening opportunities for certain types of crime. Routine activities theories predict lower crime in societies with active guardianship norms, decentralized populations, low levels of youth mobility and independence, and women engaged in homemaking roles rather than involved in the paid labor market. Kick and LaFree (1985) and Gartner (1990) have provided explicit applications of this perspective to explain variations in cross-national rates of homicide.

Neuman and Berger (1988) argue that situational or ecological approaches have also been largely ignored in cross-national criminology research. In support of their contention, only five of the studies summarized in Table 9.1 include direct references to situational or opportunity perspectives (Bennett, 1991a, 1991b; Gartner, 1990; Kick & LaFree, 1985; Ortega et al., 1992).

■ *GENERALIZATIONS OF FINDINGS FROM CROSS-NATIONAL COMPARATIVE STUDIES*

Despite the formidable methodological challenges involved in cross-national comparative analyses of homicide, there are now enough published studies to allow for some generalizations about findings from this area of research. Based mostly on the studies summarized in Table 9.1, eight of these findings are discussed in the following sections.

Homicides Versus Property Crimes

The methodological difficulties of measuring property crime across nations are even more daunting than those for homicide. Still, it is worth noting that of the 15 studies in Table 9.1 that included both rates of homicide and property crime or theft, 14 find no evidence that homicide and property crimes are produced by the same processes (Bennett, 1991a, 1991b; Hartnagel, 1982; Kick & LaFree, 1985; Krohn, 1976, 1978; Krohn & Wellford, 1977; LaFree & Kick, 1986; Landau, 1984; McDonald, 1976; Neapolitan, 1996; Steffensmeier et al., 1989; Wellford, 1974; Wolf, 1971). The lone exception is Ortega et al. (1992), whose pooled time-series analysis of Interpol data finds a significant positive relationship between economic development (per capita gross national product) and both homicide and theft rates. Ortega et al.'s *cross-sectional* analysis in the same study, however, shows no significant effect of economic development on homicide.

Economic Development and Industrialization

Variables testing for connections between economic development and industrialization on homicide rates are among the most common in the studies summarized in Table 9.1. Measured on a per capita basis, indicators of economic development have included the following:

1. Gross national product or gross domestic product (Bennett, 1991b; Braithwaite & Braithwaite, 1980; Fiala & LaFree, 1988; Groves et al., 1985; Hansmann & Quigley, 1982; Hartnagel, 1982; Krahn et al., 1986; Krohn, 1976; Krohn & Wellford, 1977; McDonald, 1976; Messner, 1980, 1982, 1985; Neapolitan, 1994, 1996; Ortega et al., 1992; Wellford, 1974; Wolf, 1971)

2. Telephones or radios (Conklin & Simpson, 1985; McDonald, 1976; Steffensmeier et al., 1989; Wolf, 1971)
3. Newspapers (McDonald, 1976; Shichor, 1990; Wolf, 1971)
4. Energy consumption (Avison & Loring, 1986; Conklin & Simpson, 1985; Krohn, 1976, 1978)
5. Industrialization and development indexes (Bennett, 1991a; Hartnagel, 1982; Kick & LaFree, 1985; LaFree & Kick, 1986; Messner, 1989; Messner & Rosenfeld, 1997; Quinney, 1965)
6. The proportion of the population in agricultural jobs (Bennett, 1991a; Groves et al., 1985; Krahn et al., 1986; Wolf, 1971)

Remarkably, only one study to date—Ortega et al. (1992)—has found significant positive effects of industrialization or development variables on homicide rates, and this was only for a pooled time-series analysis, not for a cross-sectional analysis of individual countries. Instead, and counter to most theoretical expectations, there is far more support for a *negative* relationship between homicide rates and economic development or industrialization (Krohn, 1976, 1978; Krohn & Wellford, 1977; LaFree & Kick, 1986; McDonald, 1976; Messner & Rosenfeld, 1997; Neapolitan, 1994, 1996; Quinney, 1965; Shichor, 1990; Wellford, 1974; Wolf, 1971).

The finding of a null or negative relationship between economic development measures and homicide rates has important theoretical implications in that two of the major theoretical perspectives outlined above, modernization and economic stress perspectives, predict that increasing economic development should lead to increases in homicide rates. A full discussion of this finding is beyond the scope of this chapter but is definitely a topic that deserves further consideration in cross-national homicide research.

Economic Inequality

A positive association between economic inequality and homicide rates is among the most consistent findings in the cross-national homicide literature (Avison & Loring, 1986; Braithwaite, 1979; Braithwaite & Braithwaite, 1980; Kick & LaFree, 1985; Krahn et al., 1986; Krohn, 1976; LaFree & Kick, 1986; McDonald, 1976; Messner, 1980, 1982, 1985, 1989; Messner & Rosenfeld, 1997; Neapolitan, 1994, 1996). Only three studies in Table 9.1 (Fiala & LaFree, 1988; Groves et al., 1985; Rosenfeld & Messner, 1991) report no effect; plausible explanations, however, exist for all three of those anomalous findings.

Unemployment and Homicide

Three studies included in Table 9.1 examined the effect of aggregate unemployment on general homicide rates—Avison and Loring (1986), Krohn (1976), and McDonald (1976). Another study (Fiala & LaFree, 1988) used child homicide victimization as the dependent variable. Despite expectations to the contrary, not one of the multivariate studies reviewed in Table 9.1 has found a significant positive relationship between homicide rates and simple measures of percentage unemployed, especially when controlling for the effect of other variables.

Urbanism and Homicide

Most studies summarized in Table 9.1 have operationalized urbanism as either total population size or total percentage of the population living in urban areas. In either case, the expectation has been that larger, more urbanized countries are likely to have higher murder rates. Comparative research has generally failed to support this expectation (Avison & Loring, 1986; Conklin & Simpson, 1985; Hansmann & Quigley, 1982; Hartnagel, 1982; Kick & LaFree, 1985; Krahn et al., 1986; Krohn, 1978; Krohn & Wellford, 1977; McDonald, 1976; Messner, 1980, 1982; Ortega et al., 1992; Quinney, 1965; Wellford, 1974; Wolf, 1971). There is some evidence that nations with a higher proportion of residents living in urban areas, and nations with greater populations, have lower homicide rates (Conklin & Simpson, 1985;

Krohn, 1978; Messner, 1989; Neapolitan, 1996; Ortega et al., 1992; Quinney, 1965).

Other authors in Table 9.1 have examined population density, which has also been related to urbanism (Webb, 1972). The common expectation has been that nations with high density (usually defined as number of persons per square mile) will have higher rates of homicide. None of the studies in Table 9.1 found a significant relationship between population density and homicide rates (Avison & Loring, 1986; Conklin & Simpson, 1975; Hansmann & Quigley, 1982; Messner, 1982, 1989; Neapolitan, 1994, 1996). Krahn et al. (1986), however, found evidence that population density may intensify the effects of inequality on homicide; income inequality was found to have stronger effects on homicide rates in more densely populated countries.

Disaggregated Homicide Rates

Of the 34 studies summarized in Table 9.1, 6 have examined disaggregated homicide rates. Messner (1985) and Gartner, Baker, and Pampel (1990) considered homicide rates for men and women; one (Fiala & LaFree, 1988) examined homicide victimization rates for children less than 1 year of age and children 1 to 4 years old; Hartnagel (1982) conducted research on homicide rates for female offenders; Steffensmeier et al. (1989) used the percentage of female homicide arrests; and Gartner (1990) and Gartner et al. (1990) examined homicide victimization rates separately for men, women, male adults, female adults, children, and infants. The few studies that have used disaggregated rates as dependent variables suggest that the dynamics of homicide may be different across specific gender and age groups. For example, Gartner (1990) found that the proportion of women in the labor force by country had significant effects on homicide victimization rates for women and children but no effects on male victimization homicide rates.

Population Structure

Nine of the studies listed in Table 9.1 include a measure of the proportion of young people or young men in each nation. Their results are mixed regarding the impact of this measure on cross-national homicide rates. Three studies (Conklin & Simpson, 1985; Hansmann & Quigley, 1982; Ortega et al., 1992) report a positive relationship; five (Avison & Loring, 1986; Bennett, 1991b; Gartner, 1990; Messner, 1989; Neapolitan, 1994) find no significant relationship; and one (Bennett, 1991a) reports a negative relationship. Hansmann and Quigley (1982) conclude that homicide rates increase significantly with the proportion of the population aged 15 to 24 and that this measure is one of the best predictors of cross-national rates. Similar findings are reported by Conklin and Simpson (1985) for the proportion of young males aged 15 to 29 and Ortega et al. (1992) for the proportion of youths 15 to 19. By contrast, multivariate analyses examining the impact of youths aged 15 to 24 (Avison & Loring, 1986), youths or males aged 15 to 29 (Gartner, 1990; Messner, 1989), youths aged 15 to 19 (Krahn et al., 1986), and total population less than 15 years of age (Bennett, 1991b; Messner, 1989; Neapolitan, 1994) find no significant effects on cross-national homicide rates. Bennett (1991a) reports a negative relationship based on a measure of the total proportion of juveniles (14 and younger).

Compared with the proportion of youths in the population, population growth appears as a more consistent predictor of homicide rates. Multivariate analyses (Krahn et al., 1986; LaFree & Kick, 1986; Messner, 1980) all found that increasing population growth is associated with higher homicide rates. None of the studies summarized in Table 9.1 provide contradictory evidence. The analysis by Krahn et al. (1986) compared specific age measures (e.g., percentage aged 15 to 19) with the population growth measure and found more consistent results for the population growth measure.

Social and Cultural Heterogeneity

Measures of linguistic, racial or ethnic, and religious heterogeneity also have been frequently included in cross-national comparative studies of homicide. Results, however, are far from consistent. Three studies found a significant relationship for racial/ethnic heterogeneity (Avison & Loring, 1986; Braithwaite & Braithwaite, 1980; Gartner, 1990), and three did not (Krahn et al., 1986; McDonald, 1976; Messner, 1989). McDonald (1976) reports that linguistic heterogeneity increases homicide rates but that racial and religious heterogeneity do not; Hansmann and Quigley (1982) report that cultural heterogeneity increases crime but that linguistic and religious heterogeneity do not. Consequently, definitive evidence for an effect of heterogeneity on homicide rates has not yet been found.

Implications for Theories of Cross-National Homicide

It is clear in reviewing the literature that some of the most popular theoretical ideas about cross-national rates of homicide have not been systematically supported. Although modernization/social disorganization theories have probably been the most common perspectives explored, research consistently shows that economic development has no effect or a negative effect on national homicide rates.

Similarly, support for simple economic stress models has been limited. For example, studies examining the cross-national impact of unemployment rates on homicide have been largely unsupported. In contrast, the concept of economic inequality has been a more fruitful area of investigation; a number of studies have reported a relationship between cross-national homicide rates and levels of inequality among the countries examined.

More complex economic models that include the impact of global economic relationships on national homicide rates might be useful in future research. Also, more attention to situational perspectives and cultural differences seems worthwhile. Neither of these topics, however, has yet generated enough research to allow reliable conclusions.

■ *CONCLUSIONS*

Of the three international agencies now collecting homicide statistics, two appear to have little direct interest in valid cross-national crime data. Interpol's principal interest appears to be in providing crime intelligence information to member nations, whereas WHO's main concern is in cataloging causes of death across nations. The UN crime surveys, which began only in the late 1970s, seem to be the most appropriate source for providing valid cross-national data on homicide. Thus far, the utility of UN data has been severely limited by classification and validity problems, the low number of participating nations, and the timeliness with which data are reported.

Cross-national studies of homicide clearly are becoming more methodologically and theoretically sophisticated through time. Early studies relied heavily on bivariate comparisons, but later studies have increasingly incorporated sophisticated statistical methods. Also, although several early efforts to analyze cross-national homicide data were essentially atheoretical, many of the more recent studies offer fairly complex theoretical models. By subjecting these models to systematic empirical tests, knowledge of the variables influencing cross-national homicide has been expanded considerably.

The practice of systematically collecting cross-national homicide data for the world's nations is only 50 years old. Although progress has been slow, researchers clearly have learned a great deal about collecting valid comparative data, the methods for analyzing the data collected, and the underlying relationships between homicide rates and other variables across a wide range of countries. Our knowledge of homicide will continue to be enhanced as we build on this foundation in the years ahead.

■ *NOTES*

1. In addition, several individual researchers have collected cross-national comparative data sets with fewer countries, including Gurr (1977), Christiansen (1967), and Verkko (1951).

2. The most recent report issued by Interpol as this chapter was being prepared, however, included data only for 1993.

3. Messner (1992) provides an analysis of whether the practice of including nations with incomplete data in this estimation of levels of homicide for several years affects results. He concludes that for both Interpol and WHO data, such practices are unlikely to affect results for samples of nations that regularly report data.

■ *REFERENCES*

Ancel, M. (1952). Observations on the international comparison of criminal statistics. *International Journal of Criminal Policy, 1,* 41-48.

Archer, D., & Gartner, R. (1984). *Violence and crime in cross-national perspective.* New Haven, CT: Yale University Press.

Avison, W. R., & Loring, P. L. (1986). Population diversity and cross-national homicide: The effects of inequality and heterogeneity. *Criminology, 24,* 733-749.

Bennett, R. R. (1991a). Development and crime: A cross-national time series analysis of competing models. *Sociological Quarterly, 32,* 343-363.

Bennett, R. R. (1991b). Routine activities: A cross-national assessment of a criminological perspective. *Social Forces, 70,* 147-163.

Bennett, R. R., & Lynch, J. P. (1990). Does a difference make a difference? Comparing cross-national crime indicators. *Criminology, 28,* 153-181.

Bernard, T. J. (1981). The distinction between conflict and radical criminology. *Journal of Criminal Law and Criminology, 71,* 363-379.

Braithwaite, J. (1979). *Inequality, crime and public policy.* London: Routledge & Kegan Paul.

Braithwaite, J., & Braithwaite, V. (1980). The effect of income inequality and social democracy on homicide. *British Journal of Criminology, 20,* 45-57.

Bursik, R. J., Jr. (1988). Social disorganization and theories of crime and delinquency: Problems and prospects. *Criminology, 26,* 519-552.

Campion, H. (1949). International statistics. *Journal of the Royal Statistical Society, 112,* 105-143.

Chirot, D. (1977). *Social change in the twentieth century.* New York: Harcourt.

Christiansen, K. O. (1967). *The post-war trends of crime in selected European countries.* Copenhagen, Denmark: Kriminalistiriske Institute.

Cohen, L. E., & Felson, M. (1979). Social change and crime rate trends: A routine activity approach. *American Sociological Review, 44,* 588-608.

Cohen, L. E., Felson, M., & Land, K. (1980). Property crime rates in the United States: A macrodynamic analysis 1947-1977 with *ex ante* forecasts for the mid-1980s. *American Journal of Sociology, 86,* 90-118.

Conklin, G. H., & Simpson, M. E. (1985). A demographic approach to the cross-national study of homicide. *Comparative Social Research, 8,* 171-185.

Durkheim, E. (1947). *The division of labor in society* (G. Simpson, Trans.). Glencoe, IL: Free Press. (Original work published 1893)

Federal Bureau of Investigation. (1995). *Crime in the United States 1994: Uniform crime reports.* Washington, DC: Government Printing Office.

Fiala, R., & LaFree, G. (1988). Cross-national determinants of child homicide. *American Sociological Review, 53,* 432-445.

Gartner, R. (1990). The victims of homicide: A temporal and cross-national comparison. *American Sociological Review 55,* 92-106.

Gartner, R., Baker, K., & Pampel, F. C. (1990). Gender stratification and the gender gap in homicide victimization. *Social Problems, 37,* 593-612.

Gartner, R., & McCarthy, B. (1991). The social distribution of femicide in urban Canada, 1921-1988. *Law and Society Review, 25,* 287-312.

Greenberg, D. F. (Ed.). (1981). *Crime and capitalism.* Palo Alto, CA: Mayfield.

Groves, W. B., McCleary, R., & Newman, G. R. (1985). Religion, modernization, and world crime. *Comparative Social Research, 8,* 59-78.

Gurr, T. (1977). Crime trends in modern democracies since 1945. *International Annals of Criminology and Penology, 1,* 151-160.

Hansmann, H. B., & Quigley, J. M. (1982). Population heterogeneity and the sociogenesis of homicide. *Social Forces, 61,* 206-224.

Hartnagel, T. F. (1982). Modernization, female social roles, and female crime: A cross-national investigation. *Sociological Quarterly, 23,* 477-490.

Huang, W. S. W., & Wellford, C. F. (1989). Assessing indicators of crime among international crime data series. *Criminal Justice Policy Review, 3,* 28-47.

International Criminal Police Organization (Interpol). (1960). *International crime statistics for 1959-60.* N.p.: Author.

International Criminal Police Organization. (1993). *International crime statistics for 1993.* N.p.: Author.

Kalish, C. B. (1988, May). *International crime rates* (Bureau of Justice Statistics Special Report). Washington, DC: Government Printing Office.

Kick, E. L., & LaFree, G. (1985). Development and the social context of murder and theft. *Comparative Social Research, 8,* 37-58.

Krahn, H., Hartnagel, T. F., & Gartrell, J. W. (1986). Income inequality and homicide rates: Cross-national data and criminological theories. *Criminology, 24,* 269-295.

Krohn, M. D. (1976). Inequality, unemployment and crime: A cross-national analysis. *Sociological Quarterly, 17,* 303-313.

Krohn, M. D. (1978). A Durkheimian analysis of international crime rates. *Social Forces, 57,* 654-670.

Krohn, M. D., & Wellford, C. F. (1977). A static and dynamic analysis of crime and the primary dimensions of nations. *International Journal of Criminology and Penology, 5,* 1-16.

LaFree, G., & Kick, E. L. (1986). Cross-national effects of developmental, distributional, and demographic variables on crime: A review and analysis. *International Annals of Criminology, 24,* 213-236.

Landau, S. F. (1984). Trends in violence and aggression: A cross-cultural analysis. *International Journal of Comparative Sociology, 25,* 133-158.

Landau, S. F., & Pfeffermann, D. (1988). A time series analysis of violent crime and its relation to prolonged states of warfare: The Israeli case. *Criminology, 26,* 489-504.

Lynch, J. (1995). Crime in international perspective. In J. W. Wilson & J. Petersilia (Eds.), *Crime* (pp. 16-38). San Francisco: Institute for Contemporary Studies.

McDonald, L. (1976). *The sociology of law and order.* Boulder, CO: Westview.

Messner, S. F. (1980). Income inequality and murder rates: Some cross-national findings. *Comparative Social Research, 3,* 185-198.

Messner, S. F. (1982). Societal development, social equality, and homicide: A cross-national test of a Durkheimian model. *Social Forces, 61,* 225-240.

Messner, S. F. (1985). Sex differences in arrest rates for homicide: An application of the general theory of structural strain. *Comparative Social Research, 8,* 187-201.

Messner, S. F. (1989). Economic discrimination and societal homicide rates: Further evidence on the cost of inequality. *American Sociological Review, 54,* 597-611.

Messner, S. F. (1992). Exploring the consequences of erratic data reporting for cross-national research on homicide. *Journal of Quantitative Criminology, 8,* 155-173.

Messner, S. F., & Rosenfeld, R. (1997). Political restraint of the market and levels of criminal homicide: A cross-national application of institutional-anomie theory. *Social Forces, 75,* 1393-1416.

Neapolitan, J. L. (1994). Cross-national variation in homicides: The case of Latin America. *International Criminal Justice Review, 4,* 4-22.

Neapolitan, J. L. (1996). Cross-national crime data: Some unaddressed problems. *Journal of Criminal Justice, 19,* 95-112.

Neuman, W. L., & Berger, R. J. (1988). Competing perspectives on cross-national crime: An evaluation of theory and evidence. *Sociological Quarterly, 29,* 281-313.

Ortega, S. T., Corzine, J., Burnett, C., & Poyer, T. (1992). Modernization, age structure and regional context: A cross-national study of crime. *Sociological Spectrum, 12,* 257-277.

Pears, E. (Ed.). (1872). *Prisons and reformatories at home and abroad.* London: Transactions of the International Penitentiary Congress.

Quinney, R. (1965). Suicide, homicide, and economic development. *Social Forces, 43,* 401-406.

Riedel, M. (1990). Nationwide homicide data sets: An evaluation of the uniform crime reports and National Center for Health Statistics data. In D. L. MacKenzie, P. J. Baunach, & R. R. Roberg (Eds.), *Measuring crime: Large-scale, long-range efforts* (pp. 175-205). Albany: State University of New York Press.

Rosenfeld, R., & Messner, S. F. (1991). The social sources of homicide in different types of societies. *Sociological Forum, 6,* 51-70.

Shichor, D. (1990). Crime patterns and socioeconomic development: A cross-national analysis. *Criminal Justice Review, 15,* 64-77.

Sellin, T., & Wolfgang, M. (1964). *Measuring delinquency.* New York: John Wiley.

Steffensmeier, D., Allan, E., & Streifel, C. (1989). Development and female crime: A cross-national test of alternative explanations. *Social Forces, 68,* 262-283.

United Nations. (1950). *Statistical report on the state of crime: 1937-1946.* New York: Author.

United Nations. (1966, July 18-August 7). *Report on the inter-regional meeting on research in criminology: Denmark-Norway-Sweden.* New York: Author.

United Nations. (1977, September 22). *Crime prevention and control: Report to the secretary general* (Report No. A/32/199). New York: Author.

Verkko, V. (1951). *Homicides and suicides in Finland and their dependence on national character.* Copenhagen, Denmark: G.E.C. Gads Forlag.

Vetere, E., & Newman, G. (1977). International crime statistics: An overview from a comparative perspective. *Abstracts on Criminology and Penology, 17,* 251-267.

Vigderhous, G. (1978). Methodological problems confronting cross-cultural criminological research using official data. *Human Relations, 31,* 229-247.

Wallerstein, I. (1974). *The modern world system: Capitalist agriculture and the origins of the European world economy in the sixteenth century.* New York: Academic Press.

Webb, S. (1972). Crime and the division of labor: Testing a Durkheimian model. *American Journal of Sociology, 78,* 643-656.

Wellford, C. F. (1974). Crime and the dimensions of nations. *International Journal of Criminology and Penology, 2,* 1-10.

Wolf, P. (1971). Crime and development: An international comparison of crime rates. *Scandinavian Studies in Criminology, 3,* 107-120.

World Health Organization. (1994). *World health statistics annual, 1993.* Geneva, Switzerland: Author.

World Health Organization. (1995). *World health statistics annual, 1994.* Geneva, Switzerland: Author.

PART IV

Special Issues in the Study of Homicide

CHAPTER 10

Homicide Between Intimate Partners

A 20-Year Review

■ *Angela Browne, Kirk R. Williams, & Donald G. Dutton*

Until the 1980s, studies of homicide in the United States did not focus on homicides between intimate partners or on differences in the risks of intimate homicide for women and men. Some studies disaggregated homicide into various subtypes, such as family, acquaintance, or stranger homicide, but none disaggregated couple homicides by the type of relationship (married vs. nonmarried) and gender of the perpetrator. This practice tended to mask gender and relationship differences as well as trends that through time differed from the larger national trends.

The years since the mid-1970s are especially important for examining trends of lethal violence in marital and dating relationships. Prior to 1974, assaults against wives were considered misdemeanors in most states, even when the same actions would have been considered a felony if perpetrated against an acquaintance or stranger, and little other recourse existed (for a review, see Browne & Williams, 1989). Police were not empowered to arrest on misdemeanor charges, emergency orders of protection were typically unavailable and carried no provisions for penalties or enforcement, and traditional pleas of self-defense were not applied to cases of spousal homicide (Fagan & Browne, 1994; Gillespie, 1988; U.S. Commission on Civil Rights, 1978, 1982). Although societal protections were almost nonexistent, rates of violence between partners were actually quite high. The first national survey conducted in 1975 found that 28% of all married couples reported at least one physical assault occurring in their relationship.

The next decade saw sweeping changes in law, police practices, social resources, and public awareness (Fagan & Browne, 1994; Schechter, 1982). Between 1974, when the first battered woman's shelter was established, and 1980, when findings from the first National

Family Violence Survey were published (Straus, Gelles, & Steinmetz, 1980), a wave of new social and legal resources came into being. By 1980, 47 states had passed some type of domestic violence legislation (Kalmuss & Straus, 1983; Lerman & Livingston, 1983); counseling programs were developed for both victims and perpetrators (Saunders & Azar, 1989; Sonkin, 1989; Sonkin, Martin, & Walker, 1985); police practices were revised to provide emergency response and arrest in cases of assaults between marital or dating partners (Fagan & Browne, 1994); and the self-defense plea for cases of partner homicide was gaining judicial acceptance (Sonkin, 1987; Thyfault, 1984). During the late 1970s and the 1980s, empirical and clinical research expanded to examine patterns of violence and threat in couple relationships (see Fagan & Browne, 1994, for a review) and motives for the killing of intimate partners by women and men (e.g., Barnard, Vera, & Newman, 1982; Browne, 1987; Daly & Wilson, 1988).

In this chapter, we briefly review trends in intimate partner homicide since the mid-1970s, when the first social changes were instituted. We also discuss some of the theories offered for changes in partner homicide rates through time and for different motivations by gender. Throughout this discussion, the term *partner homicide* will be used to connote *homicides occurring between current or former dating, cohabiting, common-law, and formally married heterosexual couples.*

■ *AN OVERVIEW OF PARTNER HOMICIDE*

Gender Differences in Homicide Perpetration

Males are overwhelmingly the perpetrators of homicide, typically accounting for about 90% of all homicides occurring in the United States. Most homicides by men are directed against strangers or acquaintances. In contrast, when women kill, the victim is more likely to be an intimate partner, another acquaintance, or a family member, but rarely a stranger. Almost two thirds (about 63%) of all homicides by women were against intimates (family members and relationship partners) in recent years, with a little more than 40% of all female-perpetrated homicide involving partners (this information was computed from unpublished Supplementary Homicide Reports [SHR] data made available by the Federal Bureau of Investigation [FBI]).

Spousal homicides represent more than half (about 60%) of all murders occurring between family members in the United States (see also Kellermann & Mercy, 1992). The deaths of almost 2,000 persons in 1995—or about 10% of all homicides in that year—were homicides between current or former marital, common-law, or dating partners. Only in the area of partner homicides do women's perpetration rates approach that of men. Even within couple relationships, however, women are more than *two times more likely* to be killed by their male partners as men are by their female partners; of all fatalities from partner homicide in recent years, about 70% of the victims were women killed by male partners, and 30% were men killed by female partners. Women are more likely to be killed by intimate male partners than by any other type of assailant (Browne & Williams, 1989; Kellermann & Mercy, 1992; Wilson, Johnson, & Daly, 1995; Zahn, 1989). Indeed, nationally, the killing of women by strangers is relatively rare. In their analysis of gender-specific rates of fatal violence among U.S. victims and perpetrators over the age of 15, Kellermann and Mercy (1992) note that during 1976 through 1987, more than twice as many women were shot and killed by their husband or intimate acquaintance as were murdered by strangers using guns, knives, or any other means.

Links Between Physical Abuse and Threat and Partner Homicide

SHR data do not provide information about the prior interactions of specific couples; thus, no national estimates are available on the number of partner homicides that involve a *history* of physical assault and threat prior to the lethal incident. Studies of homicide cases for which more detail was available, however, indicate that a substantial majority of homicides committed by women occur in response to male aggression and threat (Chimbos, 1978; Daly & Wilson, 1988; Daniel & Harris, 1982; Goetting, 1987; Rosenfeld, 1997; Totman, 1978; Wilbanks, 1983). Similarly, clinical and research studies document a history of physical abuse and threat by men who eventually kill their victims (e.g., Campbell, 1992; Crawford & Gartner, 1992; Dutton & Kerry, 1996).

Cross-Cultural and Regional Studies of Partner Homicide

As discussed by Gary LaFree in Chapter 9, the level of nonlethal and lethal aggression in the United States is unique among industrialized Western nations, and this distinction is not new. In a comparison of U.S. homicide rates for all victims more than 14 years of age from 1950 to 1980, U.S. rates were nearly three times as high as the next highest country (Gartner, 1990). Not only are rates of assault, homicide, and victimization higher in the United States than in other Western countries, the rate of homicide within U.S. families is higher than the *total* homicide rate in most other Western nations. The use of guns is also radically different than in other Western nations and is particularly implicated in the high rates of homicide (Kellermann et al., 1993; see also Philip Cook and Mark Moore's discussion of guns and homicide in Chapter 18).

Comparison studies on homicides between intimate partners across cultures also document U.S. leadership in this area. Wilson and Daly (1993) reviewed spousal murders for Chicago (1,758 during 1965 through 1990), all of Canada (1,748 from 1974 to 1990), and New South Wales, Australia (398 from 1968 to 1986). The highest rate recorded was for male-perpetrated partner homicides in Chicago by husbands who were estranged from their wives; this rate was more than twice the rate of homicides by estranged male spouses in New South Wales and nearly twice the rate for Canada. Differences in rates for intact couples (for perpetrators of either gender) were even more marked; the Chicago rate of spousal homicide was more than four times as high as in New South Wales and more than three times as high as the national rate for Canada.[1]

Other studies have concentrated on specific populations within the United States. For example, Kellermann et al. (1993) examined 1,860 homicides in three counties in Tennessee, Washington, and Ohio for 1987 through 1992, obtaining data from police and medical examiners and interviewing proxy respondents acquainted with the victims. Only 3.6% of these homicides were committed by a stranger; the majority (51%) occurred in the context of an intimate relationship. In other research, Block and Christakos (1995) created a data set focusing specifically on intimate partners, based on all reported homicides in Chicago for 1965 to 1993. Chicago averages 799 homicides per year; of these, 10% were found to occur between intimates. (In this data set, "perpetrators" were those deemed by the police to have committed the homicide, whether or not they were eventually found guilty). During this period, 2,556 deaths were due to one partner killing another; 58 of these murders occurred in gay relationships.

■ *TEMPORAL TRENDS IN HOMICIDE BETWEEN INTIMATES*

Although studies reporting on homicides for a single year or aggregating statistics during a multiyear period are informative for comparison purposes, *trends* in homicide rates through time are most helpful for examining correlates between macrosocial conditions and lethal violence, especially for planning future policy directions. On the basis of data from St. Louis for 1970 to 1990, Rosenfeld (1997) computed rates (per 100,000 persons) for all homicides involving current or former marital, common-law ("marital"), and current or former dating ("nonmarital") partners aged 14 and older. Rosenfeld reported an overall decrease in intimate partner homicide rates in St. Louis since 1980, a trend he attributes primarily to the declining marriage rate among the age group at most risk for offending as well as a pronounced drop in the rate of intimate partner homicides against Black women in the St. Louis sample. Findings from Rosenfeld's study (including high rates of homicides against women by nonintimates) sometimes run counter to patterns in national homicide statistics. Rosenfeld rightly notes that discrepancies in his findings from studies on national trends may be partly attributable to differences in the life experiences and changing homicide patterns among African Americans, factors that become obscured in reporting of aggregate national-level data.

A study with states as the unit of analysis (Browne & Williams, 1989) used SHR data to examine national homicide rates during some of these same years (1976-1984) among individuals aged 15 and older. The analysis disaggregated the perpetration of partner homicide by gender and compared changes in offending rates through time with changes in the presence of domestic violence legislation and extralegal resources for battered women (e.g., funding for shelters, crisis lines, and legal aid). The initial study included both married and unmarried partners (including ex-partners) in the partner homicide category. Percentage of population that was Black, geographic location, and population mobility were used as control variables. (Because of their possible influence on the estimated effects of resources for abused women and the perpetration of partner homicides, trend analyses were not further disaggregated by ethnicity.)

Controlling for the above demographic variables and the rate of male aggression against female partners, these analyses revealed a surprisingly sharp decrease—more than a 25% decline—in the rates of women killing male partners during this period. This decline began in 1979, at about the time that legal and extralegal resources for abused women were becoming established in most of the 50 states. Rates of female-perpetrated homicide were negatively associated with both resource indexes, indicating that the rate of partner homicide for *all* women was lower in those states in which domestic violence legislation and other resources for abused women were available. There were stronger inverse (negative) correlations, however, between an extralegal resources index (e.g., shelters and crisis lines) and rates of female-perpetrated partner homicide than for a domestic violence legislation index.

Given research establishing the link between male aggression and the perpetration of partner homicides by women, the study authors (Browne & Williams, 1989) theorized that simply the known presence of resources that would enable women to escape or be protected from a partner's violence might have acted to offset at least a portion of those homicides that occur in desperation and self-defense. They also concluded that such resources might have symbolic as well as tangible significance by providing a social statement that confirms victims' perceptions of the seriousness of violent attack and the need for sanctions and protections.

Unfortunately, although there was a slight decrease in the rate of husbands killing their wives during this period, the steep decline in partner homicides by women *was not* matched by a similar decline for men. Further, there was only a weak negative association between the presence of extralegal resources and male-perpetrated partner homicide and no association with the presence of state-level domestic violence legislation intended primarily to deter and protect.

Although these overall trends for partner homicide were supported by later findings of a decrease in lethal violence for married couples (e.g., Mercy & Saltzman, 1989), *failure to disaggregate partner homicides by type of intimate relationship gives a false sense of well-being if only declining rates are emphasized.* A study again using SHR data (Browne & Williams, 1993) analyzed trends in partner homicide from 1976 through 1987 both by gender and by type of intimate relationship (married versus unmarried couples). For this analysis, *marital* was used to indicate formally married, common-law, and ex-married partners. These categories were combined for two reasons: (a) Common-law and ex-married partner homicides accounted for a relatively small percentage of lethal violence between intimate partners during this period (11% and 4%, respectively), and

(b) initial analyses revealed that trends for common-law homicides were similar to those for formal marriages and that rates for homicides involving ex-partners showed no consistent trend. *Unmarried* was used to refer to individuals who were or had been dating or living with their partners but who had not resided together long enough to meet general criteria for common-law marriages as determined by the police at the time of the incident.

Using these categories, analyses of trends in homicide perpetration revealed different patterns for married and unmarried couples; a slight *decrease* in lethal violence for *married couples* was confirmed, but an *increase* in homicides between *women and men in unmarried relationships* was found. Analyses of these data by gender again highlighted the higher risks for women in partner relationships, *regardless* of relationship type. For married couples, although the rate of lethal victimization declined for both women and men during the 12-year period, the drop in the rate at which husbands were killed by their wives was greater than the drop in the rate at which wives were killed by their husbands. For unmarried couples, the rate of women killing their male partners varied unsystematically during the period; the rate of boyfriends killing their current or former girlfriends, however, increased significantly. This increase occurred, moreover, in the face of intensified social control attempts (e.g., sanctions and shelter) during those same years.

The study authors (Browne & Williams, 1993) speculated that one reason for this divergence might be that the general decrease in the rates of marital homicide—as well as the increase in lethal victimization rates for unmarried women—was related to the targeting of societal interventions primarily toward women and men in formal or marriagelike relationships. For example, in many states, domestic violence legislation focuses primarily on addressing problems of safety and access for those who are married or in common-law relationships. Few, if any, services (except on a handful of high school or college campuses) are structured specifically for individuals in dating or living-together relationships in which serious assaults occur. Thus, it is possible that a failure to emphasize the dangers for unmarried couples may leave out those relationships that potentially have the highest risk for lethal violence against women.

■ *AN UPDATED ANALYSIS: TRENDS IN PARTNER HOMICIDE IN THE UNITED STATES, 1980 TO 1995*

For this chapter, the analyses just discussed were expanded to cover from 1980 to 1995. (Readers are referred to Browne & Williams, 1993, for a full discussion of the methods used and methodological issues involved in the analysis.) The purpose was to determine whether the previously documented trends in homicide offending within intimate relationships have continued through the most recent years of available data. In addition, 1980 marked a peak year in overall lethal violence in the United States. Homicides declined through the mid-1980s, began accelerating through the latter part of the decade and into the early 1990s, then began to decline again. An increase in rates of homicide were especially pronounced for young males. Given these changes, an issue to be addressed is how trends in partner homicide were affected by these broader shifts in homicide rates.

As in the earlier analysis, national data on partner homicides were drawn from annual incident files in the SHR for 1980 to 1995. (The data were derived from unpublished data files supplied by the FBI.) These reports are filed by local law enforcement agencies voluntarily on all reported homicide incidents including murder, nonnegligent manslaughter, and manslaughter by negligence. The present analysis focuses exclusively on murder and nonnegligent manslaughter because they constitute the most common form of lethal violence (about 95% of all known incidents) in the United States. The SHR data provide detailed information on the age, gender, and race of homicide perpetrators and victims; circumstances of the incidents; weapons used; geographic location of homicides; and information on the relationship between victims and offenders if known. Thus, incidents involving partners (current and former marital and common-law and unmarried men and women) can be identified and analyzed. Because the focus is on violence among heterosexual couples, the current sample was restricted to single-offender and single-victim cases (about 90% of all incidents), rather than those involving multiple offenders or victims.

The use of SHR data requires that two important problems be addressed. First, SHR forms suffer from missing data, primarily on offender characteristics, which results from local police agencies failing to report or filing incomplete records (see Williams & Flewelling, 1987; also, see Chapter 6 by Marc Riedel). For example, information on offenders is based on arrest data. Approximately 31% of homicides may still be under investigation at the time an SHR form is filed (Kellermann & Mercy, 1992), and, in cases for which an arrest has not been made, the identity of those offenders may be listed as "unknown." If variations in missing data are purely random, the problem can be ignored. Preliminary analysis of time trends in the percentage missing, however, show systematic changes between 1980 and 1994, thus increasing the likelihood of biased estimates of trends. For this analysis, this problem was addressed by a rate calculation method that compensates for nonreporting and incomplete records. The FBI reports estimates of the total number of homicide incidents for geographic locations and time periods in its annual publication, *Crime in the United States: Uniform Crime Reports.* These estimates then can be used to determine the extent of underestimation in the SHR by comparing the two sources, then adjusting SHR data accordingly. Consequently, the analyses discussed here were conducted with data that had been weighted (adjusted) to account for information missing in the SHR. For a full discussion of the adjustment methodology, see Williams & Flewelling (1987).[2]

Second, the likelihood of biased estimation is also increased by incomplete information on victim or offender characteristics. To compensate for this problem, information from incidents with known characteristics were extrapolated to those having missing data on such characteristics.[3]

Homicide offending rates were calculated using gender- and age-specific incidents and respective demographic information. For example, the rate of marital homicide perpetrated by women includes all incidents involving heterosexual married couples in which a woman is the perpetrator and the victim is a man. This total is divided by the total number of women in the United States 15 years of age or older and then multiplied by 100,000. The number of women is used as the denominator in this case because the focus is on perpetration, not victimization. Hence, the rate should express the incidence of married partner homicide perpetrated by women per 100,000 women 15 years of age or older in the U.S. population. The reverse is appropriate when documenting trends in married partner homicide perpetrated by men. Ideally, married women or married men would be used as denominators, but a comparable denominator for unmarried couples by gender is not available. Moreover, trends using rates based on married women or men compared with those using total women or men are similar. The absolute level of the rate is lowered because of the reduced size of the denominator (i.e., married women are a subset of the total number of women), but conclusions about trends during 1980 through 1995 remain unchanged.

Because the focus of the analysis is on *homicide perpetration,* not victimization, a word of caution is in order. The SHR data come from police reports. Hence, information about perpetrators is based on individuals charged with homicide by the police, that is, suspected perpetrators. No official determination of guilt has been made at the point of filing such information to the FBI. This will introduce some error into the analysis, but the SHR data remain the best national source of information on homicide perpetration that is publicly available.

All gender and partner trends are smoothed by calculating 3-year running averages for the trend analyses. This analytical procedure involves leaving the end points in the time series (e.g., 1980 and 1995) unchanged, but the intervening points are average values calculated for

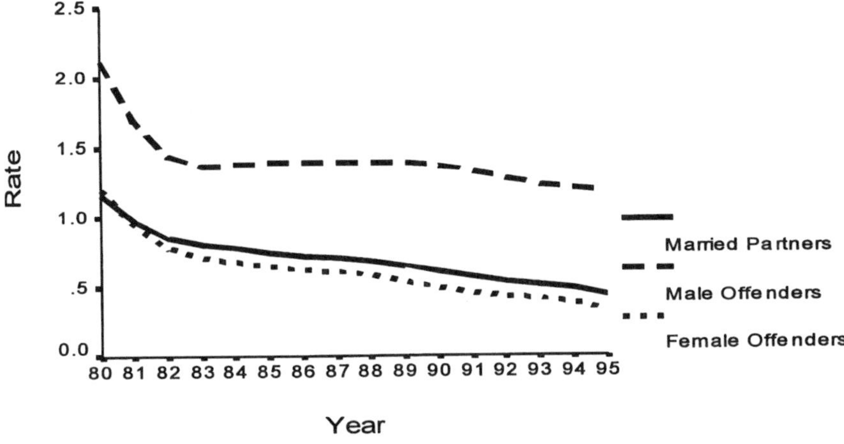

Figure 10.1. Married Partner Homicide Offending Rates: 1980 to 1995, by Gender
NOTE: Rates per 100,000.

3 consecutive years. For example, the smoothed value for 1981 is the average of the values in 1980, 1981, and 1982; the smoothed value for 1982 is the average of the values for 1981, 1982, and 1983. This procedure is followed throughout the entire time series. Smoothing is done to reduce the random year-to-year fluctuations, so that the time trends are readily visible (e.g., Hamilton, 1992, pp. 121-123). For these analyses, trends in intimate partner homicides were disaggregated by relationship type (married and unmarried), gender of perpetrator (male or female), and the perpetrator's age. Again, disaggregation reveals different patterns. Without an examination of these categories, variation in homicide trends would be lost.

Homicides Between Intimate Partners by Relationship Type and Gender

As noted in other studies, after a sharp peak in 1980, the *total* rate of homicide between heterosexual married partners (i.e., those currently or formerly married as well as common-law partners) dropped fairly sharply until 1982, then gradually declined through the remainder of the period. When marital homicide rates are broken down by gender, however, important differences emerge. As shown in Figure 10.1, the downward trend is primarily for female perpetrators; in contrast, for male perpetrators, after a sharp drop between 1980 and 1982, the trend remains fairly constant. Moreover, marital homicide rates for men are significantly higher than those for women during the period, and, by the end of the period, the gap appears to be widening. In short, the decrease in the perpetration of marital homicide is greater for women than for men.

Trends in homicide rates for unmarried partners can be seen in Figure 10.2. As for rates for marital homicide, from 1980 to 1995 there was a slight decline in the rate of homicide involving unmarried partners (individuals who were or had been dating or living periodically with each other but did not meet the general criteria of common-law marriages). The most striking aspect of trends by gender in this case is that the rate involving men as perpetrators *increased* between 1982 and 1992, after a decline between 1980 and 1982. The last few years of the period, however, show another decline in the rate of men killing their female partners. The rate involving women as perpetrators *steadily declined* through the period, again resulting in a widening gender gap in the homicide rate.

General Trends of Homicide by Gender

One might argue that the trends discussed merely reflect the more general patterns of men's and women's involvement in homicide

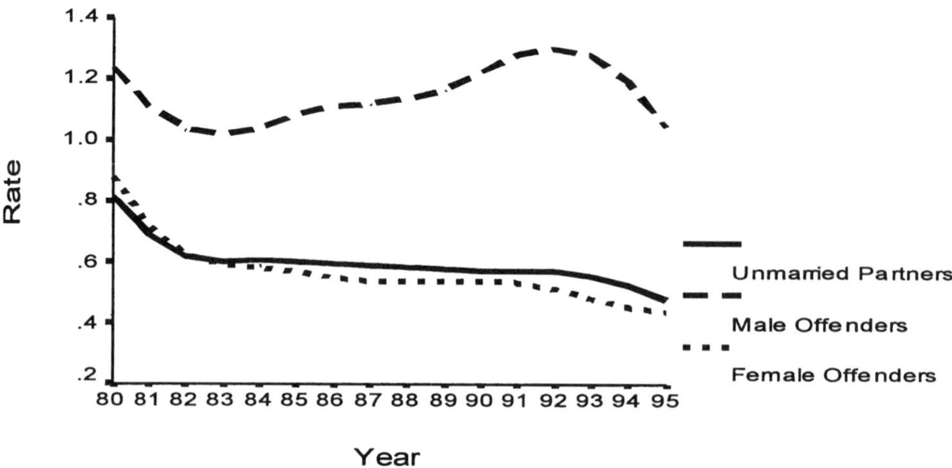

Figure 10.2. Unmarried Partner Homicide Offending Rates: 1980 to 1995, by Gender
NOTE: Rates per 100,000.

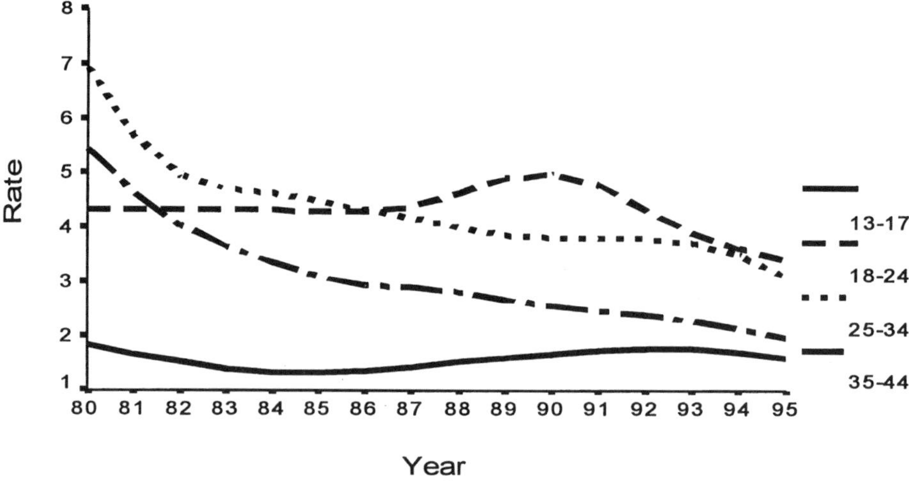

Figure 10.3. Female Homicide Rates by Age of Offender: 1980 to 1995
NOTE: Rates per 100,000.

nationally. To address this issue, we analyzed overall homicide trends for the United States by gender and age. Age-specific rates are analyzed because of the known different levels of involvement for persons in late adolescence and early adulthood. When overall homicide trends are examined for age differences, different trends in rates of homicide perpetration become evident.

Trends in female homicide are displayed in Figure 10.3. As this figure indicates, the overall *decline* noted for the perpetration of lethal partner violence by women is also found for female-perpetrated homicide in general, and this decline occurs in *all* age groups of women except for adolescents 13 to 17 years old, a group for which rates have remained low, even with slight increases since the mid-1980s. The greatest decreases in homicide perpetration occur among women 25 to 34 and 35 to 44 years old, the age groups most likely to be affected by the presence of legal and social resources for

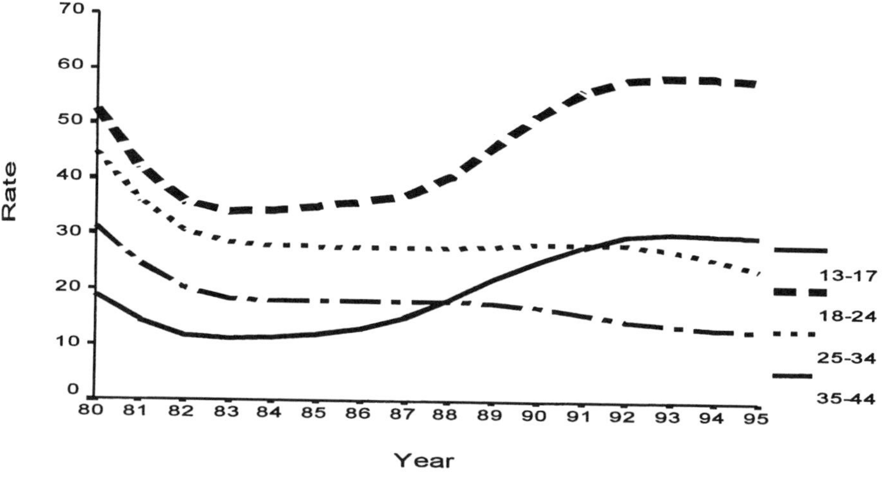

Figure 10.4. Male Homicide Rates by Age of Offender: 1980 to 1995

NOTE: Rates per 100,000.

abused women if faced with a violent or threatening partner.

Contrasting trends are shown for male perpetrators in Figure 10.4. For the total rate of overall homicides by men, sharp *increases* during the period are seen in the 13- to 17- and 18- to 24-year-old age brackets, although rates for 25- to 34- and 35- to 44-year-old men have gradually *declined* since 1980. Clearly, the general increase for men has resulted from increases among the younger age groups, which may partially explain the increase in partner homicide involving unmarried couples.

In sum, total rates of homicides between intimate partners dropped sharply between 1980 and 1982 and then continued to decline through the rest of the period. The greatest proportion of the decline in overall rates was accounted for by decreases in women killing their male partners; there was no period during which partner killings by women increased. After a sharp drop from 1980 to 1982, partner homicides by husbands against their wives also decreased, although much more slowly; the result is a widening gender gap during the period. Conversely, rates of homicide by men against unmarried partners *increased* between 1982 and 1992, with only the first 2 and the last 3 years of the period showing a decline. As noted, some of the increase from 1982 to 1992 may be accounted for by increases in homicide rates among young males in general. Unmarried relationships, however, are not confined only to those in late adolescence and early adulthood. An issue for future research is to determine what types of relationships are more common across the life span and whether there is an association between these relationship types and patterns of partner homicide.

Gender Differences in the Perpetration of Partner Homicide

In addition to differences in rates and trends through time, studies of intimate partner homicides by women and men also reveal different patterns in *circumstances* prior to and at the time of the homicide, *motivations* for the lethal assault, and *location* of the homicide (e.g., Jurik & Winn, 1990; Wilson & Daly, 1993). Men are much less likely than women to have been physically attacked by the victim prior to the homicide; further, they are much more likely to commit the homicide away from a shared dwelling, to kill others in addition to women during the incident (e.g., the women's children or other relatives), and to kill themselves after the homicide is completed (e.g., Marzuk, Tardiff, & Hirsch, 1992). In contrast, women rarely track down and kill partners from whom they are separated. Partner homicides by women most often occur in the couple's shared residence or at the woman's private residence if an estranged partner threatens her there (Browne, 1997).

Theories on Motivations for Partner Homicide

Partner Homicides by Women

One explanation for why women kill primarily their male partners rather than strangers or acquaintances is that, as seen earlier, it is their *partners* from whom they are most at risk. Research since the late 1970s suggests that partner homicides by women are more likely to be in self-defense than are homicides by men (Chimbos, 1978; Daniel & Harris, 1982; Totman, 1978). Women who perpetrate partner homicide are likely to kill during an incident in which they believe they or a child will be seriously hurt or killed (Browne, 1987; Jurik & Winn, 1990) and, contrary to popular images of catching a partner unaware, to kill while a violent or threatening incident is occurring (Maguigan, 1991). Women who kill male partners are often experiencing severe levels of violence and threat by the time a homicide occurs (Browne, 1987; Gillespie, 1988).

For example, a comparison of relationships of women charged with the death of assaultive mates with those of women in violent relationships in which no lethal incidents occurred (Browne, 1987) found several distinctions between the two groups. Women who eventually killed their assailants (a) were assaulted more frequently than women in the "abuse only" group; (b) sustained more and more severe injuries; (c) were subjected to a much higher frequency of rape and other forced sexual activities; (d) were in relationships with men who were much more likely to severely abuse alcohol and other drugs than men in the abuse-only groups (80% of men in the homicide group were intoxicated nearly every day by the end of the relationship, compared with 40% of men in the nonhomicide group); and (e) were much more likely to experience death threats against themselves or others than were women in the abuse-only group (80% vs. 59%). Possibly as a result of the severity of their experiences, women in the homicide group also were more likely to have threatened or actually attempted suicide than were women in the abuse-only group.

Early studies with female perpetrators suggest that one factor common in incidents of lethal violence by women against their male intimates is the women's inability or perceived inability to effectively protect themselves from severe aggression. In an early study of incarcerated female offenders, Totman (1978) noted that a major contributing factor to partner homicides by women was physical aggression by male intimates, coupled with a lack of safe alternatives to an overwhelming and entrapping life situation. A pretrial sample of women charged with the death or attempted murder of their husbands or common-law partners produced similar observations (Browne, 1987). In comparing a sample of women with physically violent and threatening mates who eventually killed their assailants and women with assaultive partners who took no lethal action, it was found that women killed at the point when they felt trapped in an escalating and life-threatening situation without hope for improvement or safe escape. Patterns of nonlethal and lethal physical assault by men against partners from whom they are estranged, discussed below, give some support to women's fears that merely leaving a violent partner may provide no escape from the danger (Browne, 1993, 1997).

Partner Homicides by Men

Research on dyadic interactions in couples in which the husband is violent also sheds light on a possible origin for the difference in homicide motivation by gender. Jacobson et al. (1994) noted that although both physically abusive husbands and their wives used verbal abuse and threats during escalation of an argument, only the wives were fearful. In the Jacobson et al. sample, wife violence was largely reactive to husband violence, whereas husband violence seemed to self-escalate, often reaching a point at which there was nothing the wife could do to stop it.

Severe physical abuse or neglect in childhood has been suggested as a possible pathway leading to partner homicides by men. Although later involvement in violence is only one of many potential outcomes of growing up in a violent home, two decades of research on nonlethal assaults by men against female partners documents a sharply increased risk of assaultiveness among men who have experienced or witnessed physical abuse in childhood (e.g., Fagan, Stewart, & Hanson, 1983; Hamberger & Hastings, 1991; Hotaling & Sugarman, 1986; Kalmuss, 1984; Straus et al., 1980). Although the base rates are small, rigorous empirical analyses of cases involving substantiated reports of severe childhood physical abuse, sexual molestation, or neglect and later juvenile or adult criminal behavior (on the basis of official arrest records) also verify an increased risk of arrests for physical and sexual violence in men. Physically abused children have substantially higher rates of arrest for violence than do any of the other groups (Widom, 1989; Widom & Ames, 1994).

Estrangement and Male-Perpetrated Partner Homicide

One dynamic that appears disproportionately by gender in data on homicide is the threat of or actual separation from a dating or marital partner, and a perception among some men that they are entitled to control the lives of their dating or marital partners (e.g., Wilson et al., 1995). In early studies, a theme of control over intimate partners was expressed predominantly by male versus female perpetrators of couple homicide. In an early study of this phenomenon, Barnard et al. (1982), interviewing small samples of both male and female perpetrators of partner homicide, found that the reason most often given by men for killing their mates was their "inability to accept what they perceived to be a rejection of them or their role of dominance over their eventual victim" (p. 278). A walkout or threat of separation was especially provoking, representing "intolerable desertion, rejection, or abandonment" (p. 278). In killing their female partners, male partners in this study believed that they were reacting to a previous offense against them (e.g., the woman's leaving) on the part of their wives. More than half (57%) of the male perpetrators in this study were separated from their wives when they killed them.

These more qualitative findings have been supported through the years by empirical studies with more varied and larger databases. In a study of 896 killings of women by known male perpetrators in Ontario from 1974 to 1990, Crawford and Gartner (1992) found that 551 (62%) were killed by an intimate male partner. Of all male-perpetrated homicides of women for which a motive for the killing could be established from police records, 32% were "estrangement killings"; another 11% were based on beliefs that the female partner was sexually unfaithful, whether or not that fear was otherwise substantiated. Similar findings were obtained by Campbell (1992) in a study of 73 murders of women in Dayton, Ohio, from 1975 to 1979. More than half of these women (52%) were killed by intimate partners, half of them by men from whom they were estranged. Goetting (1995), comparing 123 murders of women in Detroit for 1982 to 1983 with other homicides in the city during those years, found similar results. Goetting further noted that homicides by male intimates in response to relationship termination or jealousy seemed to dissipate the angry sentiments of many perpetrators, leaving a sense of despair at the loss of the loved one. Finally, research by Stout (1991, 1993) echoed the risk for women estranged from their partners. In a study of 23 men incarcerated for killing female partners in Missouri, she found that 52% of their murders occurred when the men were separated from their intimates.

The duration of estrangement is also noteworthy. In Stout's (1991, 1993) study, the modal period of separation was less than 1 month (25%). Similarly, in an earlier study, Wallace (1986) reported that 39% (15 of 38) of slain wives in Australia were killed within the first 2 months of relational separation; 76% (29 of 38) were killed within the first year. Comparable data are reported for Wilson and Daly's (1993) study of spousal murders. In both Chicago and New South Wales, they found that half of all separated women victims were killed by their estranged husbands within 2 months of final separation, and 87% were killed within 1 year. Although these studies indicate that the several months immediately after estrangement are especially high-risk times for women, homicides by estranged male partners may occur months or even years after couples are separated or divorced.

One perspective on the motivational basis for the killing of estranged wives comes from a study of nonlethal males who had been convicted of wife assault (Dutton & Browning, 1988). After viewing videotaped conflict scenarios with a theme of a wife "abandoning" her husband, maritally violent men reported significantly more anger and anxiety than did nonviolent controls. Dutton (1995) suggested that such "abandonment rage" has its origins in early childhood development involving events affecting attachment and object relations. As found by Wilson and Daly (1993) and Barnard et al. (1982), homicide case descriptions often make it clear that the link between separation and murder is more than incidental. Homicidal husbands often did exactly what they had threatened to do should their wives leave them, and they often explained their homicides as responses to the intolerable stimulus of the wife's departure.

As the foregoing discussion indicates, a number of factors may influence men's decisions to kill their partners. Although theories such as those discussed may help explain the motivations for males to engage in partner homicide, virtually no research has addressed the fundamental question of why a few individuals should have such extreme reactions to experiences that are common to many.

Predicting Homicide in Couple Relationships

In an effort to predict relationships at particular risk for lethal violence, lethality checklists have been developed to assess the risk of homicides between intimate partners. These checklists typically inquire about the presence and use of weapons, threats to kill, and the most severe violence level enacted in the past (e.g., Sonkin et al., 1985, p. 80). In early research that foreshadowed later predictors of risk markers to subsequent spousal homicide, Wilt and Breedlove (1977) examined risk markers associated with homicides and aggravated assaults in Kansas City, Missouri. An analysis of prior police attendance at the homes of homicide victims and perpetrators revealed that 90% of these residences had at least one prior police visit (presumably on a domestic disturbance complaint); 50% had five or more police responses. The three most prevalent precursors of violence were the presence of a gun, prior police attendance, and the presence of alcohol. Most physical force (79%) had been preceded by threats.

Sonkin (1987) published a lethality checklist based on Browne's (1987) findings on partner homicides, using reports of severity from women in the homicide group as guides for risk markers. Sonkin's list includes the man's frequency of violence, severity of violence, frequency of intoxication, drug use other than alcohol, threats to kill, forced sexual acts, and the woman's suicide threats as factors that discriminate between lethal and nonlethal cases of domestic violence. The lethality criterion in Browne's study was for female-perpetrated homicide in self-defense, whereas the predictors on Sonkin's checklist are primarily used to assess risk of lethal violence in men. In light of other research on precursors of homicide incidents, however, this use has empirical support.

For example, Kellermann et al. (1993), in their study of 1,860 homicides in Tennessee, Washington, and Ohio, interviewed proxy respondents who knew the victim and compared this information with selected controls who were matched demographically for each case, generating a set of 388 matched pairs of homicide cases. By contrasting the pairs, they were able to generate odds ratios for intimate homicides through linear comparisons of homicide and control respondents. Homicide cases more commonly involved illicit drug users (odds ratio [o.r.] = 9.0), alcoholism problems (o.r. = 20.0), persons with prior arrests (o.r. = 4.2), and cases in which domestic violence had occurred previously (o.r. = 7.9). Keeping a gun in the home increased risk by a factor of 2.7.

Some interpretative problems, however, arise with case control studies such as this. It could be that this research design generates conservative results, in that proxy respondents may underreport through not having as complete information on another person (for example, about physical abuse or gun ownership) as do control respondents, who report on themselves. Alternatively, when compared with proxy respondents who report only on others, control respondents may underreport negative aspects of their behavior such as physical violence and substance abuse to appear more socially acceptable (see Dutton & Hemphill, 1992).

In sum, the obvious problem with lethality prediction is that homicide is a rare event. Given the difficulties inherent in the prediction of rare events, researchers have turned to retrospective studies to examine risk factors associated with spousal homicide. On the basis of these retrospective studies, the greatest risk factor for partner homicide by men appears to be estrangement and prior assaultive and controlling behavior. Post hoc analyses of cases in which a partner homicide has occurred, however helpful in identifying general risk factors, still do not help us understand why only a *few* cases of those with similar risk factors result in murder.

Overkill

Killings that are motivated by rage and/or revenge might be expected to involve greater violence than other murders. Wolfgang (as cited in Straus, 1976), in an early study of homicide, defined "violent" homicides (or, as we term it, *overkill*) as "involving two or more acts of stabbing, cutting, or shooting or a severe beating" (p. 455). Studies since then have found a pattern of overkill to be characteristic of many partner homicides. For instance, Crawford and Gartner (1992) noted overkill as a frequent feature of homicides with female victims. In almost 60% of the cases they studied, men who killed female partners stabbed, bludgeoned, beat, or strangled their victims or slashed their throats. Often these assaults involved lengthy and excessive violence far beyond what would have been necessary to cause death. Almost one fifth of the cases involved multiple methods of killing (pp. 45-46). In other work, Cazanave and Zahn (1992) studied 83 homicides between intimate partners, finding that 46% of male-perpetrated homicides involved acts of overkill, compared with only 12% of female-perpetrated murders. In Campbell's (1992) study of 73 murders of women in Dayton, Ohio, overkill was found to be present in 61% of the cases. Even more dramatic findings were reported by Dutton and Kerry (1996), who interviewed and examined institutional records for 90 incarcerated men convicted of spousal homicide in Canada. They reported that overkill occurred in 90% of the cases they studied, with the number of blows or stabs administered by offenders falling in the 5 to 25 range.

■ *CONCLUDING THOUGHTS*

Despite a general decline in couple homicides during the last few years, the high rate of homicides between intimate partners in the United States compared with other Westernized nations represents a challenge still in urgent need of preventive solutions. As discussed in this chapter, *rates* of partner homicide, *changes* in offending through time, and *motivations* for these homicides all reveal different patterns by gender, type of relationship, or both. Failure to evaluate these dimensions of homicide masks important differences and forecloses the opportunity for grappling with alternative explanations or prevention possibilities when significant differences are found (Browne & Williams, 1993).

The widening gap in homicide trends for men and women in intimate relationships during the past 16-year period remains troubling. Each homicide, regardless of the gender of the perpetrator and victim, represents a tragedy affecting family members, acquaintances, the community, and society. Earlier speculations (Browne & Williams, 1989) about the sharp decline in rates of women killing male partners suggested that the presence of legal and extralegal resources for battered women had given women more alternatives when faced with violent assault or threat and that some women thus refrained from taking lethal defensive actions or were able to ensure at least temporary safety (e.g., by using emergency or other resources). As shown in the updated statistics presented here, however, although women are killing their male partners less and therefore men are indeed safer, the picture for women is different. There has been only a slight decline in homicide perpetration by husbands and, although there has been a decline in homicides perpetrated by current or former boyfriends since 1993, the level of risk is still high.

Although dating or cohabiting relationships may appear to be more open than marital situations (ostensibly, they are easier to leave), this very openness of structure may threaten the perceived power of men over their female partners, thus intensifying the risk for serious and sometimes lethal violence. In Canada during 1974 to 1992, the rate of partner homicides by men was eight times higher in coresiding common-law relationships than in coresiding marital relationships, and the rate of nonfatal violence was about four times higher (Wilson et al., 1995). Although this may be a function of both the younger age and economically poorer status of common-law, compared with marriage, relationships, it calls our attention to an especially at-risk population—women in nonmarital relationships—in need of a new level of protection and intervention when faced with violence and threat from male intimates.

In a review of empirical studies of dating violence by Sugarman and Hotaling (1989), male respondents were most likely to report that the primary purpose of their violence was to "intimidate," "frighten," or "force the other person to do something" (p. 13). Women most often gave self-defense or retaliation as the motive for their aggression. This maintenance of lethal violence by boyfriends against current and former girlfriends signifies that we are not yet reaching a critical population of potential homicide offenders. It is also possible that the high level of nonlethal violence and threats by men against their female intimate partners, and a lack of interventions perceived as relevant to their lifestyles, contributed to the more modest decline in the rates of lethal violence by unmarried women against their male intimates when compared with their married counterparts.

The lack of a sharper decline in married men killing their partners since 1982 also suggests that even with the last two decades' surge in social and criminal justice responses to partner violence, societal remedies are still not sufficient to address underlying causes of male violence against their female intimates, at least at the most extreme level. Existing studies of men who are violent toward female partners (and of the efficacy of interventions) are limited by small sample sizes, often composed of repeatedly assaultive men who are involved in treatment programs or the criminal justice system or who have volunteered or self-selected for research. Thus, findings from these studies cannot necessarily be considered representative of abusive men in the general population, the majority of whom are not involved in either community or criminal justice interventions. At the level of homicide perpetration, the ability to generalize to a wider population is even more limited. Clearly, more refined research is needed to facilitate a better understanding and possible prevention of this socially cost-intensive, painful, and personally tragic act.

■ *NOTES*

1. The rate for male-perpetrated partner homicides in Chicago for 1965 to 1990 by estranged men was 100 per million couples. Rates in Canada and New South Wales were 54 and 43, respectively. For intact couples, the U.S. rate was 30 (per million), compared with 8 in Canada and 7 in New South Wales.

2. Adjusting is done by calculating the following ratio: weight factor = a/b, where a = incidents reported in *Uniform Crime Reports* and b = incidents reported in the SHR. Complete reporting in the SHR produces a ratio of 1.0, and underestimation produces a ratio greater that 1.0. Adjusted incidents are derived by multiplying unadjusted incidents per year in the SHR by this weight factor and aggregating across states to yield national trends.

3. Extrapolation for missing data was accomplished by applying the following formula: Adjusted rate = [a +

$(a/n) \times (N - n)/p] \times 100{,}000$, where a = the number of incidents with a specific characteristic, n = the number of relevant incidents having complete information for the type of rate being calculated, N = the total number of incidents (with and without complete information), and p = the size of the relevant population. To illustrate the application of this formula, consider the adjustment of gender-specific rates of partner homicide. Suppose 1,000 incidents are reported by police in a given area, and the known gender distribution of perpetrators is 60% male and 40% female. But 200 (i.e., 20%) of the 1,000 incidents have missing information on gender. Given this known information, the components of the formula would be as follows: a = 480 (i.e., 0.60 × 800) for men and 320 (i.e., 0.40 × 800) for women, n = 800, and N = 1,000. Hence, the 200 incidents with missing data on perpetrator characteristics are assumed to have a similar gender distribution as those for which such characteristics are known (i.e., the 800 incidents), and they are assigned accordingly to adjust the gender specific homicide rates.

■ *REFERENCES*

Barnard, G. W., Vera, M., & Newman, G. (1982). "Till death do us part?" A study of spouse murder. *Bulletin of the American Academy of Psychiatry and Law, 10,* 271-280.

Block, C. R., & Christakos, A. (1995). Intimate partner homicide in Chicago over 29 years. *Crime & Delinquency, 41,* 496-526.

Browne, A. (1987). *When battered women kill.* New York: Macmillan/Free Press.

Browne, A. (1993). Violence against women by male partners: Prevalence, outcomes, and policy implications. *American Psychologist, 48,* 1077-1087.

Browne, A. (1997). Violence in marriage: Until death do us part? In A. P. Cardarelli (Ed.), *Violence between intimate partners: Patterns, causes, and effects* (pp. 48-69). Needham Heights, MA: Allyn & Bacon.

Browne, A., & Williams, K. R. (1989). Exploring the effect of resource availability and the likelihood of female-perpetrated homicides. *Law and Society Review, 23,* 75-94.

Browne, A., & Williams, K. R. (1993). Gender, intimacy, and lethal violence: Trends from 1976 through 1987. *Gender & Society, 7,* 78-98.

Campbell, J. (1992). "If I can't have you, no one can": Power and control in homicide of female partners. In J. Radford & D. E. H. Russell (Eds.), *Femicide: The politics of woman killing* (pp. 99-113). New York: Twayne.

Cazanave, N. A., & Zahn, M. A. (1992). Women, murder and male domination: Police reports of domestic violence in Chicago and Philadelphia. In E. C. Viano (Ed.), *Intimate violence: Interdisciplinary perspectives* (pp. 83-97). Washington, DC: Hemisphere.

Chimbos, P. D. (1978). *Marital violence: A study of interspousal homicide.* San Francisco: R & E Research Associates.

Crawford, M., & Gartner, R. (1992). *Woman killing: Intimate femicide in Ontario 1974-1990.* Toronto, Canada: Government of Ontario, Ministry of Social Services, Woman's Directorate.

Daly, M., & Wilson, M. (1988). *Homicide.* New York: Aldine de Gruyter.

Daniel, A. E., & Harris, P. W. (1982). Female homicide offenders referred for pre-trial psychiatric examination: A descriptive study. *Bulletin of the American Academy of Psychiatry and Law, 10,* 86-101.

Dutton, D. G. (1995). *The domestic assault of women: Psychological and criminal justice perspectives.* Vancouver, Canada: University of British Columbia Press.

Dutton, D. G., & Browning, J. J. (1988). Concern for power, fear of intimacy and aversive stimuli for wife assault. In G. T. Hotaling, D. Finkelhor, J. T. Kirkpatrick, & M. A. Straus (Eds.), *Family abuse and its consequences: New directions in research* (pp. 163-175). Newbury Park, CA: Sage.

Dutton, D. G., & Hemphill, K. J. (1992). Patterns of socially desirable responding among perpetrators and victims of wife assault. *Violence and Victims, 7,* 29-39.

Dutton, D. G., & Kerry, G. (1996). *Modus operandi and psychological profiles of uxoricidal males.* Unpublished manuscript, University of British Columbia, Department of Psychology, Vancouver, Canada.

Fagan, J., & Browne, A. (1994). Violence between spouses and intimates: Physical aggression between women and men in intimate relationships. In A. J. Reiss, Jr., & J. A. Roth (Eds.), *Understanding and preventing violence: Vol. 3. Social influences* (pp. 115-292). Washington, DC: National Academy Press.

Fagan, J., Stewart, D., & Hanson, K. (1983). Violent men or violent husbands: Background factors and situational correlates of domestic and extra-domestic violence. In D. Finkelhor, R. J. Gelles, G. T. Hotaling, & M. A. Straus (Eds.), *The dark side of families* (pp. 49-67). Beverly Hills, CA: Sage.

Gartner, R. (1990). The victims of homicide: A temporal and cross-national comparison. *American Sociological Review, 55,* 92-106.

Gillespie, C. K. (1988). *Justifiable homicide.* Columbus: Ohio State University Press.

Goetting, A. (1987). Homicidal wives: A profile. *Journal of Family Issues, 8,* 332-341.

Goetting, A. (1995). *Homicide in families and other special populations.* New York: Springer.

Hamberger, L. K., & Hastings, J. E. (1991). Personality correlates of men who batter and nonviolent men: Some continuities and discontinuities. *Journal of Family Violence, 6,* 131-147.

Hamilton, L. C. (1992). *Regression with graphics.* Pacific Grove, CA: Brooks/Cole.

Hotaling, G. T., & Sugarman, D. B. (1986). An analysis of risk markers in husband to wife violence: The current state of knowledge. *Violence and Victims, 1,* 101-124.

Jacobson, N. S., Gottman, J. M., Waltz, J., Rushe, R., Babcock, J., & Holtzworth-Munroe, A. (1994). Affect, verbal content and psychophysiology in the arguments of couples with a violent husband. *Journal of Consulting and Clinical Psychology, 62,* 982-988.

Jurik, N., & Winn, R. (1990). Gender and homicide: A comparison of men and women who kill. *Violence and Victims, 5,* 227-242.

Kalmuss, D. S. (1984). The intergenerational transmission of marital aggression. *Journal of Marriage and the Family, 46,* 16-19.

Kalmuss, D. S., & Straus, M. A. (1983). Feminist, political, and economic determinants of wife abuse services. In D. Finkelhor, R. J. Gelles, G. T. Hotaling, & M. A. Straus (Eds.), *The dark side of families* (pp. 363-376). Beverly Hills, CA: Sage.

Kellermann, A. L., & Mercy, J. A. (1992). Men, women, and murder: Gender-specific differences in rates of fatal violence and victimization. *Journal of Trauma, 33,* 1-5.

Kellermann, A. L., Rivara, F. P., Rusforth, N. B., Banton, J. G., Reay, D. T., Francisco, J. T., Locchi, A. B., Prosdzinski, B. A., Hackman, B. B., & Somes, G. (1993). Gun ownership as a risk factor for homicide in the home. *New England Journal of Medicine, 329,* 1084-1090.

Lerman, L. G., & Livingston, F. (1983). State legislation on domestic violence. *Response, 6,* 1-27.

Maguigan, H. (1991). Battered women and self-defense: Myths and misconceptions in current reform proposals. *University of Pennsylvania Law Review, 140,* 379-486.

Marzuk, P. M., Tardiff, K., & Hirsch, C. S. (1992). The epidemiology of murder-suicide. *Journal of the American Medical Association, 267,* 3179-3183.

Mercy, J. A., & Saltzman, L. E. (1989). Fatal violence among spouses in the United States. *American Journal of Public Health, 79,* 595-599.

Rosenfeld, R. (1997). Changing relationships between men and women: A note on the decline in intimate partner homicide. *Homicide Studies, 1,* 72-83.

Saunders, D. G., & Azar, S. (1989). Family violence treatment programs: Descriptions and evaluation. In L. Ohlin & M. Tonry (Eds.), *Family violence, crime and justice: A review of research* (Vol. 2, pp. 481-546). Chicago: University of Chicago Press.

Schechter, S. (1982). *Women and male violence.* Boston: South End.

Sonkin, D. J. (1987). The assessment of court mandated batterers. In D. J. Sonkin (Ed.), *Domestic violence on trial: Psychological and legal dimensions of family violence* (pp. 174-196). New York: Springer.

Sonkin, D. J. (1989). *Learning to live without violence.* Volcano, CA: Volcano Press.

Sonkin, D. J., Martin, D., & Walker, L. (1985). *The male batterer: A treatment approach.* New York: Springer.

Stout, K. D. (1991). Intimate femicide: An ecological analysis. *Journal of Interpersonal Violence, 6,* 29-46.

Stout, K. D. (1993). Intimate femicide: A study of men who have killed their mates. *Journal of Offender Rehabilitation, 19,* 81-94.

Straus, M. A. (1976). Domestic violence and homicide antecedents. *Bulletin of the New York Academy of Medicine, 62,* 446-465.

Straus, M. A., Gelles, R. J., & Steinmetz, S. K. (1980). *Behind closed doors.* New York: Doubleday.

Sugarman, D. B., & Hotaling, G. T. (1989). Dating violence: Prevalence, context, and risk markers. In M. A. Pirog-Good & J. E. Stets (Eds.), *Violence in dating relationships* (pp. 3-32). New York: Praeger.

Thyfault, R. K. (1984). Self-defense: Battered women syndrome on trial. *California Western Law Review, 20,* 485-510.

Totman, J. (1978). *The murderesses: A psychosocial study of criminal homicide.* San Francisco: R & E Associates.

U.S. Commission on Civil Rights. (1978). *Battered women: Issues of public policy.* Washington, DC: Government Printing Office.

U.S. Commission on Civil Rights. (1982). *Under the rule of thumb: Battered women and the administration of justice.* Washington, DC: Government Printing Office.

Wallace, A. (1986). *Homicide: The social reality.* Sydney, Australia: New South Wales Bureau of Crime and Statistics.

Widom, C. S. (1989). The cycle of violence. *Science, 244,* 160-166.

Widom, C. S., & Ames, M. A. (1994). Criminal consequences of childhood sexual victimization. *Child Abuse and Neglect, 18,* 303-318.

Wilbanks, W. (1983). The female homicide offender in Dade County, Florida. *Criminal Justice Review, 8,* 9-14.

Williams, K. R., & Flewelling, R. L. (1987). Family, acquaintance, and stranger homicide: Alternative procedures for rate calculation. *Criminology, 25,* 543-560.

Wilson, M., & Daly, M. (1993). Spousal homicide risk and estrangement. *Violence and Victims, 8,* 3-16.

Wilson, M., Johnson, H., & Daly, M. (1995). Lethal and nonlethal violence against wives. *Canadian Journal of Criminology, 37,* 331-361.

Wilt, M., & Breedlove, R. K. (1977). *Domestic violence and the police: Studies in Detroit and Kansas City.* Washington, DC: Police Foundation.

Zahn, M. A. (1989). Homicide in the twentieth century: Trends, types and causes. In T. R. Gurr (Ed.), *Violence in America: Vol. 1. The history of violence* (pp. 216-234). Newbury Park, CA: Sage.

CHAPTER 11

Serial Murder

Popular Myths and Empirical Realities

■ *James Alan Fox & Jack Levin*

Since the early 1980s, Americans have become more aware of and concerned about a particularly dangerous class of murderers, known as serial killers. Characterized by the tendency to kill repeatedly (at least three or four victims) and often with increasing brutality, serial killers stalk their victims, one at a time, for weeks, months, or years, generally not stopping until they are caught.

The term *serial killer* was first used in the early 1980s (see Jenkins, 1994), although the phenomenon of repeat killing existed, of course, throughout recorded history. In the late 1800s, for example, Hermann Webster Mudgett (aka H. H. Holmes) murdered dozens of attractive young women in his Chicago "house of death," and the infamous Jack the Ripper stalked the streets of London, killing five prostitutes. Prior to the 1980s, repeat killers such as Mudgett and Jack the Ripper were generally described as mass murderers. The need for a special classification for repeat killers was later recognized because of the important differences between multiple murderers who kill simultaneously and those who kill serially (Levin & Fox, 1985). *Mass killers*—those who slaughter their victims in one event—tend to target people they know (e.g., family members or coworkers), often for the sake of revenge, using an efficient weapon of mass destruction (e.g., a high-powered firearm). As we shall describe below, serial murderers are different in all these respects, typically killing total strangers with their hands to achieve a sense of power and control over others.

A rising concern with serial killing has spawned a number of media presentations, resulting in the perpetrators of this type of murder becoming a regular staple of U.S. popular culture. A steady diet of television and movie productions could lead viewers to believe that serial killing is a common type of homicide. An

AUTHORS' NOTE: We contributed equally to this work; the order of authorship was determined alphabetically. We wish to acknowledge the able assistance of Stephanie Flagg.

increasing interest in serial homicide, however, has not been limited solely to the lay public. During the past two decades, the number, as well as the mix, of scholars devoting their attention to this crime has dramatically changed. Until the early 1980s, the literature exploring aspects of multiple homicide consisted almost exclusively of bizarre and atypical case studies contributed by forensic psychiatrists pertaining to their court-assigned clients. More recently, there has been a significant shift toward social scientists examining the cultural and social forces underlying the late 20th-century rise in serial murder as well as law enforcement operatives developing research-based investigative tools for tracking and apprehending serial offenders.

Despite the shift in disciplinary focus, some basic assumptions of psychiatry appear to remain strong in the public mind. In particular, it is widely believed that the serial killer acts as a result of some individual pathology produced by traumatic childhood experiences. At the same time, a developing law enforcement perspective holds that the serial killer is a nomadic, sexual sadist who operates with a strict pattern to victim selection and crime scene behavior; this model has also contributed to myopic thinking in responding to serial murder. Unfortunately, these assumptions from both psychiatry and law enforcement may have retarded the development of new and more effective approaches to understanding this phenomenon. In an attempt to present a more balanced view, this chapter examines (serially, of course) several myths about serial killing/killers, some long-standing and others of recent origin, that have been embraced more on faith than on hard evidence.

■ *MYTH 1: THERE IS AN EPIDEMIC OF SERIAL MURDER IN THE UNITED STATES*

Although interest in serial murder has unquestionably grown, the same may not necessarily be true for the incidence of this crime itself. Curiously enough, there may actually be more scholars studying serial murder than there are offenders committing it. Regrettably, it is virtually impossible to measure with any degree of precision the prevalence of serial murder today, or even less so to trace its long-term trends (see Egger, 1990, 1998; Kiger, 1990). One thing for certain, however, is that the problem is nowhere near epidemic proportions (Jenkins, 1994).

It is true that some serial killers completely avoid detection. Unlike other forms of homicide, such as spousal murder, many of the crimes committed by serial killers may be unknown to authorities. Because serial murderers usually target strangers and often take great care in covering up their crimes by disposing of their victims' bodies, many of the homicides may remain as open missing persons reports. Moreover, because the victims frequently come from marginal groups, such as persons who are homeless, prostitutes, and drug users, disappearances may never result in any official reports of suspicious activity.

Even more problematic than the issue of missing data in measuring the extent of serial murder, law enforcement authorities are often unable to identify connections between unsolved homicides separated through time or space (Egger, 1984, 1998). Even if communication between law enforcement authorities were improved (as it has become in recent years), the tendency for some serial killers to alter their *modus operandi* frustrates attempts to link seemingly isolated killings to the same individual.

The lack of any hard evidence concerning the prevalence of serial homicide has not prevented speculation within both academic and law enforcement fields. The "serial killer panic of 1983-85," as it has been described by Jenkins (1988), was fueled by some outrageous and unsupportable statistics promulgated by the U.S. Department of Justice to buttress its claim that the extent of serial murder was on the rise. Apparently, some government officials reasoned that because the number of unsolved homicides had surged from several hundred per year in the early 1960s to several thousand per year in the 1980s, the aggregate body count produced by serial killers could be as high as 5,000 annually (Fox & Levin, 1985; for commentary on homicide clearance rates, see Chapter 6 by Marc Riedel). Unfortunately, this gross exaggeration was endorsed in some academic publications as well (see Egger, 1984; Holmes & DeBurger, 1988).

More sober thinking on the prevalence issue has occurred in recent years (Egger, 1990, 1998; Holmes & Holmes, 1998). Although still subject to the methodological limitations noted above in the identification of serial crimes, Hickey (1997) has attempted the most exhaustive measurement of the prevalence and trends in serial murder. In contrast to the Justice Department's estimate of thousands of victims annually, Hickey (1997) enumerated only 2,526 to 3,860 victims slain by 399 serial killers between 1800 and 1995. Moreover, between 1975 and 1995, the highest levels in the two centuries, Hickey identified only 153 perpetrators and as many as 1,400 victims, for an average annual tally of far less than 100 victims. Although Hickey's data collection strategy obviously ignored undetected cases, the extent of the problem is likely less than 1% of homicides in the country. Of course, that as much as 1% of the nation's murder problem can potentially be traced to but a few dozen individuals reminds us of the extreme deadliness of their predatory behavior.

■ *MYTH 2: SERIAL KILLERS ARE UNUSUAL IN APPEARANCE AND LIFESTYLE*

As typically portrayed, television and cinematic versions of serial killers are either sinister-appearing creatures of the night or brilliant-but-evil master criminals. In reality, however, most tend to fit neither of these descriptions. Serial killers are generally White males in their late 20s or 30s who span a broad range of human qualities including appearance and intelligence.

Some serial killers are high school dropouts, and others might indeed be regarded as unappealing by conventional standards. At the same time, a few actually possess brilliance, charm, and attractiveness. Most serial killers, however, are fairly average, at least to the casual observer. In short, they are "extraordinarily ordinary"; ironically, part of the secret of their success is that they do not stand out in a crowd or attract negative attention to themselves. Instead, many of them look and act much like "the boy next door"; they hold full-time jobs, are married or involved in some other stable relationship, and are members of various local community groups. The one trait that tends to separate prolific serial killers from the norm is that they are exceptionally skillful in their presentation of self so that they appear beyond suspicion. This is part of the reason why they are so difficult to apprehend (Levin & Fox, 1985).

A related misconception is that serial killers, lacking stable employment or family responsibilities, are full-time predators who roam far and wide, often crossing state and regional boundaries in their quest for victims. Evidence to the contrary notwithstanding, serial killers have frequently been characterized as nomads whose compulsion to kill carries them hundreds of thousands of miles a year as they drift from state to state and region to region leaving scores of victims in their wake. This may be true of a few well-known and well-traveled individuals, but not for the vast majority of serial killers (Levin & Fox, 1985). According to Hickey (1997), only about a third of the serial killers in his database crossed state lines in their murder sprees. John Wayne Gacy, for example, killed all of his 33 young male victims at his Des Plaines, Illinois, home, conveniently burying most of them there as well. Gacy had a job, friends, and family but secretly killed on a part-time, opportunistic basis.

■ *MYTH 3: SERIAL KILLERS ARE ALL INSANE*

What makes serial killers so enigmatic—so irrational to many casual observers—is that they generally kill not for love, money, or revenge but for the fun of it. That is, they delight in the thrill, the sexual satisfaction, or the dominance that they achieve as they squeeze the last breath of life from their victims. At a purely superficial level, killing for the sake of pleasure seems nothing less than "crazy."

The basis for the serial killer's pursuit of pleasure is found in a strong tendency toward sexual sadism (Hazelwood, Dietz, & Warren, 1992) and an interest reflected in detailed fantasies of domination (Prentky, Burgess, & Rokous, 1989). Serial killers tie up their victims to watch them squirm and torture their victims to hear them scream. They rape, mutilate, sodomize, and degrade their victims to feel powerful, dominant, and superior.

Many individuals may have fantasies about torture and murder but are able to restrain themselves from ever translating their sadistic dreams into reality. Those who do not contain their urges to kill repeatedly for no apparent motive are assumed to suffer from some extreme form of mental illness. Indeed, some serial killers have clearly been driven by psychosis, such as Herbert Mullen of Santa Cruz, California, who killed 13 people during a 4-month period to avert an earthquake—at least that is what the voices commanded him to do (the voices also ordered him to burn his penis with a cigarette).

In either a legal or a medical sense, however, most serial killers are not insane or psychotic (see Levin & Fox, 1985; Leyton, 1986). They know right from wrong, know exactly what they are doing, and can control their desire to kill—but choose not to. They are more cruel than crazy. Their crimes may be sickening, but their minds are not necessarily sick. Most apparently do not suffer from hallucinations, a profound thought disorder, or major depression. Indeed, those assailants who are deeply confused or disoriented are generally not capable of the level of planning and organization necessary to conceal their identity from the authorities and, therefore, do not amass a large victim count.

Many serial killers seem instead to possess a personality disorder known as sociopathy (or antisocial personality). They lack a conscience, are remorseless, and care exclusively for their own needs and desires. Other people are regarded merely as tools to be manipulated for the purpose of maximizing their personal pleasure (see Harrington, 1972; Magid & McKelvey, 1988). Thus, if given to perverse sexual fantasy, sociopaths simply feel uninhibited by societal rules or by conscience from literally chasing their dreams in any way necessary for their fulfillment (see Fox, 1989; Levin & Fox, 1985; Vetter, 1990).

Serial killers are not alone in their sociopathic tendencies. The American Psychiatric Association estimates that 3% of all males in our society could be considered sociopathic (for a discussion of the prevalence of antisocial personality disorder, see American Psychiatric Association, 1994). Of course, most sociopaths do not commit acts of violence; they may lie, cheat, or steal, but rape and murder are not necessarily appealing to them—unless they are threatened or they regard killing as a necessary means to some important end.

■ *MYTH 4: ALL SERIAL KILLERS ARE SOCIOPATHS*

Although many serial killers tend to be sociopaths, totally lacking in concern for their victims, some actually do have a conscience but are able to neutralize or negate their feelings of remorse by rationalizing their behavior. They feel as though they are doing something good for society, or at least nothing that bad.

Milwaukee's cannibalistic killer, Jeffrey Dahmer, for example, actually viewed his crimes as a sign of love and affection. He told Tracy Edwards, a victim who managed to escape, that if he played his cards right, he too could give his heart to Jeff. Dahmer meant it quite literally, of course, but according to Edwards, he said it affectionately, not threateningly.

The powerful psychological process of *dehumanization* allows many serial killers to slaughter scores of innocent people by viewing them as worthless and therefore expendable. To the dehumanizer, prostitutes are seen as mere sex machines, gays are AIDS carriers, nursing home patients are vegetables, and homeless alcoholics are nothing more than human trash.

In a process related to this concept of dehumanization, many serial killers compartmentalize the world into two groups—those whom they care about versus everyone else. "Hillside Strangler" Kenneth Bianchi, for example, could be kind and loving to his wife and child as well as to his mother and friends yet be vicious and cruel to those he considered meaningless. He and his cousin started with prostitutes, but later, when they grew comfortable with killing, branched out to middle-class targets.

■ *MYTH 5: SERIAL KILLERS ARE INSPIRED BY PORNOGRAPHY*

Could Theodore Bundy have been right in his death row claim that pornography turned him into a vicious killer, or was he just making excuses to deflect blame? It should be no surprise that the vast majority of serial killers do have a keen interest in pornography, particularly sadistic magazines and films (Ressler, Burgess, & Douglas, 1988). Sadism is the source of their greatest pleasure, and so, of course, they experience it vicariously in their spare time, when not on the prowl themselves. That is, a preoccupation with pornography is a reflection, not the cause, of their own sexual desires. At most, pornography may reinforce sadistic impulses, but it cannot create them.

There is experimental evidence that frequent and prolonged exposure to violent pornography tends to desensitize "normal" men to the plight of victims of sexual abuse (Malamuth & Donnerstein, 1984). In the case of serial killers, however, it takes much more than pornography to create such an extreme and vicious personality.

■ *MYTH 6: SERIAL KILLERS ARE PRODUCTS OF BAD CHILDHOODS*

Whenever the case of an infamous serial killer is uncovered, journalists and behavioral scientists alike tend to search for clues in the killer's childhood that might explain the seemingly senseless or excessively brutal murders. Many writers have emphasized, for example, Theodore Bundy's concerns about being illegitimate, and biographers of Hillside Strangler Kenneth Bianchi capitalized on his having been adopted.

There is a long tradition of research on the childhood correlates of homicidal proneness. For example, several decades ago, Macdonald (1963) hypothesized a triad of symptoms—enuresis, fire setting, and cruelty to animals—that were seen as reactions to parental rejection, neglect, or brutality. Although the so-called Macdonald's Triad was later refuted in controlled studies (see Macdonald, 1968), the connection between parental physical/sexual abuse or abandonment and subsequent violent behavior has remained a continuing focus of research (Sears, 1991). It is often suggested that because of such deep-rooted problems, serial killers suffer from a profound sense of powerlessness that they compensate for through extreme forms of aggression in which they exert control over others.

It is true that the biographies of most serial killers reveal significant physical and psychological trauma at an early age. For example, based on in-depth interviews with 36 incarcerated murderers, Ressler et al. (1988) found evidence of psychological abuse (e.g., public humiliation) in 23 cases and physical trauma in 13 cases. Hickey (1997) reported that among a group of 62 male serial killers, 48% had been rejected as children by a parent or some other important person in their lives. Of course, these same types of experiences can be found in the biographies of many "normal" people as well. More specifically, although useful for characterizing the backgrounds of serial killers, the findings presented by Ressler at al. and Hickey lack a comparison group drawn from nonoffending populations for which the same operational definitions of trauma have been applied. Therefore, it is impossible to conclude that serial killers have suffered as children to any greater extent than others.

As a related matter, more than a few serial killers—from New York City's David Berkowitz to Long Island's Joel Rifkin—were raised by adoptive parents. In the adopted child syndrome, an individual displaces anger for birth parents onto adoptive parents as well as other authority figures. The syndrome is often expressed early in life in "provocative antisocial behavior" including fire setting, truancy, promiscuity, pathological lying, and stealing. Deeply troubled adopted children may, in fantasy, create imaginary playmates who represent their antisocial impulses. Later, they may experience a dissociative disorder or even the development of an alter personality in which their murderous tendencies become situated (Kirschner, 1990, 1992).

The apparent overrepresentation of adoption in the biographies of serial killers has been exploited by those who are looking for simple explanations for heinous crimes, without fully recognizing the mechanisms behind or value of the link between adoption and criminal behavior. Even if adoption plays a role in the making of a serial murderer, the independent variable remains to be specified—that is, for example, rejection by birth parents, poor health and prenatal care of birth mother, or inadequate bonding to adoptive parents.

Some neurologists and a growing number of psychiatrists suggest that serial killers have incurred serious injury to the limbic region of the brain resulting from severe or repeated head trauma, generally during childhood. As an example, psychiatrist Dorothy Lewis and neurologist Jonathan Pincus, along with other colleagues, examined 15 murderers on Florida's death row and found that all showed signs of neurological irregularities (Lewis, Pincus, Feldman, Jackson, & Bard, 1986). In addition, psychologist Joel Norris (1988) reported excessive spinal fluid found in the brain scan of serial killer Henry Lee Lucas. Norris argued that this abnormality reflected the possible damage caused by an earlier blow or a series of blows to Lucas's head.

It is critical that we place in some perspective the many case studies that have been used in an attempt to connect extreme violence to neurological impairment. Absent from the case study approach is any indication of the prevalence of individuals who did not act violently despite a history of trauma. Indeed, if head trauma were as strong a contributor to serial murder as some suggest, then we would have many times more of these killers than we actually do.

It is also important to recognize that neurological impairment must occur in combination with a host of environmental conditions to place an individual at risk for extreme acts of brutality. Dorothy Lewis cautions, "The neuropsychiatric problems alone don't make you violent. Probably the environmental factors in and of themselves don't make you a violent person. But when you put them together, you create a very dangerous character" ("Serial Killers," 1992). Similarly, Ressler asserts that no single childhood problem indicates future criminality: "There are a whole pot of conditions that have to be met" for violence to be predictable (quoted in Meddis, 1987, p. 3A). Head trauma and abuse, therefore, may be important risk factors, but they are neither necessary nor sufficient to make someone a serial killer. Rather, they are part of a long list of circumstances—including adoption, shyness, disfigurement, speech impediments, learning and physical disabilities, abandonment, death of a parent, academic and athletic inadequacies—that may make a child feel frustrated and rejected enough to predispose, but not predestine, him or her toward extreme violence.

Because so much emphasis has been placed on early childhood, developmental factors in making the transition into adulthood and middle age are often overlooked. Serial killers tend to be in their late 20s and 30s, if not older, when they first show outward signs of murderous behavior. If only early childhood and biological predisposition were involved, why do they not begin killing as adolescents or young adults? Many individuals suffer as children, but only some of them continue to experience profound disappointment and detachment regarding family, friends, and work. For example, Danny Rolling, who murdered several college students in Gainesville, Florida, may have had a childhood filled with frustration and abuse, but his eight-victim murder spree did not commence until he was 36 years old. After experiencing a painful divorce, he drifted from job to job, from state to state, from prison to prison, and finally from murder to murder (Fox & Levin, 1996).

■ *MYTH 7: SERIAL KILLERS CAN BE IDENTIFIED IN ADVANCE*

Predicting dangerousness, particularly in an extreme form such as serial homicide, has been an elusive goal for those investigators who have attempted it. For example, Lewis, Lovely, Yeager, and Femina (1989) suggest that the interaction of neurological/psychiatric impairment and a history of abuse predicts violent crime, better even than previous violence itself. Unfortunately, this conclusion was based on retrospective "postdiction" with a sample of serious offenders, rather than a prospective attempt to predict violence within a general cross section.

It is often said that "hindsight is 20/20." This is especially true for serial murder. Following the apprehension of a serial killer, we often hear mixed reports that "he seemed like a nice guy, but there was something about him that wasn't quite right." Of course, there is often something about most people that may not seem "quite right." When such a person is exposed to be a serial murderer, however, we tend to focus on those warning signs in character and biography that were previously ignored. Even the stench emanating from Jeffrey Dahmer's apartment, which he had convincingly explained to the neighbors as the odor of spoiled meat from his broken freezer, was unexceptional until after the fact.

The methodological problems in predicting violence in advance are well known (Chaiken, Chaiken, & Rhodes, 1994). For a category of violence as rare as serial murder, however, the low base rate and consequent false-positive dilemma are overwhelming. Simply put, there are thousands of White males in their late 20s or 30s who thirst for power, are sadistic, and lack strong internal controls; most emphatically, however, the vast majority of them will never kill anyone.

■ *MYTH 8: ALL SERIAL KILLERS ARE SEXUAL SADISTS*

Serial killers who rape, torture, sodomize, and mutilate their victims attract an inordinate amount of attention from the press, the public, and professionals as well. Although they may be the most fascinating type of serial killer, they are hardly the only type.

Expanding their analysis beyond the sexual sadist, Holmes and DeBurger (1988) were among the first to assemble a motivational typology of serial killing, classifying serial murderers into four broad categories: visionary (e.g., voices from God), mission-oriented (e.g., ridding the world of evil), hedonistic (e.g., killing for pleasure), and power/control-oriented (e.g., killing for dominance). Holmes and DeBurger further divided the hedonistic type into three subtypes: lust, thrill, and comfort (see also Holmes & Holmes, 1998).

Although we applaud Holmes and DeBurger for their attempt to provide some conceptual structure, we must also note a troubling degree of overlap among their types. For example, Herbert Mullen, believing that he was obeying God's commandment, "sacrificed" (in his mind) more than a dozen people to avert catastrophic earthquakes; his motivation was both "visionary" and "mission-oriented." Furthermore, the typology is somewhat misaligned: Both the "lust" and "thrill" subtypes are expressive motivations, whereas "comfort" (e.g., murder for profit or to eliminate witnesses) is instrumental or a means toward an end.

Modifying the Holmes-DeBurger framework, we suggest that serial murders can be reclassified into three categories, each with two subtypes:

1. Thrill
   a. Sexual sadism
   b. Dominance
2. Mission
   a. Reformist
   b. Visionary
3. Expedience
   a. Profit
   b. Protection

Most serial killings can be classified as thrill motivated, and the *sexual sadist* is the most common of all. In addition, a growing number of murders committed by hospital caretakers have been exposed in recent years; although not sexual in motivation, these acts of murder are perpetrated for the sake of *dominance* nevertheless.

A less common form of serial killing consists of mission-oriented killers who murder to further a cause. Through killing, the *reformist* attempts to rid the world of filth and evil, such as by killing prostitutes, gays, or homeless persons. Most self-proclaimed reformists are also motivated by thrill seeking but try to rationalize their murderous behavior. For example, Donald Harvey, who worked as an orderly in Cincinnati-area hospitals, confessed to killing 80 or more patients through the years. Although he was termed a mercy killer, Harvey actually enjoyed the dominance he achieved by playing God with the lives of other people.

In contrast to pseudoreformists, *visionary* killers, as rare as they may be, genuinely believe in their missions. They hear the voice of the devil or God instructing them to kill. Driven by these delusions, visionary killers tend to be psychotic, confused, and disorganized. Because their killings are impulsive and even frenzied, visionaries rarely remain on the street long enough to become prolific serial killers.

The final category of serial murder includes those who are motivated by the expedience of either profit or protection. The *profit-oriented* serial killer systematically murders as a critical element of the overall plan to dispose of victims to make money (e.g., Sacramento landlady Dorothea Puente murdered 9 elderly tenants to cash their social security checks). By contrast, the *protection-oriented* killer uses murder to cover up criminal activity (e.g., the Lewington brothers systematically robbed and murdered 10 people throughout Central Ohio).

■ *MYTH 9: SERIAL KILLERS SELECT VICTIMS WHO SOMEHOW RESEMBLE THEIR MOTHERS*

Shortly after the capture of Hillside Strangler Kenneth Bianchi, psychiatrists speculated that he tortured and murdered young women as an expression of hatred toward his mother, who had allegedly brutalized him as a youngster (Fox & Levin, 1994). Similarly, the execution of Theodore Bundy gave psychiatrists occasion to suggest that his victims served as surrogates for the real target he sought, his mother.

Although unresolved family conflicts may in some cases be a significant source of frustration, most serial killers have a more opportunistic or pragmatic basis for selecting their victims. Quite simply, they tend to prey on the most vulnerable targets—prostitutes, drug users, hitchhikers, and runaways, as well as older hospital patients (Levin & Fox, 1985). Part of the vulnerability concerns the ease with which these groups can be abducted or overtaken. Children and older persons are defenseless because of physical stature or disability; hitchhikers and prostitutes become vulnerable as soon as they enter the killer's vehicle; hospital patients are vulnerable in their total dependency on their caretakers.

Vulnerability is most acute in the case of prostitutes, which explains their relatively high rate of victimization by serial killers. A sexual sadist can cruise a red-light district, seeking out the woman who best fits his deadly sexual fantasies. When he finds her, she willingly complies with his wishes—until it is too late.

Another aspect of vulnerability is the ease with which the killers can avoid being detected following a murder. Serial killers of our time are often sly and crafty, fully realizing the ease with which they can prey on streetwalkers and escape detection, much less arrest. Because the disappearance of a prostitute is more likely to be considered by the police, at least initially, as a missing person rather than a victim of homicide, the search for the body can be delayed weeks or months. Also, potential witnesses to abductions in red-light districts tend to be unreliable sources of information or distrustful of the police.

Frail older persons, particularly those in hospitals and nursing homes, represent a class of victims that is at the mercy of a different type of serial killer, called "angels of death." Revelations by a Long Island nurse who poisoned his patients in a failed attempt to be a hero by resuscitating them and of two Grand Rapids nurses aides who murdered older patients to form a lovers' pact have horrified even the most jaded observers of crime.

Not only are persons who are old and infirm vulnerable to the misdeeds of their caretakers who may have a particularly warped sense of mercy, but hospital homicides are particularly difficult to detect and solve. Death among older patients is not uncommon, and suspicions are rarely aroused. Furthermore, should a curiously large volume of deaths occur within a short time on a particular nurse's shift, hospital administrators feel in a quandary. Not only are they reluctant to bring scandal and perhaps lawsuits to their own facility without sufficient proof, but most of the potentially incriminating evidence against a suspected employee is long buried with the victim.

■ *MYTH 10: SERIAL KILLERS REALLY WANT TO GET CAUGHT*

Despite the notion that serial killers are typically lacking in empathy and remorse, some observers insist that deeply repressed feelings of guilt may subconsciously motivate them to leave telltale clues for the police. Although this premise may be popular in media portrayals, most serial killers go to great lengths to avoid detection, such as carefully destroying crime scene evidence or disposing of their victims' bodies in hard-to-find dump sites.

There is an element of self-selection in defining serial killing. Only those offenders who have sufficient cunning and guile are able to avoid capture long enough to accumulate the number of victims necessary to be classified as serial killers. Most serial killers are careful, clever, and, to use the FBI's typology (see Ressler et al., 1988), organized. Of course, disorganized killers, because of their carelessness, tend to be caught quickly, often before they surpass the serial killer threshold of victim count.

Murders committed by a serial killer are typically difficult to solve because of lack of both motive and physical evidence. Unlike the usual homicide that involves an offender and a victim who know one another, serial murders are almost exclusively committed by strangers. Thus, the usual police strategy of identifying suspects by considering their possible motive, be it jealousy, revenge, or greed, is typically fruitless.

Another conventional approach to investigating homicides involves gathering forensic evidence—fibers, hairs, blood, and prints—from the scene of the crime. In the case of many serial murders, however, this can be rather difficult, if not impossible. The bodies of the victims are often found at desolate roadsides or in makeshift graves, exposed to rain, wind, and snow. Most of the potentially revealing crime scene evidence remains in the unknown killer's house or car.

Another part of the problem is that unlike those shown in the media, many serial killers do not leave unmistakable and unique "signatures" at their crime scenes. As a result, the police may not recognize multiple homicides as the work of the same perpetrator. Moreover, some serial killings, even if consistent in style, traverse jurisdictional boundaries. Thus, "linkage blindness" is a significant barrier to solving many cases of serial murder (Egger, 1984).

To aid in the detection of serial murder cases, the FBI operationalized in 1985 the Violent Criminal Apprehension Program (VICAP), a computerized database for the collection and collation of information pertaining to unsolved homicides and missing persons around the country. It is designed to flag similarities in unsolved crimes that might otherwise be obscure (Howlett, Haufland, & Ressler, 1986).

Although an excellent idea in theory, VICAP has encountered significant practical limitations. Complexities in the data collection forms have limited the extent of participation of local law enforcement agencies in completing VICAP questionnaires. More important, pattern recognition is far from a simple or straightforward task, regardless of how powerful the computer or sophisticated the software. Furthermore, even the emergence of a pattern among a set of crime records in the VICAP database does not ensure that the offender will be identified.

In addition to the VICAP clearinghouse, the FBI, on request, assembles criminal profiles of the unknown offenders, based on behavioral clues left at crime scenes, autopsy reports, and police incident reports. Typically, these profiles speculate on the killer's age, race, sex, marital status, employment status, sexual maturity, possible criminal record, relationship to the victim, and likelihood of committing future crimes. At the core of its profiling strategy, the FBI distinguishes between *organized nonsocial* and *disorganized asocial* killers. According to Hazelwood and Douglas (1980), organized killers typically are intelligent, are socially and sexually competent, are of high birth order, are skilled workers, live with a partner, are mobile, drive late model cars, and follow their crimes in the media. In contrast, disorganized killers generally are unintelligent, are socially and sexually inadequate, are of low birth order, are unskilled workers, live alone, are nonmobile, drive old cars or no car at all, and have minimal interest in the news reports of their crimes.

According to the FBI analysis, these types tend to differ also in crime scene characteristics (Ressler et al., 1988). Specifically, organized killers use restraints on the victim, hide or transport the body, remove the weapon from the scene, molest the victim prior to death, and are methodical in their style of killing. Operating differently, disorganized killers tend not to use restraints, leave the body in full view, leave a weapon at the scene, molest the victim after death, and are spontaneous in their manner of killing. The task of profiling involves, therefore, drawing inferences from the crime scene to the behavioral characteristics of the killer.

Despite the Hollywood hype that exaggerates the usefulness of criminal profiling, it is an investigative tool of some, albeit limited, value. Even when constructed by the most experienced and skillful profilers, such as those at the FBI, profiles are not expected to solve a case; rather, they provide an additional set of clues in cases found by local police to be unsolvable. Simply put, a criminal profile cannot identify a suspect for investigation, nor can it eliminate a suspect who does not fit the mold. An overreliance on the contents of a profile can misdirect a serial murder investigation, sometimes quite seriously (see, for example, Fox & Levin, 1996). Clearly, a criminal profile can assist in assigning subjective probabilities to suspects whose names surface through more usual investigative strategies (e.g., interviews of witnesses, canvassing of neighborhoods, and "tip" phone lines). There is, however, no substitute for old-fashioned detective work and, for that matter, a healthy and helpful dose of luck.

■ *FROM MYTH TO REALITY*

The study of serial homicide is in its infancy, less than two decades old (O'Reilly-Fleming, 1996). The pioneering scholars noted the pervasiveness and inaccuracy of long-standing psychiatric misconceptions regarding the state of mind of the serial killer (see Levin & Fox, 1985; Leyton, 1986; Ressler et al., 1988). More recently, these unfounded images have been supplanted by newer myths, including those concerning the prevalence and apprehension of serial killers.

The mythology of serial killing has developed from a pervasive fascination with a crime about which so little is known. Most of the scholarly literature is based on conjecture, anecdote, and small samples, rather than rigorous and controlled research. The future credibility of this area of study will depend on the ability of criminologists to upgrade the standards of research on serial homicide. Only then will myths about serial murder give way to a reliable foundation of knowledge.

■ *REFERENCES*

American Psychiatric Association. (1994). *Diagnostic and statistical manual of mental disorders* (4th ed.). Washington, DC: American Psychiatric Association.

Chaiken, J., Chaiken, M., & Rhodes, W. (1994). Predicting violent behavior and classifying violent offenders. In A. J. Reiss Jr. & J. A. Roth (Eds.), *Understanding and preventing violence* (Vol. 4, pp. 217-295). Washington, DC: National Academy Press.

Egger, S. A. (1984). A working definition of serial murder and the reduction of linkage blindness. *Journal of Police Science and Administration, 12,* 348-357.

Egger, S. A. (1990). *Serial murder: An elusive phenomenon.* Westport, CT: Praeger.

Egger, S. A. (1998). *The killers among us: An examination of serial murder and its investigation.* Upper Saddle River, NJ: Prentice Hall.

Fox, J. A. (1989, January 29). The mind of a murderer. *Palm Beach Post,* p. 1E.

Fox, J. A., & Levin, J. (1985, December 1). Serial killers: How statistics mislead us. *Boston Herald,* p. 45.

Fox, J. A., & Levin, J. (1994). *Overkill: Mass murder and serial killing exposed.* New York: Plenum.

Fox, J. A., & Levin, J. (1996). *Killer on campus.* New York: Avon Books.

Harrington, A. (1972). *Psychopaths.* New York: Simon & Schuster.

Hazelwood, R. R., Dietz, P. E., & Warren, J. (1992). The criminal sexual sadist. *FBI Law Enforcement Bulletin, 61,* 12-20.

Hazelwood, R. R., & Douglas, J. E. (1980). The lust murderer. *FBI Law Enforcement Bulletin, 49,* 1-5.

Hickey, E. W. (1997). *Serial murderers and their victims* (2nd ed.). Belmont, CA: Wadsworth.

Holmes, R. M., & DeBurger, J. (1988). *Serial murder.* Newbury Park, CA: Sage.

Holmes, R. M., & Holmes, S. T. (1998). *Serial murder* (2nd ed.). Thousand Oaks, CA: Sage.

Howlett, J. B., Haufland, K. A., & Ressler, R. J. (1986). The violent criminal apprehension program—VICAP: A progress report. *FBI Law Enforcement Bulletin, 55,* 14-22.

Jenkins, P. (1988). Myth and murder: The serial killer panic of 1983-85. *Criminal Justice Research Bulletin* (No. 3). Huntsville, TX: Sam Houston State University.

Jenkins, P. (1994). *Using murder: The social construction of serial homicide.* New York: Walter de Gruyter.

Kiger, K. (1990). The darker figure of crime: The serial murder enigma. In S. A. Egger (Ed.), *Serial murder: An elusive phenomenon* (pp. 35-52). New York: Praeger.

Kirschner, D. (1990). The adopted child syndrome: Considerations for psychotherapy. *Psychotherapy in Private Practice, 8,* 93-100.

Kirschner, D. (1992). Understanding adoptees who kill: Dissociation, patricide, and the psychodynamics of adoption. *International Journal of Offender Therapy & Comparative Criminology, 36,* 323-333.

Levin, J., & Fox, J. A. (1985). *Mass murder: America's growing menace.* New York: Plenum.

Lewis, D. O., Lovely, R., Yeager, C., & Femina, D. D. (1989). Toward a theory of the genesis of violence: A follow-up study of delinquents. *Journal of the American Academy of Child and Adolescent Psychiatry, 28,* 431-436.

Lewis, D. O., Pincus, J. H., Feldman, M., Jackson, L., & Bard, B. (1986). Psychiatric, neurological, and psychoeducational characteristics of 15 death row inmates in the United States. *American Journal of Psychiatry, 143,* 838-845.

Leyton, E. (1986). *Compulsive killers: The story of modern multiple murderers.* New York: New York University Press.

Macdonald, J. M. (1963). The threat to kill. *American Journal of Psychiatry, 120,* 125-130.

Macdonald, J. M. (1968). *Homicidal threats.* Springfield, IL: Charles C Thomas.

Magid, K., & McKelvey, C. A. (1988). *High risk: Children without a conscience.* New York: Bantam.

Malamuth, N. M., & Donnerstein, E. (1984). *Pornography and sexual aggression.* Orlando, FL: Academic Press.

Meddis, S. (1987, March 31). FBI: Possible to spot, help serial killers early. *USA Today,* p. 3A.

Norris, J. (1988). *Serial killers: The growing menace.* New York: Doubleday.

O'Reilly-Fleming, T. (1996). *Serial and mass murder: Theory, research and policy.* Toronto, Ontario: Canadian Scholars' Press.

Prentky, R. A., Burgess, A. W., & Rokous, F. (1989). The presumptive role of fantasy in serial sexual homicide. *American Journal of Psychiatry, 146,* 887-891.

Ressler, R. K., Burgess, A. W., & Douglas, J. E. (1988). *Sexual homicide: Patterns and motives.* Lexington, MA: Lexington Books.

Sears, D. J. (1991). *To kill again.* Wilmington, DE: Scholarly Resources Books.

Serial killers. (1992, October 18). NOVA. Boston: WGBH-TV.

Vetter, H. (1990). Dissociation, psychopathy, and the serial murderer. In S. A. Egger (Ed.), *Serial murder: An elusive phenomenon* (pp. 73-92). New York: Praeger.

CHAPTER 12

Drugs, Alcohol, and Homicide

Issues in Theory and Research

■ *Robert Nash Parker & Kathleen Auerhahn*

There has been a growing interest in the relationship between alcohol, drugs, and violence during the past decade. In addition to what has been mostly misguided attention in mass media and in political circles to the relationship between illegal drugs and violence, a number of studies have examined the relationship between alcohol, drugs, and violence, and a number of studies have critically examined the conceptualization of this relationship. This effort, however, has resulted in little in the way of systematic growth in the knowledge base about how and why alcohol and other drugs are related to violence in general and homicide in particular. The major reason for this lack of growth in the knowledge base, despite a great deal of effort, is the lack of critical theorizing about this relationship and how any relationship between alcohol, drugs, and homicide is linked inextricably with the relationships of a number of important factors that contribute to the causation of homicide.

Kai Pernanen, a scholar who has devoted a great deal of attention both to the conceptual link between alcohol (1976, 1981) and to the empirical study of alcohol's role in certain types of violence (1991), has observed that any relationship between alcohol use and homicide is likely to be a complex one, embedded as both of these behaviors are in a fully articulated web of human behavior (1981, p. 15). This complexity underscores the need for specific theoretical models that link drugs and alcohol with other factors in the causation of violence, such as poverty, family breakdown, ethnic and racial inequality, and routine activities. Before this work can be advanced successfully, however, there is a need to think critically about how alcohol and other drugs relate to human behavior in general.

Promising avenues are being explored in regard to alcohol and behavior. For example, advances have been made in the study of psychological expectancies concerning alcohol's effect on behavior (Brown, 1993; Grube, Ames, & Delaney, 1994), the relationship between alcohol and cognitive functioning (Pihl, Peterson, & Lau, 1993), the impact of alcohol on aggressive behavior (Leonard & Taylor, 1983), and the dynamic developmental effects of early exposure to alcohol and violence among young people (White, Hansell, & Brick, 1993) and among women who have been victimized as children and as adults (Miller & Downs, 1993; Widom & Ames, 1994). As will be demonstrated in this chapter, however, the lack of theoretical analysis of the general links between drugs, alcohol, and behavior and the failure of researchers to develop specific conceptualizations of how drugs and alcohol might relate to homicide and its causes have weakened the cumulative contribution of the empirical work to date. This explains in large part why, despite the increased attention devoted to such research, little gain in the understanding of this relationship has been realized.

Partly as a result of the lack of theorizing about the relationship between homicide and alcohol and other drugs, and partly as a result of other aspects of social science research practice, a number of other difficulties with the current research will be discussed here. Most of the studies published during the past decade have one or more major design problems.[1] For example, most studies of drugs or alcohol and homicide suffer from *selection bias,* in that individuals whose behavior constitutes the dependent variable either have committed homicide (e.g., the empirical tests of Goldstein's approach to be discussed below) or have been victims of homicide (e.g., Welte & Abel, 1989). That such studies show that a significant number, or even a majority, of individuals in the sample used alcohol or other drugs prior to the homicide is not helpful in ascertaining the risk of homicide among all persons who drink alcohol or take drugs. In fairness to those researchers who have conducted these studies, this is not an easy problem to solve. Ultimately, homicide is a relatively rare event, even in a violence-prone nation such as the United States. One approach to this problem is to generate a comparison group, either matched on various characteristics or analyzed with statistical controls (i.e., a case and control model as applied to the study of violence; see Loftin, McDowall, & Wiersema, 1992). Such an approach is rarely found in this literature, however.

Finally, because research efforts in this area are rarely informed by carefully specified theoretical models, the majority of studies of drugs, alcohol, and homicide lack even a rudimentary notion of the impact of other potentially important factors. The result is often a failure to isolate the unique effects that drug and alcohol use might have in contributing to homicide (for a discussion of this issue, see Parker, 1995).

Despite these methodological problems, significant advances have been made in the knowledge of how drug and alcohol use may be related to homicide. Therefore, this chapter is devoted to a review and critique of the major research efforts that have contributed to the current level of understanding. We approach the drugs, alcohol, and homicide literature as a single body of research, but we acknowledge that an important contextual difference exists between *illegal* drug use and use of alcohol, a substance that can be legally obtained and consumed by adults in a variety of social settings. Although recognizing that there may be some overlap between the social worlds in which drugs and alcohol are used, we treat separately the two substances and their possible connections to homicide.

Because research on the relationship between drugs and homicide is less developed, we will review this area first, followed by a consideration of the existing research on alcohol and homicide. In both cases, our discussion will (a) assess the state of specific theorizing and theoretical models that have been advanced; (b) review empirical research that tests these approaches; (c) provide our critique of the models, their tests, and what we can infer from the research reviewed; and (d) consider the implications of this research for public policy and for research and design.

■ *DRUGS AND HOMICIDE*

The relationship between drugs and homicide has not been investigated widely. Homicide is a relatively rare occurrence that must necessarily be studied after the fact, making it difficult to assign causality. In addition, attempts to develop systematic theories about illicit drugs as an etiological factor in homicide are hindered by the lack of reliable information about the extent of illicit drug use in the population. For this reason, the research efforts in this area have been primarily descriptive. Yet these studies offer insight into the possible dynamics of a drug-homicide linkage.

The Goldstein Typology

In 1985, Paul J. Goldstein attempted to develop a theoretical framework to describe and explain the relationship of drugs and violence, including homicide. He developed a typology of three ways in which drug use and drug trafficking may be causally related to violence; these were termed psychopharmacological, economic-compulsive, and systemic violence.

Psychopharmacological violence stems from properties of the drug itself. Despite debate about the issue of the psychopharmacological effects of drugs on aggression and violent behavior, evidence shows that there may be such effects associated with alcohol, cocaine, and PCP. Psychopharmacological violence also may be associated with opiate drugs when the user is experiencing physical withdrawal. In Goldstein's framework, an escalated risk of violence can be associated with drug ingestion by the victim, the perpetrator, or both.

Economic-compulsive violence is associated with the high costs of illicit drug use. This type of violence does not stem directly from the effects of the drug but is motivated by the need or desire to obtain drugs. Because of the high prices and the capacity to induce physical and psychological dependencies, one expects opiates (particularly heroin) and cocaine (in both powder and "rock" form) to be most often associated with economic-compulsive violence.

Systemic violence is defined by Goldstein (1985) as that type of violence associated with "traditionally aggressive patterns of interaction within the system of drug distribution and use" (p. 497). He maintains that the risks of violence are greater to those involved in distribution than to those who are only users (see also Goldstein, Brownstein, Ryan, & Bellucci, 1989). Although the first two categories in this typology are primarily associated with drug *use,* systemic violence is violence that arises as a direct result of involvement in *trafficking.*

Empirical Evaluations of the Goldstein Tripartite Framework

Although Goldstein's (1985) original explication of the tripartite conceptual framework was intended to apply to the causal role that drugs play in all types of violence, most of the research that uses Goldstein's classificatory scheme has dealt with homicide. In recent years, Goldstein and his associates have undertaken several empirical tests in an attempt to understand the relationship between drugs and homicide. One such study (Goldstein et al., 1989) was primarily concerned with the relationship between the crack epidemic that took place in the 1980s and homicide. To ascertain the nature of this relationship, information from 414 homicides in New York City was gathered for the researchers by police officers investigating the crime. This was done to obtain specific information that might not ordinarily be collected in a homicide investigation, such as victim-offender relationship, type of drug involved, whether the perpetrator or victim appeared to be under the influence of drugs, and other similar information.

Goldstein et al. (1989) concluded that slightly more than half of the sampled homicides were drug related. Of these, the overwhelming majority (74.3% of all drug-related homicides) were classified as systemic. Of drug-related homicides, 65% involved crack cocaine as the primary substance involved (26% of all sampled homicides in New York); another 22% were related to other forms of cocaine. Surprisingly, alcohol was said to be involved as the primary drug in only 9.6% of drug-related cases. Goldstein et al. speculated that this may have been a result of undercounting alcohol. Given the legal status of alcohol, it is likely that police officers are less sensitive to the presence of alcohol than they are to illegal drugs. *All* homicides in which alcohol was the primary substance involved were classified as psychopharmacological. For all other drug categories, a majority of drug-related homicides were classified as systemic.

When Goldstein and his colleagues (1989) applied this model to actual data, they found that it was possible for more than one of these relationships to be present in any specific homicide. When more than one dimension seemed to be equally associated with the homicide event, the case was coded as "multidimensional." In most cases, however, the circumstances were clear enough for the researchers to assign a primary dimension to the case.

Comparison of the circumstances of homicides classified as drug-related to the circumstances of nondrug cases yielded some interesting findings. Homicides involving intimate partners (spouse, significant other) were much less likely to be drug related, as were stranger homicides. The vast majority of drug-related homicides, however, involved victims and perpetrators who were known to each other, although presumably not in the context of intimate relationships. Nearly half of all systemic crack-related homicides involved territorial disputes (44%); another 18% of such homicides involved the robbery of a dealer, whereas 11% were related to the collection of drug-related debts. Goldstein et al. (1989) concluded that the high proportion of crack-related systemic homicides related to territorial disputes was due largely to the relative ease of entry by individuals into the crack market, mainly because of lower costs than those associated with other drugs (see also Abadinsky, 1994). Goldstein et al. also commented that although at the time of the study crack was a relatively new drug, the large number of crack-related homicides did not increase the homicide rate in New York City: "In both nature and number, crack-related homicides largely appear to be replacing other types of homicides rather than just adding to the existing homicide rate" (p. 683).

The data set collected by Goldstein et al. (1989) has been the basis for several other analyses exploring various dimensions of the drug-homicide relationship. In one study, the data gathered in 1988 were compared with official case records for 1984 on 1,768 homicides throughout New York state (Goldstein, Brownstein, & Ryan, 1992). A lower percentage of 1984 homicides than 1988 homicides were classified as drug related (42% vs. 53%). The most striking difference between the 2 years is the classification of the homicide events according to the tripartite conceptual framework. The majority (59%) of drug-related cases in 1984 were classified as psychopharmacological in nature; of these, nearly 80% involved alcohol as the primary substance. Goldstein et al. attribute these differences to a real difference between the 2 years (1984 was prior to the crack epidemic in New York City), as well as the nature of the data.

Another analysis of the Goldstein et al. (1989) data was designed to determine the specific relationship between drug trafficking and homicide in New York City. Brownstein, Baxi, Goldstein, and Ryan (1992) analyzed a subset of offenders and victims from the data set for whom prior criminal histories were available. They found that both victims and perpetrators of drug-related homicides were substantially more likely than their counterparts in non-drug-related homicides to be known to the police as either drug users (67.5% of those involved in drug-related homicides vs. 22.7% of those involved in non-drug-related homicides) or drug traffickers (59.3% vs. 5.1%). Similarly, victims and perpetrators of drug-related homicides were much more likely to have prior arrests and convictions for drug offenses than were those involved in non-drug-related homicides. Not surprisingly, more than half of the drug-related homicides took place in areas known to be locales for drug sales, whereas only 10% of non-drug-related homicides did. From this analysis, Brownstein et al. concluded,

> Almost no innocent bystanders were victims of homicide. This is not to say that citizens not involved in crime or drugs are never the victims of homicide, but only that the extent of the threat to their safety has been exaggerated. It is the people who live in or near drug-involved communities that are at the greatest risk. (p. 41)

The Drug Relationships in Murder Project

Only one other data set has been used extensively to examine the relationship of drugs and homicide according to Goldstein's tripartite framework. The Drug Relationships in Murder project (DREIM) involved extensive interviews with 268 offenders who committed a homicide in 1984 and were incarcerated in New York state correctional facilities. Police records for the cases were examined to compare information recorded at the time of the arrest with the self-report data obtained in the interviews. One of the purposes of the DREIM project was to attempt to correct the deficiencies observed in other forms of data based on official records (for a review of these shortcomings, see Brownstein et al., 1992; Goldstein et al., 1992; Goldstein et al., 1989).

Several analyses have been conducted using the DREIM data. For instance, Spunt, Goldstein, Brownstein, Fendrich, and Langley (1994) and Spunt, Brownstein, Goldstein, Fendrich, and Liberty (1995) found that the drug most likely to be used by homicide offenders was, overwhelmingly, alcohol. Offenders were likely to have used alcohol in the 24 hours prior to commission of the crime. Thirty-two percent were inebriated at the time of the offense, an incidence nearly twice as high as that of any other drug category. Marijuana and cocaine, respectively, were the drugs next most implicated in the lives of homicide offenders, as well as in the offense itself.

In the DREIM study, offenders who were experiencing the effects related to the use of any drug at the time of the offense (in most cases this was intoxication, but included "coming down from" and "in need of" a drug) were specifically asked whether they felt that the homicide was related to their drug use. Overall, 86% of those who were experiencing drug effects at the time of the homicide believed that the homicide was related to their drug use. Of offenders who were inebriated at the time of the homicide, 59% believed that the alcohol had something to do with the homicide; 56% of those who were high on cocaine believed the homicide to be related to their intoxication.

Two analyses by Spunt and his colleagues approached the drug-homicide nexus in different ways. In one (Spunt et al., 1994), the dimensions of homicides related to alcohol were considered using Goldstein's (1985) tripartite framework. A majority of alcohol-related homicides (86%) were classified as psychopharmacological in nature, which was consistent with earlier findings (Goldstein et al., 1992). The other study by Spunt et al. (1995) was broader and addressed the relationship of homicide to all types of drugs but did not specifically classify cases according to the tripartite conceptual framework. Many detailed excerpts of offender accounts were provided, however, and if one takes these to be representative of the sample of offenders, it appears that the majority of drug-related homicides committed by these offenders were psychopharmacological as well.

How can these seemingly contradictory findings be explained? A possible answer is that the method of data collection may have significantly influenced the findings. Interview data supported the conclusion that the preponderance of drug-related homicides are psychopharmacological, as did analysis of official records. The only support for a systemic link between drugs and homicide derived from the data collected at the time of the homicide investigation via the instrument designed by Goldstein et al. (1989). Consequently, the introduction of bias by the data collection instrument must be considered as a source contributing to the contradictory outcomes discussed above.

More rigorous data collection will be required to use Goldstein's tripartite framework as an effective classificatory tool. Several empirical analyses have been undertaken, but all this work used the same two data sources. That analyses of the two data sources yielded internally consistent but opposing results indicates that the issue will not be resolved until more and better data become available.

There are also problems inherent in Goldstein's typology. It is often assumed that a great deal of violent crime that would be classified as economic-compulsive is associated with illicit drug use. Goldstein's and Spunt's research teams, however, classified few homicides as economic-compulsive. There are several reasons for this. In the case of a homicide that is committed in the process of a robbery, the robbery may be drug motivated but may not be perceived as a drug-related homicide by the police officer collecting data. In addition, many of the situations coded as systemic are economic in nature. "Robbery of a drug dealer" seems to be an economically motivated crime but is classified as systemic on the basis of drug-trafficking involvement of the victim and/or perpetrator. Interpretations of the classificatory scheme seem biased toward support of the systemic model of drug-effected violence. If support for the economic-compulsive model is to be found, it will be found through the process of interviewing offenders. At present, however, the available research using in-depth interviews (Spunt et al., 1995; Spunt et al., 1994) indicates that most drug-related homicides are psychopharmacological in nature.

As stated earlier, because of the nature of homicide, most research concerning the relationship of drugs to homicide is necessarily descriptive, rather than explanatory, and lacks a coherent theoretical framework. Some interesting findings, however, have emerged as a result of these descriptive studies that may aid in the process of theory construction.

Homicide, Drugs, and Women

In recent years, some research has focused on female homicide offenders. In one of those studies, Blount, Silverman, Sellers, and Seese (1994) compared two groups of battered women, those who had killed their abusers and those who had not. They found that the partners of abused women who had been killed were almost twice as likely to engage in daily alcohol use than were the partners of women who did not kill. An analysis of homicide victims in upstate New York yielded a similar finding; 61% of male homicide victims killed by women had alcohol in their blood at the time of death (Welte & Abel, 1989). These results lend support to the observation that homicides committed by females are more likely to be what Wolfgang (1958) called *victim-precipitated* than are homicides committed by male offenders (Daly, 1994).

The Blount et al. (1994) comparison study described above found that homicidal battered women were more likely than nonhomicidal battered women to use alcohol as well as other drugs. In an analysis of the general population of incarcerated females, however, Blount, Danner, Vega, and Silverman (1991) found an inverse relationship between drug or alcohol use and homicide; the homicide offenders in their sample were significantly *less* likely to use and/or abuse drugs or alcohol than female inmates incarcerated for other crimes. It appears, therefore, that drugs and alcohol play a more significant role in the causation of female-perpetrated *intimate homicide* than in other types of homicides committed by women. Other studies indicate that this relationship does not hold for men. Specifically, Lindqvist (1991) and Brownstein et al. (1992) determined from male-dominated samples that drugs were less implicated in intimate homicides than in other forms of homicide.

Other Approaches to the Drugs-Homicide Relationship

Brumm and Cloninger (1995) took a different approach in attempting to define the relationship between illicit drugs and homicide. Using a rational choice/opportunity cost framework that assumes that violent crime rates will vary in inverse proportion to the costs of committing such offenses relative to the costs of committing other crimes, Brumm and Cloninger hypothesized that if a greater proportion of law enforcement activity is directed at drug enforcement, then the costs of committing violent crime will decrease proportionately. Consequently, the incidence of violent crime may actually increase. Using cross-sectional data from 59 U.S. cities in 1985, Brumm and Cloninger developed a simultaneous equation model from which they estimated that a 1% increase in drug enforcement activities results in a 0.17% increase in the homicide rate, a finding confirming their hypothesis. Follow-up studies will be necessary to develop confidence in these findings.

Given the current concern surrounding street gangs, violence, and drugs, Klein, Maxson, and Cunningham (1991) attempted to determine whether gang involvement influenced the relationship between crack and homicide in Los Angeles. The research team analyzed a nonrepresentative sample of police records of homicide cases in South Central Los Angeles, an area characterized by high levels of drug activity and gang violence. They found that gang-related homicides were more likely than nongang homicides to involve drugs—nearly 70% of gang-related homicides were drug related, whereas slightly more than half of other homicides were. A comparison of drug-involved gang homicides and gang homicides in which drugs were not involved yielded no significant differences in characteristics such as location, number of participants, and firearm involvement. When the same comparison was made for the nongang homicides, however, differences were found, with drug-related nongang homicides closely resembling gang homicides. Klein et al. concluded that the involvement of drugs in a homicide is more relevant as a primary characteristic than is gang involvement and that their "results do not support the notion that gangs have unique and strong drug/violence connections" (p. 644).

The research of Klein et al. (1991) also reveals a difference through time. Although the incidence of drug involvement in gang homicides showed virtually no change from 1984 to 1985, the incidence of drug involvement in nongang homicides nearly doubled during the year, to approximately the same level as gang-related homicide. This is consistent with the finding that cocaine became increasingly implicated in homicides throughout the 1980s (Garriott, 1993; Hanzlick & Gowitt, 1991).

Summaries of Drug and Homicide Research

Given this diversity of research and findings, what can we say with reasonable certainty about the relationship between drugs and homicide? To address this question, we offer some generalities that have emerged from the drugs-homicide literature.

Studies consistently report that approximately half of all homicide offenders are intoxicated on drugs and/or alcohol at the time of the crime; similar percentages of homicide victims test positive for alcohol or drugs as well.[2] The preponderance of the evidence indicates that when homicides are related to substance use at all, the substance most likely to be implicated is alcohol, for both victims and offenders.[3] The next most frequently implicated substance in homicide is cocaine, a drug that appeared in an increasing percentage of homicides during the 1980s (Hanzlick & Gowitt, 1991).

Evidence is mixed regarding demographic differences in substance use and how it relates to homicide; one study found that Black males with low socioeconomic status had significantly higher rates of both alcohol and illicit drug use than other demographic groups (Barr, Farrell, Barnes, & Welte, 1993). This may be significant, given the disproportional representation of this group as both offenders and victims of homicide. Other studies are contradictory on the issue of racial and ethnic patterns of substance involvement in homicide. Some researchers report greater drug involvement in homicide for Blacks, Hispanics, and Native Americans (Abel, 1987; Bachman, 1991; Garriott, 1993; Goodman et al., 1986; Tardiff et al., 1995; Welte & Abel, 1989), whereas others find significantly lower substance involvement for Black homicide offenders (Wieczorek,

Welte, & Abel, 1990). It has also been observed that patterns of substance use vary across age groupings. In both the general population and in homicide-offender studies, persons aged 18 to 25 (the age grouping that also shows the greatest criminality) show the highest rates of both alcohol and illicit drug use (Fendrich, Mackesy-Amiti, Goldstein, Spunt, & Brownstein, 1995; Meiczkowski, 1996; Tardiff et al., 1995).

Limited data are available to estimate the prevalence of illicit drug use in the U.S. population (Meiczkowski, 1996). Even if generous estimates are considered, however, it appears that both *perpetrators* and *victims* of homicide are more drug involved than is the general population (Abel, 1987; Brownstein et al., 1992; Garriott, 1993; Goldstein et al., 1992; Goldstein et al., 1989; Hanzlick & Gowitt, 1991; Klein et al., 1991; Spunt et al., 1995). In addition, there is substantial evidence that polydrug use is common among drug-involved homicide offenders (Fendrich et al., 1995; Garriott, 1993; Ray & Simons, 1987; Spunt et al., 1995; Spunt et al., 1994).

Findings that link drugs to victim-offender relationships in homicide are also mixed. There is some evidence that the overall trend is for drugs to be less implicated in intimate homicides than in other types of homicide (Brownstein et al., 1992; Lindqvist, 1991). But as discussed earlier, there is also evidence that drug (and alcohol) involvement is disproportionately associated with intimate homicide among female offenders (Blount et al., 1994).

Despite the considerable amount that researchers have learned about drugs and alcohol, there is still a great deal that we *do not know* about their relationship. Hampered by a paucity of theory, there are no explanations for the patterns of substance use that seem to surround the homicide event as well as the lives of homicide offenders. Researchers who questioned a national sample of incarcerated felony offenders about their criminal histories determined that "homicide, which is often depicted as a unique sort of crime, appears to be merely one more aspect of a generally violent and criminal life" (Wright & Rossi, 1986, p. 72). If this is true, then it is apparent that drugs are also a part of this lifestyle.

That said, we simply do not know the extent to which any drug use operates in a causal fashion to influence homicide events. There do seem to be correlates between socioeconomic status, age, crime rates, and drug and alcohol use. The simultaneous occurrence of high crime rates and high rates of drug and alcohol use for certain groups in the population, however, can be considered only a coincidence in the absence of carefully developed theories and of rigorous empirical tests of those theories.

Directions for Future Research

The direction that future research should take depends on the desired outcome or result to be obtained from the knowledge gained. If we assume that one of the main reasons we want to understand the relationship of drugs to homicide is to prevent homicide or reduce homicide rates, then we clearly need an understanding of the way drugs and homicide are interrelated. For example, if Goldstein's systemic model is supported by empirical tests, this would indicate dramatically different public policy approaches than would support for a psychopharmacological model that links drugs and homicide.

Future research also needs to examine the different dimensions of victim drug involvement in homicide as well as offender drug involvement. How is victim drug use implicated in homicide? Does offender drug use interact with victim drug use? If so, in what ways? Which is more important to the outcome of the homicide event, victim drug use or offender drug use? How can we reconcile these questions with the notion of victim precipitation? The answers to these questions are needed to form a coherent theoretical explanation of the relationship between drugs and homicide.

In-depth interviews with homicide offenders seem to be the most promising direction in which to move for understanding the relationship between drugs and homicide. Problems with this approach, however, include the reluctance of homicide offenders to talk with researchers, as well as the possibility of unreliable information being provided by offenders because of upcoming trials or appeals. Addressing this issue, interviewers in the DREIM study were asked to determine how certain they were that the participants were truthful in their responses. In 13% of the cases, the researcher felt that the respondent was dishonest; most of the remaining cases were coded as "honest" (52%) or "somewhat honest" (29%). Overall, these results seem to indicate considerable room for unreliable information. Nevertheless, given the problems inherent in existing studies that use police records, as well as that homicide victims *cannot* be interviewed, the offenders are the best source we have for information about the circumstances that led up to the crime and the way that drug use may have been related. The types of questions posed above represent a considerable challenge to the social science community. Until we have answers to questions of this nature, however, the state of knowledge about the relationship between drugs and homicide will remain as it is now—largely descriptive and speculative.

■ *ALCOHOL AND HOMICIDE*

As suggested earlier, theorizing about the relationship between alcohol and homicide has fared somewhat better than that with regard to drugs and homicide. In part, this has been because of the legality, as opposed to the illegality, of alcohol as compared with most other drugs (although the relationship between prescription drugs and violence is understudied). Thus, it is possible to assess the extent of alcohol use and the distribution of alcohol outlets in a way that is not possible with regard to illegal drugs. In addition, alcohol is far more prominent in violence and homicide than are other drugs, perhaps because alcohol is so widely available as a legal drug. That alcohol seems to be more frequently involved in homicide than other drugs, however, does help to explain why research on this topic is more developed than that concerning the relationship between homicide and other drugs (Parker, 1993b). Two major efforts have theorized the link between alcohol and violence, one of which was specifically directed at homicide (Parker, 1993a, 1995; Parker & Rebhun, 1995), whereas the other was devoted to "intoxication and interpersonal aggression" (Fagan, 1990, p. 302).

Selective Disinhibition: Parker's Approach

Parker and Rebhun (1995) attempt to specifically link alcohol to homicide in an overall conceptual model that includes both a set of assumptions about how alcohol affects behavior and specific descriptions of how alcohol consumption interacts with other theories and models of homicide causation. Attempting to specify the underlying relationship between alcohol and violent behavior, Parker and Rebhun advance a theory of *selective disinhibition* (for an earlier statement of this model, see Parker, 1993a). This approach differs from that taken by earlier researchers who advanced a "disinhibition" model that was biologically based (see Room & Collins, 1983, for a review of that literature and the widespread criticisms applied to this notion). In the earlier conceptualization, alcohol as a biochemical agent had a universal effect on social behavior, thus ignoring evidence of the differential impact of alcohol, depending on the social and cultural contexts in which it is consumed (see Marshall, 1979, for examples of this point).

Parker and Rebhun (1995) advance their social disinhibition approach as one that endeavors to explain why violent behavior is "disinhibited" in relatively few cases, especially in light of the wide spectrum of behavior that takes place under the influence of alcohol. Instead, it appears that alcohol *selectively* disinhibits violence, depending on the characteristics of the situation, the actors involved and their relationships, the impact of bystanders, and so on. To place disinhibition into its cultural and social context, Parker and Rebhun's argument focuses on norms regarding the appropriateness of violence and on alcohol's role in determining which norms will be followed and which will become disinhibited. In U.S. society, norms about the appropriateness of violence in solving interpersonal disputes argue both for and against such behavior. Parker and Rebhun speculate that other things being equal, norms that have the least institutional support are the most likely to be disinhibited in a given situation. This aspect may, for instance, explain the frequent association between alcohol and spousal violence that has been noted in the family violence literature (e.g., Stets, 1990).

How does this interplay of conflicting norms about the use of violence in interpersonal disputes and alcohol work? We begin to address this question by assuming that behavior is goal directed, even under the influence of alcohol (see Parker & Rebhun, 1995; Pernanen, 1991); alcohol does have an impact on one's ability to pursue goals in a social situation, however, particularly in its impact on brain activity and thus on judgment and perception (see Leonard & Taylor, 1983; Pihl et al., 1993). In general, individuals are constrained from engaging in certain behaviors in a social situation by the norms that they have internalized; nevertheless, people do violate norms or, as this argument implies, have conflicting sets of norms to draw on in some situations.

With this in mind, Parker and Rebhun introduce the concept of *active and passive constraint.* In potentially violent situations, it takes active constraint—that is, a proactive and conscious decision not to use violence to "solve" the dispute—to constrain or preclude violence. Given alcohol's impact on judgment, in these situations alcohol will disinhibit norms that otherwise might prevent or constrain individuals from engaging in violent behavior. This is the case especially in situations in which violence is judged (albeit from an impaired viewpoint) as likely to result in successful resolution of a dispute. Thus, the *selective* nature of alcohol-related homicide is dependent on the interaction of an impaired rationality *and* the nature of the social situation. In many interpersonal disputes, including those under the influence of alcohol, even an impaired rationality dictates that violence not be used. This is an example of the operation of passive constraint and explains why most alcohol-involved interpersonal disputes do not result in violence and homicide.

Although these arguments have not been directly tested, Parker and Rebhun (1995) applied the logic of the selective disinhibition framework to some detailed case summaries of actual homicides from Wilbanks (1984); they found that these summaries by and large fit the selective disinhibition framework. In addition, Parker (1993a) and Parker and Rebhun examined the way alcohol relates to other theoretical concepts thought to cause homicide. For example, the relationship between homicide and economic deprivation, in both its absolute (poverty) and relative (inequality) forms, was reviewed, and hypotheses were advanced to explain the role alcohol might play in this relationship (see especially, Parker, 1993a). Similar arguments were made for subcultural theories (both southern and African American varieties), deterrence via capital punishment, and routine activities. Parker and Rebhun (pp. 44-48) further refined arguments about the link between poverty and alcohol as well as the link between routine activity and alcohol; they also advanced a perspective that linked social bonds (Hirschi, 1969; Krohn, 1991), alcohol use, and homicide. Ultimately, this approach includes both general theorizing about the relationship between alcohol and behavior, especially violent behavior, and specific theorizing about the role alcohol plays in concert with other important factors to cause homicide.

Empirical Tests of the Selective Disinhibition Framework

Several empirical tests of the approach taken by Parker (1993a) and Parker and Rebhun (1995) have been conducted to date. Using state-level data in a cross-sectional design circa 1980, Parker (1995) attempted to test the hypotheses generated earlier (1993a) concerning subcultural, deprivation, deterrence, and routine activities approaches. Parker further refined these hypotheses by making specific predictions about how five types of homicide—

robbery, other felony homicides, family intimate (spouse or partner) homicide, other family homicide, and primary nonintimate (friends, neighbors, and acquaintances) homicide—would respond to the newly integrated models. The models were tested for the main effects of alcohol consumption and for interactions between alcohol consumption and the theoretical concepts being analyzed.

The results of these analyses (Parker, 1995) indicated that alcohol consumption was a significant predictor of family intimate and primary nonintimate homicide, the two types of violence involving the closest interpersonal relationships. These are also relationships in which institutional support for norms against violence are, at best, moderate to weak. Thus, the results confirm the prediction that normative structures discouraging acts of violence in close personal relationships are most subject to breaking down under conditions of alcohol consumption.

In addition, a number of the specific interactions between alcohol and other factors were found to be statistically significant. For example, the impact of poverty on robbery and other felony homicides was stronger in states with above-average rates of alcohol consumption (Parker, 1995). It was also found that deterrence via capital punishment was most effective in states that had below-average rates of alcohol consumption, thus supporting the general notion that rational assessment of the costs and benefits of violence, including the possibility of a death sentence and an execution, was undermined by higher-than-average rates of alcohol consumption in a population. Support *was not* found, however, for the subcultural hypotheses advanced earlier (Parker, 1993a), suggesting that alcohol consumption could not be used to account for the observed relationships between region, racial composition, and homicide. Similarly, no support was found for the predictions based on routine activities.

Two additional and better-specified tests of the selective disinhibition approach have been provided (Parker & Rebhun, 1995). First, using city-level data in a longitudinal design to analyze data from 256 American cities, Parker and Rebhun reported evidence that alcohol availability helped to explain why homicide nearly tripled in these cities between 1960 and 1980. Also, the study found evidence of an interaction between alcohol availability and three factors—poverty, routine activities, and a lack of social bonds. The general thrust of these findings is that when alcohol availability is greater, the mechanisms linking homicide to these factors are strengthened, thus leading to higher-than-expected rates of homicide in those places with elevated alcohol availability.

In a second test of the general hypothesis that alcohol has a causal impact on homicide, Parker and Rebhun (1995) reported the results of a dynamic test of the impact of increases in the minimum drinking age on youth homicide at the state level. Using data from 1976 through 1983, Parker and Rebhun estimated a pooled cross section and time-series model in which two general types of homicide, primary and nonprimary (based on the prior relationship between victim and offender), in three age categories (15-18, 19-20, and 21-24) were analyzed. In the presence of other important variables, beer consumption was found to be a significant predictor in five of the six categories (two types by three age categories) of homicide rates; also, increases in the minimum drinking age were found to have a negative and significant impact on primary homicides. Both these outcomes were predicted by Parker and Rebhun from the theoretical model and the prior results described above.

In a final study of note, the selective disinhibition model was supported in a recent analysis of gender-specific homicide rates across 17 nations (Parker, 1998). This research investigated the relationships among drinking cultures, nature of alcohol consumption, the integration (or lack thereof) of alcohol into daily life, and the constellation of beverage types consumed in a society. The study argued that divorce rates would interact with drinking culture and alcohol consumption to increase homicide victimization because these relationships would increase the opportunities for active constraint to be overcome. The results indicated that divorce rates interacted with spirits consumption to increase homicide victimization rates among males and that divorce rates interacted with drinking culture to increase female homicide victimization.

Intoxication and Aggression: Fagan's Approach

In an attempt to cast the alcohol, drugs, and violence relationship in a broader light, Fagan (1990) presented a comprehensive approach by reviewing research and theoretical arguments from biological and physiological research, psychopharmacological studies, psychological and psychiatric approaches, and social and cultural perspectives. The review and ensuing discussion were framed to explore the effects of *intoxication* on violent behavior, rather than focusing on the effects of specific substances (alcohol, PCP, heroin, etc.).

Following an extensive review of studies from biological, physiological, and psychopharmacological approaches, Fagan (1990) concluded that this body of literature yielded little conclusive evidence of a link between the physiological impact of intoxicants and aggressive or violent behavior. Fagan found the literature on psychological approaches to be more fruitful, however, and identified areas in which a relationship between intoxication and violence is evident. In particular, he suggested that experimental studies have provided the strongest evidence of a relationship between psychological traits and aggression. Whether couched in the "teacher-learner" or "competition" paradigms, these studies administer doses, usually fairly low doses, to participants who then engage in a task that may elicit an aggressive response from the participant (see Taylor, 1993). In studies using a competitive design, alcohol use is consistently associated with increased aggression, whereas no association between alcohol and aggression is found in those using the noncompetitive teacher-learner paradigm. Fagan (1990) argued that these studies show the importance of social mediation, such that if the social situation provides an aggressive cue, alcohol (or other intoxicant) use leads to increased aggression. If the situation is nonconfrontational, alcohol is not associated with increases in aggression.

Having conducted this extensive review of a variety of research literatures and theoretical approaches to the intoxication and aggression relationship, Fagan (1990) then proposed an *integrated model* of the intoxicant-violence linkage. He argued that the most important areas of consensus from these different perspectives are that (a) intoxication has a significant impact on cognitive abilities and functioning and (b) the nature of this impact varies according to the substance used and is further moderated by social and cultural understandings of cognitive functioning, as well as understandings about the impact of intoxication on such abilities (e.g., expectancies). Fagan urged that these understandings be supplemented with a recognition of the importance of personality traits in mediating the relationship between intoxication and its impact on cognitive abilities and for the tendency of intoxicated individuals to have limited response sets to social interaction. In addition, Fagan maintained that two other intervening processes between intoxication and violence are the nature of the setting and social interaction itself and the absence or presence of formal and informal means of social control.

In critiquing Fagan's (1990) work, we note that despite the assertions that "understanding the intoxication-aggression relation may require several explanatory frameworks" and "theories that might explain the interaction of substance and expectancy should incorporate pharmacological, physiological, social psychological, cultural, and emotional (or cognitive) factors" (p. 288), his attempt at an integrative approach takes little from nonpsychosocial approaches. In addition, Fagan has proposed a general theoretical model that requires substantial revision to permit empirical testing. For example, arguing that intoxication results in changes in cognitive processing that condition physiological approaches and behavioral responses, or that cognitive changes are influenced by cultural and situational factors, is some distance from what would be required conceptually to design a test of this approach or to make a specific prediction about the nature of the relationship between cognitive processes, aggression, and intoxication. Arguing that the model is reciprocal in its processes is theoretically plausible and increases the face validity of Fagan's approach, but it also makes it difficult to properly specify a model to be estimated, even if some of the other specification and logical issues were to be resolved. Finally, the nature of *aggression,* the outcome measure to which Fagan continually refers, is a long way conceptually from specific acts of homicide, although there is certainly some relationship between these concepts. Further theoretical specification is needed to establish the linkages from aggression to homicide as well as from the antecedents of aggression to actual demonstrations of aggressive behavior.

Alcohol and Homicide: A Summary

What do we know about the relationship between alcohol and homicide? The state of knowledge here is more advanced than that reviewed previously with regard to drugs and homicide. In the case of alcohol, there have been at least two major attempts to develop a systematic, theoretical model based on prior research and on logical and careful theoretical analysis. First, Parker's (1993a) and Parker and Rebhun's (1995) attempts to specify the relationship with specific predictions about the relationship in various settings, relationships, and social contexts have resulted in a number of empirical tests. Findings from these suggest that alcohol is a causal agent, albeit one among many, in the genesis of homicide.

Second, Fagan's (1990) approach provides a more general explanation of Parker's selective disinhibition approach, given that both approaches argue that situational factors are paramount in understanding the impact of alcohol on individuals, on their behavior toward others, and on their interpretation of the meaning of the behavior of others with whom they interact. The majority of Fagan's best research evidence for his comprehensive model of the relationship between intoxication and aggression provides support for the Parker/Parker-Rebhun interpretation. Specifically, measures of alcohol availability, which are consistently predictors of individual consumption patterns, have been shown in longitudinal study designs to be related to changes in homicide rates at the aggregate level.

What we *do not* know about the alcohol and homicide relationship is the way in which the theoretical models just discussed operate in individual cases of homicide and other outcomes of interpersonal disputes, both violent and nonviolent. For example, if variation in alcohol availability influences homicide and other forms of violence, we need to examine in detail the places in which homicide and other violence occur in geographic space, with similarly detailed measures of the nature and level of social activities at or near these locations. The "hot spots" literature in criminology (e.g., Roncek & Maier, 1991; Sherman, Gartin, & Buerger, 1989) has confirmed that rates of violence vary dramatically across relatively small distances and spaces within communities. The extent to which this variation is due in part to alcohol availability and use has not been adequately addressed theoretically or empirically.

Needed to significantly advance our understanding of the alcohol-homicide relationship is a major data collection effort guided by a comprehensive model involving social, psychological, economic, cultural, and cognitive domains. Such a study should include extensive measures of alcohol (and other drug) use and abuse and allow researchers to follow respondents from adolescence into adulthood. Although an expensive undertaking, and one requiring careful design and measurement, such a study is feasible and would provide an excellent opportunity to examine the framework developed by Fagan. We need to know more about how cognitive functions are impaired and mediated in social settings and also about interactions involving drugs and alcohol that both did and *did not* result in violence. This type of design would address the selection bias present in almost all the empirical studies cited in this review and would help to more precisely delineate the impact of substance use and intoxication on the likelihood of homicide and other forms of violence.

■ *ISSUES IN RESEARCH AND POLICY*

We have argued that a major shortcoming of the current literature on the relationship between alcohol, drugs, and homicide is the lack of theoretical development. Discussions of the three major exceptions to this generalization, those of Goldstein (1985), Parker (1993a) and Parker and Rebhun (1995), and Fagan (1990), demonstrated both the advantages of such research and the difficulties that arise because more research has not been done on this relationship. In the case of Goldstein and Parker/Parker-Rebhun, the existence of some theoretical development resulted in empirical tests and a significant increase in knowledge about the relationship between homicide, drugs, and alcohol. Problems in these and in Fagan's approaches show that much more of this work is needed; the shortcomings of the empirical studies reviewed further underscore the utility of such work.

Our review of empirical studies further demonstrates the need to devote more energy to research design issues in the study of the relationship between drugs, alcohol, and violence. Despite the presence of earlier reviews indicating the same basic problems in this literature (e.g., Greenberg, 1981; Pernanen, 1981), weaknesses such as selection bias, too much aggregation, too little focus on context, a lack of controls, and, even more important, a lack of comprehensive and theoretically well-specified competing hypotheses models continue to characterize most research on this relationship.

On the other hand, the state of the field has advanced to the extent that we now have findings that relate changes in consumption and availability to rates of homicide. We thus can begin to make statements relevant to policy and predictions about the impact of changing policies on outcomes such as homicide and other forms of violence. As an example, the well-documented decreases in homicide rates and other forms of violence in large cities such as New York during the early and mid-1990s were preceded by a gradual and eventually significant decline in alcohol consumption in the United States that began in the early 1980s. Given some of the findings cited here, could we expect that some part of this decline in homicide is explained by the decline in alcohol consumption? In addition, the equally well documented change in police tactics suggests a connection between rates of violence (including homicide), public drunkenness, and street-level retail drug markets that encourage both sales and consumption. If the anticipated upswing in the numbers of young people that will begin in the late 1990s leads to an increase in homicide, will this be preceded by an increase in alcohol and drug consumption, as was the case in the 1960s and 1970s?

In short, researchers now have some evidence about the relationship between the use and abuse of substances such as alcohol and other drugs, and we can begin to advise policymakers and others about the likelihood that changes in the rates of use and abuse will have specific impacts on the rates of homicide and other forms of violence. A great deal of the detailed knowledge needed to appropriately advise policymakers and devise effective strategies, however, is dependent on our gaining a better understanding of both the theoretical linkages between alcohol and drugs and homicide and the increase in our empirical knowledge base that will result from such theoretical analyses. We have outlined in this chapter potentially fruitful avenues along both theoretical and empirical dimensions, and it is with considerable optimism that we look to the future of research on drugs, alcohol, and homicide.

■ *NOTES*

1. It is telling that Greenberg (1981) made an assessment of these methodological shortcomings in the then current research on alcohol and violence considerably prior to the current upswing in research interests on this relationship.

2. See Abel (1987); Fendrich et al. (1995); Garriott (1993); Kratcoski (1990); Langevin, Paitich, Orchard, Handy, and Russon (1982); Ray and Simons (1987); Spunt et al. (1995); Spunt et al. (1994); Tardiff et al. (1995); Welte and Abel (1989); and Wieczorek et al. (1990).

3. See Abel (1987); Fendrich et al. (1995); Goldstein et al. (1992); Spunt et al. (1995); Spunt et al. (1994); Yarvis (1994).

■ REFERENCES

Abadinsky, H. (1994). *Organized crime* (4th ed.). Chicago: Nelson-Hall.

Abel, E. L. (1987). Drugs and homicide in Erie County, New York. *International Journal of the Addictions, 22,* 195-200.

Bachman, R. (1991). The social causes of American Indian homicide as revealed by the life experiences of thirty offenders. *American Indian Quarterly, 15,* 468-492.

Barr, K. M., Farrell, M. P., Barnes, G. M., & Welte, J. W. (1993). Race, class, and gender differences in substance abuse: Evidence of middle-class polarization among Black males. *Social Problems, 40,* 314-327.

Blount, W. R., Danner, T. A., Vega, M., & Silverman, I. J. (1991). The influence of substance use among adult female inmates. *Journal of Drug Issues, 21,* 449-467.

Blount, W. R., Silverman, I. J., Sellers, C. S., & Seese, R. A. (1994). Alcohol and drug use among abused women who kill, abused women who don't, and their abusers. *Journal of Drug Issues, 24,* 165-177.

Brown, S. A. (1993). Drug effect expectancies and addictive behavior change. *Experimental and Clinical Psychopharmacology, 1,* 55-67.

Brownstein, H. H., Baxi, H., Goldstein, P., & Ryan, P. (1992). The relationship of drugs, drug trafficking, and drug traffickers to homicide. *Journal of Crime and Justice, 15,* 25-44.

Brumm, H. J., & Cloninger, D. O. (1995). The drug war and the homicide rate: A direct correlation? *Cato Journal, 14,* 509-517.

Daly, K. (1994). *Gender, crime, and punishment.* New Haven, CT: Yale University Press.

Fagan, J. (1990). Intoxication and aggression. In M. Tonry & J. Q. Wilson (Eds.), *Crime and justice: A review of research* (Vol. 13, pp. 241-320). Chicago: University of Chicago Press.

Fendrich, M., Mackesy-Amiti, M. E., Goldstein, P., Spunt, B., & Brownstein, H. (1995). Substance involvement among juvenile murderers: Comparisons with older offenders based on interviews with prison inmates. *International Journal of the Addictions, 30,* 1363-1382.

Garriott, J. C. (1993). Drug use among homicide victims: Changing patterns. *American Journal of Forensic Medicine and Pathology, 14,* 234-237.

Goldstein, P. J. (1985). The drugs-violence nexus: A tripartite conceptual framework. *Journal of Drug Issues, 14,* 493-506.

Goldstein, P. J., Brownstein, H. H., & Ryan, P. J. (1992). Drug-related homicide in New York: 1984 and 1988. *Crime & Delinquency, 38,* 459-476.

Goldstein, P. J., Brownstein, H. H., Ryan, P. J., & Bellucci, P. A. (1989). Crack and homicide in New York City, 1988: A conceptually based event analysis. *Contemporary Drug Problems, 16,* 651-687.

Goodman, R., Mercy, J. A., Loya, F., Rosenberg, M. L., Smith, J. C., Allen, N. N., Vargas, L., & Kolts, R. (1986). Alcohol use and interpersonal violence: Alcohol detected in homicide victims. *American Journal of Public Health, 76,* 144-149.

Greenberg, S. W. (1981). Alcohol and crime: A methodological review of the literature. In J. J. Collins, Jr. (Ed.), *Drinking and crime: Perspectives on the relationship between alcohol consumption and criminal behavior* (pp. 1-69). New York: Guilford.

Grube, J., Ames, G. M., & Delaney, W. (1994). Alcohol expectancies and workplace drinking. *Journal of Applied Social Psychology, 24,* 646-660.

Hanzlick, R., & Gowitt, G. T. (1991). Cocaine metabolite detection in homicide victims. *Journal of the American Medical Association, 265,* 760-761.

Hirschi, T. (1969). *Causes of delinquency.* Berkeley: University of California Press.

Klein, M. W., Maxson, C. L., & Cunningham, L. C. (1991). Crack, street gangs, and violence. *Criminology, 29,* 623-650.

Kratcoski, P. C. (1990). Circumstances surrounding homicides by older offenders. *Criminal Justice and Behavior, 17,* 420-430.

Krohn, M. D. (1991). Control and deterrence theories. In J. Sheley (Ed.), *Criminology: A contemporary handbook* (pp. 295-314). Belmont, CA: Wadsworth.

Langevin, R., Paitich, D., Orchard, B., Handy, L., & Russon, A. (1982). The role of alcohol, drugs, suicide attempts, and situational strains in homicide committed by offenders seen for psychiatric assessment. *Psychiatrica Scandivavica, 66,* 229-242.

Leonard, K. E., & Taylor, S. P. (1983). Exposure to pornography, permissive and nonpermissive cues, and male aggression toward females. *Motivation and Emotion, 7,* 291-299.

Lindqvist, P. (1991). Homicides committed by abusers of alcohol and illicit drugs. *British Journal of Addiction, 86,* 321-326.

Loftin, C. K., McDowall, D., & Wiersema, B. (1992). A comparative study of the preventive effects of mandatory sentencing laws for gun crimes. *Journal of Criminal Law and Criminology, 83,* 378-394.

Marshall, M. (Ed.). (1979). *Beliefs, behaviors, and alcoholic beverages: A cross-cultural survey.* Ann Arbor: University of Michigan Press.

Meiczkowski, T. M. (1996). The prevalence of drug use in the United States. In M. Tonry (Ed.), *Crime and justice: A review of research* (Vol. 20, pp. 349-414). Chicago: University of Chicago Press.

Miller, B. A., & Downs, W. R. (1993). The impact of family violence on the use of alcohol by women: Research indicates that women with alcohol problems have experienced high rates of violence during their childhoods and as adults. *Alcohol Health and Research World, 17,* 137-142.

Parker, R. N. (1993a). Alcohol and theories of homicide. In F. Adler & W. Laufer (Eds.), *Advances in criminological theory* (Vol. 4, pp. 113-142). New Brunswick, NJ: Transaction Publishing.

Parker, R. N. (1993b). The effects of context on alcohol and violence. *Alcohol Health and Research World, 17,* 117-122.

Parker, R. N. (1995). Bringing "booze" back in: The relationship between alcohol and homicide. *Journal of Research in Crime and Delinquency, 32,* 3-38.

Parker, R. N. (1998). Alcohol, homicide, and cultural context. *Homicide Studies, 2,* 6-30.

Parker, R. N., & Rebhun, L. (1995). *Alcohol and homicide: A deadly combination of two American traditions.* Albany: State University of New York Press.

Pernanen, K. (1976). Alcohol and crimes of violence. In B. Kissin & H. Beglieter (Eds.), *The biology of alcoholism: Social aspects of alcoholism* (pp. 351-444). New York: Plenum.

Pernanen, K. (1981). Theoretical aspects of the relationship between alcohol use and crime. In J. J. Collins, Jr. (Ed.), *Drinking and crime: Perspectives on the relationship between alcohol consumption and criminal behavior* (pp. 1-69). New York: Guilford.

Pernanen, K. (1991). *Alcohol in human violence.* New York: Guilford.

Pihl, R. O., Peterson, J. B., & Lau, M. A. (1993). A biosocial model of the alcohol-aggression relationship. *Journal of Studies on Alcohol* (Suppl. 11), 128-139.

Ray, M. C., & Simons, R. L. (1987). Convicted murderers' accounts of their crimes: A study of homicide in small communities. *Symbolic Interaction, 10,* 57-70.

Roncek, D. W., & Maier, P. A. (1991). Bars, blocks, and crimes revisited: Linking the theory of routine activities to the empiricism of hot spots. *Criminology, 29,* 725-754.

Room, R., & Collins, G. (Eds.). (1983). *Alcohol and disinhibition: Nature and meaning of the link* (Research Monograph 12). Washington, DC: National Institute on Alcohol Abuse and Alcoholism.

Sherman, L. W., Gartin, R. P., & Buerger, M. E. (1989). Hot spots of predatory crime: Routine activities and the criminology of place. *Criminology, 27,* 27-56.

Spunt, B., Brownstein, H., Goldstein, P., Fendrich, M., & Liberty, H. J. (1995). Drug use by homicide offenders. *Journal of Psychoactive Drugs, 27,* 125-134.

Spunt, B., Goldstein, P., Brownstein, H., Fendrich, M., & Langley, S. (1994). Alcohol and homicide: Interviews with prison inmates. *Journal of Drug Issues, 24,* 143-163.

Stets, J. E. (1990). Verbal and physical aggression in marriage. *Journal of Marriage and the Family, 43,* 721-732.

Tardiff, K., Marzuk, P. M., Leon, A. C., Hirsch, C. S., Stajik, M., Portera, L., & Hartwell, N. (1995). Cocaine, opiates, and ethanol in homicides in New York City: 1990 and 1991. *Journal of Forensic Sciences, 40,* 387-390.

Taylor, S. P. (1993). Experimental investigation of alcohol-induced aggression in humans. *Alcohol Health and Research World, 17,* 108-112.

Welte, J. W., & Abel, E. L. (1989). Homicide: Drinking by the victim. *Journal of Studies on Alcohol, 50,* 197-201.

White, H. R., Hansell, S., & Brick, J. (1993). Alcohol use and aggression among youth. *Alcohol Health and Research World, 17,* 144-150.

Widom, C. S., & Ames, M. A. (1994). Criminal consequences of childhood sexual victimization. *Child Abuse and Neglect, 18,* 303-318.

Wieczorek, W., Welte, J., & Abel, E. (1990). Alcohol, drugs, and murder: A study of convicted homicide offenders. *Journal of Criminal Justice, 18,* 217-227.

Wilbanks, W. (1984). *Murder in Miami: An analysis of homicide patterns and trends in Dade County, Florida, 1917–1983.* Lanham, MD: University Press of America.

Wolfgang, M. E. (1958). *Patterns in criminal homicide.* Philadelphia: University of Pennsylvania Press.

Wright, J. D., & Rossi, P. H. (1986). *Armed and considered dangerous: A survey of felons and their firearms.* Hawthorne, NY: Aldine.

Yarvis, R. M. (1994). Patterns of substance abuse and intoxication among murderers. *Bulletin of the American Academy of Psychiatry and the Law, 22,* 133-144.

PART V

Homicide Among Selected Populations

CHAPTER 13

What Can We Learn From Data Disaggregation?

The Case of Homicide and African Americans

■ *Darnell F. Hawkins*

When one surveys the numerous studies of homicide that have appeared during the last several decades, there is evidence of enormous advances in the knowledge of the nature and distribution of lethal violence within the United States. Investigations that span diverse social and geographic spaces and varying times have been conducted by criminologists, economists, geographers, historians, psychologists, sociologists, and others. Such studies have documented the spatial and temporal patterning of acts of homicide and the characteristics of individual perpetrators. More recently, public health professionals have made important contributions to this research tradition through their focus on the distribution of homicide victimization, a concern sometimes only implicitly addressed in earlier research. What has emerged is a vibrant, multidisciplinary enterprise that is likely to expand even further the knowledge of the etiology of homicide and what can be done to prevent it.

At the same time, a review of homicide studies also reveals unexpected patterns of redundancy and omission. Despite much progress, homicide studies have repeatedly covered the same ground while ignoring topics of potential significance. Few have achieved any of the great leaps forward envisioned by the earliest analysts of homicide such as Harrington Brearley (1932/1969) and Marvin Wolfgang (1958), whose research tradition is thoughtfully assessed in articles by Derral Cheatwood, Margaret Zahn, Carolyn and Richard Block, and Per-Olof Wikstrom in the *Journal of Crime and Justice* (1991).

Nowhere is the seeming lack of progress in homicide studies more evident than in that portion of the literature examining ethnic, racial, and social class differences in homicide victimization and offending. This literature is replete with studies at the national, state, and local levels that document comparatively high rates of homicide among some ethnic, racial, or class groups and lower rates among others. A close reading of that literature, however, reveals that researchers generally have failed to move beyond mere documentation to a more systematic examination of the causes of these disparities. Reasons for this failure range from the politics of American intergroup relations, to ideological and methodological blinders found among researchers, to the form in which official data are collected and reported (Hawkins, 1983, 1990).

The data and research to be discussed in this chapter are intended to address this void in the literature by providing examples of how future research on homicide might examine more thoroughly the nature and causes of ethnic, racial, and social class differences. These examples are focused largely on African Americans, a group whose patterns of homicide have been a frequent topic in homicide studies. In consistency with trends beginning to emerge in recent years, I suggest that the thoughtful disaggregation of homicide data into group-specific measures can provide useful and sometimes unexpected insights into the nature and causes of lethal violence. Ultimately, these insights can challenge conventional wisdom regarding the distribution of homicide within and across ethnic, racial, and social class lines.[1]

Some form of data disaggregation is a normal and expected part of the scientific research process. For example, in the social sciences, the search for subgroup and regional differences within larger populations and geographic areas is a disciplinary trademark. Social researchers are keenly aware that the building and testing of sound theory depend largely on the logic and integrity of such disaggregation. But it is also true that social researchers inevitably fall victim to the influences of prevailing societal norms and biases, disciplinary conventions and paradigms, and public policy mandates that permit and encourage some forms of comparison, disaggregation, and concomitant lines of inquiry while discouraging others. These same ideological and institutional forces lead the media and political figures to ignore findings from studies that avoid the problems that sometimes result from data aggregation. The effects of these societal and disciplinary forces are particularly evident for homicide studies that document Black-White disparities.

■ *BLACK-WHITE HOMICIDE DIFFERENCES: AN OLD AND NEW STORY*

For nearly a century, studies of homicide and crime in the United States have shown disproportionately high rates of homicide victimization and offending among African Americans as compared with other racial groupings. In one of the earliest investigations of homicide as a distinct form of social/criminal behavior, Brearley (1932/1969) reported that for the decade between 1918 and 1927, the mean annual homicide victimization rate for "colored" persons was almost seven times higher than the rate for Whites (p. 97). The White death rate was 5.32 per 100,000 persons as compared with a rate of 36.93 for the colored population. Because persons of African ancestry constituted about 96% of the colored population during this period and later, this composite non-White group statistic is often used as a proxy for the rate of homicide among African Americans. Whether Black homicide rates are estimated from rates for the colored population or calculated using the population of African Americans alone, the size of the Black-White gap has remained large during the nearly 80 years since 1918.

During most decades of the 20th century, there has been considerably more variability in homicide rates among Blacks than among Whites, with annual Black rates ranging from five to nine times the rates for Whites (e.g., Farley, 1980; Shin, Jedlicka, & Lee, 1977). The full range of this homicide victimization differential is evident even during the last 25 years. The Centers for Disease Control and Prevention (CDC) reported that for 1972, a year characterized by a rather sharp rise in the Black homicide rate, Blacks were about nine times more likely than Whites to be victims of homicide (43.3 versus 4.8 per 100,000). By 1983, following a decade of declining rates for Blacks and rate increases for Whites, the differential was 29.9 versus 5.6. For that year, Blacks were only five and one half times more likely than Whites to be homicide victims (CDC, 1986, p. 18). This ratio was maintained through 1988, when the Black rate was roughly six times that for Whites at 34.4 versus 5.9 per 100,000 (CDC, 1992, p. 7).

These rates were derived from death certification data provided to the CDC by the National Center for Health Statistics. Similar racial differentials, however, are observed in arrest and offender data supplied by the Federal Bureau of Investigation in its *Supplemental Homicide Reports* (*SHR*). Comparisons of *SHR* and death certification data by Rokaw, Mercy, and Smith (1990) and the CDC (1992) show that these two data sources provide similar calculations of the magnitude of racial differences in involvement in homicide. Both sources of homicide data will be used in this chapter to provide illustrations of the benefits of disaggregation.

The large homicide gap between Blacks and Whites is one of the most consistently and widely reported findings within homicide studies. Yet as the end of the 20th century approaches, discussions of the causes and correlates of racial disparities in homicide are similar to those taking place more than six decades ago. For example, before examining homicide rates and trends in the United States during the early 20th century, Brearley (1932/1969) offered these now familiar questions and public perceptions of the period:

> If homicide is a fairly accurate index of crime, do the people of the United States really live in "the most lawless of civilized nations," as is so frequently asserted? (p. 8)
>
> A citizen of the United States, especially one from the South, is likely to defend the homicide record of his country by laying a part of the blame upon the Negro. (p. 5)
>
> Is the high rate of homicide in the South due to the warm climate, to the presence of the Negro, or to other causes? (p. 8)

In response to these types of queries and others, Brearley and researchers such as Lottier (1938) and Pettigrew and Spier (1962) observed the following:

1. Homicide rates calculated for the entire United States conceal state, regional, and intergroup differences of substantial significance.
2. The South and border states have traditionally constituted one of the two geographic regions with above-average rates of homicide. The other region is the Far West.
3. States in New England and the northern part of the Middle West have comparatively low rates of homicide.
4. The statistical extraction of the colored population from death certification and offender statistics for the South and border states lowers their overall homicide rates but does little to alter the ranking of White southerners vis-à-vis Whites in other regions.
5. Blacks living in states in which the White population has a comparatively low rate of homicide have lower rates of homicide than Blacks living in states with high rates of homicide among Whites. The overall Black rate is consistently higher than the White rate, however. The lowest state rates for Blacks typically exceed the highest state rates for Whites.
6. Across all regions and among both Whites and non-Whites, homicide rates are generally higher in urban than in rural areas.

These observations have greatly influenced the direction of those homicide studies that have been the most attentive to matters of ethnicity, race, and class. The southern subculture of violence thesis is an obvious outgrowth of research in this tradition (Gastil, 1971; Hackney, 1969; Loftin & Hill, 1974; Reed, 1971; Smith & Parker, 1980). Although much controversy still surrounds the notion of a southern subculture of violence, the regional differences noted by Brearley and explored by advocates and opponents of the regional subculture thesis are still relevant for late 20th-century homicide studies.

Indeed, recent studies of youth violence by public health researchers echo many of the themes found in those investigations. An example is Fingerhut and Kleinman's (1990) use of mortality data to provide international and interstate comparisons of 1987 homicide rates among young males aged 15 to 24. Like Brearley (1932/1969), Fingerhut and Kleinman begin with the observation of higher rates of homicide among youths in the United States as compared with other nations. For the United States as a whole, they report a homicide rate of 21.9 per 100,000 youths in this age range. Among 21 other industrialized countries to which the United States was compared, Scotland, with a rate of 5 per 100,000, ranked a distant second. Austria and Japan's rates were lowest at less than 0.5 per 100,000.

Also like Brearley, Fingerhut and Kleinman (1990) noted that much of the difference between the United States and other countries can be attributed to the high rates of homicide found among Blacks. For example, the 1987 homicide victimization rate among 15- to 24-year-old Black males was 85.6 per 100,000, more than seven times the White rate of 11.2. The authors noted, however, that in only four states—Massachusetts, Ohio, Wisconsin, and Minnesota—were rates for young, White males as low as rates in the 21 comparison countries. Because most of these countries were in Europe, these data show that youthful Americans of European ancestry are more prone to lethal violence than their European counterparts.

In addition to these international contrasts, Fingerhut and Kleinman (1990) reported significant differences within the United States in rates of homicide among Black youths. Homicide rates for young Black males were found to be highest in Michigan, California, the District of Columbia, New York, and Missouri. They were lowest in North Carolina, Kentucky, Mississippi, South Carolina, and Ohio.

These findings are surprisingly similar to those of Brearley (1932/1969); among those states with reasonably large Black populations, rates of homicide for 1920 and 1925 ranged from a low of 18.52 per 100,000 in South Carolina to 88.91 in Michigan. Similar state differences in the rate of homicide among Blacks three decades later were also reported by Pettigrew and Spier (1962).

Studies such as these remind us that African American homicide rates and patterns are not uniform and invariable across geographic space. Yet most analyses of homicide have paid relatively little attention to explaining these types of regional variations. For example, nothing comparable with the southern subculture of violence theory has emerged to explain state differences in homicide for the Black population, although that thesis is said by some researchers to apply to the study of Blacks as well as Whites (Harries, 1990; Rose & McClain, 1990; Wolfgang & Ferracuti, 1967). When attention has been paid to the variability of Black homicide across states, attempts at explanation often appear to incorporate a type of "imitation" theory in which Blacks are seen to borrow the values and norms of those Whites with whom they have contact (Pettigrew & Spier, 1962). Other differences that distinguish sectors of the Black population are seldom considered.

Especially worthy of careful examination in this regard is the relationship between regional differences in rates of homicide and varying levels of socioeconomic well-being among both Blacks and non-Blacks. Hindering such an analysis, as every researcher in this area quickly finds, is a lack of official data that would allow researchers to incorporate indicators of socioeconomic status (SES) into their research designs. For example, apart from a recently incorporated measure of educational status of the deceased person on death certification reports, researchers are not able to ascertain the SES of homicide victims. Federal offender data sources contain no information on the SES of either offenders or victims. Similarly, the absence of census data that incorporate measures of ethnicity makes it impossible to identify and calculate population-based rates of homicide for those segments of both White and non-White populations in the United States who have historically shared a common nationality or culture.

The preceding discussion should make clear that we have much to learn about homicide within specific social groupings of people. Before discussing further the value of intragroup analyses for expanding our knowledge of homicide, let us examine in greater detail the problem of an overuse of Black-White comparisons among homicide investigators.

■ *MOVING BEYOND BLACK-WHITE COMPARISONS*

As in so many other areas of social research, homicide studies in the United States frequently have incorporated racial comparisons, but these have been limited largely to contrasts between Blacks and Whites. This has had an enormous impact on the way that homicide analysts, politicians, the media, and the general public tend to view the etiology and ecology of lethal acts of violence. That African Americans are the nation's largest non-White minority and in recent decades have been concentrated in urban areas helps explain this tendency, as well as the decision of official record keepers to compile data that encourage frequent use of a Black-White racial dichotomy. Also, the heyday of European immigration to the United States ended many decades ago, carrying with it the public interest in White ethnic differences that existed near the turn of the century.

Yet as several commentators have noted, the frequent use among social scientists of Black-White comparisons is as much a product of political exigency as a result of canons of science (Hagan & Peterson, 1995; Hawkins, 1993, 1994). As a tool of scientific investigation, the dichotomy has never been fully justified, especially in light of the ethnic and racial diversity that has historically existed in the United States. Further, as a research tool, comparisons of undifferentiated masses of Whites and Blacks limit our knowledge of differences both between and within groups in their rates of homicide. For instance, there is no clear theoretical basis to expect that race is a more significant predictor of group differences in homicide than are ethnicity, SES, place of residence, and similar attributes of offenders and victims and the environments in which they live. Also, it is unclear why some racial/ethnic comparisons are used much more frequently than others for the purposes of research.[2]

Although useful in some instances, Black-White contrasts as the mainstay of U.S. homicide studies are even less valid today than in the past. Racial and ethnic diversity has increased substantially in the nation during the last three decades. In many regions, non-Blacks and non-Whites now compose large segments of local populations. Clearly, samples and populations used in homicide studies should begin to reflect this increasing diversity.[3]

The value of including the diverse array of ethnic and racial groups found in the United States in homicide studies is obvious. Beyond the mere documentation of behavior differences across a wider array of groups, their inclusion will have important implications for the construction and testing of theory—especially those theories that have arisen in response to Black-White comparisons during the past. For instance, various theories (largely untested) have long held that Black-White differences in crime, violence, and other social behaviors can be attributed to differences in SES, cultural values, patterns of socialization, family life, levels of discrimination and oppression, place of residence, and so forth. The inclusion of multiple ethnic and racial groups will allow researchers to determine the extent to which these and other factors do or do not account for homicide rates currently found among Whites and various non-White groups in the United States and in other societies.

■ *COMPARISONS OF AFRICAN AMERICANS WITH OTHER NON-WHITE GROUPS*

Although relatively uncommon in the homicide literature, longitudinal and historical analyses may offer the best tests of the validity of competing explanations for group differences. It has long been noted, for example, that Americans of Chinese and Japanese ancestry living in the United States today and during the recent past tend to have relatively low rates of crime and violence (see Bonger, 1943; Flowers, 1988). Such rates are sometimes seen as incongruent because these groups, like African Americans, have been the frequent targets of racist and politically motivated discrimination and have encountered their own share of economic disadvantages (Flowers, 1988). How are the different homicide rates of these groups explained, especially in light of their seemingly similar experiences? A closer look at the social history of these groups offers us some insight.

In contrast to those of today, past studies of crime and social control among Chinese, Japanese, and African Americans painted a somewhat different picture of their comparative rates of crime and violence. Brearley (1932/1969) reported a homicide victimization rate of 22.7 per 100,000 for Japanese Americans during 1924, a rate slightly higher than that of American Indians (22.2). Rates for both groups were substantially higher than the rate for White Americans (5.3) but lower than that of African Americans (39.8). Brearley also found, however, that these same rates for Japanese Americans and American Indians were higher than those for the relatively large, colored (mostly Black) populations of Maryland, New Jersey, Massachusetts, Connecticut, Delaware, North Carolina, South Carolina, and Virginia in 1920 and 1925. Brearley also observed that as a result of tong warfare among Chinese Americans during 1924, their rate of homicide victimization for that year was 87.4 per 100,000 (pp. 98-99). Although this rate represented an unusual wave of conflict within the Chinese American community, it is a rate similar to that found among young Black males in the United States during recent years.

The historical record also provides other evidence of high levels of crime and punishment for Asian Americans. For example, DuBois (1904) reported Chinese Americans to have imprisonment rates higher than those of Blacks but similar to those of American Indians in 1890. Although some of the excess of Asian American criminality and punishment may be linked to a disproportionate presence of young males within their populations during these periods, as well as the adoption of laws and criminal justice practices specifically aimed at their social control, it also likely reflects their greater involvement in crime.

The studies cited above and others suggest that rates of crime, violence, and punishment among Asian Americans were closer to those of African Americans than to Whites during the late 1800s and into the early 20th century. Victimization data for both Japanese and Chinese Americans show that comparatively high rates of homicide have existed at various points in their history, despite the relatively low rates found among these groups today. Similarly, studies of White ethnic groups in the United States, such as the Irish, Greeks, and Italians, have shown substantially higher rates of violence in the past than today (Lane, 1979; Monkkonen, 1995). These changes through time also suggest a need for researchers to move beyond simple cross-sectional, Black-White quantitative analyses to explore the full range of social dynamics that are associated with varying levels of lethal aggression among a variety of ethnic and racial groups. Clearly, theories and explanations of ethnic and racial group differences must account for the rise and fall of crime and violence among Americans of both Asian and European ancestry as well as the continuing high rates among those of African, Latin American, and Native American ancestry (Hawkins, 1993).

Latino Homicide

An increasing trend toward including Latinos in contemporary studies of homicide may offer a similar check on the validity of theories that have been developed to explain high rates of Black homicide (for further discussion of Latino homicide, see Chapter 14 by Ramiro Martinez Jr. and Matthew Lee). Like Blacks, some groups of Latinos, particularly Mexican Americans, have a long history of economic and social marginality in the United States. During recent decades, homicide rates among Latinos, unlike those of most Asian Americans, have been closer to the rates of Blacks than to those of Whites. For example, the *Uniform Crime Reports* (*UCR*) for 1985 (as cited in Flowers, 1988, p. 45) showed the following homicide arrest rates per 100,000:

Black	28.5
Hispanic	15.1
Native American	7.7
White	4.1
Asian/Pacific	3.6

Similar racial differences in levels of homicide victimization were reported by the CDC (1986, p. 28). A CDC study of ethnic differences in states with large numbers of Hispanics—Arizona, California, Colorado, New Mexico, and Texas—reported the following homicide victimization rates per 100,000:

Black	46.0
Hispanic	21.6
Anglo	7.9

In some urban areas of the United States, rates of homicide offending and victimization among Latinos are even closer to those of Blacks, especially when only males are considered. For example, Block (1988) reported a victimization rate of 68.9 per 100,000 for Latino (mostly Mexican and Puerto Rican) males in Chicago during 1980; a rate of 84.5 was reported for non-Latino Black males. Rodriguez (1988) reported rates of 67.8 for Latino males and 95.3 for Black males in New York City during the same year (p. 78). Like rates for Whites and Blacks, those for Latinos also show variability across regions. Valdez and Nourjah (1988) found rates of only 46.0 per 100,000 Latino males in Southern California during 1980, as compared with a rate of 114.0 for Black males.

■ *EXPLAINING RACIAL AND ETHNIC DIFFERENCES*

Given the argument that a thoughtful disaggregation of data is important for the development and testing of credible theory, let us consider some of the theoretical implications of moving beyond Black-White analyses. I believe that the statistics presented above highlight the relevance (and reasons for the lack of closure) of the social structure versus culture/subculture debate perennially found among social scientists. A part of the logic of Black-White and other intergroup comparisons in U.S. homicide studies is that identifiable ethnic and racial groups vary in ways that are important for the differential social production of violent conduct. As the historical and contemporary data presented above attest, commonly held notions of what group attributes are most salient for the etiology of violence are not always supported.

One of the dominant etiological orientations evident in the work of those who study group differences in crime and violence is the tendency to focus on the importance of cultural and subcultural differences. That orientation is logical because researchers regularly use cultural markers to define, identify, and distinguish social groupings. Structural theorists, however, prefer to move beyond cultural identities and stress the need for understanding differences in socioeconomic inequality as a primary feature that separates and distinguishes various groupings of people.

Careful attention to group differences in rates of homicide, such as that advocated in this chapter, often reveals patterns of offending and victimization that challenge both subcultural and structural views. For instance, many groups that appear to share similar cultural attributes have dissimilar rates of crime and violence. A pertinent example is that both Asians and Hispanics in the United States have been described by social scientists as having more communal cultures than Americans of either European or African ancestry (Parrillo, 1994; Schaefer, 1993). Their family life is said to reflect this orientation and to differ from that of other ethnic/racial groups in the United States. This communalism is often cited as the source of the low rates of crime (including homicide) currently reported among persons of Asian ancestry in the United States. This same communalism, however, cannot account for the relatively high rates of Asian American crime and violence during the past or the contemporary rates seen among some groups of Hispanic ancestry.

Structural theorists, on the other hand, are quick to remind us that in modern, ethnically heterogeneous societies, minority groups, regardless of their racial, cultural, or ethnic backgrounds, have a lot in common. These commonalities include shared experiences of social and economic disadvantage and marginality, intergroup conflict, and exposure to hierarchies of political dominance and subordination. To the extent that these experiences and statuses are linked to the etiology of homicide, they are said to explain the comparatively high levels of violence found among many diverse subordinate groups, including White southerners and many White ethnic minorities in the United States. Similarly, as its status and exposure to disadvantage change through time, so may a group's disproportionate involvement in lethal violence. But it is also true that many groups who share seemingly similar levels of social control and economic disadvantage sometimes have dissimilar rates of involvement in crime and violence.

These types of observations and speculation are reminiscent of ideas emanating from Shaw and McKay's (1942) study of Chicago neighborhoods. They argued that factors associated with groups displaying above-average rates are not necessarily cultural in nature; instead, these groups are often characterized by social conditions that shape the lives of group members at given times and ecologic space. As Shaw and McKay documented, inner-city life was associated with high rates of crime among a variety of ethnic and racial groups in Chicago and other urban areas during the 1920s and 1930s. Groups who resided in "disorganized" areas tended to have high rates of involvement in crime regardless of their ethnic or racial backgrounds.[4]

The Utility of Within-Group Comparisons

The work of Brearley (1932/1969), Shaw and McKay (1942), and Wolfgang (1958) has shown the usefulness of both intergroup and within-group comparisons for the study of homicide. Although the intergroup studies have sometimes been flawed because of their overreliance on Black-White contrasts easily drawn from official homicide data, they are quite numerous. Within-group comparisons, however, have received much less scholarly and public attention. This is unfortunate, because knowledge of the causes of high rates of homicide among African Americans can be significantly improved through the use of well-designed studies of the distribution and patterning of homicide *within* the Black population (Hawkins, 1983). A similar call has been made for greater attention to comparative rates of homicide and crime for subgroups *within* populations of Americans of European, Asian, Native, and Latin American ancestry as a means of improving knowledge of the homicide phenomenon (Hawkins, 1993).

Given their preoccupation with Black-White differences, homicide studies of the last half century have largely ignored the considerable variation in rates of violence found among Blacks. This is somewhat surprising because as previously noted, many of these intragroup differences were among those cited by the earliest analysts of homicide. As discussed above, these include varying rates within the Black population that are associated with place of residence—southern versus nonsouthern and urban versus rural. Similarly, the now numerous studies of homicide in cities and metropolitan areas have shown considerably different rates for Blacks within or across these units of analysis. Some cities have *much* higher rates than others, revealing a range of variability that does not always comport to a contrast between the South (or West) and other areas.[5]

As Wilson (1987) and others have noted, these spatial contrasts in homicide rates among African Americans appear to be associated with the increasing socioeconomic differentiation that is evident in Black communities. The disappearance of jobs for unskilled workers has produced a large underclass. At the same time, civil rights reforms of the last three decades have led to an increasingly stable and larger Black middle class. Also largely unnoticed by many homicide researchers is the increasing ethnic diversification that has occurred in Black urban areas during the last two decades. Immigration from the Caribbean, Latin America, and Africa has led to large and distinctive subgroups within the Black population. Despite these unprecedented changes in the composition of the Black population in the United

States, little notice of such change and its implications for the study of lethal violence can be seen in most recent homicide studies. Clearly, measures of ethnic identity need to become a vital part of any serious attempt to understand the variations in homicide among Blacks in many U.S. cities.

The Effects of Place

The work of Rose and McClain (1990) represents one of the few within-group comparisons of the incidence of homicide among Blacks. Their studies of homicide trends and patterns in several large cities offer unique insights into the etiology of homicide within the Black population. As did Brearley (1932/1969) and Pettigrew and Spier (1962) in their studies of states, Rose and McClain discovered considerable variation in Black rates of homicide across various cities and areas *within* those cities. They posed a theory that emphasized the importance of place-specific sociopsychoeconomic stressors as contributing to higher rates of homicide by Blacks in some cities than in others and in some predominantly Black neighborhoods as compared with others. Like the work of earlier analysts, this study represents an innovation in homicide studies that deserves to be replicated and extended.

The value of pursuing further the empirical research and theory-building efforts of Rose and McClain (1990) can be seen in an informative study of youth violence by Fingerhut, Ingram, and Feldman (1992). As shown in Table 13.1, they too found substantial geographic and spatial variation in their analysis of homicide victimization for 15- to 19-year-old Black males in the United States during 1989.

Although victimization rates among Blacks were found to be considerably higher than those for Whites (not shown in Table 13.1) in all geographic areas, the firearm homicide rate for Black youths living in nonmetropolitan areas was *lower* than the rate for White youths found in the inner cities (15.5 versus 21.5). The elevated rates for inner-city White youths can be

Table 13.1 Homicide Victimization Rates for U.S. Black Males Aged 15 to 19, 1989

Area of Residence	*Firearm Homicides: Rate per 100,000*	*Nonfirearm Homicides: Rate per 100,000*
Metropolitan		
Core	143.9	10.4
Fringe	54.0	6.4
Medium size	63.1	7.4
Small	48.2	6.5
Nonmetropolitan	15.5	7.1

SOURCE: Fingerhut, Ingram, and Feldman, 1992, Table 1, p. 3049.

partly attributed to the practice of labeling both Anglos and Hispanics as Whites. It may also signal the emergence in some cities of concentrations of poor, non-Hispanic Whites who are plagued by the typical ills of inner-city life.

The public policy relevance of disaggregated analyses is suggested even more strongly by other findings reported in Fingerhut et al. (1992). For instance, the overall rate of firearm homicide for Black youths was 85.3 per 100,000 in 1989. This was 11.4 times the overall rate of 7.5 per 100,000 for White youths. Yet Black inner-city youths had a rate that was 9.3 times greater than that for nonmetropolitan Black youths, a sizeable within-group difference. To the extent that Black-White differences require explanation, so too does the large gap between inner-city, rural, and small-town Black youths. Does this gap result from urban-rural differences in levels of drug trafficking and associated gun-carrying behavior, as Blumstein (1995) has argued, or must other factors be considered?[6] Answers to questions of this nature await future research.

The Effects of Social Class

As previously noted, many attempts at explaining racial differences in rates of homicide stress the importance of socioeconomic inequality. Indeed, most of the ecological and areal studies of homicide that have shown the value of disaggregation (see note 1) use measures of socioeconomic inequality to attempt to explain Black-White differences in levels of offending and victimization. In comparison with Whites, Blacks are said to be more economically disadvantaged; therefore, they are more likely to be involved in acts of lethal aggression that arise from the psychosocial dynamics related to this disadvantage (e.g., Reiss & Roth, 1993). Researchers have shown far less interest in SES differences *within* the Black population, however, than in attempting to determine whether Blacks and Whites of similar SES have comparable rates of crime and violence. Reiss and Roth could locate only a handful of studies that probed the relationship between SES and homicide across racial groups, all of which were conducted by public health researchers rather than criminologists (Centerwall, 1984; Lowry, Hassig, Gunn, & Mathison, 1988; Muscat, 1988). On the basis of these studies, Reiss and Roth conclude, "At low socioeconomic levels, Blacks have much higher risks of becoming homicide victims than do Whites. At higher socioeconomic levels, the difference between Blacks and Whites disappears and even reverses in one of the studies" (p. 130).

The failure of researchers to probe more fully the link among race, social class, and homicide stems partly from a lack of consensus regarding the significance of socioeconomic inequality as a predictor of criminal involvement. Buttressed by evidence of weak correlations between measures of criminal offending, poverty, and inequality, Tittle and Villemez (1977) called into question the long-standing belief that persons who are poor commit crime at higher rates than do persons who are not poor. Sampson and Wilson (1995) labeled the evidence showing a relationship between social class and crime "weak at best" (p. 38), a conclusion many others have also reached. On the other hand, much of the weakness of the evidence can be attributed to a failure of researchers to design research protocols that are capable of adequately operationalizing and measuring the effects of socioeconomic inequality. Until such studies are conducted, the extent to which differences in social class explain racial and ethnic differences in rates of homicide will remain a matter of academic speculation and political debate.

Recently, researchers have begun to use traditional ecological approaches to provide new insights into the effects of socioeconomic disparities on ethnic and racial differences in rates of homicide and other violence. Most of these analysts also are attentive to the study of within-group differences, especially those found across segments of the Black population. Much of this work has been inspired by the observations of William Julius Wilson (1987) on the plight and criminality of the Black urban underclass. The effort to link the economic conditions of these communities with high levels of involvement in crime is clearly evident in a recent chapter in which Sampson and Wilson (1995) advance a theory of race and crime that incorporates both structural and cultural concepts. Support for their theory has been provided through Krivo and Peterson's (1996) finding that the sources of violent and property crime are invariant across race and are rooted largely in the structural differences among communities that they studied in Columbus, Ohio. Also, Parker and McCall (1997) report similar results when studying the differential effects of economic deprivation, racial inequality, segregation, and labor market opportunities on racially disaggregated homicide rates in 80 U.S. cities. (For related work in this area, see Shihadeh & Flynn, 1996; Shihadeh & Steffensmeier, 1994.)

■ *RACE AND HOMICIDE: RESULTS FROM A COUNTY-LEVEL ANALYSIS*

Disaggregation of data to the county level has been used only rarely by criminologists to study homicide. Most homicide studies have used states or cities as units of analysis, although recent investigations have sometimes compared multicounty metropolitan areas. Given their focus on the victims of homicide and their use of death certification statistics, county-level analyses currently are more likely to be conducted by public health researchers or government agencies such as the CDC. Results from some of this work suggest that county-

Table 13.2 Counties With Less Than 10,000 Persons: Highest 10 Age-Adjusted Homicide Rates per 100,000, 1979 to 1987

County	*State*	*Rate*
1. Todd	South Dakota	48.03
2. Corson	South Dakota	33.22
3. Wolfe	Kentucky	25.22
4. Menominee	Wisconsin	24.72
5. Lafayette	Arkansas	24.70
6. Sioux	North Dakota	24.68
7. Stewart	Georgia	24.38
8. Atkinson	Georgia	23.56
9. Jefferson	Mississippi	22.89
10. Treutlen	Georgia	22.82

Table 13.3 Counties With Populations Between 10,001 and 20,000: Highest 10 Adjusted Homicide Rates per 100,000, 1979 to 1987

County	*State*	*Rate*
1. Shannon	South Dakota	41.93
2. Lowndes	Alabama	33.41
3. Marion	Texas	27.04
4. Early	Georgia	26.72
5. East Carroll	Louisiana	26.57
6. Glacier	Montana	26.52
7. Wilcox	Alabama	25.26
8. Terrell	Georgia	24.22
9. Greene	Alabama	24.12
10. Alexander	Illinois	23.87

Table 13.4 Counties With Population Between 20,001 and 30,000: Highest 10 Adjusted Homicide Rates per 100,000, 1979 to 1987

County	*State*	*Rate*
1. Okeechobee	Florida	25.30
2. Burke	Georgia	25.23
3. Hendry	Florida	24.74
4. Pemiscot	Missouri	24.25
5. Holmes	Mississippi	24.12
6. Grenada	Mississippi	22.58
7. Clay	Kentucky	22.40
8. Macon	Alabama	20.91
9. Toombs	Georgia	19.95
10. Yazoo	Mississippi	19.74

Table 13.5 Counties With Population Between 30,001 and 50,000: Highest 10 Adjusted Homicide Rates per 100,000, 1979 to 1987

County	*State*	*Rate*
1. Perry	Kentucky	27.46
2. Coahoma	Mississippi	24.12
3. Rio Arriba	New Mexico	23.49
4. LeFlore	Mississippi	23.29
5. McCurtain	Oklahoma	21.94
6. Bolivar	Mississippi	21.19
7. Phillips	Arkansas	20.63
8. Rusk	Texas	20.42
9. Crittenden	Arkansas	20.38
10. Franklin	North Carolina	20.07

level analyses represent an underused and potentially useful tool to enhance the understanding of the social determinants and correlates of homicide, including the ethnic, race, and social class dimensions of lethal violence.

In 1992, I obtained from the CDC a set of county-level homicide victimization data for 1979 through 1987. Using the total number of homicides for the entire period and average annual population figures, I calculated homicide rates per 100,000 persons for all U.S. counties. Because a large number of counties reported no deaths during this period, the most informative analysis involved the study of counties with the highest homicide rates. The investigation reported here involved comparisons among all U.S. counties with rates of victimization that exceeded the 90th percentile for the nation. Further, because these counties varied considerably along the dimension of population size, they were grouped from smallest to largest.

Tables 13.2 through 13.8 provide a listing and characteristics of the 10 counties with the highest rates of homicide in each of seven population size groupings. In the smallest population category (Table 13.2), states with less than eight total deaths during the period were excluded from the analysis to avoid the rate calculation distortion that results from a small number of cases.

For context, it is useful to compare these county rates with total and race-specific rates

Table 13.6 Counties With Population Between 50,001 and 250,000: Highest 10 Adjusted Homicide Rates per 100,000, 1979 to 1987

County	*State*	*Rate*
1. Chatham	Georgia	21.17
2. Washington	Mississippi	20.26
3. Lauderdale	Mississippi	19.94
4. Wyandotte	Kansas	19.52
5. Tangipahoa	Louisiana	19.20
6. Robeson	North Carolina	18.83
7. Liberty	Texas	18.54
8. Ector	Texas	18.51
9. Collier	Florida	18.01
10. Potter	Texas	17.90

Table 13.7 Counties With Population Between 250,000 and 1,000,000: Highest 10 Adjusted Rates per 100,000, 1979 to 1987

County	*State*	*Rate*
1. St Louis City*	Missouri	51.68
2. Orleans	Louisiana	40.58
3. Baltimore City*	Maryland	31.41
4. Fulton	Georgia	29.15
5. Washington*	D.C.	28.84
6. St. Clair	Illinois	23.38
7. Caddo	Louisiana	21.64
8. Lake	Indiana	21.59
9. Mobile	Alabama	20.79
10. Jefferson	Alabama	20.28

*Some cities are units of analysis in the federal mortality (NCHS) data set.

for the entire United States during the same period. The CDC (1992, p. 7) reported the following rates per 100,000 for 1979 to 1987:

	Highest Rates	Lowest Rates
Nation	10.7	8.3
Whites	7.0	5.4
Blacks	38.4	28.7

Given these figures, Tables 13.2 and 13.3 reveal a pattern of high rates of mortality in some of the nation's small, rural counties. Rates for counties with less than 20,000 are much closer to those of large metropolitan counties (Tables 13.7 and 13.8) than they are to the more intermediate-sized counties (Tables 13.4 through 13.6). Consistent with past research, a

Table 13.8 Counties With Population Over 1,000,000: Highest 10 Adjusted Rates per 100,000, 1979 to 1987

County	*State*	*Rate*
1. Bronx	New York	36.73
2. Wayne	Michigan	32.84
3. Dade	Florida	29.50
4. Kings	New York	27.45
5. New York	New York	27.01
6. Harris	Texas	25.54
7. Philadelphia	Pennsylvania	23.26
8. Dallas	Texas	21.33
9. Bexar	Texas	19.71
10. Los Angeles	California	19.70

disproportionate number of these counties are found in the South. Although elevated rates of homicide in some counties can be linked to the presence of Blacks, in other counties they result from White southern violence. Further, county-level data on the extent of poverty on these counties reveal patterns of socioeconomic distress similar to that found in the nation's inner cities. For example, among the 10 counties listed in Table 13.2, the proportion of residents in poverty ranged from 15% in Menominee County, Wisconsin, to 39% in Todd County, South Dakota.

The figures shown in Tables 13.2 and 13.3 also highlight to a much greater extent than state- or city-level data the relatively high rates of homicide found among Native Americans. Rates for counties in the Dakotas, Montana, and Wisconsin reflect the incidence of homicide on Indian reservations or other enclaves. Additional race-specific data obtained from the CDC also illustrate the extent to which relatively high rates among some groups of Latinos may contribute to the rates observed in Table 13.8.

The question of the contribution that the presence of African Americans makes to the rates observed in Tables 13.2 through 13.8 has been a critical issue in homicide studies. As noted earlier, however, researchers must begin to pay more attention to the distribution of homicide within the Black population. The importance of this strategy is illustrated in Table 13.9. Computed from the same CDC county-level information, Table 13.9 shows the

Table 13.9 Counties With the 25 Highest Rates of Age-Adjusted Homicide Rates per 100,000 Among Blacks, 1979 to 1987

*County**	*State*	*Average Annual Black Population*	*Rate*
1. Wayne	Michigan	827,416	72.13
2. St. Clair	Illinois	76,728	69.73
3. Lubbock	Texas	18,821	66.17
4. Montgomery	Kansas	2,378	64.83
5. Pemiscot	Missouri	6,730	64.28
6. Dade	Florida	322,318	63.05
7. Lake	Indiana	127,105	62.68
8. Potter	Texas	8,336	61.99
9. Okeechobee	Florida	2,240	61.58
10. Los Angeles	California	997,579	61.16
11. Jackson	Georgia	2,614	58.61
12. St. Lucie	Florida	23,341	58.16
13. Indian River	Florida	7,937	57.86
14. Madera	California	2,238	57.62
15. Hot Spring	Arkansas	3,224	57.50
16. Henderson	North Carolina	2,088	56.76
17. Randolph	Alabama	4,861	56.47
18. Jackson	Missouri	130,300	56.24
19. Early	Georgia	5,871	55.65
20. Rusk	Texas	8,851	55.64
21. Gwinnett	Georgia	4,506	55.46
22. Mahoning	Ohio	41,563	54.95
23. Dallas	Texas	316,796	54.72
24. Treutlen	Georgia	2,056	54.51
25. Bibb	Alabama	3,546	54.16

*This listing excludes three units that are essentially cities or a portion of a city: St. Louis with a rate of 92.56, New Orleans with a rate of 59.03, and New York City (Manhattan only) with a rate of 56.84.

25 counties with the highest rates of homicide victimization among Blacks. Perhaps the most notable finding to emerge from this table is the considerable diversity of regions and population sizes that characterizes these counties. As well, many of the counties in Table 13.9 are found in Tables 13.2 through 13.8 and include counties in which Native Americans and Whites (a classification that includes Latinos) also suffer disproportionately high rates of deaths from homicide.

This diversity clearly is at odds with contemporary media coverage and perceptions of the distribution of homicide in the United States. The rates shown in Table 13.9 suggest that although the disproportionate incidence of homicide among urban, inner-city Blacks is a serious problem that warrants concern, a more complete and accurate portrait and analysis of homicide among Blacks must include attention to similar levels of offending and victimization in small towns and rural America. Greater scrutiny of such areas will also reveal the plight of other groups whose high levels of homicide go unnoticed because they do not live in metropolitan areas that are subject to both the glare of the media and intense scrutiny by academic researchers. Ultimately, these statistics should remind us that the problem of homicide in America extends far beyond the boundaries of the inner rings of the nation's largest cities and well beyond the experiences of just the African American community.

■ *CONCLUSION*

A recurrent theme of this chapter is that more complex analytic approaches are needed to probe many of the conceptual and theoretical issues surrounding the study of homicide, particularly among African Americans. Analyses such as the county-level research discussed here can serve a potentially useful purpose by demonstrating that homicide in the United States is characterized by considerably more spatial and etiological complexity, ethnic and racial diversity of victims and offenders, and potentially competing public policy demands than are commonly evident in either mass media accounts or in some media-driven homicide studies conducted by academic researchers.

At the same time, these studies also remind us that lethal violence is not a random event; death from homicide appears to be a much more likely event among some groups than others, only one of which is the racial/ethnic category of African American. Attention to this theoretical and methodological complexity through the use of disaggregated analyses should become a feature that regularly guides future research.

■ *NOTES*

1. A substantial literature has appeared during the last several decades in which various forms of disaggregation and reaggregation were used to examine the distribution and

correlates of crime in the United States. In the most recent period, such studies have taken the form of multivariate analyses of crime patterns across states, metropolitan areas, or cities. These largely have been ecological or areal analyses. Representative works that have been particularly attentive to the study of homicide are Bailey (1984); Blau and Blau (1982); Corzine and Huff-Corzine (1992); Land, McCall, and Cohen (1990); Loftin and Hill (1974); Messner (1983); Messner and Golden (1992); Parker and Smith (1979); Sampson (1985, 1987); Sampson and Groves (1989); Smith (1992); and Williams and Flewelling (1988). Inevitably, most of these studies have had to confront the question of what accounts for ethnic, race, and social class differences. In doing so, they have provided useful insights into the nature and causes of such differences. Nevertheless, I suggest that future studies of this type might benefit from many of the observations made in this chapter.

2. Social researchers frequently blame governmental agencies for the absence of data on ethnic background and SES. Researchers often portray themselves as unable to significantly alter the bureaucratic forces that shape data collection efforts. But the true relationship between scientific research and official record-keeping practices may be said to resemble a Catch-22 decision-making pattern with which researchers are not completely uninvolved. For example, although most researchers would like a greater variety of information concerning the characteristics of homicide victims and offenders, a more frequent use by these analysts of diverse comparisons may encourage the collection by agencies of data in that form.

3. The value of including a diverse array of gender, racial, and ethnic groups is becoming evident in biomedical research. So is attentiveness to intragroup variation. A recent study on the regional and social class distribution of cardiovascular disease for the first time showed the extent to which ethnicity, place of birth, and social class affected death rates found among sectors of the African American population (Fang, Madhavan, & Alderman, 1996).

4. Informative and innovative empirical and theoretical work on the link between social disorganization and crime is currently being conducted; for example, see Bursik (1988), Sampson and Groves (1989), Sampson and Lauritsen (1993), and Sampson and Wilson (1995). Although most of this work has maintained the traditional focus on explaining Black-White differences, it has much potential as an approach by which to study other ethnic and racial contrasts.

5. Some recent homicide analysts have turned their attention to the problem of inner-city violence. Rather than contrasting inner- versus outer-city or suburban differences within the Black population, however, these areal contrasts frequently are used only to compare the Black population with Whites.

6. It is widely accepted among criminologists that rates of crime are higher in urban than in rural areas. It is also known that homicide rates are often high in some rural areas, especially in the South and West, particularly among Blacks. Brearley (1932/1969), for instance, found that Black rural rates were near or exceeded urban rates in 6 of the 40 states for which he was able to obtain data (p. 99).

■ *REFERENCES*

Bailey, W. C. (1984). Poverty, inequality, and city homicide rates: Some not so unexpected findings. *Criminology, 22,* 531-550.

Blau, J. R., & Blau, P. M. (1982). The cost of inequality: Metropolitan structure and violent crime. *American Sociological Review, 14,* 114-129.

Block, C. R. (1988). Lethal violence in the Chicago Latino community, 1965 to 1981. In J. Kraus, S. Sorenson, & P. Juarez (Eds.), *Proceedings of research conference on violence and homicide in Hispanic communities, September 14-15, 1987* (pp. 31-66). Los Angeles: University of California.

Block, C. R., & Block, R. L. (1991). Beginning with Wolfgang: An agenda for homicide research. *Journal of Crime and Justice, 14,* 31-70.

Blumstein, A. (1995). Youth violence, guns, and the illicit-drug industry. *Journal of Criminal Law and Criminology, 86,* 10-36.

Bonger, W. (1943). *Race and crime.* New York: Columbia University Press.

Brearley, H. C. (1969). *Homicide in the United States.* Montclair, NJ: Patterson Smith. (Original work published 1932)

Bursik, R. J., Jr. (1988). Social disorganization and theories of crime and delinquency: Problems and prospects. *Criminology, 26,* 519-552.

Centers for Disease Control and Prevention. (1986). *Homicide surveillance: High-risk racial and ethnic groups: Blacks and Hispanics, 1970 to 1983.* Atlanta, GA: Author.

Centers for Disease Control and Prevention. (1992, May 29). Homicide surveillance: United States, 1979-1988. *CDC Surveillance Summaries, 41*(SS-3), 1-34. (Suppl. to *Morbidity and Mortality Weekly*)

Centerwall, B. S. (1984). Race, socioeconomic status, and domestic homicide, Atlanta, 1971-2. *American Journal of Public Health, 74,* 813-815.

Cheatwood, D. (1991). Doing the work of research: Wolfgang's foundation and beyond. *Journal of Crime and Justice, 14,* 3-15.

Corzine, J., & Huff-Corzine, L. (1992). Racial inequality and Black homicide: An analysis of felony, nonfelony, and total rates. *Journal of Contemporary Criminal Justice, 8,* 150-165.

DuBois, W. E. B. (Ed.). (1904). Some notes on Negro crime, particularly in Georgia. *Proceedings of the Ninth Atlanta Conference for the Study of Negro Problems.* Atlanta, GA: Atlanta University Press.

Fang, J., Madhavan, S., & Alderman, M. H. (1996). The association between birthplace and mortality from cardiovascular causes among Black and White residents of New York City. *New England Journal of Medicine, 335,* 1545-1551.

Farley, R. (1980). Homicide trends in the United States. *Demography, 17,* 177-188.

Fingerhut, L. A., Ingram, D. D., & Feldman, J. J. (1992). Firearm and nonfirearm homicide among persons 15 through 19 years of age: Differences by level of urbanization, United States, 1979 through 1989. *Journal of the American Medical Association, 267,* 3048-3053.

Fingerhut, L. A., & Kleinman, J. C. (1990). International and interstate comparisons of homicide among young males. *Journal of the American Medical Association, 263,* 3292-3295.

Flowers, R. B. (1988). *Minorities and criminality.* New York: Greenwood.

Gastil, R. (1971). Homicide and a regional culture of violence. *American Sociological Review, 36,* 412-427.

Hackney, S. (1969). Southern violence. *American Historical Review, 39,* 906-925.

Hagan, J., & Peterson, R. D. (1995). Criminal inequality in America. In J. Hagan & R. D. Peterson (Eds.), *Crime and inequality* (pp. 14-36). Stanford, CA: Stanford University Press.

Harries, K. D. (1990). *Serious violence.* Springfield, IL: Charles C Thomas.

Hawkins, D. F. (1983). Black and White homicide differentials: Alternatives to an inadequate theory. *Criminal Justice and Behavior, 10,* 407-440.

Hawkins, D. F. (1990). Explaining the Black homicide rate. *Journal of Interpersonal Violence, 5,* 151-163.

Hawkins, D. F. (1993). Crime and ethnicity. In B. Forst (Ed.), *The socio-economics of crime and justice* (pp. 89-120). Armonk, NY: M. E. Sharpe.

Hawkins, D. F. (1994). The analysis of racial disparities in crime and justice: A double-edged sword. In *Enhancing capacities and confronting controversies in criminal justice* (NCJ-145318; pp. 48-49). Washington, DC: U.S. Department of Justice.

Krivo, L. J., & Peterson, R. D. (1996). Extremely disadvantaged neighborhoods and urban crime. *Social Forces, 75,* 619-648.

Land, K. C., McCall, P. L., & Cohen, L. E. (1990). Structural covariates of homicide rates: Are there any invariances across time and social space? *American Journal of Sociology, 95,* 922-963.

Lane, R. (1979). *Violent death in the city: Suicide, accident and murder in nineteenth century Philadelphia.* Cambridge, MA: Harvard University Press.

Loftin, C., & Hill, R. H. (1974). Regional subculture and homicide: An examination of the Gastil-Hackney thesis. *American Sociological Review, 39,* 714-724.

Lottier, S. (1938). Distribution of criminal offenses in sectional regions. *Journal of Criminal Law, Criminology and Police Science, 29,* 329-344.

Lowry, P. W., Hassig, S., Gunn, R., & Mathison, J. (1988). Homicide victims in New Orleans: Recent trends. *American Journal of Epidemiology, 128,* 1130-1136.

Messner, S. F. (1983). Regional and racial effects on the urban homicide rate: The subculture of violence revisited. *American Journal of Sociology, 88,* 997-1007.

Messner, S. F., & Golden, R. M. (1992). Racial inequality and racially disaggregated homicide rates: An assessment of alternative theoretical explanations. *Criminology, 30,* 421-447.

Monkkonen, E. (1995). Racial factors in New York City homicides. In D. F. Hawkins (Ed.), *Ethnicity, race, and crime: Perspectives across time and place* (pp. 99-120). Albany: State University of New York Press.

Muscat, J. E. (1988). Characteristics of childhood homicide in Ohio, 1974-84. *American Journal of Public Health, 78,* 822-824.

Parker, K. F., & McCall, P. L. (1997). Adding another piece to the inequality-homicide puzzle: The impact of structural inequality on racially disaggregated homicide rates. *Homicide Studies, 1,* 35-60.

Parker, R. N., & Smith, M. D. (1979). Deterrence, poverty, and type of homicide. *American Journal of Sociology, 85,* 614-624.

Parrillo, V. N. (1994). *Strangers to these shores: Race and ethnic relations in the United States* (4th ed.). New York: Macmillan.

Pettigrew, T. F., & Spier, R. B. (1962). The ecological structure of Negro homicide. *American Journal of Sociology 67,* 621-629.

Reed, J. (1971). To live and die in Dixie: A contribution to the study of southern violence. *Political Science Quarterly, 86,* 429-443.

Reiss, A. J., Jr., & Roth, J. A. (Eds.). (1993). *Understanding and preventing violence: Vol. 3. Social influences.* Washington, DC: National Academy Press.

Rodriguez, O. (1988). Hispanics and homicide in New York City. In J. Kraus, S. Sorenson, & P. Juarez (Eds.), *Proceedings of research conference on violence and homicide in Hispanic communities, September 14-15, 1987* (pp. 67-84). Los Angeles: University of California.

Rokaw, W. M., Mercy, J., & Smith, J. C. (1990). Comparing death certificate data with FBI crime reporting statistics on U.S. homicides. *Public Health Reports, 105,* 447-555.

Rose, H. M., & McClain, P. D. (1990). *Race, place, and risk: Black homicide in urban America.* Albany: State University of New York Press.

Sampson, R. J. (1985). Race and criminal violence: A demographically disaggregated analysis of urban homicide. *Crime & Delinquency, 31,* 47-82.

Sampson, R. J. (1987). Urban Black violence: The effect of male joblessness and family disruption. *American Journal of Sociology, 93,* 348-382.

Sampson, R. J., & Groves, W. B. (1989). Community structure and crime: Testing social disorganization theory. *American Journal of Sociology, 94,* 774-802.

Sampson, R. J., & Lauritsen, J. (1993). Violent victimization and offending: Individual-, situational-, and community-level risk factors. In A. J. Reiss Jr. & J. A. Roth (Eds.), *Understanding and preventing violence: Vol. 3. Social influences* (pp. 1-114). Washington, DC: National Academy Press.

Sampson, R. J., & Wilson, W. J. (1995). Toward a theory of race, crime, and urban inequality. In J. Hagan & R. D. Peterson (Eds.), *Crime and inequality* (pp. 37-54). Stanford, CA: Stanford University Press.

Schaefer, R. T. (1993). *Racial and ethnic groups* (5th ed.). New York: HarperCollins.

Shaw, C., & McKay, H. (1942). *Juvenile delinquency and urban areas.* Chicago: University of Chicago Press.

Shihadeh, E. S., & Flynn, N. (1996). Segregation and crime: The effect of Black social isolation on the rates of Black urban violence. *Social Forces, 74,* 1325-1352.

Shihadeh, E. S., & Steffensmeier, D. J. (1994). Economic inequality, family disruption, and urban Black violence: Cities as units of stratification and social control. *Social Forces, 73,* 729-751.

Shin, Y., Jedlicka, D., & Lee, E. S. (1977). Homicide among Blacks. *Phylon, 39,* 399-406.

Smith, M. D. (1992). Variations in correlates of race-specific urban homicide rates. *Journal of Contemporary Criminal Justice, 8,* 137-149.

Smith, M. D., & Parker, R. N. (1980). Type of homicide and variation in regional rates. *Social Forces, 59,* 136-147.

Tittle, C., & Villemez, W. J. (1977). Social class and criminality. *Social Forces, 56,* 474-502.

Valdez, R. B., & Nourjah, P. (1988). Homicide in Southern California, 1966-1985: An examination based on vital statistics data. In J. Kraus, S. Sorenson, & P. Juarez (Eds.), *Proceedings of research conference on violence and homicide in Hispanic communities, September 14-15, 1987* (pp. 85-100). Los Angeles: University of California.

Wikstrom, P. H. (1991). Cross-national comparisons and context specific trends in criminal homicide. *Journal of Crime and Justice, 14,* 71-95.

Williams, K. R., & Flewelling, R. L. (1988). The social production of criminal homicide: A comparative study of disaggregated rates in American cities. *American Sociological Review, 54,* 421-431.

Wilson, W. J. (1987). *The truly disadvantaged: The inner city, the underclass and public policy.* Chicago: University of Chicago Press.

Wolfgang, M. E. (1958). *Patterns in criminal homicide.* Philadelphia: University of Pennsylvania Press.

Wolfgang, M. E., & Ferracuti, F. (1967). *The subculture of violence.* London: Tavistock.

Zahn, M. A. (1991). The Wolfgang model: Lessons for homicide research in the 1990s. *Journal of Crime and Justice, 14,* 17-30.

CHAPTER 14

Extending Ethnicity in Homicide Research

The Case of Latinos

■ *Ramiro Martinez Jr. & Matthew T. Lee*

In the preceding chapter, Darnell Hawkins presents a compelling argument for the disaggregation of appropriate data to fully comprehend patterns and correlates of homicide among African Americans. A similarly powerful argument can be made for the case of Latino[1] homicide. Despite their figuring prominently in some pioneering crime and homicide studies (Bullock, 1955; see also National Commission on Law Observance and Enforcement, 1931), Latinos have been largely ignored in the recent proliferation of research on homicide in the United States.

Although the "long history and large numbers of Latinos in the United States" (Moore & Pinderhughes, 1993, p. xix) are well recognized within the social science literature, researchers have paid little attention to the extent and seriousness of the Latino homicide problem. Prominent public health agencies identify homicide as a major contributor to death among Latinos (Baker, 1996; Mercy, 1988), yet few criminological studies have focused on murders committed by and against members of this group (Zahn & Sagi, 1987). Thus, not only is the extent of Latino homicide unknown, there is little understanding of its unique determinants (Martinez, 1996).

The purpose of this chapter is to provide a better understanding of Latino homicide in the United States. In pursuing this discussion, we propose that the combined impact of immigration and economic deprivation on Latino communities creates a social milieu that varies sub-

AUTHORS' NOTE: This chapter was made possible, in part, by funding to the first author from the National Science Foundation (SBR-9515235), a Ford Foundation Postdoctoral Fellowship, and the National Consortium on Violence Research. We thank Ronet Bachman, Richard Lundman, Amie Nielsen, and Frank Scarpitti for comments on previous versions that culminated in the present chapter. Special thanks are extended to S. Fernando Rodriguez for providing city of El Paso homicide data. Views and errors are our own and do not reflect those of any official agency.

stantially from the experiences of most other ethnic groups (e.g., Anglo and Black); this social milieu, in turn, influences violence within the Latino community. To illustrate this, we compare and contrast the small number of Latino homicide studies, paying special attention to the context within which Latino homicide occurs. Finally, we suggest future directions for the study of homicide among the Latino population of the United States.

■ *EXTENDING ETHNIC CATEGORIES IN THE STUDY OF HOMICIDE*

Despite the tremendous growth of Latinos in almost every city in the United States, contemporary research on ethnic variation in urban homicide has typically focused on Anglo and Black killings (Moore & Pinderhughes, 1993; see also Chapter 13 by Darnell Hawkins). Yet according to the 1990 U.S. census, Latinos composed 9% of the total population, or 22.4 million people, a 53% increase from 1980 (Rumbaut, 1995). Indeed, the Census Bureau projects that Latinos will emerge as the nation's largest minority group by 2005 (see Aponte & Siles, 1996). It is surprising, then, that relatively little research has been devoted to understanding patterns of homicide among this third largest ethnic group in the United States.

The exclusion of Latinos from research on the relationship between ethnicity and violence, especially homicide, raises the possibility—or, as we argue, the likelihood—that contemporary assumptions regarding Black and Anglo violence are not applicable to Latinos. Consequently, treating Latinos as a distinct ethnic category is necessary to advance the understanding of homicide among this significant and unique group (Martinez, 1996; Sampson & Wilson, 1995).

Among the prominent barriers to studying Latino homicides, one frequently noted issue is the unique history of Latinos across the United States (Flowers, 1990). The U.S. census currently highlights four Latino groups—Mexican Americans (the largest group), Puerto Ricans, Cubans, and "Other Hispanics," typically persons from Spanish-speaking Central and South American countries. Most persons in these categories, however, are grouped together and generically identified as "Hispanic origin" in census demographic profiles. This practice obscures the fact that each Latino group, as widely recognized by other scholars, has its unique pattern of settlement into the United States, further distinguishing Latinos from other racial/ethnic groups and potentially influencing their criminal activity (Mann, 1993).[2]

Another difficulty derives from inconsistent definitions of Latinos across time (Flowers, 1990). The Census Bureau in the early 1900s classified persons of Mexican origin as an "other" or "nonwhite" race. In one census count, "Mexican" was noted as an ethnic category, but other Latino groups were ignored (Samora & Simon, 1977). Later in this century, Latinos were categorized as either "Black" or "White" and therefore aggregated with non-Latino persons. Even as recently as 1970, Latinos were tabulated as "Spanish heritage," "Spanish speaking," or "Spanish surname," but only in a few states. These changing definitions thwarted attempts to disaggregate Latinos from other groups. This has presented problems for researchers, not the least of which are difficulties in calculating estimates of criminal offending and victimization rates for Latinos, resulting in a surprisingly limited amount of crime and violence research on this population (Samora & Simon, 1977, pp. 8-13).

Further complicating attempts to sort out Latino homicide victims and offenders is limited official data collection, most notably, that reported (or, more accurately, *not* reported) in the Federal Bureau of Investigation's (FBI) publication, *Crime in America: Uniform Crime Reports* (*UCR*). Lane (1997) describes how "the FBI lives in a world more Black and White than most of us" (p. 312), as reflected by the sporadic use of the "Hispanic" category in the early 1980s (see also Mann, 1993). The *UCR* listed "Hispanic" for the first time in 1980 but quickly dropped this designation because of police agency inattention. One consequence of this practice is an inaccurate portrait of murder in the United States (Nelsen, Corzine, & Huff-

Table 14.1 Comparison of 10 Highest Total City Homicide Rates and Latino Homicide Rates, 1980

City	*Rate*	*City*	*Latino Rate*
Compton, CA	69	Dallas, TX	68
Miami, FL	60	Houston, TX	64
Las Vegas, NV	57	Compton, CA	52
Inglewood, CA	54	Hollywood, FL	47
St. Louis, MO	51	Fort Worth, TX	45
Detroit, MI	47	Galveston, TX	45
Cleveland, OH	47	San Bernardino, CA	44
Oakland, CA	38	Miami, FL	43
Dallas, TX	36	Chicago, IL	42
Los Angeles, CA	34	Odessa, TX	38

SOURCE: Adapted from Martinez (1996).
NOTE: City rate is per 100,000 residents. Latino rate is per 100,000 Latino residents.

Corzine, 1994). For example, Lane (1997) notes that in 1980, Latinos accounted for 16% of arrestees nationwide, a proportion almost three times that of their population size. Because the *UCR* has been restricted to "Black" or "White" categories since then, most Latinos will be counted in one of these designations, inflating the group-specific rates for Black and White victims and offenders.

Unfortunately, no consistently reliable data exist for Latino murder arrests or victimization rates. According to Rick Florence, a statistician with the FBI's Uniform Crime Reporting Program, a policy board of police chiefs suggested mandatory collection of "Hispanic ethnicity" for the UCR Program's 1980 Supplemental Homicide Reports (*SHR*). Some police agencies, however, were in locales with few Latinos, so after 1980, collection of the Hispanic ethnicity variable was made voluntary. As a consequence, most agencies dropped the designation, and most Latinos are recorded as White or another racial category (R. Florence, personal communication, June 1996). Because these data are not forwarded to the UCR Program, most of the Latino homicide research discussed below was conducted by directly examining internal police homicide reports that include a Hispanic or Latino category.

In sum, the UCR Program's current data collection practices create barriers to conducting national-level studies of Latino homicides, and the *UCR* racial category clouds the true picture of Black and White homicides by including Latinos in these categories. The result is to obscure the Latino population in official crime reports, thereby ignoring a large and visible segment of American society in many major cities with high rates of violence, especially those cities with growing, and in some cases, majority, Latino populations (e.g., Chicago, Dallas, Houston, Los Angeles, Miami, New York City, and Washington, D.C.).

■ *RECENT STUDIES OF LATINO HOMICIDE RATES*

Despite the methodological difficulties that face researchers, some studies have attempted to concentrate on homicides involving Latinos. Recent research by Martinez (1996) provides some perspective on how Latino homicide may differ from that of other groups. In this study, 1980 rates of Latino homicide (per 100,000) were estimated for 111 cities of varying population sizes with at least 5,000 Latinos and one Latino homicide victim.[3] The 10 cities with the highest total rates and Latino homicide rates are shown in Table 14.1. As can be seen, a majority of the cities with high rates of homicide for the total population were not those with predominantly Latino populations. The cities in Table 14.1 with the highest rates of Latino homicide tend to be concentrated in the southwestern United States, an area with large numbers of Mexican-origin residents. In contrast, cities with high total homicide rates are much more diverse in their geographic locations.

Other interesting patterns are evident in Table 14.1. Among the cities shown, Miami had the second highest homicide rate, but the rate for Latinos in Miami was lower than that of Latinos in a number of southwestern cities. In contrast, the Latino rate in Dallas was twice that of the general population in the same city. These results suggest that the homicide rates of Latinos may be different from those of other groups in the same cities. Therefore, it is possible that

Table 14.2 Comparison of Anglo, Black, and Latino Homicide Rates in El Paso and Miami, 1980 to 1984 and 1990 to 1994

	El Paso, TX	*Miami, FL*
1980 to 1984		
Anglo (*N*)	83	113
Average rate	11.4	34.4
Black (*N*)	10	362
Average rate	14.9	83.1
Latino (*N*)	99	515
Average rate	7.5	53.1
1990 to 1994		
Anglo (*N*)	37	46
Average rate	5.4	25.3
Black (*N*)	21	390
Average rate	25.8	79.4
Latino (*N*)	173	244
Average rate	9.7	21.8

SOURCE: Adapted from Martinez (1996).
NOTE: Rates are per 100,000 and are group specific.

unique factors may influence the involvement in homicide by the Latino residents of these cities.

Ethnic group differences were further illustrated by examining homicides at two times (1980-1984 and 1990-1994) in two predominantly Latino cities: El Paso, Texas, and Miami, Florida (Martinez, 1996). This comparison is shown in Table 14.2; El Paso has lower homicide rates across all ethnic groups, despite having a much larger total population (in 1990, 515,342 vs. 358,458).[4] This pattern holds true for both time frames.

Table 14.2 also shows the differences found to exist both *between* and *within* ethnic groups. Latinos in El Paso, primarily Mexican, not only had a lower rate than Miami's Cuban Latinos but in the early 1980s had a rate lower than Anglos. Ten years later, however, the Latino homicide rate increased and even surpassed the Anglo rate, although never reaching the level of their Latino counterparts in Miami.

Also noteworthy is the positioning of Latino homicide rates relative to those of Blacks and Whites. In both cities, Black homicide rates are the highest of all groups, with Latino rates tending to fall in the middle. By the early 1990s, however, the Latino homicide rate was the lowest of the three groups in Miami. In contrast, Latino rates rose slightly in El Paso between the two periods but fell rather dramatically in Miami.

These findings, like those from the sample of 111 cities, suggest that Latino homicide has some unique qualities that justify its study apart from general rates and with the same interest as that shown Black and White homicide. Because few studies have attempted to do this, the following section is devoted to a brief overview of those research efforts.

■ *EARLIER STUDIES OF LATINO HOMICIDE*

A 1931 report for the National Commission on Law Observance and Enforcement was among the first to acknowledge the importance of studying Latino crime, especially among native and foreign-born "Mexicans." A supplement to the report noted that as victims and offenders, Mexican arrests and convictions varied widely by type of crime, locale, and nativity status. In some U.S. cities along the Texas-Mexico border, Latinos were actually *underrepresented* in arrests and convictions for violent crime; in other cities such as San Antonio, they engaged in crime proportionately to their population size. In still other places (Los Angeles), they were arrested at a proportionately high rate.

Specific to homicide, however, little was noted except that a higher proportion of foreign-born, as opposed to native-born, Mexicans (25% vs. 18%) were incarcerated in Texas penitentiaries for committing murder. Although the commission study was purely descriptive, it was instructive in at least two ways. First, it highlighted the diversity of Latino engagement in crime. Contrary to common stereotypes at the time, immigrant Mexicans were rarely the deadly "bandits" as widely portrayed in the popular media at the time. Clearly, Mexican involvement in violence and homicide was a relatively rare event. Second, many commission authors, much like other researchers for several decades, lamented the lack of census data on the "Mexican" population. To estimate ethnic group size, the contributors relied on school surveys that listed the students' race/ethnicity. These findings, in turn, were used to calculate the Mexican proportion in the authors' respective locales. Although less than fully precise, the authors had no other alternative to estimate ethnic population size in the early 1930s (National Commission on Law Observance and Enforcement, 1931).

It took more than 20 years for criminologists to again recognize Latinos. A 1955 article by Henry A. Bullock was among the first to acknowledge the importance of studying Latino homicide. Examining killings in Houston, Texas, for 1945 to 1949, Bullock found that Latinos were concentrated in high-homicide areas adjacent to the central business district, reflecting a relationship between crime and census-level economic conditions originally found by Shaw and McKay (1942) in their classic study of Chicago neighborhoods. The Bullock study illustrated that Latinos were settling in areas with characteristics similar to those of Blacks and White immigrants in Chicago. Although this study demonstrated again the important linkage between community conditions and crime, it was the first time that this relationship was documented for Latinos.

Several other homicide studies from Houston were important in noting the influence of Latinos. For example, Pokorny (1965) provided a descriptive analysis of Anglo, Black, and Latino lethal violence during 1960. He discovered that Latino homicide victim and offender rates fell between other ethnic groups—Latino rates were twice those of Anglos but a third less than Blacks. Pokorny's research thus served as an early indicator that potentially important differences existed for Latino homicide patterns, thus warranting further study.

Other studies of Houston found Beasley and Antunes (1974) and Mladenka and Hill (1976) incorporating "percent Mexican American" as a predictor of index crimes (including murder) in Houston police districts; these studies, however, did not directly examine killings among Latinos or any other ethnic group. (See Martinez, 1996, for a complete description of their methodologies.) Findings from both studies concerning Latinos were rather modest, largely because the "percent Mexican American" variable was found to have limited use because of its high correlation with population density and income. Nevertheless, the authors were among the first to acknowledge that a distinct ethnic group other than Blacks and Whites existed in a major urban city.

Research by Wilbanks (1984) in Dade County (Miami), Florida, provides a descriptive account of the extent and severity of Anglo and Black killings in that community from 1917 to 1983. Perhaps the most notable characteristic of this study was that it was the first to provide information on murders by and of Cubans, the third largest Latino group after Mexican Americans and Puerto Ricans, although data were limited to the 1980s. Apparently, both numerically and proportionally in 1980, a year focused on by Wilbanks, Latino victims constituted the majority of all ethnic group killings, although they were not overrepresented relative to population size.

McBride, Burgman-Habermehl, Alpert, and Chitwood (1986) also examined all homicides committed in Dade County between 1978 and 1982. A main finding was that Latinos, in particular Cubans and Colombians, were overrepresented as victims. After categorizing different types of murders, however, Latinos were found to dominate the drug-related homicides but not other types such as domestic and robbery-related killings.

In another study, Block (1985) considered the contributions of Latino killings to the overall patterns of homicide in Chicago from 1965 to 1981. She found that Latino homicide had increased at a much faster rate than the Latino population size. In contrast, Anglo and Black homicides paralleled respective group increases, or decreases, through time. Block speculated that the rapid Latino increase might have overwhelmed community structures in Latino communities, rendering them unable to accommodate the relatively large number of newcomers and, in turn, contributing to homicide. Later, Block (1993) reported that teenage Latino males were at far greater risk of homicide victimization than any other Latino group (e.g, females and adult males). Indeed, the homicide rate for Latin males 15 to 19 years of age rivaled that of their Black counterparts. Most categories of Latino homicide victimization rates, however, were found to fall in between Anglo and Black rates.

The studies just discussed notwithstanding, research on Latino homicide remains rather sparse. The exclusion of Latinos from this area of research is even more frustrating given that attempts were made to highlight Latino homicide. A workshop on Latino violence and homicide was convened at the University of California, Los Angeles, in 1987, sponsored by the Department of Health and Human Services and the National Institute of Mental Health, to compile papers on this topic. Evidence emerged that the patterns of Latino homicide victim rates and circumstances surrounding those killings were distinct from non-Latino groups. Although the results from this workshop were primarily descriptive, they did expand the literature on Latino homicide by highlighting the higher rate of killings, relative to the total population, in diverse areas of the United States. Almost as important was the collective call in the published proceedings for future research on Latino violence (see Kraus, Sorenson, & Juarez, 1988).

Missing from most of this research is a consideration of two factors that distinguish the experience of Latinos from other ethnic groups—immigration and distinct forms of economic deprivation. A full understanding of Latino homicide demands a comprehension of the impact of these factors, so we now turn our attention to these issues.

■ *LATINO IMMIGRATION AND HOMICIDE*

Immigration to the United States has reemerged as a controversial social issue in recent years (Moore & Pinderhughes, 1993). Contemporary studies report that most immigrants reside in urban areas and are disproportionately of Latino origin (Rumbaut, 1995). The result is a markedly different social milieu for the U.S. Latino population as a group from that for Anglos or Blacks.

Low levels of education and income characterize many immigrant Latinos (Bean & Tienda, 1987). Similarly, strained public resources, including poorly funded schools, pervade predominantly Latino communities, particularly areas in which most immigrant Latinos are concentrated (Portes & Rumbaut, 1996). Thus, large numbers of foreign-born Latinos live in areas that are impoverished and typically substantially inferior to surrounding neighborhoods.

Despite these conditions, some scholars note that immigrants have also become a constructive force in many cities. For example, Moore and Pinderhughes (1993) note that immigrants have revitalized areas, strengthened traditional social controls, and created new community institutions. The "hard work" ethic of many immigrants and numerous resources provided in part through kinship networks proved to be positive forces in many Latino communities. Thus, the impact of immigration can vary considerably from city to city; few scholars, unfortunately, have directly examined this aspect of the Latino experience.

Although immigration is potentially problematic for the Latino population, it has seldom been directly considered in contemporary criminological research. If, as Moore and Pinderhughes (1993) note, immigration has a significant impact on poor Latino communities across the United States, then analyses of homicide should incorporate this important influence on Latino conditions. The notion that immigration is linked with violence certainly is not recent; indeed, it was discussed at length in the early research of Shaw and McKay (1931, 1942; see also Shaw, 1930). They reported that urban neighborhoods with high concentrations of foreign-born families (as well as African American families) were also places with the highest rates of urban juvenile crime. Shaw and McKay also argued that areas close to downtown were continuously populated by successive waves of recent immigrants. The result of this influx was a host of social problems, ranging from infant mortality to crime.

Some contemporary researchers also have posited a link between immigration and violence through social disorganization theory. The best example is that of Wilson (1987, pp. 35-39), who highlights a common theme in sociological writings, specifically, how community disruption contributes to rates of serious crime. Drawing on the urban poverty literature, Wilson outlines some of the mechanisms by which immigration could have a critical influence on homicide. He suggests that Latino movement to many urban areas contributed to increased joblessness, violent crime, and welfare dependency. Thus, the Latino community, growing in part from rapid increases in immigration, also experienced greater rates of social dislocation. One offshoot from the growing community disruption was an increase in homicide.

Despite the apparent connection, few studies have systematically examined the relationship between immigration and violence. Although a handful of exceptions exist, they have added little to the understanding of connections between immigration and homicide. For instance, Pennell and Curtis (as cited in Muller, 1993) noted how undocumented workers were involved in a disproportionate share of arrests in some southern California communities (p. 215). Also, Valdez (1993) has reported that many drug-related crimes and murders in a U.S./Mexican border city were linked to an influx of Mexican immigrants. In both cases, however, the anecdotal, largely descriptive evidence used to substantiate these claims does not systematically link the incidence of crime to immigrants. More promising is the study of Alba, Logan, and Bellair (1994), who found that foreign-born Latinos were more exposed to property and violent crime than were other Latinos in the greater New York City metropolitan region for 1980. These effects were not direct measures of Latino victim rates, however, limiting the study's use for developing generalizations about the impact of immigration itself.

In neglecting the study of immigration, social scientists have largely failed to address some common but erroneous notions about crime among immigrants. For instance, during the 1980s, a focus on immigrant crime, in particular violence, emerged with a vengeance in the popular news media (Hufker & Cavender, 1990). This issue was sparked by the arrival of 125,000 refugees from the Mariel harbor in Cuba, some of whom were reportedly violent criminals released from Cuban prisons (Portes, Clark, & Manning, 1985). The "Mariels" arrived in Miami at a time when the city's homicide rate was already reaching record highs. The rate continued to rise during a period of intense social turmoil in which the Mariels absorbed most of the blame for this trend (Muller, 1993).

A recent examination of this period (Martinez, 1997b) has revealed that the Mariel refugees were rarely the "dangerous" offenders portrayed by the media. In most cases, non-Mariel Cubans engaged at a higher level of offending throughout the 1980s than the newcomers. Relative to their group size, however, the Mariels were the *victims* of crime at a disproportionately high proportion; they were at far greater risk of being murder victims than were the more established Cuban Americans who had been residing in the area for a longer time.

Although the research just discussed has been suggestive, the extent of the positive or negative manner in which immigration influences Latino communities remains unclear, especially its potential linkage to homicide. Because few other ethnic groups in the United States are influenced by immigration as much as Latinos, further research in this area is definitely needed.

■ *ECONOMIC DEPRIVATION PERSPECTIVES ON LATINO HOMICIDE*

Although the research on immigration and violence is limited, the linkage between economic deprivation and homicide has been the topic of numerous studies (see Parker, 1989, for a discussion of much of this literature). The postulate that motivates this area of research is that certain groups within the United States, especially racial and ethnic groups, are deprived of social status and economic resources. As a result, feelings of alienation and frustration are particularly high in disadvantaged groups. One response to their situation is increased aggression, including high levels of violent criminality. Thus, economic disadvantage and racial inequality are viewed as strongly influencing criminal violence in urban areas.

Latinos should figure prominently in this debate. Economic conditions among the Latino population rapidly worsened between 1970 and 1980. By 1995, Latino household income lagged behind every other ethnic group in the United States. Despite rising incomes for Anglos and Blacks, income has declined among Latinos, regardless of their nativity status, and the proportion of Latino poor recently surpassed that of Blacks (Goldberg, 1997; Holmes, 1996).

The relationship between economic conditions and Latino homicide across a large number of cities was first examined in a study described earlier in this chapter (Martinez, 1996). The results of that study revealed that Latinos' homicide rates were consistently linked with their socioeconomic conditions. In particular, economic inequality and low educational attainment in the Latino population were strongly correlated with Latino homicide across the U.S. cities in the sample.

Another recent study (Martinez, 1997a) showed that despite a constant flow of Latino immigrants and declining homicide rates throughout the 1980s, contemporary Miami is characterized by low levels of homicide among Latinos but a high rate of Black homicide that reflects largely Black-on-Black killings. Anglo and Latino homicide rates were found to be reasonably similar to one another. The study argues that because of the relatively well-off economic standing of Cubans, the gap between Latinos and Anglos is much less than that found for Blacks. Therefore, the results could be seen as corresponding to the literature concerning economic disadvantage and homicide; in this case, however, the findings help to explain the relative *lack* of homicide among a specific Latino population.

Another point deserving attention is that the primary predictors of Latino homicide across cities probably differ from those of Anglo or Blacks. For example, Latino joblessness is not as widespread among most Latino groups as for Blacks. Latinos have high rates of labor force participation but are concentrated in lower-paying blue-collar occupations, suggesting that Latinos are characterized more as the working poor than the chronically unemployed (see Rumbaut, 1995). Also, Latino households have a higher percentage of female-headed households than do Anglos (21.6% vs. 11.8%) but a substantially lower percentage than that of Black female-headed households (43.2%). Thus, traditional indicators of urban homicide rates may need refinement for Latinos.

In sum, there are important empirical and theoretical reasons to expect that immigration should influence violence among Latinos, hand in hand with socioeconomic conditions. A full understanding of Latino homicide will require that future research engage in a more thorough examination of the separate and combined roles of these two factors.

■ *FUTURE DIRECTIONS FOR THE STUDY OF LATINO HOMICIDE*

A major theme of this chapter has been the need for an expanded consideration of Latino homicide by researchers. As stressed earlier, a particular emphasis should be placed on the role of immigration in shaping the Latino experience with homicide in the United States. Lane (1986) notes that high homicide rates for European immigrants in turn-of-the-century Philadelphia fell sharply in the second generation as immigrants were integrated into the economy of the city and were provided more economic opportunities (p. 174). Latino immigrants face a different situation, with potentially different results. Unlike the economy that welcomed unskilled White immigrants at the turn of this century, it has proved difficult for newly arrived groups to advance in contemporary U.S. society, especially in light of economic restructuring. As the Latino population continues to grow, in part because of greater numbers of immigrants, the relationship between Latino immigration and Latino violent crime will remain an important issue.

Further, the possible varying experiences of specific Latino immigrant groups (Mexican, Cuban, Salvadoran, etc.) have not been sufficiently explored. The impact of immigration in particular cities (e.g., Miami, El Paso, and Washington, D.C.) requires additional attention. Also, the effects of Latino immigration on other violent crimes such as rape and robbery, and the linkages of these to homicide, have not been investigated.

In sum, these questions are only a few that homicide scholars might examine. Addressing them, however, would represent some movement toward acknowledging the increasing diversity among ethnic groups in the United States. Understanding this diversity will ultimately improve our understanding of the patterns and causes of homicide, as well as our attempts to provide means by which the incidence of homicide may be reduced among *all* ethnic groups.

■ *NOTES*

1. We define *Latinos* as persons whose national origin is Mexico, Cuba, or any other Latin American country, regardless of skin color (see Bean & Tienda, 1987). When possible, we will distinguish between Latino groups: Mexican, Puerto Rican, Cuban, and so on. The term *Latino* is used in lieu of *Hispanic* because the latter is more properly used to describe persons of Spanish descent, although both terms are used synonymously (see Sampson, Raudenbush, & Earls, 1997). We also use the heading of *Anglo* to refer to non-Hispanic/Latino Whites or persons of European American descent. The census label *Black* is used to describe persons of African American and Caribbean Black descent.

2. Regardless of origin, however, most Latinos display a great deal of cultural similarities (e.g., language and religion) and regional concentration. To highlight the latter point, consider that 75% of *all* Latinos reside in five mainland states: California, Texas, New York, Florida, and Illinois (see Rumbaut, 1995). The notable exception, of course, is the island of Puerto Rico.

3. See Martinez (1996) for a complete description of the methodology. This strategy precludes directly comparing ethnic homicide differences. In the 1996 study, Anglos were the largest group, net of Latinos, in almost every city. SHR racial codes (White and Black), however, are not mutually exclusive and include Latinos in both categories, making comparisons difficult. Also, in applying the 5,000-person criterion to other racial groups in the 111 cities, we discovered that 35% of the cities had less than 5,000 Blacks. Again, making direct comparisons could provide unreliable figures.

4. All rates are group specific and mutually exclusive. For example, the Anglo rate is the number of Anglo killings per 100,000 Anglos.

■ *REFERENCES*

Alba, R. D., Logan, J. R., & Bellair, P. (1994). Living with crime: The implications of racial/ethnic differences in suburban location. *Social Forces, 73,* 395-434.

Aponte, R., & Siles, M. (1996). Latinos to emerge as largest U.S. minority in the coming decade. *NEXO: Newsletter of the Julian Samora Research Institute, 4,* 1-8.

Baker, S. G. (1996). Demographic trends in the Chicana/o population: Policy implications for the twenty-first century. In D. R. Maciel & I. D. Ortiz (Eds.), *Chicanas/Chicanos at the crossroads* (pp. 5-24). Tucson: University of Arizona Press.

Bean, F., & Tienda, M. (1987). *The Hispanic population of the United States.* New York: Russell Sage.

Beasley, R. W., & Antunes, G. (1974). The etiology of urban crime: An ecological analysis. *Criminology, 22,* 531-550.

Block, C. R. (1985). Race/ethnicity and patterns of Chicago homicide, 1965-1981. *Crime & Delinquency, 31,* 104-116.

Block, C. R. (1993). Lethal violence in the Chicago Latino community. In A. V. Wilson (Ed.), *Homicide: The victim/offender connection* (pp. 267-342). Cincinnati, OH: Anderson.

Bullock, H. A. (1955). Urban homicide in theory and fact. *Journal of Criminal Law, Criminology and Police Science, 45,* 565-575.

Flowers, R. (1990). *Minorities and criminality.* New York: Praeger.

Goldberg, C. (1997, January 30). Hispanic households struggle as poorest of the poor in U.S. *New York Times,* p. A1.

Holmes, S. A. (1996, October 13). For Hispanic poor, no silver lining. *New York Times,* p. E5.

Hufker, B., & Cavender, G. (1990). From freedom flotilla to America's burden: The social construction of the Mariel immigrants. *Sociological Quarterly, 31,* 321-335.

Kraus, J., Sorenson, S., & Juarez, P. (Eds.). (1988). *Research conference on violence in Hispanic communities.* Washington, DC: U.S. Department of Health and Human Services.

Lane, R. (1986). *Roots of violence in Black Philadelphia, 1860-1900.* Cambridge, MA: Harvard University Press.

Lane, R. (1997). *Murder in America: A history.* Columbus: Ohio State University Press.

Mann, C. R. (1993). *Unequal justice: A question of color.* Bloomington: Indiana University Press.

Martinez, R., Jr. (1996). Latinos and lethal violence: The impact of poverty and inequality. *Social Problems, 43,* 131-146.

Martinez, R., Jr. (1997a). Homicide among Miami's ethnic groups: Anglos, Blacks, and Latinos in the 1990s. *Homicide Studies, 1,* 17-34.

Martinez, R., Jr. (1997b). Homicide among the 1980 Mariel refugees in Miami: Victims and offenders. *Hispanic Journal of Behavioral Sciences, 19,* 107-122.

McBride, D. C., Burgman-Habermehl, C., Alpert, J., & Chitwood, D. (1986). Drugs and homicide. *Bulletin of the New York Academy of Medicine, 62,* 497-508.

Mercy, J. A. (1988). Assaultive injury among Hispanics: A public health problem. In J. Kraus, S. Sorenson, & P. Juarez (Eds.), *Research conference on violence in Hispanic communities* (pp. 1-12). Washington, DC: U.S. Department of Health and Human Services.

Mladenka, K. R., & Hill, K. Q. (1976). A reexamination of the etiology of urban crime. *Criminology, 13,* 491-506.

Moore, J., & Pinderhughes, R. (1993). Introduction. In J. Moore & R. Pinderhughes (Eds.), *In the barrios: Latinos and the underclass debate* (pp. xi-xxxix). New York: Russell Sage.

Muller, T. (1993). *Immigrants and the American city.* New York: New York University Press.

National Commission on Law Observance and Enforcement. (1931). *Report on crime and the foreign born.* Washington, DC: Government Printing Office.

Nelsen, C., Corzine, J., & Huff-Corzine, L. (1994). The violent West reexamined: A research note on regional homicide rates. *Criminology, 32,* 149-161.

Parker, R. N. (1989). Poverty, subculture of violence, and type of homicide. *Social Forces, 67,* 983-1007.

Pokorny, A. (1965). Human violence: A comparison of homicide, aggravated assault, suicide, and attempted suicide. *Journal of Criminal Law, Criminology and Police Science, 56,* 488-497.

Portes, A., Clark, J. M., & Manning, R. (1985). After Mariel: A survey of the resettlement experiences of 1980 Cuban refugees in Miami. *Cuban Studies, 15,* 37-59.

Portes, A., & Rumbaut, R. G. (1996). *Immigrant America* (2nd ed.). Berkeley: University of California Press.

Rumbaut, R. (1995). *Immigrants from Latin America and the Caribbean: A socioeconomic profile* (Statistical Brief No. 6). East Lansing: Michigan State University, Julian Samora Research Institute.

Samora, J., & Simon, P. V. (1977). *A history of the Mexican-American people.* South Bend, IN: University of Notre Dame Press.

Sampson, R. J., Raudenbush, S. W., & Earls, F. (1997). Neighborhoods and violent crime: A multilevel study of collective efficacy. *Science, 277,* 918-924.

Sampson, R. J., & Wilson, W. J. (1995). Toward a theory of race, crime, and urban inequality. In J. Hagan & R. D. Peterson (Eds.), *Crime and inequality* (pp. 37-54). Stanford, CA: Stanford University Press.

Shaw, C. R. (1930). *The jack-roller: A delinquent boy's own story.* Chicago: University of Chicago Press.

Shaw, C. R., & McKay, H. D. (1931). *Social factors in juvenile delinquency* (Vol. 2 of Report on the Causes of Crime: National Commission on Law Observance and Enforcement Report No. 13). Washington, DC: Government Printing Office.

Shaw, C. R., & McKay, H. D. (1942). *Juvenile delinquency and urban areas.* Chicago: University of Chicago Press.

Valdez, A. (1993). Persistent poverty, crime, and drugs: U.S.-Mexican border region. In J. Moore & R. Pinderhughes (Eds.), *In the barrios: Latinos and the underclass debate* (pp. 195-210). New York: Russell Sage.

Wilbanks, W. (1984). *Murder in Miami: An analysis of homicide patterns and trends in Dade County, Florida, 1917–1983.* Lanham, MD: University Press of America.

Wilson, W. J. (1987). *The truly disadvantaged: The inner city, the underclass, and public policy.* Chicago: University of Chicago Press.

Zahn, M. A., & Sagi, P. C. (1987). Stranger homicides in nine American cities. *Journal of Criminal Law and Criminology, 78,* 377-397.

CHAPTER 15

Youth Homicide

An Integration of Psychological, Sociological, and Biological Approaches

■ *Kathleen M. Heide*

In August 1993, U.S. Attorney General Janet Reno characterized youth violence as "the greatest single crime problem in America today" (Kantrowitz, 1993, p. 43). Motivated by fears associated with this perceived problem, federal legislation has been proposed that lowers the age at which juveniles can be tried as adults to 13 years in some cases. This same legislation would tie federal funding to states' willingness to impose "get tough" policies toward juvenile crime, including the provision that youths may be placed in adult facilities to serve any assigned sentences (Gray, 1997).

Attorney General Reno's assessment, as well as support for the punitive legislation under consideration, is bolstered in part when youth involvement in murder is examined through time. Dramatic increases in youth arrests for homicide are apparent, whether the frame of reference is youths under 18 or those in their middle to late teenage years.

The terms *juvenile* and *adolescent* are often used interchangeably in the professional literature. Nevertheless, they can be distinguished from each other. Juvenile or minority status is determined on the basis of age and is a legislative decision (Heide, 1992). The federal government and the majority of the states designate youths under 18 as juveniles (Bortner, 1988). The Federal Bureau of Investigation (FBI) classifies arrests of children 17 and under as juvenile arrests.

Adolescence, in contrast to juvenile status, is based on human development and varies across individuals. It is a stormy period characterized by hormonal changes, growth spurts, psychological changes, and enhancement of intellectual abilities and motor skills. According to child development experts, adolescence begins with puberty around age 12 or 13 (although earlier in some children) and extends through the teen years to age 19 or 20 (Solomon, Schmidt, & Ardragna, 1990).

Perusal of FBI arrest data for 1984 through 1993 revealed that the number of youths under 18 arrested for homicide and their proportionate representation among homicide arrestees in the United States increased for 10 consecutive years. The dramatic escalation in killings by juveniles during this period put this nation in the grips of fear. In 1993, the number of juveniles arrested for murder—3,284—had reached an all-time high (Heide, 1996).

The recent problem of juvenile involvement in homicide has been especially troubling in America's cities. From 1984 to 1993, the mean percentages of homicide arrestees who were under 18 were 12.8 in urban areas, 7.5 in suburban areas, and 6.2 in rural areas. The percentage involvement of juveniles in homicide arrests in the nation's cities has risen steadily from a low of 8.3 in 1984 to a high of 17.6 in 1993. In 1993, about 1 of 6 homicide arrests in cities involved juveniles. The comparable figures in suburban and rural areas were 1 in 8 and 1 in 12, respectively (Heide, 1996).

A modest decline in the number of juvenile homicide arrests was observed for the first time in more than a decade in 1994 when 182 fewer juveniles were arrested for murder (FBI, 1995). The percentage of homicide arrestees who were juveniles, however, continued to spiral upward from 16.2 in 1993 to 16.7 in 1994. In the cities, the percentage of youths arrested for murder increased from 17.6 to 18.1. Clearly, these data do not indicate that juvenile homicide is a less pressing concern.

The increase in murders committed by youths under 18 since the mid-1980s occurred during a period when the percentage of young Americans had generally been declining (Blumstein, 1995; Cornell, 1993; Ewing, 1990; Fox, 1996; Gest & Friedman, 1994; Heide, 1994b). Aware that the juvenile population would be growing at a substantially higher rate than the total population during the 1990s, some experts predicted that murders by juveniles, if they continued at the same pace, could become a national epidemic (Ewing, 1990; Fox, 1996). Fortunately, recent years have seen a stabilization in juvenile homicide rates, albeit at relatively high levels (see the section on the 1990s in Chapter 2 by Margaret Zahn and Patricia McCall).

The seriousness of the youth homicide problem is underscored when the unit of analysis is 15- to 19-year-olds. Smith and Feiler (1995) computed the *absolute* and *relative* levels of youth involvement in arrests for murder during 1958 to 1993. Absolute involvement was estimated by the calculation of rates of homicide arrests for different age groups. Relative involvement was determined by calculating the ratio of arrests for 15- to 19-year-olds to arrest rates for other age groups in the population through age 45 to 49. Examination of trends in arrest rates revealed a striking escalation in homicides by youths in their late teens beginning in the mid-1980s. The arrest rates for 15- to 19-year-olds recorded in 1992 (42.4 per 100,000) and 1993 (42.2) were the highest rates recorded for *any* age group during the 36 years covered by the data. Similarly, Smith and Feiler concluded that "the ratio for 15- to 19-year-olds in 1993 marks the greatest relative involvement in murder arrests for any age group during the period under study" (p. 330).

When youths kill today, adults ask "why?"—just as they have for centuries (Zagar, Arbit, Sylvies, Busch, & Hughes, 1990). The question, however, has become more complex since the mid-1980s because there are really two issues involved: Why are youths killing, *and* why are more youths killing today than in previous generations? This chapter attempts to provide some answers to these questions by synthesizing the literature on clinical and empirical findings related to youth homicide. Thereafter, it addresses factors operating today that appear to be contributing to a high rate of murders by youths.

■ *CHILDREN WHO KILL: A SYNTHESIS OF THE LITERATURE*

Many clinicians and researchers have examined cases of youths killing during the last 50 years in an effort to determine the causes of juvenile homicide. Statements about juvenile murderers in the professional literature are typically about male adolescents who kill. Although some studies of adolescent homicide have included both females and males (Malmquist, 1990), most research has focused on male adolescents because they constitute the overwhelming majority of juvenile homicide offenders.

A few publications report case studies of girls who have murdered (Benedek & Cornell, 1989; Ewing, 1990; Gardiner, 1985; Heide, 1992; McCarthy, 1978; Medlicott, 1955; Russell, 1986). These studies reveal that girls are more likely than boys to kill family members and to use accomplices to effect these murders. Girls are also more likely to perform secondary roles when the killings are gang related or occur during the commission of a felony, such as robbery. Their accomplices are generally male. Pregnant unmarried girls who kill their offspring at birth or shortly thereafter, in contrast, often appear to act alone. Girls' motives for murder are varied. Instrumental reasons include ending abuse meted out by an abusive parent, eliminating witnesses to a crime, and concealing a pregnancy. Expressive reasons include acting out psychological conflict or mental illness, supporting a boyfriend's activities, and demonstrating allegiance to gang members.

Homicides Involving Young Children as Offenders

Research specifically investigating "little kids" who kill also has been sparse, partly because of its low incidence and the difficulty of obtaining access to younger children as research participants (Bender, 1959; Carek & Watson, 1964; Ewing, 1990; Goetting, 1989, 1995; Petti & Davidman, 1981; Pfeffer, 1980; Tooley, 1975). The importance of distinguishing between preadolescents and adolescents in understanding what motivates youths to kill and in designing effective treatment plans was recognized by clinicians as early as 1940 (Bender & Curran, 1940). Subsequent investigators, however, consistently have not used age as a criterion in selecting samples of youths who kill (Easson & Steinhilber, 1961; Goetting, 1989; Sargent, 1962). In one frequently cited report, for example, the juvenile killers ranged in age from 3.5 to 16 years (Sargent, 1962).

Physically healthy children under age 9 who kill, in contrast to older youths, typically do not fully understand the concept of death (Bender & Curran, 1940; Cornell, 1989; Heide, 1992; O'Halloran & Altmaier, 1996). They have great difficulty comprehending that their actions are irreversible (Bender & Curran, 1940). Prepubescent children who kill often act impulsively and without clear goals in mind (Adelson, 1972; Carek & Watson, 1964; Goetting, 1989). Preadolescent murderers are also more likely to kill than are older youths in response to the unstated wishes of their parents (Tooley, 1975; Tucker & Cornwall, 1977). In addition, the incidence of severe conflict (Bernstein, 1978; Paluszny & McNabb, 1975) or severe mental illness (Bender, 1959; Heide, 1984; Pfeffer, 1980; Tucker & Cornwall, 1977; Zenoff & Zients, 1979) tends to be higher among little kids who kill than among their adolescent counterparts. Adolescent killers are more likely to kill because of the lifestyles that they have embraced or in response to situational or environmental constraints that they believe to be placed on them (Heide, 1984, 1992; Sorrells, 1977; Zenoff & Zients, 1979).

■ *CASE STUDY RESEARCH PERTAINING TO ADOLESCENT MURDERERS*

In recognition of reporting practices in the professional literature, the terms *juvenile* and *adolescent* are treated as equivalent terms in the discussion that follows. Similarly, the terms *murder* and *homicide* are used synonymously, although the intended legal meaning is that of *murder.* Accordingly, terms such as *juvenile homicide offender, adolescent murderer,* and *young killer* are used interchangeably throughout the remainder of this chapter.

Cornell (1989) and Ewing (1990) have published two critiques of the literature on adolescent murderers. Both scholars cited methodological problems with most of the available research on juvenile homicide and suggested that findings reported from such research be viewed with caution.

Much of the difficulty with this literature arises because most published accounts of adolescent murderers derive from case studies. The cases discussed were often drawn from psychiatric populations referred to the authors for evaluation and/or treatment after the youths committed homicides. The conclusions drawn from these cases, although interesting and suggestive, cannot provide precise explanations regarding why youths kill because it is unknown to what extent the youths examined are typical of the population of juvenile murderers. In addition, in the absence of control groups of any type, it is unknown how these young killers differ from nonviolent juvenile offenders, violent juvenile offenders who do not kill, and juveniles with no prior records.

The following sections address various areas covered in case studies of adolescent murderers. It is important to keep in mind the caveats discussed above regarding the shortcomings of this body of literature.

Psychological Disorder and Youth Homicide

Several scholars have also synthesized existing scientific publications relating to various types of juvenile homicide offenders (Adams, 1974; Busch, Zagar, Hughes, Arbit, & Bussell, 1990; Cornell, 1989; Ewing, 1990; Haizlip, Corder, & Ball, 1984; Lewis, Lovely, et al., 1988; Lewis et al., 1985; Myers, 1992). Much of the literature, particularly during the 1940s, 1950s, 1960s, and 1970s, suggested that psychodynamic factors propelled youths to kill (Lewis et al., 1985). These factors included impaired ego development, unresolved Oedipal and dependency needs, displaced anger, the ability to dehumanize the victim, and narcissistic deficits (Cornell, 1989; see also Bender & Curran, 1940; Mack, Scherl, & Macht, 1973; Malmquist, 1971, 1990; McCarthy, 1978; Miller & Looney, 1974; Scherl & Mack, 1966; Smith, 1965; Washbrook, 1979).

Many studies have investigated the extent of severe psychopathology, such as psychosis, organic brain disease, and neurological impairments (Cornell, 1989; Ewing, 1990). The findings, particularly with respect to the presence of psychosis among juvenile homicide offenders, are mixed and may be the result of how the samples were generated. Individuals who are diagnosed as psychotic have lost touch with reality, often experience hallucinations (seeing or hearing things that are not occurring) and delusions (bizarre beliefs), and behave inappropriately. Most studies report that juvenile homicide offenders are rarely psychotic (Cornell, 1989; Cornell, Benedek, & Benedek, 1987b, 1989; Corder, Ball, Haizlip, Rollins, & Beaumont, 1976; Ewing, 1990; Hellsten & Katila, 1965; King, 1975; Malmquist, 1971; Myers & Kemph, 1988, 1990; Patterson, 1943; Petti & Davidman, 1981; Russell, 1979; Sorrells, 1977; Stearns, 1957; Walsh-Brennan, 1974, 1977; Yates, Beutler, & Crago, 1984). Some studies, however, do posit a high incidence of psychosis (Bender, 1959; Lewis, Pincus, et al., 1988; Rosner, Weiderlight, Rosner, & Wieczorek, 1978; Sendi & Blomgren, 1975); episodic psychotic symptomatology (Lewis, Lovely, et al., 1988; Lewis et al., 1985); and other serious mental illness, such as mood disorders (Lewis, Pincus, et al., 1988; Malmquist, 1971, 1990).

Several case reports have suggested that juvenile murderers suffered from brief psychotic episodes, which remitted spontaneously after the homicides (Cornell, 1989; McCarthy, 1978; Miller & Looney, 1974; Mohr & McKnight, 1971; Sadoff, 1971; Smith, 1965). This phenomenon, known as *episodic dyscontrol syndrome,* is characterized by incidents of severe loss of impulse control in individuals with impaired ego development (Menninger & Mayman, 1956). Diagnosing psychosis in homicide offenders who kill impulsively, brutally, and apparently senselessly, in the absence of clear psychotic symptoms, has been strongly challenged by juvenile homicide experts (Cornell, 1989; Ewing, 1990).

Although there is considerable variation in diagnoses given to adolescent murderers within

(Malmquist, 1971; Rosner et al., 1978; Russell, 1979) as well as across studies, personality disorders and conduct disorders rank among the more common diagnoses (Ewing, 1990; Malmquist, 1971; Myers & Kemph, 1988, 1990; Rosner et al., 1978; Russell, 1979; Sendi & Blomgren, 1975; Sorrells, 1977; Yates et al., 1984). Significant disagreement also exists with respect to the prevalence of neurological problems in juvenile killers (Cornell, 1989; Ewing, 1990), which may be partly due to differences in assessment and reporting practices used by various clinicians (Restifo & Lewis, 1985). Neurological impairment may be indicated by brain or severe head injuries, past and present seizure disorders, abnormal head circumferences or electroencephalogram (EEG) findings, soft neurological signs, and deficits on neurological testing (Myers, 1992). Several researchers have found significant neurological impairment or abnormalities among young killers (Bender, 1959; Busch et al., 1990; Lewis, Lovely, et al., 1988; Lewis et al., 1985; Michaels, 1961; Woods, 1961; Zagar et al., 1990), particularly those on death row (Lewis, Pincus, et al., 1988). Others maintain that neurological difficulties are absent or rare among the juvenile murderers assessed in their studies (Hellsten & Katila, 1965; Petti & Davidman, 1981; Russell, 1986; Scherl & Mack, 1966; Walsh-Brennan, 1974, 1977).

The Intelligence of Young Homicide Offenders

The findings with respect to intelligence are also mixed. Several studies reported that there were mentally retarded youths (IQ scores below 70) among their samples of adolescent homicide offenders (Bender, 1959; Busch et al., 1990; Lewis, Pincus, et al., 1988; Patterson, 1943; Solway, Richardson, Hays, & Elion, 1981; Zagar et al., 1990). There is a consensus across many studies, however, that few young killers are mentally retarded (Ewing, 1990).

In contrast, there is considerable disagreement regarding the intelligence of the majority of young offenders. Some researchers report that the average IQ scores of the juvenile homicide offenders in their samples were in the below-average range of 70 to 99 (Busch et al., 1990; Hays, Solway, & Schreiner, 1978; Lewis, Pincus, et al., 1988; Petti & Davidman, 1981; Solway et al., 1981; Zagar et al., 1990). Others, however, have reported that the IQ scores of their participants were typically in the average to above-average ranges (100-129; Bender, 1959; King, 1975; Patterson, 1943).

The literature indicates that many adolescent offenders, regardless of their intelligence, struggle in educational settings. As a group, they tend to perform poorly academically (Bernstein, 1978; Hellsten & Katila, 1965; Scherl & Mack, 1966; Sendi & Blomgren, 1975; Stearns, 1957); have cognitive and language deficits (King, 1975; Myers & Mutch, 1992); experience severe educational difficulties (Busch et al., 1990; Zagar et al., 1990); and suffer from learning disabilities (Bender, 1959; King, 1975; Lewis, Pincus, et al., 1988; Patterson, 1943; Sendi & Blomgren, 1975).

Home Environments of Youths Who Murder

Case studies of adolescents who killed biological parents and stepparents have appeared far more often in the professional literature than case studies of other types of juvenile homicide offenders (Ewing, 1990; Zenoff & Zients, 1979). These studies have indicated that youths who killed parents or stepparents, particularly fathers or stepfathers, were typically raised in homes in which child abuse, spouse abuse, and parental chemical dependency were common (Heide, 1992). Recent research on the "adopted child syndrome" suggests that adopted youths who kill their fathers may be driven by other psychodynamic factors, including unresolved loss, extreme dissociation of rage, hypersensitivity to rejection, and confusion about their identity (Kirschner, 1992).

With few exceptions (Fiddes, 1981; King, 1975), published research and case studies report that the majority of adolescent homicide offenders are raised in broken homes (Ewing, 1990; see also Easson & Steinhilber, 1961; McCarthy, 1978; Patterson, 1943; Petti & Davidman, 1981; Rosner et al., 1978; Russell,

1986; Scherl & Mack, 1966; Sorrells, 1977; Smith, 1965; Woods, 1961). Recent studies suggest that the majority are likely to come from criminally violent families (Busch et al., 1990; Zagar et al., 1990).

Parental alcoholism, mental illness, and other indicators of parental psychopathology are commonly found in the histories of juvenile murderers (Ewing, 1990; see also Corder et al., 1976; Heide, 1992; Hellsten & Katila, 1965; Lewis, Lovely, et al., 1988; Lewis et al., 1985; Lewis, Pincus, et al., 1988; Petti & Davidman, 1981; Sorrells, 1977). Child maltreatment and spouse abuse are also repeatedly encountered in the homes of adolescent homicide offenders (Ewing, 1990). Young killers as a group (King, 1975; Woods, 1961), and youths who kill parents in particular (Corder et al., 1976; Duncan & Duncan, 1971; Heide, 1992, 1994a; Malmquist, 1971; Mones, 1991; Patterson, 1943; Post, 1982; Russell, 1984; Sargent, 1962; Tanay, 1973, 1976), have frequently witnessed one parent, typically the mother, being abused by the other parental figure. Juvenile murderers (King, 1975; Lewis et al., 1985; Lewis, Pincus, et al., 1988; Sendi & Blomgren, 1975), especially adolescent parricide offenders (Corder et al., 1976; Duncan & Duncan, 1971; Heide, 1992, 1994a; Malmquist, 1971; Scherl & Mack, 1966; Tanay, 1976), have often been physically abused. Sexual abuse has also been documented in the lives of juvenile murderers (Corder et al., 1976; Lewis, Pincus, et al., 1988; Sendi & Blomgren, 1975), including those who kill parents (Heide, 1992, 1994a).

Involvement in Other Anti-Social Behavior

Juvenile homicide offenders had typically engaged in several types of deviant behavior prior to committing homicide (Ewing, 1990). Several studies have reported that the majority of adolescent murderers have had a prior arrest history (Cornell, Benedek, & Benedek, 1987a; Ewing, 1990; Fiddes, 1981; Rosner et al., 1978; Sorrells, 1977). Findings regarding whether young killers have had a lengthy history of fighting and other violent or antisocial behavior have been mixed. Some researchers have reported extensive antisocial behavior (Lewis, Lovely, et al., 1988; Lewis et al., 1985; McCarthy, 1978); others have uncovered little or none (Malmquist, 1971; Patterson, 1943; Walsh-Brennan, 1974); and still others claim that previous delinquency varied significantly by the type of juvenile homicide offender (Zenoff & Zients, 1979) or the nature of the relationship between the offender and the victim (Corder et al., 1976). Gang participation has also been found among juvenile homicide offenders (Busch et al., 1990; Zagar et al., 1990).

Substance Abuse

The literature on substance abuse among juvenile homicide offenders has been sparse (Ewing, 1990). Earlier studies indicated that between 20% and 25% of young killers abused alcohol or drugs (Corder et al., 1976; Malmquist, 1971) or were under the influence of alcohol or drugs at the time of the killing (Sorrells, 1977). More recent studies of juvenile homicide offenders indicated that 45% abused alcohol (Zagar et al., 1990) and that 50% were evaluated as substance dependent (Myers & Kemph, 1990). Some research has reported that more than 40% of juvenile killers had killed while they were high on substances (Cornell et al., 1987a; Fendrich, Mackesy-Amiti, Goldstein, Spunt, & Brownstein, 1995; U.S. Department of Justice, 1987).

Other Social Difficulties

Studies have reported that significant proportions of juvenile murderers do not attend school regularly (Ewing, 1990) because of truancy (Smith, 1965), dropping out, or expulsion (Cornell, 1989). Running away is a common response of adolescent parricide offenders (Heide, 1992; Sadoff, 1971; Scherl & Mack, 1966; Tanay, 1976). Enuresis (bed wetting; Easson & Steinhilber, 1961; Michaels, 1961; Russell, 1986; Sendi & Blomgren, 1975) and difficulties relating to peers (Corder et al., 1976; Marten, 1965; Zenoff & Zients, 1979) also have been found in the histories of youths who kill.

Summary: A Case Study Portrait of Adolescents Who Kill

In consideration of the methodological problems in the literature cited earlier, generalizations from many of these studies to the population of juvenile murderers must be made with caution. Some consensus among the studies reported, however, suggests that the portrait of the typical adolescent murderer might be drawn as follows. The adolescent murderer tends to be a male who is unlikely to be psychotic or mentally retarded, to do well in school, or to come from a home in which his biological parents live together in a healthy and peaceful relationship. Rather, he is likely to have experienced or to have been exposed to violence in his home and to have a prior arrest record. More so than juvenile homicide offenders in the past, he is likely to use/abuse drugs and alcohol.

■ *EMPIRICAL STUDIES OF JUVENILE HOMICIDE OFFENDERS*

Well-designed empirical studies of juvenile murderers that attempt to compensate for the weaknesses of case studies are relatively few in number, but they do exist. In one study, for example, 71 adolescent homicide offenders were matched with 71 nonviolent delinquents with respect to age, race, gender, and socioeconomic class. Both groups were assessed on numerous educational, psychiatric and psychological, social, and physical dimensions. Four significant differences were found between the two groups. Compared with nonviolent delinquents, juvenile homicide offenders were more likely to come from criminally violent families, to participate in a gang, to have severe educational deficits, and to abuse alcohol (Busch et al., 1990). The same results were obtained when the study was replicated with different groups of juveniles matched in the same way (Zagar et al., 1990).

Lewis and her colleagues have also conducted several investigations of juvenile homicide offenders (Lewis, Lovely, et al., 1988; Lewis et al., 1985; Lewis, Pincus, et al., 1988; Lewis, Shanok, Grant, & Ritvo, 1983). In one of their studies, they compared 13 juvenile murderers evaluated after the homicide with 14 violent delinquents and 18 nonviolent youths. All three groups were incarcerated at the time of the evaluation and were compared in regard to a set of neurological, psychiatric, psychological, and social variables. Analyses revealed that the adolescent homicide offenders did not differ from violent delinquents. The juvenile murderers, however, were significantly more likely than the nonviolent delinquents to be neuropsychiatrically impaired, to have been raised in violent homes, and to have been physically abused (Lewis, Lovely, et al., 1988).

Other empirical studies have looked for distinguishing characteristics among youths who commit murder (Corder et al., 1976; Cornell et al., 1987b; Cornell, Miller, & Benedek, 1988). Corder and her colleagues compared 10 youths charged with killing parents with 10 youths charged with killing other relatives or close acquaintances and 10 youths charged with killing strangers. Individuals in the three groups had been sent to the hospital for evaluation and were matched with one another by age, gender, intelligence, socioeconomic status, and date of hospital admission. The three groups differed significantly from one another on several variables. Those who killed parents, for example, were significantly more likely than those who killed others to have been physically abused, to have come from homes in which their mothers were beaten by their fathers, and to have amnesia regarding the murder.

Several other researchers, as highlighted earlier, have proposed typologies of youths who kill. Attempts to validate typologies of juvenile homicide offenders, however, have often failed because they consisted of small samples or lacked control groups. In contrast, the typology proposed by Cornell et al. (1987b, 1989) has shown remarkable promise. This scheme classifies juvenile homicide offenders into three categories based on circumstances of the offense: (a) *psychotic* (youths who had symptoms of severe mental illness such as hallucinations or delusions), (b) *conflict* (youths who were engaged in an argument or dispute with the victim when the killing occurred), and (c) *crime* (youths who killed during the commission of another felony, such as rape or robbery).

The Cornell et al. (1987b, 1989) typology was tested using 72 juveniles charged with murder and a control group of 35 adolescents charged with larceny. Both groups were referred for pretrial evaluation and were assessed with respect to eight composite categories: "family dysfunction, school adjustment, childhood problems, violence history, delinquent behavior, substance abuse, psychiatric problems, and stressful life events prior to the offense" (1987b, p. 386). On the basis of information pertaining to the offense, 7% of the juvenile homicide offenders were assigned to the psychotic subgroup, 42% to the conflict subgroup, and 51% to the crime subgroup.

Analyses revealed significant differences on all eight categories between those youths charged with homicide and the group charged with larceny. In addition, significant differences emerged among the three subgroups of juvenile homicide offenders. Psychotic homicide offenders were significantly more likely to score higher on the psychiatric history composite and lower on the index of criminal activity than the nonpsychotic groups. In relation to the conflict group, the crime group scored significantly higher on school adjustment problems, substance abuse, and criminal activity and lower on stressful life events. This study provided preliminary support that juvenile homicide offenders could be distinguished from other groups of offenders and from one another. Cornell et al. (1987b, 1989) correctly advised that further studies were needed to determine whether the differences among the homicide subgroups would hold up when group assignment is not determined by offense circumstances.

Subsequent research has found important differences between the crime and conflict groups. The crime group youths had higher levels of psychopathology on the Minnesota Multiphasic Personality Inventory (an objective measure of personality; Cornell et al., 1988) and more serious histories of substance abuse and prior delinquent behavior than the conflict group adolescents (Cornell, 1990). The crime group adolescents were more likely than the conflict group youths to act with others and to be intoxicated on drugs at the time of the murder. Also, they showed poorer object differentiation and more of a victim orientation in responses to a Rorschach analysis (a projective measure of personality) than the conflict group youths. The Rorschach responses suggest that crime group youths are more likely to dehumanize other people, to respond violently when frustrated, and to have more severe developmental deficits than conflict group youths (Greco & Cornell, 1992).

Distinctions also emerged within the conflict group between youths who murdered parents and those who killed other victims, none of whom were family members. Juvenile parricide offenders scored lower on school adjustment problems and prior delinquent history than those who killed nonfamily victims but were higher on a family dysfunction measure. Cornell's (1990) findings regarding youths who kill parents are similar to those in clinical case studies and provide further empirical support that these youths may represent a distinct type of homicide offender.

■ *FACTORS CONTRIBUTING TO THE RISE IN JUVENILE HOMICIDE*

The existent literature on juvenile homicide rarely addresses the factors fueling the recent rise in juveniles murders. Several reasons account for the gap. Most of the studies of adolescent murderers were published prior to 1990 and were restricted to the analysis of individual and family characteristics. Many of these variables were relatively easy to obtain and to verify. Regardless of their findings, however, these studies often have lacked any connection to broad societal changes that have occurred during the past several decades. The following section attempts to supplement the existing literature on young murderers with a perspective that

Table 15.1 Summary of Primary Factors Involved in Murder by Juveniles in the 1990s

Situational Factors	• Child abuse
	• Child neglect
	• Absence of positive male role models
Societal Influences	• Crisis in leadership and lack of heroes
	• Exposure to violence
Resource Availability	• Access to guns
	• Involvement in alcohol and drugs
	• Poverty and lack of resources
Personality Characteristics	• Low self-esteem
	• Inability to deal with strong negative feelings
	• Boredom and nothing constructive to do
	• Poor judgment
	• Prejudice and hatred
Cumulative Effect	• Feelings of little or nothing left to lose
	• Possible biological connection

SOURCE: From "Juvenile Homicide in America: How Can We Stop the Killing," by K. M. Heide, 1997, *Behavioral Sciences and the Law, 15,* p. 205. Copyright © by John Wiley & Sons, Limited. Reproduced with permission.

offers explanations for the increase in younger offenders' involvement in acts of homicide.[1]

I am convinced, after evaluating 90 adolescents involved in murder, that many factors often act in concert when youths kill. Some of these factors are difficult to measure in the individual case, yet their effects on a society and on a generation of children growing up today are more visible. As depicted in Table 15.1, these variables can be grouped into five main categories: situational factors, societal influences, resource availability, personality characteristics, and the cumulative effects of these factors.

Situational Factors

Many of today's youths grow up in families that foster violent and destructive behaviors. Despite a decrease in the number of young Americans, reports of *child abuse* have greatly increased in recent years (Florida Center for Children and Youth, 1993; Snyder, Sickmund, & Poe-Yamagata, 1997; U.S. Advisory Board on Child Abuse and Neglect, 1993; Willis, 1995).

Although the majority of children who are victims or witnesses of family violence do not grow up to victimize others (Gelles & Conte, 1990; Scudder, Blount, Heide, & Silverman, 1993; Smith & Thornberry, 1995), a growing body of research indicates that children who are subjected to such behavior are at greater risk of engaging in delinquent behavior. Retrospective studies of violent adolescents and young killers have repeatedly found child abuse, neglect, and exposure to parental violence in their backgrounds (Cornell, 1989; Ewing, 1990; Heide, 1992; Lewis, Lovely, Yeager, & Femina, 1989; Lewis, Lovely, et al., 1988; Lewis et al., 1985; Lewis, Pincus, et al., 1988; Sendi & Blomgren, 1975). Research that has compared maltreated youths with matched groups of nonmaltreated youths also suggests that abused and neglected youths suffer an increased risk of becoming juvenile delinquents or adult criminals and engaging in violent criminal behavior (Smith & Thornberry, 1995; Widom, 1989a, 1989b, 1989c, 1989d).

Increasing evidence indicates that exposure to parental violence is also related to violent behavior, particularly by men toward their spouses or partners (Briere, 1992; Browne, 1987; Gelles & Conte, 1990; Hotaling & Sugarman, 1986; Howell, Krisberg, & Jones, 1995; Silvern et al., 1994; Thornberry, 1994). Smith and Thornberry (cited in Howell et al., 1995) found that children who witnessed and experienced many violent acts in their homes (child abuse, spouse abuse, and family conflict) were twice as likely to engage in violent acts themselves.

Some children who are physically, sexually, verbally, and psychologically abused kill the abusive parent because they are afraid or see no other way out to escape this situation or to end the abuse (Heide, 1992). Other youths who are abused do not bond with others. Consequently, they develop no values or empathy to insulate them from killing innocent human beings. Still other abused juveniles are angry and in pain and vent their rage by destroying others (Magid & McKelvey, 1988).

Neglect frequently accompanies abuse, but it can also exist independently, often manifesting itself as the common failure of parents to supervise their children (Heide, 1992). During the last 25 years, several significant changes in family structures have contributed to decreasing levels of child supervision and have placed adolescents at greater risk of getting into serious trouble.

As one indicator, the number of children born to unmarried mothers has nearly tripled—from 398,700 in 1970 to 1,165,384 in 1990 (National Center for Health Statistics, 1994). During the same period, the divorce rate (Bynum & Thompson, 1996; National Center for Health Statistics, 1990) and percentage of single-parent households (Magid & McKelvey, 1988) also increased. Today, more than 50% of all marriages end in divorce. The Carnegie Council on Adolescent Development (1995) noted in its concluding report that more than 50% of all children in the United States in the mid-1990s will be raised for at least part of their childhood and adolescent years in single-parent households, a far greater percentage than a few decades ago.

The number of mothers in the workforce has also increased significantly during the last two decades. In 1970, 30% of married women with children under age 6 were gainfully employed; in 1990, 59% of women in this category were working. The percentage of married women with children ages 6 to 17 who were working rose from 49% in 1970 to 74% in 1990. Figures for single mothers with children are not available for 1970 to permit comparisons across the two decades. Data for 1990, however, indicate that among single mothers, 49% with children aged 6 to 17 were working (U.S. Bureau of the Census, 1994, Table no. 626).

Given these familial changes, the time that youths spend with their parents and the amount of supervision and guidance that they receive have significantly decreased during the past several decades (Carnegie Council on Adolescent Development, 1995). In 1970, 37% of families with children under 18 lacked full-time parental supervision. In 1992, the proportion had risen to 57% (Fox, 1996). Many adolescent homicide offenders I examine are not in school during the day and are out late at night. Their parents do not know where they are, what they are doing, or with whom they are associating.

Often accompanying abuse or lack of supervision is the *absence of positive male role models*. In some cases, the identities or whereabouts of fathers are unknown. In others, fathers are present only to be uninvolved, violent, or both. Boys need same-sex role models to define themselves as male. When fathers are absent, young males are more likely to exaggerate their purported masculinity (Messerschmidt, 1993; Silverman & Dinitz, 1974). Mothers, although typically loved and often revered by their sons, all too frequently cannot control their sons' behavior.

Societal Influences

On a larger scale, youths who kill today are also affected by our country's *crisis in leadership and lack of heroes*. In the past, U.S. presidents, successful entertainers, and legendary sports figures were presented to the youths of America as people to emulate. In the 1990s, the personal ethics and behavior of many of these individuals have been seriously questioned. Government leaders who break campaign promises and involve themselves in money and sex scandals have shown that many politicians today deny responsibility for their behavior and their decisions. When leaders of our country are no longer expected to keep their word and are not held accountable, some youths become cynical about their futures. When police officers are viewed on nationwide television repeatedly beating an African American in their custody and are proved to be lying on the witness stand in the case of another African American man, adolescents from minority groups increasingly lose faith in a criminal justice system that is supposed to protect them and to dispense equal justice. When world-class boxing champion Mike Tyson and rap performers such as Snoop Doggy Dogg (Dunn, 1996) are accused of violent crimes, some youths feel free to adopt similar courses of behavior.

Adolescent deviance and decreased inhibitions to violence have also been correlated to *witnessing violence* (Prothrow-Stith & Weissman, 1991). During the last two decades, films and television shows, including the evening news, have become increasingly violent (Fox & Levin, 1994; Levin & Fox, 1985; Prothrow-Stith & Weissman, 1991). Experts estimate that the average youth in the United States watches

45 violent acts on television *every day,* with most of them committed with handguns (Myers, 1992).

An impressive body of research spanning more than 30 years indicates that exposure to television violence is related to violent behavior (Wheeler, 1993). For example, research shows that aggressive children who have difficulty in school and in relating to peers tend to watch more television (Sleek, 1994).

Perhaps even more troubling than the thousands of children watching violent programs are the scores of youths who see violence firsthand in their neighborhoods, schools, and homes. The exposure to violence among inner-city youths is particularly prevalent (Jenkins & Bell, 1994). Of 203 African American students in a Chicago inner-city high school, 43% reported that they had seen a killing, and 59% reported that someone close to them had been killed. The percentages of children who reported exposure to shootings were even higher: 61% had seen a shooting, 66% indicated that someone who was close to them had been shot, and 48% had been shot at themselves (*Breaking the Cycles of Violence,* 1994).

To many children and teens, the world is a violent place. Accordingly, many youths who eventually kill carry guns and are prepared to use violence when they perceive the situation as warranting it. This image is particularly extolled in the music known as "gangsta rap." These rappers sing about robbing, killing, and raping, activities that they maintain are part of everyday life in "the hood" for low-income members of society, particularly African Americans. The words in gangsta rap music, similar to the scenes in televised violence, appear likely to have a disinhibiting and desensitizing effect on those who listen to them repeatedly. Although the link between gangsta rap music and violence has not been proved, a recent study provided some evidence that misogynous (hateful toward women) rap music was related to sexually aggressive behavior against women by men (Barongan & Hall, 1995). In several of my recent cases, violent music lyrics appeared to provide the additional impetus needed for unbonded youths to kill (Heide, 1997a).

Resource Availability

The substantial majority of juvenile homicide offenders whom I see used *guns* to kill their victims. Many of these kids did not have the physical ability or the emotional detachment to use other weapons such as knives or fists. Young killers frequently reported that guns were cheap and easy to get in their neighborhoods.

Indeed, not only do our youths grow up in a world that encourages violence, they are increasingly finding themselves surrounded with the tools that make acts of violence quick and easy (Sheley & Wright, 1995). The increase in murders by juveniles in recent years has been linked to an escalated presence of firearms, particularly handguns, in the possession of young people (Blumstein, 1995; Fox, 1996). Analyses by the FBI indicate that gun homicides by juveniles nearly tripled from 1983 to 1991. In contrast, murders by juveniles using other weapons declined during the same period. In 1976, 59% of young homicide offenders killed their victims with firearms. Twenty-five years later, 78% selected firearms as their weapons of destruction (Howell et al., 1995).

Blumstein (1995) has argued that the increase in killings by juveniles is a result of the rapid growth in the crack markets in the mid-1980s. Juveniles who were recruited into illicit drug marketing armed themselves with guns for protection. Other juveniles in these communities, aware of what was happening, armed themselves for protection (usually from the young drug carriers) and for status. Consequently, guns became more prevalent in the larger community. When guns are easily accessible, youths, who often are impulsive and unskilled in conflict resolution, may decide to use them as a means of retaliation. The presence of firearms increases the likelihood that an act of lethal violence will occur under these conditions.

Of the adolescents involved in felony homicides whom I have evaluated, most are using *alcohol and drugs.* These observations are consistent with findings from a growing number of studies of a substantial relationship between adolescent violence and substance abuse (Elliott, Huizinga, & Menard, 1989; Johnston, O'Malley, & Bachman, 1993; Office of National Drug Control Policy, 1995; Osgood, 1995). Drug use surveys indicate that the rates of illicit drug use by adolescents, which had declined during the 1980s (Osgood, 1995), are again rising in the 1990s and are much higher than they were a generation ago. The percentage of youths reporting past-month use of marijuana, stimulants, hallucinogens, and inhalants rose from 1991 through 1994. A 1993-1994 survey of junior high (grades 6 through 8) and high school students (grades 9 through 12) found a strong link in both groups between use of alcohol and marijuana and several measures of violent behavior, including carrying a gun to school and threatening to harm another person (Office of National Drug Control Policy, 1995).

Although few of the young killers I have interviewed claim that alcohol or drugs caused them to commit murder, it is likely that chemical abuse affected their judgment about engaging in criminal activity as well as their perceptions during the homicidal event. In addition, it is highly probable, in light of prior research, that the use of alcohol and drugs by many adolescent murderers is "more a reflection of shared influences on a wide variety of deviant behavior than of any causal relationship" (Osgood, 1995, p. 32).

Regarding resource availability factors other than guns and drugs, the majority of the young killers I have met are *poor and lacking in resources.* This finding, to some extent, reflects the rising percentage of Americans under age 18 being raised in families with incomes below the poverty line in recent years (Heide, 1998). Many are from lower-class areas in which violent crimes are commonplace. Robbery and burglary provide a means to acquire money, drugs, and other goods, as well as an opportunity for fun. When asked how he could afford to buy drugs, for example, one young killer I evaluated stated matter-of-factly that he was "stealing anything that I can get my hands on" from "any place."

Personality Characteristics

Changes in the personality characteristics of youths during the last two or three decades are difficult to measure. Unlike the variables discussed under situational factors, societal influences, and resource availability, no indicators are available that systematically chart differences in how youths today perceive the world and respond to it, relative to their counterparts 20 and 30 years ago. On the basis of the above discussion, it seems fair to say that adolescents today in many ways encounter greater challenges at a younger age than youths in the past. Many of these juveniles face these difficulties with parents who cope maladaptively themselves. Other youths confront problems alone. Some youths under such constraints fare well; unfortunately, too many do poorly.

The personalities of youths who kill are almost always marked by *low self-esteem.* They may appear tough and cool, but deep down they typically feel insecure and do not believe they can succeed in conventional activities such as school, sports, or work.

Another common trait of adolescents who kill is an *inability to deal with strong negative emotions* such as anger or jealousy. When wronged, they become consumed with rage and feel compelled to strike back. In addressing "the young male syndrome" and homicide, Wilson and Daly (1985) noted that "the precipitating insult may appear petty, but it is usually a deliberate provocation (or is perceived to be), and hence constitutes a public challenge that cannot be shrugged off" (p. 69). To some male adolescents, nothing less than murder is considered an appropriate response.

Other youths are more *bored* than angry. Engaging in violent behavior becomes a way to amuse themselves, to pass the time. Many of the young killers whom I evaluated were not involved in conventional and prosocial activities, such as school, sports, or work. Robbing and using guns often seemed like fun and a way to reduce boredom. A number of them explained that on the night of the homicide, they were hanging out with other boys drinking and doing drugs, when one suggested that they rob somebody. Although most of the boys had participated in robberies several times in the past, this time was different. Something happened in the interchange, typically quite unexpectedly, that turned the robbery into a homicide.

This scenario also reflects that many adolescent murderers simply have *poor judgment.* They become involved in felony homicides not so much from anger or reckless thrill seeking but because they choose to be at the wrong place at the wrong time. When invited to accompany a group of boys "out for a night of fun," they are sent cues that something bad might happen, but these indications go undetected or are ignored.

Although many groups of children and youths commit acts of violence from generalized anger or "for kicks," still others do so from *prejudice and hatred.* Despite the civil rights movement of the 1960s, the United States has encountered increasing struggles with issues of cultural diversity in recent years. Affirmative action, sexual harassment policies, gender equity, political correctness, and hate crime statutes were once presented as means to move our nation toward a society of peacefulness and equity. Today, these concepts are interpreted by some Americans as threats, reverse discrimination, and detrimental to First Amendment rights. Youths today, as in the past, search for their identities through causes in which to believe. Those with fragile self-esteem tend to be attracted to groups that accept and exalt them on the basis of superficial characteristics, such as skin color. Two teenage Caucasian brothers about whom I was consulted were members of a skinhead group. One evening, they came across a homeless African American man who had passed out in a public garage. Unprovoked, they beat him until he died.

The Cumulative Effect in Context

For many youths, the effect of these factors is cumulative. Put succinctly, many young killers growing up in the 1990s have felt that they have *little or nothing left to lose.* These are the kids who are angry, frequently in pain, and often unattached to other human beings because of experiences in their home and neighborhood environments. More than in other generations, adolescents today are growing up in an era beset by "an overall decline of the extent and influence of the family from the extended multigenerational family, to the nuclear family, to the single parent family, to the 'no parent' family of street children" (Friedman, 1993, p. 509). Many of these youngsters lack self-esteem and the resources to improve their lives. They are living in a society experiencing increases in youths having sex and babies outside marriage (Friedman, 1992), using drugs, participating in criminal violence, and dying violently whether through homicide or suicide. As a result, many young people today are severely alienated (Lerner, 1994; Wynne & Hess, 1986). They do not hold conventional values or dreams. Often chronically bored, they use drugs, alcohol, and sex to numb themselves and commit crimes for fun. They live in the moment. To them, thrills—and lives—are cheap.

In summary, changes in situational factors, societal influences, and resource availability in the 1990s appear to be significant factors in the rising involvement of youths in homicides. These variables likely interact with the personality characteristics of particular adolescents, making some youths more likely to engage in violent behavior than others.

Biological Factors

Biological factors have not been considered under any of the variables discussed so far, yet in many cases, they may be intricately entwined in the homicidal equation. Research suggests that criminal behavior may be linked at least in some cases to genetics, neurological factors, and biochemical reactions (for recent examples, see Fishbein, 1990; Lewis, 1992; Pincus, 1993; Widom, 1991; Wilson & Herrnstein, 1985).

Sociobiologists have maintained that criminal behavior is influenced by both individual biological factors and social and environmental conditions (Jeffery, 1979). Lewis's (1992;

Lewis et al., 1989; Lewis et al., 1991) extensive studies on juvenile murderers led her to conclude that genetic factors and biological vulnerabilities, particularly when severe, predispose certain individuals to respond violently. Her research suggests that if these individuals are subjected to intense psychological, social, and environmental stressors that exceed their ability to cope, violent expression is more likely to result, particularly among males. This theory of neuropsychiatric vulnerability also received support in a larger study involving urban delinquents in Chicago (Hughes, Zagar, Arbit, & Busch, 1991).

■ *CONCLUDING THOUGHTS*

This chapter has been prepared in the hope that the discussion will aid in understanding why youths are involved in murder and why youths of today are more likely to kill than in prior years. Neutralizing or eliminating the variables that contribute to youths' involvement in homicidal incidents may require years to accomplish and will require some rather broad societal changes (Heide, 1996, 1998). My clinical experiences with violent youths have convinced me that participants in these changes must include parents, the educational system, communities, government leaders, medical and mental health professionals, the media, and individuals. Ultimately, all these forces must work together to raise a healthier next generation and to build a more peaceful society.

■ *NOTE*

1. Portions of this section were originally published in the *Stanford Law and Policy Review* (Heide, 1996) and in a special edition of *Behavioral Sciences and the Law* (Heide, 1997b).

■ *REFERENCES*

Adams, K. A. (1974). The child who murders: A review of theory and research. *Criminal Justice and Behavior, 1,* 51-61.

Adelson, L. (1972). The battering child. *Journal of the American Medical Association, 222,* 159-161.

Barongan, C., & Hall, G. C. N. (1995). The influence of misogynous rap music on sexual aggression against women. *Psychology of Women Quarterly, 19,* 195-207.

Bender, L. (1959). Children and adolescents who have killed. *American Journal of Psychiatry, 116,* 510-513.

Bender, L., & Curran, F. J. (1940). Children and adolescents who kill. *Criminal Psychopathology, 1,* 297-321.

Benedek, E. P., & Cornell, D. G. (1989). Clinical presentations of homicidal adolescents. In E. P. Benedek & D. G. Cornell (Eds.), *Juvenile homicide* (pp. 37-57). Washington, DC: American Psychiatric Press.

Bernstein, J. I. (1978). Premeditated murder by an eight year old boy. *International Journal of Offender Therapy & Comparative Criminology, 22,* 47-56.

Blumstein, A. (1995). Youth violence, guns, and the illicit-drug industry. *Journal of Criminal Law and Criminology, 86,* 10-36.

Bortner, M. A. (1988). *Delinquency and justice.* New York: McGraw-Hill.

Breaking the cycles of violence: Hearing of the Subcommittee on Juvenile Justice of the United States Senate Committee on Juvenile Crime, 103d Cong., 2d Sess. (1994, November 29) (testimony of C. C. Bell and E. Jenkins).

Briere, J. N. (1992). *Child abuse trauma.* Newbury Park, CA: Sage.

Browne, A. (1987). *When battered women kill.* New York: Free Press.

Busch, K. G., Zagar, R., Hughes, J. R., Arbit, J., & Bussell, R. E. (1990). Adolescents who kill. *Journal of Clinical Psychology, 46,* 472-485.

Bynum, J. E., & Thompson, W. E. (1996). *Juvenile delinquency: A sociological approach* (3rd ed.). Boston: Allyn & Bacon.

Carek, D. J., & Watson, A. S. (1964). Treatment of a family involved in fratricide. *Archives of General Psychiatry, 16,* 533-542.

Carnegie Council on Adolescent Development. (1995, October). *Great transitions: Preparing adolescents for a new century.* New York: Carnegie Corporation.

Corder, B. F., Ball, B. C., Haizlip, T. M., Rollins, R., & Beaumont, R. (1976). Adolescent parricide: A comparison with other adolescent murder. *American Journal of Psychiatry, 133,* 957-961.

Cornell, D. G. (1989). Causes of juvenile homicide: A review of the literature. In E. P. Benedek & D. G. Cornell (Eds.), *Juvenile homicide* (pp. 3-36). Washington, DC: American Psychiatric Press.

Cornell, D. G. (1990). Prior adjustment of violent juvenile offenders. *Law and Human Behavior, 14,* 569-577.

Cornell, D. G. (1993). Juvenile homicide: A growing national problem. *Behavioral Sciences and the Law, 16,* 389-396.

Cornell, D. G., Benedek, E. P., & Benedek, D. M. (1987a). Characteristics of adolescents charged with homicide. *Behavioral Sciences and the Law, 5,* 11-23.

Cornell, D. G., Benedek, E. P., & Benedek, D. M. (1987b). Juvenile homicide: Prior adjustment and a proposed typology. *American Journal of Orthopsychiatry, 57,* 383-393.

Cornell, D. G., Benedek, E. P., & Benedek, D. M. (1989). A typology of juvenile homicide offenders. In E. P. Benedek & D. G. Cornell (Eds.), *Juvenile homicide* (pp. 59-84). Washington, DC: American Psychiatric Press.

Cornell, D. G., Miller, C., & Benedek, E. P. (1988). MMPI profiles of adolescents charged with homicide. *Behavioral Sciences and the Law, 6,* 401-407.

Duncan, J. W., & Duncan, G. M. (1971). Murder in the family. *American Journal of Psychiatry, 127,* 74-78.

Dunn, M. (1996, February 21). No ordinary trial for no ordinary rapper. *Tampa Tribune,* Metro section, p. 4.

Easson, W. M., & Steinhilber, R. M. (1961). Murderous aggression by children and adolescents. *Archives of General Psychiatry, 4,* 27-35.

Elliott, D. S., Huizinga, D., & Menard, S. (1989). *Multiple problem youth: Delinquency, substance use, and mental health problems.* New York: Springer-Verlag.

Ewing, C. P. (1990). *When children kill.* Lexington, MA: Lexington Books.

Federal Bureau of Investigation. (1995). *Crime in the United States 1994: Uniform crime reports.* Washington, DC: Government Printing Office.

Fendrich, M., Mackesy-Amiti, M. E., Goldstein, P., Spunt, B., & Brownstein, H. (1995). Substance involvement among juvenile murderers: Comparisons with older offenders based on interviews with prison inmates. *International Journal of the Addictions, 30,* 1363-1382.

Fiddes, D. O. (1981). Scotland in the seventies: Adolescents in care and custody: A survey of adolescent murder in Scotland. *Journal of Adolescence, 4,* 47-58.

Fishbein, D. H. (1990). Biological perspectives in criminology. *Criminology, 28,* 27-72.

Florida Center for Children and Youth. (1993). *Key facts about the children: A report on the status of Florida's children: Vol 4. The 1993 Florida kids count data book.* Tallahassee, FL: Author.

Fox, J. A. (1996). *Trends in juvenile violence: A report to the United States attorney general on current and future rates of juvenile offending.* Washington, DC: Bureau of Justice Statistics.

Fox, J. A., & Levin, J. (1994). *Overkill: Mass murder and serial killing exposed.* New York: Plenum.

Friedman, H. L. (1992). Changing patterns of adolescent sexual behavior: Consequences for health and development. *Journal of Adolescent Health, 13,* 345-350.

Friedman, H. L. (1993). Promoting the health of adolescents in the United States of America: A global perspective. *Journal of Adolescent Health, 14,* 509-519.

Gardiner, M. (1985). *The deadly innocents: Portraits of children who kill.* New Haven, CT: Yale University Press.

Gelles, R. J., & Conte, J. R. (1990). Domestic violence and sexual abuse of children: A review of research in the eighties. *Journal of Marriage and the Family, 52,* 1045-1058.

Gest, T., & Friedman, D. (1994, August 29). The new crime wave. *U.S. News & World Report, 117,* 26.

Goetting, A. (1989). Patterns of homicide among children. *Criminal Justice and Behavior, 16,* 63-80.

Goetting, A. (1995). *Homicide in families and other special populations.* New York: Springer.

Gray, J. (1997, May 9). Bill to combat juvenile crime passes House. *New York Times,* pp. A1, A32.

Greco, C. M., & Cornell, D. G. (1992). Rorschach object relations of adolescents who committed homicide. *Journal of Personality Assessment, 59,* 574-583.

Haizlip, T., Corder, B. F., & Ball, B. C. (1984). Adolescent murderer. In C. R. Keith (Ed.), *Aggressive adolescent* (pp. 126-148). New York: Free Press.

Hays, J. R., Solway, K. S., & Schreiner, D. (1978). Intellectual characteristics of juvenile murderers versus status offenders. *Psychological Reports, 43,* 80-82.

Heide, K. M. (1984, November). *A preliminary identification of types of adolescent murderers.* Paper presented at the annual meeting of the American Society of Criminology, Cincinnati, OH.

Heide, K. M. (1992). *Why kids kill parents: Child abuse and adolescent homicide.* Columbus: Ohio State University Press. [(1995) paperback ed., Thousand Oaks, CA: Sage]

Heide, K. M. (1994a). Evidence of child maltreatment among adolescent parricide offenders. *International Journal of Offender Therapy & Comparative Criminology, 38,* 151-162.

Heide, K. M. (1994b). Homicide: 25 years later. In M. Moore (Ed.), *Economic and social issues in the New South: Perspectives on race and ethnicity conference proceedings* (pp. 64-84). Tampa: University of South Florida, Institute on Black Life.

Heide, K. M. (1996). Why kids keep killing: The correlates, causes, and challenge of juvenile homicide. *Stanford Law and Policy Review, 71,* 43-49.

Heide, K. M. (1997a). Associate editor's editorial: Killing words. *International Journal of Offender Therapy & Comparative Criminology, 41,* 3-8.

Heide, K. M. (1997b). Juvenile homicide in America: How can we stop the killing. *Behavioral Sciences and the Law, 15,* 203-220.

Heide, K. M. (1998). *Young killers: The challenge of juvenile homicide.* Thousand Oaks, CA: Sage.

Hellsten, P., & Katila, O. (1965). Murder and other homicide, by children under 15 in Finland. *Psychiatric Quarterly Supplement, 39,* 54-74.

Hotaling, G. T., & Sugarman, D. B. (1986). An analysis of risk markers in husband to wife violence: The current state of knowledge. *Violence and Victims, 1,* 101-124.

Howell, J. C., Krisberg, B., & Jones, M. (1995). Trends in juvenile crime and youth violence. In J. C. Howell, B. Krisberg, J. D. Hawkins, & J. J. Wilson (Eds.), *A sourcebook: Serious, violent, and chronic juvenile offenders* (pp. 1-35). Thousand Oaks, CA: Sage.

Hughes, J. R., Zagar, R., Arbit, J., & Busch, K. G. (1991). Medical, family, and scholastic conditions in urban delinquents. *Journal of Clinical Psychology, 47,* 448-464.

Jeffery, C. R. (1979). *Biology and crime.* Beverly Hills, CA: Sage.

Jenkins, E., & Bell, C. (1994). Violence among inner city high school students and post-traumatic stress disorder. In S. Friedman (Ed.), *Anxiety disorders in African Americans* (pp. 76-88). New York: Springer.

Johnston, L. D., O'Malley, P. M., & Bachman, J. G. (1993). *National survey results on drug use from the monitoring the future study, 1975-1992: Vol. 1. Secondary school students.* Rockville, MD: National Institute on Drug Abuse.

Kantrowitz, B. (1993, August 2). Teen violence: Wild in the streets. *Newsweek, 122,* 40-46.

King, C. H. (1975). The ego and the integration of violence in homicidal youth. *American Journal of Orthopsychiatry, 45,* 134-145.

Kirschner, D. (1992). Understanding adoptees who kill: Dissociation, patricide, and the psychodynamics of adoption. *International Journal of Offender Therapy & Comparative Criminology, 36,* 323-333.

Lerner, R. M. (1994). *America's youth in crisis.* Thousand Oaks, CA: Sage.

Levin, J., & Fox, J. A. (1985). *Mass murder: America's growing menace.* New York: Plenum.

Lewis, D. O. (1992). From abuse to violence: Psychophysiological consequences of maltreatment. *Journal of the American Academy of Child and Adolescent Psychiatry, 31,* 383-391.

Lewis, D. O., Lovely, R., Yeager, C., & Femina, D. D. (1989). Toward a theory of the genesis of violence: A follow-up study of delinquents. *Journal of the American Academy of Child and Adolescent Psychiatry, 28,* 431-436.

Lewis, D. O., Lovely, R., Yeager, C., Ferguson, G., Friedman, M., Sloane, G., Friedman, H., & Pincus, J. H. (1988). Intrinsic and environmental characteristics of juvenile murderers. *Journal of the American Academy of Child and Adolescent Psychiatry, 27,* 582-587.

Lewis, D. O., Moy, E., Jackson, L. D., Aaronson, R., Restifo, N., Serra, S., & Simos, A. (1985). Biopsychosocial characteristics of children who later murder: A prospective study. *American Journal of Psychiatry, 142,* 1161-1167.

Lewis, D. O., Pincus, J. H., Bard, B., Richardson, E., Feldman, M., Prichep, L. S., & Yeager, C. (1988). Neuropsychiatric, psychoeducational, and family characteristics of 14 juveniles condemned to death in the United States. *American Journal of Psychiatry, 145,* 584-589.

Lewis, D. O., Shanok, S. S., Grant, M., & Ritvo, E. (1983). Homicidally aggressive young children: Neuropsychiatric and experimental correlates. *American Journal of Psychiatry, 140,* 148-153.

Lewis, D. O., Yeager, C., Cobham-Portorreal, C. S., Klein, N., Showalter, C., & Anthony, A. (1991). A follow-up of female delinquents: Maternal contributions to the perpetuation of deviance. *Journal of the American Academy of Child Psychiatry, 302,* 197-201.

Mack, J., Scherl, D., & Macht, L. (1973). Children who kill their mothers. In A. J. Anthony & C. Koupernik (Eds.), *The child and his family: The impact of disease and death* (pp. 319-332). New York: Wiley Interscience.

Magid, K., & McKelvey, C. A. (1988). *High risk: Children without a conscience.* New York: Bantam.

Malmquist, C. P. (1971). Premonitory signs of homicidal aggression in juveniles. *American Journal of Psychiatry, 128,* 461-465.

Malmquist, C. P. (1990). Depression in homicidal adolescents. *Bulletin of the American Academy of Psychiatry and the Law, 18,* 23-36.

Marten, G. W. (1965). Adolescent murderers. *Southern Medical Journal, 58,* 1217-1218.

McCarthy, J. B. (1978). Narcissism and the self in homicidal adolescents. *American Journal of Psychoanalysis, 38,* 19-29.

Medlicott, R. W. (1955). Paranoia of the exalted type in a setting of "folie a deux": A study of two adolescent homicides. *British Journal of Medical Psychology, 28,* 205-223.

Menninger, K., & Mayman, M. (1956). Episodic dyscontrol: A third order of stress adaptation. *Bulletin of the Menninger Clinic, 20,* 153-165.

Messerschmidt, J. W. (1993). *Masculinities and crime: Critique and reconceptualization.* Lanham, MD: Rowman & Littlefield.

Michaels, J. J. (1961). Enuresis in murderous aggressive children and adolescents. *Archives of General Psychiatry, 5,* 94-97.

Miller, D., & Looney, J. (1974). The prediction of adolescent homicide: Episodic dyscontrol and dehumanization. *American Journal of Psychoanalysis, 34,* 187-198.

Mohr, J. W., & McKnight, C. K. (1971). Violence as a function of age and relationship with special reference to matricide. *Canadian Psychiatric Association Journal, 16,* 29-32.

Mones, P. (1991). *When a child kills: Abused children who kill their parents.* New York: Pocket.

Myers, W. C. (1992). What treatments do we have for children and adolescents who have killed? *Bulletin of the American Academy of Psychiatry and the Law, 20,* 47-58.

Myers, W. C., & Kemph, J. P. (1988). Characteristics and treatment of four homicidal adolescents. *Journal of the American Academy of Child and Adolescent Psychiatry, 27,* 595-599.

Myers, W. C., & Kemph, J. P. (1990). DSM-IIIR classification of homicidal youth: Help or hindrance. *Journal of Clinical Psychiatry, 51,* 239-242.

Myers, W. C., & Mutch, P. A. (1992). Language disorders in disruptive behavior disordered homicidal youth. *Journal of Forensic Sciences, 37,* 919-922.

National Center for Health Statistics. (1994). *Vital statistics of the United States 1990* (Vol. 1. Natality). Washington, DC: Government Printing Office.

Office of National Drug Control Policy. (1995). *National drug control strategy: Executive summary.* Washington, DC: Author.

O'Halloran, C. M., & Altmaier, E. M. (1996). Awareness of death among children: Does a life-threatening illness alter the process of discovery? *Journal of Counseling and Development, 74,* 259-262.

Osgood, D. W. (1995). *Drugs, alcohol, and violence.* Boulder: University of Colorado, Institute of Behavioral Science.

Paluszny, M., & McNabb, M. (1975). Therapy of a six-year-old who committed fratricide. *Journal of the American Academy of Child Psychiatry, 14,* 319-336.

Patterson, R. M. (1943). Psychiatric study of juveniles involved in homicide. *American Journal of Orthopsychiatry, 13,* 125-130.

Petti, T. A., & Davidman, L. (1981). Homicidal school-age children: Cognitive style and demographic features. *Child Psychiatry and Human Development, 12,* 82-89.

Pfeffer, C. R. (1980). Psychiatric hospital treatment of assaultive homicidal children. *American Journal of Psychotherapy, 342,* 197-207.

Pincus, J. H. (1993). Neurologists' role in understanding violence. *Archives of Neurology, 8,* 867-869.

Post, S. (1982). Adolescent parricide in abusive families. *Child Welfare, 61,* 445-455.

Prothrow-Stith, D., & Weissman, M. (1991). *Deadly consequences.* New York: HarperCollins.

Restifo, N., & Lewis, D. O. (1985). Three case reports of a single homicidal adolescent. *American Journal of Psychiatry, 142,* 388.

Rosner, R., Weiderlight, M., Rosner, M. B. H., & Wieczorek, R. R. (1978). Adolescents accused of murder and manslaughter: A five year descriptive study. *Bulletin of the American Academy of Psychiatry and Law, 7,* 342-351.

Russell, D. H. (1979). Ingredients of juvenile murder. *International Journal of Offender Therapy & Comparative Criminology, 23,* 65-72.

Russell, D. H. (1984). A study of juvenile murderers of family members. *International Journal of Offender Therapy & Comparative Criminology, 28,* 177-192.

Russell, D. H. (1986). Girls who kill. *International Journal of Offender Therapy & Comparative Criminology, 30,* 171-176.

Sadoff, R. L. (1971). Clinical observations on parricide. *Psychiatric Quarterly, 45,* 65-69.

Sargent, D. (1962). Children who kill: A family conspiracy? *Social Work, 7,* 35-42.

Scherl, D. J., & Mack, J. E. (1966). A study of adolescent matricide. *Journal of the American Academy of Child Psychiatry, 5,* 569-593.

Scudder, R. G., Blount, W. R., Heide, K. M., & Silverman, I. J. (1993). Important links between child abuse, neglect, and delinquency. *International Journal of Offender Therapy & Comparative Criminology, 37,* 315-323.

Sendi, I. B., & Blomgren, P. G. (1975). A comparative study of predictive criteria in the predisposition of homicidal adolescents. *American Journal of Psychiatry, 132,* 423-427.

Sheley, J. F., & Wright, J. D. (1995). *In the line of fire: Youth, guns, and violence in urban America.* New York: Aldine de Gruyter.

Silverman, I. J., & Dinitz, S. (1974). Compulsive masculinity and delinquency. *Criminology, 11,* 498-515.

Silvern, L., Waelde, L. C., Karyl, J., Hodges, W. F., Starke, J., Heidt, E., & Min, K. (1994). Relationships of parental abuse to college students' depression, trauma symptoms, and self-esteem. *Child, Youth, and Family Services Quarterly, 17,* 7-9.

Sleek, S. (1994, January). APA works to reduce violence in media. *The Monitor,* pp. 6-7.

Smith, C., & Thornberry, T. P. (1995). The relationship between childhood maltreatment and adolescent involvement in delinquency. *Criminology, 33,* 451-481.

Smith, M. D., & Feiler, S. M. (1995). Absolute and relative involvement in homicide offending: Contemporary youth and the baby boom cohorts. *Violence and Victims, 10,* 327-333.

Smith, S. (1965). The adolescent murderer: A psychodynamic interpretation. *Archives of General Psychiatry, 13,* 310-319.

Snyder, H. N., Sickmund, M., & Poe-Yamagata, E. (1997). *Juvenile offenders and victims: 1997 update on violence.* Washington, DC: Office of Juvenile Justice and Delinquency Prevention.

Solomon, E., Schmidt, R., & Ardragna, P. (1990). *Human anatomy and physiology.* Philadelphia: Saunders College Publishing.

Solway, I. S., Richardson, L., Hays, J. R., & Elion, V. H. (1981). Adolescent murderers: Literature review and preliminary research findings. In J. R. Hays, T. K. Roberts, & K. Solway (Eds.), *Violence and the violent individual* (pp. 193-210). Jamaica, NY: Spectrum.

Sorrells, J. M. (1977). Kids who kill. *Crime & Delinquency, 23,* 313-320.

Stearns, A. (1957). Murder by adolescents with obscure motivation. *American Journal of Psychiatry, 114,* 303-305.

Tanay, E. (1973). Adolescents who kill parents: Reactive parricide. *Australian and New Zealand Journal of Psychiatry, 7,* 263-277.

Tanay, E. (1976). Reactive parricide. *Journal of Forensic Sciences, 21,* 76-82.

Thornberry, T. P. (1994). *Violent families and youth violence* (Fact Sheet No. 21). Washington, DC: Office of Juvenile Justice and Delinquency Prevention.

Tooley, K. (1975). The small assassins. *Journal of the American Academy of Child Psychiatry, 14,* 306-318.

Tucker, L. S., & Cornwall, T. P. (1977). Mother-son "folie a deux": A case of attempted patricide. *American Journal of Psychiatry, 134,* 1146-1147.

U.S. Advisory Board on Child Abuse and Neglect. (1993). *Neighbors helping neighbors: A new national strategy for the protection of children.* Washington, DC: National Clearinghouse on Child Abuse and Neglect.

U.S. Bureau of the Census. (1994). *Statistical abstract of the United States.* Washington, DC: Government Printing Office.

U.S. Department of Justice. (1987). *Survey of youth in custody* (Bureau of Justice Statistics special report). Washington, DC: Government Printing Office.

Walsh-Brennan, K. S. (1974). Psychopathology of homicidal children. *Royal Society of Health, 94,* 274-276.

Walsh-Brennan, K. S. (1977). A socio-psychological investigation of young murderers. *British Journal of Criminology, 17,* 53-63.

Washbrook, R. A. H. (1979). Bereavement leading to murder. *International Journal of Offender Therapy & Comparative Criminology, 23,* 57-64.

Wheeler, J. L. (1993). *Remote controlled: How TV affects you and your family.* Hagerstown, MD: Review and Herald Publishing Association.

Widom, C. S. (1989a). Child abuse, neglect, and adult behavior: Research design and findings on criminality, violence, and child abuse. *American Journal of Orthopsychiatry, 59,* 355-366.

Widom, C. S. (1989b). Child abuse, neglect, and violent criminal behavior. *Criminology, 27,* 251-271.

Widom, C. S. (1989c). The cycle of violence. *Science, 244,* 160-166.

Widom, C. S. (1989d). Does violence beget violence? A critical examination of the literature. *Psychological Bulletin, 106,* 3-28.

Widom, C. S. (1991). A tail on an untold tale: Response to "Biological and genetic contributors to violence—Widom's untold tale." *Psychological Bulletin, 109,* 130-132.

Willis, D. J. (1995). Psychological impact of child abuse and neglect. *Journal of Clinical Child Psychology, 24,* 2-4.

Wilson, J. Q., & Herrnstein, R. J. (1985). *Crime and human nature.* New York: Simon & Schuster.

Wilson, M., & Daly, M. (1985). Competitiveness, risk taking, and violence: The young male syndrome. *Ethology and Sociobiology, 6,* 59-73.

Woods, S. M. (1961). Adolescent violence and homicide: Ego disruption and the 6 and 14 dysrhythmia. *Archives of General Psychiatry, 5,* 528-534.

Wynne, E., & Hess, M. (1986). Long-term trends in youth conduct and the revival of traditional value patterns. *Educational Evaluation and Policy Analysis, 8,* 294-308.

Yates, A., Beutler, L. E., & Crago, M. (1984). Characteristics of young, violent offenders. *Journal of Psychiatry and Law, 16,* 137-149.

Zagar, R., Arbit, J., Sylvies, R., Busch, K., & Hughes, J. R. (1990). Homicidal adolescents: A replication. *Psychological Reports, 67,* 1235-1242.

Zenoff, E. H., & Zients, A. B. (1979). Juvenile murderers: Should the punishment fit the crime? *International Journal of Law and Psychiatry, 2,* 533-553.

CHAPTER 16

Gang Homicide

A Review and Extension of the Literature

■ *Cheryl L. Maxson*

A large number of studies have documented the higher offending profiles of gang members compared with similar-aged youths (Esbensen & Huizinga, 1993; Fagan, 1989; Klein, Maxson, & Cunningham, 1991; Thornberry, Krohn, Lizotte, & Chard-Wierschem, 1993; Tracy, 1979). Recent analysis of longitudinal data from interviews with a representative sample of youths in Rochester, New York, found that gang members, who constituted 30% of the sample, committed 69% of violent offenses reported by all youths studied during a 4-year period (Thornberry & Burch, 1997). Similar findings are reported in Denver (14% gang members, 79% of serious violent offenses [Huizinga, 1997]) and Seattle (15% gang members, 85% of robberies [Battin, Hill, Abbott, Catalano, & Hawkins, 1998]).

Analyses from these types of studies generally support a *facilitation* model; gang members have higher offending patterns during their periods of active gang membership than either before they join or after they leave (Esbensen & Huizinga, 1993; Hill et al., 1996; Thornberry et al., 1993). Not known, as yet, however, is *how* gang membership facilitates violent offending. For example, it is not clear whether membership places youths in riskier situations, alters individual assessments of appropriate or alternative behaviors, or exposes the youths to group processes (e.g., initiation rituals, internal status struggles, or territorial threats from rival gangs) that encourage violent behavior (Dodge, 1997). The increased access to and ownership of firearms by gang members are other considerations in determining this relationship (Lizotte, Tesoriero, Thornberry, & Krohn, 1994; Sheley & Wright, 1995).

Youth participation in homicide has increased during the past several years (Fox,

1996; see also Chapter 15 by Kathleen Heide). Whether increased levels of youth involvement are the result of higher levels of participation in street gangs is a matter of some debate. The proliferation of gangs across the country, however, means that joining gangs is an option faced by more of our nation's youths than ever before (Klein, 1995; Maxson, 1996; Miller, 1996; National Youth Gang Center [NYGC], 1997).

Although it is recognized that violent activity represents a small portion of crime committed by gang members (Decker & Van Winkle, 1996; Esbensen, Huizinga, & Weiher, 1993; Klein, 1995; Short, 1996) and that gang violence is often overrepresented by sensationalist portrayals in the media (Hagedorn, in press), few dispute the contention that violence committed in the gang context is an appropriate concern. As will be discussed below, data from the gang-entrenched cities of Chicago and Los Angeles document that increasing proportions of homicides reflect aspects of gang membership and, consequently, dramatically increased risks of homicide victimization among those demographic groups disproportionately involved in gang activities.

Several comprehensive reviews on the gang homicide literature are available elsewhere (see Howell, 1995, for the most recent). Therefore, the objective of this chapter is to offer a variety of information about gang homicide by discussing the research literature and, where possible, extending it by presenting previously unpublished data.[1] Major aspects to be discussed here are (a) the national prevalence of gang homicide, (b) changes in the prevalence and in the proportion of all homicides that are gang related in the cities for which these data are available, and (c) comparisons of characteristics of gang homicides with other homicides, using data from several areas within Los Angeles County and deciphering whether these patterns have changed during the last 15 years. Before turning to the data on gang homicide, I first will discuss some methodological issues that affect efforts to better understand the scope and nature of gang homicide.

■ *METHODOLOGICAL ISSUES IN THE STUDY OF GANG HOMICIDE*

Interviews with representative samples of youth are not useful in investigating the characteristics of homicide because, fortunately, homicide is a rare outcome among all potentially lethal encounters (Block & Block, 1993). Therefore, interviews with incarcerated or chronic offenders, as well as ethnographic studies of individual street gangs, have generated little generalizable knowledge about gang homicides (but see Moore, 1991).

Much homicide research is conducted with national databases such as the Supplementary Homicide Reports (SHR) provided by the Uniform Crime Reporting Program and the mortality data in *Vital Statistics* reported by the National Center for Health Statistics (see Chapter 6 by Marc Riedel). These are rich sources for answers to other questions, but gang information either is unavailable (as in the death certificate file) or is of questionable use (as in SHR data[2]). Instead, gang homicide scholars must turn to databases maintained by local law enforcement agencies or extract information themselves from homicide case investigation files. Usually, this means that data are available for just one city or police jurisdiction. Studies of homicide that consider multiple cities are the exception, rather than the rule.

Although law enforcement typically devotes more resources to the investigation of homicide than any other crime, the information available in records is limited to that which is known and documented by law enforcement investigators. Information on some coded items may be missing, conflicting, or otherwise so confusing as to challenge the skills of even the most skilled data collectors.[3] Cases involving gang members are among the most difficult to research because the dynamics in these incidents are frequently chaotic and, because of intimidation factors, information from witnesses is often only minimally available. These features, coupled with low levels of gang participation in homicide in most U.S. cities, have discouraged most researchers from investigating the gang aspects of homicide. Chicago and Los Angeles are the most notable exceptions. This lack of attention to gang homicide seems to be changing, however, with studies currently under way in Pittsburgh, Boston, and the three cities included in the work of Zahn and Jamieson (1997).

The most critical methodological issue facing researchers concerns the specific definition of what one calls a *gang-related homicide.* As Huff (1996) notes, "In the history of research and public policy discussions regarding gangs, no single issue has been as controversial as that of defining 'gangs' and what constitutes 'gang-related' crime" (pp. xxi-xxii). It is standard practice for gang researchers to caution their audiences about definitional issues; typically, these are directed to what is meant by *gang, gang membership,* and *gang crime.* Recent extended discussions of gang definitions appear in Klein (1995), Spergel (1995), and Ball and Curry (1995).

Ultimately, the controversy on gang-related crime definitions can be summarized thus: Is gang member *participation* sufficient to designate a crime as gang-related, or is it necessary that the *motive* of the crime be linked to gang function? Law enforcement agencies in Los Angeles and the rest of California have tended to embrace the former approach; the Chicago Police Department is the most cited advocate of the latter. This is not just an academic concern; law enforcement agencies across the country have debated the relative merits of one approach or the other (Spergel, 1988). Generally, gang member-based designation practices place more reliance on adequate listings of active gang members. Motive-based policies require more thorough investigation of the dynamics of the particular incident, a practice that can be problematic for crimes other than homicide. Studies of the implications of the two approaches (Maxson & Klein, 1990, 1996) have found that the choice of approach has substantial effects on prevalence estimates but few differences in the general depictions of incident and participant characteristics. Following the practice adopted in earlier work on this topic in which I was involved, however, the terms *gang member* and *gang motive* will be used for the remainder of this chapter to alert the reader to the two definitional styles.

The reliability of designations made by law enforcement agencies is a matter of concern in the study of gang homicides. When describing the scope and nature of gang homicide, the critical issue is the *type of definition* used in any particular study. Fortunately, considerable consistency has been found in Los Angeles data (Klein, Gordon, & Maxson, 1986). Suggestions of gang motives are quite rare in nongang cases in Los Angeles (Maxson & Klein, 1996) and in Chicago (C. R. Block, personal communication, January 13, 1997). Offenders or victims with gang affiliations explicitly noted in the case file appeared in about 6% and 3%, respectively, of nongang homicides in Los Angeles. Whether the designator of gang incidents is a law enforcement official or researchers, the validity of the designation depends on the case material available.

■ *NATIONAL PREVALENCE OF GANG HOMICIDE*

As yet, there is no national register of gang homicides, although President Clinton's reactivation of the federal effort to establish a national gang tracking network may provide the foundation for such a database (Jackson, Lopez, & Connell, 1997). Walter Miller (1982/1992) provided the first set of tabulations of gang homicides in selected cities across the country. Noting the limitations of definitional variations, dubious recording practices, and considerable missing data, he presented counts of gang homicides for nine gang cities (plus others in aggregate form) for 1967 through 1979.[4] Despite these limitations, Miller's work should be credited as the first effort to document variations in gang homicides between major U.S. cities, to compare rates per population, and to note the vulnerability of law enforcement definitional and reporting procedures to social and political pressures.

National surveys of U.S. cities and towns with street gangs customarily request information about homicide incidence (Curry, Ball, & Decker, 1996; Maxson, 1996; NYGC, 1997). Although such surveys have made great strides in documenting the scope of gang problems in this country, the data gathered on gang homicides remain largely unanalyzed and/or unreported in the literature. In part, this may be due to researchers' reluctance to report such data because of the definitional ambiguities discussed earlier. For instance, the Curry et al. (1996) surveys requested annual counts of gang homicides based on whatever definitional approach was adopted by the reporting agency; in contrast, the NYGC survey asked for the number of homicides involving gang members as perpetrators and, separately, as victims.

The study to be discussed at length here is a survey by Malcolm Klein and me that asked for the number of homicides occurring in 1991 that *involved gang members* (see Maxson, Woods, & Klein, 1995). Findings from this survey are presented in the spirit of offering preliminary baseline information and illustrating various approaches to reporting national prevalence data. No claim is made regarding the validity of this particular approach to measurement or to its superiority of the coverage of U.S. cities and towns with street gangs. On the contrary, the NYGC (1997) survey is more recent and identified 1,492 cities and 515 counties with street gangs. Also, in discussing these results, I readily acknowledge the limitations of law enforcement tabulations of gang members that were used in the survey, limitations that are discussed in detail by Curry and his colleagues in several publications (Curry, Ball, & Decker, 1995; Curry et al., 1996; Curry, Ball, & Fox, 1994).

The Maxson-Klein survey, conducted in 1992, identified 792 cities that reported local street gangs.[5] Four hundred and fifty-three gang cities (60% of 752 responding to this item) stated that they had *no* gang homicides during 1991.[6] Of the 299 cities with gang homicides, 247—more than 80% of cities with gang homicides—had less than 10 incidents in the targeted year. Another 40 cities had between 10 and 25 homicides, while just 12 reported between 30 and 371 incidents. The homicides reported by these 12 cities represent 40% of the total (2,166 incidents) tallied for the entire sample. Selected characteristics of these cities with relatively high levels of gang homicide are listed in Table 16.1.

Table 16.1 Cities With Highest Levels of Gang Homicide: Selected Characteristics

City	*Gang Homicides (1991)*	*City Population (1990)*	*Gang Members*	*Gang Emergence*
Los Angeles, CA	371	3,485,398	55,927	1922
Chicago, IL	129	2,783,726	28,500	1920
Long Beach, CA	53	429,433	11,200	1970
Inglewood, CA	44	109,602	6,500	1961
Commerce, CA	40	12,135	9,000	1925
Cleveland, OH	37	505,616	1,900	1987
San Bernardino, CA	37	164,164	1,550	1988
Kansas City, MO	35	435,146	420	1988
Compton, CA	30	90,454	3,000	1970
Fresno, CA	30	354,202	1,750	1988
Milwaukee, WI	30	628,088	5,000	1976
Oakland, CA	30	372,242	2,500	1966

SOURCE: Adapted from Maxson et al. (1995).

The emergence of Los Angeles and Chicago[7] as standouts in the gang homicide arena will be surprising to no one. The city of Commerce, California, might be, because it is highly industrial with a small residential population. Large numbers of gang members living in surrounding communities, however, claim territory in Commerce and thus are identified as Commerce gang members. Most of the cities on this list have the large populations reflective of our nation's urban centers. Three quarters of these cities have chronic, rather than emerging, gang problems (Spergel & Curry, 1990); just four reported the onset of gangs in their communities during or after the 1980s.

A summary description of the U.S. cities with the highest volume of gang homicides is that they tend to be large urban centers with long-standing gang problems. This is hardly a novel statement, yet in the midst of current widespread concern about the prolifera-

Table 16.2 Cities With Highest Rates of Gang Homicide per 100,000 Population: Selected Characteristics

City	*Gang Homicides per 100,000 Population*	*Gang Homicides (1991)*	*City Population (1990)*	*Gang Members*	*Gang Emergence*
Commerce, CA	329.62	40	12,135	9,000	1925
Hawaiian Gardens, CA	109.98	15	13,639	800	1950
East Palo Alto, CA	81.02	19	23,451	375	1984
Artesia, CA	64.67	10	15,464	300	1955
Harvey, IL	63.82	19	29,771	70	1985
East St. Louis, IL	56.17	23	40,944	50	1968
Inglewood, CA	40.14	44	109,602	6,500	1961
Paramount, CA	39.86	19	47,669	1,200	1950
Compton, CA	33.17	30	90,454	3,000	1970
Huntington Park, CA	32.11	18	56,065	1,500	1958

SOURCE: Adapted from Maxson et al. (1995).

tion of street gangs to small, less populated areas (Klein, 1995; Maxson, 1996; Quinn, Tobolowsky, & Downs, 1994), it is important to remember that the majority of the most violent gang episodes occur in large cities with a long history of gang problems, most notably, Los Angeles and Chicago.

A closer inspection of Table 16.1 reveals apparent anomalies in addition to the Commerce situation already mentioned. The Southern California cities of Compton, Inglewood, and San Bernardino have far lower residential populations than the other cities. Also, Kansas City (Missouri) appears to have relatively few gang members to generate 35 gang homicides. Thus, to compensate for the erroneous impressions that can be conveyed by the use of raw numbers, we computed *rates* of gang homicides per 100,000 population and per 1,000 gang members.[8] These two measures provide a different perspective from the sheer numbers of gang homicides.

The cities with the 10 highest gang homicide rates, as calculated by general population figures, are listed in Table 16.2. The high-incidence cities of Commerce, Compton, and Inglewood represent the only overlap with the cities listed in Table 16.1. With the exception of Compton and Inglewood, all the high-rate cities have relatively low city populations, ranging from around 50,000 to just under 10,000. Seven of these cities are in the county of Los Angeles. All are chronic, rather than emergent, gang cities. The historical nature of gang problems in these cities, like those with high levels of incidents, suggests that their law enforcement agencies may be more attuned to *tabulating gang indicators* through such tactics as assigning officers to special gang units, building gang intelligence, listing gang members, and systematically reviewing all homicides for signs of gang involvement. Given this approach, there is a strong likelihood that gang-related homicides will be detected and identified as such. The infrastructure for systematic reporting, particularly among smaller cities with fewer resources, more likely is provided by locations with long-standing concerns about gang violence. For instance, law enforcement agencies within the Los Angeles region have a well-developed infrastructure, and this may explain why so many of these cities appear in Table 16.2. In contrast, newer gang cities might still have been in the assessment phase or in the process of building intelligence capacities at the time of the survey.

With this caveat in mind, the final set of data on homicide rates per 1,000 gang members should be viewed with considerable skepticism. The list of 10 cities with the highest homicide rates per gang population is provided in Table 16.3. All these cities have low counts of gang members (ranging from 50 to 420 individuals), which are particularly questionable among the six cities with populations greater

Table 16.3 Cities With Highest Rates of Gang Homicide per 1,000 Gang Members: Selected Characteristics

City	*Gang Homicides per 1,000 Gang Members*	*Gang Homicides (1991)*	*City Population (1990)*	*Gang Members*	*Gang Emergence*
East St. Louis, IL	460.00	23	40,944	50	1968
Harvey, IL	271.43	19	29,771	70	1985
Baton Rouge, LA	133.33	20	219,531	150	1989
Saginaw, MI	125.00	20	69,512	160	1986
Durham, NC	110.00	11	136,611	100	1982
Kansas City, MO	83.33	35	435,146	420	1988
New Orleans, LA	76.67	23	496,938	300	1986
Rochester, NY	75.00	15	231,636	200	1985
East Palo Alto, CA	50.67	19	23,451	375	1984
Flint, MI	50.00	15	140,761	300	1978

SOURCE: Adapted from Maxson et al. (1995).

than 100,000. It is interesting to note that no Southern California city appears on this list. Although two cities (Baton Rouge and Kansas City) report the more recent emergence of gangs, and as a group these cities have more recent onset dates than the prior two groups, a number of cities listed in Table 16.3 had gang activity at least 5 years prior to the survey completion. Although some of these cities may have narrow definitions of street gangs and members, this would be inconsistent with the relatively high numbers of gang homicides they reported. It was not possible to pursue such anomalies with all survey respondents,[9] and until more information becomes available, the generalizability of these data is highly suspect.

Despite the limitations noted, these data provide a glimpse of the prevalence of gang homicide across the country in 1992. Most gang cities do not report any homicides involving gang members; two fifths of all gang homicides occur in just a dozen cities, mostly urban centers, with gang problems spanning several decades. Cities with the highest homicide rates per city population also have chronic gang problems, but these tend to be smaller cities and towns and are disproportionately located in the Los Angeles region.

Gang violence is a substantial challenge to law enforcement in cities where well-entrenched gang traditions couple with high volumes of lethal gang activity in communities with limited resources. The attempt to identify gang cities with particularly lethal gang populations generated such mixed findings that it is best viewed as a cautionary note for users of law enforcement estimates of gang membership. On the other hand, these data will provide an opportunity for comparison with the NYGC survey when that source's 1996 gang homicide data become available.[10]

Changes in the Prevalence and Proportions of Gang Homicides in Selected U.S. Cities

Coincidental with the proliferation of street gangs and attendant concerns about gang violence, homicide researchers have begun to pay closer attention to gang issues when gathering data from homicide cases. Earlier interest in this topic, however, can be found in the work of C. Rebecca Block and colleagues regarding Chicago and my studies with Malcolm Klein in Los Angeles that extend well through the last decade. The volume of lethal gang activity, its intransigence during an extended period, and the level of law enforcement resources and expertise devoted to gang issues in these two cities have provided the foundation of information that makes such recent research possible. The following section draws from these and other studies to describe the nature of gang homicides, how they contrast with nongang events, and what is known about the proportion of homicides attributable to gang matters. The definitional approach to determining which crimes are designated as "gang" is critical, so I discuss only those studies that provide this information.

Chicago

The Chicago homicide data set maintained by the Illinois Criminal Justice Information Authority (ICJIA) contains information coded from all homicides committed in Chicago between 1965 and 1995. Researchers at the ICJIA code the designation generated by investigators from the Chicago Police Department, applying that department's definition of street gang-related homicide based on the *motive of the offender.* Thus, in Chicago, there must be strong indication that the incident grew from a street gang function (see Block, Christakos, Jacob, & Przybylski, 1996, for a detailed description of possible street gang motives). Thus, *by definition,* Chicago and other jurisdictions employing motive-based categories will report lower volumes of gang-related homicides (and consequently, lower proportions of all homicides as gang related) than departments such as Los Angeles that adopt the broader member-involvement criterion. About 50% to 60% (depending on period and law enforcement agency) of Los Angeles gang homicides meet the more restrictive gang-motivated definition used in Chicago (Maxson & Klein, 1990, 1996).

The trend data on Chicago gang homicides shown in Figure 16.1 reveal several peaks and troughs that Block and her colleagues have noted as characteristic of the spurts or bursts of rival gang activity (Block & Block, 1993; Block & Christakos, 1995).[11] During this period, the total number of homicides in Chicago—gang and nongang combined—showed generally higher numbers in the 1970s than in the 1980s, with marked increases to unprecedented levels in the 1990s, except for the peak year of 962 killings in 1974 (Block & Christakos, 1995). The proportion of all homicides found to be gang motivated averaged 5% during the 1970s, averaged just under 9% during the 1980s, and then nearly doubled to 17% during the first half of the 1990s. Even with year-to-year fluctuations, the trend shown in Figure 16.1 suggests that street gangs have claimed an increasing share of all Chicago homicides since the mid-1970s; in 1994 and 1995, more than one fourth of Chicago homicides were attributed to gang motives.

Los Angeles

Trend data are also available on gang homicides for the Los Angeles area, although several differences from the Chicago data are noted. The Los Angeles data are provided by the Los Angles Sheriff's Department (LASD), which provides *countywide* gang statistics based on the broader, member-involved definitional approach.[12] The *city* of Los Angeles contributed roughly one half of the countywide gang homicide figures.

The Los Angeles County data for 1978 to 1995 are presented in Figure 16.2. The larger area covered and broader definitions of gang homicides yield substantially more gang events than in Chicago. In Los Angeles County, gang homicides decreased during the early 1980s but began to increase steadily from 1985 to 1992, when they leveled off to around 800 incidents per year (with a dip in 1993 and 1994). Preliminary data for 1996 (not shown in Figure 16.2) indicate a dramatic drop in gang homicides; both the Los Angeles Police Department (LAPD) and LASD report a decrease of 20% in the number of gang incidents for that year. In Chicago, gang homicides were rising in the early 1980s, and that city's data do not show the plateau pattern in the first half of the 1990s that is evident in Los Angeles County.

In Los Angeles County, all homicides decreased from 1980 to 1984, whereas the proportion of gang homicides declined also from 19% (1980) to less than 15% (1984). The period from 1985 to 1992 saw a steady increase in total homicides, but the proportion of these homicides with gang aspects increased from 2% to 5% *each* year through 1991. The 1991 proportion of 37% dipped slightly in 1992 and 1993 before jumping to 43% and 45% in 1994 and 1995, respectively. That nearly half of the homi-

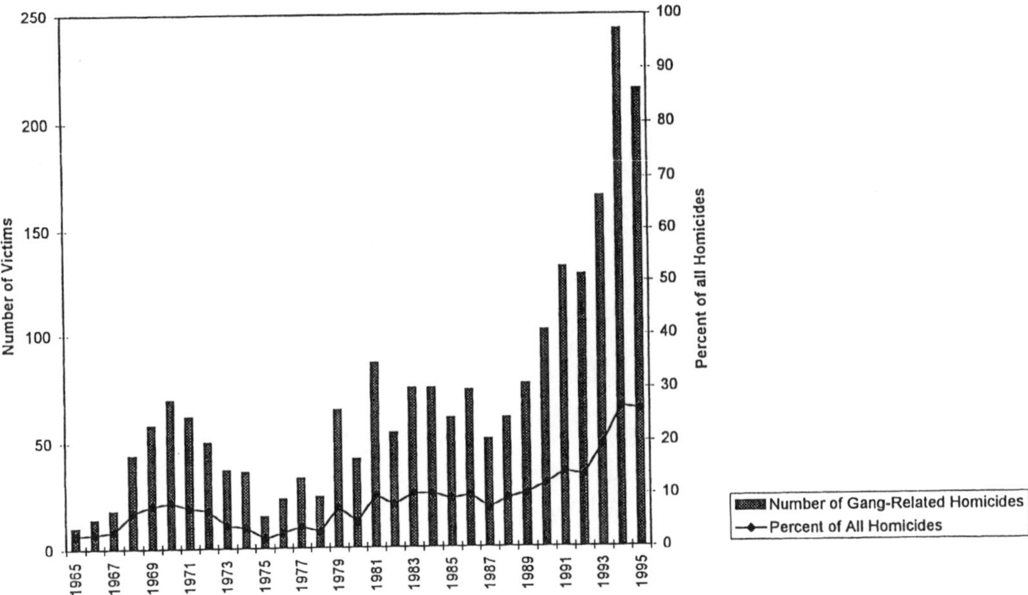

Figure 16.1. Gang-Motivated Homicides in Chicago, 1965 to 1995

SOURCE: Figures provided by C. Rebecca Block, Illinois Criminal Justice Information Authority.

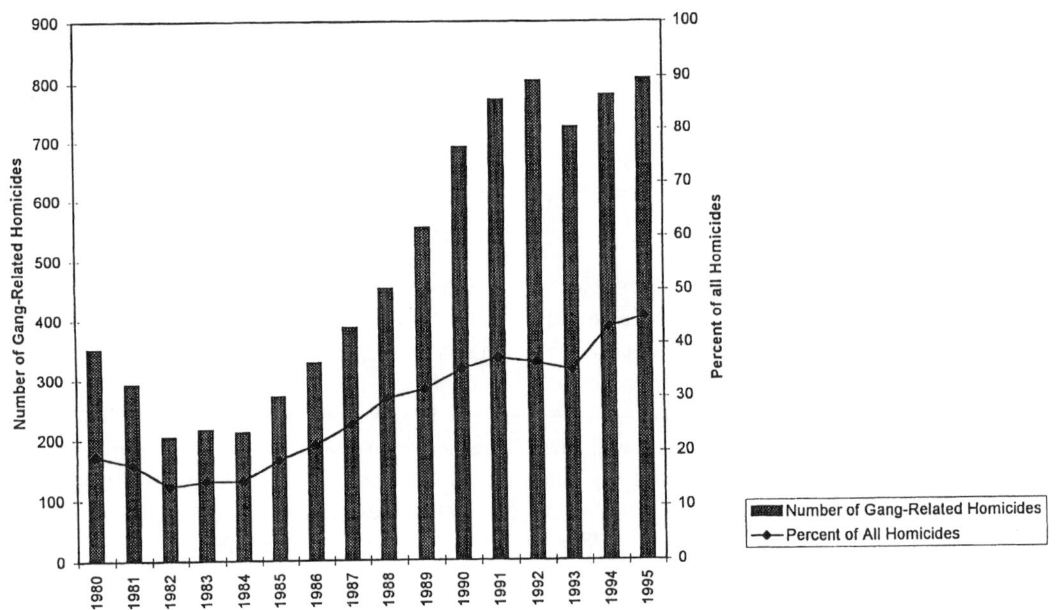

Figure 16.2. Gang-Related Homicides in Los Angeles County, 1980 to 1995

SOURCE: Figures provided by Los Angeles County Sheriff's Department.

cides in Los Angeles County evidence some type of gang involvement is a statistic not lost on the area's law enforcement, politicians, and social service agencies. This figure is somewhat deceptive, however, because it results largely from declines in the overall number of killings from 1993 to 1995, declines that are *not* mirrored in reduced levels of lethal gang activity. In short, the proportion of gang homicides has increased because the incidence of gang homicides has remained relatively stable at a time that the incidence of nongang homicides has been declining.

The foregoing analysis cannot answer the question of which urban area faces the more severe problem; quite simply, definitional variations preclude such a comparison. Other comparisons can be made, however. For instance, it appears that Chicago figures fluctuate more from year to year. I have discussed elsewhere reported differences in the *structure* of street gangs in the two locations as well as the dangers of comparing the two (Maxson & Klein, 1997). The more organized depictions of Chicago gangs argue for more stability in that city's homicide numbers, but that seems not to be the case. As evidence, African American and Latino gang homicides have been shown to display different patterns, but the overall pattern of fluctuation is evident in gang victimization data for both groups (Block & Christakos, 1995).

Other Cities

As mentioned earlier, researchers in cities other than Chicago and Los Angeles are beginning to investigate levels of gang involvement in homicide. As part of the Boston Gun Project, a team of police, probation officers, and street workers examined lists of homicide victims and offenders, as well as incident locations for 1990 to 1994 to designate incidents as "gang-related" according to a shared consensus of what this meant. According to the researchers' description of this process, the assigned meaning of gang homicides more closely approximated the Chicago than the Los Angeles definition (Kennedy, Braga, & Piehl, 1997).[13] With this definition, nearly 60% of the 155 homicides with victims aged 21 years and younger were attributed to Boston gangs.

Tita, Cohen, and Blumstein (1996) have reported preliminary findings on gang aspects in homicides in Pittsburgh. Data were collected from the Pittsburgh Police Department homicide files for 362 incidents that occurred between 1987 and 1994. Incidents were coded as "gang-motivated" and "gang-involved" (i.e., at least one participant was known to be a gang member, but homicide was not gang motivated). The researchers identified 27 (7%) incidents as gang-involved and 65 (18%) as gang-motivated. Eighteen of the 74 homicides coded as drug-motivated included gang members; these are included in the gang-involved (11 cases) and gang-motivated (7 cases) counts above. The researchers found that gang homicides were more likely to involve multiple offenders and large-caliber automatic weapons than were drug homicides. Altogether, 92 (25%) of Pittsburgh homicides would be designated as "gang" according to the "gang member" definition. These figures are surprising for a city whose police department reported *no* local gang activity on my 1992 survey with Malcolm Klein.

■ *THE NATURE OF GANG HOMICIDE IN LOS ANGELES*

In Los Angeles, data have been gathered from police investigation files for samples of gang and nongang homicides for three periods: 1978 to 1982, 1984 to 1985, and 1988 to 1989. Elsewhere, characteristics of these two types of incidents for the first two periods have been discussed, especially the remarkable consistency in the features that distinguish gang from nongang homicides (Klein et al., 1991; Maxson, Gordon, & Klein, 1985). In this section, I offer updated information from the 1988-1989 incidents to address whether the incident and participant descriptors of gang and nongang cases have changed since the earlier period. The 1988-1989 data come from the five station areas in South Central Los Angeles that were studied in 1984 to 1985.[14] Three of the five stations were within the jurisdiction of the LAPD, and two were county areas handled by the LASD; about three fourths of these cases, however, were from LAPD.

Gang and nongang homicides occurring in the five station areas during 1988 and 1989 were sampled using a random stratified approach to yield equal numbers of each type of homicide. Lists of "gang-involved" cases were supplied by each jurisdiction's specialized gang unit. The sampling procedures resulted in 201 gang and 201 nongang homicides, reflecting about two thirds of the population of gang-related homicides and slightly less of the nongang population.[15]

A team of data collectors extracted information from extensive homicide investigation files. Coded items included descriptors of the incident (e.g., setting, automobile involvement, weapons, related case charges, additional injuries, and gang motives); participants (e.g., numbers on each side, relationship, demographics of designated victims and suspects, and stated gang affiliations); and an extensive list of drug indicators (use/sales paraphernalia, drugs found in investigation, autopsy results, drug use or sales by participants, aspects of the location, and drug motives).[16]

Table 16.4 Incident and Participant Characteristics in Gang and Nongang Homicides, 1988 to 1989

	Gang (N = 201)	*Nongang (N = 201)*	*Association and Significance*[a]
Incident Characteristics:			
Setting			
Street	57% (114)	34% (68)	
Residence	30% (60)	50% (101)	.237***
Other	13% (27)	16% (32)	
Firearms present	95% (191)	75% (150)	.284***
Participants on suspect side	2.75	1.71	.302***
(Missing)	(6)	(28)	
Homicide Victims:[b]			
All victims male	90% (180)	77% (155)	.167**
Mean age of victims	24.2	34.4	-.391***
(Missing)	(4)	(4)	
Proportion Black victims	.80	.75	*ns*
Proportion Hispanic victims	.18	.23	*ns*
Homicide Suspects:			
All suspects male	93% (139)	83% (124)	.163**
(Missing)	(52)	(51)	
Mean age of suspects	20.5	31.3	-.523***
(Missing)	(52)	(52)	
Proportion Black suspects	.86	.81	*ns*
(Missing)	(52)	(51)	
Proportion Hispanic suspects	.14	.17	*ns*
(Missing)	(52)	(51)	

SOURCE: Adapted from Maxson, Klein, and Cunningham (1992).
a. Levels of association reported are Phi or Pearson's *r*. Significance levels determined by chi-squares or *t* tests. $*p < .05$; $**p < .01$; $***p < .001$.
b. Participant characteristics are computed across all homicide victims, or suspects, within a case. Additional victims, or suspects charged with associated case offenses rather than for homicide, are deleted from these calculations. Note that 26% of the homicide cases have no identified homicide suspect.

Differences in Gang and Nongang Homicides

In previous studies (Klein et al., 1991; Maxson et al., 1985), it was found that gang cases were more likely to take place on the street, to involve firearms, and to have more participants (see also Spergel, 1983). Gang homicide suspects were of younger ages and more likely to be male, although ethnicity did not produce significant gang-nongang differences. The same demographic distinctions hold for homicide victims.

A descriptive comparison of gang and nongang homicides for 1988-1989 is shown in Table 16.4. As expected, each of the variables tested shows significant gang-nongang differences, with the exception of the ethnicity variables.[17] The patterns of differences are similar to those found in the 1984-1985 homicides; the same variables distinguish gang and nongang cases, and there are no directional changes.

Data that are not shown in Table 16.4, however, reveal a pattern of *slightly diminishing differences between gang and nongang cases through time.* The percentage of gang cases occurring on the street decreased slightly (67% in 1984-1985; 57% in 1988-1989). Firearms presence remained about the same in gang cases, although it increased slightly in nongang cases (64% in 1984-1985; 75% in 1988-1989). The average number of suspected participants decreased by about one person in gang cases (3.71 in 1984-1985; 2.75 in 1988-1989) and increased slightly in nongang cases (1.50 in 1984-1985; 1.71 in 1988-1989). Victim gender and average age figures remained constant in both type of cases, as did the victim ethnicity in gang cases. In contrast, there was a slight decrease in the percentage of nongang Black victims (85% in 1984-1985; 75% in 1988-1989). Nongang suspects were about 2 years older (29 in 1984-1985; 31.3 in 1988-1989), whereas gang ages remain constant at 20 years. Suspect gender is the same in the two types of cases for the two periods. The only notable ethnic difference is an increase in Hispanic nongang suspects (11% in 1984-1985; 17% in 1988-1989).

Overall, the changes noted are minor and insubstantial relative to the generally consistent patterns of gang-nongang differences through the two periods. Further, this similarity extends to findings derived from the much earlier data collection of homicides occurring from 1978 to 1982 that were drawn from more than 20 station areas within LASD and LAPD (Maxson et al., 1985).

Drug Involvement in Gang and Nongang Homicides

The level and type of drug involvement in gang as compared with nongang homicides have been matters of concern for the last decade (for a review of this literature, see Howell, 1995; Klein & Maxson, 1994). To provide special attention to this facet of homicide incidents, gang-nongang comparisons for 1988 to 1989 are shown in Table 16.5. In the following discussion, these results will be compared with findings from the 1984-1985 homicide data.

The first question raised is the proportion of cases with drug involvement. The notion of drug involvement was approached quite broadly, and cases mentioning any aspect of drugs were labeled as drug involved. Later analyses will examine the specific nature of the drug involvement.

Of the 402 homicide cases, 64% have some aspect of drugs mentioned, but there are no gang-nongang differences ($p = .350$). The gang

Table 16.5 Drug Characteristics in Gang and Nongang Homicides, 1988 to 1989

All Homicides	*Gang (N = 201)*	*Nongang (N = 201)*	*Association and Significance*[a]
Drug mention	62% (124)	66% (133)	*ns*
Crack mention	19% (39)	30% (60)	–.121*
Cocaine mention	34% (68)	48% (97)	–.147**
Sales mention	40% (81)	33% (66)	*ns*
Drug motive mention	17% (34)	27% (55)	–.126*
Drug Homicides	*Gang (N = 124)*	*Nongang (N = 133)*	*Association and Significance*[a]
Crack mention	31% (39)	45% (60)	–.140*
Cocaine mention	55% (68)	73% (97)	–.189**
Sales mention	65% (81)	50% (66)	.159**
Drug motive mention	27% (34)	41% (55)	–.146*

SOURCE: Adapted from Maxson, Klein, and Cunningham (1992).
a. Levels of association reported are Phi. Significance levels determined by chi-squares. *$p < .05$; **$p < .01$; ***$p < .001$.

figure (124; 62% of cases) is similar to that found in gang cases in 1984 to 1985. On the other hand, the nongang figure (133; 60% of cases) has increased somewhat from the earlier figure of 56%. It appears that the pattern of increasing proportions of drug-involved nongang cases observed earlier in 1984 and 1985 has stabilized to the levels recorded in gang cases (Klein et al., 1991).

Given the similar levels of any drug mention in gang and nongang cases, it is appropriate to look more closely at the nature of drug involvement in these cases. Drug information was collected on specific items, most of which did not produce sufficiently high frequencies to support analyses of gang-nongang differences. Alternatively, variables were computed that represent more general aspects of drug involvement and reflect the gang-drug issues in South Central Los Angeles. Most drug mentions were coded to indicate the type of drug involved. From these, a variable was computed for any mention of crack/rock in the case and, because the form of cocaine is often not specified, also any mention of cocaine. The presence of any type of sales or distributional aspect of the case could derive from the nature of the incident location, sales involvement by participants on either side, or motives related to drug distribution. Finally, mention of any drug-related motive for the homicide includes conflicts about drug use, although these are far less frequent than motives stemming from drug distribution.

These aspects of drug involvement are reported in Table 16.5, first for all cases in the sample, then separately for only those homicides with drug involvement. The lower half of the table presents the different percentages and significance tests derived from computations on the smaller set of drug-involved homicides. The patterns in the two halves of Table 16.5 are, of course, similar; the only difference appears in the statistical significance attained by the higher level of drug sales mentions in gang cases when the numbers are reduced to drug-involved cases only.

Specific mentions of crack, or cocaine of any type, are more common in *nongang* than in gang homicides. Both types of drug mentions have increased proportionally over the 1984-1985 figures for nongang cases with drug involvement and have remained stable in gang cases.

On the other hand, presence of drug sales as an aspect of homicide has decreased slightly from the 1984-1985 levels, and in the 1988-1989 homicides, sales are mentioned more commonly in gang drug cases than in the nongang incidents. Finally, drug motives were recorded in about one third of these cases, similar to the findings for 1984 and 1985. *Mentions of drug motives remain proportionally more common in nongang than in gang homicides.*

Overall, 22% of the homicide cases studied had drug motives mentioned in the investigation file. Meehan and O'Carroll (1992) reported the same figure in the Centers for Disease Control and Prevention (CDC) study of 2,162 homicides occurring in the city of Los Angeles between January 1, 1986, and August 31, 1988. Although the CDC study covered a larger area and a slightly earlier (although overlapping) period, neither study provides confirmation of media reports of high levels of drug-motivated homicide in Los Angeles.

In other studies of gang, drugs, and homicide, Block et al. (1996) found that just 2.2% of Chicago street gang-related homicides between 1965 and 1994 involved a drug motive. Equally low proportions are reported by Kennedy et al. (1997) for Boston. Tita et al. (1996) found that 20% of all Pittsburgh gang homicides had a drug component and that 25% of all drug homicides had a gang component. In contrast to these studies, Sanders (1994) attributed an increase in gang-related homicides in San Diego between 1985 and 1988 to competition for turf in cocaine trafficking, but data are not presented to support this contention.

■ *CONCLUSIONS*

Investigations into the nature of gang homicide in several large but otherwise diverse U.S. cities find that these homicides most often reflect the dynamics of gang membership such as continuing intergroup rivalries, neighborhood turf battles, identity challenges, and occasional intragroup status threats. The victims in gang homicides are usually other gang members. The commonly stated myths of gang homicides—that they are steeped in drug distribution systemic processes or random acts of expressive outrage against innocent citizens—simply do not hold up. Instead, there is much continuity in findings about the character of gang homicide, despite the growth in numbers. This increase, in the face of the current declining trend in other types of homicide, suggests that the *unique* aspects of gang violence are especially deserving of more attention.

Far less common, although much more publicized, are the deaths of innocent bystanders. These victims represent collateral tragedies of gang rivalries and membership dynamics, yet mobilize community groups and government officials in ways that the numbing annual statistics of gang homicides apparently do not. The 1995 death of 3-year-old blond-haired and blue-eyed Stephanie Kuhen in Los Angeles was the catalyst for establishing a citywide collaborative task force. The group's findings led local government officials to reassess long-standing practices of allocating funds to unevaluated gang prevention programs in an uncoordinated manner. Recently, the city council launched a new comprehensive prevention effort, the L.A. Bridges project. This program has generated a much-enhanced funding pool ($11 million per year), a longer time commitment to funded programs, and an integrated evaluation component to determine the effectiveness of funded programs.

More often, such catalyzing events provoke large increments in law enforcement responses intended to suppress gang activity. Social scientists, however, can help local policymakers avoid simplistic, ill-designed crisis management reactions (Hagedorn, in press). A small but growing body of alternative efforts uses research knowledge and local empirical data to formulate coordinated and well-targeted responses. The Boston Gun Project, the geographic mapping of crime hot spots in Chicago, and Irving Spergel's Little Village project, also in Chicago, are just a few examples of promising efforts currently under way. Unquestionably, annual tabulations of gang homicides in cities across the country are an important component in recognizing the scope of gang violence. Let us hope, however, that analysts can move rapidly to a better assessment of the character of these lethal (and also nonlethal) events and that these assessments will contribute to the development of solutions targeted to the specific nature of gang-related problems in their communities.

■ *NOTES*

1. Previously unpublished data were gathered with support from the Harry Frank Guggenheim Foundation, the Southern California Injury Prevention Center (under the auspices of the Public Health Service Centers for Disease Control and Injury Prevention Grant No. R49/CCR903622) and the National Institute of Justice (No. 91-IJ-CX-K004). Malcolm W. Klein was a coprincipal investigator on all three grants. Views expressed herein are solely mine and do not represent the official position of any of the agencies providing support. I appreciate comments by Mac Klein on an earlier draft and the computer assistance of Karen Sternheimer and Brianna Garcia.

2. Periodically, researchers have attempted to use the gang information (i.e., victim-offender relationship and gang circumstances) recorded in the Supplementary Homicide Reports but have obtained less than desirable results. In general, the SHR data are thought to underestimate levels of gang involvement, particularly in the past (Bailey & Unnithan, 1994; P. Lattimore, personal communication, January 9, 1997; Riedel & Lewitt, 1996).

3. I have previously detailed many of the challenges in coding data from gang homicide investigation files, particularly with reference to victim-offender relationships, motives or circumstances, and number of participants (Maxson, 1992).

4. Wild variations exist between figures provided for Chicago by Miller (1982/1992) and by Block et al. (1996), although both obtained their figures from the Chicago Police Department. For example, Block and her colleagues report 18 gang homicides for 1967, whereas Miller's number is 150. Miller notes the political dimensions of gang homicide reporting (see Appendix D in his 1982 report), a factor that likely accounts for the discrepancy. Convergence between the sources is evident during 1970 to 1974 and 1977 to 1979.

5. The survey population was 1,019 cities of all sizes, including all U.S. cities with populations greater than 100,000 and other locations with reported gang problems, drawn from a variety of sources. For a detailed description of the study methods and definitions of street gangs, see Maxson et al. (1995), especially Appendix A.

6. These data were first reported in Klein (1995, p. 116).

7. Despite the request for counts of homicides involving gang members, the figure of 129 gang homicides in Chicago is consistent with the Chicago Police Department's policy of designating crimes as gang-related only if they are tied directly to a gang function (Maxson & Klein, 1996, but see footnote 2 in that work). Data are not available to assess whether respondents in other cities on this list reported gang homicide figures based on definitional approaches other than those they were requested to use.

8. In recognition of the fluctuation of gang homicides from one year to the next (Block et al., 1996), rates were calculated only for those cities with at least 10 homicides.

9. Approximately 5% of all survey respondents were telephoned to clarify ambiguities or conflicting information, but the counts of gang homicides were not a priority item for this process.

10. The wording of this item on the 1996 NYGC survey (covering homicides in 1995) is not comparable with any other survey. The request of counts of homicides that involved gang members as perpetrators separate from counts of incidents with gang members as victims is problematic. If the NYGC data are limited to city agencies that report at least one homicide in which a gang member was a perpetrator or victim, a simple comparison with the Maxson-Klein 1991 homicide data is possible. NYGC staff identified 366 cities with at least one homicide so defined (J. Moore, personal communication, January 16, 1997). This number represents about one fourth of all gang cities in the NYGC database. In the Maxson-Klein 1992 survey, just under 300 cities, or about 40% of all gang cities, reported gang homicides during 1991. Thus, the NYGC survey identified nearly twice the number of gang cities in 1995 but just 25% more cities with gang homicides than the earlier survey. A revision of this item on the upcoming NYGC survey of 1996 gang

homicides will produce data directly comparable with that gathered in the 1992 survey.

11. For Figure 16.1, gang homicide tabulations for each year between 1965 and 1994 are taken from Block et al. (1996). The proportions of all homicides were calculated from annual homicide figures printed in Block and Christakos (1995). Data for 1995 were provided by C. Rebecca Block.

12. Most of the gang homicides in Los Angeles County occur in jurisdictions patrolled by the LAPD and the LASD. The Sheriff Department's Operation Safe Streets gang unit gathers counts of gang homicides that occur in the more than 70 independent police jurisdictions in the county. Uniform definitional practices are used throughout the county.

13. According to Kennedy et al. (1997),

> Gang-related, as the group understood it, meant in practice that the incident was either the product of gang behavior such as drug dealing, turf protection, a continuing "beef" with a rival gang or gangs, or a product of activity that was narrowly and directly connected with gang membership such as a struggle for power within a particular gang. Not all homicide involvement by gang members counted under this definition. (p. 222)

14. Case sampling and data collection procedures were similar in the two studies.

15. The five stations were characterized by high levels of gang activity, with a high proportion of all homicides occurring in their areas being gang related.

16. Intercoder reliability was assessed by duplicate coding of 10% of the sample; overall, reliabilities were high (greater than .90), but the data collection was closely supervised, with heavy involvement by senior staff in coding decisions.

17. The high proportion of African American involvement in these cases is a reflection of the ethnic composition of these five station areas and is *not* representative of homicides in Los Angeles County. Hutson, Anglin, Kyriacou, Hart, and Spears (1995) found that 57% of victims of gang homicides from 1979 through 1994 in the county were Hispanic and 37% were African American. The study of 1978 to 1982 gang and nongang homicides occurring in all unincorporated areas of the county and within three high-activity stations in LAPD, 1979 to 1981, also found that Hispanics were more often victims in gang, than in nongang, homicides (Maxson et al., 1985).

■ *REFERENCES*

Bailey, G. W., & Unnithan, N. P. (1994). Gang homicides in California: A discriminant analysis. *Journal of Criminal Justice, 22,* 267-275.

Ball, R. A., & Curry, G. D. (1995). The logic of definition in criminology: Purposes and methods for defining "gangs." *Criminology, 33,* 225-245.

Battin, S. R., Hill, K. G., Abbott, R. D., Catalano, R. F., & Hawkins, J. D. (1998). The contribution of gang membership to delinquency beyond delinquent friends. *Criminology, 36,* 93-115.

Block, C. R., & Christakos, A. (1995). *Major trends in Chicago homicide: 1965-1994* (Research bulletin). Chicago: Illinois Criminal Justice Information Authority.

Block, C. R., Christakos, A., Jacob, A. P., & Przybylski, R. (1996). *Street gangs and crime: Patterns and trends in Chicago* (Research bulletin). Chicago: Illinois Criminal Justice Information Authority.

Block, R. L., & Block, C. R. (1993). *Street gang crime in Chicago* (Research in Brief: NCJ-144782). Washington, DC: National Institute of Justice.

Curry, G. D., Ball, R. A., & Decker, S. H. (1995). *An update on gang crime and law enforcement record keeping.* St. Louis: University of Missouri, Department of Criminology and Criminal Justice.

Curry, G. D., Ball, R. A., & Decker, S. H. (1996). Estimating the national scope of gang crime from law enforcement data. In C. R. Huff (Ed.), *Gangs in America* (2nd ed., pp. 21-36). Thousand Oaks, CA: Sage.

Curry, G. D., Ball, R. A., & Fox, R. J. (1994). *Gang crime and law enforcement record keeping* (Research in Brief: NCJ-148345). Washington, DC: National Institute of Justice.

Decker, S. H., & Van Winkle, B. (1996). *Life in the gang: Family, friends and violence.* New York: Cambridge University Press.

Dodge, K. A. (1997). *How gang membership increases violent behavior* (National Consortium on Violence Research grant proposal). Nashville, TN: Vanderbilt University, Department of Psychology and Human Development.

Esbensen, F., & Huizinga, D. (1993). Gangs, drugs and delinquency in a survey of urban youth. *Criminology, 31,* 565-589.

Esbensen, F., Huizinga, D., & Weiher, A. (1993). Gang and non-gang youth: Differences in explanatory factors. *Journal of Contemporary Criminal Justice, 9,* 94-116.

Fagan, J. (1989). The social organization of drug use and drug dealing among urban gangs. *Criminology, 27,* 633-669.

Fox, J. A. (1996). *Trends in juvenile violence: A report to the United States attorney general on current and future rates of juvenile offending.* Washington, DC: Bureau of Justice Statistics.

Hagedorn, J. (in press). Gang violence in the post industrial era. In M. Tonry (Ed.), *Youth violence.* Chicago: University of Chicago Press.

Hill, K. G., Hawkins, D., Catalano, R. F., Kosterman, R., Abbott, R., & Edwards, T. (1996, November). *The longitudinal dynamics of gang membership and problem behavior: A replication and extension of the Denver and Rochester gang studies in Seattle.* Paper presented at the annual meeting of the American Society of Criminology, Chicago.

Howell, J. C. (1995). Gangs and youth violence: Present research. In J. C. Howell, B. Krisberg, J. D. Hawkins, &

J. J. Wilson (Eds.), *Serious, violent, and chronic juvenile offenders* (pp. 261-274). Thousand Oaks, CA: Sage.

Huff, C. R. (1996). Introduction. In C. R. Huff (Ed.), *Gangs in America* (2nd ed., pp. xxi-xxvii). Thousand Oaks, CA: Sage.

Huizinga, D. (1997, February). *Gangs and volume of crime.* Paper presented at the annual meeting of the Western Society of Criminology, Honolulu, HI.

Hutson, H. R., Anglin, D., Kyriacou, D. M., Hart, J., & Spears, K. (1995). The epidemic of gang-related homicides in Los Angeles County from 1979 through 1994. *Journal of the American Medical Association, 274,* 1031-1036.

Jackson, R. L., Lopez, R. J., & Connell, R. (1997, January 12). Clinton puts priority on curtailing gang crime. *Los Angeles Times,* p. A1.

Kennedy, D. M., Braga, A. A., & Piehl, A. M. (1997). The (un)known universe: Mapping gangs and gang violence in Boston. In D. Weisburd & T. McEwen (Eds.), *Crime mapping and crime prevention* (pp. 219-262). New York: Criminal Justice Press.

Klein, M. W. (1995). *The American street gang: Its nature, prevalence, and control.* New York: Oxford University Press.

Klein, M. W., Gordon, M. A., & Maxson, C. L. (1986). The impact of police investigations on police-reported rates of gang and nongang homicides. *Criminology, 24,* 489-512.

Klein, M. W., & Maxson, C. L. (1994). Gangs and crack cocaine trafficking. In D. L. MacKenzie & C. D. Uchida (Eds.), *Drugs and crime* (pp. 42-58). Thousand Oaks, CA: Sage.

Klein, M. W., Maxson, C. L., & Cunningham, L. C. (1991). "Crack," street gangs, and violence. *Criminology, 29,* 623-650.

Lizotte, A. J., Tesoriero, J. M., Thornberry, T. P., & Krohn, M. D. (1994). Patterns of adolescent firearms ownership and use. *Justice Quarterly, 16,* 51-73.

Maxson, C. L. (1992). Collecting data from investigation files: Descriptions of three Los Angeles gang homicide projects. In C. R. Block & R. L. Block (Eds.), *Questions and answers in lethal and non-lethal violence* (pp. 87-95). Washington, DC: National Institute of Justice.

Maxson, C. L. (1996). *Street gang members on the move: The role of migration in the proliferation of street gangs in the U.S.* Tallahassee, FL: National Youth Gang Center.

Maxson, C. L., Gordon, M. A., & Klein, M. W. (1985). Differences between gang and nongang homicides. *Criminology, 23,* 209-222.

Maxson, C. L., & Klein, M. W. (1990). Street gang violence: Twice as great, or half as great? In C. R. Huff (Ed.), *Gangs in America* (pp. 71-100). Newbury Park, CA: Sage.

Maxson, C. L., & Klein, M. W. (1996). Defining gang homicide: An updated look at member and motive approaches. In C. R. Huff (Ed.), *Gangs in America* (2nd ed., pp. 3-20). Thousand Oaks, CA: Sage.

Maxson, C. L., & Klein, M. W. (1997). Urban street gangs in Los Angeles. In M. Dear & P. Ethington (Eds.), *Los Angeles versus Chicago: Re-envisioning the urban process.* Unpublished report, University of Southern California, Southern California Studies Center, Los Angeles.

Maxson, C. L., Klein, M. W., & Cunningham, L. (1992). *Definitional variations affecting drug and gang homicide issues.* Los Angeles: University of Southern California, Center for the Study of Crime and Social Control, Social Science Research Institute.

Maxson, C. L., Woods, K. J., & Klein, M. W. (1995). *Street gang migration in the United States.* Los Angeles: University of Southern California, Center for the Study of Crime and Social Control, Social Science Research Institute.

Meehan, P. J., & O'Carroll, P. W. (1992). Gangs, drugs, and homicide in Los Angeles. *American Journal of Disease Control, 146,* 683-687.

Miller, W. B. (1992). *Crime by youth gangs and groups in the United States.* Washington, DC: Office of Juvenile Justice and Delinquency Prevention. (Original report issued 1982)

Miller, W. B. (1996). *The growth of youth gang problems in the U.S.: 1970-1995.* Tallahassee, FL: National Youth Gang Center, Institute for Intergovernmental Research.

Moore, J. (1991). *Going down to the barrio: Homeboys and homegirls in change.* Philadelphia: Temple University Press.

National Youth Gang Center. (1997). *1995 National youth gang survey.* Washington, DC: Office of Juvenile Justice and Delinquency Prevention.

Quinn, J. F., Tobolowsky, P. M., & Downs, W. T. (1994). The gang problem in large and small cities: An analysis of police perceptions in nine states. *The Gang Journal, 2,* 13-22.

Riedel, M., & Lewitt, K. N. (1996, November). *Hispanic homicides in Los Angeles: A study of racial and ethnic patterns.* Paper presented at the annual meeting of the American Society of Criminology, Chicago.

Sanders, W. (1994). *Gangbangs and drive-bys: Grounded culture and juvenile gang violence.* New York: Aldine de Gruyter.

Sheley, J. F., & Wright, J. D. (1995). *In the line of fire: Youth, guns, and violence in urban America.* New York: Aldine de Gruyter.

Short, J. F., Jr. (1996). *Gangs and adolescent violence.* Boulder: University of Colorado, Center for the Study and Prevention of Violence.

Spergel, I. A. (1983). *Violent gangs in Chicago: Segmentation and integration.* Chicago: University of Chicago, School of Social Service Administration.

Spergel, I. A. (1988). *Report of the Law Enforcement Youth Gang Symposium.* Chicago: University of Chicago, School of Social Service Administration.

Spergel, I. A. (1995). *The youth gang problem: A community approach.* New York: Oxford University Press.

Spergel, I. A., & Curry, D. G. (1990). Strategies and perceived agency effectiveness in dealing with the youth gang problem. In C. R. Huff (Ed.), *Gangs in America* (pp. 288-309). Newbury Park, CA: Sage.

Thornberry, T. P., & Burch, J. H., II. (1997). *Gang members and delinquent behavior* (NCJ-165154). Washington,

DC: Office of Juvenile Justice and Delinquency Prevention.

Thornberry, T. P., Krohn, M. D., Lizotte, A. J., & Chard-Wierschem, D. (1993). The role of juvenile gangs in facilitating delinquent behavior. *Journal of Research in Crime and Delinquency, 30,* 55-87.

Tita, G. E., Cohen, J., & Blumstein, A. (1996, November). *Exploring the gang-drug-gun nexus: Evidence from homicides in Pittsburgh.* Paper presented at the annual meeting of the American Society of Criminology, Chicago.

Tracy, P. E. (1979). *Subcultural delinquency: A comparison of the incidence and seriousness of gang and nongang member offensivity.* Philadelphia: University of Pennsylvania, Center for Studies in Criminology and Criminal Law.

Zahn, M. A., & Jamieson, K. M. (1997). Changing patterns of homicide and social policy. *Homicide Studies, 1,* 190-196.

PART VI

Preventing Homicide: Proposed Solutions

CHAPTER 17

Capital Punishment, Homicide, and Deterrence

An Assessment of the Evidence and Extension to Female Homicide

■ *William C. Bailey & Ruth D. Peterson*

Scholars have devoted a great deal of attention to the role of capital punishment in the criminal justice system. Concerns about the death penalty were at the forefront of interest for a number of the early founders of criminology (Beccaria, 1764/1963; Bentham, 1962), and the debate continues today as the United States maintains the distinction of being the only Western nation to retain capital punishment for common murder. Currently, 38 states and the federal government authorize capital punishment for murder and various other crimes. As of the last Bureau of Justice Statistics census (December 1996), more than 3,000 persons were on death row awaiting execution (Snell, 1997). One core empirical issue is whether the death penalty is more effective than alternative sanctions, namely, long terms of imprisonment, in preventing (deterring) murder. In this chapter, we review and assess the empirical literature regarding the marginal deterrent effect of capital punishment for murder. To set the stage for this discussion, however, we first briefly review the deterrence argument.

Deterrence theory is rooted in the classical and neoclassical schools of criminology (Beccaria, 1764/1963; Bentham, 1962). Two basic assumptions underlie these perspectives. First is the view that the fundamental purpose of state-imposed sanctions is to prevent crime. Second is the reliance on a rationalistic view of human behavior. Here, persons are seen as rationally weighing the costs and rewards of alternative actions and choosing behaviors that yield the greatest gain at the least cost.

AUTHORS' NOTE: Correspondence regarding this article should be addressed to William C. Bailey, College of Graduate Studies, Cleveland State University, Euclid Avenue at 24th Street, Cleveland, OH 44115.

As an outgrowth of these schools of thought, deterrence theory holds that preventing crime requires the development of a system of punishment that will teach the lesson that "crime does not pay." To be effective, punishments must be perceived as sufficiently severe to outweigh the pleasure or profits gained from the crimes in question, must occur with a high level of certainty so that the punishments are perceived as real, must be administered promptly, and must be made known to the public so that it is clear to would-be offenders that there is a cause-and-effect link between the commission of the crime and the sanctioning of the offender. Proponents of deterrence contend that under such conditions, the threat and application of sanctions can be effective in discouraging would-be offenders from breaking the law (*general deterrence*) and reducing repeat offending (*specific deterrence*) by those who have been punished.

Applied to capital punishment and homicide, deterrence theory assumes that murder is a rational act and that in calculating the gains and losses from killing, potential offenders not only are cognizant of the death penalty but also identify with the executed offender. That is, people are able to put themselves in the shoes of the offender and thereby assume that they will likely suffer the same consequences for killing (i.e., execution). Because the threat of one's own death presumably outweighs the reward from killing another, the would-be killer rationally refrains from murder. In short, as a result of the rationalizing and identification processes, capital punishment reduces the likelihood that murder will occur beyond that achieved by alternative sanctions (Berns, 1979, 1980; Lehtinen, 1977; van den Haag, 1975). In addition to directly deterring potential offenders, proponents of the death penalty believe that this sanction provides an educative function in morally validating the sanctity of human life (Berns, 1979, 1980; van den Haag, 1975).

In light of the proposed application of deterrence principles to capital punishment, the purpose of this chapter is to assess the state of knowledge regarding the deterrent effectiveness of capital punishment. Given the quantity of such research, we note the following considerations in our examination of the literature:

1. Our analysis is restricted to deterrence investigations conducted in the United States. Readers should consult works by Bowers (1988), Chandler (1976), Fattah (1972), Jayewardene (1977), and Phillips (1980) for a sampling of deterrence research for other countries.

2. We are concerned solely with deterrence studies in which murder is the dependent variable. Historically, in the United States, the death penalty has been authorized for various other crimes, including kidnapping, treason, espionage, rape, robbery, arson, and train wrecking (Bowers, 1984). Executions, however, have been restricted largely to convicted murderers. Indeed, since the mid-1960s, no one in the United States has been executed for a crime other than murder.

3. Our assessment of the literature focuses on studies of capital punishment and general, rather than specific, deterrence (Andenaes, 1974). The concern is with how capital punishment influences *potential* homicide offenders, rather than assessing the relative merits of long terms of imprisonment versus executions in preventing convicted murderers from killing again.

4. Although our specific focus is deterrence, we will also consider works on the *brutalization effect* of the death penalty. These studies test the long-held hypothesis that capital punishment *encourages,* rather than discourages, murder by setting a "savage example" for society to follow (Beccaria, 1764/1963). In contrast to the deterrence argument, the brutalization thesis does not assume that would-be murderers identify with the executed person. Rather, the assumption is that observers identify the person who is executed with someone who has offended them greatly. As such, they identify with the state as executioner and thus justify and reinforce the desire for lethal vengeance (Bowers & Pierce, 1980). Most studies of brutalization are virtually identical to deterrence analyses in their methodology; they differ only in the direction of the expected relationship between capital punishment and murder.

5. Finally, because of the large volume of work on deterrence and capital punishment, our review of the literature will be selective, rather

than exhaustive. In selecting studies to present, we will provide a sampling of the different methodological approaches and research designs that have been employed.

■ *AN OVERVIEW OF THE CAPITAL PUNISHMENT AND HOMICIDE LITERATURE*

In the discussion that follows, we organize studies according to their focus on one or more of the four dimensions of punishment that are central to the deterrence thesis—severity, certainty, celerity, and publicity. We also address as separate topics deterrence investigations that have considered specific types of murder.

Comparative Studies and the Severity Hypothesis

From early in this century through the 1960s, the comparative methodology provided the most common means of testing for the deterrent effect of the death penalty. Here, the punishment measure of concern was the statutory provision or absence of the death penalty. One approach involved comparing average homicide rates for jurisdictions with (i.e., retentionist states) and without (i.e., abolitionist states) capital punishment (Bye, 1919; Savitz, 1958; Sellin, 1955, 1959, 1961, 1967, 1980; Sutherland, 1925). An extension of this methodology involved comparing murder rates for clusters of contiguous, and presumably similar, abolitionist and retentionist jurisdictions. This latter strategy was based on the recognition that death penalty and non-death penalty states may differ in other respects that might influence murder rates, such as population composition, region, and socioeconomic conditions. Contiguous state comparisons provide a method of controlling for how such factors may differentiate abolitionist and retentionist jurisdictions and, thereby, distort simple analyses of average homicide rates for the two types of states. The deterrence hypothesis in cross-state comparative analyses is that murder rates should be higher in abolitionist jurisdictions.

An alternative comparative strategy involved examining rates for states before and after the abolition and/or reinstatement of the death penalty (Bedau, 1967; Schuessler, 1952; Sellin, 1955, 1959, 1967). Here, the deterrence thesis predicts that abolition should be followed by an increase in murder rates and that reinstatement should result in a decrease in killings.

Through the decades, the findings of comparative studies were consistent and contrary to the deterrence thesis. Simple comparative analyses revealed that average homicide rates were consistently higher for death penalty jurisdictions. Studies of changes in murder rates before and after the abolition and/or reinstatement of capital punishment revealed that states that abolished the death penalty did not experience unusual increases in homicides. Rather, abolition and/or reintroduction of capital punishment was sometimes followed by an increase in murders and sometimes not. Moreover, changes in rates paralleled almost exactly changes in homicides in neighboring states in which no statutory change had occurred. Also contrary to the deterrence thesis, contiguous state comparisons of retentionist and abolitionist jurisdictions showed that the provision for the death penalty had no discernible effect on murder.

This nondeterrence pattern holds for the contemporary period as well. To illustrate, murder rates for six groupings of neighboring death penalty and abolitionist states for 1980 to 1995 are presented in Table 17.1. Abolitionist states are indicated with an asterisk (*).

For most of the six groupings, the evidence is contrary to the deterrence hypothesis. For New England states, New Hampshire is the only state that prescribes the death penalty for murder. Rates consistently are lower for New Hampshire than for abolitionist Rhode Island and Massachusetts during 1980 through 1995. The pattern for New Hampshire, however, is similar to that for Maine and Vermont, neither of which is a death penalty jurisdiction. Rates are lower for abolitionist North Dakota compared with retentionist South Dakota, Montana, and Wyoming. In the South, murder rates are lower each year for abolitionist West Virginia

Table 17.1 Rates of Murder and Nonnegligent Manslaughter for Neighboring Death Penalty and Abolitionist States, 1980 to 1995

State	*Abolition Period*	*1980*	*1981*	*1982*	*1983*	*1984*	*1985*	*1986*	*1987*	*1988*	*1989*	*1990*	*1991*	*1992*	*1993*	*1994*	*1995*
Maine*	1980-1995	3	3	2	2	2	2	2	3	3	3	2	1	2	2	2	2
Vermont*	1980-1995	2	4	2	4	2	3	2	2	2	2	2	2	2	4	1	5
New Hampshire		3	3	2	2	1	2	2	3	2	3	2	4	2	2	1	2
Rhode Island*	1980-1995	4	4	4	3	3	4	4	4	4	5	5	4	4	4	4	3
Massachusetts*	1980-1982 1984-1995	4	4	4	4	4	4	3	4	4	4	4	4	4	4	4	4
Michigan*	1980-1995	10	9	9	10	10	11	11	12	11	11	10	11	10	10	10	9
Ohio*	1980	8	7	6	6	5	5	6	6	5	6	6	7	7	6	6	5
Indiana		9	7	7	5	6	6	6	6	6	6	6	8	8	8	8	8
Wisconsin*	1980-1995	3	3	3	3	3	3	3	4	3	4	5	5	4	4	5	4
Iowa*	1980-1995	2	3	2	2	2	2	2	2	2	2	2	2	2	2	2	2
Illinois		11	11	9	10	9	8	9	8	9	8	8	11	11	11	12	10
North Dakota*	1980-1995	1	2	1	2	1	1	1	2	2	1	1	1	2	2	0	1
South Dakota		1	2	3	2	2	2	4	2	3	1	2	2	1	3	1	2
Montana		4	3	4	2	4	6	3	4	3	4	5	3	4	3	3	2
Wyoming		6	6	9	6	3	4	5	2	3	4	5	3	4	3	3	2
West Virginia*	1980-1995	7	6	5	5	4	4	6	5	5	7	6	6	6	7	5	5
Virginia		9	9	7	7	8	7	7	7	8	8	9	9	9	8	9	8
Oregon*	1981-1983	5	4	5	4	5	5	7	6	5	5	4	5	5	5	5	4
Washington		6	5	4	5	5	5	5	6	6	4	5	4	4	5	6	5
Idaho		3	4	3	4	3	2	3	3	4	3	3	2	4	3	4	4

SOURCE: Compiled from data from Federal Bureau of Investigation (1981-1996), *Crime in the United States: Uniform Crime Reports* (annual editions); Snell (1996).
NOTE: Murder rates (per 100,000 population) are rounded to whole numbers.
*States without capital punishment for the periods indicated. Death penalty status determined as of December 31 of the years indicated.

compared with Virginia, a death penalty state during the period. For the three Northwest states, the period during which rates for death penalty states and an abolitionist state (Oregon) can be compared is short (1981-1983). Still, there is no indication of a deterrent effect for capital punishment. In addition, the murder rate did not decline with Oregon's return to capital punishment in 1984.

The two groupings of states in the Midwest provide more ambiguous results. Compared with Indiana and Ohio (Ohio was without the death penalty in 1980), homicide rates are consistently higher for abolitionist Michigan. This, on the surface, is consistent with the deterrence argument. In the opposite direction, however, murder rates are consistently higher in Illinois than in neighboring Wisconsin and Iowa, which were abolitionist states throughout the period. Unfortunately, these opposing patterns can result in misleading conclusions. It is well recognized that Illinois's high homicide rate is largely a function of killings in one city—Chicago. There is no counterpart to Chicago in Wisconsin and Iowa.

The case is similar for contiguous Michigan, Indiana, and Ohio. Throughout the period, the homicide rate in abolitionist Michigan was dominated by killings in a single city, Detroit. When Detroit's killings are excluded in calculating the Michigan homicide rate, there is no indication of an added measure of protection afforded by the death penalty in neighboring Ohio or Indiana. Excluding a community with high homicide rates from one type of state (Detroit in Michigan) but ignoring the effect of similar atypical communities in neighboring retentionist states (e.g., Cleveland in Ohio and Indianapolis in Indiana), however, is to betray the intent of contiguous state comparisons—to control for those "other" factors influencing homicides.

In sum, earlier comparative studies provided little evidence that capital punishment gives residents of retentionist jurisdictions an added measure of protection against criminal homicide. Applying this methodology to the most recent period shows that for the majority of comparisons, this remains true today. This illustrative analysis also reveals, however, that in some cases neighboring death penalty and abolitionist states are not similar enough to warrant drawing reasonable conclusions from comparative analyses. In addition, relying on contiguous state comparisons means that we ignore the death penalty question for some jurisdictions. Notably, less West Virginia, there are no abolitionist states in the southern or border regions of the country. Finally, the contiguous state approach does not differentiate properly between neighboring death penalty jurisdictions that vary in their actual use (i.e., certainty) of capital punishment.

The Certainty Hypothesis

Exploring the issue of certainty requires examining the relationship between levels of actual execution and murder rates. With the exception of a study by Schuessler (1952), the certainty hypothesis did not receive systematic attention until the 1970s. Schuessler correlated average execution rates (the ratio of executions to criminal homicides) with homicide rates for 1937 to 1941 for 41 U.S. death penalty states. Contrary to deterrence predictions, he observed only a slight negative relationship ($r = -.26$, $R^2 = .067$) between executions and homicides. As a check on the consistency of this pattern, Schuessler examined execution and homicide rates for four groupings of death penalty states divided according to the size of the homicide rate. This analysis showed that homicide rates do not consistently fall as the risk of execution increases. These observations led Schuessler to conclude that "the death penalty has little if anything to do with the relative occurrence of murder" (p. 61). A replication and an extension of Schuessler's analysis for 1967 to 1968 (Bailey, 1975) also found no evidence of a significant deterrent effect for the certainty of execution.

The Ehrlich Analysis

An important contribution to understanding the deterrent effect of the certainty of capital punishment came from a study by Isaac Ehrlich (1975) in the mid-1970s. Ehrlich dismissed previous death penalty research as simplistic and inadequate because investigators largely ignored the certainty of execution hypothesis. He also complained that previous studies did not consider appropriate control variables to guard against spurious results for the death penalty factors. Ehrlich sought to address these shortcomings by conducting a statistical analysis that explicitly recognized the fundamental importance of the certainty hypothesis, considered multiple measures of the certainty of capital punishment, recognized the possible importance of the severity and certainty of alternative sanctions (imprisonment) in deterring murder, and considered a variety of law enforcement and sociodemographic factors associated with murder rates as formal control variables in examining U.S. homicide rates for various periods between 1933 and 1969. Aggregating his data on a national and annual basis, Ehrlich found a significant decline in executions and a general rise in the homicide rate during this period. The observed trade-off between homicide rates and different measures of execution certainty varied somewhat, but the pattern was convincing for Ehrlich. On the basis of his analyses, Ehrlich claimed that each execution that was performed during the period may have prevented, on average, seven to eight murders.

Ehrlich's analysis brought to the forefront the complexity of the deterrence and death penalty issue and the need for a more sophisticated methodology than found in earlier studies. Indeed, his article stimulated a new round of research in the 1970s and 1980s that addressed important, but traditionally neglected, questions regarding deterrence and capital punishment.

Reactions to Ehrlich's Study

The reaction to Ehrlich's study was a series of replications of his national time-series analysis (Bowers & Pierce, 1975; Klein, Forst, &

Filatov, 1978; Layson, 1985; Passell & Taylor, 1977; Yunker, 1976). With the exceptions of Layson and Yunker, these efforts did not support Ehrlich's claims. Rather, scholars detected theoretical and technical problems with his investigation. First, critics noted that such time-series analyses are subject to serious problems of aggregation error/bias when the unit of analysis is the entire nation and when an obvious factor such as dramatic changes in the percentage of the U.S. population subject to the death penalty is ignored as either a deterrence or a control variable. As an example, the proportion of the U.S. population residing in retentionist and abolitionist jurisdictions was far from uniform from 1933 through 1969. Ignoring this fact renders extremely suspect national aggregate studies such as Ehrlich's. Problems of interpretation also arise because Ehrlich aggregated his homicide and control variables on a national level, thus also ignoring the tremendous variation in these factors from state to state.

Second, some critics took issue with Ehrlich for operationalizing his main independent variable as execution risk and ignoring the legal status of the death penalty (Baldus & Cole, 1975). Although measuring execution risk takes into account the use of the death penalty (in retentionist states), Ehrlich's analysis ignores the policy issue of deterrence and abolition (or reinstatement) of capital punishment on the state level.

Third, critics debated the relative merits of econometric modeling versus other means of controlling for important etiological factors in attempting to isolate the possible deterrent effect of capital punishment. With this approach, there is the risk that important variables might be overlooked or used improperly (Baldus & Cole, 1975). If important predictor variables are excluded, or if irrelevant variables are included in the model, the apparent precision in estimating the impact of a given variable (such as executions) on homicide rates will result in misleading conclusions.

Finally, Ehrlich's findings of deterrence do not hold when other factors are considered. This is evident in two ways. Some of the statistical models he specified suggested a possible deterrent effect and some did not, but Ehrlich chose to emphasize the former models over the latter. There is no a priori theoretical reason, however, for viewing the models that suggest a possible deterrent effect as superior to those models that produced no indication of deterrence (Klein et al., 1978). In addition, Ehrlich's findings of deterrence are dependent on the period being examined, 1933 to 1969. When the time series ends in the *early to mid*-1960s, the deterrent effect disappears. The obvious question is this: Why was the death penalty a significant deterrent to murder from 1933 to 1969 but not from 1933 through the mid-1960s? These and other unanswered questions cause the results of the Ehrlich study to be highly suspect.

Building on the Ehrlich Analysis

Ehrlich's (1975) study inspired a renewed interest in the deterrence issue and a number of efforts aimed at addressing the difficulties with his investigation. For example, to address aggregation problems associated with a nationwide analysis, researchers examined time-series data for individual states for various periods extending back to the turn of the century. Among the jurisdictions examined were California (Bailey, 1979c), Illinois (Decker & Kohfeld, 1984), New York (Bowers & Pierce, 1980), North Carolina (Bailey, 1979a), Ohio (Bailey, 1979d), Oregon (Bailey, 1979b), Utah (Bailey, 1978), and Washington, D.C. (Bailey, 1984b). None of these analyses produced consistent evidence of a deterrent effect for the certainty of capital punishment.

Using states as the unit of analysis, several researchers (including Ehrlich himself) also conducted cross-sectional studies of the relationship between executions and murder rates while controlling for various sociodemographic factors associated with homicide. In some of these analyses, measures of the certainty and length of *imprisonment* for murder were incorporated as additional deterrence variables (Bailey, 1975, 1977, 1980b, 1983; Ehrlich, 1977; Forst, 1977; Passell, 1975; Peterson & Bailey, 1988). Among these studies, Ehrlich was the only researcher to report evidence of a deterrent effect for executions. Because no other investigators observed a deterrence pattern, Ehrlich's work was once again subject to scrutiny. As before, scholars found serious theoretical and methodological difficulties with his analysis, rendering Ehrlich's cross-sectional findings suspect as well (Barnett, 1981; Beyleveld, 1982; Brier & Feinberg, 1980; Friedman, 1979; McGahey, 1980).

The Celerity of Capital Punishment

Proponents of deterrence long have argued that for legal sanctions to be effective, they must be administered swiftly. Jeffery (1965), for example, has emphasized the importance of the *celerity* (as well as certainty) of sanctions in accounting for the negative evidence for the death penalty:

> The *uncertainty* of capital punishment is one major factor in the system. Another factor is the *time* element. A consequence [the death penalty] must be applied immediately if it is to be effective. . . . The lesson to be learned from capital punishment is not that punishment does not deter, but that the improper and sloppy use of punishment does not deter. (p. 299)

The issue of the celerity of executions has seldom been examined in the empirical literature. Indeed, our search produced only a single study of the celerity question (Bailey, 1980a). In that study, a cross-state analysis was conducted for 1956 through 1960 that examined the relationship between homicide rates for death penalty states and (a) the certainty of execution for homicide, (b) the certainty and severity of imprisonment for homicide, and (c) the celerity of the death penalty—the elapsed time between the sentencing and execution of convicted murderers. The analysis controlled for a number of sociodemographic factors to avoid spurious results for the sanction variables. Also, it was confined to death penalty states because the celerity of executions is not an issue for abolitionist jurisdictions. Contrary to theoretical expectations, the study found no evidence that speedy executions discourage murder. At the bivariate level, there was a near-zero correlation ($r = -.01$) between 1960 murder rates and the average elapsed time between sentencing and executions for 1956 through 1960. This statistically nonsignificant pattern persisted in a multivariate analysis as well.

Analyses of Execution Publicity

Another fundamental premise of deterrence theory is that to prevent crime, the threat and application of the law must be communicated to the public. In addition, deterrence theorists have long contended that the publicity surrounding punishment serves important educative, moralizing, and normative validation functions (Andenaes, 1974; Gibbs, 1975, 1986). If this premise is applied to capital punishment, high levels of execution publicity should result in lower homicide rates.

Research examining the effects of execution publicity dates to the 1930s. In the first such investigation, Dann (1935) examined the number of homicides for 60 days before and after five highly publicized Philadelphia executions in 1927, 1929, 1930, 1931, and 1932. He found an *increase,* not a decline, in killings following each execution. In another study, Savitz's (1958) examination of four highly publicized death sentences in Philadelphia in 1944, 1946 (two sentences), and 1947 revealed no change in definite and possible capital homicides during the 8 weeks before and after each event. These early execution publicity studies are informative but limited because they are confined to a single location and a limited period.

Most research examining the deterrent impact of execution publicity has focused on recent periods. After a 10-year moratorium on capital punishment (1968-1976), executions resumed in the United States in January 1977. The first few executions after the moratorium received considerable print and electronic media coverage. For example, the execution of Gary Gilmore in Utah on January 17, 1977, was front-page news across the country and was the lead story for the evening news for the three major television networks.

McFarland (1983) examined whether the tremendous amount of news coverage given the

Gilmore execution and the three executions to follow (John Spinkelink [Florida, 1979], Jesse Bishop [Nevada, 1979], and Steven Judy [Indiana, 1981]) produced a significant decline in U.S. homicides. Examining weekly public health statistics for homicide for various periods leading up to and following each of the four "celebrated" executions, McFarland uncovered no evidence of a significant downward (or upward) shift in weekly killings. The Gilmore execution was followed by a decline in the level of U.S. weekly homicides for 2 weeks following the execution, but homicides during the next few weeks seemed to be unaffected. The dip in killings immediately following Gilmore's execution suggests a possible short-term deterrent effect, but McFarland rejects this interpretation. Via a disaggregated regional analysis, he demonstrates that the significant decline in killings following the Gilmore execution was confined to parts of the country that experienced abnormally severe winter conditions during that period. Of particular note, following the Gilmore execution in Utah, weather conditions were normal for the western states; there was not a notable decline in homicides, however, in these jurisdictions.

Stack (1987) took a different approach in examining the deterrent effect of media coverage of executions. He conducted a time-series analysis for 1950 to 1980 in which monthly rates of murder were regressed against measures indicating the *amount* of newspaper coverage devoted to executions (high, medium, or low), with statistical controls being introduced for two factors associated with murder rates—the level of unemployment and the percentage of the population aged 16 to 34 years. Executions recorded in *Facts on File* (a comprehensive national index of major news stories) and appearing in the *New York Times* were classified as receiving high levels of publicity. Those appearing in the *New York Times* but not in *Facts* were classified as receiving moderate media attention. Executions not receiving coverage in either source were considered as low-publicity cases. Stack found a significant decline in homicide rates for months with highly publicized executions but little impact for cases receiving moderate or low publicity. This led him to estimate that during the three decades, "16 [highly] publicized executions may have saved as many as 480 lives" (p. 538), amounting to an average of 30 persons saved per execution.

A number of problems with the Stack analysis have been described (Bailey & Peterson, 1989). For example, we found that Stack (a) failed to control for changes in the proportion of the U.S. population not legally subject to capital punishment, which ranged from approximately 10% to 45% during the period; (b) ignored the frequency of monthly executions for murder (which ranged from 0 to 16 during the period); (c) failed to control for structural variables found to be associated with homicide rates (such as those in Bailey, 1976; Ehrlich, 1975; Kleck, 1979; Logan, 1982); and (d) classified 23 executions (occurring during 16 months) as receiving high levels of publicity, when 26 executions spread throughout 19 months met his criteria of high-publicity executions.

In light of these problems, we (Bailey & Peterson, 1989) replicated Stack's investigation for 1950 to 1980 and conducted an additional analysis with a more extended period (1940-1986). The replication revealed that these problems had a devastating effect on Stack's findings. For example, merely correcting the coding errors for the execution publicity variables eliminated the reported significant association between execution publicity and homicide rates. This nondeterrence pattern remained when the monthly analysis was extended from 1940 through 1986.

Television News Coverage of Executions

For the periods considered by Stack (1950-1980) and by us (1940-1986), newspapers provided an important source of news for the U.S. population. During that time, however, the percentage of homes with television sets grew dramatically from less than 10% in 1950 to more than 98% by the early 1980s, with the American public coming to view television as providing the most "complete," "intelligent," and "unbiased" source of news (Bower, 1985, p. 17).

Because of the growing importance of television news, I (Bailey, 1990) extended deterrence publicity research by examining the relationship between monthly murder rates and evening television news coverage devoted to executions in the United States from 1976 through 1987. I used monthly homicide (murder and nonnegligent manslaughter) data from yearly editions of the Federal Bureau of Investigation's (FBI) *Crime in America: Uniform Crime Reports* and news coverage data from the Vanderbilt Television News Archives (1968-1992). Both the amount and type of news coverage devoted to each execution during the period were coded.

Little association was found between homicide rates and the *amount* of television news coverage of executions (Bailey, 1990). Similarly, the study did not find consistent evidence of deterrence when different *types* of coverage were aired, such as graphic versus matter-of-fact presentation of the execution or, as another example, murderers being presented as fully deserving of execution versus those for whom concerns were raised about the fairness of the execution (as in cases in which youths or persons with mental retardation were executed).

In sum, studies of execution publicity have produced results that are in line with analyses of severity, certainty, and celerity. They provide no creditable evidence that the level of print or electronic media attention devoted to executions significantly discourages (deters) murder.

■ *DETERRENCE AND DIFFERENT TYPES OF MURDER*

Although support for deterrence has been negligible, researchers largely have examined general homicide rates. Thus, some critics of the deterrence literature have noted that neither in theory nor in policy has the death penalty been aimed at deterring all types of killing (van den Haag, 1969, 1975, 1978; van den Haag & Conrad, 1983). Most death penalty jurisdictions restrict capital punishment to planned, intentional killings (i.e., premeditated murder, first-degree murder, and aggravated murder) and/or killings that result from the commission of another felony crime (i.e., felony murders). Thus, it would be most appropriate to use only *capital* murders—those eligible for the death penalty—when conducting investigations of possible deterrence effects.

Because of data limitations, addressing this criticism has been a formidable task. Most researchers have made use of either police data for murder and nonnegligent manslaughter or public health figures for homicide derived from coroners and medical examiners. Unfortunately, neither police nor public health figures allow researchers to differentiate capital from noncapital killings.[1] In deterrence investigations, the use of a broad category of homicides is acceptable if it could be assumed (a) for time-series analyses that the proportion of capital-to-total homicides remained constant during the period so that the more inclusive homicide data accurately reflect changes in capital offenses and (b) for cross-sectional analyses that the ratio of capital-to-total homicides is the same across states such that observed variations in general rates reflect comparable variations in capital murder. Most death penalty investigators have been willing to accept these assumptions, but the empirical basis for doing so is questionable. Sellin's (1967) early observation that no one has succeeded in accurately identifying and counting capital offenses hidden in the available aggregate homicide figures still holds.

Studies of Capital Murder

Despite the difficulty of identifying capital homicides, a few attempts have examined directly the impact of capital punishment on death-eligible killings. Earlier, we presented briefly the results of Savitz's (1958) short-term impact study of the influence of four highly publicized death sentences in Philadelphia. From an analysis of police and judicial records, Savitz was able to count what he termed "definite" and "possible" capital homicides that occurred during the 8 weeks before and after the death sentences. As indicated, Savitz did not find support for either deterrence or brutalization arguments.

Another study also mentioned above (Bailey, 1975) examined *first-degree murder* rates in 1967 and 1968 for death penalty and abolitionist jurisdictions, controlling for a variety of sociodemographic factors associated with homicide. Figures for first-degree murder (the number of prison admissions for first-degree murder) came from a survey of state correctional authorities. Consistent with studies of general homicides, this analysis provided no indication of deterrence. Average rates of first-degree murder were not higher for abolitionist (1967 = .18 per 100,000 population, 1968 = .21) than for death penalty (1967 = .47, 1968 = .58) jurisdictions, and there was only a slight negative correlation between executions and rates of first-degree murder (1967, r = -.137; 1968, r = -.194).

In another investigation (Bailey, 1984a), a monthly time-series analysis of executions and first-degree murders was conducted in Chicago, Illinois, for 1915 through 1921. Simple and multiple regression analyses were performed with various execution measures and time-lag structures being considered. For 1915 through 1921, monthly (N = 84) first-degree murder figures were taken from the annual statistical reports of the Chicago Police Department. Executions (N = 26) were drawn from the records of the Cook County Prison.

At the bivariate level, a slight positive relationship (r = .158) was found between rates of first-degree murder and the number of monthly executions. A slight and statistically nonsignificant relationship for these two variables generally persisted when a variety of control variables were incorporated into multivariate analyses. In no instance was there evidence of a significant decline in killings resulting from executions. There was a tendency in some models for executions to be associated with significantly higher levels of first-degree murder, a pattern that is consistent with the brutalization argument. Because the analysis is so time and place bound, it is not clear whether this possible brutalization effect is generalizable.

A recent analysis (Peterson & Bailey, 1991) calls into question the possibility of both brutalization and deterrence for the most common type of capital homicide—killings that occur during the commission of certain felony crimes. Felony murders and suspected felony murders constitute a quarter to a third of homicides annually, and they also account for a majority of executions. There were 93 executions during the period of concern (1976-1987) in this analysis. Of these, 67 (72%) were for murders associated with robbery, rape, burglary, and kidnapping. On the basis of these figures, the study concluded that for recent years, a felony murder analysis provides the most direct test of the deterrent effect of the death penalty for *capital murder.*

Using felony murder data drawn from unpublished Supplementary Homicide Reports (SHR) information supplied by the FBI, we (Peterson & Bailey, 1991) replicated the earlier analysis (Bailey, 1990) of monthly homicide rates and television news coverage of executions but used different dependent variables—overall felony murder rates and rates for particular types of felony murder. Included in these rates were killings resulting from rape, robbery, burglary, larceny, vehicle theft, and arson. The study examined the impact of the volume of executions and the amount and type of news coverage the executions received on monthly felony murder rates, while controlling for selected law enforcement and sociodemographic control variables.

Consistent with studies of general homicides, our study (Peterson & Bailey, 1991) produced negative findings regarding deterrence. With one minor exception, the overall rate and rates for different types of felony murder were not responsive to levels of execution or television news coverage of executions for 1976 to 1987. Rates of narcotics-related murders, however, were found to be significantly lower during months when there was television news coverage of what might be considered "questionable" executions—those in which the person who was put to death was young or retarded and in which there were appeals for mercy from prominent figures. We were not able to offer a plausible explanation for this unique finding.

Finally, Cochran, Chamlin, and Seth (1994) conducted an interrupted time-series analysis to examine the possible deterrent effect of Oklahoma's return to capital punishment after a 25-year moratorium. On September 10, 1990, Charles Coleman was executed at the Oklahoma State Penitentiary, an event generating a great deal of media coverage in the state. Cochran and his associates reasoned that if the death penalty has an effect on homicide, any such effect should be evident in comparing weekly rates of felony and other types of murder before and after the Coleman execution.

Examining the period of January 1989 through December 1991 (N = 156 weeks), Cochran et al. did not find a statistically significant decline in felony murder following the Coleman execution. The average number of weekly felony murders was only slightly higher for the pre- versus postintervention period (.73 versus .65). Cochran et al. observed, however, what they termed a strong brutalization effect for the Coleman execution for killings involving strangers. For the preexecution period, the mean number of weekly killings involving persons not known to one another was .42, compared with an average of .76 for the postexecution period. This increase in stranger killings (+.34) was statistically significant and was not due to any nonexecution factor that Cochran and his associates could detect.

Police Killings and Capital Punishment

Police killings are also capital crimes in most death penalty jurisdictions. Thus, the question arises, do the threat and application of the death penalty afford the police an added measure of protection against being slain in the line of duty? Scholars have sought to address this issue in several ways. The formats of their analyses parallel the evolution of deterrence studies of general homicides, moving from simple comparative investigations to increasingly complex multivariate analyses. Sellin (1955) conducted the first police killings study. On the basis of a survey of police departments in U.S. cities with a population of at least 10,000 (in 1950) in 17 death penalty and 6 abolitionist jurisdictions, he examined annual police killing rates per 10,000 population from 1919 to 1954. Sellin did not find support for the deterrence hypothesis. Rather, he observed that the average police homicide rates for cities in death penalty (1.3) and abolitionist (1.2) states were virtually identical.

The length of the period (1919-1954) and the number of jurisdictions (265) examined by Sellin are impressive, but he used an unorthodox measure of police killings: the total number of police homicides per 10,000 *general,* not police, population. Correcting for this problem, I (Bailey, 1982) examined abolitionist and death penalty states (1961-1971) using annual police homicide rates computed on the basis of the number of police killings per 1,000 *police officers.* I also examined the relationship between the certainty of execution for murder and police killings, employing a number of control variables to avoid possibly spurious relationships. Like Sellin, I did not find policing to be less hazardous in death penalty states or in jurisdictions in which executions were at higher levels. Further, a later extension of this analysis for 1973 to 1984 revealed no statistically significant associations between state-level police killing rates and states' use of capital punishment (Bailey & Peterson, 1987).

A recent investigation (Bailey & Peterson, 1994) provides a more refined analysis of police killings by examining the effects of an alternative certainty measure on different types of police killings in a national, monthly time-series analysis for 1976 to 1989. Certainty was operationalized as the ratio of police killings to the number of monthly executions of "cop killers." We considered a general police killing rate (the number of officers killed per 100,000 police personnel) *and* rates for killings involving (a) on-duty and (b) off-duty police and killings of (c) general jurisdiction and (d) special function police. During the period, 1,204 law enforcement officers were killed feloniously, and there were 120 executions in the United States, 12 of which involved cop killers. Because of their relatively small number (N = 12), we also considered a broader execution rate measure—the ratio of total executions to total criminal homicides. Despite the added features of this study, we found no evidence that overall and specific types of police killings are responsive to changes in the provision for capital punishment, the certainty of execution, or the amount and type of television news coverage devoted to executions.

■ *EXTENDING THE LITERATURE: DETERRENT EFFECTS OF CAPITAL PUNISHMENT ON FEMALE HOMICIDE OFFENDING*

Examining whether capital punishment discourages (or encourages) women from committing murder may seem like an odd question because murder is by and large not a female activity. For example, in 1995, women constituted slightly more than 52% of the U.S. population but only 9.5% of persons arrested for murder (FBI, 1996). Nonetheless, women may be good candidates for a study of capital punishment and deterrence because of their likely greater general deterrability compared with men. General deterrence is a "communication theory" whereby the threat and application of sanctions are thought to influence persons' perceptions of the severity, certainty, and celerity of the punishment that would result from violating the law (Gibbs, 1975). It is presumed that where "objective" sanction levels are severe, certain, and prompt, persons will refrain from rule breaking. Individuals' perceptions of sanctions, however, and not the objective characteristics of penalties, are important for general deterrence. Unfortunately, little is known about the factors that influence perceived probabilities of official sanctions and the perceptions of sanctions that might result from breaking the law and/or being detected officially. It is clear, however, that not all segments of the population perceive equally the types and probabilities of official and unofficial sanctions that would result from engaging in illegal conduct. As a consequence, some population groups may be more or less deterrable.

Deterrence researchers barely have begun to explore the experiences, life situations, and circumstances that influence selectively the link between objective and perceived sanctions. A number of sociological and psychological theories of deviance, however, lead to the prediction of significant gender differences in the way sanction risks are perceived (Richards & Tittle, 1981), and gender differences have been observed in a number of studies. These investigations indicate that compared with men, women perceive a higher probability of being apprehended by the authorities if they were to break the law and anticipate more severe consequences as a result. Indeed, Richards and Tittle note that in criminology, "one of the most intriguing potential differences between males and females is that of deterrability," not only for property and public order offenses but also for assault, "physically harming someone on purpose" (pp. 1182, 1186).

It is beyond the scope of this chapter to discuss the various theoretical explanations that may account for why women perceive their possible misdeeds as more likely to be detected and punished more severely (we refer readers to Richards and Tittle [1981] for a summary of such perspectives). Nor is it possible to present the various studies that document this pattern. Here, we draw on this body of work simply to establish that women *do* perceive a higher probability of detection and apprehension for violating the law, and, as a result, capital punishment may be a more effective deterrent for women than for men.

Of course, this is not to suggest that *differential deterrability* is the sole factor that differentiates men from women in their level of homicidal behavior. We propose only that the homicide rate of women may be more responsive to deterrence factors such as the level of death sentences handed down by the courts, level of execution, and amount of media coverage devoted to executions. These three deterrence variables have been examined in previous studies of general homicide but with null results. These negative findings may be a consequence of men (by a margin of about 90%) being the dominant homicide offender population. As a result, any deterrence effects that might stem from capital punishment for women may have gone unnoticed by researchers examining only general homicide rates.

Methods and Procedures

To examine the possible deterrent (and brutalization) effect of capital punishment for female homicide offending, we extend the methodology employed in recent investigations (Bailey, 1990; Peterson & Bailey, 1991). The former study was a national monthly time-series analysis (1976-1987) of executions, general homicide rates, and television news coverage of executions. The latter study considered the impact of news coverage of executions on different types of felony murder (1976-1987) for the general population. The research to follow is a national monthly time-series analysis of female homicide for 1976 to 1991. We use 1976 as a baseline year because the first execution in the United States since 1967 took place in January 1977. The time series ends with December 1991 because adequate monthly homicide figures for the United States are not available from the FBI for some years after 1991.

Dependent Variables

The dependent variable of the analysis is the overall monthly female homicide offending rate, measured as the number of female homicides per 100,000 female population. The homicide data are drawn from the FBI's Supplementary Homicide Reports (SHR). For 1976 through 1991, the SHR files include approximately 33,500 female offenders. In addition, we compute female offending rates for killings involving (a) felony murders (n = 3,345); (b) lover's triangle killings (n = 987); (c) arguments about money or property (n = 868) and "other" arguments (n = 17,532); and (d) alcohol-related "brawl" killings (n = 1,079). We select these types of female killings because there are a sufficient number (at least three per month on average—192 × 3 = 576) to permit a reliable statistical analysis.

The SHR program has received considerable attention in the professional literature (see Chapter 6 by Marc Riedel for a review), so there is no need to detail the general features of these data. Three points regarding them, however, should be noted. First, fewer police departments participate in the SHR reporting program than in the annual Uniform Crime Reporting (UCR) Program. For example, for 1976 to 1991, the average number of monthly UCR murders was 1,736, compared with an average of 1,586 SHR criminal homicides. Nonetheless, the 1976 to 1991 monthly UCR and SHR homicide counts are highly correlated (r = .83) such that the resulting undercounts of the SHR do not pose a major concern for the analyses to follow.

A second and more serious problem is that gender information for offenders is not available for all killings that do appear in the SHR files. For example, for 1976, the gender of homicide offenders is classified as "unknown" for 3,455 (19.4%) cases. At the other end of the time series, for 1991, the gender of the homicide offender is classified as "unknown" for 29.6% (n = 7,264) of cases. Because of missing gender information, male and female offending rates based on SHR data underestimate the actual level with which these respective groups commit murder.

A third concern is missing homicide circumstance information in the SHR files. On the basis of reports submitted by the police, FBI statisticians code murders into 25 circumstance categories. Among the codes is an "unknown" category. For 1976 to 1991, 1,887 (5.6%) killings involving female offenders were coded as "unable to determine circumstance." Maxfield (1989) has argued that SHR data submitted by the police often reflect only preliminary information about killings and that "murders initially coded as (circumstances) 'unknown' tend to be 'transformed' into felony murders . . . when the investigation is completed" (p. 691). Thus, to control for the likely undercount of female felony murders, in our analysis of these killings we include the percentage of monthly SHR homicide incidents involving "missing" circumstance information. The time-series analyses were also conducted without the "percentage missing" control variable; both analyses yielded the same results for the death penalty variables.

Independent Variables

The following independent variables were included in the analysis:

1. *Levels of execution:* To consider the effect of the frequency of executions on female killings, monthly execution figures were drawn from the NAACP Legal Defense and Educational Fund, Inc.'s (1992) *Death Row, U.S.A.* From 1976 through 1991, there were 157 executions, with a range of 0 to 6 per month.

2. *Death sentences:* As an additional measure of the level of capital punishment, we tallied the number of women admitted to death row in penal institutions ($n = 76$). Female death row admissions ranged from 0 to 3 per month.

3. *Execution publicity:* We also examined the possible deterrent impact of national television news coverage of executions. As measures of the amount of television execution publicity, we (a) differentiated (as a dummy variable) between months during which there was none versus some execution publicity, and totaled the number of (b) minutes and (c) days of news coverage of executions for each month. News coverage data were drawn from the Vanderbilt Television News Archive, which began abstracting the ABC, CBS, and NBC evening news programs in 1968. Of the 157 executions between 1977 and 1991, 39 (distributed through 31 months) received coverage by one or more of the three networks. Following the practice of previous investigators, we coded media coverage that occurred after the 23rd of the month as taking place the following month. The assumption here is that executions aired at the end of the month will have their greatest impact on homicides the next month.

Control Variables

To isolate the effect of capital punishment, the following selected control variables were introduced into the multivariate analyses: *percentage of women* who are (a) Black, (b) 15 to 34 years of age, and (c) divorced. Also, (d) the female unemployment rate was included. In addition, the (e) percentage of the U.S. population receiving Aid to Families With Dependent Children (AFDC) benefits was used as an indicator of changes in general socioeconomic conditions. Monthly AFDC figures were taken from the *Annual Statistical Supplement to the Social Security Bulletin.* The *Statistical Abstract of the United States* and *Current Population Reports* provided figures for the sociodemographic variables.

We also included as control variables (f) the homicide arrest clearance rate and (g) the percentage of the population residing in jurisdictions without the death penalty for common murder (i.e., abolitionist jurisdictions). During 1976 to 1991, there was significant variation in the murder clearance rate (e.g., 1976 = 78%, 1989 = 67%) and the proportion of the U.S. population not subject to capital punishment for murder (12% to 28%). For some types of female homicide, (h) dummy variables were included to control for months during which rates were significantly higher or lower than for other months.

Multicollinearity

We employed a series of auxiliary regressions to explore possible collinearity problems for the capital punishment variables. Specifically, each death penalty variable was regressed against (a) the homicide arrest rate, (b) the sociodemographic factors, and (c) the other death penalty variables included in the models. Findings indicate that multicollinearity is not a problem for the central independent variables. Results of the collinearity analyses are available on request.

Findings

The first step in the analysis was to examine for each type of female homicide the autoregressive structure for lag periods ranging from t-1 through t-12 months. Yule-Walker estimates are reported where there is significant autoregression; ordinary least squares estimates are

Table 17.2 Autoregression Analysis of Death Sentences, Executions, Execution Publicity, and Rates of Total Female Murder, Female Felony Murder, and Female Killings Resulting From Arguments About Money and Property, 1976 to 1991

Predictor Variable	*(I) Total Female Murder*		*(II) Female Felony Murder*		*III) Female Argument Killings About Money or Property*	
	β (SE)	*β (SE)*	*β (SE)*	*β (SE)*	*β (SE)*	*β (SE)*
Percentage Black population	–.0048	.0143	.0373*	.0368*	–.0019	–.0021
	(.0030)	(.0301)	(.0088)	(.0089)	(.0037)	(.0037)
Percentage age 15-34	.0000*	.0000*	.0000*	.0000*	–.0000	–.0000
	(.0000)	(.0000)	(.0000)	(.0000)	(.0000)	(.0000)
AFDC population	.0004	.0024	–.0007	–.0004	–.0016	–.0015
	(.0091)	(.0098)	(.0024)	(.0024)	(.0010)	(.0010)
Unemployment rate	.0051*	.0045*	.0015*	.0015*	.0002	.0001
	(.0021)	(.0021)	(.0006)	(.0006)	(.0002)	(.0002)
Divorce rate	–.0286*	–.0254*	–.0102*	–.0102*	–.0000	–.0000
	(.0076)	(.0077)	(.0021)	(.0022)	(.0009)	(.0009)
Arrest rate	–.0024*	-.0022*	.0000	.0000	–.0000	–.0000
	(.0009)	(.0009)	(.0003)	(.0003)	(.0001)	(.0000)
Percentage abolitionist population	.0002	.0002	.0002	.0002	–.0000	–.0000
	(.0006)	(.0006)	(.0002)	(.0002)	(.0001)	(.0001)
No. of death sentences	–.0009	–.0010	–.0003	–.0002	.0003	.0003*
	(.0017)	(.0017)	(.0004)	(.0005)	(.0002)	(.0002)
No. of executions	.0006	.0001	.0002	.0002	.0001	.0001
	(.0011)	(.0011)	(.0003)	(.0003)	(.0001)	(.0001)
Television coverage of executions (0/1)	–.0035	—	–.0016*	—	–.0004	—
	(.0032)		(.0008)		(.0004)	
No. of days of TV coverage	—	.0008	—	–.0007	—	–.0002
		(.0018)		(.0005)		(.0002)
Intercept	.2686	.3445	–.4294	–.4270	.0459	.0462
R^2	.739	.663	.189	.182	.208	.208

$*p \leq .05$.

presented where autoregression is not a problem. As shown by the results displayed in Table 17.2, total female homicide rates (Panel I), female rates of felony murder (Panel II), and argument-related killings (Panel III) were regressed against the death sentence, execution, and control variables. Unstandardized regression coefficients are presented along with their standard errors (in parentheses). For each dependent variable, two models are presented. The first uses the 0/1 dummy variable for television news coverage of executions; the second examines the number of *days* of media coverage of executions. We also considered a third measure of media coverage of executions (the number of minutes of airtime), but this variable was not found to have a statistically significant relationship with any type of female homicide and therefore is not reported. Also, for reasons of brevity, we do not report in Table 17.2 the results for the high/low monthly control variables.

Total Female Homicides

Panel I of Table 17.2 shows the results of the analysis whereby the total female homicide rate is regressed against the death sentence, execution, and control variables. The results reveal that the number of death sentences is associated negatively with rates for both models, but the coefficients are slight (β = –.0009 and –.0010) and are not statistically significant. Conversely, there is a slight, but nonsignificant, positive association between the number of executions and female homicide rates (β = .0006 and .0001). Finally, the coefficients for the television news variables are mixed in sign (β = –.0035 and

.0008), slight in magnitude, and not statistically significant. In sum, Table 17.2 provides no evidence that capital punishment produces either a deterrence or brutalization effect for overall female homicides.

Felony Murder

Shown in Panel II of Table 17.2 are the findings where rates for known and suspected felony murder are the dependent variable. For each model, there is a slight, statistically nonsignificant, positive or negative association between female felony murders and the level of death sentences, the number of executions, and the number of days of news coverage of executions. The negative association between felony murder and the execution publicity dummy variable, however, is statistically significant ($\beta = -.0016$, $SE = .0008$, $p < .031$). When the coefficient for the relationship between these two variables is converted from a monthly to an annual basis ($\beta = -.00157 \times 12 = [\beta = -.01884]$), the common metric in homicide research, the relationship between the media variable and felony murders remains slight. Nonetheless, it is the case that for 1976 to 1991, there were significantly fewer felony murders committed by women during months when there was at least some television news coverage of executions.

The findings for the television news dummy variable are suggestive of deterrence, but the above analysis does not indicate which type(s) of felony murder might be responsive to capital punishment. We explored this issue by examining robbery-related killings ($n = 1,678$), the one type of felony murder for which there were on average at least three incidents per month. To conserve space, we do not present the negative findings for robbery-related killings in tabular form but report that the analysis revealed no indication of a significant deterrent (or brutalization) effect for this type of felony murder.

Argument-Related Killings

During 1976 to 1991, most female killings (55%) were an outgrowth of arguments. FBI data distinguish between two types of argument killings—those involving money or property ($n = 868$) and other arguments ($n = 17,532$). Rates for each type of argument killing were formed, and the same regression analyses were conducted. Although not presented in table form, for the broad category of other arguments, the null hypothesis holds for all the death penalty variables. This is not the case for killings resulting from arguments about money or property, findings from which are shown in Panel III of Table 17.2.

For both models, the results show a statistically nonsignificant positive or negative association between the rates and the execution and news coverage variables. When the number of days of news coverage is the media variable, however, the coefficient ($\beta = .0003$) for the number of death sentences is positive and reaches statistical significance. (Although not shown here, the same pattern prevailed for this type of homicide when the media variable was operationalized as the number of minutes of television news coverage.) This result suggests a possible brutalization effect for death sentences for killings resulting from arguments about money or property.

Killings Involving Other Circumstances

During 1976 to 1991, two other types of female homicide were sufficient in number to be considered here: lover's triangle killings and homicides resulting from a "brawl due to the influence of alcohol." It seems unlikely that alcohol-related killings would be subject to deterrence because of their expressive nature, but this type of murder may be subject to brutalization because of alcohol's effect in reducing inhibitions against violence. For lover's triangle killings, some of which are expressive but others instrumental in nature, both deterrence *and* brutalization are possible. We conducted analyses to assess these possibilities (results not shown here) but found no indication that either triangle or alcohol-related killings are responsive to any of the three dimensions of capital punishment.

Summary and Implications of the Findings

Consistent with the dominant finding in studies of the general homicide rate, this analysis has provided no indication that any aspect of capital punishment is associated significantly with the overall rate of female homicide offending. Female felony murder rates proved to be significantly lower, however, for months during which executions received at least some degree of television news coverage (Panel II of Table 17.2). This is consistent with deterrence predictions, but a deterrence pattern did not hold for robbery-related killings, the most common type of felony murder for women. Because other types of felony murder were so infrequent during 1976 to 1991, it was not possible to examine how female felony murders other than robbery-related killings might have contributed to the significant relationship between total felony murder rates and the television dummy variable ($\beta = -.0016$). Consequently, the meaning of our findings for felony murder is ambiguous.

We speculated at the outset of this investigation that some types of female homicide might be subject to brutalization. We found evidence of a possible brutalization effect for one type of female homicide. The greater the level of monthly death sentences for female homicide offenders, the higher the rate of female killings involving arguments about money or property, and significantly so when number of days (or minutes) of television coverage of executions is the media variable. The reader is cautioned that this positive trade-off is slight.

Our analysis provides the first examination of deterrence and brutalization arguments for female homicide offending. Thus, the significant deterrence finding for felony murder, brutalization results for argument-related killings, and our null findings for the other types of female homicide offending cannot be compared with the results of previous investigations. Consequently, we are hesitant to draw any firm conclusions from this analysis. Rather, we regard our work as pointing to the need for further research examining the possible impact of capital punishment on female homicide offending.

■ *RECOMMENDATIONS FOR FUTURE RESEARCH*

On the basis of the overwhelmingly negative evidence regarding any deterrent effect of capital punishment on the incidence of homicide, it is tempting to conclude, as many have (Zimring & Hawkins, 1986), that further deterrence research would be a waste of time. We agree that little of value will likely result from additional studies of the general homicide rate, the felony murder rate for the general population, or the police killing victimization rate. We believe, however, that advancements are possible if researchers use available census data and police data on homicides to provide more refined analyses of the possible differential impact of capital punishment for different types of homicide offenders. This differentiation should include variations in economic and social circumstances of offenders. As well, researchers have not systematically explored the circumstances and situations under which capital punishment may generate a brutalization effect (such as that reported by Cochran et al., 1994). Yet it is important for both criminological theory and criminal justice practice to know for which populations and under what conditions capital punishment might actually promote homicide.

■ *SUMMARY AND CONCLUSIONS*

This chapter has provided a selective review of deterrence and death penalty research. Detailed discussion was provided for selected studies but only when warranted because of their findings (e.g., the study finds support for deterrence) and/or the uniqueness of the question examined or the research approaches taken. In general, an overview of the literature suggests that *results have not provided support for a deterrent effect of capital punishment on homicide.* There are some noted exceptions to this pattern (Ehrlich, 1975, 1977; Layson, 1985; Stack, 1987), but they are few in number and have not stood up well under close examination. In addition, no study has produced evidence that the death penalty is an effective deterrent to specific forms of capital homicide such as felony murder and police killings, types of homicide that seem particularly risky for incurring a death penalty. Rather, limited evidence suggests that the death penalty actually may encourage (via a brutalization effect) at least some types of (i.e., stranger) killing (Cochran et al., 1994).

The failure to find evidence that capital punishment deters murder is not entirely surprising. Not all types of crimes and offenders are equally deterrable. For example, expressive acts are thought to be less deterrable than instrumental offenses (Chambliss, 1967), and select populations such as persons who are mentally ill, youths (because of their immaturity), and persons under the influence of alcohol or drugs may not be as rational as others in sorting out the costs and rewards of breaking the law. In large part, homicides are expressive, rather than instrumental. As Chambliss notes, murder is "usually shrouded with a great deal of emotional involvement on the part of the offender" (p. 400). Homicides also commonly involve alcohol or drug use or are otherwise spur-of-the-moment incidents (Luckenbill, 1977). Thus, it may well be that neither imprisonment nor the death penalty can be effective in deterring murder because "such offenses are less dictated by 'rational' considerations of gain or loss" (Chambliss, 1967, p. 400).

In brief, the studies reviewed above, and countless others that are not examined here, provide no consistent evidence that capital punishment is more effective than alternative sanctions in deterring general homicides. Our review has also revealed that most studies of deterrence (or brutalization) ignore the possibility that capital punishment may be more or less effective in preventing or promoting killings by specific population groups. Still, the strength of the evidence suggests that policymakers would do well to consider means *other* than capital punishment to significantly reduce the rate of homicide in the United States.

■ *NOTE*

1. The FBI (1992), which collects homicide incident figures from police departments and state-level law enforcement coordinating agencies across the country, defines murder and nonnegligent manslaughter as "the willful (nonnegligent) killing of one human being by another" (p. 7). Observing the World Health Organization's *International Classification of Diseases* definition, the National Center for Health Statistics (1967) defines homicide as "a death resulting from an injury purposely inflicted by another person" (p. 9).

■ *REFERENCES*

Andenaes, J. (1974). *Punishment and deterrence.* Ann Arbor: University of Michigan Press.

Bailey, W. C. (1975). Murder and capital punishment: Some further evidence. *American Journal of Orthopsychiatry, 45,* 669-688.

Bailey, W. C. (1976). Certainty of arrest and crime rates for major felonies. *Journal of Research in Crime and Delinquency, 13,* 145-154.

Bailey, W. C. (1977). Imprisonment vs. the death penalty as a deterrent to murder. *Law and Human Behavior, 1,* 239-260.

Bailey, W. C. (1978). Deterrence and the death penalty for murder in Utah: A time-series analysis. *Journal of Contemporary Law, 5,* 1-20.

Bailey, W. C. (1979a). An analysis of the deterrence effect of the death penalty in North Carolina. *North Carolina Central Law Journal, 10,* 29-51.

Bailey, W. C. (1979b). Deterrence and the death penalty for murder in Oregon. *Willamette Law Review, 16,* 67-85.

Bailey, W. C. (1979c). The deterrent effect of the death penalty for murder in California. *Southern California Law Review, 52,* 743-764.

Bailey, W. C. (1979d). The deterrent effect of the death penalty for murder in Ohio. *Cleveland State Law Review, 28,* 51-81.

Bailey, W. C. (1980a). Deterrence and the celerity of the death penalty: A neglected question in deterrence research. *Social Forces, 58,* 1308-1333.

Bailey, W. C. (1980b). A multivariate cross-sectional analysis of the deterrent effect of the death penalty. *Sociology and Social Research, 64,* 183-207.

Bailey, W. C. (1982). Capital punishment and lethal assaults against police. *Criminology, 19,* 608-625.

Bailey, W. C. (1983). The deterrent effect of capital punishment during the 1950's. *Suicide, 13,* 95-107.

Bailey, W. C. (1984a). Disaggregation in deterrence and death penalty research: The case of murder in Chicago. *Journal of Criminal Law and Criminology, 74,* 827-859.

Bailey, W. C. (1984b). Murder and capital punishment in the nation's capitol. *Justice Quarterly, 1,* 211-233.

Bailey, W. C. (1990). Murder and capital punishment: An analysis of television execution publicity. *American Sociological Review, 55,* 628-633.

Bailey, W. C., & Peterson, R. D. (1987). Police killings and capital punishment: The post-Furman period. *Criminology, 25,* 1-25.

Bailey, W. C., & Peterson, R. D. (1989). Murder and capital punishment: A monthly time-series analysis of execution publicity. *American Sociological Review, 54,* 722-743.

Bailey, W. C., & Peterson, R. D. (1994). Murder, capital punishment, and deterrence: A review of the evidence and an examination of police killings. *Journal of Social Issues, 50,* 53-74.

Baldus, D., & Cole, J. (1975). A comparison of the work of Thorsten Sellin and Isaac Ehrlich on the deterrent effect of capital punishment. *Yale Law Journal, 18,* 170-186.

Barnett, A. (1981). The deterrent effect of capital punishment: A test of some recent studies. *Operations Research, 29,* 346-370.

Beccaria, C. (1963). *On crimes and punishment* (H. Paolucci, Trans.). Indianapolis, IN: Bobbs-Merrill. (Original work published 1764)

Bedau, H. A. (1967). *The death penalty in America* (Rev. ed.). New York: Doubleday.

Bentham, J. (1962). The rationale of punishment. In J. Browning (Ed.), *Works of Jeremy Bentham* (pp. 388-524). New York: Russell & Russell.

Berns, W. (1979). *For capital punishment.* New York: Basic Books.

Berns, W. (1980). Defending the death penalty. *Crime & Delinquency, 26,* 503-511.

Beyleveld, D. (1982). Ehrlich's analysis of deterrence. *British Journal of Criminology, 22,* 101-123.

Bower, R. T. (1985). *The changing television audience in America.* New York: Columbia University Press.

Bowers, W. J. (1984). *Legal homicide: Death as punishment in America.* Boston: Northeastern University Press.

Bowers, W. J. (1988). The effect of executions is brutalization, not deterrence. In K. C. Haas & J. A. Inciardi (Eds.), *Capital punishment: Legal and social science approaches* (pp. 49-89). Newbury Park, CA: Sage.

Bowers, W. J., & Pierce, G. (1975). The illusion of deterrence in Isaac Ehrlich's research on capital punishment. *Yale Law Journal, 85,* 187-208.

Bowers, W. J., & Pierce, G. (1980). Deterrence or brutalization: What is the effect of executions? *Crime & Delinquency, 26,* 453-484.

Brier, S., & Feinberg, S. (1980). Recent econometric modeling of crime and punishment: Support for the deterrence hypothesis? *Evaluation Review, 4,* 147-191.

Bye, R. T. (1919). *Capital punishment in the United States.* Philadelphia: Committee on Philanthropic Labor of Philadelphia Yearly Meeting of Friends.

Chambliss, W. J. (1967). Types of deviance and the effectiveness of legal sanctions. In W. J. Chambliss (Ed.), *Criminal law in action* (2nd ed., pp. 398-407). New York: John Wiley.

Chandler, D. B. (1976). *Capital punishment in Canada: A sociological study of repressive law.* Ottawa, Canada: McClelland and Stewart Limited in association with Carleton University, Institute of Canadian Studies.

Cochran, J. K., Chamlin, M. B., & Seth, M. (1994). Deterrence or brutalization? An impact assessment of Oklahoma's return to capital punishment. *Criminology, 32,* 107-134.

Dann, R. (1935). *The deterrent effect of capital punishment.* Philadelphia: Committee of Philanthropic Labor of Philadelphia Yearly Meeting of Friends.

Decker, S. H., & Kohfeld, C. W. (1984). A deterrence study of the death penalty in Illinois, 1933-1980. *Journal of Criminal Justice, 12,* 367-377.

Ehrlich, I. (1975). The deterrent effect of capital punishment: A question of life or death. *American Economic Review, 65,* 397-417.

Ehrlich, I. (1977). Capital punishment and deterrence: Some further thoughts and additional evidence. *Journal of Political Economy, 85,* 741-788.

Fattah, E. A. (1972). *A study of the deterrent effect of capital punishment with special reference to the Canadian situation.* Ottawa, Canada: Department of the Solicitor General.

Federal Bureau of Investigation. (1981-1996). *Crime in the United States: Uniform crime reports* (Annual editions). Washington, DC: Government Printing Office.

Federal Bureau of Investigation. (1992). *Crime in the United States 1991: Uniform crime reports.* Washington, DC: Government Printing Office.

Federal Bureau of Investigation. (1996). *Crime in the United States 1995: Uniform crime reports.* Washington, DC: Government Printing Office.

Forst, B. (1977). The deterrent effect of capital punishment: A cross-state analysis of the 1960's. *Minnesota Law Review, 61,* 743-767.

Friedman, L. (1979). The use of multiple regression analysis to test for a deterrent effect of capital punishment: Prospects and problems. In S. Messinger & E. Bittner (Eds.), *Criminology review yearbook* (Vol. 1, pp. 61-87). Beverly Hills, CA: Sage.

Gibbs, J. P. (1975). *Crime, punishment, and deterrence.* New York: Elsevier.

Gibbs, J. P. (1986). Deterrence theory and research. In G. B. Melton (Ed.), *Nebraska Symposium on Motivation 1985: The law as a behavioral instrument* (pp. 87-130). Lincoln: University of Nebraska Press.

Jayewardene, C. H. S. (1977). *The penalty of death: The Canadian experiment.* Lexington, MA: D. C. Heath.

Jeffery, C. R. (1965). Criminal behavior and learning theory. *Journal of Criminal Law, Criminology and Police Science, 56,* 294-300.

Kleck, G. (1979). Capital punishment, gun ownership, and homicide. *American Journal of Sociology, 84,* 882-910.

Klein, L., Forst, B., & Filatov, V. (1978). The deterrent effect of capital punishment: An assessment of the estimates. In A. Blumstein, J. Cohen, & D. Nagin (Eds.), *Deterrence and incapacitation: Estimating the effects of criminal sanctions on crime rates* (pp. 336-360). Washington, DC: National Academy of Sciences.

Layson, S. K. (1985). Homicide and deterrence: An examination of the United States time-series evidence. *Southern Economic Journal, 52,* 68-89.

Lehtinen, M. (1977). The value of life: An argument for the death penalty. *Crime & Delinquency, 23,* 237-252.

Logan, C. H. (1982). Problems in ratio correlation: The case of deterrence research. *Social Forces, 60,* 791-810.

Luckenbill, D. F. (1977). Criminal homicide as a situated transaction. *Social Problems, 25,* 176-186.

Maxfield, M. G. (1989). Circumstances in Supplementary Homicide Reports: Variety and validity. *Criminology, 27,* 671-695.

McFarland, S. G. (1983). Is capital punishment a short-term deterrent to homicide? A study of the effects of four recent American executions. *Journal of Criminal Law and Criminology, 74,* 1014-1030.

McGahey, R. M. (1980). Dr. Ehrlich's magic bullet: Economic theory, econometrics, and the death penalty. *Crime & Delinquency, 26,* 485-502.

NAACP Legal Defense and Educational Fund, Inc. (1992). *Death row, U.S.A.* New York: Author.

National Center for Health Statistics. (1967). Homicide in the United States 1950-1964. *Vital and Health Statistics* (Series 20, No. 6). Washington, DC: Government Printing Office.

Passell, P. (1975). The deterrent effect of the death penalty: A statistical test. *Stanford Law Review, 28,* 61-80.

Passell, P., & Taylor, J. (1977). The deterrent effect of capital punishment. *American Economic Review, 67,* 445-451.

Peterson, R. D., & Bailey, W. C. (1988). Murder and capital punishment in the evolving context of the post-*Furman* era. *Social Forces, 66,* 774-807.

Peterson, R. D., & Bailey, W. C. (1991). Felony murder and capital punishment: An examination of the deterrence question. *Criminology, 29,* 367-395.

Phillips, D. P. (1980). The deterrent effect of capital punishment: New evidence on an old controversy. *American Journal of Sociology, 86,* 139-148.

Richards, P., & Tittle, C. R. (1981). Gender and perceived chances of arrest. *Social Forces, 59,* 1182-1199.

Savitz, L. (1958). A study of capital punishment. *Journal of Criminal Law, Criminology and Police Science, 49,* 338-341.

Schuessler, K. (1952). The deterrent effect of the death penalty. *The Annals, 284,* 54-62.

Sellin, T. (1955). *The Royal Commission on capital punishment, 1949-1953: Report of the Great Britain Parliament* (Papers by Command 8932, pp. 17-24). London: HMSO.

Sellin, T. (1959). *The death penalty.* Philadelphia: American Law Institute.

Sellin, T. (1961). Capital punishment. *Federal Probation, 25*(3), 3-11.

Sellin, T. (1967). *Capital punishment.* New York: Harper & Row.

Sellin, T. (1980). *The penalty of death.* Beverly Hills, CA: Sage.

Snell, T. L. (1996). *Capital punishment 1995* (Bureau of Justice Statistics Bulletin NCJ-162040). Washington, DC: U.S. Department of Justice.

Snell, T. L. (1997). *Capital punishment 1996* (Bureau of Justice Statistics Bulletin NCJ-167031). Washington, DC: U.S. Department of Justice.

Stack, S. (1987). Publicized executions and homicide, 1950-1980. *American Sociological Review, 52,* 532-540.

Sutherland, E. (1925). Murder and the death penalty. *Journal of the American Institute of Criminal Law and Criminology, 51,* 522-529.

van den Haag, E. (1969). On deterrence and the death penalty. *Journal of Criminal Law, Criminology and Police Science, 60,* 141-147.

van den Haag, E. (1975). *Punishing criminals: Concerning a very old and painful question.* New York: Basic Books.

van den Haag, E. (1978). In defense of the death penalty: A legal-practical-moral analysis. *Criminal Law Bulletin, 14,* 51-68.

van den Haag, E., & Conrad, J. (1983). *The death penalty: A debate.* New York: Plenum.

Vanderbilt Television News Archive. (1968-1992). *Vanderbilt television and news index and abstracts, 1977-1992.* Nashville, TN: Author.

Yunker, J. A. (1976). Is the death penalty a deterrent to homicide? Some time series evidence. *Journal of Behavioral Economics, 5,* 1-32.

Zimring, F. E., & Hawkins, G. (1986). *Capital punishment and the American agenda.* New York: Cambridge University Press.

CHAPTER 18

Guns, Gun Control, and Homicide

A Review of Research and Public Policy

■ *Philip J. Cook & Mark H. Moore*

In the search for more effective ways to reduce homicide, establishing more stringent controls on gun commerce and use has the broad support of the American public. Guns are the immediate cause of about 15,000 criminal homicides a year (Federal Bureau of Investigation, 1997) and are used to threaten or injure victims in hundreds of thousands of robberies and assaults (Bureau of Justice Statistics, 1997). It makes sense that if we could find a way to make guns less readily available, especially to those inclined toward crime and violence, we could reduce the level and seriousness of crime, including a reduction in homicide.

It is an understatement to say simply that not everyone accepts this perspective on guns. Some people argue that guns are the mere instruments of criminal intent, with no more importance than the type of shoes the criminal wears. If the type of weapon does not matter, then policy interventions focused on guns would have little use. This argument is taken another step by those who argue that although the type of weapon used by the perpetrator does not matter much, the type of weapon available to the victim for use in self-defense matters a great deal. Their conclusion is that measures depriving the public of guns would serve only to increase criminal activity.

This point and counterpoint make it appear as if the debate about gun control is primarily concerned with facts about the role of guns in crime and self-defense. If this were true, one might hope that empirical research would eventually resolve the matter, and the proper choice of gun control measures would become clear. In reality, however, deeply conflicting values are at stake here concerning the proper relationship between the individual, the community, and the state. Even a definitive empirical demonstration that a gun control measure would save lives will not persuade someone who believes that any infringement on the individual right to bear arms is tantamount to opening the door to tyranny.

Further, empirical research in this area will never resolve all the important factual issues, so the value conflict will flourish in the face of uncertainty about the consequences of proposed reforms.

The purpose of this chapter is to set out a framework for thinking about the next steps that should be taken in the search for an effective gun control policy. We begin with a review of the more or less noncontroversial facts about trends in gun ownership and use and the reasons why Americans are inclined to arm themselves. A discussion follows of the more controversial issue of whether guns influence levels or seriousness of crime. We then identify the important values at stake in adopting any gun control policy and go on to describe the existing policies and the mechanisms by which they and other such measures have their effect. Finally, we make recommendations about promising next steps.

■ *GUN OWNERSHIP: USE AND MISUSE*

Guns are versatile tools with many uses, so their broad appeal is not surprising. They are an especially common feature of rural life, where wild animals provide both a threat and an opportunity for sport. As America has become more urban and more violent, however, the demand for guns has become increasingly motivated by the need for protection against other people.

Patterns of Gun Ownership

The 1994 National Survey of the Private Ownership of Firearms (NSPOF) by the National Opinion Research Center found that 41% of American households included at least one firearm. Approximately 29% of adults say that they personally own a gun. These percentages reflect an apparent *decline* in the prevalence of gun ownership since the 1970s (Cook & Ludwig, 1996).

Although the prevalence of gun ownership has declined, it appears that the number of guns in private hands has been increasing rapidly. Since 1970, total sales of new guns have accounted for more than half of all the guns sold during this century, and the total now in circulation is on the order of 200 million (Cook & Ludwig, 1996). How can this volume of sales be reconciled with the decline in the prevalence of ownership? Part of the answer is in the growth in population (and the more rapid growth in the number of households) during this period; millions of new guns were required to arm the baby boom cohorts. Beyond that is the likelihood that the average gun owner has increased the size of his or her collection (Wright, 1981). The NSPOF estimates that gun-owning households average 4.4 guns, up substantially from the 1970s (Cook & Ludwig, 1996).[1]

One addition for many gun-owning households has been a *handgun.* The significance of this trend toward increased handgun ownership lies in that although rifles and shotguns are acquired primarily for sporting purposes, handguns are intended primarily for use against people, either in crime or self-defense. The increase in handgun prevalence corresponds to a large increase in the relative importance of handguns in retail sales; since the early 1970s, the handgun fraction of new gun sales has increased from one third to near one half (Cook, 1993).

Although the prevalence of handgun ownership has increased substantially during the past three decades, it remains true that most people who possess a handgun also own one or more rifles and shotguns. The 1994 NSPOF (see Cook & Ludwig, 1996, p. 39) found that just 20% of gun-owning individuals have only handguns, 36% have only long guns, and 44% have both. These statistics suggest that people who have acquired guns for self-protection are for the most part also hunters and target shooters. Indeed, only 46% of gun owners say that they own a gun *primarily* for self-protection against crime, and only 26% keep a gun loaded. Most (80%) grew up in a house with a gun.

The demographic patterns of gun ownership are no surprise: Most owners are men, and the men who are most likely to own a gun reside in rural areas or small towns and were reared in such small places (Kleck, 1991). The regional pattern gives the highest prevalence to the states of the Mountain Census Region, followed by the South and Midwest. Blacks are less likely to own guns than are Whites, in part because the Black population is more urban.[2] The likelihood of gun ownership increases with income and age.

That guns fit more comfortably into rural life than urban life raises a question. What will happen to gun ownership patterns as new generations with less connection to rural life come along? Hunting is already on the decline; as revealed in the National Survey of Wildlife-Associated Recreation, the absolute number of hunting licenses issued in 1990 was about the same as in 1970, despite the growth in the population, indicating a decline in the percentage of people who hunt (U.S. Department of the Interior, 1991). This trend may eventually erode the importance of the rural sporting culture that has dominated the "gun scene." In its place is an ever-greater focus on the criminal and self-defense uses of guns.

Uses of Guns Against People

A great many Americans die by gunfire. The gun death counts from suicide, homicide, and accident have totaled more than 30,000 for every year since 1972. In 1994, there were approximately 39,000 firearms deaths, a rate of 15 per 100,000 U.S. residents. All but 2,200 of these deaths were either homicides or suicides (although homicides garner the bulk of the public concern, there were actually 1,200 more gun suicides than homicides). The remaining gun deaths were classified as accidents, legal interventions, or unknown (Violence Policy Center, 1997).

There are different points of reference to make sense of these numbers. For example, for Americans killed, a year of gun killing in the United States is the equivalent of the Korean War. Another familiar reference is highway accidents: Nearly as many Americans die of gunfire as in motor vehicle crashes, with the former showing a strong secular increase, whereas the latter has declined.

Criminal homicide and other criminal uses of guns cause the greatest public concern. Gun accident rates have been declining steadily during the past two decades,[3] and suicide seems a threat only to those whose loved ones are at risk. Homicide rates have varied little since 1970, with the homicide rate per 100,000 fluctuating between 8.1 and 10.6. Of these, 60% to 70% were committed with guns, mostly (80%) handguns. The peak rates, occurring in 1980 and 1991, were about the same magnitude (Federal Bureau of Investigation, 1971-1997).

Homicide is not a democratic crime. Both victims and perpetrators are vastly disproportionately male, Black, and young. With respect to the victims, homicide is the leading cause of death for Black males aged 15 to 34, whose victimization rate (in 1994) was 9.5 times as high as for White males and Black females in this age range and nearly 50 times as high as for White females. (The evidence suggests that most victims in the high-risk category are killed by people with the same demographic characteristics.) About 75% of the homicide victims in this age group were killed with firearms. Thus, we see a remarkable disparity between the demography of gun sports and of gun crime: Sportsmen are disproportionately older White males from small towns and rural areas, whereas the criminal misuse of guns is concentrated among young urban males, especially minorities.[4] Young Black men have suffered the greatest increase in homicide rates since 1985; by 1994, the homicide victimization rate for 15- to 24-year-olds in this group had tripled, reaching 160 per 100,000[5] (Centers for Disease Control and Prevention, 1997).

Of course, most gun crimes are not fatal. For every gun homicide victim, roughly six gun crime victims receive a less than mortal wound (Cook, 1985), and many more are not wounded at all. Indeed, the most common criminal use of guns is to threaten, with the objective of robbing, raping, or otherwise gaining the victim's compliance. Relatively few of these victims are physically injured, but the threat of lethal violence and the potential for escalation necessarily make these crimes serious. According to the 1994 National Crime Victimization Survey (NCVS), 316,000 guns were used in robberies,

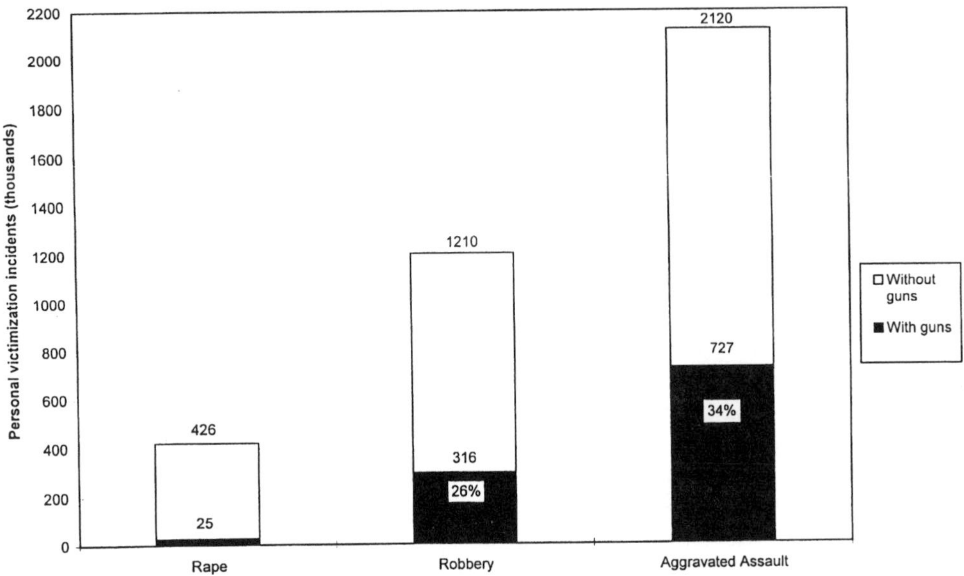

Figure 18.1. Personal Crimes of Violence, 1994
SOURCE: Bureau of Justice Statistics (1997, Table 66).

727,000 aggravated assaults (of which 94,000 caused injury), and 25,000 rapes in that year, for a total estimated volume of gun crimes of about 1,068,000 (Bureau of Justice Statistics, 1997, Table 66). For each of these crime types, guns are used in only a fraction of all cases, as shown in Figure 18.1. When a gun is used, it is almost always a handgun, which accounts for upwards of 92% of these crimes.

Gun Use as Self-Defense

Although guns do enormous damage in crime, they also provide some crime victims with the means of escaping serious injury or property loss. The NCVS is generally considered the most reliable source of information on predatory crime because it has been in the field more than two decades and incorporates the best thinking of survey methodologists. From this source, it appears that use of guns in self-defense against criminal predation is rather rare, occurring on the order of 100,000 times per year (Cook, Ludwig, & Hemenway, 1997). Of particular interest is the likelihood that a gun will be used in self-defense against an intruder. Cook (1991), using NCVS data, found that only 3% of victims were able to deploy a gun against someone who broke in (or attempted to do so) while they were at home. Remembering that 40% of all households have a gun, we conclude that it is quite rare for victims to be able to deploy a gun against intruders even when they have one available.

Gary Kleck and Marc Gertz (1995) have come up with far higher estimates of 2.5 million self-defense uses each year. Indeed, Kleck and Gertz conclude that guns are used more commonly in self-defense than in crime. Cook et al. (1997) have demonstrated that Kleck and Gertz's high estimate may result from a significant false-positive rate—in short, there is no clear sense of how many shootings were truly justifiable in the sense of being committed in self-defense. It is quite possible that most "self-defense" uses occur in circumstances that are normatively ambiguous, such as chronic violence within a marriage, gang fights, robberies of drug dealers, and encounters with groups of young men who simply *appear* threatening. In one survey of convicted felons in prison, the most common reason offered for carrying a gun was self-defense (Wright & Rossi, 1986); a similar finding emerged from a study of juveniles incarcerated for serious criminal offenses (Smith, 1996). Although self-defense conjures up an image of the innocent victim using a gun to fend off an unprovoked criminal assault, many self-defense cases are not nearly so clear-cut or so commendable.

■ *INSTRUMENTALITY AND AVAILABILITY OF FIREARMS*

An overriding issue in the gun control debate is, "Do guns kill people?" or "Do people kill people?" In murder trials, the killer's motivation and state of mind are explored thoroughly, whereas the type of weapon—usually some type of gun—is often treated as an incidental detail. Yet there is compelling evidence that the *type of weapon matters a great deal* in determining whether the victim lives or dies and therefore becomes a homicide victim. This means that depriving potentially violent people of guns probably can save lives, an essential tenet of the argument for restricting gun availability. But then a second question arises: How can we use the law to deprive violent people of guns if such people are not inclined to be law-abiding? The saying "if guns are outlawed, only outlaws will have guns" may ring true.[6] There is also some evidence on this matter suggesting that some criminals' decisions of what weapon to use are influenced by the difficulty and legal risks of obtaining and using a gun (Wright & Rossi, 1986).

We now explore the evidence on these two issues, designated *instrumentality* and *availability.* The same two issues should also be considered in an assessment of the self-defense uses of guns, and we do so in the next two sections.

Instrumentality

The first piece of evidence is that robberies and assaults committed with guns are more likely to result in the victim's death than are similar violent crimes committed with other weapons. In public health jargon, the *case fatality rates* differ by weapon type. A prime example is robbery, for which the fatality rate for *gun robbery* is 3 times as high as for robberies with knives and 10 times as high as for robberies with other weapons (Cook, 1987). It is more difficult to come up with significant probability estimates for aggravated (serious) assault because the crime itself is in part defined by the type of weapon used. We do know, however, that for assaults in which the victim sustains an injury, the case fatality rate is closely linked to the type of weapon (Kleck & McElrath, 1991; Zimring, 1968, 1972), as is also the case for family and intimate assaults known to the police (Saltzman, Mercy, O'Carroll, Rosenberg, & Rhodes, 1992).

Fatality rates do not by themselves prove that the type of weapon has an independent causal effect on the probability of death. Possibly, the type of weapon is simply an indicator of the assailant's intent, and the intent, rather than the weapon, determines whether the victim lives or dies. In this view, the gun makes the killing easier and hence is the obvious choice if the assailant's intent is indeed to kill. The overriding assumption is that if no gun were available, most would-be killers would still find a way (Wolfgang, 1958; Wright, Rossi, & Daly, 1983).

Perhaps the most telling response to this argument comes from Franklin Zimring (1968, 1972; see also Zimring & Hawkins, 1997), who concluded that there actually is a good deal of overlap between fatal and nonfatal attacks; even in the case of earnest and potentially deadly attacks, assailants commonly lack a clear or sustained intent to kill. Zimring's argument in a nutshell is that homicide is fundamentally a by-product of violent crime. Although the law determines the seriousness of the crime by whether the victim lives or dies, the outcome is not a reliable guide to the assailant's intent or state of mind. One logical implication of this perspective is that there should be a close link between the overall volume of violent crimes and the number of murders. One study provided confirmatory evidence, finding that an additional 1,000 gun robberies "produces" three times as many extra murders as an additional 1,000 robberies with other weapons (Cook, 1987). The instrumentality explanation for this result is simpler and more persuasive than an argument based on changes in the prevalence of homicidal intent among robbers.

Another study provides further evidence on the importance of reducing gun use in violent homes. In research based on six cities in three crimes, it was found that mandatory sentencing enhancements for those convicted of using a gun in a crime are effective in reducing the homicide rate (McDowall, Loftin, & Wiersema, 1992b).

Zimring's reasoning can also be extended to a comparison of different types of guns. In the gun control debate, the prime target has been the handgun, because handguns are used in most gun crimes. But rifles and shotguns tend to be more lethal than handguns; a rifle is easier to aim, and the bullet travels with higher velocity than for a short-barreled weapon, whereas a shotgun blast spreads and causes a number of wounds when it strikes. To the extent that assailants substitute rifles and shotguns for handguns in response to handgun control measures, the result may be to increase the death rate (Kleck, 1984).[7] Unfortunately, there is little evidence on the question of whether effective handgun control would lead robbers and other violent people to substitute long guns (more lethal) or, in contrast, knives (less lethal).

Other Perspectives on Instrumentality

Instrumentality effects are not limited to differences in case fatality rates among weapons. The type of weapon also appears to matter in other ways. For example, gun robbers are far less likely to attack and injure their victims than are robbers using other weapons and are less likely to incur resistance (Conklin, 1972; Cook, 1976, 1980; Skogan, 1978). We have evidence that aggravated assaults also follow similar patterns (Kleck & McElrath, 1991). The most plausible explanation for this pattern of outcomes is simply that a gun gives the assailant the power to intimidate and gain the victim's compliance without use of force, whereas with less lethal weapons, the assailant is more likely to find it necessary to back up the threat with a physical attack.

The intimidating power of a gun may also help explain the effectiveness of using one in self-defense. According to one study of NCVS data, in burglaries of occupied dwellings, only 5% of victims who used guns in self-defense were injured, compared with 25% of those who resisted with other weapons.[8] Other studies have confirmed that victims of predatory crime who are able to resist with a gun are generally successful in thwarting the crime and avoiding injury (Kleck, 1988; McDowall et al., 1992b). The interpretation of this result, however, is open to some question. In particular, other means of defense usually are attempted after the assailant threatens or attacks the victim, whereas those who use guns in self-defense are relatively likely to be the first to threaten or use force (McDowall et al., 1992b). Given this difference in the sequence of events, and the implied difference in the competence or intentions of the perpetrator, the proper interpretation of the statistical evidence concerning weapon-specific success rates in self-defense is unclear (Cook, 1986, 1991).

In sum, we postulate that the type of weapon deployed in violent confrontations appears to matter in several ways. Because guns provide the power to kill quickly, at a distance, and without much skill or strength, they also provide the power to intimidate other people and gain control of a violent situation. When there is a physical attack, then the lethality of the weapon is an important determinant of whether the victim survives. But when the assailant's purpose is robbery, intimidation, or self-defense, rather than inflicting injury, then a gun appears to be more effective than other weapons in achieving that purpose, and without actual use of violence. These hypothesized effects receive support from the empirical work that has been published in this area, but the current state of that evidence surely leaves room for doubt.

Availability

If the type of weapon transforms violent encounters in important ways, as suggested in the preceding discussion, then the extent to which guns are available to violence-prone people is a matter of public concern. *Availability* can be thought of as time, expense, and other costs. Violent confrontations often occur unexpectedly, and in such cases, the weapons that will be used are among those that are close at hand; the relevant question is whether a gun is *immediately* available. Logically, the next question concerns the likelihood that a gun will be present *when* a violent confrontation occurs. In particular, do the costs of obtaining a gun and keeping it handy influence the likelihood of gun use in violence?

Arthur L. Kellermann and his associates (1993, 1992) provide evidence on the importance of the first issue, immediate availability. In case control studies of violent events occurring in the home, they found that the likelihoods of both suicide and homicide are greatly elevated by the presence of a gun in the home. The authors selected each control from the same neighborhood as that in which the killing occurred, and through their matching criteria and use of multivariate statistical techniques, attempted to control for other differences between the suicide/homicide cases and cases used as controls. There is no guarantee that this effort to control for other factors that might be confounded with gun possession was successful, so the proper interpretation of these findings remains controversial.[9] If we accept Kellermann et al.'s interpretation, then two propositions follow.

1. If a member of the household owns a gun, then at-home suicide attempts and armed assaults are more likely to involve a gun than otherwise.
2. A gun is more deadly than other weapons would have been in these circumstances (an instrumentality effect).

Extending these propositions, we can ask whether the extent to which guns are readily available in a community influences the likelihood of weapons used in violent crime (and suicide). A recent cross-national comparison for 11 countries indicates a strong positive correlation (.72) between a country's household prevalence of gun ownership and the proportion of homicides committed with a gun (Killias, 1993). This finding suggests that the overall scarcity (or availability) of guns in a country influences weapon choice in violent events.

Within the American context, however, many commentators have expressed doubt that guns are in any sense scarce, or that anyone (including youths and violent criminals) would find it more difficult to obtain a gun than, say, a kitchen knife. Regional comparisons, however, suggest otherwise. The prevalence of gun ownership differs rather widely across urban areas, from around 10% in the cities of the Northeast to upwards of 50% in the Mountain states. (An obvious explanation for these large differences has to do with the differing importance of rural traditions in these areas.[10]) The overall prevalence of gun ownership has been found to be highly correlated with the percentage of homicides, suicides, and robberies that involve guns in these cities (Cook, 1979, 1985). Therefore, where gun ownership is prevalent in the general population, guns tend to be prevalent in violence.

A natural explanation for this pattern is differences among cities in their *scarcity* of guns. Predatory criminals obtain most of their guns from acquaintances, family members, drug dealers, thefts from homes and vehicles, and other street sources, rather than from licensed dealers (Decker, Pennell, & Caldwell, 1997; Sheley & Wright, 1995; Smith, 1996). The ease of making such a connection will be greater in a city in which guns are prevalent. Further, the black markets for guns, which are the ultimate source for perhaps half or more of the crime guns, will tend to be more active in cities in which gun ownership is prevalent (Moore, 1981; Wright & Rossi, 1986).

It helps in thinking about the availability of guns to realize how frequently they change hands. For youthful criminals, acquiring a gun is typically not a one-time decision. One statistic from a survey of inner-city male high school students helps make the point: 22% said they currently owned a gun, whereas an additional 8% indicated that they had owned one or more guns in the past but did not at the time of the interview. Further, the number who said they carried a gun on occasion exceeded the number who owned one, suggesting loans and other temporary arrangements may be important features of this scene (Wright, Sheley, & Smith, 1992). The thrust of this research certainly suggests that acquiring a firearm poses little challenge to those persons who are motivated to acquire one.

Of course, for a gun to be available for use during a violent encounter, it must also be carried. Because most violent crime occurs away from home, one important aspect of gun availability is the propensity to go armed. The majority of states allow carrying concealed handguns (if the carrier has obtained a license) but do not treat violations as serious offenses. A notable exception is the Bartley-Fox Amendment in Massachusetts, which in 1975 legislated a mandatory 1-year prison sentence for anyone convicted of carrying a gun without a license. This mandatory sentence provision received tremendous publicity at the time it was implemented. The immediate impact was that thousands of gun owners applied for the licenses required to carry a handgun legally. Several studies analyzed subsequent trends in violent crime. Among these, Pierce and Bowers (1981) concluded that the short-term impact was to reduce the fractions of assaults and robberies involving guns and, presumably, as a consequence, to reduce the criminal homicide rate (see also Deutsch, 1979). Apparently, some streetwise people were deterred from carrying a gun; as a result, they were more likely to commit their robberies and assaults, when the occasion arose, with weapons other than guns. Because of the instrumentality effect, the death rate was reduced in these attacks.

It is not just street criminals who carry guns; sometimes, their potential victims do as well. The practice of going armed in public has been facilitated in recent years by changes in state laws governing concealed-carry licensing; by 1997, a majority of states had liberal provisions that enable most adults to obtain a license to carry. A controversial study by two economists (Lott & Mustard, 1997) found evidence that states that liberalized their concealed-carry regulations enjoyed a reduction in violent crime rates, presumably because some would-be assailants feared that potential victims might be armed. Black and Nagin (1998), however, using the same data, conclude that there is no evidence of a deterrent effect (see also McDowall, Loftin, & Wiersema, 1995). Stronger conclusions will have to await better evidence.

One important question remains: Does gun availability influence the overall *volume* of violent crime? The existing evidence provides little reason to believe that robbery and assault rates are much affected by the prevalence of gun ownership (Cook, 1979; Kleck & Patterson, 1993). Consequently, that the United States is such a violent country[11] does not have much to do with guns; that our violent crimes *are so deadly*—and thus, our homicide rate so high—however, has *much* to do with availability and use of guns (see Zimring & Hawkins, 1997, for an extensive argument concerning this aspect of crime in the United States).

■ *GUNS AND PUBLIC POLICY: THE VALUES AT STAKE*

Used in the manner of our rural sporting tradition, a gun provides recreation, food, and, arguably, a way of learning a sense of responsibility. When kept behind the counter of a small grocery store in a high-crime neighborhood, a gun may serve as a means of self-defense and even a deterrent to crime. When used in a robbery, gang warfare, or domestic violence, however, a gun becomes part of the nation's nightmare of crime that terrorizes urban residents and cuts short far too many lives.

Guns have many uses, all of which have legitimacy to the people who use them in those ways. Society as a whole, however, values some uses less highly than do the individual owners. The result is a "great American gun war," a continuing debate and political struggle to determine which uses will be protected and which should be sacrificed to achieve some greater social good.

The debate about gun control policy makes broad use of both consequentialist and deontological arguments. A *consequentialist* framework is concerned with ascertaining and valuing the consequences of proposed reform, whereas the *deontological* framework is concerned with how a proposed reform measures up in its assignment of civic rights and responsibilities. Advocates on both sides tend to make use of both sets of claims. For instance, control advocates typically argue their case by pointing to the reductions in fatalities engendered by the proposed reform *and* by insisting that gun owners, as a matter of principle, should be willing to relinquish some of their rights to own guns in the interests of achieving these benefits. The anticontrol advocates argue that gun ownership reduces, rather than increases, crime *and* that it is their constitutional right to own guns.

Much of the rhetoric in the debate stems from three broad perspectives that will be considered in the following sections. Two of these, the public health and welfare economics perspectives, are predominantly consequentialist, whereas the third is primarily deontological.

The Public Health Perspective

The essence of the public health framework is whether a proposed control measure would reduce the incidence of injury and death. There is little concern with the value of sporting uses of guns. From this perspective, the modest pleasures associated with recreational shooting and the dubious benefits from self-defense should yield to society's overwhelming interest in reducing gun deaths. Preserving life is the paramount value in this scheme. (For a highly critical review of the public health literature on firearms and homicide, see Blackman, 1997.)

The Welfare Economics Framework

The welfare economics framework is similar to that of the public health framework but has a wider array of consequences and greater attention to individual preferences. It leads us to view the gun "problem" as the harm inflicted on others, with much less attention to suicides and self-inflicted accidents. The uses seen as socially detrimental are virtually the same as those that are prohibited by law. There is no presumption within this framework, however, that punishing criminal uses is an adequate response; consequently, there remains the possibility that the benefits of preemptive controls on guns, such as a ban on carrying concealed handguns, would outweigh the costs. The costs of such controls include the public costs of enforcement and the private costs of compliance (or evasion) of these regulations.

In this calculus of cost and benefit, where does self-defense fit in? For most gun owners, the possibility that the gun will prove useful in fending off a robber or burglar is one source of its value.[12] Indeed, if guns had no value in self-protection, a ban on possession of guns in the home would quite likely be worthwhile, because sporting uses of guns could be preserved by allowing people to store firearms in shooting clubs and use them under regulated conditions. Given this, the self-defense uses of guns ultimately are more important than sporting uses in assessing the costs of restrictions on home possession and carrying in urban areas.

Some writers have even argued that the private valuation of guns in this respect understates their public value because the widespread possession of guns has a *general* deterrent effect on crime (Kleck, 1991; Snyder, 1993). Indeed, one survey of imprisoned felons found that a paramount concern in doing their crimes was the prospect of meeting up with an armed victim (Wright & Rossi, 1986). We do not know, however, whether the predominant effect on criminal behavior is desisting, displacement to victims who are not likely to be armed, or a change in technique. If the latter two predominate, then the overall impact is negative, rather than positive (Clotfelter, 1993).

The "Rights and Responsibilities" Perspective

The welfare economics framework helps organize the arguments pro and con gun controls and suggests a procedure for assigning values. But for those who believe in the "right" to bear arms, it is not a completely satisfactory approach. The debate about gun control can and should be conducted, at least in part, in the context of a framework that defines the appropriate relationship between the individual, the community, and the state.

Much in the foreground of this debate lies the Second Amendment, which states, "A well regulated militia, being necessary to the security of a free State, the right of the people to keep and bear arms, shall not be infringed." The proper interpretation of this statement has been contested in recent years. The U.S. Supreme Court has not chosen to clarify the matter, having ruled only once during this century on a Second Amendment issue, and that on a rather narrow technical basis.[13] Indeed, no federal court has ever overturned a gun control law on Second Amendment grounds.

For most people, the crucial issue concerns self-defense. Some commentators go so far as to assert that there is a public duty for private individuals to defend against criminal predation now, just as there was in 1789 when there were no police. The argument is that if all reliable people were to equip themselves with guns both in the home and out, there would be far less predatory crime (Polsby, 1993; Snyder, 1993). Other commentators, less optimistic about the possibility of creating a more civil society by force of arms, also stress the public duty of gun owners but with an emphasis on responsible use: storing them safely away from children and burglars, learning how to operate them properly, exercising good judgment in deploying them when feeling threatened, and so forth (Karlson & Hargarten, 1997). In any event, the right to bear arms, like the right of free speech, is not absolute but is subject to reasonable restrictions and carries with it certain civic responsibilities. The appropriate extent of those restrictions and responsibilities, however, remains an unresolved issue.

In conclusion, each of these three perspectives—public health, welfare economics, and civic rights and responsibilities—provides arguments about the public interest that seem familiar and important. Each is well represented in the debate about the appropriate regulation of firearms. In practice, the public health perspective helps focus greater attention on suicide, whereas the perspective that stresses civic rights strengthens the case for protecting self-defense uses of guns. We are not inclined to argue the relative merits of these differing perspectives in the abstract but will have more to say about policy evaluation in the next sections.

■ *ALTERNATIVE GUN CONTROL POLICIES*

Commerce in guns and the possession and use of guns are regulated by federal, state, and local governments. To assess the options for reform, it is first helpful to understand the current array of controls and why they fail to achieve an acceptably low rate of gun violence.

The Current Array of Policies

The primary objective of federal law in regulating firearms is to insulate the states from one another, so that restrictive laws adopted in some states are not undercut by the greater availability of guns in other states. The Gun Control Act of 1968 established the framework for the current system of controls on gun transfers. All shipments of firearms (including mail-order sales) are limited to federally licensed dealers who are required to obey applicable state and local ordinances. There are also restrictions on sales of guns to out-of-state residents.[14]

Federal law also seeks to establish a minimum set of restrictions on acquisition and possession of guns. The Gun Control Act of 1968 stipulates several categories of people who are denied the right to receive or possess a gun, including illegal aliens, convicted felons and those under indictment, and people who have at some time been involuntarily committed to a mental institution. Persons with a history of substance abuse are also prohibited from possessing a gun. Dealers are not allowed to sell handguns to people younger than 21 years old or to sell long guns to those younger than 18, although there is no federal prohibition of gun *possession* by youth. These various prohibitions are implemented by a requirement that the buyer sign a form stating that he or she does not fall into any of the proscribed categories.

A number of states have adopted significant restrictions on commerce in firearms, especially handguns. As of 1993, a majority of states require that handgun buyers obtain a permit or license before taking possession of a handgun. All but a few state transfer-control systems are "permissive" in the sense that most people are legally entitled to obtain a gun. In a few jurisdictions, however, it is difficult to obtain a handgun legally. The most stringent is Washington, D.C., where only law enforcement officers and security guards are entitled to obtain a handgun (Jones, 1981). In 1993, Congress adopted the Brady Bill, which requires dealers in states without screening systems for handgun buyers to enforce a 5-day waiting period between the purchase and transfer of a handgun. The dealers are required to notify law enforcement officials shortly after the purchase in order that a background check can be run on the buyer.[15]

State and local legislation tends to make a sharp distinction between keeping a gun in one's home or business and carrying a gun in public. All but a few states either ban concealed weapons entirely or require a special license for carrying concealed weapons (although many states have recently eased the requirements for obtaining a license). Local ordinances typically place additional restrictions on carrying and discharging guns inside city limits.

Some sense of the variety of possibilities here is suggested by this list of recent efforts, proposed or adopted, to extend additional control over firearms commerce and use:

1. Imposing a heavy federal tax on ammunition
2. Banning the sale and possession of assault rifles at the state level
3. Limiting handgun sales to no more than one per month per customer
4. Requiring that gun buyers pass a test demonstrating their knowledge of law and good practice in handling a gun
5. Raising the fees charged to acquire a federal license for gun dealing
6. Trying local drug dealers in the federal courts if they are in possession of a gun at the time of their arrest
7. Offering cash, tickets to sporting events, or even toys in exchange for guns
8. Establishing minimum mandatory sentences for illegally carrying guns
9. Using public education campaigns and the cooperation of the television industry to stigmatize storing unlocked, loaded guns in households
10. Giving the police power to revoke licenses and search intensively for guns in residences for which court restraining orders have been issued against spouses
11. Using magnetometers to keep guns out of schools
12. Developing a "parents' compact" to promote parents' efforts to prevent their children from possessing or carrying guns

Facing such a daunting array of possibilities for legislation, policymakers need guidance on which approaches hold the most promise of reducing firearms violence, and at what cost to legitimate owners. Reliable information is difficult to obtain; still, some evidence is available concerning which general approaches show the most promise. In searching for worthwhile reforms, we find it useful to classify alternative gun control measures into three categories: (a) those designed to affect the supply and overall availability of guns, (b) those designed to influence who has these weapons, and (c) those designed to affect how the guns are used by the people who have them.

On the basis of combined empirical evidence and logic, the generic strengths and weaknesses of each category can be sketched. The result is a rough map of the relevant terrain with some of the details missing, but it is nonetheless a useful guide.

Reducing Overall Supply and Availability

Many gun control measures focus on the supply and availability of the guns themselves (or, in one imaginative leap, on the ammunition that makes them deadly). The basic idea is that if guns (or ammunition) become less readily available, or more expensive to purchase, then some violence-prone people will decide to rely on other weapons instead, and gun violence will be reduced.

Many commentators have suggested that this approach is doomed by the huge arsenal of guns currently in private hands. How can we discourage violence-prone people from obtaining guns when there are already enough in circulation to arm every teenager and adult in the country? In response, we note that the number of guns in circulation is only indirectly relevant to whether supply restrictions can hope to succeed; of direct consequence is the *price* and *difficulty* of obtaining a gun. Our discussion of availability in a previous section helps establish the evidence on these matters—availability *does* seem to matter, even within the current context of widespread private ownership.

Basic economic reasoning suggests that if the price of new guns is increased by amending the federal tax or other means, the effects will ripple through all the markets in which guns are transferred, including the black market for stolen guns (Cook & Leitzel, 1996). If the average prices of guns go up, some people—including some violence-prone people—will decide that there are better uses for their money. Others will be discouraged if, in addition to raising the money price, the amount of time or risk required to obtain a gun increases. Although there are no reliable estimates of the elasticity of demand for guns by youths, we believe that youths, in particular, are likely to be more responsive to price than to more remote costs (such as the possibility of arrest and punishment). Those who argue that youthful offenders will do whatever is necessary to obtain their guns may have some hard-core group of violent gang members and drug dealers in mind, but surely not the much larger group of kids who rarely get into serious trouble (see Sheley & Wright, 1995; Smith, 1996).

At present, a substantial increase in the federal tax on the purchase of firearms is under discussion for the first time in memory. Potentially even more important is the growing possibility of successful tort litigation against manufacturers of cheap concealable handguns, which, if successful, would raise the price of even the cheapest guns (Teret, 1986). Another approach to raising prices, however, is to impose safety requirements on gun manufacturers. Proposals in this area include "childproofing" guns so that they are inoperable by children; requiring that domestically manufactured guns meet the same safety requirements as imports, including protections against accidental discharge; and requiring safety devices such as trigger locks and loaded chamber indicators (Teret & Wintemute, 1993). As it is now, firearms manufacturers are remarkably free of safety regulation, in part because the Consumer Product Safety Commission has no authority over personal firearms. Although such regulations may be welcomed by gun buyers who are seeking some protection against gun accidents, they would have little direct effect on suicide and criminal misuse of firearms. To the extent that complying with such regulations made guns more costly, however, there could be some indirect effect comparable with raising the federal tax (Cook & Leitzel, 1996).

A more far-reaching proposal is to encourage the manufacture of guns that are "personalized," in the sense that they would be equipped with an electronic sensing device that would recognize a ring on the owner's finger, or even the owner's fingerprint. Such devices are currently under development. If they prove reliable, law enforcement agencies may adopt them to protect officers from being assaulted with their own guns. Equipping all new handguns with such devices would gradually reduce the number of gun accidents and reduce the profitability of stealing guns.

Restricting Access

The second broad class of gun control policy instruments includes those designed to influence who has access to different types of weapons. The intuitive notion here is that if we could find a way to keep guns out of the hands of the "bad guys" without denying access to the "good guys," then gun crimes would decrease without infringing on the legitimate uses of guns. The challenges for this type of policy are, first, to decide where to draw the line and, second, to develop effective barriers to prevent guns from crossing this line.

Who should be trusted with a gun? Federal law rules out several large groups, including drug users and illegal aliens, but there are no ready means of identifying those who fall into these categories. Public records provide more information on criminal background, and there is an important debate concerning what sort of criminal record should be disqualifying. Any felony conviction strips an individual of the right to own a gun under federal law, although many felons are able to obtain court orders allowing them to possess guns after they have served their sentences.

A fundamental premise underlying much gun legislation holds that owning a gun is a right granted to all adults[16] unless they do something to disqualify themselves, such as committing a serious crime. A different approach would be to treat gun ownership as a privilege, as is the case, say, with driving a vehicle on public highways. Similar to driving privileges, one eminently sensible requirement for those who seek to acquire a gun is that they demonstrate knowledge of how to use it safely and legally. An intriguing possibility is that such a requirement would engender considerable growth in the National Rifle Association's safety training programs because many of those wishing to qualify for a license would need to enroll in such a course.

Wherever the line is drawn, there is the serious problem of defending it against illegal transfers. That task is currently being done poorly. The major loopholes stem from the widespread abuse of the federal licensing system, the lack of effective screening of those who seek to buy guns from dealers, a vigorous and largely unregulated "gray" market by which used guns change hands, and an active black market supplied by theft, scofflaw gun dealers (those who knowingly violate the terms of their license on a frequent basis), and interstate gunrunning operations.

Federal Licensing System

The U.S. Bureau of Alcohol, Tobacco, and Firearms (ATF) is the agency charged with the regulation of federally licensed gun dealers. It is a small agency whose jurisdiction includes not only regulatory inspections of gun dealers but also criminal investigations of violations of federal gun laws. As well, it is responsible for the regulatory surveillance and criminal investigation of the explosives, alcohol, and tobacco industries. Obtaining a federal dealer's license from ATF was formerly just a matter of paying a small fee and filling out a form, and in 1993, there were 260,000 people who had done so—far more than were genuinely in the business of selling guns to the public. At that time, ATF lacked the authority and resources to screen applicants effectively or to inspect their operations after issuing the license (Violence Policy Center, 1992). In response to this problem, recent changes in application requirements, combined with the hefty increase in fee mandated by the Brady Law, have had the effect of reducing the number of federal licensees to about 100,000 (as of 1997) and of greatly enhancing ATF's ability to serve its regulatory function.

Screening

People who seek to buy handguns from a dealer are required to submit to state permit requirements or, if there are none, a 5-day waiting period required by federal law. If the dealer and purchaser comply with this requirement, there is some chance that disqualified buyers will be identified and screened out. But felons, youths, and others who are not permitted to purchase a gun can ask a qualified friend or relative to make a "straw man" purchase from a dealer on their behalf or find a scofflaw dealer who is willing to sell guns off the books. Most common of all is simply to purchase a gun from a nondealer.

Black and Gray Markets

There is a remarkably active and open market for used guns that is largely unregulated, a market in which buyers and sellers find each other through gun shows, word of mouth, or the classified ads. These transactions are often entirely legal; someone who sells a gun or two on occasion is not subject to any federal requirements except that they not knowingly sell to a felon, illicit drug user, or other person prohibited from possessing a gun.[17]

In considering intervention strategies, it is useful to distinguish between transfers that move guns from the licit to the illicit sectors and transfers within the illicit sector (Koper & Reuter, 1996). In the former category are sales by scofflaw dealers and theft from legitimate owners, whereas the latter includes the active but highly disorganized black market for guns in which kids and criminals frequently buy and sell (Cook, Molliconi, & Cole, 1995; Kennedy, 1994).

Perhaps the best hope for reducing gun trafficking to youths and criminals is a multifaceted enforcement and regulatory effort aimed primarily at reducing the flow of guns from the licit to the illicit sector. On the regulatory side, the main objective is to rein in scofflaw dealers, which most states have left to the ATF. ATF's capacity to act effectively has been strengthened in recent years by the great reduction in the number of licensed dealers resulting from changes in ATF licensing procedures and the increase in the initial license fee from $30 to $200 that was required in the Brady Law. ATF is also beginning to exploit gun tracing data to identify dealers who are frequently involved in selling guns that are used in crime. Further regulatory efforts to discourage gunrunning include the requirement that dealers report multiple purchases and the prohibition adopted by several states on sale of more than one handgun to a customer per month.

Designing policies to reduce theft is conceptually more difficult, yet with an estimated 500,000 guns a year being transferred this way (Cook & Ludwig, 1996), it is just as important. To reduce this source of crime guns, it may be possible to impose some obligation on gun dealers and gun owners to store their weapons securely (as we now do on pharmacists who sell abusable drugs) and to step up enforcement against fences who happen to deal in stolen guns.

Interdicting transfers *within* the illicit sector falls most naturally to local police, although this has been a low-priority mission for most police departments. Because there has been so little experience with local investigations directed at stopping the redistribution of guns among youths, drug dealers, and others in the illicit sector, it is not clear what can be accomplished in this arena. The analogy to drug enforcement may provide some guidance, but gun markets appear different from heroin and cocaine markets for several reasons, so the effectiveness of similar strategies is open to question (Koper & Reuter, 1996; Moore, 1981).

Considering its various components, the illicit gun market is best seen as a relatively large number of persons engaging in relatively unspecialized enterprises. It is filled with burglars who happen to find some guns next to the household items they wish to steal, some small entrepreneurs who brought a small stock of guns back from the South, gangs who have accumulated an arsenal for their own purposes, and those persons who sometimes are willing to sell a gun to a colleague barred from making a legal purchase. The type of enforcement that would be appropriate in attacking such markets is probably a high-volume "buy and bust" operation (Moore, 1983). Law enforcement agencies may be reluctant to launch an operation of this sort, given the danger inherent in dealing with guns and the legal difficulties in proving that the guns they are buying are actually stolen and being sold illegally. Consequently, the possibilities for choking off supply to the illicit sector appear more promising than attempting to disrupt their activities.

Controlling Uses

The third broad class of gun control policy instruments is concerned with limiting unsafe and criminal uses of guns. Most prominent are provisions for increasing prison sentences when a gun is used in a crime. One clear advantage of this approach as compared with other gun policies is that it does not impinge on legitimate uses of guns. A recent analysis of crime trends in jurisdictions that adopted such sentencing provisions provides evidence that they may be effective in reducing the homicide rate (McDowall, Loftin, & Wiersema, 1992a).

Another and far more controversial tactic is to focus local law enforcement efforts on illegal possession and carrying. As discussed earlier, the potential effectiveness of this approach is suggested by the success of the Bartley-Fox Amendment in Massachusetts. This sort of gun enforcement typically requires proactive police efforts, and there is considerable variation among police departments in how much effort they direct to halting illegal possession and gun carrying (Moore, 1980). The controversy about enforcement stems in part from the concern that police, if sufficiently motivated, may conduct illegal searches in the effort to get guns off the street. More fundamentally, treating illegal carrying as a serious crime puts in jeopardy millions of otherwise law-abiding people who carry guns for self-protection. Nonetheless, gun-oriented patrol tactics appear to have the potential to reduce gun violence (Sherman, Shaw, & Rogan, 1995).

Rather than a general effort to get guns off the streets, a more focused effort can be directed at prohibiting guns in particularly dangerous locations such as homes with histories of domestic violence, bars with histories of drunken brawls, parks in which gang fights tend to break out, and schools in which teachers and students have been assaulted.[18] Often, in seeking to reduce the presence of weapons in these particularly dangerous places, groups other than the police may be mobilized to help make the laws effective. Victimized spouses or their advocates might help enforce rules against guns in violence-prone households, liquor-licensing agencies might be enlisted to help keep guns out of bars, the recreation department might be mobilized to reduce gun carrying in public parks, and so on. The point is that there may be some particular hot spots for gun offenses that could be targeted as places to concentrate gun enforcement efforts much as we focus on keeping guns and bombs out of airplanes.

■ *CONCLUSION: WHAT'S TO BE DONE?*

Given the important value conflicts and empirical uncertainties surrounding gun control policies, some caution in recommending public or governmental action is warranted. But recommending caution is far from recommending *inaction*. Indeed, we think that it is time to get on with the business of actively exploring alternative gun control initiatives to develop more effective interventions than those on which we now rely. The goal of gun control policy during the next decade should be to develop and evaluate specific gun control measures that can reduce gun crimes, suicides, and accidents, while preserving as much legitimate use of guns as possible. There is no reason to believe that there is a single best policy. Rather, we should be looking for a combination of policies that address the full array of gun "problems." To some extent, these policies should differ according to local circumstances and values, with an emphasis ranging from suicide prevention in Iowa to street violence in Washington, D.C. The following suggestions are organized according to the level of government at which the appropriate action should occur.

Action at the Federal Level

The federal government is best positioned to make guns more valuable and harder to obtain while insulating the states from one another's supply of guns. Among the next steps that appear most promising are these:

1. Raise the tax on guns and ammunition to make the cost of acquiring and owning particular types of guns more accurately reflect the social costs and benefits of having them. For instance, we favor converting the current excise tax, which is proportional to the wholesale price, to a flat tax. Cheap handguns do as much damage as expensive ones. On the one hand, we recognize that this tax is regressive and will be particularly burdensome on poorer people who want a gun. On the other hand, the benefit of such a tax, reductions in gun crimes and accidents, will be disproportionately experienced by the poor, who are vastly overrepresented among the victims of gunshot wounds and deaths.
2. Require all gun transfers to pass through federally licensed dealers, with the same screening and paperwork provisions as if the gun were being sold by the dealer.

3. Step up criminal enforcement efforts against gunrunning operations.
4. Provide funding and technical know-how to enhance the quality and completeness of state and federal criminal records files and facilitating access by law enforcement agencies to these files.[19]
5. Enhance cooperation with the local law enforcement efforts in investigating and prosecuting those who deal in stolen guns.
6. Mandating that new guns meet minimum safety requirements to reduce gun accidents, while encouraging research in devices to personalize guns.

The federal government is also in the best position to accumulate the national experience with gun control policy initiatives. For instance, the National Institute of Justice could expedite the search for more effective gun control policies by noting and evaluating the large number of diverse policy interventions that will be launched at different levels of government during the next few years. As well, the surgeon general and attorney general together could use their offices to help create an environment in which local governments, community groups, and private individuals would begin to change their attitudes and behaviors with respect to guns. The message should be clear: Guns are dangerous, particularly in an urban environment, and it is important that owners learn how to store them safely and use them responsibly.

Action at the State Level

The agenda for each state will and should depend on its circumstances. In the past, the states have been the laboratory for instituting a variety of licensing and regulatory programs, as well as establishing different sentencing schemes for use of guns in crime and for carrying illegally. Technology transfer can take place only if these innovations are subjected to careful evaluation.

A battle in the state arena looms over the extent of liability for manufacturers, sellers, and owners of guns when a gun is used to injure someone. Lawsuits based on a variety of liability theories are moving through the courts. The implicit threat posed by these lawsuits is that if manufacturers and sellers are held responsible for the damage done by handguns, the monetary liability would be prohibitive. This possibility is appealing to those who are impatient with the more moderate results achievable through the political process.

Action at the Metropolitan or Municipal Level

Perhaps the greatest opportunities to work on reducing gun violence in the immediate future lie in the cities in which the toll of gun violence is so high. It is there that the scales balancing the competing values of rights to gun ownership on one hand, and the social interest in reducing gun violence on the other, tilt decidedly toward reducing gun violence. Working against effective gun legislation at this level, however, is a persistent fear of crime and the fervent belief by some that a gun will provide protection. Thus, one significant goal of gun control policy at the local level should be not simply to reduce the availability of guns but to find other, less socially costly means that people can use to produce security and reduce fear. In many cities, this is one of the important goals of shifting to a strategy of community policing. To the extent that efforts associated with this strategy help to diminish fear of crime, these measures might also reduce the perceived need for individual gun ownership; with that accomplished, an increase in the range of feasible and desirable gun control policies might become possible.

The particular targets of city efforts against gun violence that seem important to us are these:

1. Reducing gun carrying by offenders on city streets
2. Reducing youth access to and use of all types of weapons[20]
3. Keeping guns out of places that have records of violent conflicts, such as rowdy bars, homes in which domestic violence often occurs, and other community hot spots

Exactly how to accomplish these particular objectives remains unclear, but it is not hard to list particular actions one could imagine police departments undertaking. Indeed, bringing gun crime down is a good exercise in problem solving to turn over to an innovative police agency.

Action at the Community and Household Level

Through the long run, effective gun control may be best achieved by action at the community and household level, rather than at the governmental level. Just as the battles against the costly social consequences of smoking and drinking (and to some degree, drug abuse) are now being advanced through volunteer community initiatives, so may the problem of gun violence be eased as the public demands that individuals become more responsible gun owners. For instance, in particularly risky circumstances, such as continuing domestic violence or if a member of the household is suicidal, neighbors, counselors, and social workers must be prepared to insist that any guns be removed from those premises.

The challenge of implementing effective gun control measures in the United States is daunting in the face of our considerable uncertainty about what works, especially when coupled with the profound national disagreement about which values concerning guns are most important. Still, with continuing attention to the evidence generated by the state and local innovations, and a vigorous public dialogue on the importance of both rights and responsibilities in this arena, therę is every hope of doing better. There is little doubt that one of the benefits of such success would a reduced rate of homicide in the United States.

■ *NOTES*

1. Kleck (1991, Appendix 2) offers another explanation, that gun ownership increased during the past couple of decades but that survey respondents have become increasingly reluctant to admit to gun ownership during this period. We favor our explanation because it is supported by the survey evidence on the number of guns per household as well as by the growth in household disposable income during this period.

2. These patterns are based on surveys and are subject to potential biases induced by the sensitivity of the topic and the difficulty of contacting a representative sample of young urban males.

3. Much has been made of the unintentional firearm deaths of children, but tragic as such cases are, they are quite rare. Between 1985 and 1990, the annual average number of deaths for children less than 10 years old was 94 (Fingerhut, 1993).

4. On the other hand, the demography of gun suicide looks much more like that of gun sports, with victims coming disproportionately from the ranks of older White men.

5. Pierce and Fox (1992) demonstrate that between 1985 and 1991, the homicide arrest rate for males more than doubled for those under age 21, while actually declining for those age 30 and older (see also Blumstein, 1995; Smith & Feiler, 1995).

6. It is, after all, a tautology.

7. Kleck, like Wright et al. (1983), claims that Zimring and others have not succeeded in demonstrating that guns are more lethal than knives but accept with confidence the claim that long guns are more lethal than handguns. See Cook (1991) for a discussion of this paradox.

8. The source is unpublished data provided by the Bureau of Justice Statistics. See Cook (1991) for details.

9. The authors of the case-control study of homicide discuss the possibility that their results are due in part to reverse causation, noting that in a limited number of cases, people may have acquired a gun in response to a specific threat, which eventually led to their murder. They also note that both gun ownership and homicide may be influenced by a third, unidentified factor (Kellermann et al., 1993). From those characteristics that were observed in this study, it is clear that the victims differed from the controls in ways that may have contributed to the likelihood that there was a gun in the house. In comparison with their controls, the cases or the people they lived with were more likely to have a criminal record, to use illicit drugs, and to have a drinking problem.

10. Kleck and Patterson (1993) assert that the intercity differences in the prevalence of gun ownership are influenced by crime rates. Although this may explain some small part of the variance, it could not reasonably be considered the dominant explanation. For one thing, the vast majority of gun owners in the United States are sportsmen, for whom self-defense is a secondary purpose at most.

11. A recent comparison of victim survey estimates found that the U.S. robbery rate was substantially higher than that of England, Germany, Hungary, Hong Kong, Scotland, and Switzerland. On the other hand, Canada's robbery rate was nearly twice as high as that of the United States (Block, 1993).

12. This is true not just for law-abiding citizens but is felt even more keenly by drug dealers and other criminals who are frequently threatened by the bad company they keep (Wright & Rossi, 1986).

13. William Van Alstyne (1994) argues that the Second Amendment has generated almost no useful body of law to date, substantially because of the Supreme Court's inertia on this subject. In his view, Second Amendment law is currently as undeveloped as First Amendment law was up until Holmes and Brandeis began taking it seriously in a series of opinions in the 1920s.

14. The McClure-Volkmer Amendment of 1986 eased the restriction on out-of-state purchases of rifles and shotguns. Such purchases are now legal as long as they comply with the regulations of both the buyer's state of residence and the state in which the sale occurs.

15. On June 27, 1997, the Supreme Court ruled that the federal requirement that local law enforcement agencies conduct background searches on the purchasers of handguns could not be enforced.

16. Although federal law does not prohibit gun possession by youths, a number of states have placed limits on when youths can carry guns in public.

17. A provision of the 1986 McClure-Volkmer Amendments to the Gun Control Act creates a federal criminal liability for individuals who transfer a gun to a person they know or have reasonable cause to believe falls into one of the seven high-risk categories specified in the act.

18. Surprisingly, it is a *federal* crime (under the Gun-Free School Zones Act of 1990) for an individual to carry a gun in a school zone.

19. Upgrading criminal history files will of course have value in a variety of other law enforcement tasks as well.

20. Boston has implemented a comprehensive strategy of this sort. The Boston Gun Project was designed to curb the city's epidemic of youth gun violence and has met with considerable success. See Kennedy, Piehl, and Braga (1996) for a description and analysis of the program.

■ *REFERENCES*

Black, D., & Nagin, D. (1998). Do "right-to-carry" laws deter violent crime? *Journal of Legal Studies, 26,* 209-220.

Blackman, P. H. (1997). A critique of the epidemiologic study of firearms and homicide. *Homicide Studies, 1,* 169-189.

Block, R. L. (1993). A cross-section comparison of the victims of crime: Victim surveys of twelve countries. *International Review of Criminology, 2,* 183-207.

Blumstein, A. (1995). Youth violence, guns, and the illicit-drug industry. *Journal of Criminal Law and Criminology, 86,* 10-36.

Bureau of Justice Statistics. (1997). *Criminal victimization in the United States, 1994* (NCJ-162126). Washington, DC: Government Printing Office.

Centers for Disease Control and Prevention. (1997). CDC WONDER [On-line]. Available: http://wonder.cdc.gov/WONDER

Clotfelter, C. T. (1993). The private life of public economics. *Southern Economic Journal, 59,* 579-596.

Conklin, J. E. (1972). *Robbery and the criminal justice system.* Philadelphia: J. B. Lippincott.

Cook, P. J. (1976). A strategic choice analysis of robbery. In W. Skogan (Ed.), *Sample surveys of the victims of crimes* (pp. 173-187). Cambridge, MA: Ballinger.

Cook, P. J. (1979). The effect of gun availability on robbery and robbery murder: A cross section study of fifty cities. In R. H. Haveman & B. B. Zellner (Eds.), *Policy studies review annual* (Vol. 3, pp. 743-781). Beverly Hills, CA: Sage.

Cook, P. J. (1980). Reducing injury and death rates in robbery. *Policy Analysis, 6,* 21-45.

Cook, P. J. (1985). The case of the missing victims: Gunshot woundings in the National Crime Survey. *Journal of Quantitative Criminology, 1,* 91-102.

Cook, P. J. (1986). The relationship between victim resistance and injury in noncommercial robbery. *Journal of Legal Studies, 15,* 405-416.

Cook, P. J. (1987). Robbery violence. *Journal of Criminal Law and Criminology, 78,* 357-376.

Cook, P. J. (1991). The technology of personal violence. In M. H. Tonry (Ed.), *Crime and justice: A review of research* (Vol. 14, pp. 1-71). Chicago: University of Chicago Press.

Cook, P. J. (1993). Notes on the availability and prevalence of firearms. *American Journal of Preventive Medicine, 9,* 33-38.

Cook, P. J., & Leitzel, J. A. (1996). Perversity, futility, jeopardy: An economic analysis of the attack on gun control. *Law and Contemporary Problems, 59,* 91-118.

Cook, P. J., & Ludwig, J. (1996). *Guns in America: Results of a comprehensive national survey on firearms ownership and use.* Washington, DC: Police Foundation.

Cook, P. J., Ludwig, J., & Hemenway, D. (1997). The gun debate's new mythical number: How many defensive gun uses per year? *Journal of Policy Analysis and Management, 16,* 463-469.

Cook, P. J., Molliconi, S., & Cole, T. B. (1995). Regulating gun markets. *Journal of Criminal Law and Criminology, 86,* 59-92.

Decker, S. H., Pennell, S., & Caldwell, A. (1997). *Illegal firearms: Access and use by arrestees* (NCJ-163496). Washington, DC: Bureau of Justice Statistics.

Deutsch, S. J. (1979). Lies, damn lies, and statistics: A rejoinder to the comment by Hay and McCleary. *Evaluation Quarterly, 3,* 315-328.

Federal Bureau of Investigation. (1971-1997). *Crime in the United States: Uniform crime reports.* Washington, DC: Government Printing Office.

Fingerhut, L. A. (1993). Firearm mortality among children, youth, and young adults 1-34 years of age, trends and current status: United States, 1985-90. *Advance data from vital and health statistics* (No. 231). Hyattsville, MD: National Center for Health Statistics.

Jones, E. D., III. (1981). The District of Columbia's Firearms Control Regulations Act of 1975: The toughest handgun control law in the United States—or is it? *Annals of the American Academy of Political and Social Sciences, 455,* 138-149.

Karlson, T. A., & Hargarten, S. W. (1997). *Reducing firearm injury and death: A public health sourcebook on guns.* New Brunswick, NJ: Rutgers University Press.

Kellermann, A. L., Rivara, F. P., Rushforth, N. B., Banton, J. G., Reay, D. T., Francisco, J. T., Locci, A. B., Prodzinski, J. P., Hackman, B. B., & Somes, G. (1993). Gun ownership as a risk factor for homicide in the home. *New England Journal of Medicine, 329,* 1084-1091.

Kellermann, A. L., Rivara, F. P., Somes, G., Reay, D. T., Francisco, J. T., Banton, J. G., Prodzinski, J. P., Fligner, C., & Hackman, B. B. (1992). Suicide in the home in relation to gun ownership. *New England Journal of Medicine, 327,* 467-472.

Kennedy, D. M. (1994). Can we keep guns away from kids? *The American Prospect, 18,* 74-80.

Kennedy, D. M., Piehl, A. M., & Braga, A. A. (1996). Youth violence in Boston: Gun markets, serious youth offenders, and a use-reduction strategy. *Law and Contemporary Problems, 59,* 147-196.

Killias, M. (1993). Gun ownership, suicide, and homicide: An international perspective. In A. Del Frate, U. Zvekic, & J. J. M. van Dijk (Eds.), *Understanding crime: Experiences of crime and crime control* (pp. 289-302). Rome: United States Interregional Crime and Justice Research Institute.

Kleck, G. (1984). Handgun-only control: A policy disaster in the making. In D. B. Kates, Jr. (Ed.), *Firearms and violence: Issues of public policy* (pp. 167-199). Cambridge, MA: Ballinger.

Kleck, G. (1988). Crime control through the private use of armed force. *Social Problems, 35,* 1-22.

Kleck, G. (1991). *Point blank: Guns and violence in America.* New York: Aldine de Gruyter.

Kleck, G., & Gertz, M. (1995). Armed resistance to crime: The prevalence and nature of self-defense with a gun. *Journal of Criminal Law and Criminology, 86,* 150-187.

Kleck, G., & McElrath, K. (1991). The effects of weaponry on human violence. *Social Forces, 69,* 669-692.

Kleck, G., & Patterson, E. B. (1993). The impact of gun control and gun ownership levels on violence rates. *Journal of Quantitative Criminology, 9,* 249-287.

Koper, C. S., & Reuter, P. (1996). Suppressing illegal gun markets: Lessons from drug enforcement. *Law and Contemporary Problems, 59,* 119-143.

Lott, J. R., Jr., & Mustard, D. B. (1997). Crime, deterrence and right-to-carry concealed handguns. *Journal of Legal Studies, 26,* 1-68.

McDowall, D., Loftin, C., & Wiersema, B. (1992a). A comparative study of the preventive effects of mandatory sentencing laws for gun crimes. *Journal of Criminal Law and Criminology, 83,* 378-394.

McDowall, D., Loftin, C., & Wiersema, B. (1992b). *The incidence of civilian defensive firearm use.* Unpublished manuscript, University of Maryland-College Park, Institute of Criminal Justice.

McDowall, D., Loftin, C., & Wiersema, B. (1995). Easing concealed firearms laws: Effects on homicide in three states. *Journal of Criminal Law and Criminology, 86,* 193-206.

Moore, M. H. (1980). Police and weapons offenses. *Annals of the American Academy of Political and Social Science, 452,* 22-32.

Moore, M. H. (1981). Keeping handguns from criminal offenders. *Annals of the American Academy of Political and Social Science, 455,* 92-109.

Moore, M. H. (1983). The bird in hand: A feasible strategy for gun control. *Journal of Policy Analysis and Management, 2,* 185-195.

Pierce, G. L., & Bowers, W. J. (1981). The Bartley-Fox Gun Law's short-term impact on crime in Boston. *Annals of the American Academy of Political and Social Science, 455,* 120-137.

Pierce, G. L., & Fox, J. A. (1992). *Recent trends in violent crime: A closer look.* Unpublished manuscript, Northeastern University, Boston.

Polsby, D. D. (1993, October). Equal protection. *Reason, 25,* 35-38.

Saltzman, L. E., Mercy, J. A., O'Carroll, P. W., Rosenberg, M. L., & Rhodes, P. H. (1992). Weapon involvement and injury outcomes in family and intimate assaults. *Journal of the American Medical Association, 267,* 3043-3047.

Sheley, J. F., & Wright, J. D. (1995). *In the line of fire: Youth, guns, and violence in urban America.* New York: Aldine de Gruyter.

Sherman, L., Shaw, J. W., & Rogan, D. P. (1995). *The Kansas City gun experiment.* Washington, DC: National Institute of Justice.

Skogan, W. (1978). *Weapon use in robbery: Patterns and policy implications.* Unpublished manuscript, Northwestern University, Evanston, IL.

Smith, M. D. (1996). Sources of firearm acquisition among a sample of inner-city youths: Research results and policy implications. *Journal of Criminal Justice, 24,* 361-367.

Smith, M. D., & Feiler, S. M. (1995). Absolute and relative involvement in homicide offending: Contemporary youth and the baby boom cohorts. *Violence and Victims, 10,* 327-333.

Snyder, J. R. (1993). A nation of cowards. *The Public Interest, 113,* 40-55.

Teret, S. P. (1986). Litigating for the public's health. *American Journal of Public Health, 76,* 1027-1029.

Teret, S. P., & Wintemute, G. (1993). Policies to prevent firearm injuries. *Health Affairs, 12*(4), 96-108.

U.S. Department of the Interior. (1991). *Survey of fishing, hunting, and wildlife-associated recreation.* Washington, DC: Government Printing Office.

Van Alstyne, W. (1994). *The Second Amendment and the personal right to arms.* Durham, NC: Duke University School of Law.

Violence Policy Center. (1992). *More gun dealers than gas stations.* Washington, DC: Author.

Violence Policy Center. (1997). *Who dies?* Washington, DC: Author.

Wolfgang, M. E. (1958). *Patterns in criminal homicide.* Philadelphia: University of Pennsylvania Press.

Wright, J. D. (1981). Public opinion and gun control: A comparison of results from two recent national surveys. *An-*

nals of the American Academy of Political and Social Science, 455, 24-39.

Wright, J. D., & Rossi, P. H. (1986). *Armed and considered dangerous: A survey of felons and their firearms.* Hawthorne, NY: Aldine.

Wright, J. D., Rossi, P. H., & Daly, K. (1983). *Under the gun: Weapons, crime, and violence in America.* Hawthorne, NY: Aldine.

Wright, J. D., Sheley, J. F., & Smith, M. D. (1992). Kids, guns, and killing fields. *Society, 30*(1), 84-89.

Zimring, F. E. (1968). Is gun control likely to reduce violent killings? *University of Chicago Law Review, 35,* 21-37.

Zimring, F. E. (1972). The medium is the message: Firearm caliber as a determinant of death from assault. *Journal of Legal Studies, 1,* 97-124.

Zimring, F. E., & Hawkins, G. (1997). *Crime is not the problem: Lethal violence in America.* New York: Oxford University Press.

CHAPTER 19

Combining Action and Analysis to Prevent Homicide

A Public Health Perspective

■ *James A. Mercy & W. Rodney Hammond*

There is overwhelming evidence that homicide and nonfatal assaultive violence are major contributors to premature death, injury, and disability in the United States and around the world. Although few in the fields of research, government, and criminal justice dispute the impact of violence on public health, many question whether public health can make significant contributions toward preventing and mitigating the health consequences of violence. Some skeptics argue that the primary causes of violence are deeply rooted cultural, social, and economic phenomena over which public health institutions have little or no control. Others argue that swift and certain punishment for violent behavior through criminal justice systems is the only effective and just response to the problem. Our aim in this chapter is to allay such skepticism by describing a public health approach to violence and discussing how public health can contribute to effective solutions. We will discuss briefly the global health impact of homicide and assaultive violence, the public health process for finding solutions, and a conceptual framework for organizing potential prevention strategies to address this problem.

Two caveats are important in framing this chapter. First, we feel it is necessary to consider homicide in the context of the larger problem of assaultive violence when discussing solutions. Some preventive approaches, such as improving the health care response to trauma, may reduce homicide without affecting the general level of assaultive violence, but most solutions cannot be targeted specifically at homicide. Consequently, we will discuss preventive approaches that go beyond those that specifically target prevention of homicide as the health outcome to include approaches that address specific types of violence (e.g., domestic violence), behavior (e.g., fighting), or environments (e.g., concentrated poverty) that could lead or contribute to homicide. Second, we assume that there is no one solution to the problem of homicide and assaultive violence. Rather, a combination of effective approaches that address different types of violence, behavior, and environments and that are appropriate for different target groups (e.g., children, adolescents, and women) is needed.

■ *THE PUBLIC HEALTH CONTRIBUTION*

A public health approach can contribute to finding solutions to the problem of homicide and assaultive violence in several key ways. First and most important, public health brings an emphasis and commitment to identifying policies and programs aimed at preventing violence. The predominant response to violence has been a reactive one; overwhelming attention and resources in our society and throughout the world have been given to the deterrence and incapacitation of violent offenders through criminal justice systems and the medical treatment of injuries resulting from violence. Little attention has been given, however, to the development and implementation of strategies aimed at preventing violent behavior and its associated injuries from occurring in the first place. From a public health perspective, we should shift the way societies deal with violence from a focus limited to reacting to the problem after it occurs to a focus that includes changing the social, behavioral, and environmental factors that lead to violence (Mercy, Rosenberg, Powell, Broome, & Roper, 1993).

Second, the development and implementation of effective policies and programs for preventing violence must be firmly grounded in science. Scientific research provides information essential to developing effective public policies, programs, and methods for testing their effectiveness. Although many scientific disciplines have advanced our understanding of violence, the scientific basis for developing effective prevention policies and programs remains rudimentary. Public health brings something that has been missing from this field: a multidisciplinary scientific approach that is directed explicitly toward identifying effective approaches to prevention.

Third, public health brings a tradition of integrative leadership by which we can organize a broad array of scientific disciplines, organizations, and communities to work together to solve the problem of violence. This approach is in direct contrast to traditional responses to violence that have been fragmented along disciplinary lines and narrowly focused in the criminal justice sector. By unifying the various scientific disciplines pertinent to violence prevention and by establishing links with education, labor, public housing, media, business, medicine, criminal justice, and other entities, public health can help to forge responses that are more efficient and complementary.

Fourth, public health also has an essential role in ensuring that necessary health services are provided to victims of violence to reduce the severity of physical or psychological injuries and to rehabilitate the physical, sensory, and mental capacities of injured persons (Committee for the Study of the Future of Public Health, 1988). Unless death occurs immediately, the outcome of an injury depends not only on its severity but also on the speed and appropriateness of treatment (Committee on Trauma Research, 1985). Public health helps in building the scientific foundation for the development of effective treatments and therapies for mitigating the consequences of injury.

Finally, public health brings a long-standing commitment to supporting and facilitating the central role of communities in solving health problems. Successful community-based health promotion efforts have improved dietary habits, reduced teenage pregnancy rates, and lowered prevalence of smoking among adolescents (Bruvold, 1993; Johnson et al., 1993; Vincent, Clearie, & Schluchter, 1987). Local communities and their governments are in direct contact with their citizens and thus are uniquely well placed to identify and solve the problems that affect people's health and the environment. The full participation of communities in violence prevention is critical to engendering a sense of ownership for this problem and its solutions. Public health seeks to empower people and their communities to see violence not as an inevitable consequence of modern life but as a problem that can be understood and changed.

An important point that flows from this discussion is that public health approaches to violence prevention are defined not by the sector or discipline that carries them out but by whether the prevention strategy or policy has the potential to reduce the physical or mental health consequences of violence. For example, police help reduce the public health burden of motor vehicle injuries by enforcing speeding and drunk-driving laws; they may also contribute to the public's health by virtue of their efforts to prevent violence through the enforcement of gun laws and curfews and by initiating other preventive activities through community policing. The criminal justice sector, therefore, may be viewed as an agent for public health. Similarly, media, business, labor, education, and other sectors may play critical roles in a public health vision of violence prevention. The public health perspective provides a new way of looking at violence, one that seeks to transcend existing bureaucratic and disciplinary boundaries that have impeded progress in finding and implementing effective solutions.

■ *GLOBAL HEALTH BURDEN OF VIOLENCE*

The starting point for public health involvement in violence is, of course, its impact on physical and emotional health. In considering the health impact of violence, it is useful to look at the problem globally. Although the United States has high rates of homicide and assaultive violence in comparison with other industrialized countries, the problem is even greater in many parts of the world. Estimates of the relative and absolute contribution of assaultive violence to the global health burden recently have become available through a comprehensive assessment of mortality and disability from disease and injuries in 1990; these estimates are projected to 2020 (Murray & Lopez, 1996b). The burden of assaultive violence is quantified by measures of two general types of health consequences: (a) premature mortality as measured by numbers, rates, and years of life lost from homicide and (b) combined burden of fatal and nonfatal health outcomes as indicated by a new measure called Disability Adjusted Life Years Lost (DALYs).

One limitation of these estimates is a slight inflation because of the combining of unintentional firearm-related injuries with homicide/assaultive violence. Our estimates of the global incidence of deaths from unintentional firearm-related injury, however, based on data from 40 nations around the world—between 6,000 and 7,000 fatalities from unintentional firearm-related injury annually throughout the world (E. Krug, M.D., Division of Violence Prevention, National Center for Injury Control and Prevention, Centers for Disease Control and Prevention, personal communication, February 15, 1997)—indicate these fatalities would have only a slight effect on estimates of the health burden of homicide and assaultive violence. Deaths from war are separated from estimates of homicide in these data.

The DALY is a new method of measuring disease burden; it is based on a quantification of years of life lost through death and years of life expected to be lived with disability. Disability is derived from the incidence, duration, and severity of the morbidity and complications associated with specific conditions (Murray, 1996). The method was developed by the World Health Organization and the World Bank to overcome the limitations of using mortality as the sole measure of health impact. Although the DALY measure is an advance in assessing the burden of disease, it has limited application. The information needed to calculate the DALY is often incomplete, particularly in many developing countries, and suitable indicators to measure such factors as the psychological consequences of violence have not yet been developed or made generally available. Nevertheless, it is useful as a crude indicator of the total health burden of assaultive violence across different regions of the world and relative to other health problems (for details on how DALYs are calculated, see Murray, 1996).

In 1990, an estimated 563,000 homicides occurred throughout the world (Murray & Lopez, 1996b, Annex Table 6i), representing about

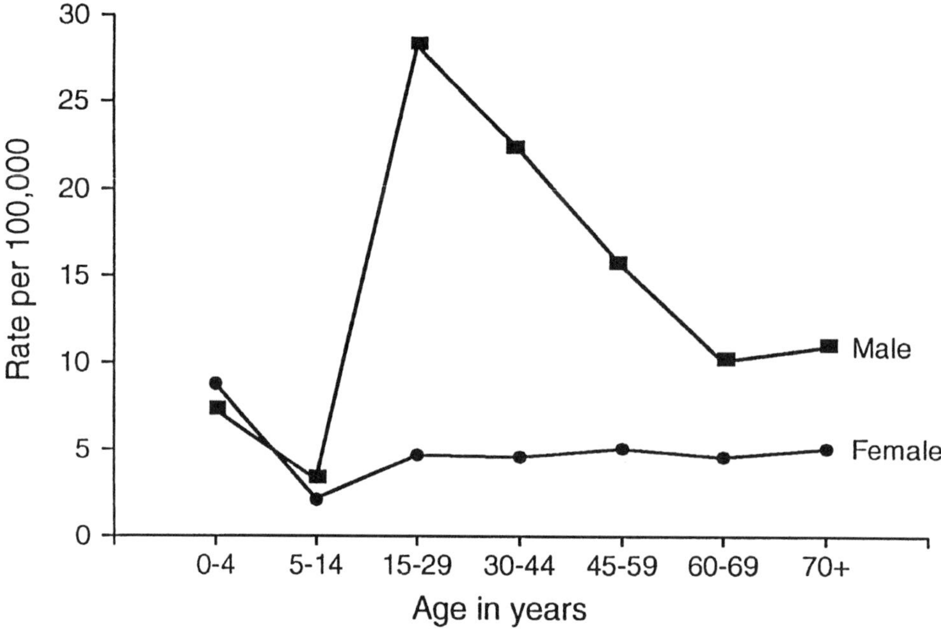

Figure 19.1. Homicide Rates by Age and Sex, World, 1990

SOURCE: Murray and Lopez (1996b, Annex Tables 6a-6i and 11).

NOTE: These rates may be slightly inflated because on average, about 1.2% of the fatalities included in these rate calculations are due to unintentional firearm-related injury deaths.

Table 19.1 Homicide Rates by Region and Sex: World, 1990

Region	Rate per 100,000		
	Total	*Male*	*Female*
Sub-Saharan Africa	40.2	69.8	11.2
Latin America	23.0	40.1	5.8
Former socialist economies	8.7	13.3	4.4
Middle Eastern Crescent	7.6	9.4	5.7
Other Asia and Pacific Islands	7.5	12.0	2.9
India	6.6	7.5	5.6
China	4.5	5.1	3.6
Established market economies	3.8	5.9	2.0
United States	10.0	16.2	4.2
World	10.7	16.5	4.7

SOURCE: Murray and Lopez (1996b, Annex Tables 6a-6i and 11).
NOTE: These rates may be slightly inflated because on average, about 1.2% of the fatalities in these rate calculations are due to unintentional firearm-related injuries.

1.1% of all the deaths occurring in that year. The global homicide rate was 10.7 per 100,000 persons; as can be seen in Figure 19.1, however, rates of homicide varied considerably by age and sex. Rates for males were 3.5 times those for females. Rates peaked in the 15- to 29-year-old age group for males and in the 0- to 4-year-old age group for females.

Patterns in the risk of homicide also were subject to substantial regional variation. As shown in Table 19.1, homicide rates were highest in those nations of Sub-Saharan Africa (40.2) and Latin America (23.0). They were lowest in the nations with established market economies (3.8) and in China (4.5). Although the United States was an outlier among the countries with established market economies (10.0 in 1990), U.S. homicide rates were substantially lower than those typical for nations in Sub-Saharan Africa and Latin America. The peak in global, age-specific homicide rates for females in the 0- to 4-year-old age category seems to be driven by high rates of female infanticide in China, India, and countries in the Middle Eastern Crescent. On the other hand, the global age-specific male homicide rate, which

Table 19.2 DALYs Attributable to Violence and Percentage of All Health-Related DALYs Attributable to Violence by Region and Sex, 1990

Region	*Total Violence DALYs* (1000s)*	*Percentage of All DALYs*	*Male Violence DALYs (1000s)*	*Percentage of All Male DALYs*	*Female Violence DALYs (1000s)*	*Percentage of All Female DALYs*
Latin America/Caribbean	3,172	3.2 2,751	5.1	421	0.9	
Sub-Saharan Africa	6,576	2.2 5,657	3.7	918	0.7	
Former socialist economies	847	1.4 652	1.8	195	0.7	
Established market economies	993	1.0 756	1.4	237	0.5	
Other Asia and Pacific Islands	1,534	0.9 1,197	1.3	337	0.4	
China	1,638	0.8 984	0.9	654	0.7	
Middle Eastern Crescent	1,201	0.8 772	1.0	429	0.6	
India	1,510	0.5 893	0.6	618	0.4	
World	17,472	1.3 13,662	1.9	3,810	0.6	

SOURCE: World Health Organization (1996).
NOTE: Numbers in this table have been rounded, leading to rounding errors that prevent summed totals for the regions from exactly matching the world totals.
*DALYs: Disability Adjusted Life Years Lost.

peaks among adolescents and young adults, is similar to that for the United States and represents a more consistent pattern worldwide. In China and countries of the Middle Eastern Crescent, however, male homicide rates peak among 0- to 4-year-olds, although the contrast with older age groups is not as great as it is for females in those regions.

For both developed and developing regions, homicide was not among the 10 leading causes of death or, when considered separately, among the leading causes of death for males or females (Murray & Lopez, 1996a). Homicide, however, was the 3rd leading cause of death for 15- to 44-year-old males in the world, accounting for 8.8% of all deaths among males in that age category. In contrast, homicide was the 10th leading cause of death in the United States in 1990, both as a whole and for males specifically. Similar to the global pattern, homicide was the 3rd leading cause of death among males aged 15 to 44 years in the United States; in contrast to the global pattern, homicide was the 4th leading cause of death among females aged 15 to 44 years in the United States. Homicide was the 10th leading cause of years of life lost in the world for males in both developed and developing regions.

On the basis of knowledge of epidemiologic transition and the assumption that the secular increases in the rate of violence will continue, it is estimated that in 2020, there will be more than 1 million homicides; the global homicide rate would increase from 10.7 in 1990 to 13.3 in 2020. Given this scenario, by 2020, homicide would become the 10th leading cause of death among *all* males in the world.

Another way in which to view the impact of violence is to view the distribution of DALYs on a worldwide basis. In 1990, assaultive violence was estimated to account for 1.3% of the total global health burden, or 17.5 million DALYs worldwide. It is estimated that males lost about 13.7 million DALYs to violence, compared with 3.8 million for females. As shown in Table 19.2, violence posed a relatively greater health burden in Latin America/Caribbean countries, in Sub-Saharan Africa, and in European countries with formerly socialist economies than in other regions of the world. This regional variation was similar for both males and females.

In 1990, violence ranked as the 19th leading cause of DALYs. Projections to the year 2020 suggest that 29.5 million DALYs will be lost to violence, thus increasing the contribution of violence to the burden of disability to 2.4%. If this scenario of the global burden of disability were to prevail, violence would move up to become the 12th leading cause of DALYs in the world.

These patterns in the relative burden of homicide and assaultive violence suggest that the risk of violence in many areas of the world far exceeds that in the United States, but so does the burden of other health problems. In part, assaultive violence has emerged as a significant public health problem in the United States because the burden of other health problems is much less, relative to that in other parts of the world. Nevertheless, despite the heavy health burden attributable to communicable and chronic diseases, violence remains a serious health problem in other parts of the world, particularly in countries in Sub-Saharan Africa and Latin America.

Statistics on the global and regional burden of violence obscure its disproportionate impact on specific subgroups throughout the world, most notably, youths, women, children, and the poor. Adolescent and young adult males are the primary victims and perpetrators of violence throughout the world. Violence against women, including rape, domestic violence, genital mutilation, homicide, and sexual abuse, is a major public health problem for women worldwide. The World Bank (1993) estimates that in established market economies, gender-based victimization is responsible for 1 of every 5 healthy days of life lost to women of reproductive age. The health burden imposed by rape and domestic violence in the industrial world is roughly equivalent to that in the developing world on a per capita basis; because the total disease burden is so much greater in developing nations, however, the proportion attributable to gender-based violence is smaller (Heise, 1994).

Children are particularly vulnerable to violence, and they become unwitting agents in the perpetuation and amplification of the problem. Child abuse and neglect are worldwide problems with dimensions and consequences that are only beginning to be understood. Moreover, violence has profound psychological implications for victims and witnesses that are not captured in these statistics. Victims of violence exhibit a variety of psychological symptoms that are similar to those of victims of other types of trauma such as motor vehicle crashes and natural disasters. Although a single incident can lead to emotional scars, continuing and repetitive violence such as that often associated with intimate partner violence and child abuse can have profound effects on psychological well-being (Follingstad, Brennen, Hause, Polek, & Rutledge, 1991).

Clearly, violence is a global health problem of major and increasing proportions. The magnitudes of the health consequences and the social and economic repercussions point directly to the need to develop effective strategies to prevent violence as well as strategies to mitigate the severity of its physical and emotional consequences.

■ *A PROCESS FOR FINDING EFFECTIVE SOLUTIONS*

Historically, public health has made a difference in the quality of life for all Americans through the application of its fundamental problem-solving capacity (Committee for the Study of the Future of Public Health, 1988). Public health actions such as water quality control, immunization programs, and food inspection have prevented many deaths and illnesses. These successes exemplify what is possible as a result of an organized effort based on technical knowledge. Similarly, success in solving the problem of homicide and assaultive violence must be firmly grounded in science. It is counterproductive to separate a discussion of solutions to violence from the scientific process through which we generate knowledge that, in turn, leads to policies and programs that are effective in reducing the toll of violence. Greater investment in science is particularly important because our understanding of the patterns, causes, and prevention of homicide and assaultive violence remains limited.

The public health approach described in Figure 19.2 provides a multidisciplinary, scientific approach that is explicitly directed toward identifying effective approaches to prevention (Mercy et al., 1993). The approach starts with defining the problem and progresses to identifying associated risk factors and causes, developing and evaluating interventions, and implementing intervention programs. Although the

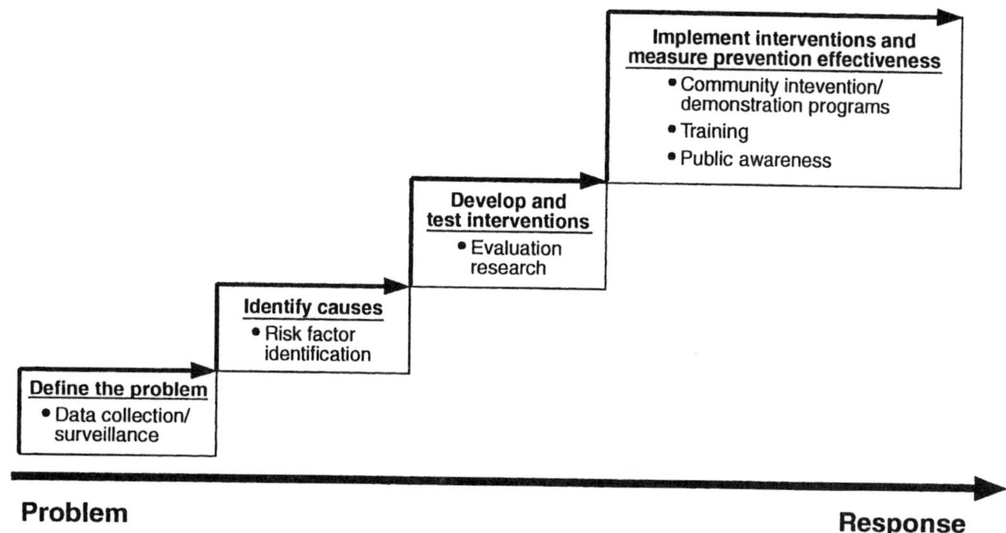

Figure 19.2. Public Health Model of a Scientific Approach to Prevention
SOURCE: Mercy et al. (1993).

figure suggests a linear progression from the first step to the last, the reality is that many of these steps are likely to occur simultaneously. In addition, information systems used to define the problem can also be useful in evaluating programs, and information gained in program evaluation and implementation can lead to new and promising interventions.

Defining the Problem

The first step, defining the problem, includes delineating incidents of homicide and related morbidity but goes beyond simply counting cases. This step includes obtaining such information as the demographic characteristics of the persons involved, the temporal and geographic characteristics of the incident, the victim-perpetrator relationship, and the severity and cost of the injury. The information collected should be useful for answering questions such as these: How often does homicide and assaultive violence occur? When and under what circumstances? What are the characteristics of the social environment in which the event took place? Were drugs or alcohol involved? What types of weapons were used? These and other variables can be important in defining discrete subsets of homicide for which various interventions may be appropriate. Because each community is unique, it is important to collect information that will give an accurate picture of homicide and assaultive violence and related problems in specific communities. Focus groups, incident reports, and surveys are all potential sources of information for problem definition.

Surveillance Systems

One method for better defining the problem and establishing data on trends is to create surveillance systems for the systematic and continuing collection, analysis, and interpretation of data on homicide and assaultive violence. This need is particularly acute at the state and local levels, where most prevention programs and policies are implemented. States and local communities need data to determine the extent and nature of the problem in their community, develop appropriate preventive responses, and evaluate progress toward reducing the problem.

Fortunately, useful surveillance systems do exist. For example, the final mortality data from the national Vital Statistics system and the Supplemental Homicide Reports from the Uniform Crime Reporting Program are available for examining patterns of homicide victimization and perpetration nationally and at the state and local levels (Annest, Conn, & James, 1996). These systems, however, have limited use for states and localities because the data are not timely or sufficiently detailed. National surveillance systems such as the National Crime Victimization Survey are available for examining nonfatal assaultive violence, but these data cannot be used to characterize state or local patterns. Consequently, greater investment is needed to build an infrastructure of state and local surveillance systems for homicide and assaultive violence that can provide a foundation for research, preventive action, and evaluation.

Identifying Causes

The second step in the public health approach involves identifying causes. Whereas the first step considers the questions of who, when, where, what, and how, the second step looks at why an incident occurred. This latter step also can be used to define populations at high risk and to suggest specific interventions. Risk and protective factors can be identified by a variety of scientific research methodologies including rate calculations, cohort studies, and case control studies. Recent reviews by the National Research Council have established useful agendas for guiding further scientific inquiry into the etiology of homicide and the various types of assaultive violence (Crowell & Burgess, 1996; Panel on Research on Child Abuse and Neglect, 1993; Reiss & Roth, 1993). Investment in this type of research is essential for helping to identify new avenues for prevention by providing a better picture of the biological, behavioral, and social mechanisms leading to violence.

Developing and Testing Interventions

The next step is based in large part on information obtained from the previous steps and involves developing and testing interventions. This step includes evaluating the efficacy of existing programs, policies, and other strategies. Methods for testing include prospective randomized controlled trials, comparison of intervention and comparison populations for occurrence of health outcomes, time-series analysis of trends in multiple areas, and observational studies such as case control studies.

Although little is known about the efficacy of most interventions to prevent violence, the severe and persistent impact of violence on many communities makes it necessary to initiate programs based on our best knowledge of what is likely to work. Two principles follow from this: (a) We must assess and improve our programs and interventions on a continuous basis, and (b) we must push hard to complete rigorous evaluations of existing interventions. There is a critical need to make sure that interventions are evaluated before they are adopted on a large scale.

Implementing Interventions and Measuring Prevention Effectiveness

The final stage is to implement interventions that have been proved (or are highly likely) to achieve the goal of violence reduction. It is important that data be collected to measure the program's effectiveness, particularly because an intervention that has been found to have an impact in a clinical trial or an academic study can perform differently at the community or state level. An essential component of this data gathering is to conduct a cost analysis of the programs. Balancing the costs of a program against the cases prevented by it can help policymakers determine optimal public health practice.

The implementation phase also includes developing guidelines and procedures for putting programs in place. How do we build viable coalitions across traditionally separate sectors such as criminal justice, education, and public health? How do we continuously assess and improve the programs that are put into place? How do we involve parents and youths in programs designed to prevent violence in their communities? How do we adopt interventions appropriate to particular community values, cultures, and standards and, at the same time, allow for and benefit from racial and culturally diverse participation from all parts of the community? Such questions must be answered to develop programs that work on a large scale.

Developing a Typology of Violence Prevention Strategies

There is increased recognition that violence is caused by a complex interaction among biological, psychological, and social factors. Ultimately, public policies to reduce the health burden of violence will need to be multifaceted to have measurable effects on the problem. A typology of violence prevention strategies can be useful when considering the range of prevention strategies that might make up an effective public policy. We propose such a typology based on two key dimensions: (a) a classification system based on the population groups toward which interventions are directed and (b) an ecological model of the multiple influences that play a role in explaining violence. To better understand the resulting typologies, these two dimensions are discussed in the following sections.

Classification of Violence Reduction Strategies

The traditional system for classifying disease prevention is based on three types of strategies: primary, secondary, and tertiary. *Primary prevention* strategies are designed to prevent new occurrences of disease or injury, *secondary strategies* seek to reduce the rate of established diseases or disorders in a population, and *tertiary strategies* focus on reducing the amount of disability associated with existing diseases or injuries (Commission on Chronic Illness, 1957). This typology, however, assumes an understanding of the mechanisms leading to the disease or injury that lies beyond the current state of scientific knowledge about many diseases and certainly violence (Mrazek & Haggerty, 1994).

Population Groups

Recognition of the complex interaction between risk and protective factors and many disease outcomes has given rise to an alternative typology organized around the population groups toward which interventions are directed (Gorden, 1983). The three categories of this typology are universal, selective, and indicated preventive measures. *Universal preventive measures* are directed at everyone in an eligible population (e.g., laws requiring seat belt use, the promotion of healthy diets and nonsmoking, and the maintenance of safe drinking water). *Selective preventive measures* are directed at those members of a population whose risk of injury, disease, or unhealthy behavior is above average. These subgroups may be distinguished by demographic factors or factors that characterize the environment in which they live. Examples of selective measures are restricted driving hours for teenagers and mammograms for women with a family history of breast cancer. *Indicated preventive measures* are directed at persons in a population who manifest a risk factor, condition, or abnormality that identifies them as at high risk for injury, the development of disease, or unhealthy behaviors. Examples of indicated preventive measures are dietary restrictions for persons with high cholesterol and revoking driver's licenses away from persons convicted of driving under the influence.

Ecological Model of Violence

Tolan and Guerra (1994) have proposed an ecological model for classifying adolescent violence prevention programs that can be applied to other forms of violence. Their model conceptualizes the multiple factors that can influence violence as different environmental systems affecting human behavior; these include individual factors, close interpersonal relationships, proximal social contexts, and societal macrosystems. Programs that target *individual factors* attempt to modify risk or protective factors associated with violence such as poor peer relation skills, low academic achievement, and inappropriate beliefs about the use of violence against others. Strategies addressing *close*

Table 19.3 Examples of Violence Prevention Strategies by Type of Preventive Measure and Systems Influencing Violence

Systems Influencing Violence	*Type of Preventive Measure*		
	Universal	*Selective*	*Indicated*
Individual factors	• Provide violence risk education for all students • Teach children to recognize and report sexual abuse • Provide enriched preschool education for all children	• Provide therapy for children who witness violence • Teach convenience store clerks techniques to avoid injury during robberies	• Treat sex offenders • Provide psychotherapy for violent offenders • Use former perpetrators to influence nonconforming peers through social marketing programs
Close interpersonal relationships	• Provide parenting education for all new parents • Teach adolescents how to form healthy relationships with the opposite sex	• Use peer mediation to resolve disputes in schools • Increase adult mentoring of high-risk youths • Visit homes of families at high risk of child abuse	• Improve parent management strategies and parent-child bonding in the families of violent children
Proximal social contexts	• Use metal detectors to keep weapons out of schools • Initiate after-school programs to extend adult supervision of youths	• Create safe havens for children in homes and businesses on high-risk routes to and from school • Establish violence prevention coalitions in high-risk neighborhoods	• Provide adequate shelter space for battered women • Disrupt illegal gun markets in communities • Train health care professionals in identification and referral of family violence victims
Social macrosystems	• Reduce violence in media • Reduce income inequality	• Deconcentrate lower-income housing • Establish meaningful job creation programs for inner-city youths	• Increase severity of penalties for violent crime • Reduce illegal interstate transfers of firearms by limiting purchases to one gun a month

interpersonal relationships might include attempts to influence factors such as poor emotional bonding between parents and children, intense peer pressure to engage in violence, and the absence of a strong relationship with a caring adult. *Proximal social context* interventions are designed to change factors such as the family setting in which a victim resides, elements of the physical environment that affect the likelihood of assault (e.g., outdoor lighting and presence of security guards), and the lack of opportunities to engage in prosocial activities in neighborhood institutions such as schools or churches. Strategies that take into account the *societal macrosystem* address risk or protective factors such as norms or values embedded in the culture that promote violence, economic conditions, and low levels of general deterrence for violent behavior.

A Typology of Violence Reduction Strategies

Examples of specific strategies that emerge from the integration of the two key dimensions just discussed are presented in Table 19.3. The ecological model is one axis of the typology (individual, close interpersonal relations, etc.). The interventions classified along this dimension attempt to influence violence through the ecological level identified (universal, etc.). So, as one example shown, at the universal level, parenting programs attempt to influence violence by affecting the way parents (a close interpersonal relation) interact with and raise their children.

These examples provided in this typology are not intended to be exhaustive, nor do they all represent strategies that have proved to be effective. Rather, they are listed to illustrate the breadth of potential solutions and to emphasize the need to address the problem simultaneously for various populations and through different systems of influence.

At least two limitations of this typology should be acknowledged. First, the typology does not differentiate between strategies directed at preventing violent *behavior* and those designed to prevent violent *victimization.* Although this important distinction is not immediately obvious, both are useful approaches to violence prevention and are intermixed among the array of strategies. Second, the typology does not differentiate among specific types of violence. For example, there is a consensus that distinguishes among at least three types of violence: (a) primary, expressive, or relationship violence; (b) secondary, predatory, or instrumental criminal violence; and (c) psychopathological violence that is associated with severe mental illness. One could imagine developing an array of prevention strategies for each of these types of violence or for types organized along other dimensions (e.g., relationship between victim and offender). Although not explicitly distinguished, specific strategies that address each of these types of violence could be drawn from some of the programs suggested in Table 19.3.

The majority of existing violence prevention resources are spent trying to modify individual factors thought to contribute to violent behavior. Much less scientific and programmatic attention is given to addressing social factors that may contribute to violence such as the macrosystem influences shown in our typology. Yet scientific research suggests that marked social and economic disparities contribute to the etiology of violence in fundamental ways (Reiss & Roth, 1993). Poverty and the lack of real employment opportunities can promote violence by generating a sense of frustration, low self-esteem, hopelessness about the future, and family instability. Racism and sexism exacerbate social and economic disparities and might contribute to violence by depriving certain segments of society of the opportunities to be successful in school and work. The poor in our society, who are disproportionately African American, Hispanic, and Native American, do not have equal access to criminal justice, health care, and educational systems; thus they have more difficulty overcoming impoverished conditions that contribute to violence. More attention should be given to research and policy development that will guide us on how to reduce violence through addressing larger social and economic issues.

■ *PROMISING VIOLENCE PREVENTION STRATEGIES*

The past 5 years have been marked by significant advances in our understanding of violence and promising leads in our efforts to prevent it. For example, although the general public and the media have spoken in broad terms about violence, researchers and intervention specialists have learned to put violence into more significant categories that improve understanding of the differing risks, contributing factors, and potentially effective interventions. We know that expressive (relationship-oriented) violence is especially prevalent in the United States and that some individuals and groups are disproportionately at risk; most homicides are of this type. Other useful distinctions between types of violence (e.g., intimate, acquaintance, and stranger violence) can be made. We have learned, however, that it is extremely important to delineate clearly what form of violence is of concern before significant recommendations can be made about prevention and intervention from a public health perspective.

In the area of youth violence, we are beginning to identify and document the characteristics of effective prevention strategies based on accumulated evidence from controlled field studies (Kazdin, 1994; Lipsey & Wilson, 1993; Tolan & Guerra, 1994). Among the strategies that appear most promising are those that try to change individual behavior by enhancing educational success or addressing the development of appropriate knowledge and skills necessary to avoid expressive violence. These programs have been applied in universal, selected, and indicated populations with some success. For instance, preschool programs that seek to reduce the likelihood of school failure have been found to alter risk factors for aggressive behavior and direct involvement in violent and antisocial behavior later in life (Kazdin, 1994). An example is the Perry Preschool Project, an educational program directed at the intellectual and social development of preschool-aged children. This program has been credited with reducing the cost of delinquency and crime (including violence) through adolescence by approximately $2,400 per child (Barnett & Escobar, 1990). Evidence is mounting regarding the effectiveness of school-based programs that focus on improving problem solving, anger management, and other behavioral skills in high-risk youths (Guerra, Tolan, & Hammond, 1994).

Other promising strategies include those that address close interpersonal relations through intervening with parents and their children early in life. For instance, some programs have attempted to assist in family life (especially childhood development) by providing education, counseling, and appropriate services through home visitation and other strategies. Long-term evaluations of some of these programs have found them to reduce risk factors for youth violence (e.g., child abuse) and later involvement in violent and delinquent behavior (Kazdin, 1994). In particular, a study using controlled random trials has found that regular visits by health practitioners to the homes of unmarried, poor teenage mothers have been shown to reduce the incidence of child abuse (Olds, Henderson, Chamberlin, & Tatelbaum, 1986). Also shown to be promising is parent management training that seeks to strengthen emotional bonds between parents and their children and to enhance the ability of parents to supervise their adolescent children (Kazdin, 1994; Tolan & Guerra, 1994).

Other strategies that focus not on individual behavior change but on environmental factors such as firearms have been found to reduce homicide. For additional discussion of some prevention strategies aimed at the use of firearms, see Chapter 18 by Philip Cook and Mark Moore.

We are learning that the effectiveness of prevention programs depends a great deal on the quality of the implementation process. Problems such as poor staff training, departures from intended procedures, and the lack of administrative support may contribute to program ineffectiveness (Kazdin, 1994).

In sum, the understanding of how to change individual behavior associated with violence is rapidly advancing. The cost-effectiveness of these approaches, however, is not well understood. Further research on strategies that seek to reduce violence by altering proximal social contexts or social macrosystems is sorely needed; facilitating change through these systems may hold the greatest promise for broad-scale reductions in homicide and assaultive violence. Thus, we have a great deal more to learn about how to prevent violence, but preliminary evaluation research clearly indicates that this can be accomplished.

■ *THE PUBLIC HEALTH MODEL: CHALLENGES AND PROSPECTS*

To reiterate, we have discussed a public health perspective on finding solutions to the problem of homicide. The public health approach does not provide ready-made solutions for this problem; rather, it provides a process through which analysis and action are combined to continually improve our ability to reduce the impact of homicide and assaultive violence. The primary contributions of this approach include a focus on prevention, using science to identify effective strategies, and integrating the efforts of a broad array of people and organizations in research and programmatic efforts to find solutions. From a public health perspective, the development and implementation of effective policies for preventing violence must be firmly grounded in science and attentive to unique community perceptions and conditions. The principles and methods underlying this approach are being successfully applied in communities across the country (see Powell & Hawkins, 1996, for examples).

The public health paradigm outlined in this chapter suggests a vision for developing effective solutions to the problems of homicide and assaultive violence. This paradigm helps us visualize where additional work is needed, as in the need for more functional surveillance mechanisms at the state and local levels. We must develop ways to obtain more information, beyond what is available from crime reports, about the context of violence-related injuries and homicides. We must be committed to expanding our systems for tracking violence-related injuries in addition to homicides. We also must develop and use indicators that will help us identify the likelihood of violence (both perpetration and victimization) in different settings.

Unfortunately, the lag between basic research, risk identification, and intervention efficacy studies has outstripped our ability to inform public policy and field practice in a timely manner. That we have no clear and systematic infrastructure to facilitate the transfer of appropriate violence prevention programs, services, and technology into the community is a problem far greater than the limitations in our knowledge about violence prevention. Cost-benefit analyses of various configurations of services by setting, types of service personnel, and levels of training are sorely lacking; consequently, a vastly increased research and development investment is sorely needed in these areas. In addition, the potential roles of the private sector and combined public-private efforts need to be more seriously addressed.

There is a pressing need for more information about the effects of structural conditions in communities that contribute to violence. To name a few, these include effects of poverty, unemployment, neighborhood socioeconomic isolation, drug trafficking, the easy availability of guns, and neighborhood safety resources. Finally, we need to better understand what conditions in communities, homes, schools, and families tend to reinforce nonviolent patterns of behavior and other forms of healthy development within various at-risk groups. Much can be learned from the experiences of successful and well-adjusted youths and families who endure adverse circumstances. Just as there are natural forms of resistance to infectious disease within populations, there may be natural forms of resistance to the development of unhealthy behavior within communities and families.

Citizens of the United States have a right to expect a safe environment and, most certainly, a society that is not distinguished by excessive levels of victimization through violence, including homicide. There is every reason to believe that well-conceptualized contributions from public health, science, and technology can help achieve that goal.

In summary, the causes of and solutions to violence in the United States are complex. Reducing violence-related death and injury rates in the United States will be a long-term endeavor. On the other hand, promising opportunities for prevention already exist. If we effectively use our knowledge to strategically allocate our resources among health care, education, and research programs, there is considerable reason to believe that we can reduce significantly the prevalence of homicide and assaultive violence in this society.

■ *REFERENCES*

Annest, J. L., Conn, J. M., & James, S. P. (1996). *Inventory of federal data systems in the United States for injury surveillance, research, and prevention activities.* Atlanta, GA: Centers for Disease Control and Prevention, National Center for Injury Control and Prevention.

Barnett, W. S., & Escobar, C. M. (1990). Economic costs and benefits of early intervention. In S. J. Meisels & J. P. Shonkoff (Eds.), *Handbook of early childhood intervention* (pp. 560-582). New York: Cambridge University Press.

Bruvold, W. H. (1993). A meta-analysis of adolescent smoking prevention programs. *American Journal of Public Health, 83,* 872-880.

Commission on Chronic Illness. (1957). *Chronic illness in the United States* (Vol. 1). Cambridge, MA: Harvard University Press.

Committee for the Study of the Future of Public Health, Division of Health Care Services, Institute of Medicine. (1988). *The future of public health.* Washington, DC: National Academy Press.

Committee on Trauma Research, Commission on Life Sciences, National Research Council, and the Institute of Medicine. (1985). *Injury in America: A continuing public health problem.* Washington, DC: National Academy Press.

Crowell, N. A., & Burgess, A. W. (Eds.). (1996). *Understanding violence against women* (Panel on Research on Violence Against Women, Commission on Behavioral Social Sciences and Education, National Research Council). Washington, DC: National Academy Press.

Follingstad, D. R., Brennen, A. F., Hause, D. S., Polek, D. S., & Rutledge, L. L. (1991). Factors moderating physical and psychological symptoms of battered women. *Journal of Family Violence, 6,* 81-95.

Gorden, R. (1983). An operational classification of disease prevention. *Public Health Reports, 98,* 107-109.

Guerra, N., Tolan, P. H., & Hammond, W. R. (1994). Prevention and treatment of adolescent violence. In L. D. Eron, J. Gentry, & P. Schlegel (Eds.), *Reason to hope: A psychosocial perspective on violence and youth* (pp. 383-403). Washington, DC: American Psychological Association.

Heise, L. (1994). *Violence against women: The hidden health burden* (World Bank Discussion Paper No. 255). Washington, DC: World Bank.

Johnson, C. L., Rifkind, B. M., Sempos, C. T., Carroll, M. D., Bachorik, P. S., Briefel, R. R., Gorden, D. J., Burt, V. L., Brown, C. D., Lippel, K., & Cleeman, J. I. (1993). Declining serum total cholesterol levels among U.S. adults: The National Health and Nutrition Examination Survey. *Journal of the American Medical Association, 269,* 3002-3008.

Kazdin, A. E. (1994). Interventions for aggressive and antisocial children. In L. D. Eron, J. Gentry, & P. Schlegel (Eds.), *Reason to hope: A psychosocial perspective on violence and youth* (pp. 341-382). Washington, DC: American Psychological Association.

Lipsey, M., & Wilson, D. (1993). The efficacy of psychological, education, and behavioral treatment: Confirmation from meta-analysis. *American Psychologist, 48,* 1181-1209.

Mercy, J. A., Rosenberg, M. L., Powell, K. E., Broome, C. V., & Roper, W. L. (1993). Public health policy for preventing violence. *Health Affairs, 12*(4), 7-29.

Mrazek, P., & Haggerty, R. J. (Eds.). (1994). *Reducing risks for mental disorders: Frontiers for preventive intervention research* (Institute of Medicine, Division of Biobehavioral Sciences and Mental Disorders, Committee on the Prevention of Mental Disorders). Washington, DC: National Academy Press.

Murray, C. (1996). Rethinking DALYs. In C. Murray & A. D. Lopez (Eds.), *The global burden of disease: A comprehensive assessment of mortality and disability from disease, injuries, and risk factors in 1990 and projected to 2020* (pp. 1-98). Geneva, Switzerland: World Health Organization.

Murray, C., & Lopez, A. D. (1996a). Estimating causes of death: New methods and global and regional applications for 1990. In C. Murray & A. D. Lopez (Eds.), *The global burden of disease: A comprehensive assessment of mortality and disability from disease, injuries, and risk factors in 1990 and projected to 2020* (pp. 118-200). Geneva, Switzerland: World Health Organization.

Murray, C., & Lopez, A. D. (Eds.). (1996b). *The global burden of disease: A comprehensive assessment of mortality and disability from disease, injuries, and risk factors in 1990 and projected to 2020.* Geneva, Switzerland: World Health Organization.

Olds, D. L., Henderson, C. R., Chamberlin, R., & Tatelbaum, R. (1986). Preventing child abuse and neglect: A randomized trial of nurse home visitation. *Pediatrics, 78,* 65-78.

Panel on Research on Child Abuse and Neglect, Commission on Behavioral and Social Sciences and Education, National Research Council. (1993). *Understanding child abuse and neglect.* Washington, DC: National Academy Press.

Powell, K. E., & Hawkins, D. F. (Eds.). (1996). Youth violence prevention: Descriptions and baseline data from 13 evaluation projects [Suppl.]. *American Journal of Preventive Medicine, 12*(5).

Reiss, A. J., Jr., & Roth, J. A. (Eds.). (1993). *Understanding and preventing violence: Vol. 3. Social influences.* Washington, DC: National Academy Press.

Tolan, P., & Guerra, N. (1994). *What works in reducing adolescent violence: An empirical review of the field.* Unpublished manuscript, University of Colorado, Institute for Behavioral Sciences, Center for the Study and Prevention of Violence, Boulder.

Vincent, M. L., Clearie, A. R., & Schluchter, M. D. (1987). Reducing adolescent pregnancy through school and community-based education. *Journal of the American Medical Association, 257,* 3382-3386.

World Bank. (1993). *World development report 1993: Investing in health.* New York: Oxford University Press.

World Health Organization. (1996). *Report of the ad hoc committee on health research relating to future intervention options: Investing in health research and development* (Document TDR/Gen/06.1). Geneva, Switzerland: Author.

Comprehensive Reference List

Abadinsky, H. (1994). *Organized crime* (4th ed.). Chicago: Nelson-Hall.

Abel, E. L. (1987). Drugs and homicide in Erie County, New York. *International Journal of the Addictions, 22,* 195-200.

Abramson, L. Y., Metalsky, G. I., & Alloy, L. B. (1988). The hopelessness theory of depression: Does the research test the theory? In L. Y. Abramson (Ed.), *Social cognition and clinical psychology* (pp. 33-65). New York: Guilford.

Adams, K. A. (1974). The child who murders: A review of theory and research. *Criminal Justice and Behavior, 1,* 51-61.

Adelson, L. (1972). The battering child. *Journal of the American Medical Association, 222,* 159-161.

Agnew, R. (1992). Foundations for a general strain theory of crime and delinquency. *Criminology, 30,* 47-87.

Akiyama, Y., & Rosenthal, H. M. (1990). The future of the Uniform Crime Reporting Program: Its scope and promise. In D. L. MacKenzie, P. J. Baunach, & R. R. Roberg (Eds.), *Measuring crime: Large-scale, long-range efforts* (pp. 49-74). Albany: State University of New York Press.

Alba, R. D., Logan, J. R., & Bellair, P. (1994). Living with crime: The implications of racial/ethnic differences in suburban location. *Social Forces, 73,* 395-434.

Alexander, R. D. (1979). *Darwinism and human affairs.* Seattle: University of Washington Press.

Alexander, R. D. (1987). *The biology of moral systems.* Hawthorne, NY: Aldine.

Alloy, L. B., Abramson, L. Y., Metalsky, G. I., & Hartlage, S. (1988). The hopelessness theory of depression: Attributional aspects. *British Journal of Clinical Psychology, 27,* 5-21.

American Psychiatric Association. (1994). *Diagnostic and statistical manual of mental disorders* (4th ed.). Washington, DC: American Psychiatric Association.

Ancel, M. (1952). Observations on the international comparison of criminal statistics. *International Journal of Criminal Policy, 1,* 41-48.

Andenaes, J. (1974). *Punishment and deterrence.* Ann Arbor: University of Michigan Press.

Anderson, E. (1990). *Streetwise: Race, class, and change in an urban community.* Chicago: University of Chicago Press.

Anderson, E. (1994, May). The code of the streets. *Atlantic Monthly, 273,* 81-94.

Annest, J. L., Conn, J. M., & James, S. P. (1996). *Inventory of federal data systems in the United States for injury surveillance, research, and prevention activities.* Atlanta, GA: Centers for Disease Control and Prevention, National Center for Injury Control and Prevention.

Aponte, R., & Siles, M. (1996). Latinos to emerge as largest U.S. minority in the coming decade. *NEXO: Newsletter of the Julian Samora Research Institute, 4,* 1-8.

EDITORS' NOTE: The following list is not keyed to individual chapters but contains all references cited in the chapters of this volume.

Archer, D., & Gartner, R. (1984). *Violence and crime in cross-national perspective.* New Haven, CT: Yale University Press.

Archer, J. (1988). *The behaviourial biology of aggression.* New York: Cambridge University Press.

Athens, L. (1989). *The creation of dangerous violent criminals.* New York: Routledge & Kegan Paul.

Avakame, E. F. (1997). Urban homicide: A multilevel analysis across Chicago's census tracts. *Homicide Studies, 1,* 338-358.

Avison, W. R., & Loring, P. L. (1986). Population diversity and cross-national homicide: The effects of inequality and heterogeneity. *Criminology, 24,* 733-749.

Bachman, R. (1991a). An analysis of American Indian homicide: A test of social disorganization and economic deprivation at the reservation county level. *Journal of Research in Crime and Delinquency, 28,* 456-471.

Bachman, R. (1991b). The social causes of American Indian homicide as revealed by the life experiences of thirty offenders. *American Indian Quarterly, 15,* 468-492.

Bachman, R. (1992). *Death and violence on the reservation: Homicide, family violence and suicide in American Indian populations.* New York: Auburn House.

Bailey, G. W., & Unnithan, N. P. (1994). Gang homicides in California: A discriminant analysis. *Journal of Criminal Justice, 22,* 267-275.

Bailey, W. C. (1975). Murder and capital punishment: Some further evidence. *American Journal of Orthopsychiatry, 45,* 669-688.

Bailey, W. C. (1976). Certainty of arrest and crime rates for major felonies. *Journal of Research in Crime and Delinquency, 13,* 145-154.

Bailey, W. C. (1977). Imprisonment vs. the death penalty as a deterrent to murder. *Law and Human Behavior, 1,* 239-260.

Bailey, W. C. (1978). Deterrence and the death penalty for murder in Utah: A time-series analysis. *Journal of Contemporary Law, 5,* 1-20.

Bailey, W. C. (1979a). An analysis of the deterrence effect of the death penalty in North Carolina. *North Carolina Central Law Journal, 10,* 29-51.

Bailey, W. C. (1979b). Deterrence and the death penalty for murder in Oregon. *Willamette Law Review, 16,* 67-85.

Bailey, W. C. (1979c). The deterrent effect of the death penalty for murder in California. *Southern California Law Review, 52,* 743-764.

Bailey, W. C. (1979d). The deterrent effect of the death penalty for murder in Ohio. *Cleveland State Law Review, 28,* 51-81.

Bailey, W. C. (1980a). Deterrence and the celerity of the death penalty: A neglected question in deterrence research. *Social Forces, 58,* 1308-1333.

Bailey, W. C. (1980b). A multivariate cross-sectional analysis of the deterrent effect of the death penalty. *Sociology and Social Research, 64,* 183-207.

Bailey, W. C. (1982). Capital punishment and lethal assaults against police. *Criminology, 19,* 608-625.

Bailey, W. C. (1983). The deterrent effect of capital punishment during the 1950's. *Suicide, 13,* 95-107.

Bailey, W. C. (1984a). Disaggregation in deterrence and death penalty research: The case of murder in Chicago. *Journal of Criminal Law and Criminology, 74,* 827-859.

Bailey, W. C. (1984b). Murder and capital punishment in the nation's capitol. *Justice Quarterly, 1,* 211-233.

Bailey, W. C. (1984c). Poverty, inequality, and city homicide rates: Some not so unexpected findings. *Criminology, 22,* 531-550.

Bailey, W. C. (1990). Murder and capital punishment: An analysis of television execution publicity. *American Sociological Review, 55,* 628-633.

Bailey, W. C., & Peterson, R. D. (1987). Police killings and capital punishment: The post-Furman period. *Criminology, 25,* 1-25.

Bailey, W. C., & Peterson, R. D. (1989). Murder and capital punishment: A monthly time-series analysis of execution publicity. *American Sociological Review, 54,* 722-743.

Bailey, W. C., & Peterson, R. D. (1994). Murder, capital punishment, and deterrence: A review of the evidence and an examination of police killings. *Journal of Social Issues, 50,* 53-74.

Bailey, W. C., & Peterson, R. D. (1995). Gender inequality and violence against women. In J. Hagan & R. D. Peterson (Eds.), *Crime and inequality* (pp. 174-205). Stanford, CA: Stanford University Press.

Baker, R. K., & Ball, S. J. (1969). *Mass media and violence: Report to the National Commission on Causes and Prevention of Violence.* Washington, DC: Government Printing Office.

Baker, S. G. (1996). Demographic trends in the Chicana/o population: Policy implications for the twenty-first century. In D. R. Maciel & I. D. Ortiz (Eds.), *Chicanas/Chicanos at the crossroads* (pp. 5-24). Tucson: University of Arizona Press.

Baldus, D., & Cole, J. (1975). A comparison of the work of Thorsten Sellin and Isaac Ehrlich on the deterrent effect of capital punishment. *Yale Law Journal, 18,* 170-186.

Balkwell, J. W. (1990). Ethnic inequality and the rate of homicide. *Social Forces, 69,* 53-70.

Ball, R. A., & Curry, G. D. (1995). The logic of definition in criminology: Purposes and methods for defining "gangs." *Criminology, 33,* 225-245.

Ball-Rokeach, S. J. (1973). Values and violence: A test of the subculture of violence thesis. *American Sociological Review, 38,* 736-749.

Bankston, W. B., & Thompson, C. Y. (1989). Carrying firearms for protection: A causal model. *Sociological Inquiry, 59,* 75-87.

Barkow, J., Cosmides, L., & Tooby, J. (Eds.). (1992). *The adapted mind.* New York: Oxford University Press.

Barnard, G. W., Vera, M., & Newman, G. (1982). "Till death do us part?" A study of spouse murder. *Bulletin of the American Academy of Psychiatry and Law, 10,* 271-280.

Barnett, A. (1981). The deterrent effect of capital punishment: A test of some recent studies. *Operations Research, 29,* 346-370.

Barnett, W. S., & Escobar, C. M. (1990). Economic costs and benefits of early intervention. In S. J. Meisels & J. P. Shonkoff (Eds.), *Handbook of early childhood interven-*

tion (pp. 560-582). New York: Cambridge University Press.

Baron, L., & Straus, M. A. (1989). *Four theories of rape in American society: A state-level analysis.* New Haven, CT: Yale University Press.

Barongan, C., & Hall, G. C. N. (1995). The influence of misogynous rap music on sexual aggression against women. *Psychology of Women Quarterly, 19,* 195-207.

Barr, K. M., Farrell, M. P., Barnes, G. M., & Welte, J. W. (1993). Race, class, and gender differences in substance abuse: Evidence of middle-class polarization among Black males. *Social Problems, 40,* 314-327.

Battin, S. R., Hill, K. G., Abbott, R. D., Catalano, R. F., & Hawkins, J. D. (1998). The contribution of gang membership to delinquency beyond delinquent friends. *Criminology, 36,* 93-115.

Bean, F., & Tienda, M. (1987). *The Hispanic population of the United States.* New York: Russell Sage.

Beasley, R. W., & Antunes, G. (1974). The etiology of urban crime: An ecological analysis. *Criminology, 22,* 531-550.

Beccaria, C. (1963). *On crimes and punishment* (H. Paolucci, Trans.). Indianapolis, IN: Bobbs-Merrill. (Original work published 1764)

Bedau, H. A. (1967). *The death penalty in America* (Rev. ed.). New York: Doubleday.

Belsley, D. A., Kuh, E., & Welsch, R. E. (1980). *Regression diagnostics: Identifying influential data and sources of collinearity.* New York: John Wiley.

Bender, L. (1959). Children and adolescents who have killed. *American Journal of Psychiatry, 116,* 510-513.

Bender, L., & Curran, F. J. (1940). Children and adolescents who kill. *Criminal Psychopathology, 1,* 297-321.

Benedek, E. P., & Cornell, D. G. (1989). Clinical presentations of homicidal adolescents. In E. P. Benedek & D. G. Cornell (Eds.), *Juvenile homicide* (pp. 37-57). Washington, DC: American Psychiatric Press.

Bennett, R. R. (1991a). Development and crime: A cross-national time series analysis of competing models. *Sociological Quarterly, 32,* 343-363.

Bennett, R. R. (1991b). Routine activities: A cross-national assessment of a criminological perspective. *Social Forces, 70,* 147-163.

Bennett, R. R., & Lynch, J. P. (1990). Does a difference make a difference? Comparing cross-national crime indicators. *Criminology, 28,* 153-181.

Bensing, R. C., & Schroeder, O., Jr. (1970). *Homicide in an urban community.* Springfield, IL: Charles C Thomas.

Bentham, J. (1962). The rationale of punishment. In J. Browning (Ed.), *Works of Jeremy Bentham* (pp. 388-524). New York: Russell & Russell.

Bernard, T. J. (1981). The distinction between conflict and radical criminology. *Journal of Criminal Law and Criminology, 71,* 363-379.

Bernard, T. J. (1990). Angry aggression among the truly disadvantaged. *Criminology, 28,* 73-96.

Berns, W. (1979). *For capital punishment.* New York: Basic Books.

Berns, W. (1980). Defending the death penalty. *Crime & Delinquency, 26,* 503-511.

Bernstein, J. I. (1978). Premeditated murder by an eight year old boy. *International Journal of Offender Therapy & Comparative Criminology, 22,* 47-56.

Betzig, L. L. (1986). *Despotism and differential reproduction: A Darwinian view of history.* Hawthorne, NY: Aldine de Gruyter.

Beyleveld, D. (1982). Ehrlich's analysis of deterrence. *British Journal of Criminology, 22,* 101-123.

Black, D., & Nagin, D. (1998). Do "right-to-carry" laws deter violent crime? *Journal of Legal Studies, 27,* 209-220.

Blackman, P. H. (1997). A critique of the epidemiologic study of firearms and homicide. *Homicide Studies, 1,* 169-189.

Blau, J. R., & Blau, P. M. (1982). The cost of inequality: Metropolitan structure and violent crime. *American Sociological Review, 14,* 114-129.

Blau, P. M., & Golden, R. M. (1986). Metropolitan structure and criminal violence. *Sociological Quarterly, 27,* 15-26.

Blau, P. M., & Schwartz, J. E. (1984). *Crosscutting social circles.* New York: Academic Press.

Block, C. R. (1985). Race/ethnicity and patterns of Chicago homicide, 1965-1981. *Crime & Delinquency, 31,* 104-116.

Block, C. R. (1986). *Homicide in Chicago.* Chicago: Loyola University, Center for Urban Policy.

Block, C. R. (1988). Lethal violence in the Chicago Latino community, 1965 to 1981. In J. Kraus, S. Sorenson, & P. Juarez (Eds.), *Proceedings of research conference on violence and homicide in Hispanic communities, September 14-15, 1987* (pp. 31-66). Los Angeles: University of California.

Block, C. R. (1993). Lethal violence in the Chicago Latino community. In A. V. Wilson (Ed.), *Homicide: The victim/offender connection* (pp. 267-342). Cincinnati, OH: Anderson.

Block, C. R., & Block, R. L. (1980). *Patterns of change in Chicago homicide: The twenties, the sixties, and the seventies.* Chicago: Statistical Analysis Center, Illinois Law Enforcement Commission.

Block, C. R., & Block, R. L. (1991). Beginning with Wolfgang: An agenda for homicide research. *Journal of Crime and Justice, 14,* 31-70.

Block, C. R., & Block, R. L. (1992). Overview of the Chicago homicide project. In C. R. Block & R. L. Block (Eds.), *Questions and answers in lethal and non-lethal violence: Proceedings of the first annual workshop of the homicide research working group* (pp. 97-122). Washington, DC: National Institute of Justice.

Block, C. R., & Christakos, A. (1995a). Intimate partner homicide in Chicago over 29 years. *Crime and Delinquency, 41,* 496-526.

Block, C. R., & Christakos, A. (1995b). *Major trends in Chicago homicide: 1965-1994* (Research Bulletin). Chicago: Illinois Criminal Justice Information Authority.

Block, C. R., Christakos, A., Jacob, A. P., & Przybylski, R. (1996). *Street gangs and crime: Patterns and trends in Chicago* (Research bulletin). Chicago: Illinois Criminal Justice Information Authority.

Block, R. L. (1974, November). *Homicide in Chicago: A ten-year study, 1965-1974.* Paper presented at the annual meeting of the American Society of Criminology, Chicago.

Block, R. L. (1977). *Violent crime.* Lexington, MA: Lexington Books.

Block, R. L. (1993). A cross-section comparison of the victims of crime: Victim surveys of twelve countries. *International Review of Criminology, 2,* 183-207.

Block, R. L., & Block, C. R. (1992). Homicide syndromes and vulnerability: Violence in Chicago community areas over 25 years. *Studies on Crime and Crime Prevention, 1,* 61-87.

Block, R. L., & Block, C. R. (1993). *Street gang crime in Chicago* (Research in Brief: NCJ-144782). Washington, DC: National Institute of Justice.

Block, R. L., & Zimring, F. E. (1973). Homicide in Chicago, 1965-1970. *Journal of Research in Crime and Delinquency, 10,* 1-7.

Blount, W. R., Danner, T. A., Vega, M., & Silverman, I. J. (1991). The influence of substance use among adult female inmates. *Journal of Drug Issues, 21,* 449-467.

Blount, W. R., Silverman, I. J., Sellers, C. S., & Seese, R. A. (1994). Alcohol and drug use among abused women who kill, abused women who don't, and their abusers. *Journal of Drug Issues, 24,* 165-177.

Blumstein, A. (1995). Youth violence, guns, and the illicit-drug industry. *Journal of Criminal Law and Criminology, 86,* 10-36.

Blumstein, A., & Rosenfeld, R. L. (1998, March). *Explaining recent trends in U.S. homicide rates.* Paper presented at conference on decreasing crime rates, Northwestern University Law School, Evanston, IL.

Bock, G., & Cardew, G. (Eds.). (1997). *Characterizing human psychological adaptations.* Chichester, UK: Wiley.

Bonger, W. (1943). *Race and crime.* New York: Columbia University Press.

Bortner, M. A. (1988). *Delinquency and justice.* New York: McGraw-Hill.

Boudouris, J. (1970). *Trends in homicide: Detroit, 1926-1968.* Unpublished doctoral dissertation, Wayne State University, Detroit, MI.

Boudouris, J. (1974). A classification of homicides. *Criminology, 11,* 525-540.

Bower, R. T. (1985). *The changing television audience in America.* New York: Columbia University Press.

Bowers, W. J. (1984). *Legal homicide: Death as punishment in America.* Boston: Northeastern University Press.

Bowers, W. J. (1988). The effect of executions is brutalization, not deterrence. In K. C. Haas & J. A. Inciardi (Eds.), *Capital punishment: Legal and social science approaches* (pp. 49-89). Newbury Park, CA: Sage.

Bowers, W. J., & Pierce, G. (1975). The illusion of deterrence in Isaac Ehrlich's research on capital punishment. *Yale Law Journal, 85,* 187-208.

Bowers, W. J., & Pierce, G. (1980). Deterrence or brutalization: What is the effect of executions? *Crime & Delinquency, 26,* 453-484.

Braithwaite, J. (1979). *Inequality, crime, and public policy.* London: Routledge & Kegan Paul.

Braithwaite, J., & Braithwaite, V. (1980). The effect of income inequality and social democracy on homicide. *British Journal of Criminology, 20,* 45-57.

Breaking the cycles of violence: Hearing of the Subcommittee on Juvenile Justice of the United States Senate Committee on Juvenile Crime, 103d Cong., 2d Sess. (1994, November 29) (testimony of C. C. Bell and E. Jenkins).

Brearley, H. C. (1932). *Homicide in the United States.* Chapel Hill: University of North Carolina Press.

Brearley, H. C. (1969). *Homicide in the United States.* Montclair, NJ: Patterson Smith. (Original work published 1932)

Brewer, V. E., & Smith, M. D. (1995). Gender inequality and rates of female homicide victimization across U.S. cities. *Journal of Research in Crime and Delinquency, 32,* 175-190.

Brier, S., & Feinberg, S. (1980). Recent econometric modeling of crime and punishment: Support for the deterrence hypothesis? *Evaluation Review, 4,* 147-191.

Briere, J. N. (1992). *Child abuse trauma.* Newbury Park, CA: Sage.

Britt, C., III. (1992). Constancy and change in the U.S. distribution of crime: A test of the "invariance hypothesis." *Journal of Quantitative Criminology, 8,* 75-187.

Brown, S. A. (1993). Drug effect expectancies and addictive behavior change. *Experimental and Clinical Psychopharmacology, 1,* 55-67.

Browne, A. (1987). *When battered women kill.* New York: Macmillan/Free Press.

Browne, A. (1993). Violence against women by male partners: Prevalence, outcomes, and policy implications. *American Psychologist, 48,* 1077-1087.

Browne, A. (1997). Violence in marriage: Until death do us part? In A. P. Cardarelli (Ed.), *Violence between intimate partners: Patterns, causes, and effects* (pp. 48-69). Needham Heights, MA: Allyn & Bacon.

Browne, A., & Williams, K. R. (1989). Exploring the effect of resource availability and the likelihood of female-perpetrated homicides. *Law and Society Review, 23,* 75-94.

Browne, A., & Williams, K. R. (1993). Gender, intimacy, and lethal violence: Trends from 1976 through 1987. *Gender & Society, 7,* 78-98.

Brownstein, H. H., & Goldstein, P. (1990). Research and the development of public policy: The case of drugs and violent crime. *Journal of Applied Sociology, 7,* 77-92.

Brownstein, H. H., Baxi, H., Goldstein, P., & Ryan, P. (1992). The relationship of drugs, drug trafficking, and drug traffickers to homicide. *Journal of Crime and Justice, 15,* 25-44.

Brumm, H. J., & Cloninger, D. O. (1995). The drug war and the homicide rate: A direct correlation? *Cato Journal, 14,* 509-517.

Bruvold, W. H. (1993). A meta-analysis of adolescent smoking prevention programs. *American Journal of Public Health, 83,* 872-880.

Bullock, H. A. (1955). Urban homicide in theory and fact. *Journal of Criminal Law, Criminology and Police Science, 45,* 565-575.

Bureau of Justice Statistics. (1993). *Survey of state prison inmates, 1991.* Washington, DC: U.S. Department of Justice.

Bureau of Justice Statistics. (1997). *Criminal victimization in the United States, 1994* (NCJ-162126). Washington, DC: Government Printing Office.

Bursik, R. J., Jr. (1988). Social disorganization and theories of crime and delinquency: Problems and prospects. *Criminology, 26,* 519-552.

Busch, K. G., Zagar, R., Hughes, J. R., Arbit, J., & Bussell, R. E. (1990). Adolescents who kill. *Journal of Clinical Psychology, 46,* 472-485.

Bye, R. T. (1919). *Capital punishment in the United States.* Philadelphia: Committee on Philanthropic Labor of Philadelphia Yearly Meeting of Friends.

Bynum, J. E., & Thompson, W. E. (1996). *Juvenile delinquency: A sociological approach* (3rd ed.). Boston: Allyn & Bacon.

Campbell, J. (1992). "If I can't have you, no one can": Power and control in homicide of female partners. In J. Radford & D. E. H. Russell (Eds.), *Femicide: The politics of woman killing* (pp. 99-113). New York: Twayne.

Campion, H. (1949). International statistics. *Journal of the Royal Statistical Society, 112,* 105-143.

Cantor, D., & Cohen, L. E. (1980). Comparing measures of homicide trends: Methodological and substantive differences in the Vital Statistics and Uniform Crime Report time series (1933-1975). *Social Science Research, 9,* 121-145.

Cantor, D., & Land, K. C. (1985). Unemployment and crime rates in the post-World War II United States: A theoretical and empirical analysis. *American Sociological Review, 50,* 317-323.

Cao, L., Adams, A., & Jensen, B. J. (1997). A test of the Black subculture of violence thesis: A research note. *Criminology, 35,* 367-379.

Carek, D. J., & Watson, A. S. (1964). Treatment of a family involved in fratricide. *Archives of General Psychiatry, 16,* 533-542.

Carnegie Council on Adolescent Development. (1995, October). *Great transitions: Preparing adolescents for a new century.* New York: Carnegie Corporation.

Carver, C. M. (1987). *American regional dialects: A word geography.* Ann Arbor: University of Michigan Press.

Cazanave, N. A., & Zahn, M. A. (1992). Women, murder and male domination: Police reports of domestic violence in Chicago and Philadelphia. In E. C. Viano (Ed.), *Intimate violence: Interdisciplinary perspectives* (pp. 83-97). Washington, DC: Hemisphere.

Center, L. J., & Smith, T. G. (1973). Criminal statistics: Can they be trusted? *American Criminal Law Review, 11,* 1046-1086.

Centers for Disease Control and Prevention. (1986). *Homicide surveillance: High-risk racial and ethnic groups—Blacks and Hispanics, 1970 to 1983.* Atlanta, GA: Author.

Centers for Disease Control and Prevention. (1992, May 29). Homicide surveillance: United States, 1979-1988. *CDC Surveillance Summaries, 41*(SS-3), 1-34. (Suppl. to *Morbidity and Mortality Weekly*)

Centers for Disease Control and Prevention. (1997-1998). CDC WONDER [On-line]. Available: http://wonder.cdc.gov/WONDER and http://wonder.cdc.gov/rchtml/Convert/data/AdHoc.html

Centerwall, B. S. (1984). Race, socioeconomic status, and domestic homicide, Atlanta, 1971-2. *American Journal of Public Health, 74,* 813-815.

Chagnon, N. A. (1988). Life histories, blood revenge, and warfare in a tribal population. *Science, 239,* 958-992.

Chagnon, N. A. (1996). Chronic problems in understanding tribal violence and warfare. In G. Bock & J. Goode (Eds.), *Genetics and crime* (pp. 202-236). Chichester, UK: Wiley.

Chaiken, J., Chaiken, M., & Rhodes, W. (1994). Predicting violent behavior and classifying violent offenders. In A. J. Reiss, Jr., & J. A. Roth (Eds.), *Understanding and preventing violence* (Vol. 4, pp. 217-295). Washington, DC: National Academy Press.

Chambliss, W. J. (1967). Types of deviance and the effectiveness of legal sanctions. In W. J. Chambliss (Ed.), *Criminal law in action* (2nd ed., pp. 398-407). New York: John Wiley.

Chamlin, M. B. (1989). A macro social analysis of the change in robbery and homicide rates: Controlling for static and dynamic effects. *Sociological Focus, 22,* 275-286.

Chandler, D. B. (1976). *Capital punishment in Canada: A sociological study of repressive law.* Ottawa, Canada: McClelland and Stewart Limited in association with Carleton University, Institute of Canadian Studies.

Cheatwood, D. (1991). Doing the work of research: Wolfgang's foundation and beyond. *Journal of Crime and Justice, 14,* 3-15.

Chilton, R. (1996). Can the National Incident-Based Reporting System (NIBRS) contribute to our understanding of domestic violence? In M. Riedel & J. Boulahanis (Eds.), *Lethal violence: Proceedings of the 1995 meeting of the Homicide Research Working Group* (pp. 195-205). Washington, DC: Government Printing Office.

Chimbos, P. D. (1978). *Marital violence: A study of interspousal homicide.* San Francisco: R & E Research Associates.

Chirot, D. (1977). *Social change in the twentieth century.* New York: Harcourt.

Christiansen, K. O. (1967). *The post-war trends of crime in selected European countries.* Copenhagen, Denmark: Kriminalistiriske Institute.

Clotfelter, C. T. (1993). The private life of public economics. *Southern Economic Journal, 59,* 579-596.

Clutton-Brock, T. H. (1990). *The evolution of parental care.* Princeton, NJ: Princeton University Press.

Cochran, J. K., Chamlin, M. B., & Seth, M. (1994). Deterrence or brutalization? An impact assessment of Oklahoma's return to capital punishment. *Criminology, 32,* 107-134.

Cohen, A. K. (1955). *Delinquent boys: The culture of the gang.* New York: Free Press.

Cohen, A. K. (1985). The assumption that crime is a product of environments: Sociological approaches. In R. F.

Meier (Ed.), *Theoretical methods in criminology* (pp. 223-243). Beverly Hills, CA: Sage.

Cohen, L. E., & Felson, M. (1979). Social change and crime rate trends: A routine activity approach. *American Sociological Review, 44,* 588-608.

Cohen, L. E., Felson, M., & Land, K. C. (1980). Property crime rates in the United States: A macrodynamic analysis 1947-1977 with *ex ante* forecasts for the mid-1980s. *American Journal of Sociology, 86,* 90-118.

Cohen, L. E., & Land, K. C. (1987). Age structure and crime: Symmetry versus asymmetry and the projection of crime rates through the 1990s. *American Sociological Review, 52,* 170-183.

Commission on Chronic Illness. (1957). *Chronic illness in the United States* (Vol. 1). Cambridge, MA: Harvard University Press.

Committee for the Study of the Future of Public Health, Division of Health Care Services, Institute of Medicine. (1988). *The future of public health.* Washington, DC: National Academy Press.

Committee on Trauma Research, Commission on Life Sciences, National Research Council, and the Institute of Medicine. (1985). *Injury in America: A continuing public health problem.* Washington, DC: National Academy Press.

Conklin, G. H., & Simpson, M. E. (1985). A demographic approach to the cross-national study of homicide. *Comparative Social Research, 8,* 171-185.

Conklin, J. E. (1972). *Robbery and the criminal justice system.* Philadelphia: J. B. Lippincott.

Cook, P. J. (1976). A strategic choice analysis of robbery. In W. Skogan (Ed.), *Sample surveys of the victims of crimes* (pp. 173-187). Cambridge, MA: Ballinger.

Cook, P. J. (1979). The effect of gun availability on robbery and robbery murder: A cross-section study of fifty cities. In R. H. Haveman & B. B. Zellner (Eds.), *Policy studies review annual* (Vol. 3, pp. 743-781). Beverly Hills, CA: Sage.

Cook, P. J. (1980). Reducing injury and death rates in robbery. *Policy Analysis, 6,* 21-45.

Cook, P. J. (1983). *Robbery in the United States: An analysis of recent trends and patterns.* Washington, DC: National Institute of Justice.

Cook, P. J. (1985). The case of the missing victims: Gunshot woundings in the National Crime Survey. *Journal of Quantitative Criminology, 1,* 91-102.

Cook, P. J. (1986). The relationship between victim resistance and injury in noncommercial robbery. *Journal of Legal Studies, 15,* 405-416.

Cook, P. J. (1987). Robbery violence. *Journal of Criminal Law and Criminology, 70,* 357-376.

Cook, P. J. (1991). The technology of personal violence. In M. H. Tonry (Ed.), *Crime and justice: A review of research* (Vol. 14, pp. 1-71). Chicago: University of Chicago Press.

Cook, P. J. (1993). Notes on the availability and prevalence of firearms. *American Journal of Preventive Medicine, 9,* 33-38.

Cook, P. J., & Leitzel, J. A. (1996). Perversity, futility, jeopardy: An economic analysis of the attack on gun control. *Law and Contemporary Problems, 59,* 91-118.

Cook, P. J., & Ludwig, J. (1996). *Guns in America: Results of a comprehensive national survey on firearms ownership and use.* Washington, DC: Police Foundation.

Cook, P. J., Ludwig, J., & Hemenway, D. (1997). The gun debate's new mythical number: How many defensive gun uses per year? *Journal of Policy Analysis and Management, 16,* 463-469.

Cook, P. J., Molliconi, S., & Cole, T. B. (1995). Regulating gun markets. *Journal of Criminal Law and Criminology, 86,* 59-92.

Corder, B. F., Ball, B. C., Haizlip, T. M., Rollins, R., & Beaumont, R. (1976). Adolescent parricide: A comparison with other adolescent murder. *American Journal of Psychiatry, 133,* 957-961.

Cornell, D. G. (1989). Causes of juvenile homicide: A review of the literature. In E. P. Benedek & D. G. Cornell (Eds.), *Juvenile homicide* (pp. 3-36). Washington, DC: American Psychiatric Press.

Cornell, D. G. (1990). Prior adjustment of violent juvenile offenders. *Law and Human Behavior, 14,* 569-577.

Cornell, D. G. (1993). Juvenile homicide: A growing national problem. *Behavioral Sciences and the Law, 16,* 389-396.

Cornell, D. G., Benedek, E. P., & Benedek, D. M. (1987a). Characteristics of adolescents charged with homicide. *Behavioral Sciences and the Law, 5,* 11-23.

Cornell, D. G., Benedek, E. P., & Benedek, D. M. (1987b). Juvenile homicide: Prior adjustment and a proposed typology. *American Journal of Orthopsychiatry, 57,* 383-393.

Cornell, D. G., Benedek, E. P., & Benedek, D. M. (1989). A typology of juvenile homicide offenders. In E. P. Benedek & D. G. Cornell (Eds.), *Juvenile homicide* (pp. 59-84). Washington, DC: American Psychiatric Press.

Cornell, D. G., Miller, C., & Benedek, E. P. (1988). MMPI profiles of adolescents charged with homicide. *Behavioral Sciences and the Law, 6,* 401-407.

Corzine, J., & Huff-Corzine, L. (1989). On cultural explanations of southern homicide: Comment on Dixon and Lizotte. *American Journal of Sociology, 95,* 178-182.

Corzine, J., & Huff-Corzine, L. (1992). Racial inequality and Black homicide: An analysis of felony, nonfelony, and total rates. *Journal of Contemporary Criminal Justice, 8,* 150-165.

Corzine, J., Huff-Corzine, L., & Whitt, H. P. (1995, November). *Country music and lethal violence.* Paper presented at the annual meeting of the American Society of Criminology, Boston.

Corzine, J., Huff-Corzine, L., & Wilson, J. K. (1992, November). *Mean streets: Poverty, race, and homicide in metropolitan areas.* Paper presented at the annual meeting of the American Society of Criminology, New Orleans.

Cosmides, L., & Tooby, J. (1995). Are humans good intuitive statisticians after all? Rethinking some conclusions of the literature on judgment under uncertainness. *Cognition, 58,* 1-73.

Crawford, M., & Gartner, R. (1992). *Woman killing: Intimate femicide in Ontario 1974-1990.* Toronto, Canada: Government of Ontario, Ministry of Social Services, Woman's Directorate.

Cronin, H. (1991). *The ant and the peacock.* Cambridge, UK: Cambridge University Press.

Crowell, N. A., & Burgess, A. W. (Eds.). (1996). *Understanding violence against women* (Panel on Research on Violence Against Women, Commission on Behavioral Social Sciences and Education, National Research Council). Washington, DC: National Academy Press.

Crutchfield, R. D., Geerken, M. R., & Gove, W. R. (1982). Crime rate and social integration. *Criminology, 20,* 467-478.

Curry, G. D., Ball, R. A., & Decker, S. H. (1995). *An update on gang crime and law enforcement record keeping.* St. Louis: University of Missouri, Department of Criminology and Criminal Justice.

Curry, G. D., Ball, R. A., & Decker, S. H. (1996). Estimating the national scope of gang crime from law enforcement data. In C. R. Huff (Ed.), *Gangs in America* (2nd ed., pp. 21-36). Thousand Oaks, CA: Sage.

Curry, G. D., Ball, R. A., & Fox, R. J. (1994). *Gang crime and law enforcement record keeping* (Research in Brief: NCJ-148345). Washington, DC: National Institute of Justice.

Curtis, L. A. (1974). *Criminal violence.* Lexington, MA: Lexington Books.

Curtis, L. A. (1975). *Violence, race, and culture.* Lexington, MA: D. C. Heath.

Daly, K. (1994). *Gender, crime, and punishment.* New Haven, CT: Yale University Press.

Daly, M., Salmon, C., & Wilson, M. (1997). Kinship: The conceptual hole in psychological studies of social cognition and close relationships. In J. A. Simpson & D. Kenrick (Eds.), *Evolutionary social psychology* (pp. 265-296). Mahwah, NJ: Lawrence Erlbaum.

Daly, M., & Wilson, M. (1982). Homicide and kinship. *American Anthropologist, 84,* 372-378.

Daly, M., & Wilson, M. (1983). *Sex, evolution, and behavior* (2nd ed.). Belmont, CA: Wadsworth.

Daly, M., & Wilson, M. (1988a). Evolutionary social psychology and family homicide. *Science, 242,* 519-524.

Daly, M., & Wilson, M. (1988b). *Homicide.* Hawthorne, NY: Aldine de Gruyter.

Daly, M., & Wilson, M. (1990). Killing the competition. *Human Nature, 1,* 83-109.

Daly, M., & Wilson, M. (1994). Some differential attributes of lethal assaults on small children by stepfathers versus genetic fathers. *Ethology and Sociobiology, 15,* 207-217.

Daly, M., & Wilson, M. (1995). Discriminate parental solicitude and the relevance of evolutionary models to the analysis of motivational systems. In M. S. Gazzaniga (Ed.), *The cognitive neuroscience* (pp. 1269-1286). Cambridge: MIT Press.

Daly, M., & Wilson, M. (1996). Violence against stepchildren. *Current Directions in Psychological Science, 5,* 77-81.

Daly, M., & Wilson, M. (1997). Crime and conflict: Homicide in evolutionary psychological perspective. *Crime and Justice, 18,* 251-300.

Daly, M., Wiseman, K. A., & Wilson, M. (1997). Women with children sired by former partners incur excess risk of uxoricide. *Homicide Studies, 1,* 61-71.

Daniel, A. E., & Harris, P. W. (1982). Female homicide offenders referred for pre-trial psychiatric examination: A descriptive study. *Bulletin of the American Academy of Psychiatry and Law, 10,* 86-101.

Dann, R. (1935). *The deterrent effect of capital punishment.* Philadelphia: Committee of Philanthropic Labor of Philadelphia Yearly Meeting of Friends.

Darwin, C. (1859). *On the origin of species by means of natural selection, or, the preservation of favored races in the struggle for life.* London: John Murray.

Dawkins, R. (1986). *The blind watchmaker.* Harlow, UK: Longman.

Decker, S. H. (1993). Exploring victim-offender relationships in homicide: The role of individual and event characteristics. *Justice Quarterly, 10,* 585-612.

Decker, S. H., & Kohfeld, C. W. (1984). A deterrence study of the death penalty in Illinois, 1933-1980. *Journal of Criminal Justice, 12,* 367-377.

Decker, S. H., Pennell, S., & Caldwell, A. (1997). *Illegal firearms: Access and use by arrestees* (NCJ-163496). Washington, DC: Bureau of Justice Statistics.

Decker, S. H., & Van Winkle, B. (1996). *Life in the gang: Family, friends and violence.* New York: Cambridge University Press.

Deutsch, S. J. (1979). Lies, damn lies, and statistics: A rejoinder to the comment by Hay and McCleary. *Evaluation Quarterly, 3,* 315-328.

Division of Law Enforcement. (1994). *Homicide in California, 1994.* Sacramento, CA: Bureau of Criminal Justice Information and Analysis.

Dixon, J., & Lizotte, A. J. (1987). Gun ownership and the southern subculture of violence. *American Journal of Sociology, 93,* 383-405.

Dodge, K. A. (1997). *How gang membership increases violent behavior* (National Consortium on Violence Research grant proposal). Nashville, TN: Vanderbilt University, Department of Psychology and Human Development.

DuBois, W. E. B. (Ed.). (1904). Some notes on Negro crime, particularly in Georgia. *Proceedings of the Ninth Atlanta Conference for the Study of Negro Problems.* Atlanta, GA: Atlanta University Press.

Dugan, L., Nagin, D., & Rosenfeld, R. (1997). *Explaining the decline in intimate partner homicide: The effects of changing domesticity, women's status, and domestic violence resources* (Working paper No. 2.). Pittsburgh, PA: Carnegie Mellon University, National Consortium on Violence Research.

Duncan, J. W., & Duncan, G. M. (1971). Murder in the family. *American Journal of Psychiatry, 127,* 74-78.

Dunn, M. (1996, February 21). No ordinary trial for no ordinary rapper. *Tampa Tribune,* Metro section, p. 4.

Durkheim, E. (1947). *The division of labor in society* (G. Simpson, Trans.). Glencoe, IL: Free Press. (Original work published 1893)

Durkheim, E. (1951). *Suicide* (J. A. Spaulding & G. Simpson, Trans.). Glencoe, IL: Free Press. (Original work published 1897)

Durkheim, E. (1964). *The rules of sociological method.* New York: Free Press. (Original work published 1895)

Durkheim, E. (1966). *Suicide: A study in sociology.* New York: Free Press. (Original work published 1897)

Dutton, D. G. (1995). *The domestic assault of women: Psychological and criminal justice perspectives.* Vancouver, Canada: University of British Columbia Press.

Dutton, D. G., & Browning, J. J. (1988). Concern for power, fear of intimacy and aversive stimuli for wife assault. In G. T. Hotaling, D. Finkelhor, J. T. Kirkpatrick, & M. A. Straus (Eds.), *Family abuse and its consequences: New directions in research* (pp. 163-175). Newbury Park, CA: Sage.

Dutton, D. G., & Hemphill, K. J. (1992). Patterns of socially desirable responding among perpetrators and victims of wife assault. *Violence and Victims, 7,* 29-39.

Dutton, D. G., & Kerry, G. (1996). *Modus operandi and psychological profiles of uxoricidal males.* Unpublished manuscript, University of British Columbia, Department of Psychology, Vancouver, Canada.

Easson, W. M., & Steinhilber, R. M. (1961). Murderous aggression by children and adolescents. *Archives of General Psychiatry, 4,* 27-35.

Easterlin, R. A. (1987). *Birth and fortune: The impact of numbers on personal welfare* (2nd ed.). Chicago: University of Chicago Press.

Eckberg, D. (1995). Estimates of early twentieth-century U.S. homicide rates: An econometric forecasting approach. *Demography, 32,* 1-16.

Egger, S. A. (1984). A working definition of serial murder and the reduction of linkage blindness. *Journal of Police Science and Administration, 12,* 348-357.

Egger, S. A. (1990). *Serial murder: An elusive phenomenon.* Westport, CT: Praeger.

Egger, S. A. (1998). *The killers among us: An examination of serial murder and its investigation.* Upper Saddle River, NJ: Prentice Hall.

Ehrlich, I. (1975). The deterrent effect of capital punishment: A question of life or death. *American Economic Review, 65,* 397-417.

Ehrlich, I. (1977). Capital punishment and deterrence: Some further thoughts and additional evidence. *Journal of Political Economy, 85,* 741-788.

Elliott, D. S., Huizinga, D., & Menard, S. (1989). *Multiple problem youth: Delinquency, substance use, and mental health problems.* New York: Springer-Verlag.

Ellison, C. G. (1991). An eye for an eye? A note on the southern subculture of violence thesis. *Social Forces, 69,* 1223-1239.

Ellison, C. G., & McCall, P. L. (1989). Region and violent attitudes reconsidered: Comment on Dixon and Lizotte. *American Journal of Sociology, 95,* 174-178.

Erlanger, H. S. (1974). The empirical status of the subculture of violence thesis. *Social Problems, 22,* 280-292.

Esbensen, F., & Huizinga, D. (1993). Gangs, drugs and delinquency in a survey of urban youth. *Criminology, 31,* 565-589.

Esbensen, F., Huizinga, D., & Weiher, A. (1993). Gang and non-gang youth: Differences in explanatory factors. *Journal of Contemporary Criminal Justice, 9,* 94-116.

Ewing, C. P. (1990). *When children kill.* Lexington, MA: Lexington Books.

Fagan, J. (1989). The social organization of drug use and drug dealing among urban gangs. *Criminology, 27,* 633-669.

Fagan, J. (1990). Intoxication and aggression. In M. Tonry & J. Q. Wilson (Eds.), *Crime and justice: A review of research* (Vol. 13, pp. 241-320). Chicago: University of Chicago Press.

Fagan, J., & Browne, A. (1994). Violence between spouses and intimates: Physical aggression between women and men in intimate relationships. In A. J. Reiss, Jr., & J. A. Roth (Eds.), *Understanding and preventing violence: Vol. 3. Social influences* (pp. 115-292). Washington, DC: National Academy Press.

Fagan, J., Stewart, D., & Hanson, K. (1983). Violent men or violent husbands: Background factors and situational correlates of domestic and extra-domestic violence. In D. Finkelhor, R. J. Gelles, G. T. Hotaling, & M. A. Straus (Eds.), *The dark side of families* (pp. 49-67). Beverly Hills, CA: Sage.

Fang, J., Madhavan, S., & Alderman, M. H. (1996). The association between birthplace and mortality from cardiovascular causes among Black and White residents of New York City. *New England Journal of Medicine, 335,* 1545-1551.

Farley, R. (1980). Homicide trends in the United States. *Demography, 17,* 177-188.

Fattah, E. A. (1972). *A study of the deterrent effect of capital punishment with special reference to the Canadian situation.* Ottawa, Canada: Department of the Solicitor General.

Faulkner, R. R. (1974). Making violence by doing work: Selves, situations, and the world of professional hockey. *Sociology of Work and Occupations, 1,* 288-304.

Federal Bureau of Investigation. (1980). *Uniform crime reporting handbook.* Washington, DC: Government Printing Office.

Federal Bureau of Investigation. (1984). *Uniform crime reporting handbook.* Washington, DC: Government Printing Office.

Federal Bureau of Investigation. (1992). *Uniform crime reporting handbook: National Incident-Based Reporting System edition.* Washington, DC: Government Printing Office.

Federal Bureau of Investigation. (1993). *Age-specific arrest rates and race-specific arrest rates for selected offenses, 1965-1992.* Washington, DC: U.S. Department of Justice.

Federal Bureau of Investigation. (Selected years). *Crime in the United States: Uniform crime reports.* Washington, DC: Government Printing Office.

Felson, M., & Cohen, L. E. (1980). Human ecology and crime: A routine activity approach. *Human Ecology, 32,* 389-406.

Felson, R., Liska, A., South, S., & McNulty, T. (1994). The subculture of violence and delinquency: Individual vs. school context effects. *Social Forces, 73,* 155-174.

Felson, R., & Messner, S. F. (1996). To kill or not to kill? Lethal outcomes in injurious attacks. *Criminology, 34,* 519-545.

Fendrich, M., Mackesy-Amiti, M. E., Goldstein, P., Spunt, B., & Brownstein, H. (1995). Substance involvement among juvenile murderers: Comparisons with older offenders based on interviews with prison inmates. *International Journal of the Addictions, 30,* 1363-1382.

Ferri, E. (1934). *Omicidio-suicidio* [Homicide-Suicide] (4th ed.) (C. Pena, Trans.). Madrid, Spain: Editorial Review. (Original work published 1925)

Fiala, R., & LaFree, G. (1988). Cross-national determinants of child homicide. *American Sociological Review, 53,* 432-445.

Fiddes, D. O. (1981). Scotland in the seventies: Adolescents in care and custody: A survey of adolescent murder in Scotland. *Journal of Adolescence, 4,* 47-58.

Fine, G. A., & Kleinman, S. (1979). Rethinking subculture: An interactionist analysis. *American Journal of Sociology, 85,* 1-20.

Fingerhut, L. A. (1993). Firearm mortality among children, youth, and young adults 1-34 years of age, trends and current status: United States, 1985-90. *Advance data from Vital and Health Statistics* (No. 231). Hyattsville, MD: National Center for Health Statistics.

Fingerhut, L. A., Ingram, D. D., & Feldman, J. J. (1992). Firearm and nonfirearm homicide among persons 15 through 19 years of age: Differences by level of urbanization, United States, 1979 through 1989. *Journal of the American Medical Association, 267,* 3048-3053.

Fingerhut, L. A., & Kleinman, J. C. (1990). International and interstate comparisons of homicide among young males. *Journal of the American Medical Association, 263,* 3292-3295.

Fishbein, D. H. (1990). Biological perspectives in criminology. *Criminology, 28,* 27-72.

Fisher, R. A. (1936). The use of multiple measurements in taxonomic problems. *Annals of Eugenics, 7,* 179-188.

Flango, V. E., & Sherbenou, E. L. (1976). Poverty, urbanization, and crime. *Criminology, 14,* 331-346.

Florida Center for Children and Youth. (1993). *Key facts about the children: A report on the status of Florida's children: Vol 4. The 1993 Florida kids count data book.* Tallahassee, FL: Author.

Flowers, R. (1988). *Minorities and criminality.* New York: Greenwood.

Flowers, R. (1990). *Minorities and criminality.* New York: Praeger.

Follingstad, D. R., Brennen, A. F., Hause, D. S., Polek, D. S., & Rutledge, L. L. (1991). Factors moderating physical and psychological symptoms of battered women. *Journal of Family Violence, 6,* 81-95.

Forst, B. (1977). The deterrent effect of capital punishment: A cross-state analysis of the 1960's. *Minnesota Law Review, 61,* 743-767.

Fowles, R., & Merva, M. (1996). Wage inequality and criminal activity: An extreme bounds analysis for the United States, 1975-1990. *Criminology, 34,* 163-182.

Fox, J. A. (1978). *Forecasting crime data.* Lexington, MA: Lexington Books.

Fox, J. A. (1989, January 29). The mind of a murderer. *Palm Beach Post,* p. 1E.

Fox, J. A. (1996). *Trends in juvenile violence: A report to the United States attorney general on current and future rates of juvenile offending.* Washington, DC: Bureau of Justice Statistics.

Fox, J. A., & Levin, J. (1985, December 1). Serial killers: How statistics mislead us. *Boston Herald,* p. 45.

Fox, J. A., & Levin, J. (1994). *Overkill: Mass murder and serial killing exposed.* New York: Plenum.

Fox, J. A., & Levin, J. (1996). *Killer on campus.* New York: Avon Books.

Friedman, H. L. (1992). Changing patterns of adolescent sexual behavior: Consequences for health and development. *Journal of Adolescent Health, 13,* 345-350.

Friedman, H. L. (1993). Promoting the health of adolescents in the United States of America: A global perspective. *Journal of Adolescent Health, 14,* 509-519.

Friedman, L. (1979). The use of multiple regression analysis to test for a deterrent effect of capital punishment: Prospects and problems. In S. Messinger & E. Bittner (Eds.), *Criminology review yearbook* (Vol. 1, pp. 61-87). Beverly Hills, CA: Sage.

Furlow, B., Gangestad, S. W., & Armijo-Prewitt, T. (1998). Developmental stability and human violence. *Proceedings of the Royal Society of London: Series B, 265,* 1-6.

Gardiner, M. (1985). *The deadly innocents: Portraits of children who kill.* New Haven, CT: Yale University Press.

Garriott, J. C. (1993). Drug use among homicide victims: Changing patterns. *American Journal of Forensic Medicine and Pathology, 14,* 234-237.

Gartner, R. (1990). The victims of homicide: A temporal and cross-national comparison. *American Sociological Review, 55,* 92-106.

Gartner, R. (1991). Family structure, welfare spending, and child homicide in developed democracies. *Journal of Marriage and the Family, 53,* 231-240.

Gartner, R., Baker, K., & Pampel, F. C. (1990). Gender stratification and the gender gap in homicide victimization. *Social Problems, 37,* 593-612.

Gartner, R., & McCarthy, B. (1991). The social distribution of femicide in urban Canada, 1921-1988. *Law and Society Review, 25,* 287-312.

Gartner, R., & Parker, R. N. (1990). Cross-national evidence on homicide and the age structure of the population. *Social Forces, 69,* 351-371.

Gastil, R. (1971). Homicide and a regional culture of violence. *American Sociological Review, 36,* 412-427.

Gastil, R. (1975). *The cultural regions of the United States.* Seattle: University of Washington Press.

Govone, G. (1968). Speech to parliament by General Govone after leaving his military command in Sicily, December 3, 1863. In D. Mack Smith (Ed.), *The making of Italy, 1796-1870* (pp. 371-373). New York: Walker.

Gelles, R. J., & Conte, J. R. (1990). Domestic violence and sexual abuse of children: A review of research in the eighties. *Journal of Marriage and the Family, 52,* 1045-1058.

Gelles, R. J., & Straus, M. A. (1985). Violence in the American family. In A. J. Lincoln & M. A. Straus (Eds.), *Crime and the family* (pp. 55-110). Springfield, IL: Charles C Thomas.

Gest, T., & Friedman, D. (1994, August 29). The new crime wave. *U.S. News & World Report, 117,* 26.

Gibbs, J. P. (1975). *Crime, punishment, and deterrence.* New York: Elsevier.

Gibbs, J. P. (1986). Deterrence theory and research. In G. B. Melton (Ed.), *Nebraska Symposium on Motivation 1985: The law as a behavioral instrument* (pp. 87-130). Lincoln: University of Nebraska Press.

Gigerenzer, G., & Hoffrage, U. (1995). How to improve Bayesian reasoning without instruction: Frequency formats. *Psychological Review, 102,* 684-704.

Gillespie, C. K. (1988). *Justifiable homicide.* Columbus: Ohio State University Press.

Gillis, A. R. (1996). So long as they both shall live: Marital dissolution and the decline of domestic homicide in France, 1852-1909. *American Journal of Sociology, 101,* 1273-1305.

Goetting, A. (1987). Homicidal wives: A profile. *Journal of Family Issues, 8,* 332-341.

Goetting, A. (1989). Patterns of homicide among children. *Criminal Justice and Behavior, 16,* 63-80.

Goetting, A. (1995). *Homicide in families and other special populations.* New York: Springer.

Goldberg, C. (1997, January 30). Hispanic households struggle as poorest of the poor in U.S. *New York Times,* p. A1.

Golden, R. M., & Messner, S. F. (1987). Dimensions of racial inequality and rates of violent crime. *Criminology, 25,* 525-554.

Goldstein, J. H. (1986). *Aggression and crimes of violence* (2nd ed.). New York: Oxford University Press.

Goldstein, P. J. (1985). The drugs-violence nexus: A tripartite conceptual framework. *Journal of Drug Issues, 14,* 493-506.

Goldstein, P. J. (1989). Drugs and violent crime. In N. A. Weiner & M. E. Wolfgang (Eds.), *Pathways to criminal violence* (pp. 16-48). Newbury Park, CA: Sage.

Goldstein, P. J., Bellucci, P. A., Spunt, B. J., & Miller, T. (1991). Volume of cocaine use and violence: A comparison between men and women. *Journal of Drug Issues, 21,* 345-367.

Goldstein, P. J., Brownstein, H. H., & Ryan, P. J. (1992). Drug-related homicide in New York: 1984 and 1988. *Crime & Delinquency, 38,* 459-476.

Goldstein, P. J., Brownstein, H. H., Ryan, P. J., & Bellucci, P. A. (1989). Crack and homicide in New York City, 1988: A conceptually based event analysis. *Contemporary Drug Problems, 16,* 651-687.

Goodman, R., Mercy, J. A., Loya, F., Rosenberg, M. L., Smith, J. C., Allen, N. N., Vargas, L., & Kolts, R. (1986). Alcohol use and interpersonal violence: Alcohol detected in homicide victims. *American Journal of Public Health, 76,* 144-149.

Gorden, R. (1983). An operational classification of disease prevention. *Public Health Reports, 98,* 107-109.

Gordon, R. A. (1967). Issues in multiple regression. *American Journal of Sociology, 78,* 592-616.

Gottfredson, M. R., & Hirschi, T. (1990). *A general theory of crime.* Stanford, CA: Stanford University Press.

Gove, W. R., Hughes, M., & Geerken, M. (1985). Are Uniform Crime Reports a valid indicator of index crimes? An affirmative answer with some minor qualifications. *Criminology, 23,* 451-501.

Govone, G. (1968). Speech to parliament by General Govone after leaving his military command in Sicily, December 3, 1863. In D. M. Smith (Ed.), *The making of Italy, 1796-1870* (pp. 371-373). New York: Walker. (Original work published 1863)

Grasmick, H. G., Davenport, E., Chamlin, M. B., & Bursik, R. J., Jr. (1992). Protestant fundamentalism and the retributive doctrine of punishment. *Criminology, 30,* 21-45.

Gray, J. (1997, May 9). Bill to combat juvenile crime passes House. *New York Times,* pp. A1, A32.

Greco, C. M., & Cornell, D. G. (1992). Rorschach object relations of adolescents who committed homicide. *Journal of Personality Assessment, 59,* 574-583.

Greenberg, D. (1977). Delinquency and the age structure of society. *Contemporary Crises, 1,* 189-224.

Greenberg, D. (1985). Age, crime, and social explanation. *American Journal of Sociology, 91,* 1-21.

Greenberg, D. (Ed.). (1981). *Crime and capitalism.* Palo Alto, CA: Mayfield.

Greenberg, S. W. (1981). Alcohol and crime: A methodological review of the literature. In J. J. Collins, Jr. (Ed.), *Drinking and crime: Perspectives on the relationship between alcohol consumption and criminal behavior* (pp. 1-69). New York: Guilford.

Groves, W. B., McCleary, R., & Newman, G. R. (1985). Religion, modernization, and world crime. *Comparative Social Research, 8,* 59-78.

Grube, J., Ames, G. M., & Delaney, W. (1994). Alcohol expectancies and workplace drinking. *Journal of Applied Social Psychology, 24,* 646-660.

Guerra, N., Tolan, P. H., & Hammond, W. R. (1994). Prevention and treatment of adolescent violence. In L. D. Eron, J. Gentry, & P. Schlegel (Eds.), *Reason to hope: A psychosocial perspective on violence and youth* (pp. 383-403). Washington, DC: American Psychological Association.

Guerry, A. (1833). *Essai sur la statistique morale de la France* [Essay on the moral statistics of France]. Paris: Chez Crochard.

Gurr, T. (1977). Crime trends in modern democracies since 1945. *International Annals of Criminology and Penology, 1,* 151-160.

Gurr, T. (Ed.). (1989). *Violence in America: Vol. 1. The history of crime.* Newbury Park, CA: Sage.

Hackney, S. (1969). Southern violence. *American Historical Review, 39,* 906-925.

Hagan, J. (1990). The structuration of gender and deviance: A power-control theory of vulnerability to crime and the search for deviant exit roles. *Canadian Review of Sociology and Anthropology, 27,* 137-156.

Hagan, J., & Peterson, R. D. (1995). Criminal inequality in America. In J. Hagan & R. D. Peterson (Eds.), *Crime and inequality* (pp. 14-36). Stanford, CA: Stanford University Press.

Hagedorn, J. (in press). Gang violence in the post industrial era. In M. Tonry (Ed.), *Youth violence.* Chicago: University of Chicago Press.

Haig, D. (1993). Genetic conflicts in human pregnancy. *Quarterly Review of Biology, 68,* 495-532.

Haizlip, T., Corder, B. F., & Ball, B. C. (1984). Adolescent murderer. In C. R. Keith (Ed.), *Aggressive adolescent* (pp. 126-148). New York: Free Press.

Haller, M. H. (1989). Bootlegging: The business and politics of violence. In T. Gurr (Ed.), *Violence in America: Vol. 1. The history of crime* (pp. 146-162). Newbury Park, CA: Sage.

Hamberger, L. K., & Hastings, J. E. (1991). Personality correlates of men who batter and nonviolent men: Some continuities and discontinuities. *Journal of Family Violence, 6,* 131-147.

Hambright, T. Z. (1968). Comparability of age on the death certificate and matching census record: United States—May-August, 1960. *Vital and health statistics: Data evaluation and methods research* (Series 2, No. 29). Rockville, MD: National Center for Health Statistics.

Hambright, T. Z. (1969). Comparability of marital status, race, nativity, and country of origin on the death certificate and matching census record: United States—May-August, 1960. *Vital and health statistics: Data evaluation and methods research* (Series 2, No. 34). Rockville, MD: National Center for Health Statistics.

Hamilton, L. C. (1992). *Regression with graphics.* Pacific Grove, CA: Brooks/Cole.

Hamilton, W. D. (1964). The genetical evolution of social behavior. *Journal of Theoretical Biology, 7,* 1-52.

Hamilton, W. D. (1967). Extraordinary sex ratios. *Science, 156,* 477-488.

Hannerz, U. (1969). The roots of Black manhood. *Transaction, 6,* 12-21.

Hansmann, H. B., & Quigley, J. M. (1982). Population heterogeneity and the sociogenesis of homicide. *Social Forces, 61,* 206-224.

Hanzlick, R., & Gowitt, G. T. (1991). Cocaine metabolite detection in homicide victims. *Journal of the American Medical Association, 265,* 760-761.

Harcourt, A. H. (1988). Letter to the editor. *Science, 243,* 462-463.

Harer, M. D., & Steffensmeier, D. J. (1992). The differing effects of economic inequality on Black and White rates of violence. *Social Forces, 70,* 1035-1054.

Harer, M. D., & Steffensmeier, D. J. (1996). Race and prison violence. *Criminology, 34,* 323-355.

Harlan, H. (1950). Five hundred homicides. *Journal of Criminal Law, Criminology and Police Science, 40,* 736-752.

Harries, K. (1974). *The geography of crime and justice.* New York: McGraw-Hill.

Harries, K. (1976). Cities and crime: A geographic model. *Criminology, 14,* 369-386.

Harries, K. (1989). Homicide and assault: A comparative analysis of attributes in Dallas neighborhoods, 1981-1985. *Professional Geographer, 41,* 29-38.

Harries, K. (1990). *Serious violence.* Springfield, IL: Charles C Thomas.

Harries, K. (1993). A victim ecology of drug-related homicide. In A. V. Wilson (Ed.), *Homicide: The victim/offender connection* (pp. 397-414). Cincinnati, OH: Anderson.

Harrington, A. (1972). *Psychopaths.* New York: Simon & Schuster.

Hartnagel, T. F. (1980). Subculture of violence: Further evidence. *Pacific Sociological Review, 23,* 217-242.

Hartnagel, T. F. (1982). Modernization, female social roles, and female crime: A cross-national investigation. *Sociological Quarterly, 23,* 477-490.

Hawkins, D. F. (1983). Black and White homicide differentials: Alternatives to an inadequate theory. *Criminal Justice and Behavior, 10,* 407-440.

Hawkins, D. F. (1990). Explaining the Black homicide rate. *Journal of Interpersonal Violence, 5,* 151-163.

Hawkins, D. F. (1993). Crime and ethnicity. In B. Forst (Ed.), *The socio-economics of crime and justice* (pp. 89-120). Armonk, NY: M. E. Sharpe.

Hawkins, D. F. (1994). The analysis of racial disparities in crime and justice: A double-edged sword. In *Enhancing capacities and confronting controversies in criminal justice* (NCJ-145318; pp. 48-49). Washington, DC: U.S. Department of Justice.

Hays, J. R., Solway, K. S., & Schreiner, D. (1978). Intellectual characteristics of juvenile murderers versus status offenders. *Psychological Reports, 43,* 80-82.

Hazelwood, R. R., Dietz, P. E., & Warren, J. (1992). The criminal sexual sadist. *FBI Law Enforcement Bulletin, 61,* 12-20.

Hazelwood, R. R., & Douglas, J. E. (1980). The lust murderer. *FBI Law Enforcement Bulletin, 49,* 1-5.

Heide, K. M. (1984, November). *A preliminary identification of types of adolescent murderers.* Paper presented at the annual meeting of the American Society of Criminology, Cincinnati, OH.

Heide, K. M. (1992). *Why kids kill parents: Child abuse and adolescent homicide.* Columbus: Ohio State University Press.

Heide, K. M. (1994a). Evidence of child maltreatment among adolescent parricide offenders. *International Journal of Offender Therapy & Comparative Criminology, 38,* 151-162.

Heide, K. M. (1994b). Homicide: 25 years later. In M. Moore (Ed.), *Economic and social issues in the New South: Perspectives on race and ethnicity conference proceedings* (pp. 64-84). Tampa: University of South Florida, Institute on Black Life.

Heide, K. M. (1996). Why kids keep killing: The correlates, causes, and challenge of juvenile homicide. *Stanford Law and Policy Review, 71,* 43-49.

Heide, K. M. (1997a). Associate editor's editorial: Killing words. *International Journal of Offender Therapy & Comparative Criminology, 4,* 3-8.

Heide, K. M. (1997b). Juvenile homicide in America: How can we stop the killing. *Behavioral Sciences and the Law, 15,* 203-220.

Heide, K. M. (1998). *Young killers: The challenge of juvenile homicide.* Thousand Oaks, CA: Sage.

Heimer, K. (1997). Socioeconomic status, subcultural definitions, and violent delinquency. *Social Forces, 75,* 799-833.

Heise, D. R. (1975). *Causal analysis.* New York: Wiley-Interscience.

Heise, L. (1994). *Violence against women: The hidden health burden* (World Bank Discussion Paper No. 255). Washington, DC: World Bank.

Hellsten, P., & Katila, O. (1965). Murder and other homicide, by children under 15 in Finland. *Psychiatric Quarterly Supplement, 39,* 54-74.

Henry, A. F., & Short, J. F., Jr. (1954). *Suicide and homicide: Some economic, sociological, and psychological aspects of aggression.* Glencoe, IL: Free Press.

Hepper, P. G. (Ed.). (1991). *Kin recognition.* Cambridge, UK: Cambridge University Press.

Hickey, E. W. (1997). *Serial murderers and their victims* (2nd ed.). Belmont, CA: Wadsworth.

Hill, K. G., Hawkins, D., Catalano, R. F., Kosterman, R., Abbott, R., & Edwards, T. (1996, November). *The longitudinal dynamics of gang membership and problem behavior: A replication and extension of the Denver and Rochester gang studies in Seattle.* Paper presented at the annual meeting of the American Society of Criminology, Chicago.

Hindelang, M. (1974). The Uniform Crime Reports revisited. *Journal of Criminal Justice, 2,* 1-17.

Hirschi, T. (1969). *Causes of delinquency.* Berkeley: University of California Press.

Hirschi, T., & Gottfredson, M. R. (1983). Age and the explanation of crime. *American Journal of Sociology, 89,* 552-584.

Hitson, H. M., & Funkenstein, D. H. (1959). Family pattern and paranoidal personality structure in Boston and Burma. *International Journal of Social Psychiatry, 5,* 182-190.

Hoffman, F. (1925). *The homicide problem.* San Francisco: Prudential Press.

Holmes, R. M., & DeBurger, J. (1988). *Serial murder.* Newbury Park, CA: Sage.

Holmes, R. M., & Holmes, S. T. (1998). *Serial murder* (2nd ed.). Thousand Oaks, CA: Sage.

Holmes, S. A. (1996, October 13). For Hispanic poor, no silver lining. *New York Times,* p. E5.

Holmes, W. G., & Sherman, P. W. (1982). The ontogeny of kin recognition in two species of ground squirrels. *American Zoologist, 22,* 491-517.

Horowitz, A. V. (1990). *The logic of social control.* New York: Plenum.

Hotaling, G. T., & Sugarman, D. B. (1986). An analysis of risk markers in husband to wife violence: The current state of knowledge. *Violence and Victims, 1,* 101-124.

Howell, J. C. (1995). Gangs and youth violence: Present research. In J. C. Howell, B. Krisberg, J. D. Hawkins, & J. J. Wilson (Eds.), *Serious, violent, and chronic juvenile offenders* (pp. 261-274). Thousand Oaks, CA: Sage.

Howell, J. C., Krisberg, B., & Jones, M. (1995). Trends in juvenile crime and youth violence. In J. C. Howell, B. Krisberg, J. D. Hawkins, & J. J. Wilson (Eds.), *A sourcebook: Serious, violent, and chronic juvenile offenders* (pp. 1-35). Thousand Oaks, CA: Sage.

Howlett, J. B., Haufland, K. A., & Ressler, R. J. (1986). The violent criminal apprehension program—VICAP: A progress report. *FBI Law Enforcement Bulletin, 55,* 14-22.

Hsieh, C., & Pugh, M. D. (1993). Poverty, income inequality, and violent crime: A meta-analysis of recent aggregate data studies. *Criminal Justice Review, 18,* 182-202.

Huang, W. S. W., & Wellford, C. F. (1989). Assessing indicators of crime among international crime data series. *Criminal Justice Policy Review, 3,* 28-47.

Huff, C. R. (1996). Introduction. In C. R. Huff (Ed.), *Gangs in America* (2nd ed., pp. xxi-xxvii). Thousand Oaks, CA: Sage.

Huff-Corzine, L., Corzine, J., & Moore, D. C. (1986). Southern exposure: Deciphering the South's influence on homicide rates. *Social Forces, 64,* 906-924.

Huff-Corzine, L., Corzine, J., & Moore, D. C. (1991). Deadly connections: Culture, poverty, and the direction of lethal violence. *Social Forces, 69,* 715-732.

Hufker, B., & Cavender, G. (1990). From freedom flotilla to America's burden: The social construction of the Mariel immigrants. *Sociological Quarterly, 31,* 321-335.

Hughes, J. R., Zagar, R., Arbit, J., & Busch, K. G. (1991). Medical, family, and scholastic conditions in urban delinquents. *Journal of Clinical Psychology, 47,* 448-464.

Huizinga, D. (1997, February). *Gangs and volume of crime.* Paper presented at the annual meeting of the Western Society of Criminology, Honolulu.

Huntingford, D., & Turner, A. (1987). *Animal conflict.* London: Chapman & Hall.

Hutson, H. R., Anglin, D., Kyriacou, D. M., Hart, J., & Spears, K. (1995). The epidemic of gang-related homicides in Los Angeles County from 1979 through 1994. *Journal of the American Medical Association, 274,* 1031-1036.

Illinois State Police. (1995). *Crime in Illinois: 1994.* Springfield: State of Illinois.

Inciardi, J. A., & Faupel, C. E. (Eds.). (1980). *History and crime: Implications for criminal justice policy.* Beverly Hills, CA: Sage.

International Criminal Police Organization (Interpol). (1960). *International crime statistics for 1959-60.* N.p.: Author.

International Criminal Police Organization (Interpol). (1993). *International crime statistics for 1993.* N.p.: Author.

Jackson, R. L., Lopez, R. J., & Connell, R. (1997, January 12). Clinton puts priority on curtailing gang crime. *Los Angeles Times,* p. A1.

Jacobson, N. S., Gottman, J. M., Waltz, J., Rushe, R., Babcock, J., & Holtzworth-Munroe, A. (1994). Affect, verbal content and psychophysiology in the arguments of couples with a violent husband. *Journal of Consulting and Clinical Psychology, 62,* 982-988.

James, G., Patton, R. E., & Heslin, A. S. (1955). Accuracy of cause of death statements on death certificates. *Public Health Reports, 70,* 39-51.

Jarvis, J. P. (1992). The National Incident-Based Reporting System and its application to homicide research. In C. R. Block & R. L. Block (Eds.), *Questions and answers in lethal and non-lethal violence: Proceedings of the homicide research working group* (pp. 81-85). Washington, DC: Government Printing Office.

Jason, J., Carpenter, M. M., & Tyler, C. W., Jr. (1983). Underrecording of infant homicide in the United States. *American Journal of Public Health, 73,* 195-197.

Jason, J., Strauss, L. T., & Tyler, C. W., Jr. (1983). A comparison of primary and secondary homicides in the United States. *American Journal of Epidemiology, 117,* 309-319.

Jayewardene, C. H. S. (1977). *The penalty of death: The Canadian experiment.* Lexington, MA: D. C. Heath.

Jeffery, C. R. (1965). Criminal behavior and learning theory. *Journal of Criminal Law, Criminology and Police Science, 56,* 294-300.

Jeffery, C. R. (1979). *Biology and crime.* Beverly Hills, CA: Sage.

Jenkins, E., & Bell, C. (1994). Violence among inner city high school students and post-traumatic stress disorder. In S. Friedman (Ed.), *Anxiety disorders in African Americans* (pp. 76-88). New York: Springer.

Jenkins, P. (1988). Myth and murder: The serial killer panic of 1983-85. *Criminal Justice Research Bulletin* (No. 3). Huntsville, TX: Sam Houston State University.

Jenkins, P. (1994). *Using murder: The social construction of serial homicide.* New York: Walter de Gruyter.

Johnson, C. L., Rifkind, B. M., Sempos, C. T., Carroll, M. D., Bachorik, P. S., Briefel, R. R., Gorden, D. J., Burt, V. L., Brown, C. D., Lippel, K., & Cleeman, J. I. (1993). Declining serum total cholesterol levels among U.S. adults: The National Health and Nutrition Examination Survey. *Journal of the American Medical Association, 269,* 3002-3008.

Johnston, L. D., O'Malley, P. M., & Bachman, J. G. (1993). *National survey results on drug use from the monitoring the future study, 1975-1992: Vol. 1. Secondary school students.* Rockville, MD: National Institute on Drug Abuse.

Jones, E. D., III. (1981). The District of Columbia's Firearms Control Regulations Act of 1975: The toughest handgun control law in the United States—or is it? *Annals of the American Academy of Political and Social Sciences, 455,* 138-149.

Jurik, N., & Winn, R. (1990). Gender and homicide: A comparison of men and women who kill. *Violence and Victims, 5,* 227-242.

Kahneman, D., Slovic, P., & Tversky, A. (Eds.). (1982). *Judgment under uncertainness.* New York: Cambridge University Press.

Kalish, C. B. (1988, May). *International crime rates* (Bureau of Justice Statistics Special Report). Washington, DC: Government Printing Office.

Kalmuss, D. S. (1984). The intergenerational transmission of marital aggression. *Journal of Marriage and the Family, 46,* 16-19.

Kalmuss, D. S., & Straus, M. A. (1983). Feminist, political, and economic determinants of wife abuse services. In D. Finkelhor, R. J. Gelles, G. T. Hotaling, & M. A. Straus (Eds.), *The dark side of families* (pp. 363-376). Beverly Hills, CA: Sage.

Kantrowitz, B. (1993, August 2). Teen violence: Wild in the streets. *Newsweek, 122,* 40-46.

Karlson, T. A., & Hargarten, S. W. (1997). *Reducing firearm injury and death: A public health sourcebook on guns.* New Brunswick, NJ: Rutgers University Press.

Kazdin, A. E. (1994). Interventions for aggressive and antisocial children. In L. D. Eron, J. Gentry, & P. Schlegel (Eds.), *Reason to hope: A psychosocial perspective on violence and youth* (pp. 341-382). Washington, DC: American Psychological Association.

Kellermann, A. L., & Mercy, J. A. (1992). Men, women, and murder: Gender-specific differences in rates of fatal violence and victimization. *Journal of Trauma, 33,* 1-5.

Kellermann, A. L., Rivara, F. P., Rushforth, N. B., Banton, J. G., Reay, D. T., Francisco, J. T., Locci, A. B., Prodzinski, J. P., Hackman, B. B., & Somes, G. (1993). Gun ownership as a risk factor for homicide in the home. *New England Journal of Medicine, 329,* 1084-1091.

Kellermann, A. L., Rivara, F. P., Somes, G., Reay, D., Francisco, J., Banton, J., Prodzinski, J., Fligner, C., & Hackman, B. B. (1992). Suicide in the home in relation to gun ownership. *New England Journal of Medicine, 327,* 467-472.

Kennedy, B. P., Kawachi, I., & Prothrow-Stith, D. (1996). Income distribution and mortality: Cross sectional ecological study of the Robin Hood index in the United States. *British Medical Journal, 312,* 1004-1007.

Kennedy, D. M. (1994). Can we keep guns away from kids? *The American Prospect, 18,* 74-80.

Kennedy, D. M., Braga, A. A., & Piehl, A. M. (1997). The (un)known universe: Mapping gangs and gang violence in Boston. In D. Weisburd & T. McEwen (Eds.), *Crime mapping and crime prevention* (pp. 219-262). New York: Criminal Justice Press.

Kennedy, D. M., Piehl, A. M., & Braga, A. A. (1996). Youth violence in Boston: Gun markets, serious youth offenders, and a use-reduction strategy. *Law and Contemporary Problems, 59,* 147-196.

Keppel, R. D., Weis, J. G., & LaMoria, R. (1990). *Improving the investigation of murder: The Homicide Information and Tracking System (HITS)* (National Institute of Justice Final Report No. 87-IJ-CX-0026). Washington, DC: Government Printing Office.

Kick, E. L., & LaFree, G. (1985). Development and the social context of murder and theft. *Comparative Social Research, 8,* 37-58.

Kiger, K. (1990). The darker figure of crime: The serial murder enigma. In S. A. Egger (Ed.), *Serial murder: An elusive phenomenon* (pp. 35-52). New York: Praeger.

Killian, L. M. (1970). *White southerners.* New York: Random House.

Killias, M. (1993). Gun ownership, suicide, and homicide: An international perspective. In A. Del Frate, U. Zvekic, & J. J. M. van Dijk (Eds.), *Understanding crime: Experiences of crime and crime control* (pp. 289-302). Rome: United States Interregional Crime and Justice Research Institute.

Kim, J., & Mueller, C. W. (1985). *Introduction to factor analysis: What is it and how to do it.* Beverly Hills, CA: Sage.

King, C. H. (1975). The ego and the integration of violence in homicidal youth. *American Journal of Orthopsychiatry, 45,* 134-145.

Kirschner, D. (1990). The adopted child syndrome: Considerations for psychotherapy. *Psychotherapy in Private Practice, 8,* 93-100.

Kirschner, D. (1992). Understanding adoptees who kill: Dissociation, patricide, and the psychodynamics of adoption. *International Journal of Offender Therapy & Comparative Criminology, 36,* 323-333.

Klebba, A. (1975). Homicide trends in the United States, 1900-1974. *Public Health Reports, 90,* 195-204.

Klebba, A., Dolman, J., & Dolman, A. B. (1975). Comparability of mortality statistics for the seventh and eighth revision of the International Classification of Diseases: United States. *Vital and health statistics: Data evaluation and methods research* (Series 2, No. 66). Rockville, MD: National Center for Health Statistics.

Kleck, G. (1979). Capital punishment, gun ownership, and homicide. *American Journal of Sociology, 84,* 882-910.

Kleck, G. (1984). Handgun-only control: A policy disaster in the making. In D. B. Kates, Jr. (Ed.), *Firearms and violence: Issues of public policy* (pp. 167-199). Cambridge, MA: Ballinger.

Kleck, G. (1988). Crime control through the private use of armed force. *Social Problems, 35,* 1-22.

Kleck, G. (1991). *Point blank: Guns and violence in America.* New York: Aldine de Gruyter.

Kleck, G., & Gertz, M. (1995). Armed resistance to crime: The prevalence and nature of self-defense with a gun. *Journal of Criminal Law and Criminology, 86,* 150-187.

Kleck, G., & McElrath, K. (1991). The effects of weaponry on human violence. *Social Forces, 69,* 669-692.

Kleck, G., & Patterson, E. B. (1993). The impact of gun control and gun ownership levels on violence rates. *Journal of Quantitative Criminology, 9,* 249-287.

Klein, L., Forst, B., & Filatov, V. (1978). The deterrent effect of capital punishment: An assessment of the estimates. In A. Blumstein, J. Cohen, & D. Nagin (Eds.), *Deterrence and incapacitation: Estimating the effects of criminal sanctions on crime rates* (pp. 336-360). Washington, DC: National Academy of Sciences.

Klein, M. W. (1995). *The American street gang: Its nature, prevalence, and control.* New York: Oxford University Press.

Klein, M. W., Gordon, M. A., & Maxson, C. L. (1986). The impact of police investigations on police-reported rates of gang and nongang homicides. *Criminology, 24,* 489-512.

Klein, M. W., & Maxson, C. L. (1994). Gangs and crack cocaine trafficking. In D. L. MacKenzie & C. D. Uchida (Eds.), *Drugs and crime* (pp. 42-58). Thousand Oaks, CA: Sage.

Klein, M. W., Maxson, C. L., & Cunningham, L. C. (1991). "Crack," street gangs, and violence. *Criminology, 29,* 623-650.

Kniffin, F. B. (1965). Folk housing: Key to diffusion. *Annals of the Association of American Geographers, 55,* 549-577.

Koper, C. S., & Reuter, P. (1996). Suppressing illegal gun markets: Lessons from drug enforcement. *Law and Contemporary Problems, 59,* 119-143.

Kornhauser, R. R. (1978). *Social sources of delinquency: An appraisal of analytic models.* Chicago: University of Chicago Press.

Kposowa, A. J., & Breault, K. D. (1993). Reassessing the structural covariates of U.S. homicide rates: A county level study. *Sociological Focus, 26,* 27-46.

Krahn, H., Hartnagel, T. F., & Gartrell, J. W. (1986). Income inequality and homicide rates: Cross-national data and criminological theories. *Criminology, 24,* 269-295.

Kratcoski, P. C. (1990). Circumstances surrounding homicides by older offenders. *Criminal Justice and Behavior, 17,* 420-430.

Kraus, J., Sorenson, S., & Juarez, P. (Eds.). (1988). *Research conference on violence in Hispanic communities.* Washington, DC: U.S. Department of Health and Human Services.

Krivo, L. J., & Peterson, R. D. (1996). Extremely disadvantaged neighborhoods and urban crime. *Social Forces, 75,* 619-648.

Krohn, M. D. (1976). Inequality, unemployment and crime: A cross-national analysis. *Sociological Quarterly, 17,* 303-313.

Krohn, M. D. (1978). A Durkheimian analysis of international crime rates. *Social Forces, 57,* 654-670.

Krohn, M. D. (1991). Control and deterrence theories. In J. Sheley (Ed.), *Criminology: A contemporary handbook* (pp. 295-314). Belmont, CA: Wadsworth.

Krohn, M. D., & Wellford, C. F. (1977). A static and dynamic analysis of crime and the primary dimensions of nations. *International Journal of Criminology and Penology, 5,* 1-16.

Kurath, H. (1949). *A word geography of the eastern United States.* Ann Arbor: University of Michigan Press.

LaFree, G., & Drass, K. A. (1996). The effect of changes in intraracial income inequality and educational attainment on changes in arrest rates for African Americans and Whites, 1957 to 1990. *American Sociological Review, 61,* 614-634.

LaFree, G., Drass, K. A., & O'Day, P. (1992). Race and crime in postwar America: Determinants of African-American and White rates, 1957-1988. *Criminology, 30,* 157-188.

LaFree, G., & Kick, E. L. (1986). Cross-national effects of developmental, distributional, and demographic variables on crime: A review and analysis. *International Annals of Criminology, 24,* 213-236.

Land, K. C., McCall, P. L., & Cohen, L. E. (1990). Structural covariates of homicide rates: Are there any invariances across time and social space? *American Journal of Sociology, 95,* 922-963.

Landau, S. F. (1984). Trends in violence and aggression: A cross-cultural analysis. *International Journal of Comparative Sociology, 25,* 133-158.

Landau, S. F., & Pfeffermann, D. (1988). A time series analysis of violent crime and its relation to prolonged states of warfare: The Israeli case. *Criminology, 26,* 489-504.

Lane, R. (1979). *Violent death in the city: Suicide, accident, and murder in nineteenth century Philadelphia.* Cambridge, MA: Harvard University Press.

Lane, R. (1986). *Roots of violence in Black Philadelphia, 1860-1900.* Cambridge, MA: Harvard University Press.

Lane, R. (1997). *Murder in America: A history.* Columbus: Ohio State University Press.

Langevin, R., Paitich, D., Orchard, B., Handy, L., & Russon, A. (1982). The role of alcohol, drugs, suicide attempts, and situational strains in homicide committed by offenders seen for psychiatric assessment. *Psychiatrica Scandivavica, 66,* 229-242.

Lapidus, G. D., Gregorio, D. I., & Hansen, H. (1990). Misclassification of childhood homicide on death certificates. *American Journal of Public Health, 80,* 213-214.

Lashly, A. V. (1929). Homicide (in Cook County). In J. H. Wigmore (Ed.), *The Illinois crime survey* (pp. 589-640). Chicago: Illinois Association for Criminal Justice and Chicago Crime Commission.

Lattimore, P. K., Trudeau, J., Riley, K. J., Leiter, J., & Edwards, S. (1997). *Homicide in eight U.S. cities: Trends, context, and policy implications* (NCJ-167262). Washington, DC: U.S. Department of Justice.

Layson, S. K. (1985). Homicide and deterrence: An examination of the United States time-series evidence. *Southern Economic Journal, 52,* 68-89.

Lehtinen, M. (1977). The value of life: An argument for the death penalty. *Crime & Delinquency, 23,* 237-252.

Leonard, K. E., & Taylor, S. P. (1983). Exposure to pornography, permissive and nonpermissive cues, and male aggression toward females. *Motivation and Emotion, 7,* 291-299.

Lerman, L. G., & Livingston, F. (1983). State legislation on domestic violence. *Response, 6,* 1-27.

Lerner, R. M. (1994). *America's youth in crisis.* Thousand Oaks, CA: Sage.

Levin, J., & Fox, J. A. (1985). *Mass murder: America's growing menace.* New York: Plenum.

Lewis, D. O. (1992). From abuse to violence: Psychophysiological consequences of maltreatment. *Journal of the American Academy of Child and Adolescent Psychiatry, 31,* 383-391.

Lewis, D. O., Lovely, R., Yeager, C., & Femina, D. D. (1989). Toward a theory of the genesis of violence: A follow-up study of delinquents. *Journal of the American Academy of Child and Adolescent Psychiatry, 28,* 431-436.

Lewis, D. O., Lovely, R., Yeager, C., Ferguson, G., Friedman, M., Sloane, G., Friedman, H., & Pincus, J. H. (1988). Intrinsic and environmental characteristics of juvenile murderers. *Journal of the American Academy of Child and Adolescent Psychiatry, 27,* 582-587.

Lewis, D. O., Moy, E., Jackson, L. D., Aaronson, R., Restifo, N., Serra, S., & Simos, A. (1985). Biopsychosocial characteristics of children who later murder: A prospective study. *American Journal of Psychiatry, 142,* 1161-1167.

Lewis, D. O., Pincus, J. H., Bard, B., Richardson, E., Feldman, M., Prichep, L. S., & Yeager, C. (1988). Neuropsychiatric, psychoeducational, and family characteristics of 14 juveniles condemned to death in the United States. *American Journal of Psychiatry, 145,* 584-589.

Lewis, D. O., Pincus, J. H., Feldman, M., Jackson, L., & Bard, B. (1986). Psychiatric, neurological, and psychoeducational characteristics of 15 death row inmates in the United States. *American Journal of Psychiatry, 143,* 838-845.

Lewis, D. O., Shanok, S. S., Grant, M., & Ritvo, E. (1983). Homicidally aggressive young children: Neuropsychiatric and experimental correlates. *American Journal of Psychiatry, 140,* 148-153.

Lewis, D. O., Yeager, C., Cobham-Portorreal, C. S., Klein, N., Showalter, C., & Anthony, A. (1991). A follow-up of female delinquents: Maternal contributions to the perpetuation of deviance. *Journal of the American Academy of Child Psychiatry, 302,* 197-201.

Leyton, E. (1986). *Compulsive killers: The story of modern multiple murderers.* New York: New York University Press.

Lindqvist, P. (1991). Homicides committed by abusers of alcohol and illicit drugs. *British Journal of Addiction, 86,* 321-326.

Lipsey, M., & Wilson, D. (1993). The efficacy of psychological, education, and behavioral treatment: Confirmation from meta-analysis. *American Psychologist, 48,* 1181-1209.

Lizotte, A. J., Tesoriero, J. M., Thornberry, T. P., & Krohn, M. D. (1994). Patterns of adolescent firearms ownership and use. *Justice Quarterly, 16,* 51-73.

Loftin, C. (1986). The validity of robbery-murder classifications in Baltimore. *Violence and Victims, 1,* 191-204.

Loftin, C., & Hill, R. H. (1974). Regional culture and homicide: An examination of the Gastil-Hackney thesis. *American Sociological Review, 39,* 714-724.

Loftin, C., McDowall, D., & Wiersema, B. (1992). A comparative study of the preventive effects of mandatory sentencing laws for gun crimes. *Journal of Criminal Law and Criminology, 83,* 378-394.

Loftin, C., & Parker, R. N. (1985). An errors-in-variable model of the effect of poverty on urban homicide rates. *Criminology, 23,* 269-285.

Logan, C. H. (1982). Problems in ratio correlation: The case of deterrence research. *Social Forces, 60,* 791-810.

Logan, J. R., & Messner, S. F. (1987). Racial residential segregation and suburban violent crime. *Social Science Quarterly, 68,* 510-527.

Lott, J. R., Jr., & Mustard, D. B. (1997). Crime, deterrence and right-to-carry concealed handguns. *Journal of Legal Studies, 26,* 1-68.

Lottier, S. (1938). Distribution of criminal offenses in sectional regions. *Journal of Criminal Law, Criminology and Police Science, 29,* 329-344.

Lowry, P. W., Hassig, S., Gunn, R., & Mathison, J. (1988). Homicide victims in New Orleans: Recent trends. *American Journal of Epidemiology, 128,* 1130-1136.

Luckenbill, D. F. (1977). Criminal homicide as a situated transaction. *Social Problems, 25,* 176-186.

Lundsgaarde, H. P. (1977). *Murder in space city.* New York: Oxford University Press.

Lupfer, M., Hopkinson, P. J., & Kelley, P. (1988). An exploration of the attributional styles of Christian fundamentalists and authoritarians. *Journal of Scientific Study of Religion, 27,* 389-398.

Lynch, J. (1995). Crime in international perspective. In J. W. Wilson & J. Petersilia (Eds.), *Crime* (pp. 16-38). San Francisco: Institute for Contemporary Studies.

Macdonald, J. M. (1963). The threat to kill. *American Journal of Psychiatry, 120,* 125-130.

Macdonald, J. M. (1968). *Homicidal threats.* Springfield, IL: Charles C Thomas.

Mack Smith, D. (1969). *Italy: A modern history.* Ann Arbor: University of Michigan Press.

Mack, J., Scherl, D., & Macht, L. (1973). Children who kill their mothers. In A. J. Anthony & C. Koupernik (Eds.), *The child and his family: The impact of disease and death* (pp. 319-332). New York: Wiley Interscience.

Magid, K., & McKelvey, C. A. (1988). *High risk: Children without a conscience.* New York: Bantam.

Maguigan, H. (1991). Battered women and self-defense: Myths and misconceptions in current reform proposals. *University of Pennsylvania Law Review, 140,* 379-486.

Maguire, E. R., & Snipes, J. B. (1994). Reassessing the link between country music and suicide. *Social Forces, 72,* 1239-1243.

Malamuth, N. M., & Donnerstein, E. (1984). *Pornography and sexual aggression.* Orlando, FL: Academic Press.

Malmquist, C. P. (1971). Premonitory signs of homicidal aggression in juveniles. *American Journal of Psychiatry, 128,* 461-465.

Malmquist, C. P. (1990). Depression in homicidal adolescents. *Bulletin of the American Academy of Psychiatry and the Law, 18,* 23-36.

Mann, C. R. (1993). *Unequal justice: A question of color.* Bloomington: Indiana University Press.

Markowitz, F. E., & Felson, R. B. (1998). Social-demographic attitudes and violence. *Criminology, 36,* 117-138.

Markwardt, A. H. (1957). Principal and subsidiary dialect areas of the north-central states. *Publications of the American Dialect Society, 27,* 3-15.

Marshall, M. (Ed.). (1979). *Beliefs, behaviors, and alcoholic beverages: A cross-cultural survey.* Ann Arbor: University of Michigan Press.

Marten, G. W. (1965). Adolescent murderers. *Southern Medical Journal, 58,* 1217-1218.

Martinez, R., Jr. (1996). Latinos and lethal violence: The impact of poverty and inequality. *Social Problems, 43,* 131-146.

Martinez, R., Jr. (1997a). Homicide among Miami's ethnic groups: Anglos, Blacks, and Latinos in the 1990s. *Homicide Studies, 1,* 17-34.

Martinez, R., Jr. (1997b). Homicide among the 1980 Mariel refugees in Miami: Victims and offenders. *Hispanic Journal of Behavioral Sciences, 19,* 107-122.

Marzuk, P. M., Tardiff, K., & Hirsch, C. S. (1992). The epidemiology of murder-suicide. *Journal of the American Medical Association, 267,* 3179-3183.

Matza, D. (1964). *Delinquency and drift.* New York: John Wiley.

Maxfield, M. G. (1989). Circumstances in Supplementary Homicide Reports: Variety and validity. *Criminology, 27,* 671-695.

Maxim, P. (1985). Cohort size and juvenile delinquency: A test of the Easterlin hypothesis. *Social Forces, 63,* 661-679.

Maxson, C. L. (1992). Collecting data from investigation files: Descriptions of three Los Angeles gang homicide projects. In C. R. Block & R. L. Block (Eds.), *Questions and answers in lethal and non-lethal violence* (pp. 87-95). Washington, DC: National Institute of Justice.

Maxson, C. L. (1996). *Street gang members on the move: The role of migration in the proliferation of street gangs in the U.S.* Tallahassee, FL: National Youth Gang Center.

Maxson, C. L., Gordon, M. A., & Klein, M. W. (1985). Differences between gang and nongang homicides. *Criminology, 23,* 209-222.

Maxson, C. L., & Klein, M. W. (1990). Street gang violence: Twice as great, or half as great? In C. R. Huff (Ed.), *Gangs in America* (pp. 71-100). Newbury Park, CA: Sage.

Maxson, C. L., & Klein, M. W. (1996). Defining gang homicide: An updated look at member and motive approaches. In C. R. Huff (Ed.), *Gangs in America* (2nd ed., pp. 3-20). Thousand Oaks, CA: Sage.

Maxson, C. L., & Klein, M. W. (1997). Urban street gangs in Los Angeles. In M. Dear & P. Ethington (Eds.), *Los Angeles versus Chicago: Re-envisioning the urban process.* Unpublished report, University of Southern California, Southern California Studies Center, Los Angeles.

Maxson, C. L., Klein, M. W., & Cunningham, L. (1992). *Definitional variations affecting drug and gang homicide issues.* Los Angeles: University of Southern California, Center for the Study of Crime and Social Control, Social Science Research Institute.

Maxson, C. L., Woods, K. J., & Klein, M. W. (1995). *Street gang migration in the United States.* Los Angeles: University of Southern California, Center for the Study of Crime and Social Control, Social Science Research Institute.

Mayr, E. (1983). How to carry out the adaptationist program? *American Naturalist, 121,* 324-334.

McBride, D. C., Burgman-Habermehl, C., Alpert, J., & Chitwood, D. (1986). Drugs and homicide. *Bulletin of the New York Academy of Medicine, 62,* 497-508.

McCall, P. L., Land, K. C., & Cohen, L. E. (1992). Violent criminal behavior: Is there a general and continuing influence of the South? *Social Science Research, 21,* 286-310.

McCarthy, J. B. (1978). Narcissism and the self in homicidal adolescents. *American Journal of Psychoanalysis, 38,* 19-29.

McCarthy, M. A. (1968). Comparison of classification of place of residence on death certificates and matching census records. *Vital and health statistics: Data evaluation and methods research* (Series 2, No. 30). Washington, DC: National Center for Health Statistics.

McDonald, L. (1976). *The sociology of law and order.* Boulder, CO: Westview.

McDowall, D., Loftin, C., & Wiersema, B. (1992a). A comparative study of the preventive effects of mandatory sentencing laws for gun crimes. *Journal of Criminal Law and Criminology, 83,* 378-394.

McDowall, D., Loftin, C., & Wiersema, B. (1992b). *The incidence of civilian defensive firearm use.* Unpublished manuscript, University of Maryland-College Park, Institute of Criminal Justice.

McDowall, D., Loftin, C., & Wiersema, B. (1995). Easing concealed firearms laws: Effects on homicide in three states. *Journal of Criminal Law and Criminology, 86,* 193-206.

McFarland, S. G. (1983). Is capital punishment a short-term deterrent to homicide? A study of the effects of four recent American executions. *Journal of Criminal Law and Criminology, 74,* 1014-1030.

McGahey, R. M. (1980). Dr. Ehrlich's magic bullet: Economic theory, econometrics, and the death penalty. *Crime & Delinquency, 26,* 485-502.

Meddis, S. (1987, March 31). FBI: Possible to spot, help serial killers early. *USA Today,* p. 3A.

Medlicott, R. W. (1955). Paranoia of the exalted type in a setting of "folie a deux": A study of two adolescent homicides. *British Journal of Medical Psychology, 28,* 205-223.

Meehan, P. J., & O'Carroll, P. W. (1992). Gangs, drugs, and homicide in Los Angeles. *American Journal of Disease Control, 146,* 683-687.

Meiczkowski, T. M. (1996). The prevalence of drug use in the United States. In M. Tonry (Ed.), *Crime and justice: A review of research* (Vol. 20, pp. 349-414). Chicago: University of Chicago Press.

Menninger, K., & Mayman, M. (1956). Episodic dyscontrol: A third order of stress adaptation. *Bulletin of the Menninger Clinic, 20,* 153-165.

Mercy, J. A. (1988). Assaultive injury among Hispanics: A public health problem. In J. Kraus, S. Sorenson, & P. Juarez (Eds.), *Research conference on violence in Hispanic communities* (pp. 1-12). Washington, DC: U.S. Department of Health and Human Services.

Mercy, J. A., Rosenberg, M. L., Powell, K. E., Broome, C. V., & Roper, W. L. (1993). Public health policy for preventing violence. *Health Affairs, 12*(4), 7-29.

Mercy, J. A., & Saltzman, L. E. (1989). Fatal violence among spouses in the United States. *American Journal of Public Health, 79,* 595-599.

Merton, R. K. (1938). Social structure and anomie. *American Sociological Review, 3,* 672-682.

Messerschmidt, J. W. (1993). *Masculinities and crime: Critique and reconceptualization.* Lanham, MD: Rowman & Littlefield.

Messner, S. F. (1980). Income inequality and murder rates: Some cross-national findings. *Comparative Social Research, 3,* 185-198.

Messner, S. F. (1982a). Poverty, inequality, and the urban homicide rate: Some unexpected findings. *Criminology, 20,* 103-114.

Messner, S. F. (1982b). Societal development, social equality, and homicide: A cross-national test of a Durkheimian model. *Social Forces, 61,* 225-240.

Messner, S. F. (1983a). Regional and racial effects on the urban homicide rate: The subculture of violence revisited. *American Journal of Sociology, 88,* 997-1007.

Messner, S. F. (1983b). Regional difference in the economic correlates of the urban homicide rate: Some evidence of the importance of culture context. *Criminology, 21,* 477-488.

Messner, S. F. (1985). Sex differences in arrest rates for homicide: An application of the general theory of structural strain. *Comparative Social Research, 8,* 187-201.

Messner, S. F. (1988). Research on cultural and socioeconomic factors in criminal violence. *Psychiatric Clinics of North America, 16,* 511-525.

Messner, S. F. (1989). Economic discrimination and societal homicide rates: Further evidence on the cost of inequality. *American Sociological Review, 54,* 597-611.

Messner, S. F. (1992). Exploring the consequences of erratic data reporting for cross-national research on homicide. *Journal of Quantitative Criminology, 8,* 155-173.

Messner, S. F., & Golden, R. M. (1992). Racial inequality and racially disaggregated homicide rates: An assessment of alternative theoretical explanations. *Criminology, 30,* 421-447.

Messner, S. F., & Rosenfeld, R. (1997a). *Crime and the American dream* (2nd ed.). Belmont, CA: Wadsworth.

Messner, S. F., & Rosenfeld, R. (1997b). Political restraint of the market and levels of criminal homicide: A cross-national application of institutional-anomie theory. *Social Forces, 75,* 1393-1416.

Messner, S. F., & Sampson, R. J. (1991). The sex ratio, family disruption, and rates of violent crime: The paradox of demographic structure. *Social Forces, 69,* 693-713.

Messner, S. F., & South, S. J. (1992). Interracial homicide: A macrostructural-opportunity perspective. *Sociological Forum, 7,* 517-536.

Messner, S. F., & Tardiff, K. (1986). Economic inequality and levels of homicide: An analysis of urban neighborhoods. *Criminology, 24,* 297-319.

Mezzich, J. E., & Solomon, H. (1980). Cluster analysis of iris specimens. In P. H. Rossi (Ed.), *Taxonomy and behavioral science: Comparative performance of grouping methods* (pp. 84-107). New York: Academic Press.

Michaels, J. J. (1961). Enuresis in murderous aggressive children and adolescents. *Archives of General Psychiatry, 5,* 94-97.

Miller, B. A., & Downs, W. R. (1993). The impact of family violence on the use of alcohol by women: Research indicates that women with alcohol problems have experienced high rates of violence during their childhoods and as adults. *Alcohol Health and Research World, 17,* 137-142.

Miller, D., & Looney, J. (1974). The prediction of adolescent homicide: Episodic dyscontrol and dehumanization. *American Journal of Psychoanalysis, 34,* 187-198.

Miller, J. G. (1984). Culture and the development of everyday social explanation. *Journal of Personality and Social Psychology, 46,* 961-978.

Miller, L. S., & Block, C. R. (1983). *Illinois murder victim data 1973-1981: Guide to quality, availability, and interpretation.* Chicago: Illinois Criminal Justice Information Authority.

Miller, W. B. (1958). Lower class culture as a generating milieu in gang delinquency. *Journal of Social Issues, 14,* 5-19.

Miller, W. B. (1992). *Crime by youth gangs and groups in the United States.* Washington, DC: Office of Juvenile Justice and Delinquency Prevention. (Original report issued 1982)

Miller, W. B. (1996). *The growth of youth gang problems in the U.S.: 1970-1995.* Tallahassee, FL: National Youth Gang Center, Institute for Intergovernmental Research.

Mladenka, K. R., & Hill, K. Q. (1976). A reexamination of the etiology of urban crime. *Criminology, 13,* 491-506.

Mohr, J. W., & McKnight, C. K. (1971). Violence as a function of age and relationship with special reference to matricide. *Canadian Psychiatric Association Journal, 16,* 29-32.

Mones, P. (1991). *When a child kills: Abused children who kill their parents.* New York: Pocket.

Monkkonen, E. (1995). Racial factors in New York City homicides. In D. F. Hawkins (Ed.), *Ethnicity, race, and crime: Perspectives across time and place* (pp. 99-120). Albany: State University of New York Press.

Montell, W. L. (1986). *Killings: Folk justice in the upper South.* Lexington: University Press of Kentucky.

Moore, J. (1991). *Going down to the barrio: Homeboys and homegirls in change.* Philadelphia: Temple University Press.

Moore, J., & Pinderhughes, R. (1993). Introduction. In J. Moore & R. Pinderhughes (Eds.), *In the barrios: Latinos and the underclass debate* (pp. xi-xxxix). New York: Russell Sage.

Moore, M. H. (1980). Police and weapons offenses. *Annals of the American Academy of Political and Social Science, 452,* 22-32.

Moore, M. H. (1981). Keeping handguns from criminal offenders. *Annals of the American Academy of Political and Social Science, 455,* 92-109.

Moore, M. H. (1983). The bird in hand: A feasible strategy for gun control. *Journal of Policy Analysis and Management, 2,* 185-195.

Morenoff, J. D., & Sampson, R. J. (1997). Violent crime and the spatial dynamics of neighborhood transition: Chicago, 1970-1990. *Social Forces, 76,* 31-64.

Moriyama, I. M., Baum, W. S., Haenszel, W. M., & Mattison, B. F. (1958). Inquiry into diagnostic evidence supporting medical certifications of death. *American Journal of Public Health, 48,* 1376-1387.

Morselli, H. (1903). *Suicide: An essay in comparative moral statistics.* New York: Appleton. (Original work published 1879)

Mrazek, P., & Haggerty, R. J. (Eds.). (1994). *Reducing risks for mental disorders: Frontiers for preventive intervention research* (Institute of Medicine, Division of Biobehavioral Sciences and Mental Disorders, Committee on the Prevention of Mental Disorders). Washington, DC: National Academy Press.

Muller, T. (1993). *Immigrants and the American city.* New York: New York University Press.

Murray, C. (1996). Rethinking DALYs. In C. Murray & A. D. Lopez (Eds.), *The global burden of disease: A comprehensive assessment of mortality and disability from disease, injuries, and risk factors in 1990 and projected to 2020* (pp. 1-98). Geneva, Switzerland: World Health Organization.

Murray, C., & Lopez, A. D. (1996a). Estimating causes of death: New methods and global and regional applications for 1990. In C. Murray & A. D. Lopez (Eds.), *The global burden of disease: A comprehensive assessment of mortality and disability from disease, injuries, and risk factors in 1990 and projected to 2020* (pp. 118-200). Geneva, Switzerland: World Health Organization.

Murray, C., & Lopez, A. D. (Eds.). (1996b). *The global burden of disease: A comprehensive assessment of mortality and disability from disease, injuries, and risk factors in 1990 and projected to 2020.* Geneva, Switzerland: World Health Organization.

Muscat, J. E. (1988). Characteristics of childhood homicide in Ohio, 1974-84. *American Journal of Public Health, 78,* 822-824.

Myers, W. C. (1992). What treatments do we have for children and adolescents who have killed? *Bulletin of the American Academy of Psychiatry and the Law, 20,* 47-58.

Myers, W. C., & Kemph, J. P. (1988). Characteristics and treatment of four homicidal adolescents. *Journal of the American Academy of Child and Adolescent Psychiatry, 27,* 595-599.

Myers, W. C., & Kemph, J. P. (1990). DSM-IIIR classification of homicidal youth: Help or hindrance. *Journal of Clinical Psychiatry, 51,* 239-242.

Myers, W. C., & Mutch, P. A. (1992). Language disorders in disruptive behavior disordered homicidal youth. *Journal of Forensic Sciences, 37,* 919-922.

NAACP Legal Defense and Educational Fund, Inc. (1992). *Death row, U.S.A.* New York: Author.

National Archives of Criminal Justice Data. (1998). Mortality data [On-line]. Available: http://www.icpsr.umich.edu/nacjd/

National Center for Health Statistics. (1967). Homicide in the United States 1950-1964. *Vital and Health Statistics* (Series 20, No. 6). Washington, DC: Government Printing Office.

National Center for Health Statistics. (1976). *Vital statistics of the United States 1975* (Vol. 2, Mortality, Pt. A). Washington, DC: Government Printing Office.

National Center for Health Statistics. (1982). Annotated bibliography of cause-of-death validation studies: 1958-

1980. *Vital and health statistics* (Series 2, No. 89). Washington, DC: Government Printing Office.

National Center for Health Statistics. (1985). *Vital statistics of the United States 1980* (Vol. 2, Mortality, Pt. A, Tech. Appendix). Washington, DC: Government Printing Office.

National Center for Health Statistics. (1994). *Vital statistics of the United States 1990* (Vol. 1, Natality). Washington, DC: Government Printing Office.

National Center for Health Statistics. (1996). *Vital statistics of the United States 1992* (Vol. 2, Mortality, Pt. A, Tech. Appendix). Washington, DC: Government Printing Office.

National Center for Health Statistics. (Selected years). *Vital statistics of the United States* (Vol. 2, Mortality, Pt. A). Washington, DC: Government Printing Office.

National Commission on Law Observance and Enforcement. (1931). *Report on crime and the foreign born.* Washington, DC: Government Printing Office.

National Youth Gang Center. (1997). *1995 National youth gang survey.* Washington, DC: Office of Juvenile Justice and Delinquency Prevention.

Neapolitan, J. L. (1994). Cross-national variation in homicides: The case of Latin America. *International Criminal Justice Review, 4,* 4-22.

Neapolitan, J. L. (1996). Cross-national crime data: Some unaddressed problems. *Journal of Criminal Justice, 19,* 95-112.

Nelsen, C., Corzine, J., & Huff-Corzine, L. (1994). The violent West reexamined: A research note on regional homicide rates. *Criminology, 32,* 149-161.

Nesse, R. M. (1990). Evolutionary explanations of emotions. *Human Nature, 1,* 261-289.

Nesse, R. M., & Williams, G. C. (1994). *Why we get sick.* New York: Random House.

Neuman, W. L., & Berger, R. J. (1988). Competing perspectives on cross-national crime: An evaluation of theory and evidence. *Sociological Quarterly, 29,* 281-313.

Nisbett, R. E. (1993). Violence and U.S. regional culture. *American Psychologist, 48,* 441-449.

Nisbett, R. E., & Ross, L. (1980). *Human inference: Strategies and shortcomings of social judgment.* Englewood Cliffs, NJ: Prentice Hall.

Nisbett, R. E., & Wilson, T. D. (1977). Telling more than we can know: Verbal reports on mental processes. *Psychological Review, 84,* 231-259.

Norris, J. (1988). *Serial killers: The growing menace.* New York: Doubleday.

O'Brien, R. M. (1989). Relative cohort size and age-specific crime rates: An age-period-relative cohort size model. *Criminology, 27,* 57-78.

O'Carroll, P. W., & Mercy, J. A. (1986). Patterns and recent trends in Black homicide. In D. F. Hawkins (Ed.), *Homicide among Black Americans* (pp. 29-42). Lanham, MD: University Press of America.

O'Halloran, C. M., & Altmaier, E. M. (1996). Awareness of death among children: Does a life-threatening illness alter the process of discovery? *Journal of Counseling and Development, 74,* 259-262.

O'Reilly-Fleming, T. (1996). *Serial and mass murder: Theory, research and policy.* Toronto, Ontario: Canadian Scholars' Press.

Odum, H. W. (1936). *Southern regions of the United States.* Chapel Hill: University of North Carolina Press.

Odum, H. W., & Moore, H. E. (1966). *American regionalism.* Glouster, MA: Peter Smith. (Original work published 1938)

Office of National Drug Control Policy. (1995). *National drug control strategy: Executive summary.* Washington, DC: Author.

Ogle, R. S., Maier-Katkin, D., & Bernard, T. J. (1995). A theory of homicidal behavior among women. *Criminology, 33,* 173-193.

Olds, D. L., Henderson, C. R., Chamberlin, R., & Tatelbaum, R. (1986). Preventing child abuse and neglect: A randomized trial of nurse home visitation. *Pediatrics, 78,* 65-78.

Ortega, S. T., Corzine, J., Burnett, C., & Poyer, T. (1992). Modernization, age structure and regional context: A cross-national study of crime. *Sociological Spectrum, 12,* 257-277.

Osgood, D. W. (1995). *Drugs, alcohol, and violence.* Boulder: University of Colorado, Institute of Behavioral Science.

Paluszny, M., & McNabb, M. (1975). Therapy of a six-year-old who committed fratricide. *Journal of the American Academy of Child Psychiatry, 14,* 319-336.

Pampel, F., C., & Gartner, R. (1995). Age structure, socio-political institutions, and national homicide rates. *European Sociological Review, 16,* 243-260.

Panel on Research on Child Abuse and Neglect, Commission on Behavioral and Social Sciences and Education, National Research Council. (1993). *Understanding child abuse and neglect.* Washington, DC: National Academy Press.

Parker, K. F., & McCall, P. L. (1997). Adding another piece to the inequality-homicide puzzle: The impact of structural inequality on racially disaggregated homicide rates. *Homicide Studies, 1,* 35-60.

Parker, R. N. (1989). Poverty, subculture of violence, and type of homicide. *Social Forces, 67,* 983-1007.

Parker, R. N. (1993a). Alcohol and theories of homicide. In F. Adler & W. Laufer (Eds.), *Advances in criminological theory* (Vol. 4, pp. 113-142). New Brunswick, NJ: Transaction Publishing.

Parker, R. N. (1993b). The effects of context on alcohol and violence. *Alcohol Health and Research World, 17,* 117-122.

Parker, R. N. (1995). Bringing "booze" back in: The relationship between alcohol and homicide. *Journal of Research in Crime and Delinquency, 32,* 3-38.

Parker, R. N. (1998). Alcohol, homicide, and cultural context. *Homicide Studies, 2,* 6-30.

Parker, R. N., & Rebhun, L. (1995). *Alcohol and homicide: A deadly combination of two American traditions.* Albany: State University of New York Press.

Parker, R. N., & Smith, M. D. (1979). Deterrence, poverty, and type of homicide. *American Journal of Sociology, 85,* 614-624.

Parker, R. N., & Toth, A. T. (1990). Family, intimacy, and homicide: A macro-social approach. *Violence and Victims, 5,* 195-210.

Parrillo, V. N. (1994). *Strangers to these shores: Race and ethnic relations in the United States* (4th ed.). New York: Macmillan.

Passell, P. (1975). The deterrent effect of the death penalty: A statistical test. *Stanford Law Review, 28,* 61-80.

Passell, P., & Taylor, J. (1977). The deterrent effect of capital punishment. *American Economic Review, 67,* 445-451.

Patterson, E. B. (1991). Poverty, income inequality, and community crime rates. *Criminology, 29,* 755-776.

Patterson, R. M. (1943). Psychiatric study of juveniles involved in homicide. *American Journal of Orthopsychiatry, 13,* 125-130.

Pears, E. (Ed.). (1872). *Prisons and reformatories at home and abroad.* London: Transactions of the International Penitentiary Congress.

Pernanen, K. (1976). Alcohol and crimes of violence. In B. Kissin & H. Beglieter (Eds.), *The biology of alcoholism: Social aspects of alcoholism* (pp. 351-444). New York: Plenum.

Pernanen, K. (1981). Theoretical aspects of the relationship between alcohol use and crime. In J. J. Collins, Jr. (Ed.), *Drinking and crime: Perspectives on the relationship between alcohol consumption and criminal behavior* (pp. 1-69). New York: Guilford.

Pernanen, K. (1991). *Alcohol in human violence.* New York: Guilford.

Petee, T. A., & Kowalski, G. S. (1993). Modeling rural violent crime rates: A test of social disorganization theory. *Sociological Focus, 26,* 87-89.

Peterson, R. A., & DiMaggio, P. (1975). From region to class: The changing focus of country music. *Social Forces, 53,* 497-506.

Peterson, R. D., & Bailey, W. C. (1988). Murder and capital punishment in the evolving context of the post-*Furman* era. *Social Forces, 66,* 774-807.

Peterson, R. D., & Bailey, W. C. (1991). Felony murder and capital punishment: An examination of the deterrence question. *Criminology, 29,* 367-395.

Peterson, R. D., & Krivo, L. J. (1993). Racial segregation and Black urban homicide. *Social Forces, 71,* 1001-1026.

Petti, T. A., & Davidman, L. (1981). Homicidal school-age children: Cognitive style and demographic features. *Child Psychiatry and Human Development, 12,* 82-89.

Pettigrew, T. F., & Spier, R. B. (1962). The ecological structure of Negro homicide. *American Journal of Sociology 67,* 621-629.

Pfeffer, C. R. (1980). Psychiatric hospital treatment of assaultive homicidal children. *American Journal of Psychotherapy, 342,* 197-207.

Phillips, D. P. (1980). The deterrent effect of capital punishment: New evidence on an old controversy. *American Journal of Sociology, 86,* 139-148.

Pierce, G. L., & Bowers, W. J. (1981). The Bartley-Fox Gun Law's short-term impact on crime in Boston. *Annals of the American Academy of Political and Social Science, 455,* 120-137.

Pierce, G. L., & Fox, J. A. (1992). *Recent trends in violent crime: A closer look.* Unpublished manuscript, Northeastern University, Boston.

Pihl, R. O., Peterson, J. B., & Lau, M. A. (1993). A biosocial model of the alcohol-aggression relationship. *Journal of Studies on Alcohol* (Suppl. 11), 128-139.

Pincus, J. H. (1993). Neurologists' role in understanding violence. *Archives of Neurology, 8,* 867-869.

Poggio, E. C., Kennedy, S. D., Chaiken, J. M., & Carlson, K. E. (1985). *Blueprint for the future of the Uniform Crime Reporting Program: Final report of the UCR study.* Boston: Abt Associates.

Pokorny, A. (1965). Human violence: A comparison of homicide, aggravated assault, suicide, and attempted suicide. *Journal of Criminal Law, Criminology and Police Science, 56,* 488-497.

Polk, K., & Ranson, D. (1991). The role of gender in intimate homicide. *Australia and New Zealand Journal of Criminology, 24,* 15-24.

Polsby, D. D. (1993, October). Equal protection. *Reason, 25,* 35-38.

Portes, A., Clark, J. M., & Manning, R. (1985). After Mariel: A survey of the resettlement experiences of 1980 Cuban refugees in Miami. *Cuban Studies, 15,* 37-59.

Portes, A., & Rumbaut, R. G. (1996). *Immigrant America* (2nd ed.). Berkeley: University of California Press.

Post, S. (1982). Adolescent parricide in abusive families. *Child Welfare, 61,* 445-455.

Powell, K. E., & Hawkins, D. F. (Eds.). (1996). Youth violence prevention: Descriptions and baseline data from 13 evaluation projects [Suppl.]. *American Journal of Preventive Medicine, 12*(5).

Prentky, R. A., Burgess, A. W., & Rokous, F. (1989). The presumptive role of fantasy in serial sexual homicide. *American Journal of Psychiatry, 146,* 887-891.

Prothrow-Stith, D., & Weissman, M. (1991). *Deadly consequences.* New York: HarperCollins.

Przybylski, R. K., & Block, C. R. (1991, November). *Drug-related homicides in Chicago: Trends over twenty-five years.* Paper presented at the annual meeting of the American Society of Criminology, San Francisco.

Quinn, J. F., Tobolowsky, P. M., & Downs, W. T. (1994). The gang problem in large and small cities: An analysis of police perceptions in nine states. *The Gang Journal, 2,* 13-22.

Quinney, R. (1965). Suicide, homicide, and economic development. *Social Forces, 43,* 401-406.

Radzinowicz, L. (1966). *Ideology and crime.* New York: Columbia University Press.

Rand, M. R. (1993). The study of homicide caseflow: Creating a comprehensive homicide data set. In C. R. Block & R. L. Block (Eds.), *Questions and answers in lethal and non-lethal violence: Proceedings of the homicide research working group* (pp. 103-118). Washington, DC: Government Printing Office.

Rasche, C. E. (1993). Given reasons for violence in intimate relationships. In A. V. Wilson (Ed.), *Homicide: The victim/offender connection* (pp. 75-100). Cincinnati, OH: Anderson.

Ray, M. C., & Simons, R. L. (1987). Convicted murderers' accounts of their crimes: A study of homicide in small communities. *Symbolic Interaction, 10,* 57-70.

Reaves, B. A. (1993). *Using NIBRS data to analyze violent crime* (Bureau of Justice Statistics Tech. Rep. NCJ-144785). Washington, DC: Government Printing Office.

Redfield, H. V. (1880). *Homicide, North and South.* Philadelphia: J. B. Lippincott.

Reed, J. S. (1971). To live and die in Dixie: A contribution to the study of southern violence. *Political Science Quarterly, 86,* 429-443.

Reed, J. S. (1976). The heart of Dixie: An essay in folk geography. *Social Forces, 54,* 925-939.

Reed, J. S. (1982). *One South: An ethnic approach to regional culture.* Baton Rouge: Louisiana State University Press.

Reed, J. S. (1993). *My tears spoiled my aim and other reflections on southern culture.* Columbia: University of Missouri Press.

Reiss, A. J., Jr., & Roth, J. A. (Eds.). (1993). *Understanding and preventing violence: Vol. 3. Social influences.* Washington, DC: National Academy Press.

Ressler, R. K., Burgess, A. W., & Douglas, J. E. (1988). *Sexual homicide: Patterns and motives.* Lexington, MA: Lexington Books.

Restifo, N., & Lewis, D. O. (1985). Three case reports of a single homicidal adolescent. *American Journal of Psychiatry, 142,* 388.

Rice, T. W., & Goldman, C. R. (1994). Another look at the subculture of violence thesis: Who murders whom and under what circumstances. *Sociological Spectrum, 14,* 371-384.

Richards, P., & Tittle, C. R. (1981). Gender and perceived chances of arrest. *Social Forces, 59,* 1182-1199.

Riedel, M. (1990). Nationwide homicide data sets: An evaluation of the uniform crime reports and National Center for Health Statistics data. In D. L. MacKenzie, P. J. Baunach, & R. R. Roberg (Eds.), *Measuring crime: Large-scale, long-range efforts* (pp. 175-205). Albany: State University of New York Press.

Riedel, M. (1993). *Stranger violence: A theoretical inquiry.* New York: Garland.

Riedel, M. (1998). Counting stranger homicides: A case study of statistical prestidigitation. *Homicide Studies, 2,* 206-219.

Riedel, M. (Ed.). (1987). Symposium on stranger violence: Perspectives, issues, and problems [Special issue]. *Journal of Criminal Law and Criminology, 78*(2).

Riedel, M., & Lewitt, K. N. (1996, November). *Hispanic homicides in Los Angeles: A study of racial and ethnic patterns.* Paper presented at the annual meeting of the American Society of Criminology, Chicago.

Riedel, M., & Przybylski, R. J. (1993). Stranger murders and assault: A study of a neglected form of stranger violence. In A. V. Wilson (Ed.), *Homicide: The victim/offender connection* (pp. 359-382). Cincinnati, OH: Anderson.

Riedel, M., & Rinehart, T. A. (1996). Murder clearances and missing data. *Journal of Crime and Justice, 19,* 83-102.

Riedel, M., & Zahn, M. A. (1985). *National Institute of Justice research report: The nature and patterns of American homicide.* Washington, DC: Government Printing Office.

Rodriguez, O. (1988). Hispanics and homicide in New York City. In J. Kraus, S. Sorenson, & P. Juarez (Eds.), *Proceedings of research conference on violence and homicide in Hispanic communities, September 14-15, 1987* (pp. 67-84). Los Angeles: University of California.

Rodriquez, S. F., & Henderson, V. A. (1995). Intimate homicide: Victim-offender relationship in female-perpetrated homicide. *Deviant Behavior, 16,* 45-57.

Rojek, D. G., & Williams, J. L. (1993). Interracial vs. intraracial offenses in terms of the victim/offender relationship. In A. V. Wilson (Ed.), *Homicide: The victim/offender connection* (pp. 249-266). Cincinnati, OH: Anderson.

Rokaw, W. M., Mercy, J. A., & Smith, J. C. (1990). Comparing death certificate data with FBI crime reporting statistics on U.S. homicides. *Public Health Reports, 105,* 447-455.

Roncek, D. W., & Maier, P. A. (1991). Bars, blocks, and crimes revisited: Linking the theory of routine activities to the empiricism of hot spots. *Criminology, 29,* 725-754.

Room, R., & Collins, G. (Eds.). (1983). *Alcohol and disinhibition: Nature and meaning of the link* (Research Monograph 12). Washington, DC: National Institute on Alcohol Abuse and Alcoholism.

Rose, H. M., & McClain, P. D. (1990). *Race, place, and risk: Black homicide in urban America.* Albany: State University of New York Press.

Rose, H. M., & McClain, P. D. (1998). Race, place, and risk revisited: A perspective on the emergence of a new subcultural paradigm. *Homicide Studies, 2,* 101-129.

Rosenfeld, R. (1986). Urban crime rates: Effects of inequality, welfare dependency, region and race. In J. M. Byrne & R. J. Sampson (Eds.), *The social ecology of crime* (pp. 116-130). New York: Springer-Verlag.

Rosenfeld, R. (1997). Changing relationships between men and women: A note on the decline in intimate partner homicide. *Homicide Studies, 1,* 72-83.

Rosenfeld, R., & Messner, S. F. (1991). The social sources of homicide in different types of societies. *Sociological Forum, 6,* 51-70.

Rosner, R., Weiderlight, M., Rosner, M. B. H., & Wieczorek, R. R. (1978). Adolescents accused of murder and manslaughter: A five year descriptive study. *Bulletin of the American Academy of Psychiatry and Law, 7,* 342-351.

Rumbaut, R. (1995). *Immigrants from Latin America and the Caribbean: A socioeconomic profile* (Statistical Brief No. 6). East Lansing: Michigan State University, Julian Samora Research Institute.

Russell, D. H. (1979). Ingredients of juvenile murder. *International Journal of Offender Therapy & Comparative Criminology, 23,* 65-72.

Russell, D. H. (1984). A study of juvenile murderers of family members. *International Journal of Offender Therapy & Comparative Criminology, 28,* 177-192.

Russell, D. H. (1986). Girls who kill. *International Journal of Offender Therapy & Comparative Criminology, 30,* 171-176.

Sadoff, R. L. (1971). Clinical observations on parricide. *Psychiatric Quarterly, 45,* 65-69.

Saltzman, L. E., Mercy, J. A., O'Carroll, P. W., Rosenberg, M. L., & Rhodes, P. H. (1992). Weapon involvement and injury outcomes in family and intimate assaults. *Journal of the American Medical Association, 267,* 3043-3047.

Samora, J., & Simon, P. V. (1977). *A history of the Mexican-American people.* South Bend, IN: University of Notre Dame Press.

Sampson, R. J. (1985). Race and criminal violence: A demographically disaggregated analysis of urban homicide. *Crime & Delinquency, 31,* 47-82.

Sampson, R. J. (1986). Crime in cities: The effects of formal and informal social control. In A. J. Reiss, Jr., & M. Tonry (Eds.), *Communities and crime* (pp. 271-311). Chicago: University of Chicago Press.

Sampson, R. J. (1987). Urban Black violence: The effect of male joblessness and family disruption. *American Journal of Sociology, 93,* 348-382.

Sampson, R. J. (1991). Linking the micro- and macrolevel dimensions of community social organization. *Social Forces, 70,* 43-64.

Sampson, R. J., & Groves, W. B. (1989). Community structure and crime: Testing social disorganization theory. *American Journal of Sociology, 94,* 774-802.

Sampson, R. J., & Lauritsen, J. (1993). Violent victimization and offending: Individual, situational, and community-level risk factors. In A. J. Reiss Jr. & J. A. Roth (Eds.), *Understanding and preventing violence: Vol. 3. Social influences* (pp. 1-114). Washington, DC: National Academy Press.

Sampson, R. J., Raudenbush, S. W., & Earls, F. (1997). Neighborhoods and violent crime: A multilevel study of collective efficacy. *Science, 277,* 918-924.

Sampson, R. J., & Wilson, W. J. (1995). Toward a theory of race, crime, and urban inequality. In J. Hagan & R. D. Peterson (Eds.), *Crime and inequality* (pp. 37-54). Stanford, CA: Stanford University Press.

Sanders, W. (1994). *Gangbangs and drive-bys: Grounded culture and juvenile gang violence.* New York: Aldine de Gruyter.

Sargent, D. (1962). Children who kill: A family conspiracy? *Social Work, 7,* 35-42.

Saunders, D. G., & Azar, S. (1989). Family violence treatment programs: Descriptions and evaluation. In L. Ohlin & M. Tonry (Eds.), *Family violence, crime and justice: A review of research* (Vol. 2, pp. 481-546). Chicago: University of Chicago Press.

Savitz, L. (1958). A study of capital punishment. *Journal of Criminal Law, Criminology and Police Science, 49,* 338-341.

Savitz, L. D. (1978). Official police statistics and their limitations. In L. D. Savitz & N. Johnston (Eds.), *Crime in society* (pp. 69-82). New York: John Wiley.

Schaefer, R. T. (1993). *Racial and ethnic groups* (5th ed.). New York: HarperCollins.

Schechter, S. (1982). *Women and male violence.* Boston: South End.

Scherl, D. J., & Mack, J. E. (1966). A study of adolescent matricide. *Journal of the American Academy of Child Psychiatry, 5,* 569-593.

Schneider, V. W., & Wiersema, B. (1990). Limits and use of the Uniform Crime Reports. In D. L. MacKenzie, P. J. Baunach, & R. R. Roberg (Eds.), *Measuring crime: Large-scale, long-range efforts* (pp. 21-48). Albany: State University of New York Press.

Schuerman, C. E., & Kobrin, S. (1986). Community careers in crime. In A. J. Reiss, Jr., & M. Tonry, *Communities and crime* (pp. 67-100). Chicago: University of Chicago Press.

Schuessler, K. (1952). The deterrent effect of the death penalty. *The Annals, 284,* 54-62.

Scudder, R. G., Blount, W. R., Heide, K. M., & Silverman, I. J. (1993). Important links between child abuse, neglect, and delinquency. *International Journal of Offender Therapy & Comparative Criminology, 37,* 315-323.

Sears, D. J. (1991). *To kill again.* Wilmington, DE: Scholarly Resources Books.

Seligman, M. E. P. (1990). *Learned optimism.* New York: Pocket.

Seligman, M. E. P. (1992). *Helplessness: On development, depression and death.* New York: Freeman.

Sellin, T. (1938). *Culture conflict and crime.* New York: Social Science Research Council.

Sellin, T. (1955). *The Royal Commission on capital punishment, 1949-1953: Report of the Great Britain Parliament* (Papers by Command 8932, pp. 17-24). London: HMSO.

Sellin, T. (1959). *The death penalty.* Philadelphia: American Law Institute.

Sellin, T. (1961). Capital punishment. *Federal Probation, 25*(3), 3-11.

Sellin, T. (1967). *Capital punishment.* New York: Harper & Row.

Sellin, T. (1980). *The penalty of death.* Beverly Hills, CA: Sage.

Sellin, T., & Wolfgang, M. (1964). *Measuring delinquency.* New York: John Wiley.

Sendi, I. B., & Blomgren, P. G. (1975). A comparative study of predictive criteria in the predisposition of homicidal adolescents. *American Journal of Psychiatry, 132,* 423-427.

Serial killers. (1992, October 18). NOVA. Boston: WGBH-TV.

Shaw, C. R. (1930). *The jack-roller: A delinquent boy's own story.* Chicago: University of Chicago Press.

Shaw, C. R., & McKay, H. D. (1931). *Social factors in juvenile delinquency* (Vol. 2 of Report on the Causes of Crime: National Commission on Law Observance and Enforcement Report No. 13). Washington, DC: Government Printing Office.

Shaw, C. R., & McKay, H. D. (1942). *Juvenile delinquency and urban areas.* Chicago: University of Chicago Press.

Shaw, C. R., & McKay, H. D. (1969). *Juvenile delinquency in urban areas.* Chicago: University of Chicago Press.

Sheley, J. F., & Wright, J. D. (1995). *In the line of fire: Youth, guns, and violence in urban America.* New York: Aldine de Gruyter.

Sherman, L., Gartin, R. P., & Buerger, M. E. (1989). Hot spots of predatory crime: Routine activities and the criminology of place. *Criminology, 27,* 27-56.

Sherman, L., & Langworthy, R. H. (1979). Measuring homicide by police officers. *Journal of Criminal Law and Criminology, 70,* 546-560.

Sherman, L., Shaw, J. W., & Rogan, D. P. (1995). *The Kansas City gun experiment.* Washington, DC: National Institute of Justice.

Shichor, D. (1990). Crime patterns and socioeconomic development: A cross-national analysis. *Criminal Justice Review, 15,* 64-77.

Shihadeh, E. S., & Flynn, N. (1996). Segregation and crime: The effect of Black social isolation on the rates of Black urban violence. *Social Forces, 74,* 1325-1352.

Shihadeh, E. S., & Maume, M. O. (1997). Segregation and crime: The relationship between Black centralization and urban Black homicide. *Homicide Studies, 1,* 254-280.

Shihadeh, E. S., & Steffensmeier, D. J. (1994). Economic inequality, family disruption, and urban Black violence: Cities as units of stratification and social control. *Social Forces, 73,* 729-751.

Shin, Y., Jedlicka, D., & Lee, E. S. (1977). Homicide among Blacks. *Phylon, 39,* 399-406.

Shoemaker, D. J., & Williams, J. S. (1987). The subculture of violence and ethnicity. *Journal of Criminal Justice, 15,* 461-472.

Short, J. F., Jr. (1996). *Gangs and adolescent violence.* Boulder: University of Colorado, Center for the Study and Prevention of Violence.

Silverman, I. J., & Dinitz, S. (1974). Compulsive masculinity and delinquency. *Criminology, 11,* 498-515.

Silvern, L., Waelde, L. C., Karyl, J., Hodges, W. F., Starke, J., Heidt, E., & Min, K. (1994). Relationships of parental abuse to college students' depression, trauma symptoms, and self-esteem. *Child, Youth, and Family Services Quarterly, 17,* 7-9.

Simpson, J. A., & Kenrick, D. (Eds.). (1997). *Evolutionary social psychology.* Mahwah, NJ: Lawrence Erlbaum.

Simpson, M. E. (1985). Violent crime, income inequality, and regional culture: Another look. *Sociological Focus, 18,* 199-208.

Skogan, W. (1978). *Weapon use in robbery: Patterns and policy implications.* Unpublished manuscript, Northwestern University, Evanston, IL.

Sleek, S. (1994, January). APA works to reduce violence in media. *The Monitor,* pp. 6-7.

Smith, C., & Thornberry, T. P. (1995). The relationship between childhood maltreatment and adolescent involvement in delinquency. *Criminology, 33,* 451-481.

Smith, D. A., & Jarjoura, G. R. (1988). Social structure and criminal victimization. *Journal of Research in Crime and Delinquency, 25,* 27-52.

Smith, M. D. (1986). The era of increased violence in the United States: Age, period, or cohort effect? *Sociological Quarterly, 27,* 239-251.

Smith, M. D. (1992). Variations in correlates of race-specific urban homicide rates. *Journal of Contemporary Criminal Justice, 8,* 137-149.

Smith, M. D. (1996). Sources of firearm acquisition among a sample of inner-city youths: Research results and policy implications. *Journal of Criminal Justice, 24,* 361-367.

Smith, M. D., & Brewer, V. E. (1992). A sex-specific analysis of correlates of homicide victimization in United States cities. *Violence and Victims, 7,* 279-286.

Smith, M. D., Devine, J. A., & Sheley, J. F. (1992). Crime and unemployment: Effects across age and race categories. *Sociological Perspectives, 35,* 551-572.

Smith, M. D., & Feiler, S. M. (1995). Absolute and relative involvement in homicide offending: Contemporary youth and the baby boom cohorts. *Violence and Victims, 10,* 327-333.

Smith, M. D., & Parker, R. N. (1980). Type of homicide and variation in regional rates. *Social Forces, 59,* 136-147.

Smith, S. (1965). The adolescent murderer: A psychodynamic interpretation. *Archives of General Psychiatry, 13,* 310-319.

Snell, T. L. (1996). *Capital punishment 1995* (Bureau of Justice Statistics Bulletin NCJ-162040). Washington, DC: U.S. Department of Justice.

Snell, T. L. (1997). *Capital punishment 1996* (Bureau of Justice Statistics Bulletin NCJ-167031). Washington, DC: U.S. Department of Justice.

Snipes, J. B., & Maguire, E. R. (1995). Country music, suicide and spuriousness. *Social Forces, 74,* 327-329.

Snyder, H. N. (1995). NIBRS and the study of juvenile crime and victimization. In C. R. Block & R. L. Block (Eds.), *Trends, risks, and interventions in lethal violence: Proceedings of the homicide research working group* (pp. 309-315). Washington, DC: Government Printing Office.

Snyder, H. N., Sickmund, M., & Poe-Yamagata, E. (1997). *Juvenile offenders and victims: 1997 update on violence.* Washington, DC: Office of Juvenile Justice and Delinquency Prevention.

Snyder, J. R. (1993). A nation of cowards. *The Public Interest, 113,* 40-55.

Solomon, E., Schmidt, R., & Ardragna, P. (1990). *Human anatomy and physiology.* Philadelphia: Saunders College Publishing.

Solway, I. S., Richardson, L., Hays, J. R., & Elion, V. H. (1981). Adolescent murderers: Literature review and preliminary research findings. In J. R. Hays, T. K. Roberts, & K. Solway (Eds.), *Violence and the violent individual* (pp. 193-210). Jamaica, NY: Spectrum.

Sonkin, D. J. (1987). The assessment of court mandated batterers. In D. J. Sonkin (Ed.), *Domestic violence on trial: Psychological and legal dimensions of family violence* (pp. 174-196). New York: Springer.

Sonkin, D. J. (1989). *Learning to live without violence.* Volcano, CA: Volcano Press.

Sonkin, D. J., Martin, D., & Walker, L. (1985). *The male batterer: A treatment approach.* New York: Springer.

Sorlie, P. D., Rogot, E., & Johnson, N. J. (1992). Validity of demographic characteristics on the death certificate. *Epidemiology, 3,* 181-184.

Sorrells, J. M. (1977). Kids who kill. *Crime & Delinquency, 23,* 313-320.

Spergel, I. A. (1983). *Violent gangs in Chicago: Segmentation and integration.* Chicago: University of Chicago, School of Social Service Administration.

Spergel, I. A. (1988). *Report of the Law Enforcement Youth Gang Symposium.* Chicago: University of Chicago, School of Social Service Administration.

Spergel, I. A. (1995). *The youth gang problem: A community approach.* New York: Oxford University Press.

Spergel, I. A., & Curry, D. G. (1990). Strategies and perceived agency effectiveness in dealing with the youth gang problem. In C. R. Huff (Ed.), *Gangs in America* (pp. 288-309). Newbury Park, CA: Sage.

Spunt, B., Brownstein, H., Goldstein, P., Fendrich, M., & Liberty, H. J. (1995). Drug use by homicide offenders. *Journal of Psychoactive Drugs, 27,* 125-134.

Spunt, B., Goldstein, P., Brownstein, H., Fendrich, M., & Langley, S. (1994). Alcohol and homicide: Interviews with prison inmates. *Journal of Drug Issues, 24,* 143-163.

Stack, S. (1987). Publicized executions and homicide, 1950-1980. *American Sociological Review, 52,* 532-540.

Stack, S., & Gundlach, J. (1992). The effect of country music on suicide. *Social Forces, 71,* 211-218.

Stack, S., & Gundlach, J. (1994). Country music and suicide: A reply to Maguire and Snipes. *Social Forces, 72,* 1245-1248.

Stack, S., & Gundlach, J. (1995). Country music and suicide—individual, indirect and interaction effects: A reply to Snipes and Maguire. *Social Forces, 74,* 331-335.

Stearns, A. (1957). Murder by adolescents with obscure motivation. *American Journal of Psychiatry, 114,* 303-305.

Steffensmeier, D., & Harer, M. D. (1991). Did crime rise or fall during the Reagan presidency? The effects of an "aging" U.S. population on the nation's crime rate. *Journal of Research in Crime and Delinquency, 28,* 330-359.

Steffensmeier, D., Allan, E. A., Harer, M. D., & Streifel, C. (1989). Age and the distribution of crime. *American Journal of Sociology, 94,* 803-831.

Steffensmeier, D., Allan, E. A., & Streifel, C. (1989). Development and female crime: A cross-national test of alternative explanations. *Social Forces, 68,* 262-283.

Steffensmeier, D., Streifel, C., & Shihadeh, E. S. (1992). Cohort size and arrest rates over the life course: The Easterlin hypothesis reconsidered. *American Sociological Review, 57,* 306-314.

Stets, J. E. (1990). Verbal and physical aggression in marriage. *Journal of Marriage and the Family, 43,* 721-732.

Stout, K. D. (1991). Intimate femicide: An ecological analysis. *Journal of Interpersonal Violence, 6,* 29-46.

Stout, K. D. (1993). Intimate femicide: A study of men who have killed their mates. *Journal of Offender Rehabilitation, 19,* 81-94.

Straus, J. H., & Straus, M. A. (1953). Suicide, homicide and social structure in Ceylon. *American Journal of Sociology, 58,* 461-469.

Straus, M. A. (1976). Domestic violence and homicide antecedents. *Bulletin of the New York Academy of Medicine, 62,* 446-465.

Straus, M. A., Gelles, R. J., & Steinmetz, S. K. (1980). *Behind closed doors.* New York: Doubleday.

Sugarman, D. B., & Hotaling, G. T. (1989). Dating violence: Prevalence, context, and risk markers. In M. A. Pirog-Good & J. E. Stets (Eds.), *Violence in dating relationships* (pp. 3-32). New York: Praeger.

Sutherland, E. (1925). Murder and the death penalty. *Journal of the American Institute of Criminal Law and Criminology, 51,* 522-529.

Sutherland, E., & Gehlke, C. E. (1933). Crime and punishment. In W. C. Mitchell (Ed.), *Recent social trends in the United States* (pp. 1114-1167). New York: McGraw-Hill.

Swidler, A. (1986). Culture in action. *American Sociological Review, 51,* 273-286.

Sykes, G. M., & Matza, D. (1957). Techniques of neutralization. *American Sociological Review, 22,* 664-670.

Symons, D. (1990). Adaptiveness and adaptation. *Ethology and Sociobiology, 16,* 427-444.

Tanay, E. (1973). Adolescents who kill parents: Reactive parricide. *Australian and New Zealand Journal of Psychiatry, 7,* 263-277.

Tanay, E. (1976). Reactive parricide. *Journal of Forensic Sciences, 21,* 76-82.

Tardiff, K., Marzuk, P. M., Leon, A. C., Hirsch, C. S., Stajik, M., Portera, L., & Hartwell, N. (1995). Cocaine, opiates, and ethanol in homicides in New York City: 1990 and 1991. *Journal of Forensic Sciences, 40,* 387-390.

Taylor, S. P. (1993). Experimental investigation of alcohol-induced aggression in humans. *Alcohol Health and Research World, 17,* 108-112.

Teret, S. P. (1986). Litigating for the public's health. *American Journal of Public Health, 76,* 1027-1029.

Teret, S. P., & Wintemute, G. (1993). Policies to prevent firearm injuries. *Health Affairs, 12*(4), 96-108.

Thomas, C. K. (1958). The linguistic Mason and Dixon line. In D. C. Bryant (Ed.), *The rhetorical idiom: Essays in rhetoric, oratory, language, and drama* (pp. 251-255). Ithaca, NY: Cornell University Press.

Thompson, S. (1955). *Motif-index of folk literature.* Bloomington: University of Indiana Press.

Thornberry, T. P. (1994). *Violent families and youth violence* (Fact Sheet No. 21). Washington, DC: Office of Juvenile Justice and Delinquency Prevention.

Thornberry, T. P., & Burch, J. H., II. (1997). *Gang members and delinquent behavior* (NCJ-165154). Washington, DC: Office of Juvenile Justice and Delinquency Prevention.

Thornberry, T. P., Krohn, M. D., Lizotte, A. J., & Chard-Wierschem, D. (1993). The role of juvenile gangs in facilitating delinquent behavior. *Journal of Research in Crime and Delinquency, 30,* 55-87.

Thyfault, R. K. (1984). Self-defense: Battered women syndrome on trial. *California Western Law Review, 20,* 485-510.

Tita, G. E., Cohen, J., & Blumstein, A. (1996, November). *Exploring the gang-drug-gun nexus: Evidence from homicides in Pittsburgh.* Paper presented at the annual meeting of the American Society of Criminology, Chicago.

Tittle, C. (1988). Two empirical regularities (maybe) in search of an explanation. *Criminology, 26,* 75-85.

Tittle, C., & Villemez, W. J. (1977). Social class and criminality. *Social Forces, 56,* 474-502.

Tolan, P., & Guerra, N. (1994). *What works in reducing adolescent violence: An empirical review of the field.* Unpublished manuscript, University of Colorado, Institute for Behavioral Sciences, Center for the Study and Prevention of Violence, Boulder.

Tooby, J., & Cosmides, L. (1990). The past explains the present: Emotional adaptations and the structure of ancestral environments. *Ethology and Sociobiology, 16,* 375-424.

Tooley, K. (1975). The small assassins. *Journal of the American Academy of Child Psychiatry, 14,* 306-318.

Totman, J. (1978). *The murderesses: A psychosocial study of criminal homicide.* San Francisco: R & E Associates.

Toupin, J. (1993). Adolescent murders: Validation of a typology and study of their recidivism. In A. V. Wilson (Ed.), *Homicide: The victim/offender connection* (pp. 135-156). Cincinnati, OH: Anderson.

Tracy, P. E. (1979). *Subcultural delinquency: A comparison of the incidence and seriousness of gang and nongang member offensivity.* Philadelphia: University of Pennsylvania, Center for Studies in Criminology and Criminal Law.

Trivers, R. L. (1974). Parent-offspring conflict. *American Zoologist, 14,* 249-264.

Trivers, R. L., & Willard, D. (1973). Natural selection of parental ability to vary the sex-ratio of offspring. *Science, 179,* 90-92.

Tucker, L. S., & Cornwall, T. P. (1977). Mother-son "folie a deux": A case of attempted patricide. *American Journal of Psychiatry, 134,* 1146-1147.

United Nations. (1950). *Statistical report on the state of crime: 1937-1946.* New York: Author.

United Nations. (1966, July 18-August 7). *Report on the inter-regional meeting on research in criminology: Denmark-Norway-Sweden.* New York: Author.

United Nations. (1977, September 22). *Crime prevention and control: Report to the secretary general* (Report No. A/32/199). New York: Author.

Unnithan, N. P., Huff-Corzine, L., Corzine, J., & Whitt, H. P. (1994). *The currents of lethal violence: An integrated model of suicide and homicide.* Albany: State University of New York Press.

Unnithan, N. P., & Whitt, H. P. (1992). Inequality, economic development and lethal violence: A cross-national analysis of suicide and homicide. *International Journal of Comparative Sociology, 33,* 182-195.

U.S. Advisory Board on Child Abuse and Neglect. (1993). *Neighbors helping neighbors: A new national strategy the protection of children.* Washington, DC: National Clearinghouse on Child Abuse and Neglect.

U.S. Bureau of the Census. (1994). *Statistical abstract of the United States.* Washington, DC: Government Printing Office.

U.S. Commission on Civil Rights. (1978). *Battered women: Issues of public policy.* Washington, DC: Government Printing Office.

U.S. Commission on Civil Rights. (1982). *Under the rule of thumb: Battered women and the administration of justice.* Washington, DC: Government Printing Office.

U.S. Department of Health and Human Services. (1991, October). *International classification of diseases* (9th rev., 4th ed., Vol. 1) (DHHS Publication No. PHS 91-1260). Washington, DC: Government Printing Office.

U.S. Department of Justice. (1987). *Survey of youth in custody* (Bureau of Justice Statistics special report). Washington, DC: Government Printing Office.

U.S. Department of the Interior. (1991). *Survey of fishing, hunting, and wildlife-associated recreation.* Washington, DC: Government Printing Office.

Valdez, A. (1993). Persistent poverty, crime, and drugs: U.S.-Mexican border region. In J. Moore & R. Pinderhughes (Eds.), *In the barrios: Latinos and the underclass debate* (pp. 195-210). New York: Russell Sage.

Valdez, R. B., & Nourjah, P. (1988). Homicide in Southern California, 1966-1985: An examination based on vital statistics data. In J. Kraus, S. Sorenson, & P. Juarez (Eds.), *Proceedings of research conference on violence and homicide in Hispanic communities, September 14-15, 1987* (pp. 85-100). Los Angeles: University of California.

Van Alstyne, W. (1994). *The Second Amendment and the personal right to arms.* Durham, NC: Duke University School of Law.

van den Haag, E. (1969). On deterrence and the death penalty. *Journal of Criminal Law, Criminology and Police Science, 60,* 141-147.

van den Haag, E. (1975). *Punishing criminals: Concerning a very old and painful question.* New York: Basic Books.

van den Haag, E. (1978). In defense of the death penalty: A legal-practical-moral analysis. *Criminal Law Bulletin, 14,* 51-68.

van den Haag, E., & Conrad, J. (1983). *The death penalty: A debate.* New York: Plenum.

Vanderbilt Television News Archive. (1968-1992). *Vanderbilt television and news index and abstracts, 1977-1992.* Nashville, TN: Author.

Verkko, V. (1951). *Homicides and suicides in Finland and their dependence on national character.* Copenhagen, Denmark: G.E.C. Gads Forlag.

Vetere, E., & Newman, G. (1977). International crime statistics: An overview from a comparative perspective. *Abstracts on Criminology and Penology, 17,* 251-267.

Vetter, H. (1990). Dissociation, psychopathy, and the serial murderer. In S. A. Egger (Ed.), *Serial murder: An elusive phenomenon* (pp. 73-92). New York: Praeger.

Vigderhous, G. (1978). Methodological problems confronting cross-cultural criminological research using official data. *Human Relations, 31,* 229-247.

Vincent, M. L., Clearie, A. R., & Schluchter, M. D. (1987). Reducing adolescent pregnancy through school and community-based education. *Journal of the American Medical Association, 257,* 3382-3386.

Violence Policy Center. (1992). *More gun dealers than gas stations.* Washington, DC: Author.

Violence Policy Center. (1997). *Who dies?* Washington, DC: Author.

Voland, E. (1984). Human sex-ratio manipulation: Historical data from a German parish. *Journal of Human Evolution, 13,* 99-107.

Walinsky, A. (1995, July). The crisis of public order. *Atlantic Monthly, 276,* 39-54.

Wallace, A. (1986). *Homicide: The social reality.* Sydney, Australia: New South Wales Bureau of Crime and Statistics.

Wallerstein, I. (1974). *The modern world system: Capitalist agriculture and the origins of the European world economy in the sixteenth century.* New York: Academic Press.

Walsh-Brennan, K. S. (1974). Psychopathology of homicidal children. *Royal Society of Health, 94,* 274-276.

Walsh-Brennan, K. S. (1977). A socio-psychological investigation of young murderers. *British Journal of Criminology, 17,* 53-63.

Washbrook, R. A. H. (1979). Bereavement leading to murder. *International Journal of Offender Therapy & Comparative Criminology, 23,* 57-64.

Webb, S. (1972). Crime and the division of labor: Testing a Durkheimian model. *American Journal of Sociology, 78,* 643-656.

Wellford, C. (1973). Age composition and the increase in recorded crime. *Criminology, 16,* 61-70.

Wellford, C. (1974). Crime and the dimensions of nations. *International Journal of Criminology and Penology, 2,* 1-10.

Welte, J. W., & Abel, E. L. (1989). Homicide: Drinking by the victim. *Journal of Studies on Alcohol, 50,* 197-201.

Wheeler, J. L. (1993). *Remote controlled: How TV affects you and your family.* Hagerstown, MD: Review and Herald Publishing Association.

White, H. R., Hansell, S., & Brick, J. (1993). Alcohol use and aggression among youth. *Alcohol Health and Research World, 17,* 144-150.

White, L. K., & Booth, A. (1985). The quality and stability of remarriages: The role of stepchildren. *American Sociological Review, 50,* 689-698.

Whitt, H. P., Corzine, J., & Huff-Corzine, L. (1995). Where is the South? A preliminary analysis of the southern subculture of violence. In C. R. Block & R. L. Block (Eds.), *Trends, risks, and interventions in lethal violence* (pp. 127-148). Washington, DC: National Institute of Justice.

Whitt, H. P., Gordon, C. P., & Hofley, J. R. (1972). Religion, economic development and lethal aggression. *American Sociological Review, 37,* 193-201.

Widom, C. S. (1989a). Child abuse, neglect, and adult behavior: Research design and findings on criminality, violence, and child abuse. *American Journal of Orthopsychiatry, 59,* 355-366.

Widom, C. S. (1989b). Child abuse, neglect, and violent criminal behavior. *Criminology, 27,* 251-271.

Widom, C. S. (1989c). The cycle of violence. *Science, 244,* 160-166.

Widom, C. S. (1989d). Does violence beget violence? A critical examination of the literature. *Psychological Bulletin, 106,* 3-28.

Widom, C. S. (1991). A tail on an untold tale: Response to "Biological and genetic contributors to violence—Widom's untold tale." *Psychological Bulletin, 109,* 130-132.

Widom, C. S., & Ames, M. A. (1994). Criminal consequences of childhood sexual victimization. *Child Abuse and Neglect, 18,* 303-318.

Wieczorek, W., Welte, J., & Abel, E. (1990). Alcohol, drugs, and murder: A study of convicted homicide offenders. *Journal of Criminal Justice, 18,* 217-227.

Wikstrom, P. H. (1991). Cross-national comparisons and context specific trends in criminal homicide. *Journal of Crime and Justice, 14,* 71-95.

Wilbanks, W. (1983). The female homicide offender in Dade County, Florida. *Criminal Justice Review, 8,* 9-14.

Wilbanks, W. (1984). *Murder in Miami: An analysis of homicide patterns and trends in Dade County, Florida, 1917-1983.* Lanham, MD: University Press of America.

Williams, G. C., & Nesse, R. M. (1991). The dawn of Darwinian medicine. *Quarterly Review of Biology, 66,* 1-22.

Williams, K. R. (1984). Economic sources of homicide: Reestimating the effects of poverty and inequality. *American Sociological Review, 49,* 283-289.

Williams, K. R., & Flewelling, R. L. (1987). Family, acquaintance, and stranger homicide: Alternative procedures for rate calculations. *Criminology, 25,* 543-560.

Williams, K. R., & Flewelling, R. L. (1988). The social production of criminal homicide: A comparative study of disaggregated rates in American cities. *American Sociological Review, 54,* 421-431.

Willis, D. J. (1995). Psychological impact of child abuse and neglect. *Journal of Clinical Child Psychology, 24,* 2-4.

Wilson, J. Q., & Herrnstein, R. J. (1985). *Crime and human nature.* New York: Simon & Schuster.

Wilson, M. I., & Daly, M. (1985). Competitiveness, risk-taking and violence: The young male syndrome. *Ethology and Sociobiology, 6,* 59-73.

Wilson, M. I., & Daly, M. (1992a). The man who mistook his wife for a chattel. In J. Barkow, L. Cosmides, & J. Tooby (Eds.), *The adapted mind* (pp. 289-322). New York: Oxford University Press.

Wilson, M. I., & Daly, M. (1992b). Who kills whom in spouse killings? On the exceptional sex ratio of spousal homicides in the United States. *Criminology, 30,* 189-215.

Wilson, M. I., & Daly, M. (1993a). An evolutionary psychological perspective on male sexual proprietariness and violence against wives. *Violence and Victims, 8,* 271-294.

Wilson, M. I., & Daly, M. (1993b). The psychology of parenting in evolutionary perspective and the case of human filicide. In S. Parmigiami & F. vom Saal (Eds.), *Infanticide and parental care* (pp. 73-140). Chur, Switzerland: Harwood Academic.

Wilson, M. I., & Daly, M. (1993c). Spousal homicide risk and estrangement. *Violence and Victims, 8,* 3-16.

Wilson, M. I., & Daly, M. (1996). Male sexual proprietariness and violence against wives. *Current Directions in Psychological Science, 5,* 2-7.

Wilson, M. I., & Daly, M. (1997). Life expectancy, economic inequality, homicide, and reproductive timing in Chicago neighborhoods. *British Medical Journal, 314,* 1271-1274.

Wilson, M. I., Daly, M., & Daniele, A. (1995). Familicide: The killing of spouse and children. *Aggressive Behavior, 21,* 275-291.

Wilson, M. I., Daly, M., & Weghorst, S. J. (1980). Household composition and the risk of child abuse and neglect. *Journal of Biosocial Science, 12,* 333-340.

Wilson, M. I., Daly, M., & Wright, C. (1993). Uxoricide in Canada: Demographic risk patterns. *Canadian Journal of Criminology, 35,* 263-291.

Wilson, M. I., Johnson, H., & Daly, M. (1995). Lethal and nonlethal violence against wives. *Canadian Journal of Criminology, 37,* 331-361.

Wilson, N. K. (1993). Gendered interaction in criminal homicide. In A. V. Wilson (Ed.), *Homicide: The victim/offender connection* (pp. 43-64). Cincinnati, OH: Anderson.

Wilson, W. J. (1987). *The truly disadvantaged: The inner city, the underclass, and public policy.* Chicago: University of Chicago Press.

Wilson, W. J. (1996). *When work disappears: The world of the new urban poor.* New York: Knopf.

Wilt, M., & Breedlove, R. K. (1977). *Domestic violence and the police: Studies in Detroit and Kansas City.* Washington, DC: Police Foundation.

Wolf, P. (1971). Crime and development: An international comparison of crime rates. *Scandinavian Studies in Criminology, 3,* 107-120.

Wolfgang, M. E. (1958). *Patterns in criminal homicide.* Philadelphia: University of Pennsylvania Press.

Wolfgang, M. E. (1978). Family violence and criminal behavior. In R. L. Sadoff (Ed.), *Violence and responsibility* (pp. 87-103). New York: Spectrum.

Wolfgang, M. E., & Ferracuti, F. (1967). *The subculture of violence.* London: Tavistock.

Woods, S. M. (1961). Adolescent violence and homicide: Ego disruption and the 6 and 14 dysrhythmia. *Archives of General Psychiatry, 5,* 528-534.

World Bank. (1993). *World development report 1993: Investing in health.* New York: Oxford University Press.

World Health Organization. (1994). *World health statistics annual, 1993.* Geneva, Switzerland: Author.

World Health Organization. (1995). *World health statistics annual, 1994.* Geneva, Switzerland: Author.

World Health Organization. (1996). *Report of the ad hoc committee on health research relating to future intervention options: Investing in health research and development* (Document TDR/Gen/06.1). Geneva, Switzerland: Author.

Wright, J. D. (1981). Public opinion and gun control: A comparison of results from two recent national surveys. *Annals of the American Academy of Political and Social Science, 455,* 24-39.

Wright, J. D., & Rossi, P. H. (1986). *Armed and considered dangerous: A survey of felons and their firearms.* Hawthorne, NY: Aldine.

Wright, J. D., Rossi, P. H., & Daly, K. (1983). *Under the gun: Weapons, crime, and violence in America.* Hawthorne, NY: Aldine.

Wright, J. D., Sheley, J. F., & Smith, M. D. (1992). Kids, guns, and killing fields. *Society, 30*(1), 84-89.

Wright, R. (1994). *The moral animal.* New York: Pantheon.

Wright, R. K., & Davis, J. H. (1977). Studies in the epidemiology of murder: A proposed classification system. *Journal of Forensic Science, 22,* 464-470.

Wynne, E., & Hess, M. (1986). Long-term trends in youth conduct and the revival of traditional value patterns. *Educational Evaluation and Policy Analysis, 8,* 294-308.

Yarvis, R. M. (1994). Patterns of substance abuse and intoxication among murderers. *Bulletin of the American Academy of Psychiatry and the Law, 22,* 133-144.

Yates, A., Beutler, L. E., & Crago, M. (1984). Characteristics of young, violent offenders. *Journal of Psychiatry and Law, 16,* 137-149.

Yunker, J. A. (1976). Is the death penalty a deterrent to homicide? Some time series evidence. *Journal of Behavioral Economics, 5,* 1-32.

Zagar, R., Arbit, J., Sylvies, R., Busch, K., & Hughes, J. R. (1990). Homicidal adolescents: A replication. *Psychological Reports, 67,* 1235-1242.

Zahn, M. A. (1989). Homicide in the twentieth century: Trends, types and causes. In T. Gurr (Ed.), *Violence in America: Vol. 1. The history of violence* (pp. 216-234). Newbury Park, CA: Sage.

Zahn, M. A. (1991). The Wolfgang model: Lessons for homicide research in the 1990s. *Journal of Crime and Justice, 14,* 17-30.

Zahn, M. A. (1997, November). *Changing patterns of homicide and social policy.* Paper presented at the annual meeting of the American Society of Criminology, San Diego.

Zahn, M. A., & Bencivengo, M. (1973). Violent death: A comparison between drug users and non-drug users. *Addictive Diseases, 1,* 183-296.

Zahn, M. A., & Jamieson, K. M. (1997). Changing patterns of homicide and social policy. *Homicide Studies, 1,* 190-196.

Zahn, M. A., & Riedel, M. (1983). National versus local data sources in the study of homicide: Do they agree? In G. P. Waldo (Ed.), *Measurement issues in criminal justice* (pp. 103-120). Beverly Hills, CA: Sage.

Zahn, M. A., & Sagi, P. C. (1987). Stranger homicides in nine American cities. *Journal of Criminal Law and Criminology, 78,* 377-397.

Zahn, M. A., & Snodgrass, G. (1978). Drug use and the structure of homicide in two U.S. cities. In E. Flynn & J. Conrad (Eds.), *The new and old criminology* (pp. 134-150). New York: Praeger.

Zelinsky, W. (1951). Where the South begins: The northern limit of the CIS-Appalachian South in terms of settlement landscape. *Social Forces, 30,* 172-178.

Zelinsky, W. (1961). An approach to the religious geography of the United States: Patterns of church membership in 1952. *Annals of the Association of American Geographers, 51,* 139-193.

Zelinsky, W. (1973). *The cultural geography of the United States.* Englewood Cliffs, NJ: Prentice Hall.

Zenoff, E. H., & Zients, A. B. (1979). Juvenile murderers: Should the punishment fit the crime? *International Journal of Law and Psychiatry, 2,* 533-553.

Zimring, F. E. (1968). Is gun control likely to reduce violent killings? *University of Chicago Law Review, 35,* 21-37.

Zimring, F. E. (1972). The medium is the message: Firearm caliber as a determinant of death from assault. *Journal of Legal Studies, 1,* 97-124.

Zimring, F. E. (1979). Determinants of the death rate from robbery: A Detroit time study. In H. M. Rose (Ed.), *Lethal aspects of urban violence* (pp. 31-50). Lexington, MA: Lexington Books.

Zimring, F. E., & Hawkins, G. (1986). *Capital punishment and the American agenda.* New York: Cambridge University Press.

Zimring, F. E., & Hawkins, G. (1997). *Crime is not the problem: Lethal violence in America.* New York: Oxford University Press.

Author Index

Subject Index

About the Editors

M. Dwayne Smith is Professor and Chair of the Department of Sociology, Anthropology, and Social Work at the University of North Carolina at Charlotte. His research interests center on differences in homicide rates across U.S. communities. His publications on this topic have appeared in journals such as *American Journal of Sociology, American Sociological Review, Crime & Delinquency, Journal of Crime and Delinquency, Social Forces,* and *Violence and Victims.* He is a member of the Homicide Research Working Group and currently serves as editor of the organization's journal, *Homicide Studies: An Interdisciplinary & International Journal.*

Margaret A. Zahn is Dean of Humanities and Social Sciences and Professor of Sociology at North Carolina State University. She has published extensively in the field of homicide for more than 25 years in a variety of professional journals and edited volumes. She is a frequent commentator on issues regarding youth violence and homicide and is the principal investigator for a National Institute of Justice grant, "Homicide and Social Policy in Three American Cities." She is a member of the Homicide Research Working Group and served as President of the American Society of Criminology in 1998.

About the Contributors

Kathleen Auerhahn is a Ph.D. candidate in sociology at the University of California, Riverside. She received her B.A. degree in sociology at Tulane University in New Orleans. Her primary interests are social control, sociology of law, and criminal justice policy evaluation. Her current projects include research on offender risk management and incarceration policy. Her publications include a chapter in the 1998 edition of *Annual Review of Sociology* (with Robert Nash Parker).

William C. Bailey is a Professor of Sociology and Associate Dean of the Graduate School at Cleveland State University. He received the doctoral degree in sociology from Washington State University (1971). He has published numerous articles on crime and deterrence, capital punishment, and urban crime patterns.

Angela Browne is a Senior Soros Justice Fellow and Senior Research Scientist at the Harvard Injury Control Research Center, Harvard School of Public Health. She has published and spoken nationally on the short- and long-term effects of physical and sexual assault on women and children, patterns of assault and threat in couple relationships, and homicides between intimate partners. She has published numerous articles and book chapters and is the author of *When Battered Women Kill* (1987). She is also the author of both the American Medical Association and American Psychological Association review and policy statements on violence against women. Since 1988, she has acted as Consulting Psychologist to Bedford Hills Maximum Security Prison for women in New York State.

Philip J. Cook is ITT/Terry Sanford Distinguished Professor of Public Policy and Professor of Economics and Sociology at Duke University. He has authored a number of review articles and original research on the technology of violent crime and recently edited an issue of *Law and Contemporary Problems* titled "Kids, Guns, and Public Policy." Other recent publications include *The Winner Take All Society* (with Robert H. Frank) and *Selling Hope: State Lotteries in America* (with Charles T. Clotfelter).

Jay Corzine is Professor and Chair of the Department of Sociology and Anthropology at the University of Central Florida. He is currently editor of *Sociological Spectrum* and an associate editor of *Homicide Studies.* His long-term research interests include homicide and collective violence. He is the coauthor of *The Currents of Lethal Violence: An Integrated Model of Suicide and Homicide* (1994) and articles in numerous journals, including *Social Forces, Criminology, Deviant Behavior,* and *Sociological Inquiry.*

Martin Daly is Professor of Psychology and Biology at McMaster University in Hamilton, Ontario. He has published extensively with Margo Wilson in journals ranging from *American Anthropologist* to *Violence and Victims,* as well as coauthoring *Homicide* (1988). Their epidemiological studies of homicide have been guided by hypotheses about the who, why, where, and how of interpersonal conflict and competition. He is coeditor of *Evolution and Human Behavior* and is on the editorial board of the journal *Homicide Studies.*

Donald G. Dutton is Professor of Psychology at the University of British Columbia. Since 1979, he has served as a therapist in the Assaultive Husbands Project, a court-mandated treatment program for men convicted of wife assault. While providing therapy for these men, he developed a psychological model for intimate abusiveness. He has served as an expert witness in civil trials involving domestic abuse and in criminal trials involving family violence, including work for the prosecution in the O. J. Simpson trial. He has published more than 80 articles and three books, including *The Domestic Assault of Women, The Batterer: A Psychological Profile,* and *The Abusive Personality.*

Robert L. Flewelling is Senior Research Epidemiologist in the Health and Social Policy Division at the Research Triangle Institute. His research activities include epidemiologic studies on violence and substance use and the design and evaluation of health risk behavior prevention programs and policies. He is currently conducting an examination of patterns and trends in youth homicide in the United States and is also directing the evaluation of a community-based youth violence and substance abuse prevention program in North Carolina. He takes particular interest in the challenge of applying epidemiologic data to state and local prevention program development, needs assessment, and evaluation.

James Alan Fox is Dean of the College of Criminal Justice at Northeastern University in Boston. He has authored or coauthored 12 books, including *Mass Murder, Overkill,* and *Killer on Campus.* He has also published dozens of journal and magazine articles and newspaper columns, primarily on multiple murder, juvenile crime, workplace violence, and capital punishment. He often gives media interviews, lectures, and expert testimony, including nine appearances before the U.S. Congress and briefings with the White House and the Department of Justice on trends in juvenile violence.

W. Rodney Hammond is Director of the Division of Violence Prevention and a Senior Behavioral Scientist at the Centers for Disease Control and Prevention (CDC) in Atlanta, Georgia. He is a Fellow of the American Psychological Association and a member of the Board of Governors of the National College of Professional Psychology. His recent research interests have focused on youth homicide and violence prevention as a public health concern. He is author and Executive Producer of the series *Dealing With Anger: A Violence Prevention Program for African American Youth,* a nationally recognized resource in the field of violence prevention.

Darnell F. Hawkins is Professor of African American Studies and Sociology at the University of Illinois at Chicago, where he is also a faculty affiliate in Criminal Justice. He is editor of *Homicide Among Black Americans* (1986), *Ethnicity, Race and Crime: Perspectives Across Time and Place* (1995), and a forthcoming volume, *Violent Crimes: The Nexus of Ethnicity, Race, and Class.*

Kathleen M. Heide is Professor of Criminology at the University of South Florida, Tampa. She received her B.A. degree in psychology from Vassar College and her M.A. and Ph.D. in criminal justice from State University of New York at Albany. She is an internationally recognized consultant on homicide and family violence, as well as a court-appointed expert in matters relating to homicide, sexual battery, children, and families. In addition to her academic work, she is a licensed mental health counselor and serves as the Director of Education at the Center for Mental Health Education, Assessment and Therapy in Tampa.

Lin Huff-Corzine is Associate Professor of Sociology at the University of Central Florida, where she teaches and does research on criminological and gender-related issues. In addition to her coauthored book, *The Currents of Lethal Violence: An Integrated Model of Suicide and Homicide,* she has published in journals such as *Social Forces, Criminology, Deviant Behavior,* and *Homicide Studies.*

Gary LaFree is Professor of Sociology at the University of New Mexico, where he also directs the Institute for Social Research. His latest book, *Losing Legitimacy* (1998), examines the impact of social institutions on the rapid growth of U.S. crime rates in the 1960s and 1970s, as well as the recent downturn in crime in the 1990s. He is currently using United Nations data to study homicide trends around the world.

Kenneth C. Land is John Franklin Crowell Professor of Sociology at Duke University. His work as a social statistician and criminologist has included the articulation and testing of the crime opportunity/routine activities theory of crime rates and victimization, studies of explanations of crime rate trends and cross-sectional distributions, and the development of mixed Poisson regression models for the analysis of delinquent/criminal careers.

Matthew T. Lee received his M.A. in criminology from the University of Delaware and is currently a Ph.D. candidate in sociology. In addition to homicide studies, his research focuses on issues related to corporate and governmental deviance. His most recent research has examined the social construction of deviance associated with the Ford Pinto case and the Cold War human radiation experiments.

Jack Levin is Director of the Program for the Study of Violence and Conflict and the Brudnick Professor of Sociology and Criminology at Northeastern University in Boston. He has authored or coauthored 19 books, including *Hate Crimes, The Functions of Discrimination and Prejudice, Mass Murder, Overkill,* and *Killer on Campus.* He has published numerous articles in professional and trade journals on homicide, prejudice and violence, and social psychology. He frequently lectures, appears on national television, and is quoted by the press. He was recently honored by the Council for Advancement and Support of Education as its Professor of the Year in Massachusetts.

Ramiro Martinez Jr. received his Ph.D. from Ohio State University and is currently Associate Professor at the University of Delaware. His research interests include examining economic conditions, ethnicity, and levels of violence at the neighborhood level. He is also a member of the National Consortium on Violence Research and the Homicide Research Working Group.

Cheryl L. Maxson is Associate Research Professor at the University of Southern California. Her research interests are in delinquency and violence, street gangs, and community and justice system responses to juvenile offenders. Recent coedited books include *The Modern Gang Reader* (1995) and *Responding to Troubled Youth* (1997). Current research projects concern community responses to community policing, homicide, juvenile violence in Los Angeles, and the assessment of a firearms/violence reduction project targeting youth.

Patricia L. McCall is Associate Professor of Sociology in the Department of Sociology at North Carolina State University. Her research interests include aggregate studies of homicide and suicide, modeling criminal careers, and juvenile recidivism. Her most recent publications appear in *Social Forces, American Journal of Sociology, Theoretical Criminology,* and *Homicide Studies.*

James A. Mercy is Associate Director for Science of the Division of Violence Prevention in the National Center for Injury Prevention and Control of the Centers for Disease Control and Prevention (CDC) in Atlanta, Georgia. During his time at CDC, he has conducted and overseen numerous studies of the epidemiology of youth suicide, youth violence, homicide, and firearm injuries. Most recently, he has been working on a study testing the hypothesis that suicidal behavior may be contagious and working on a project to collate lessons learned from CDC's efforts to assist state and local health departments in establishing firearm injury surveillance systems.

Steven F. Messner is Professor of Sociology at the State University of New York at Albany. He has published numerous articles on the relationship between features of social organization and crime rates with data for neighborhoods, metropolitan communities, and nation-states. He has also been involved in research on crime in China and on the situational dynamics of violence. Currently, he is conducting research on the cultural and institutional determinants of serious crimes in market societies. He is coauthor with Richard Rosenfeld of *Crime and the American Dream* and coauthor with Allen E. Liska of *Perspectives on Crime and Deviance.*

Mark H. Moore is Guggenheim Professor of Criminal Justice Policy and Management at the John F. Kennedy School of Government, Harvard University, and Faculty Chair of the Kennedy School's Program in Criminal Justice Policy and Management. His research interests are in public management and leadership in criminal justice policy and management and in the intersection of the two. His most recent book is *Creating Public Value: Strategic Management in Government.* Other books include *Buy and Bust: The Effective Regulation of an Illicit Market in Heroin, Dangerous Offenders: Elusive Targets of Justice,* and *Beyond 911: A New Era for Policing.*

Karen F. Parker is Assistant Professor of Sociology in the Center for Studies in Criminology and Law at the University of Florida. Her current research interests include examining the effects of labor market factors and racial competition on racially disaggregated homicide rates, exploring the impact of drug-related violence on communities, and evaluating recidivism among Florida's inmates.

Robert Nash Parker is Professor of Sociology and Director of the Robert Presley Center for Crime and Justice Studies at the University of California, Riverside. His primary research interests are in the social-structural causes of violence. A recent focus involves the impact of alcohol use on homicide, especially variations in this impact across cultures and situational contexts. He is the author of *Alcohol and Homicide: A Deadly Combination of Two American Traditions* (with Linda Rebhun) and has published articles related to homicide in such journals as *American Journal of Sociology, American Sociological Review, Social Forces, Criminology,* and *Homicide Studies.*

Ruth D. Peterson is Professor of Sociology at Ohio State University. She received the doctoral degree in sociology from the University of Wisconsin in 1983. She has published a number of journal articles and book chapters that address such topics as interrelationships among racial residential segregation, social disadvantage, and crime; legal decision making and sentencing; and crime and deterrence.

Marc Riedel is Associate Professor in the Center for the Study of Crime, Delinquency, and Corrections at Southern Illinois University. He does research on prescribed and proscribed forms of violence. His articles on the death penalty and homicide have appeared in journals such as the *Annals of the American Academy of Political and Social Science, Journal of Criminal Law and Criminology,* and *Temple Law Quarterly.* His most recent book, *Stranger Violence: A Theoretical Inquiry,* was published in 1993. In 1985, he received the Herbert A. Bloch award from the American Society of Criminology for outstanding service to the society and the profession.

Richard Rosenfeld is Professor of Criminology and Criminal Justice at the University of Missouri at St. Louis. He is coauthor with Steven F. Messner of *Crime and the American Dream* (1994, 1997) as well the author of articles in various professional journals. His publications focus on the social sources of violent crime. He is a member of the National Consortium on Violence Research.

Hugh P. Whitt is Professor of Sociology at the University of Nebraska at Lincoln. As one of the architects of an integrated model of suicide and homicide in *The Currents of Lethal Violence* (1994), he focuses his homicide research on the impact of cultural and structural factors on lethal violence and on the mode in which lethal violence is expressed. He also works in the sociology of religion, exploring the sources and consequences of denominational switching.

Kirk R. Williams is Professor of Sociology and Associate Director of the Center for the Study and Prevention of Violence at the University of Colorado. His areas of interest include criminology, deviance, and social control, but the emphasis of his research is on violence, particularly intimate and youth violence. He has published widely in professional journals and has received a number of grants from national and state agencies, as well as several private foundations.

Margo Wilson is Professor of Psychology at McMaster University in Hamilton, Ontario. She was the first recipient of the University of Toronto's Master of Studies in Law degree (1987), and is President (1997-1999) of the Human Behavior & Evolution Society. She is coauthor, with Martin Daly, of *Homicide* (1988) and coeditor of *Evolution & Human Behavior,* and is on the editorial board of the journal *Homicide Studies.*